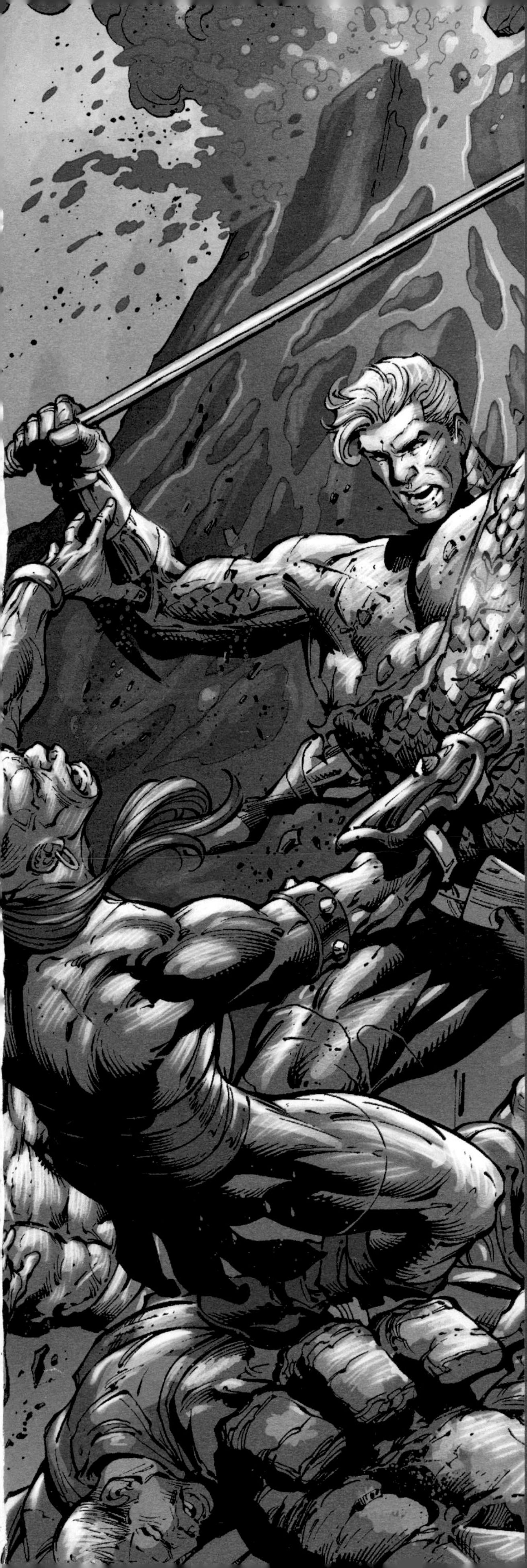

AQUAMAN

VOLUME 6
MAELSTROM

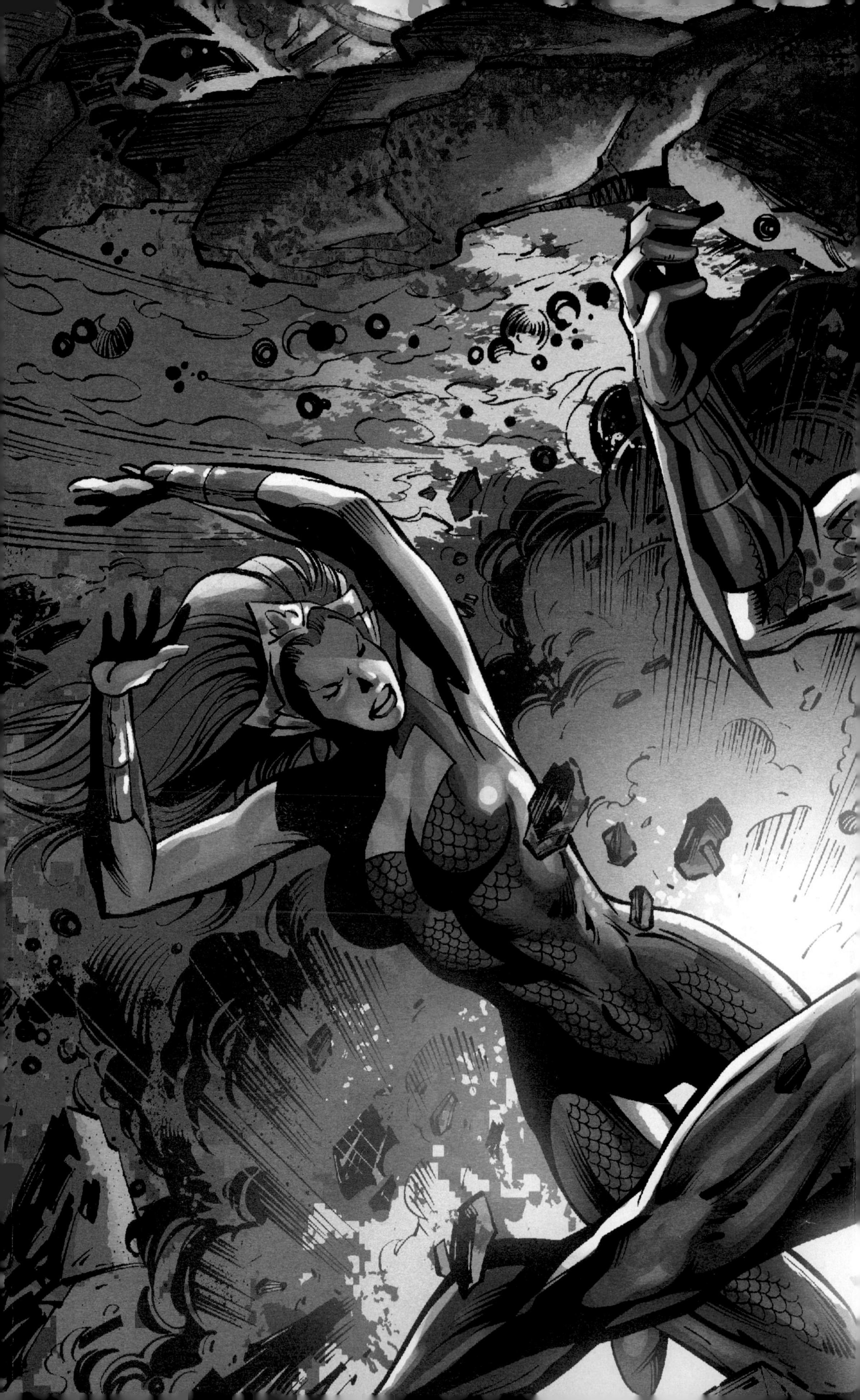

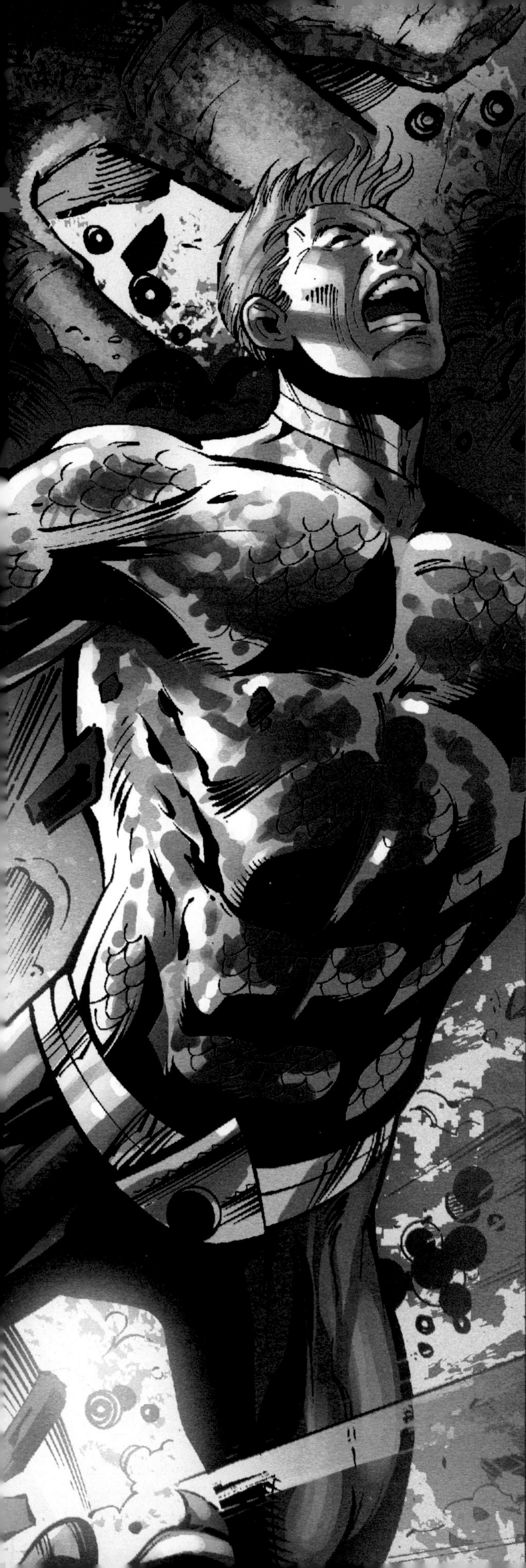

AQUAMAN

VOLUME 6
MAELSTROM

WRITTEN BY
JEFF PARKER

PENCILS BY
PAUL PELLETIER
CARLOS RODRIGUEZ
ALVARO MARTINEZ
DANIEL HDR

INKS BY
SEAN PARSONS
SANDRA HOPE
WAYNE FAUCHER
RAUL FERNANDEZ
BIT
DANIEL HDR
TONY KORDOS
RICK MAGYAR

COLOR BY
RAIN BEREDO
PETE PANTAZIS
GUY MAJOR

LETTERS BY
DEZI SIENTY
TAYLOR ESPOSITO
CARLOS M. MANGUAL
TRAVIS LANHAM
DAVE SHARPE

COLLECTION COVER ART BY
PAUL PELLETIER
and SEAN PARSONS

AQUAMAN CREATED BY
PAUL NORRIS

CHRIS CONROY FRANK PITTARESE Editors– Original Series
HARVEY RICHARDS Associate Editor – Original Series
AMEDEO TURTURRO Assistant Editor – Original Series
LIZ ERICKSON Editor
ROBBIN BROSTERMAN Design Director – Books
DAMIAN RYLAND Publication Design

BOB HARRAS Senior VP – Editor-in-Chief, DC Comics

DIANE NELSON President
DAN DIDIO and JIM LEE Co-Publishers
GEOFF JOHNS Chief Creative Officer
AMIT DESAI Senior VP – Marketing & Franchise Management
AMY GENKINS Senior VP – Business & Legal Affairs
NAIRI GARDINER Senior VP – Finance
JEFF BOISON VP – Publishing Planning
MARK CHIARELLO VP – Art Direction & Design
JOHN CUNNINGHAM VP – Marketing
TERRI CUNNINGHAM VP – Editorial Administration
LARRY GANEM VP – Talent Relations & Services
ALISON GILL Senior VP – Manufacturing & Operations
HANK KANALZ Senior VP – Vertigo & Integrated Publishing
JAY KOGAN VP – Business & Legal Affairs, Publishing
JACK MAHAN VP – Business Affairs, Talent
NICK NAPOLITANO VP – Manufacturing Administration
SUE POHJA VP – Book Sales
FRED RUIZ VP – Manufacturing Operations
COURTNEY SIMMONS Senior VP – Publicity
BOB WAYNE Senior VP – Sales

AQUAMAN VOLUME 6: MAELSTROM

DC Comics, 4000 Warner Blvd., Burbank, CA 91522
A Warner Bros. Entertainment Company
Printed by RR Donnelley, Salem, VA, USA. 5/29/15.
ISBN: 978-1-4012-5441-4
First Printing.

Library of Congress Cataloging-in-Publication Data

Parker, Jeff, 1966- author.
Aquaman. Volume 6, Maelstrom / Jeff Parker, writer ; Paul Pelletier, artist.
pages cm. — (The New 52!)
ISBN 978-1-4012-5441-4 (hardback)
1. Graphic novels. I. Pelletier, Paul, 1970- illustrator. II. Title. III. Title: Maelstrom.

PN6728.A68P37 2014
741.5'973—dc23

SUSTAINABLE FORESTRY INITIATIVE
Certified Chain of Custody
20% Certified Forest Content,
80% Certified Sourcing
www.sfiprogram.org
SFI-01042
APPLIES TO TEXT STOCK ONLY

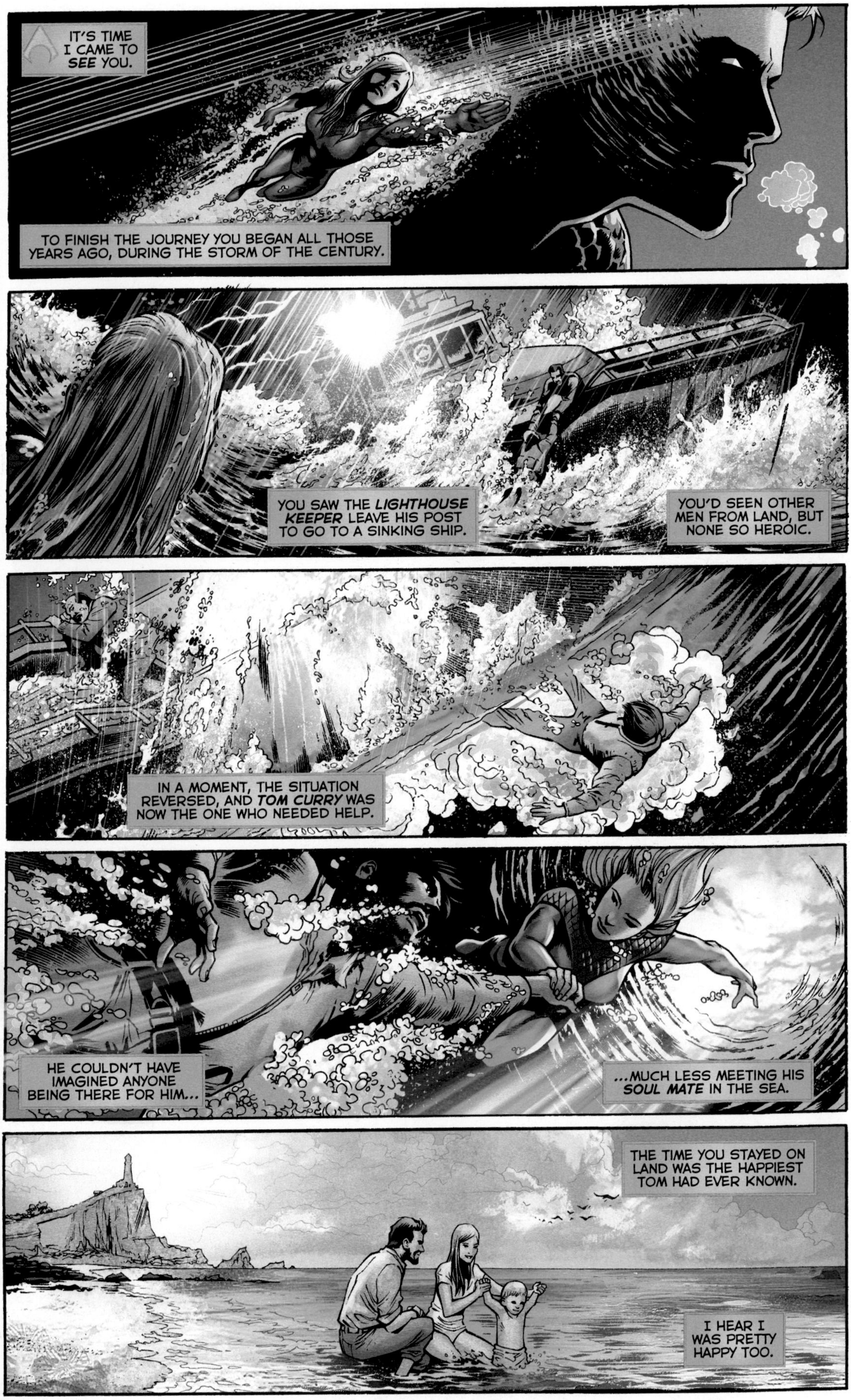
IT'S TIME I CAME TO SEE YOU.
TO FINISH THE JOURNEY YOU BEGAN ALL THOSE YEARS AGO, DURING THE STORM OF THE CENTURY.
YOU SAW THE LIGHTHOUSE KEEPER LEAVE HIS POST TO GO TO A SINKING SHIP.
YOU'D SEEN OTHER MEN FROM LAND, BUT NONE SO HEROIC.
IN A MOMENT, THE SITUATION REVERSED, AND TOM CURRY WAS NOW THE ONE WHO NEEDED HELP.
HE COULDN'T HAVE IMAGINED ANYONE BEING THERE FOR HIM...
...MUCH LESS MEETING HIS SOUL MATE IN THE SEA.
THE TIME YOU STAYED ON LAND WAS THE HAPPIEST TOM HAD EVER KNOWN.
I HEAR I WAS PRETTY HAPPY TOO.

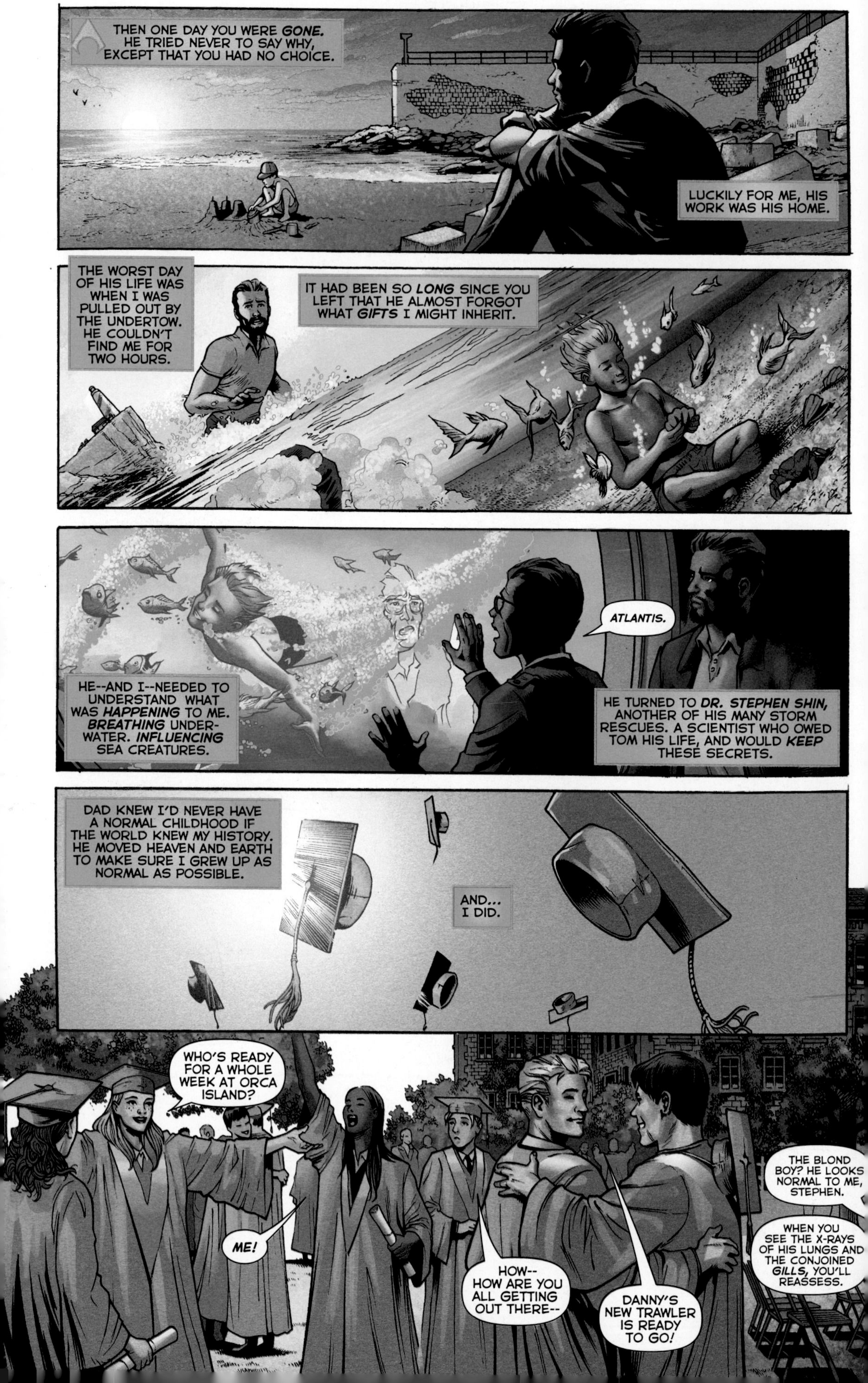
THEN ONE DAY YOU WERE GONE. HE TRIED NEVER TO SAY WHY, EXCEPT THAT YOU HAD NO CHOICE.
LUCKILY FOR ME, HIS WORK WAS HIS HOME.
THE WORST DAY OF HIS LIFE WAS WHEN I WAS PULLED OUT BY THE UNDERTOW. HE COULDN'T FIND ME FOR TWO HOURS.
IT HAD BEEN SO LONG SINCE YOU LEFT THAT HE ALMOST FORGOT WHAT GIFTS I MIGHT INHERIT.
HE--AND I--NEEDED TO UNDERSTAND WHAT WAS HAPPENING TO ME. BREATHING UNDER-WATER. INFLUENCING SEA CREATURES.
ATLANTIS.
HE TURNED TO DR. STEPHEN SHIN, ANOTHER OF HIS MANY STORM RESCUES. A SCIENTIST WHO OWED TOM HIS LIFE, AND WOULD KEEP THESE SECRETS.
DAD KNEW I'D NEVER HAVE A NORMAL CHILDHOOD IF THE WORLD KNEW MY HISTORY. HE MOVED HEAVEN AND EARTH TO MAKE SURE I GREW UP AS NORMAL AS POSSIBLE.
AND... I DID.
WHO'S READY FOR A WHOLE WEEK AT ORCA ISLAND?
ME!
HOW-- HOW ARE YOU ALL GETTING OUT THERE--
DANNY'S NEW TRAWLER IS READY TO GO!
THE BLOND BOY? HE LOOKS NORMAL TO ME, STEPHEN.
WHEN YOU SEE THE X-RAYS OF HIS LUNGS AND THE CONJOINED GILLS, YOU'LL REASSESS.

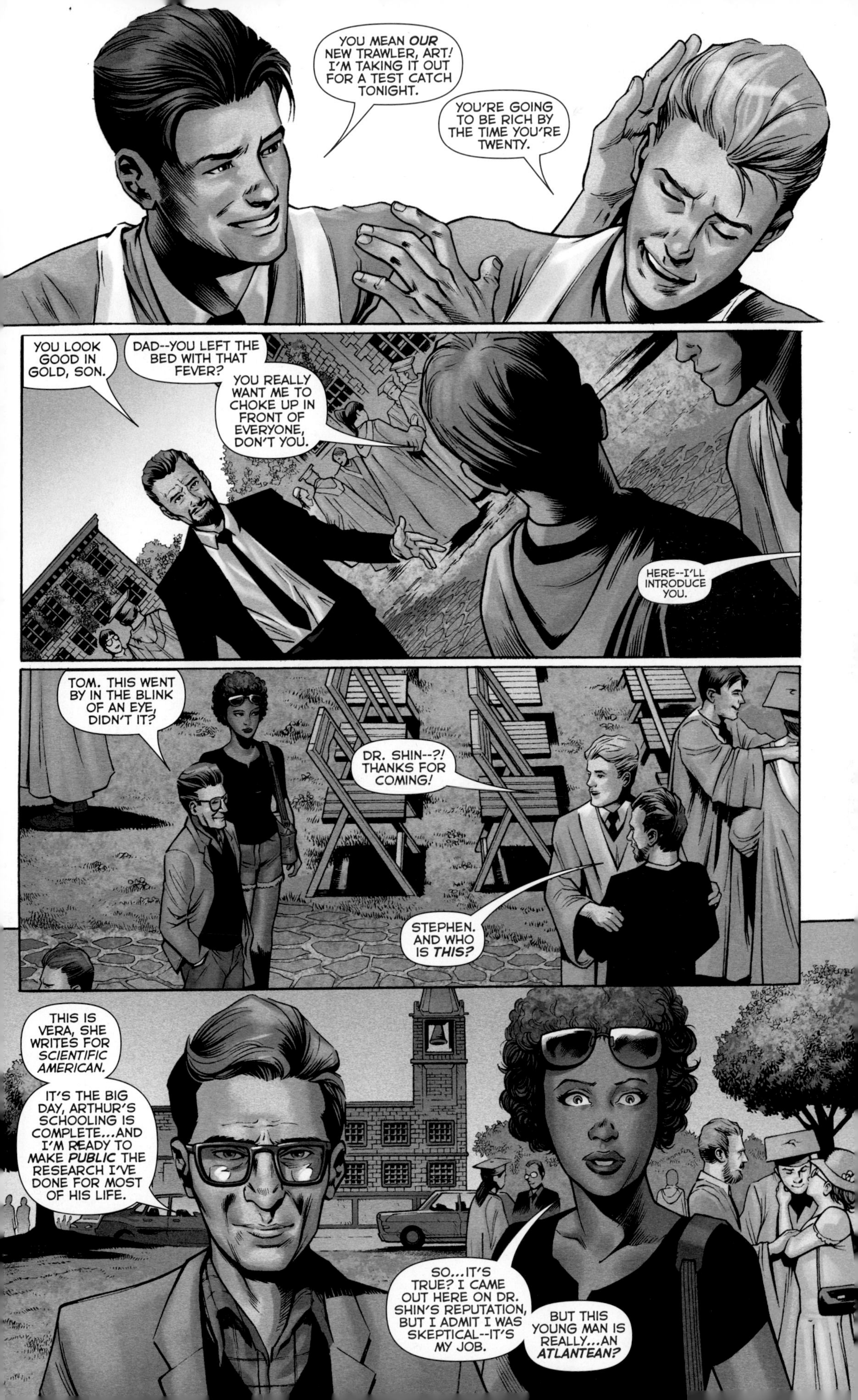
YOU MEAN OUR NEW TRAWLER, ART! I'M TAKING IT OUT FOR A TEST CATCH TONIGHT.
YOU'RE GOING TO BE RICH BY THE TIME YOU'RE TWENTY.
YOU LOOK GOOD IN GOLD, SON.
DAD--YOU LEFT THE BED WITH THAT FEVER?
YOU REALLY WANT ME TO CHOKE UP IN FRONT OF EVERYONE, DON'T YOU.
HERE--I'LL INTRODUCE YOU.
TOM. THIS WENT BY IN THE BLINK OF AN EYE, DIDN'T IT?
DR. SHIN--?! THANKS FOR COMING!
STEPHEN. AND WHO IS THIS?
THIS IS VERA, SHE WRITES FOR SCIENTIFIC AMERICAN.
IT'S THE BIG DAY, ARTHUR'S SCHOOLING IS COMPLETE...AND I'M READY TO MAKE PUBLIC THE RESEARCH I'VE DONE FOR MOST OF HIS LIFE.
SO...IT'S TRUE? I CAME OUT HERE ON DR. SHIN'S REPUTATION, BUT I ADMIT I WAS SKEPTICAL--IT'S MY JOB.
BUT THIS YOUNG MAN IS REALLY...AN ATLANTEAN?

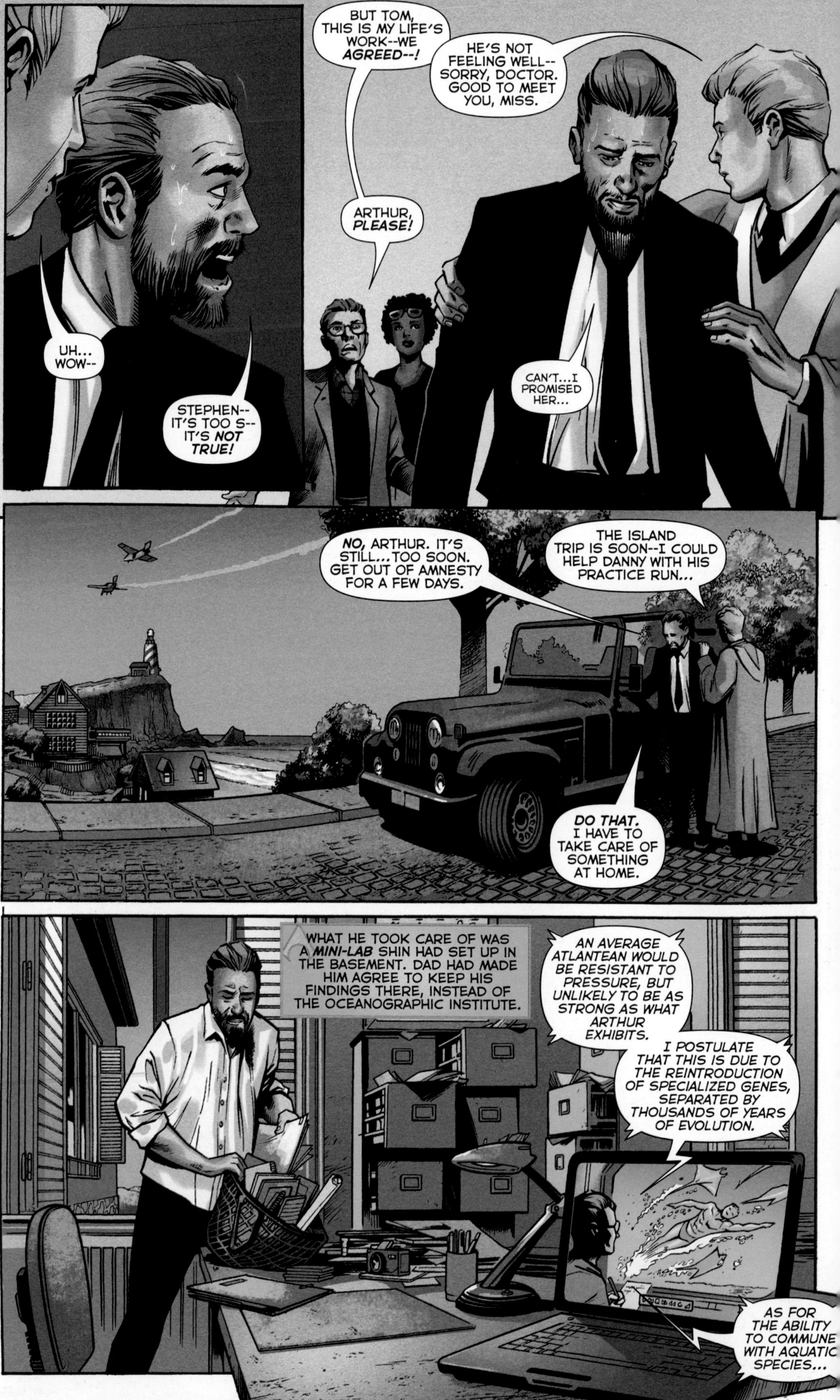

BUT TOM, THIS IS MY LIFE'S WORK--WE AGREED--!
HE'S NOT FEELING WELL--SORRY, DOCTOR. GOOD TO MEET YOU, MISS.
ARTHUR, PLEASE!
UH... WOW--
STEPHEN--IT'S TOO S--IT'S NOT TRUE!
CAN'T...I PROMISED HER...
NO, ARTHUR. IT'S STILL...TOO SOON. GET OUT OF AMNESTY FOR A FEW DAYS.
THE ISLAND TRIP IS SOON--I COULD HELP DANNY WITH HIS PRACTICE RUN...
DO THAT. I HAVE TO TAKE CARE OF SOMETHING AT HOME.
WHAT HE TOOK CARE OF WAS A MINI-LAB SHIN HAD SET UP IN THE BASEMENT. DAD HAD MADE HIM AGREE TO KEEP HIS FINDINGS THERE, INSTEAD OF THE OCEANOGRAPHIC INSTITUTE.
AN AVERAGE ATLANTEAN WOULD BE RESISTANT TO PRESSURE, BUT UNLIKELY TO BE AS STRONG AS WHAT ARTHUR EXHIBITS.
I POSTULATE THAT THIS IS DUE TO THE REINTRODUCTION OF SPECIALIZED GENES, SEPARATED BY THOUSANDS OF YEARS OF EVOLUTION.
AS FOR THE ABILITY TO COMMUNE WITH AQUATIC SPECIES...

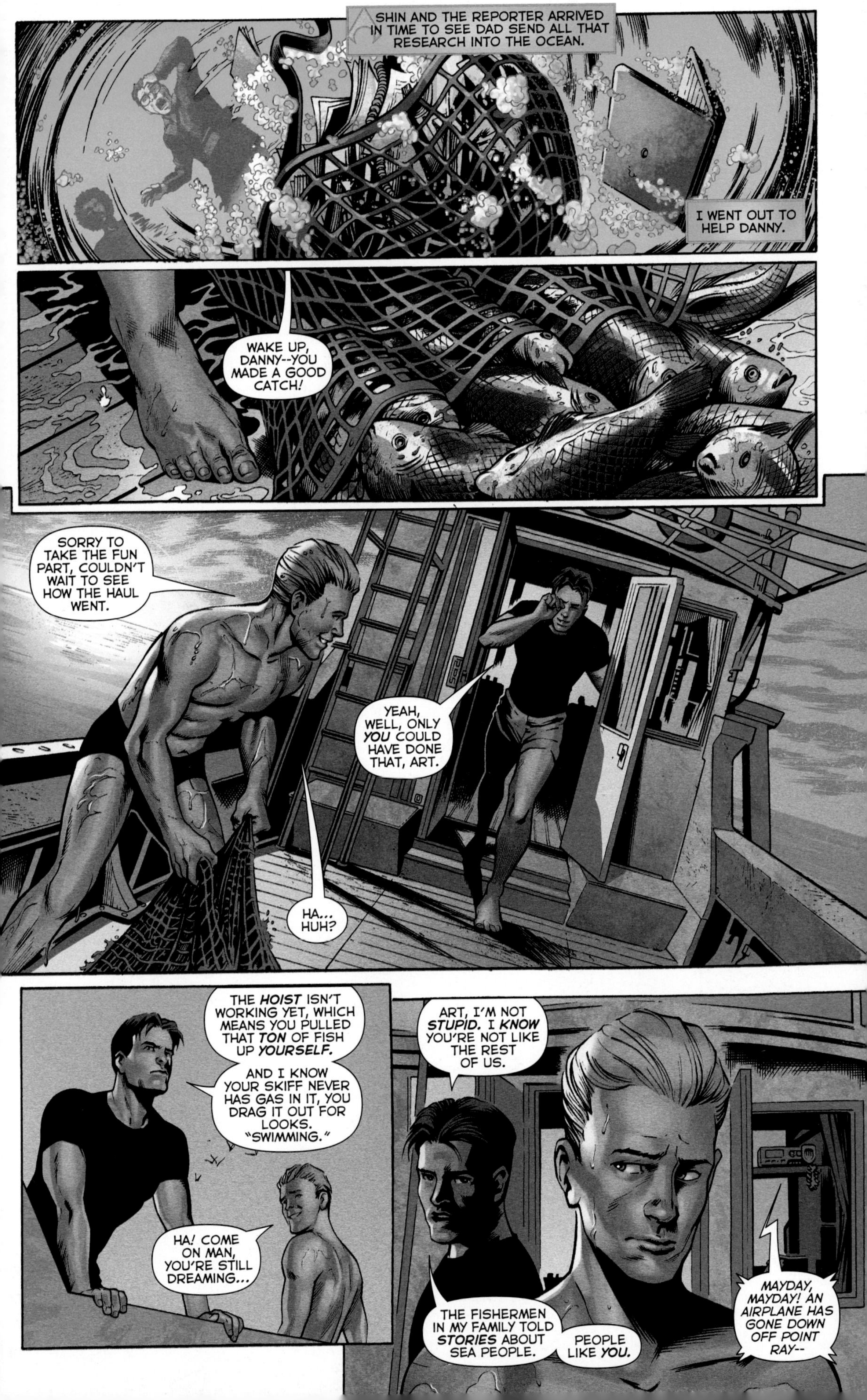
SHIN AND THE REPORTER ARRIVED IN TIME TO SEE DAD SEND ALL THAT RESEARCH INTO THE OCEAN.
I WENT OUT TO HELP DANNY.
WAKE UP, DANNY--YOU MADE A GOOD CATCH!
SORRY TO TAKE THE FUN PART, COULDN'T WAIT TO SEE HOW THE HAUL WENT.
YEAH, WELL, ONLY YOU COULD HAVE DONE THAT, ART.
HA... HUH?
THE HOIST ISN'T WORKING YET, WHICH MEANS YOU PULLED THAT TON OF FISH UP YOURSELF.
AND I KNOW YOUR SKIFF NEVER HAS GAS IN IT, YOU DRAG IT OUT FOR LOOKS. "SWIMMING."
HA! COME ON MAN, YOU'RE STILL DREAMING...
ART, I'M NOT STUPID. I KNOW YOU'RE NOT LIKE THE REST OF US.
THE FISHERMEN IN MY FAMILY TOLD STORIES ABOUT SEA PEOPLE.
PEOPLE LIKE YOU.
MAYDAY, MAYDAY! AN AIRPLANE HAS GONE DOWN OFF POINT RAY--

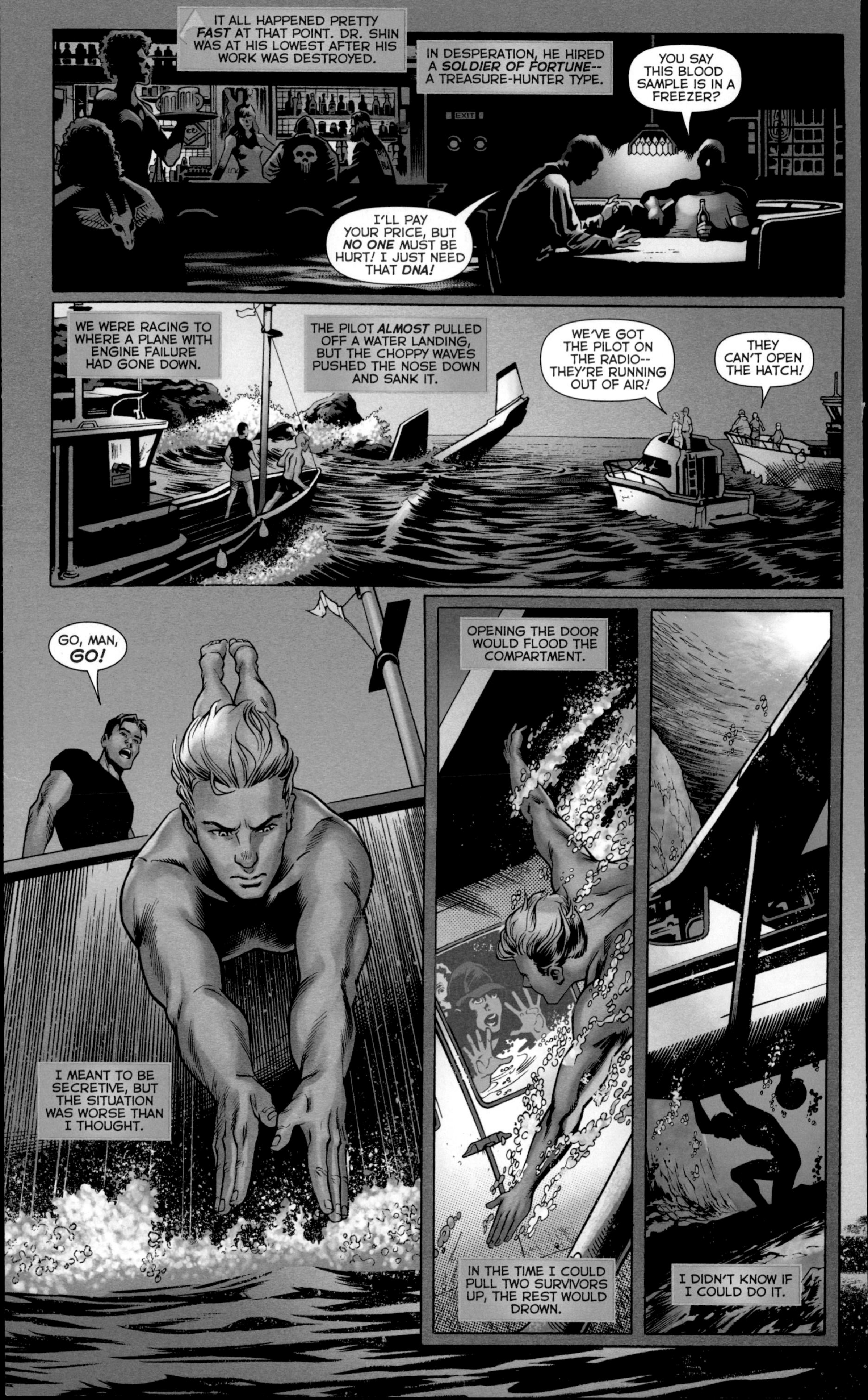

IT ALL HAPPENED PRETTY FAST AT THAT POINT. DR. SHIN WAS AT HIS LOWEST AFTER HIS WORK WAS DESTROYED.
IN DESPERATION, HE HIRED A SOLDIER OF FORTUNE-- A TREASURE-HUNTER TYPE.
YOU SAY THIS BLOOD SAMPLE IS IN A FREEZER?
I'LL PAY YOUR PRICE, BUT NO ONE MUST BE HURT! I JUST NEED THAT DNA!
EXIT
WE WERE RACING TO WHERE A PLANE WITH ENGINE FAILURE HAD GONE DOWN.
THE PILOT ALMOST PULLED OFF A WATER LANDING, BUT THE CHOPPY WAVES PUSHED THE NOSE DOWN AND SANK IT.
WE'VE GOT THE PILOT ON THE RADIO-- THEY'RE RUNNING OUT OF AIR!
THEY CAN'T OPEN THE HATCH!
GO, MAN, GO!
I MEANT TO BE SECRETIVE, BUT THE SITUATION WAS WORSE THAN I THOUGHT.
OPENING THE DOOR WOULD FLOOD THE COMPARTMENT.
IN THE TIME I COULD PULL TWO SURVIVORS UP, THE REST WOULD DROWN.
I DIDN'T KNOW IF I COULD DO IT.

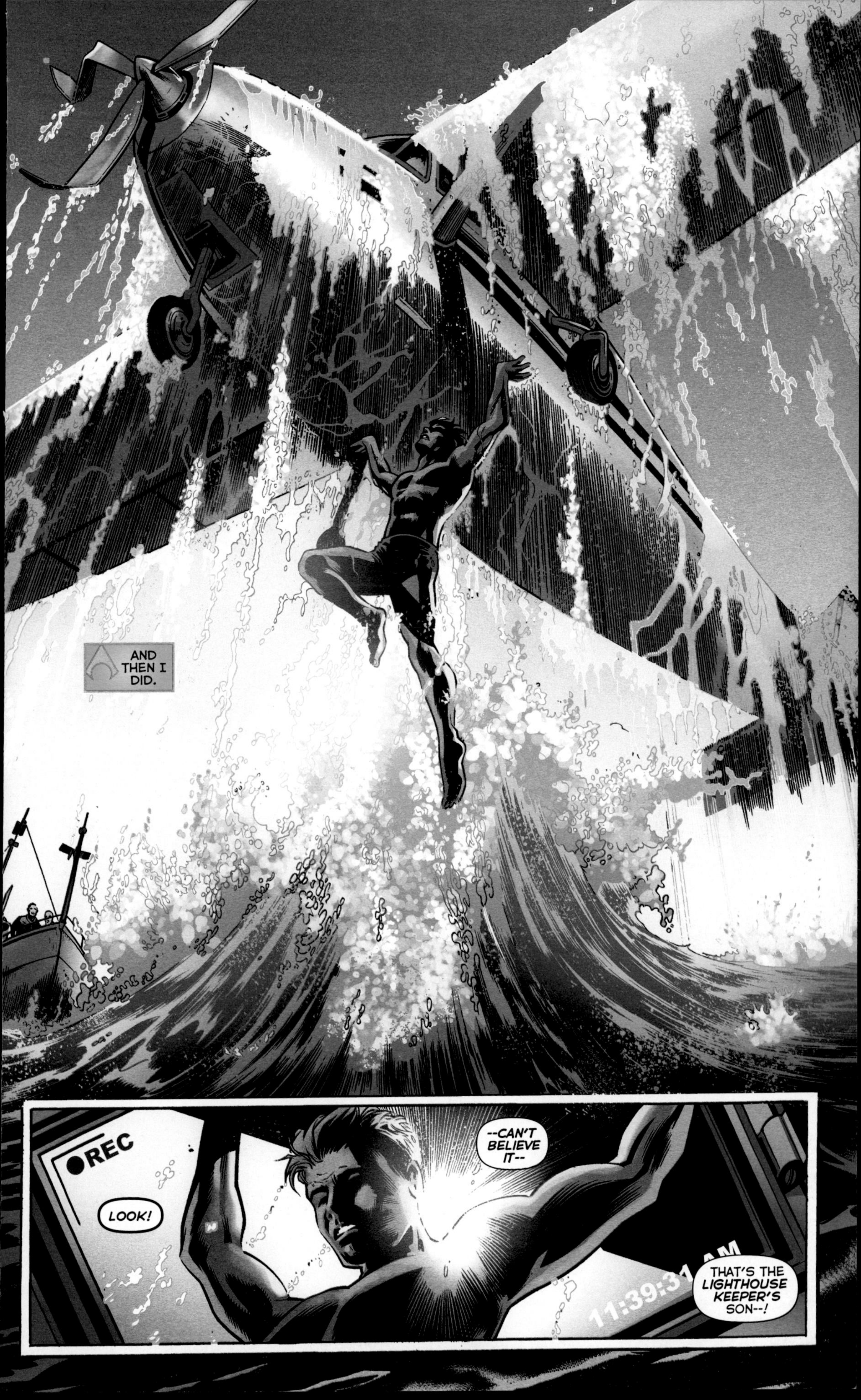
AND THEN I DID.
REC
--CAN'T BELIEVE IT--
LOOK!
11:39:31 AM
THAT'S THE LIGHTHOUSE KEEPER'S SON--!

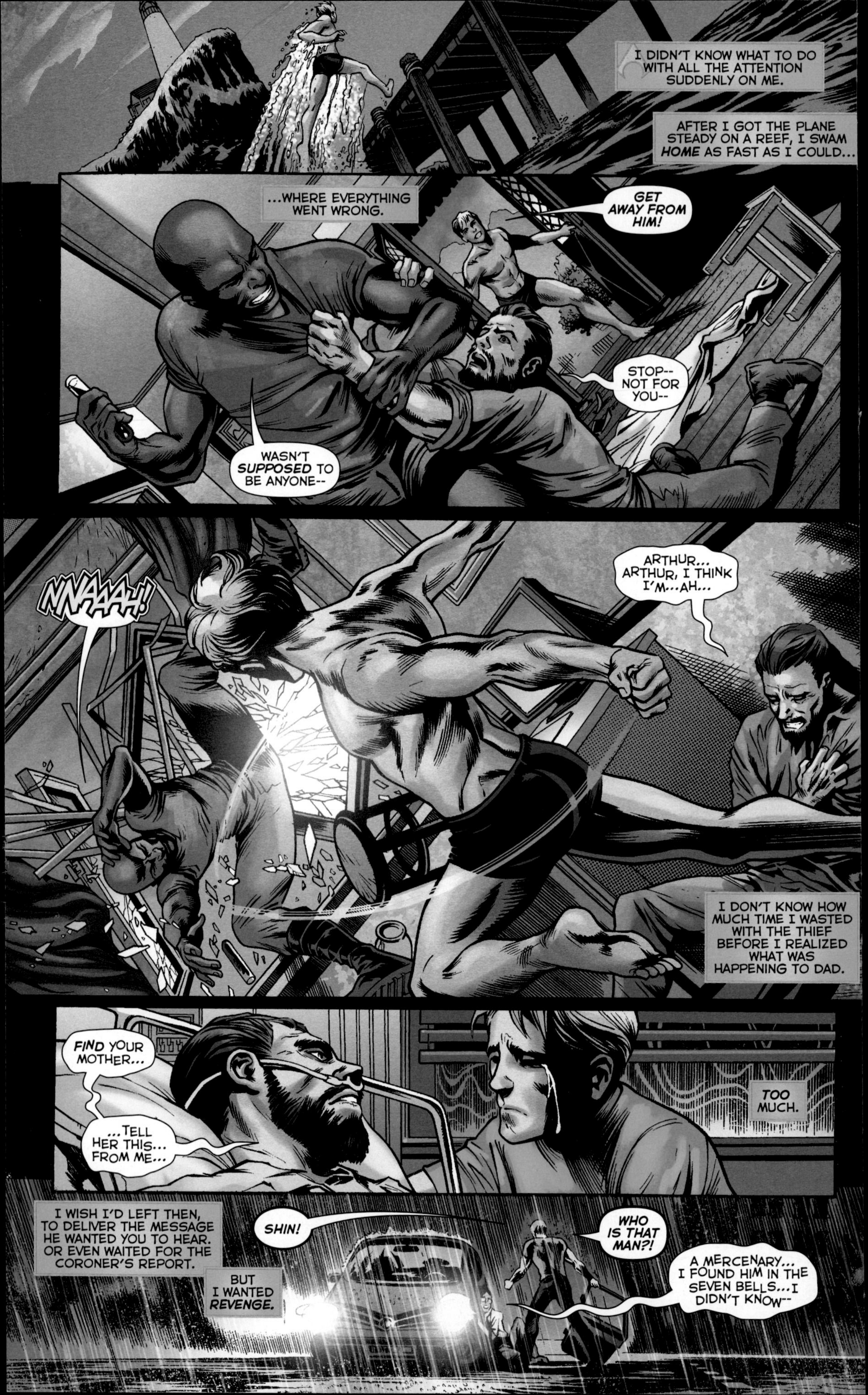
I DIDN'T KNOW WHAT TO DO WITH ALL THE ATTENTION SUDDENLY ON ME.
AFTER I GOT THE PLANE STEADY ON A REEF, I SWAM HOME AS FAST AS I COULD...
...WHERE EVERYTHING WENT WRONG.
GET AWAY FROM HIM!
STOP-- NOT FOR YOU--
WASN'T SUPPOSED TO BE ANYONE--
NNAAAH!
ARTHUR... ARTHUR, I THINK I'M...AH...
I DON'T KNOW HOW MUCH TIME I WASTED WITH THE THIEF BEFORE I REALIZED WHAT WAS HAPPENING TO DAD.
FIND YOUR MOTHER...
...TELL HER THIS... FROM ME...
TOO MUCH.
I WISH I'D LEFT THEN, TO DELIVER THE MESSAGE HE WANTED YOU TO HEAR. OR EVEN WAITED FOR THE CORONER'S REPORT.
BUT I WANTED REVENGE.
SHIN!
WHO IS THAT MAN?!
A MERCENARY... I FOUND HIM IN THE SEVEN BELLS...I DIDN'T KNOW--

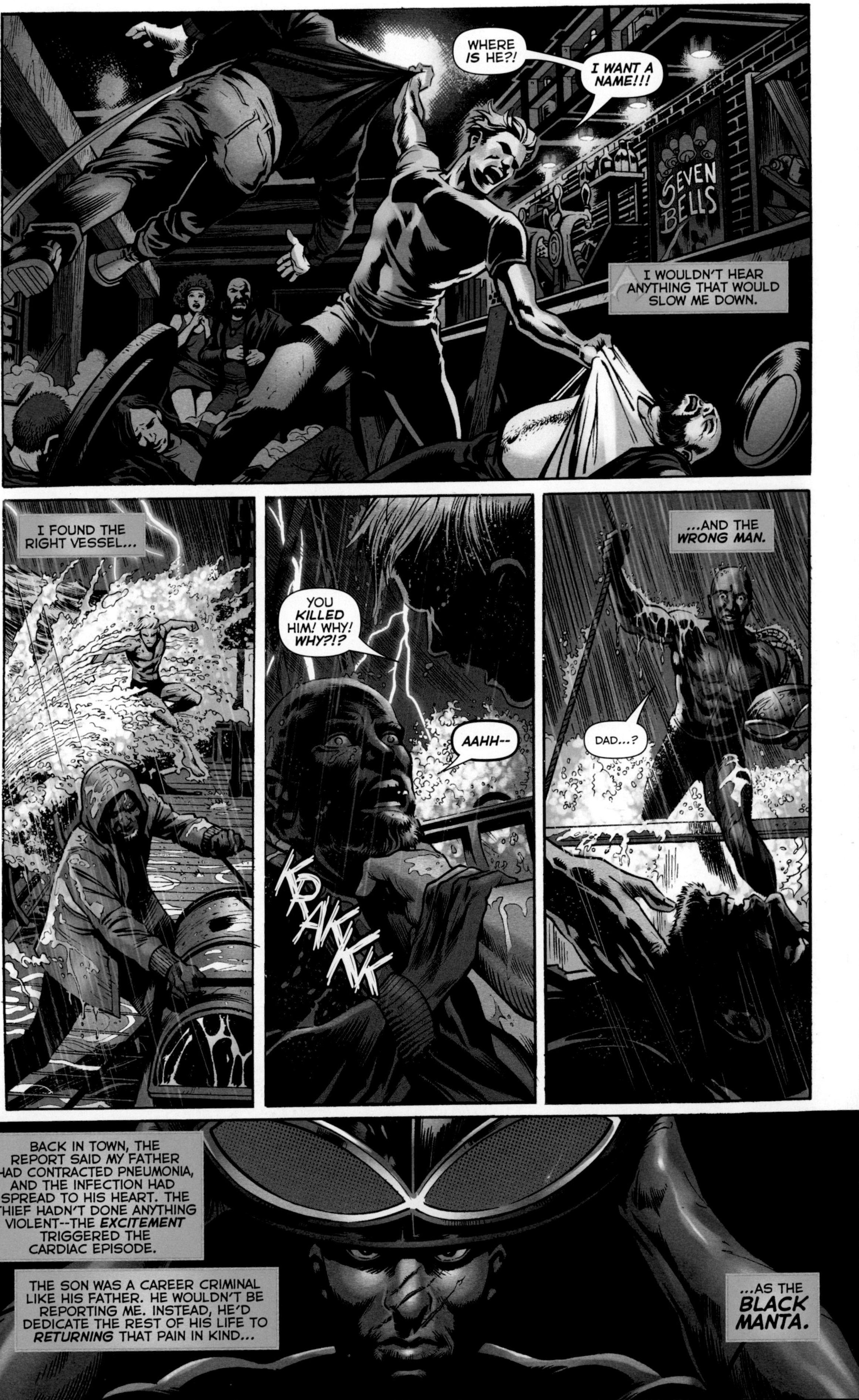
WHERE IS HE?!
I WANT A NAME!!!
SEVEN BELLS
I WOULDN'T HEAR ANYTHING THAT WOULD SLOW ME DOWN.
I FOUND THE RIGHT VESSEL...
YOU KILLED HIM! WHY! WHY?!?
AAHH--
...AND THE WRONG MAN.
DAD...?
BACK IN TOWN, THE REPORT SAID MY FATHER HAD CONTRACTED PNEUMONIA, AND THE INFECTION HAD SPREAD TO HIS HEART. THE THIEF HADN'T DONE ANYTHING VIOLENT--THE EXCITEMENT TRIGGERED THE CARDIAC EPISODE.
THE SON WAS A CAREER CRIMINAL LIKE HIS FATHER. HE WOULDN'T BE REPORTING ME. INSTEAD, HE'D DEDICATE THE REST OF HIS LIFE TO RETURNING THAT PAIN IN KIND...
...AS THE BLACK MANTA.

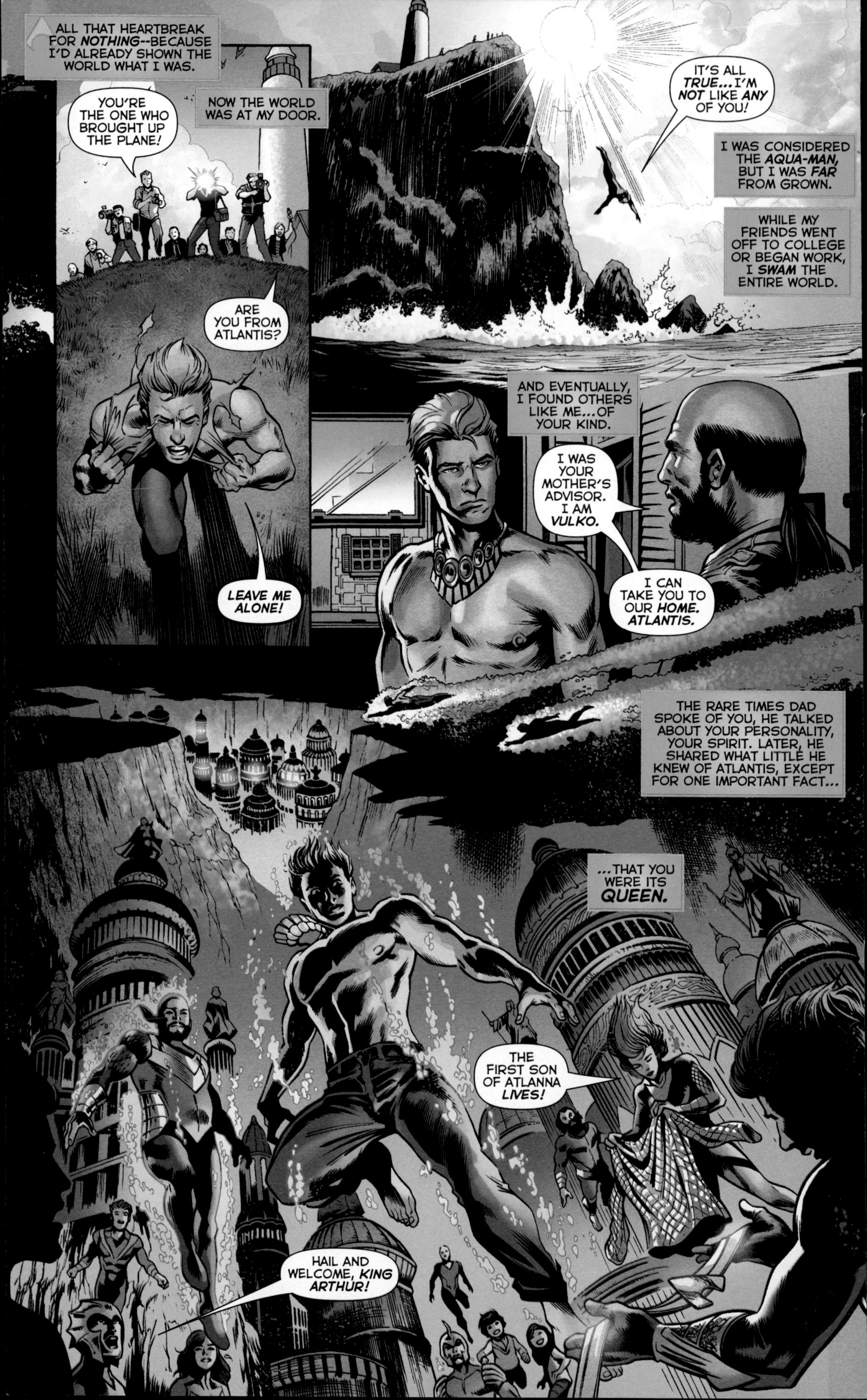
ALL THAT HEARTBREAK FOR NOTHING--BECAUSE I'D ALREADY SHOWN THE WORLD WHAT I WAS.
YOU'RE THE ONE WHO BROUGHT UP THE PLANE!
NOW THE WORLD WAS AT MY DOOR.
ARE YOU FROM ATLANTIS?
LEAVE ME ALONE!
IT'S ALL TRUE...I'M NOT LIKE ANY OF YOU!
I WAS CONSIDERED THE AQUA-MAN, BUT I WAS FAR FROM GROWN.
WHILE MY FRIENDS WENT OFF TO COLLEGE OR BEGAN WORK, I SWAM THE ENTIRE WORLD.
AND EVENTUALLY, I FOUND OTHERS LIKE ME...OF YOUR KIND.
I WAS YOUR MOTHER'S ADVISOR. I AM VULKO.
I CAN TAKE YOU TO OUR HOME. ATLANTIS.
THE RARE TIMES DAD SPOKE OF YOU, HE TALKED ABOUT YOUR PERSONALITY, YOUR SPIRIT. LATER, HE SHARED WHAT LITTLE HE KNEW OF ATLANTIS, EXCEPT FOR ONE IMPORTANT FACT...
...THAT YOU WERE ITS QUEEN.
THE FIRST SON OF ATLANNA LIVES!
HAIL AND WELCOME, KING ARTHUR!

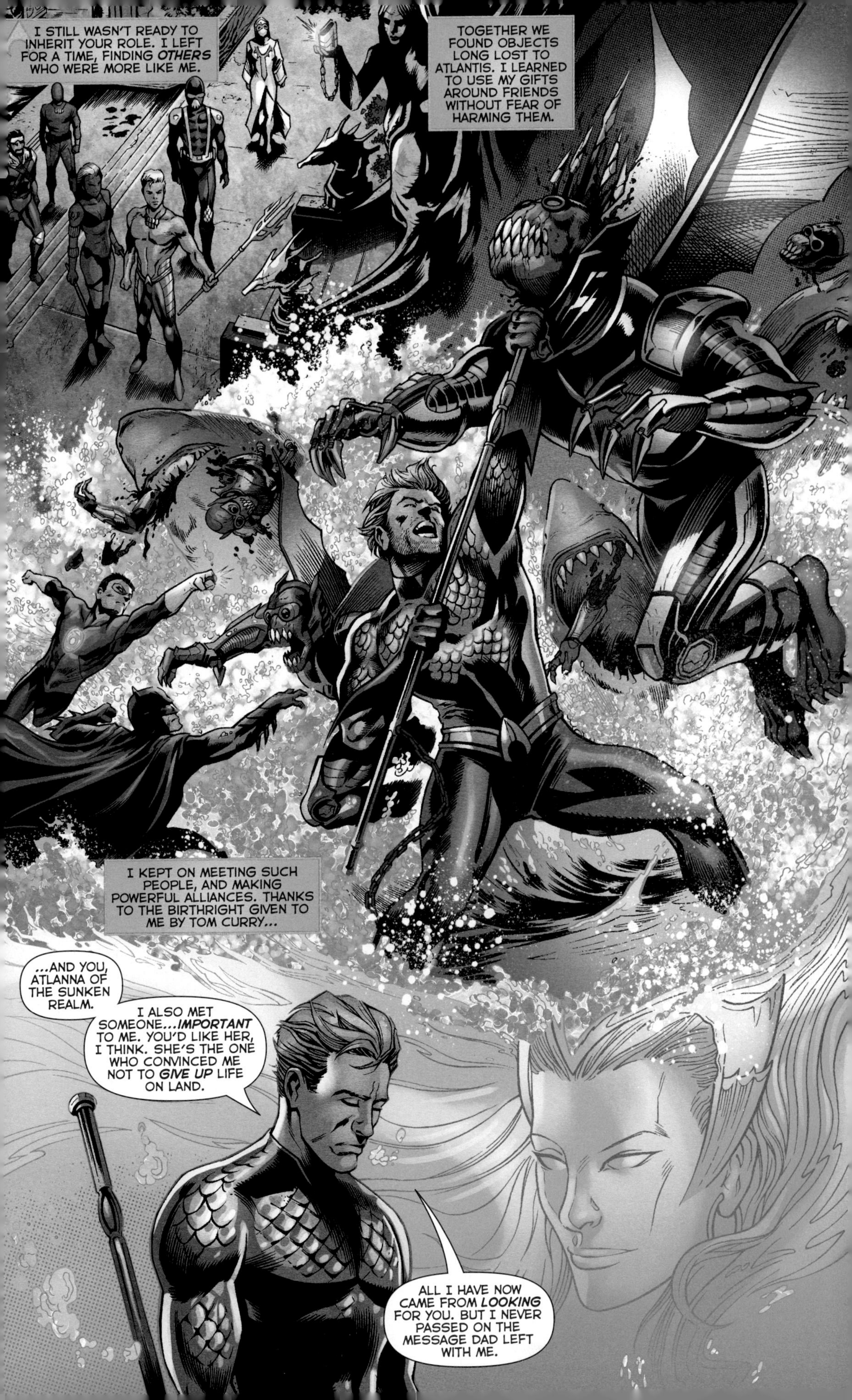
I STILL WASN'T READY TO INHERIT YOUR ROLE. I LEFT FOR A TIME, FINDING OTHERS WHO WERE MORE LIKE ME.
TOGETHER WE FOUND OBJECTS LONG LOST TO ATLANTIS. I LEARNED TO USE MY GIFTS AROUND FRIENDS WITHOUT FEAR OF HARMING THEM.
I KEPT ON MEETING SUCH PEOPLE, AND MAKING POWERFUL ALLIANCES. THANKS TO THE BIRTHRIGHT GIVEN TO ME BY TOM CURRY...
...AND YOU, ATLANNA OF THE SUNKEN REALM.
I ALSO MET SOMEONE...IMPORTANT TO ME. YOU'D LIKE HER, I THINK. SHE'S THE ONE WHO CONVINCED ME NOT TO GIVE UP LIFE ON LAND.
ALL I HAVE NOW CAME FROM LOOKING FOR YOU. BUT I NEVER PASSED ON THE MESSAGE DAD LEFT WITH ME.

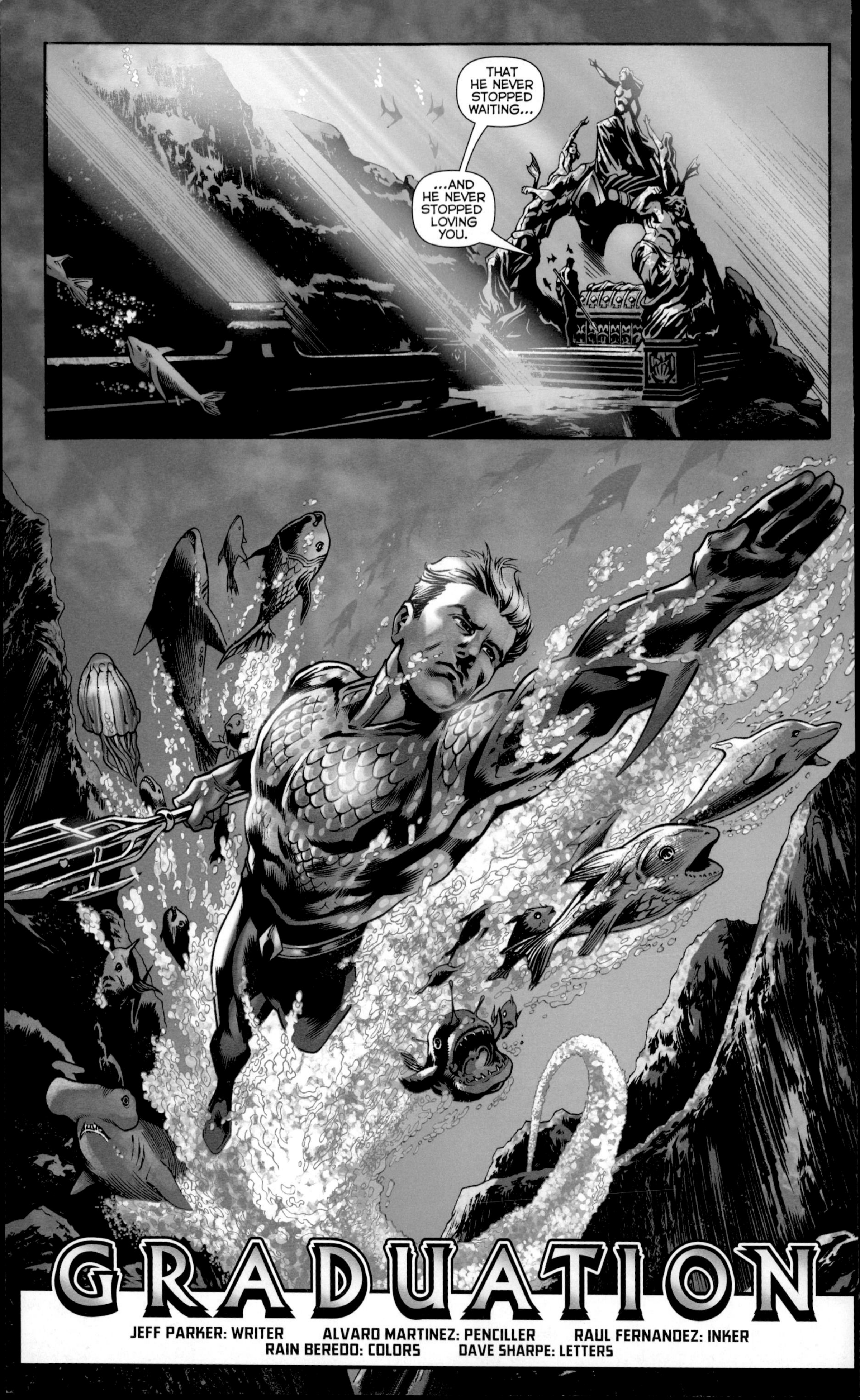
THAT HE NEVER STOPPED WAITING...
...AND HE NEVER STOPPED LOVING YOU.
GRADUATION
JEFF PARKER: WRITER
ALVARO MARTINEZ: PENCILLER
RAUL FERNANDEZ: INKER
RAIN BEREDO: COLORS
DAVE SHARPE: LETTERS

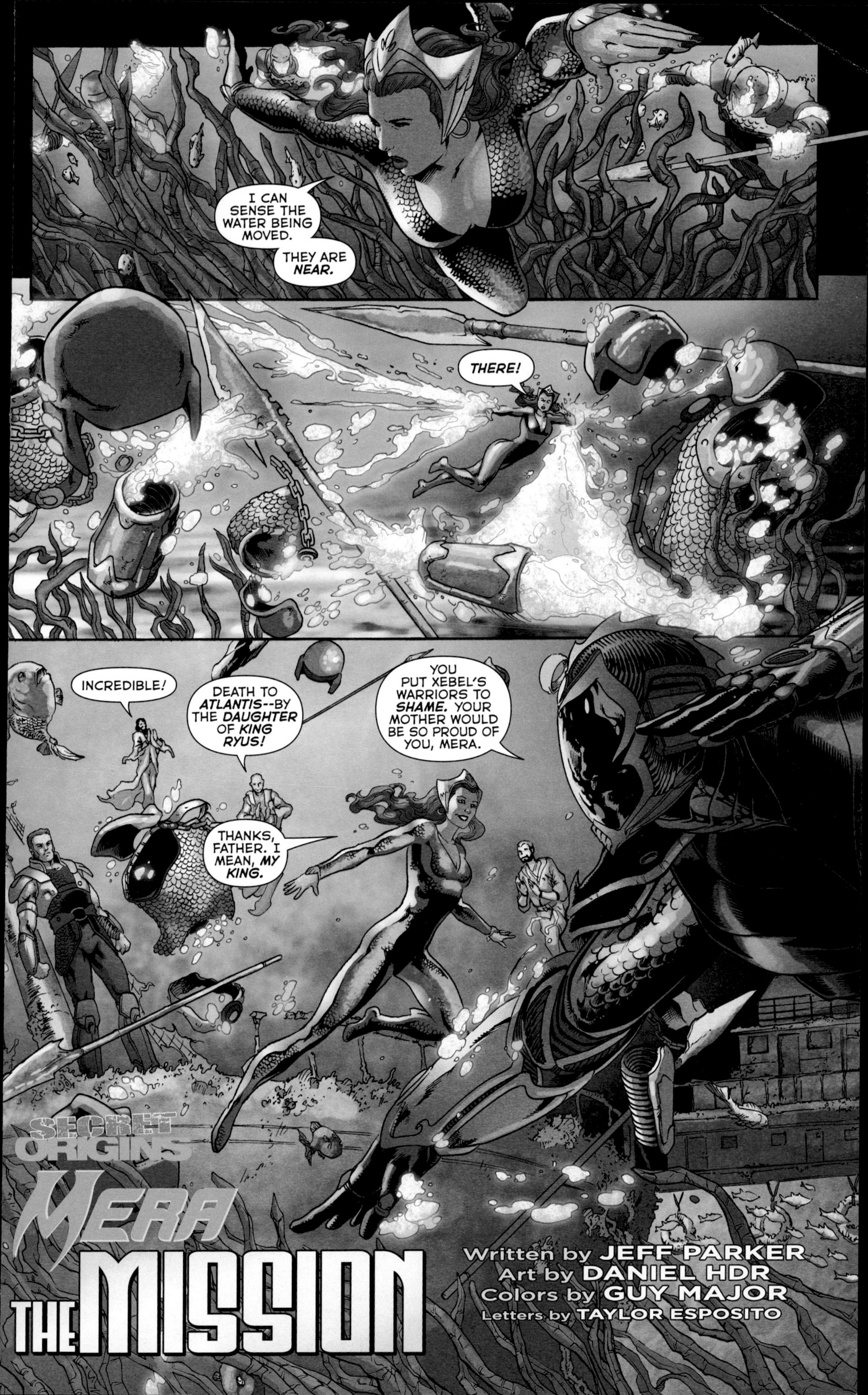
I CAN SENSE THE WATER BEING MOVED.
THEY ARE *NEAR.*
THERE!
INCREDIBLE!
DEATH TO *ATLANTIS*--BY THE *DAUGHTER* OF *KING RYUS!*
YOU PUT XEBEL'S WARRIORS TO *SHAME.* YOUR MOTHER WOULD BE SO PROUD OF YOU, MERA.
THANKS, FATHER. I MEAN, *MY KING.*
SECRET ORIGINS
MERA
THE MISSION
Written by JEFF PARKER
Art by DANIEL HDR
Colors by GUY MAJOR
Letters by TAYLOR ESPOSITO

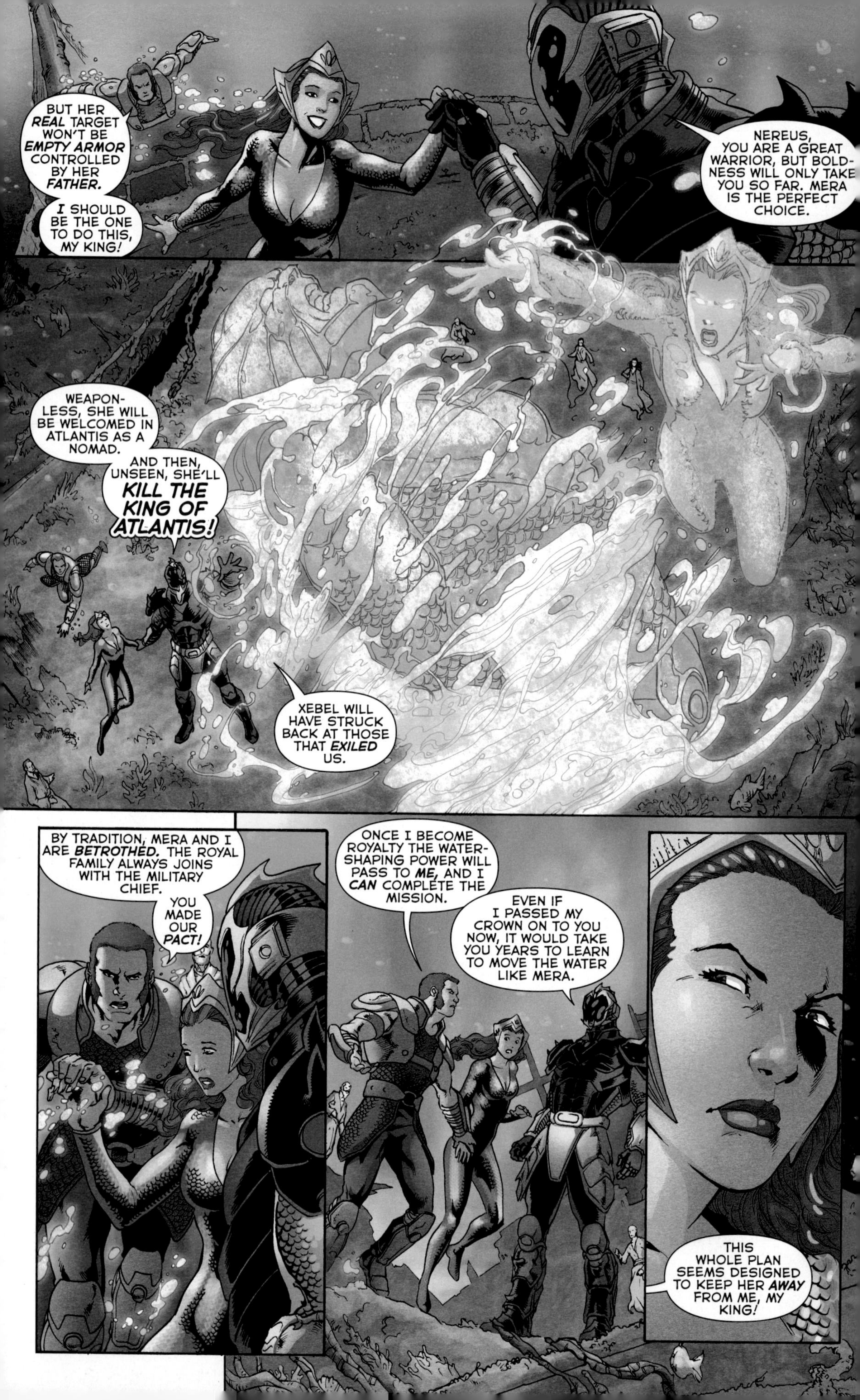

BUT HER REAL TARGET WON'T BE EMPTY ARMOR CONTROLLED BY HER FATHER.
I SHOULD BE THE ONE TO DO THIS, MY KING!
NEREUS, YOU ARE A GREAT WARRIOR, BUT BOLDNESS WILL ONLY TAKE YOU SO FAR. MERA IS THE PERFECT CHOICE.
WEAPONLESS, SHE WILL BE WELCOMED IN ATLANTIS AS A NOMAD.
AND THEN, UNSEEN, SHE'LL KILL THE KING OF ATLANTIS!
XEBEL WILL HAVE STRUCK BACK AT THOSE THAT EXILED US.
BY TRADITION, MERA AND I ARE BETROTHED. THE ROYAL FAMILY ALWAYS JOINS WITH THE MILITARY CHIEF.
YOU MADE OUR PACT!
ONCE I BECOME ROYALTY THE WATER-SHAPING POWER WILL PASS TO ME, AND I CAN COMPLETE THE MISSION.
EVEN IF I PASSED MY CROWN ON TO YOU NOW, IT WOULD TAKE YOU YEARS TO LEARN TO MOVE THE WATER LIKE MERA.
THIS WHOLE PLAN SEEMS DESIGNED TO KEEP HER AWAY FROM ME, MY KING!

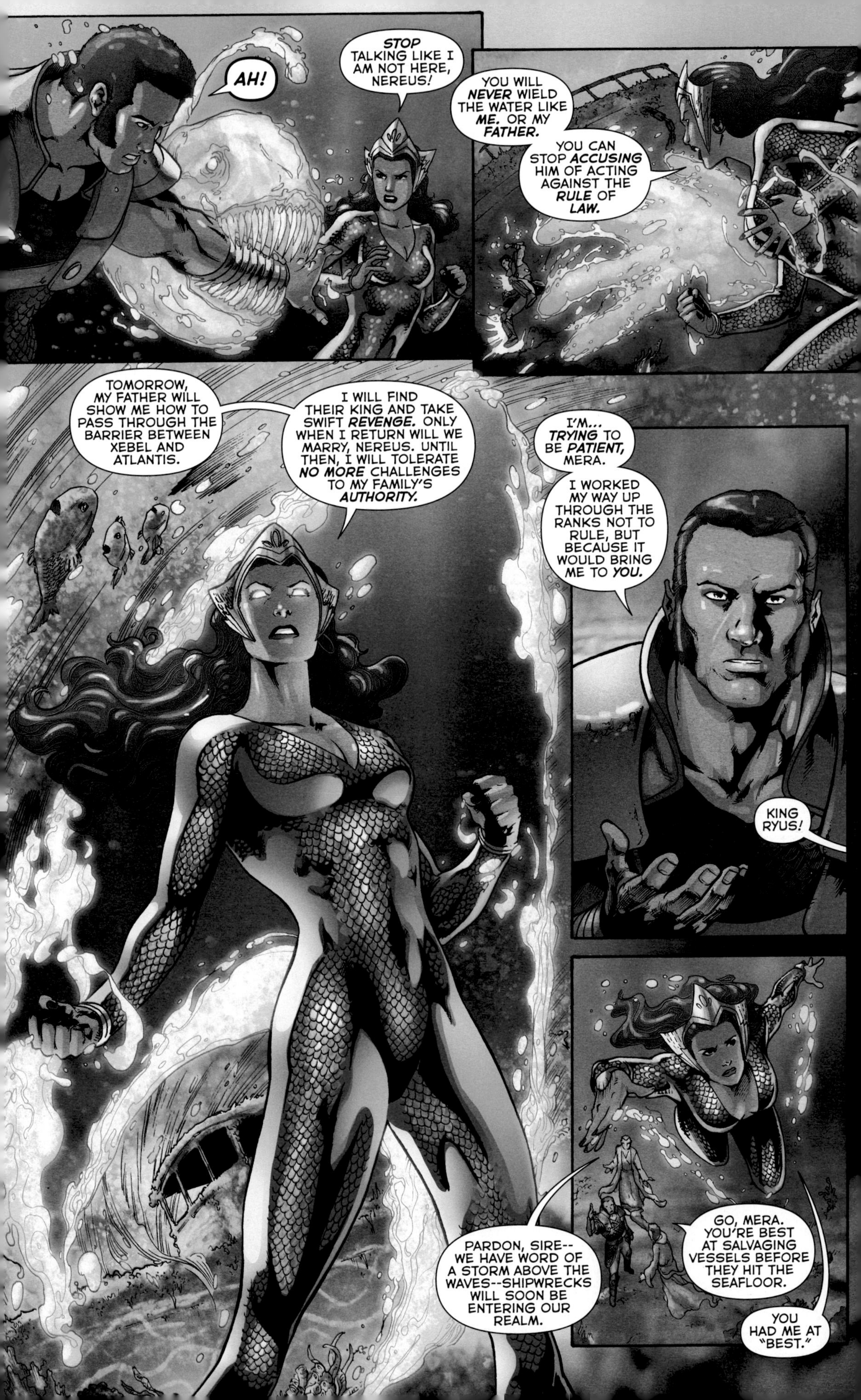
AH!
STOP TALKING LIKE I AM NOT HERE, NEREUS!
YOU WILL NEVER WIELD THE WATER LIKE ME. OR MY FATHER.
YOU CAN STOP ACCUSING HIM OF ACTING AGAINST THE RULE OF LAW.
TOMORROW, MY FATHER WILL SHOW ME HOW TO PASS THROUGH THE BARRIER BETWEEN XEBEL AND ATLANTIS.
I WILL FIND THEIR KING AND TAKE SWIFT REVENGE. ONLY WHEN I RETURN WILL WE MARRY, NEREUS. UNTIL THEN, I WILL TOLERATE NO MORE CHALLENGES TO MY FAMILY'S AUTHORITY.
I'M... TRYING TO BE PATIENT, MERA.
I WORKED MY WAY UP THROUGH THE RANKS NOT TO RULE, BUT BECAUSE IT WOULD BRING ME TO YOU.
KING RYUS!
PARDON, SIRE-- WE HAVE WORD OF A STORM ABOVE THE WAVES--SHIPWRECKS WILL SOON BE ENTERING OUR REALM.
GO, MERA. YOU'RE BEST AT SALVAGING VESSELS BEFORE THEY HIT THE SEAFLOOR.
YOU HAD ME AT "BEST."

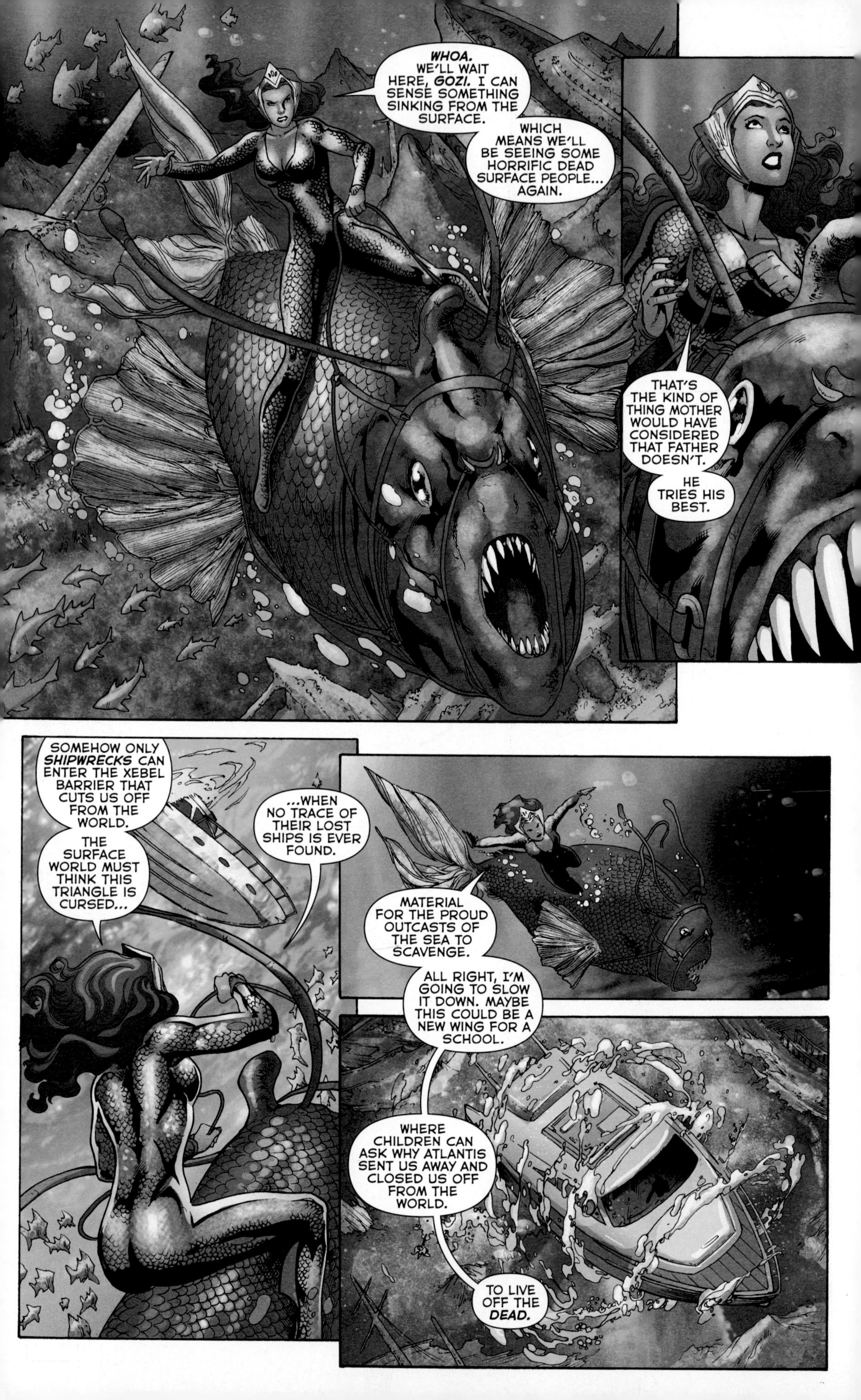
WHOA. WE'LL WAIT HERE, GOZI. I CAN SENSE SOMETHING SINKING FROM THE SURFACE.
WHICH MEANS WE'LL BE SEEING SOME HORRIFIC DEAD SURFACE PEOPLE... AGAIN.
THAT'S THE KIND OF THING MOTHER WOULD HAVE CONSIDERED THAT FATHER DOESN'T.
HE TRIES HIS BEST.
SOMEHOW ONLY SHIPWRECKS CAN ENTER THE XEBEL BARRIER THAT CUTS US OFF FROM THE WORLD.
THE SURFACE WORLD MUST THINK THIS TRIANGLE IS CURSED...
...WHEN NO TRACE OF THEIR LOST SHIPS IS EVER FOUND.
MATERIAL FOR THE PROUD OUTCASTS OF THE SEA TO SCAVENGE.
ALL RIGHT, I'M GOING TO SLOW IT DOWN. MAYBE THIS COULD BE A NEW WING FOR A SCHOOL.
WHERE CHILDREN CAN ASK WHY ATLANTIS SENT US AWAY AND CLOSED US OFF FROM THE WORLD.
TO LIVE OFF THE DEAD.

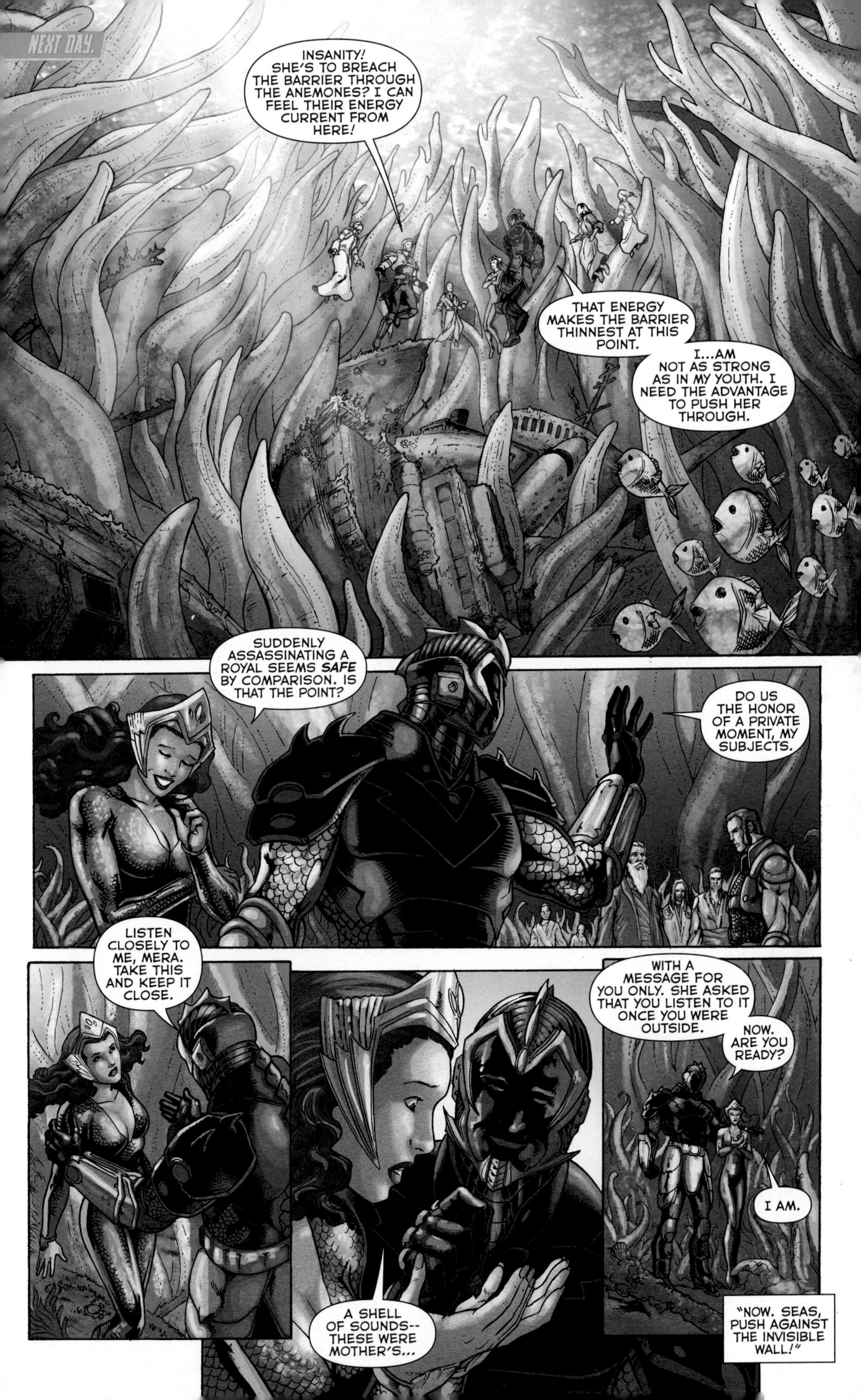
NEXT DAY.
INSANITY! SHE'S TO BREACH THE BARRIER THROUGH THE ANEMONES? I CAN FEEL THEIR ENERGY CURRENT FROM HERE!
THAT ENERGY MAKES THE BARRIER THINNEST AT THIS POINT.
I...AM NOT AS STRONG AS IN MY YOUTH. I NEED THE ADVANTAGE TO PUSH HER THROUGH.
SUDDENLY ASSASSINATING A ROYAL SEEMS *SAFE* BY COMPARISON. IS THAT THE POINT?
DO US THE HONOR OF A PRIVATE MOMENT, MY SUBJECTS.
LISTEN CLOSELY TO ME, MERA. TAKE THIS AND KEEP IT CLOSE.
A SHELL OF SOUNDS-- THESE WERE MOTHER'S...
WITH A MESSAGE FOR YOU ONLY. SHE ASKED THAT YOU LISTEN TO IT ONCE YOU WERE OUTSIDE.
NOW. ARE YOU READY?
I AM.
"NOW. SEAS, PUSH AGAINST THE INVISIBLE WALL!"

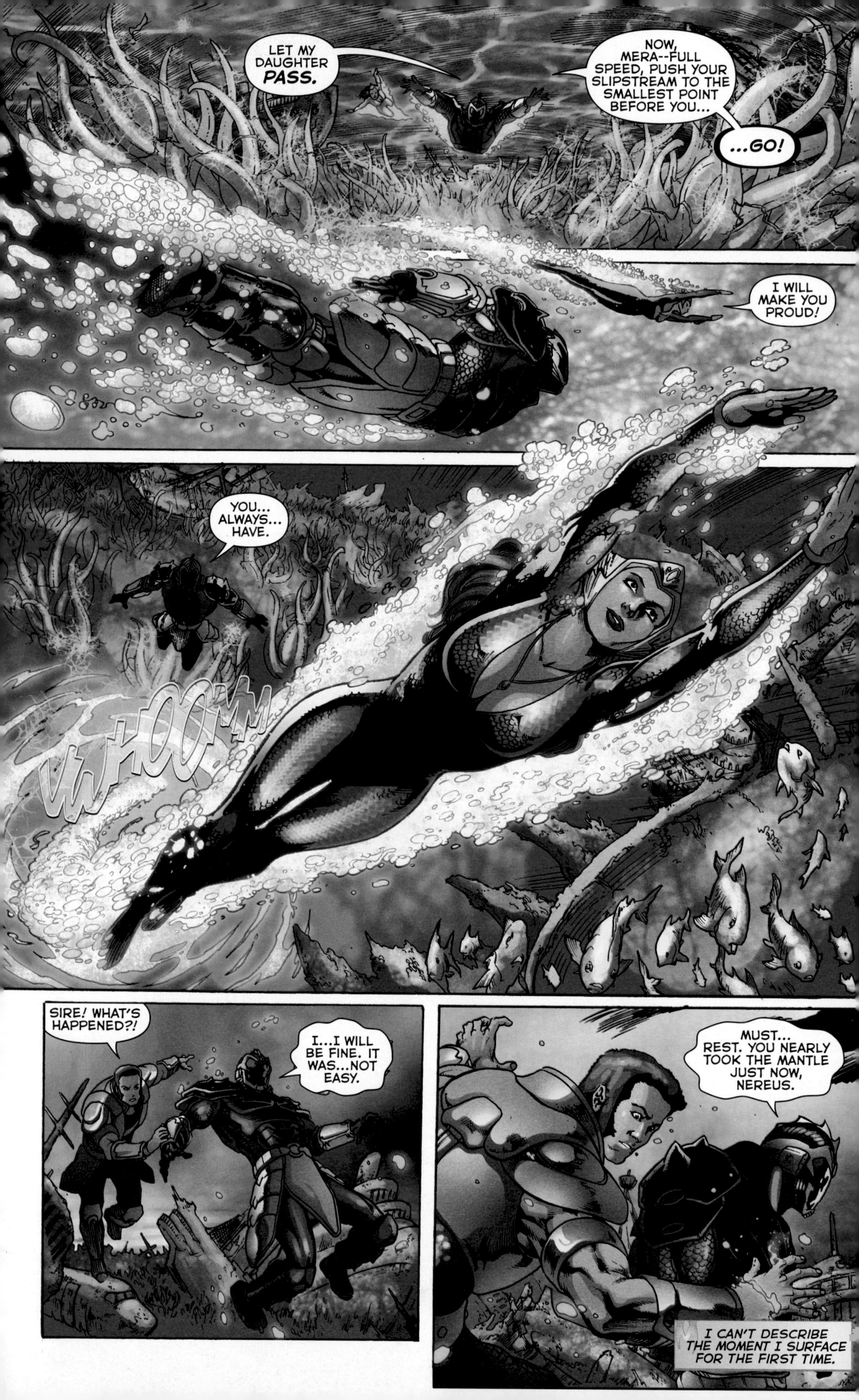
LET MY DAUGHTER PASS.
NOW, MERA--FULL SPEED, PUSH YOUR SLIPSTREAM TO THE SMALLEST POINT BEFORE YOU...
...GO!
I WILL MAKE YOU PROUD!
YOU... ALWAYS... HAVE.
WHOOM
SIRE! WHAT'S HAPPENED?!
I...I WILL BE FINE. IT WAS...NOT EASY.
MUST... REST. YOU NEARLY TOOK THE MANTLE JUST NOW, NEREUS.
I CAN'T DESCRIBE THE MOMENT I SURFACE FOR THE FIRST TIME.

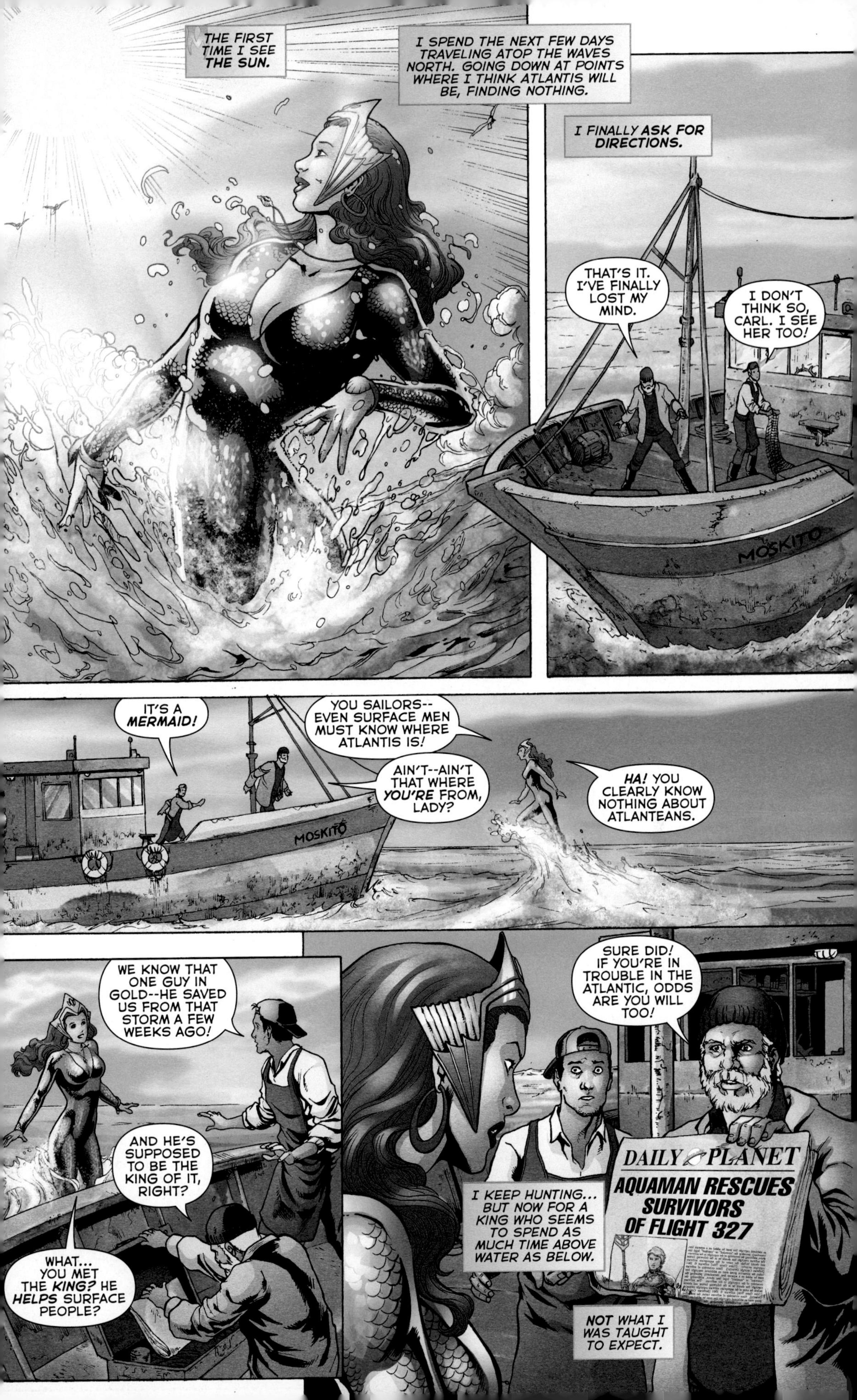

THE FIRST TIME I SEE THE SUN.
I SPEND THE NEXT FEW DAYS TRAVELING ATOP THE WAVES NORTH. GOING DOWN AT POINTS WHERE I THINK ATLANTIS WILL BE, FINDING NOTHING.
I FINALLY ASK FOR DIRECTIONS.
THAT'S IT. I'VE FINALLY LOST MY MIND.
I DON'T THINK SO, CARL. I SEE HER TOO!
MOSKITO
IT'S A MERMAID!
YOU SAILORS-- EVEN SURFACE MEN MUST KNOW WHERE ATLANTIS IS!
AIN'T--AIN'T THAT WHERE YOU'RE FROM, LADY?
HA! YOU CLEARLY KNOW NOTHING ABOUT ATLANTEANS.
MOSKITO
WE KNOW THAT ONE GUY IN GOLD--HE SAVED US FROM THAT STORM A FEW WEEKS AGO!
AND HE'S SUPPOSED TO BE THE KING OF IT, RIGHT?
WHAT... YOU MET THE KING? HE HELPS SURFACE PEOPLE?
SURE DID! IF YOU'RE IN TROUBLE IN THE ATLANTIC, ODDS ARE YOU WILL TOO!
DAILY PLANET
AQUAMAN RESCUES SURVIVORS OF FLIGHT 327
I KEEP HUNTING... BUT NOW FOR A KING WHO SEEMS TO SPEND AS MUCH TIME ABOVE WATER AS BELOW.
NOT WHAT I WAS TAUGHT TO EXPECT.

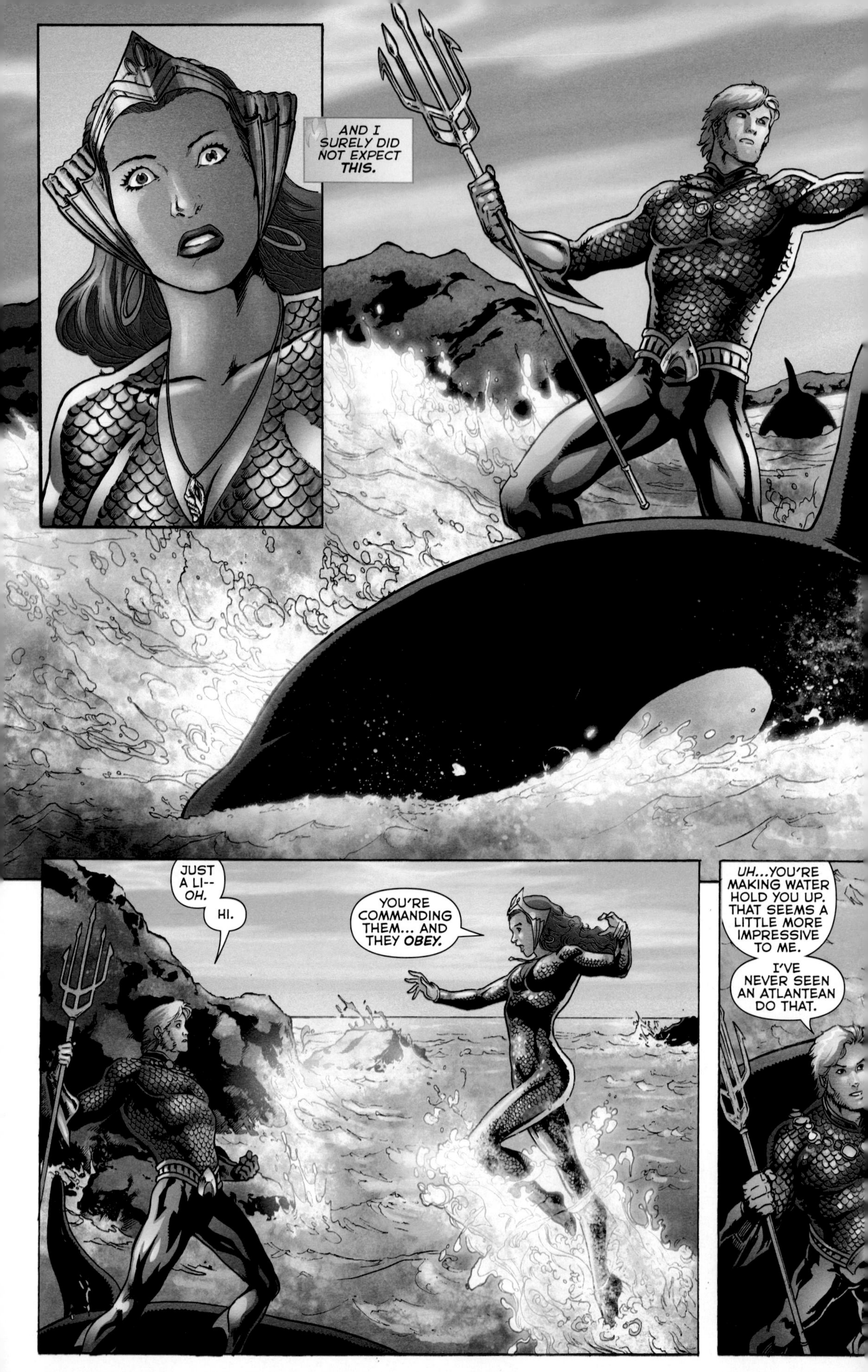
AND I SURELY DID NOT EXPECT *THIS.*
JUST A LI-- *OH.*
HI.
YOU'RE COMMANDING THEM... AND THEY *OBEY.*
*UH...*YOU'RE MAKING WATER HOLD YOU UP. THAT SEEMS A LITTLE MORE IMPRESSIVE TO ME.
I'VE NEVER SEEN AN ATLANTEAN DO THAT.

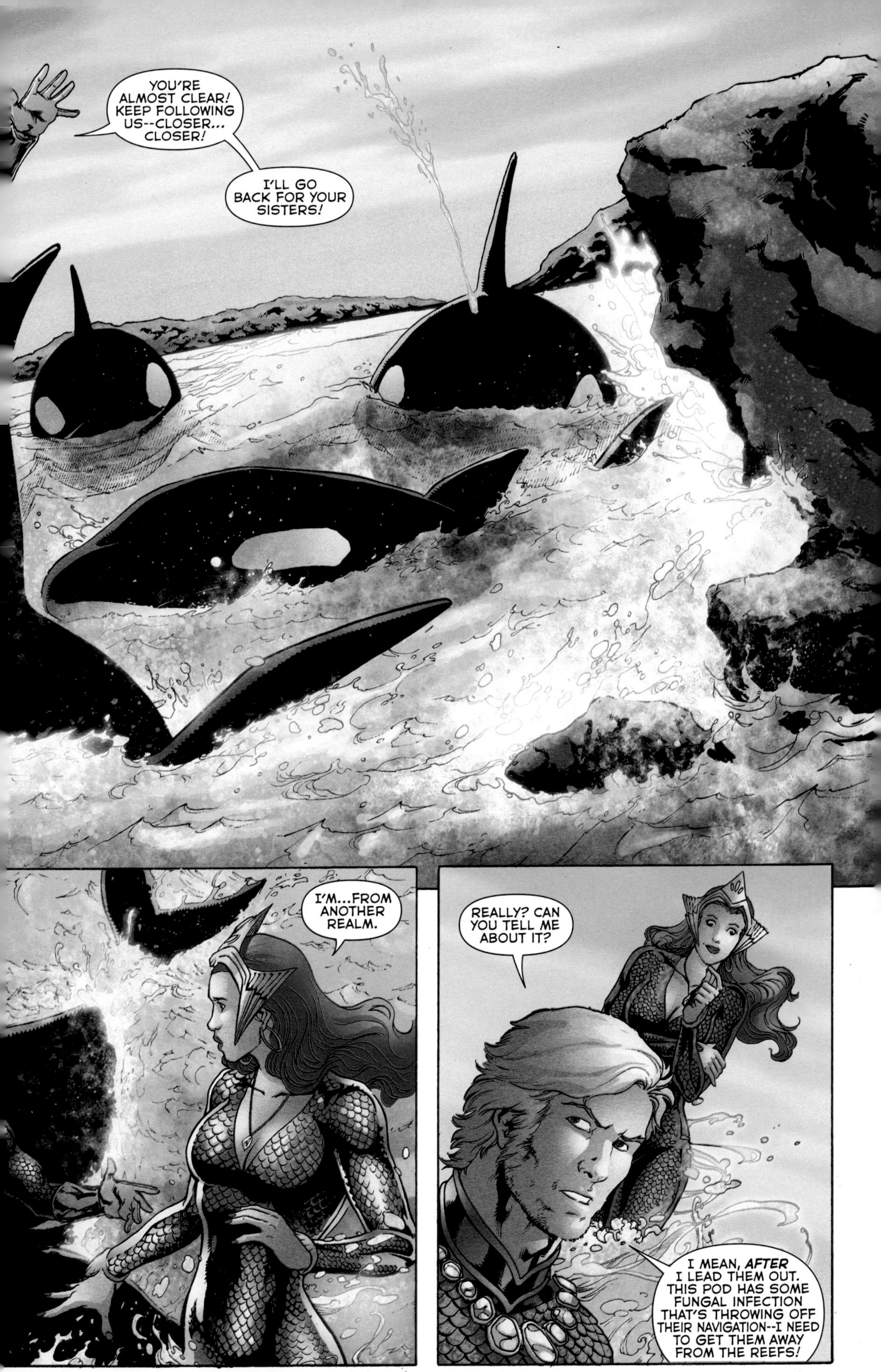
YOU'RE ALMOST CLEAR! KEEP FOLLOWING US--CLOSER... CLOSER!
I'LL GO BACK FOR YOUR SISTERS!
I'M...FROM ANOTHER REALM.
REALLY? CAN YOU TELL ME ABOUT IT?
I MEAN, AFTER I LEAD THEM OUT. THIS POD HAS SOME FUNGAL INFECTION THAT'S THROWING OFF THEIR NAVIGATION--I NEED TO GET THEM AWAY FROM THE REEFS!

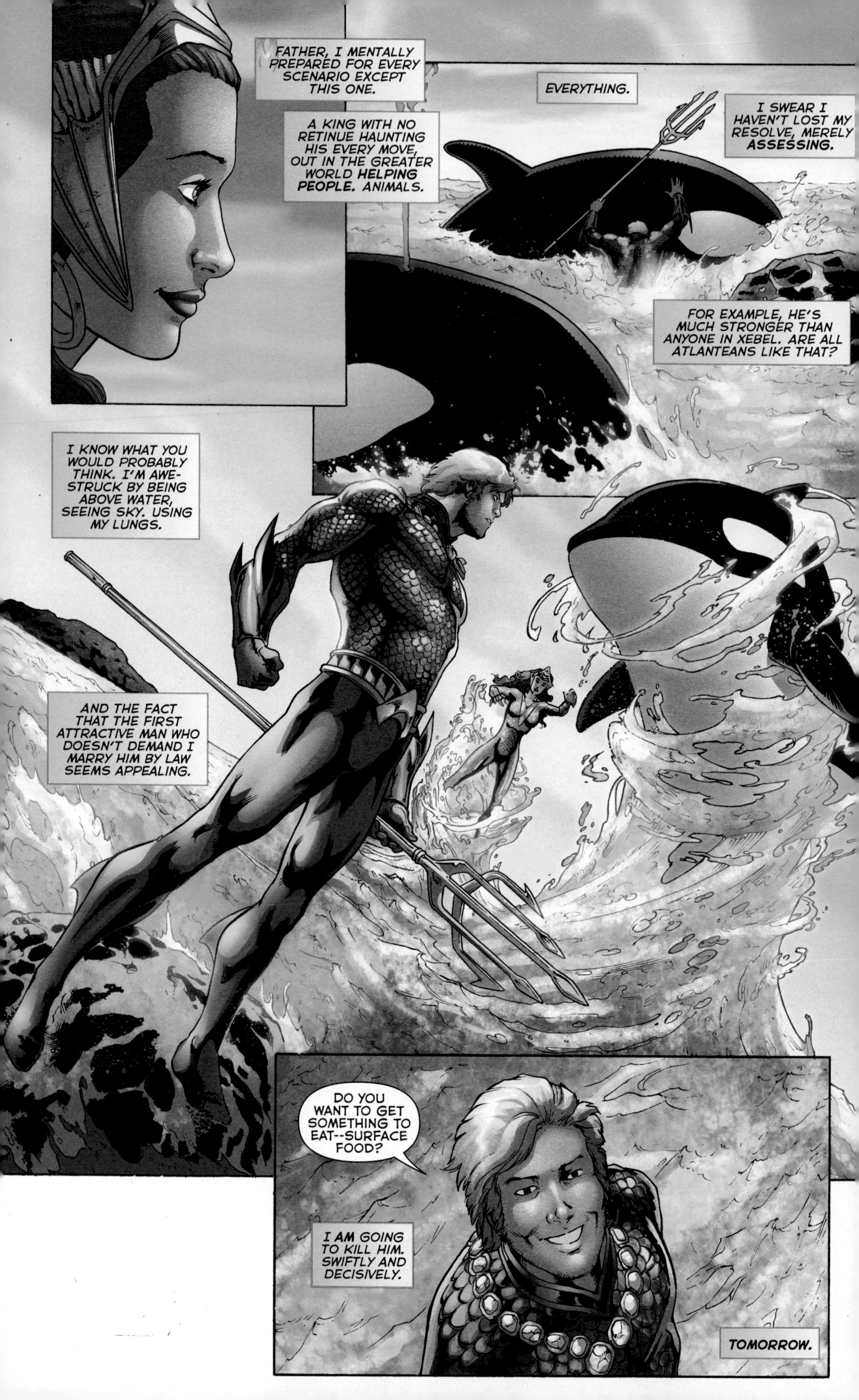

FATHER, I MENTALLY PREPARED FOR EVERY SCENARIO EXCEPT THIS ONE.
A KING WITH NO RETINUE HAUNTING HIS EVERY MOVE, OUT IN THE GREATER WORLD HELPING PEOPLE. ANIMALS.
EVERYTHING.
I SWEAR I HAVEN'T LOST MY RESOLVE, MERELY ASSESSING.
FOR EXAMPLE, HE'S MUCH STRONGER THAN ANYONE IN XEBEL. ARE ALL ATLANTEANS LIKE THAT?
I KNOW WHAT YOU WOULD PROBABLY THINK. I'M AWE-STRUCK BY BEING ABOVE WATER, SEEING SKY. USING MY LUNGS.
AND THE FACT THAT THE FIRST ATTRACTIVE MAN WHO DOESN'T DEMAND I MARRY HIM BY LAW SEEMS APPEALING.
DO YOU WANT TO GET SOMETHING TO EAT--SURFACE FOOD?
I AM GOING TO KILL HIM. SWIFTLY AND DECISIVELY.
TOMORROW.

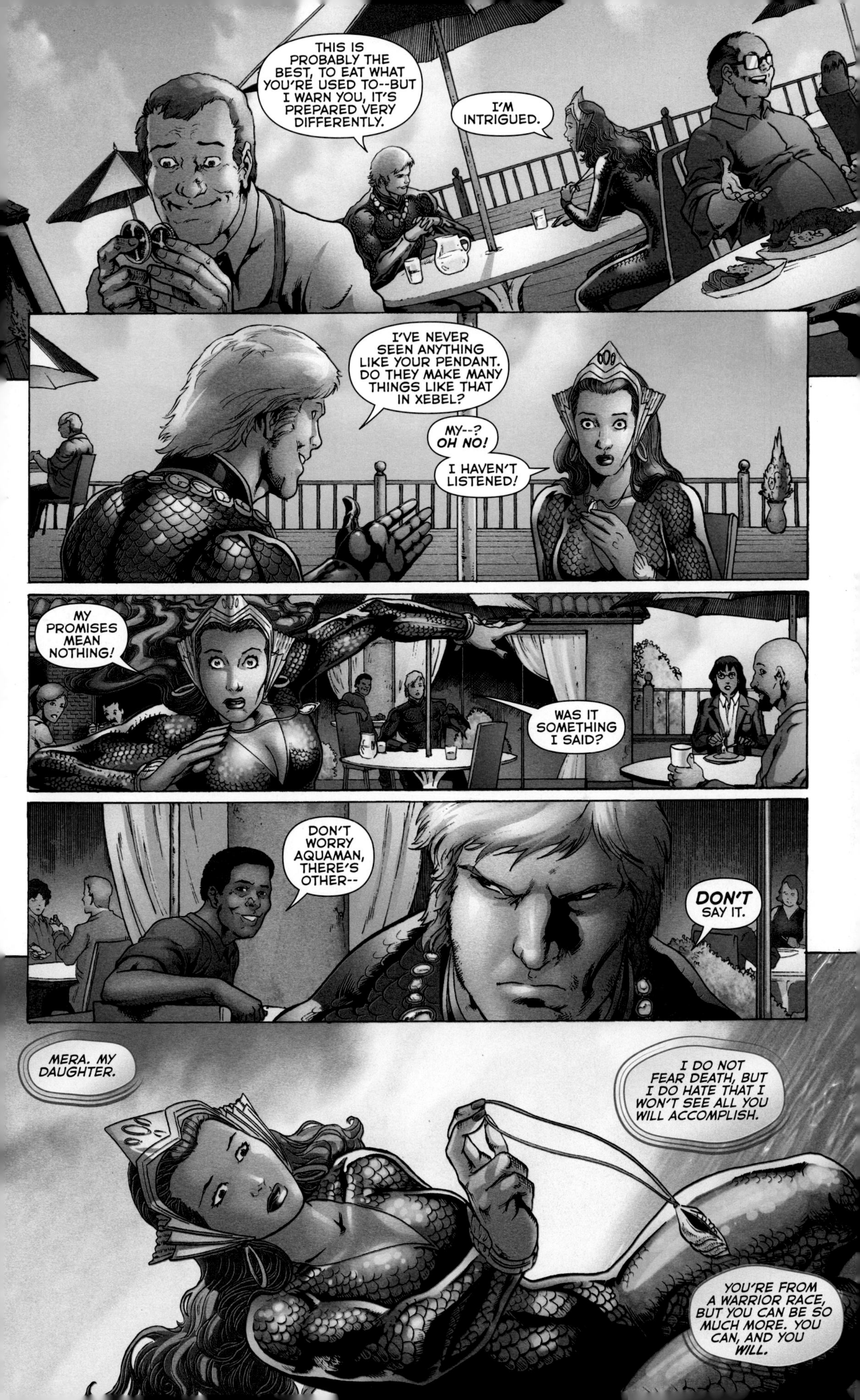
THIS IS PROBABLY THE BEST, TO EAT WHAT YOU'RE USED TO--BUT I WARN YOU, IT'S PREPARED VERY DIFFERENTLY.
I'M INTRIGUED.
I'VE NEVER SEEN ANYTHING LIKE YOUR PENDANT. DO THEY MAKE MANY THINGS LIKE THAT IN XEBEL?
MY--? OH NO!
I HAVEN'T LISTENED!
MY PROMISES MEAN NOTHING!
WAS IT SOMETHING I SAID?
DON'T WORRY AQUAMAN, THERE'S OTHER--
DON'T SAY IT.
MERA. MY DAUGHTER.
I DO NOT FEAR DEATH, BUT I DO HATE THAT I WON'T SEE ALL YOU WILL ACCOMPLISH.
YOU'RE FROM A WARRIOR RACE, BUT YOU CAN BE SO MUCH MORE. YOU CAN, AND YOU WILL.

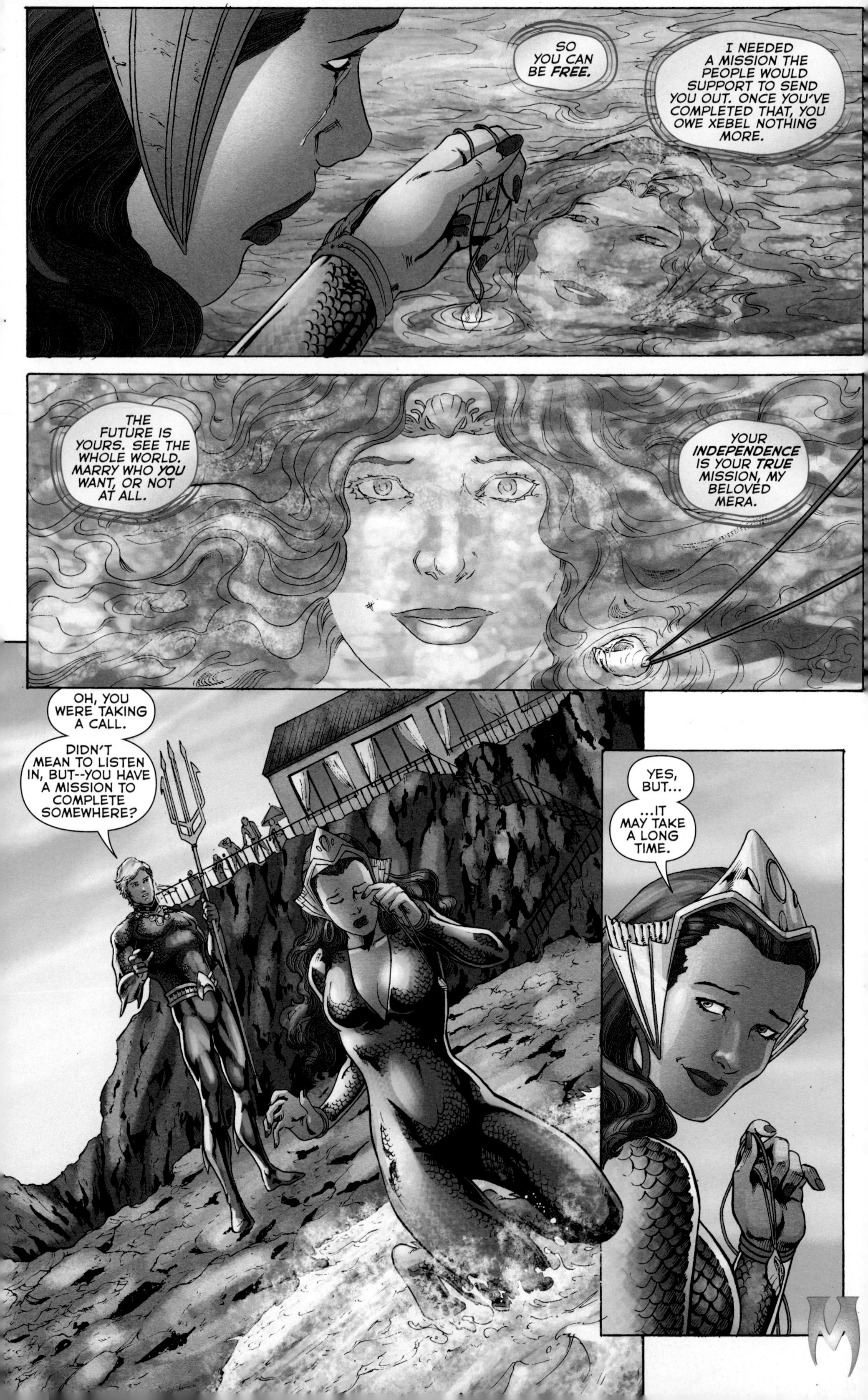
SO YOU CAN BE FREE.
I NEEDED A MISSION THE PEOPLE WOULD SUPPORT TO SEND YOU OUT. ONCE YOU'VE COMPLETED THAT, YOU OWE XEBEL NOTHING MORE.
THE FUTURE IS YOURS. SEE THE WHOLE WORLD. MARRY WHO YOU WANT, OR NOT AT ALL.
YOUR INDEPENDENCE IS YOUR TRUE MISSION, MY BELOVED MERA.
OH, YOU WERE TAKING A CALL.
DIDN'T MEAN TO LISTEN IN, BUT--YOU HAVE A MISSION TO COMPLETE SOMEWHERE?
YES, BUT...
...IT MAY TAKE A LONG TIME.

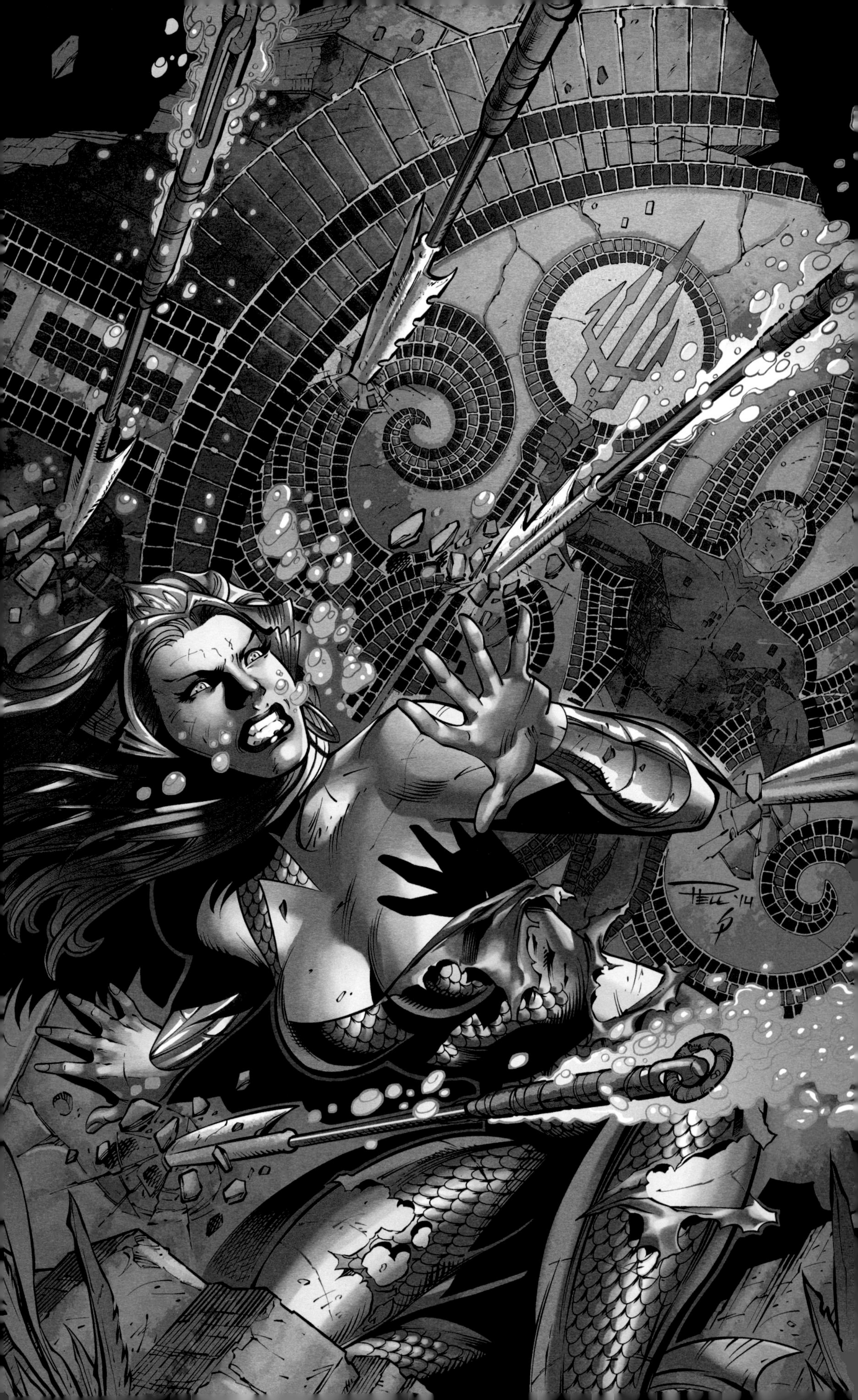

IT LIVES

JEFF PARKER writer **PAUL PELLETIER** penciller **SEAN PARSONS RICK MAGYAR (PGS. 40, 44)** inkers **RAIN BEREDO** colorist **DEZI SIENTY** letterer
PELLETIER, PARSONS and **BEREDO** cover art

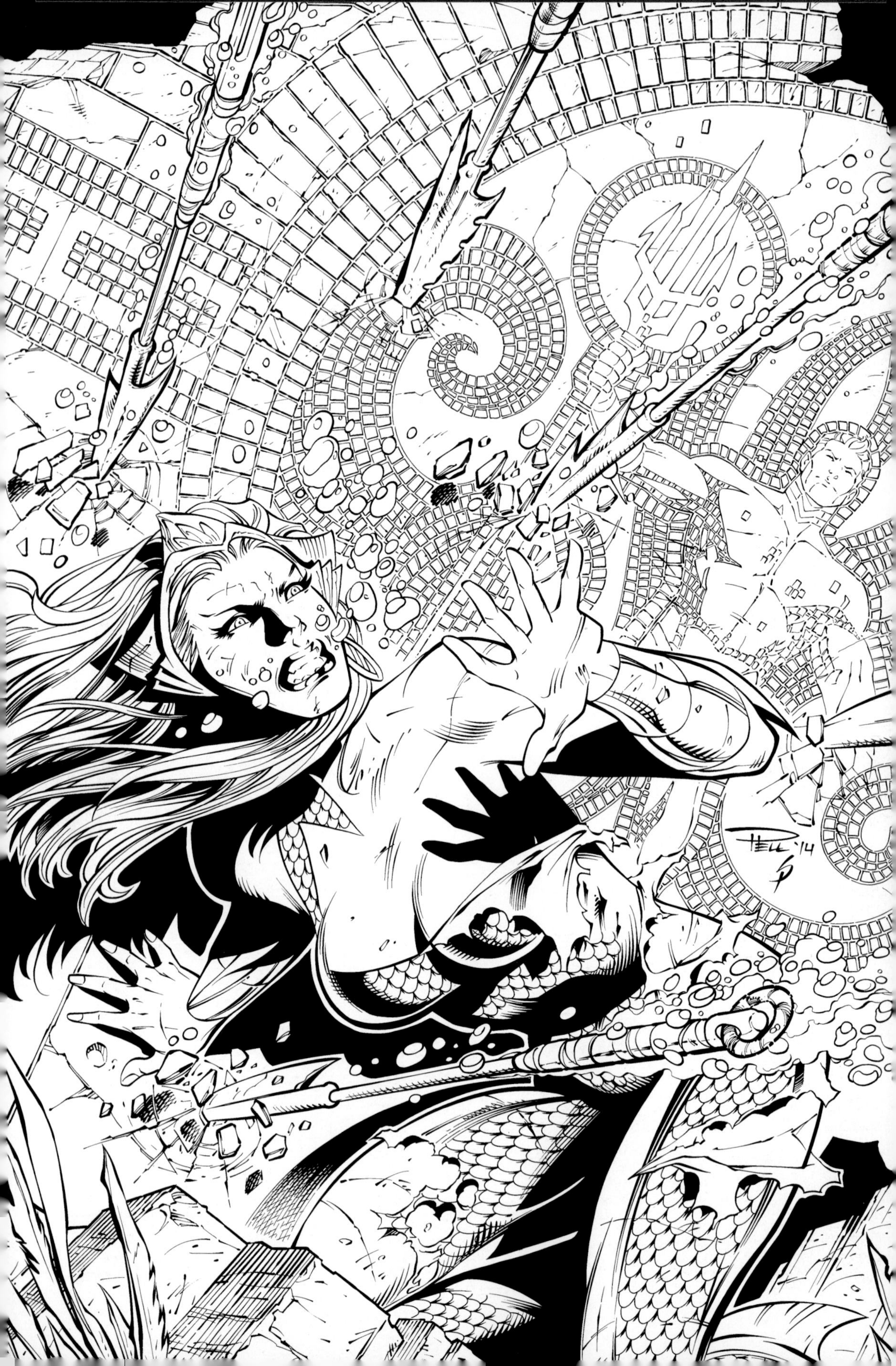

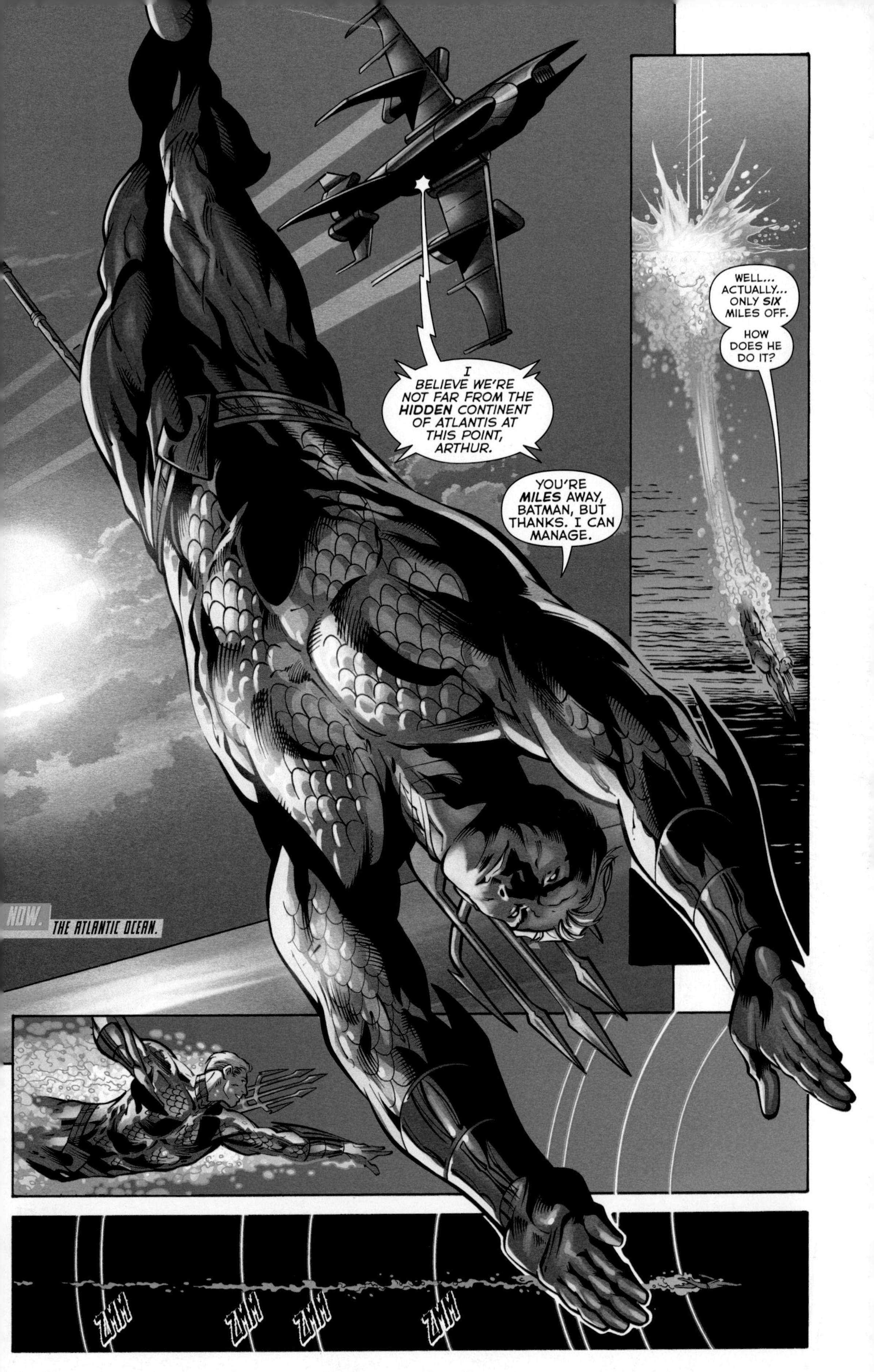
I BELIEVE WE'RE NOT FAR FROM THE HIDDEN CONTINENT OF ATLANTIS AT THIS POINT, ARTHUR.
YOU'RE MILES AWAY, BATMAN, BUT THANKS. I CAN MANAGE.
WELL... ACTUALLY... ONLY SIX MILES OFF.
HOW DOES HE DO IT?
NOW.
THE ATLANTIC OCEAN.
ZMM
ZMM
ZMM
ZMM

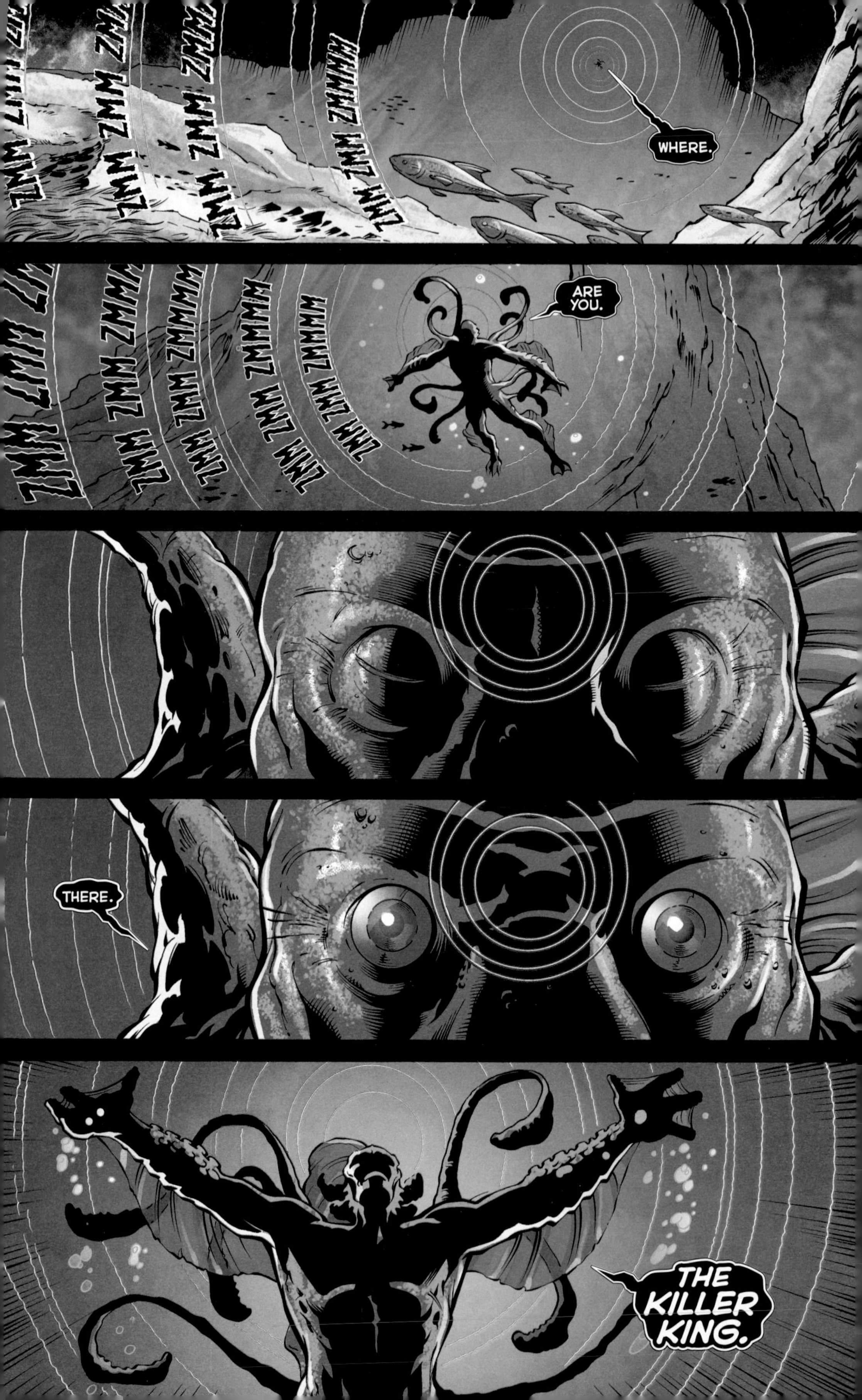
WHERE.
ARE YOU.
THERE.
THE KILLER KING.

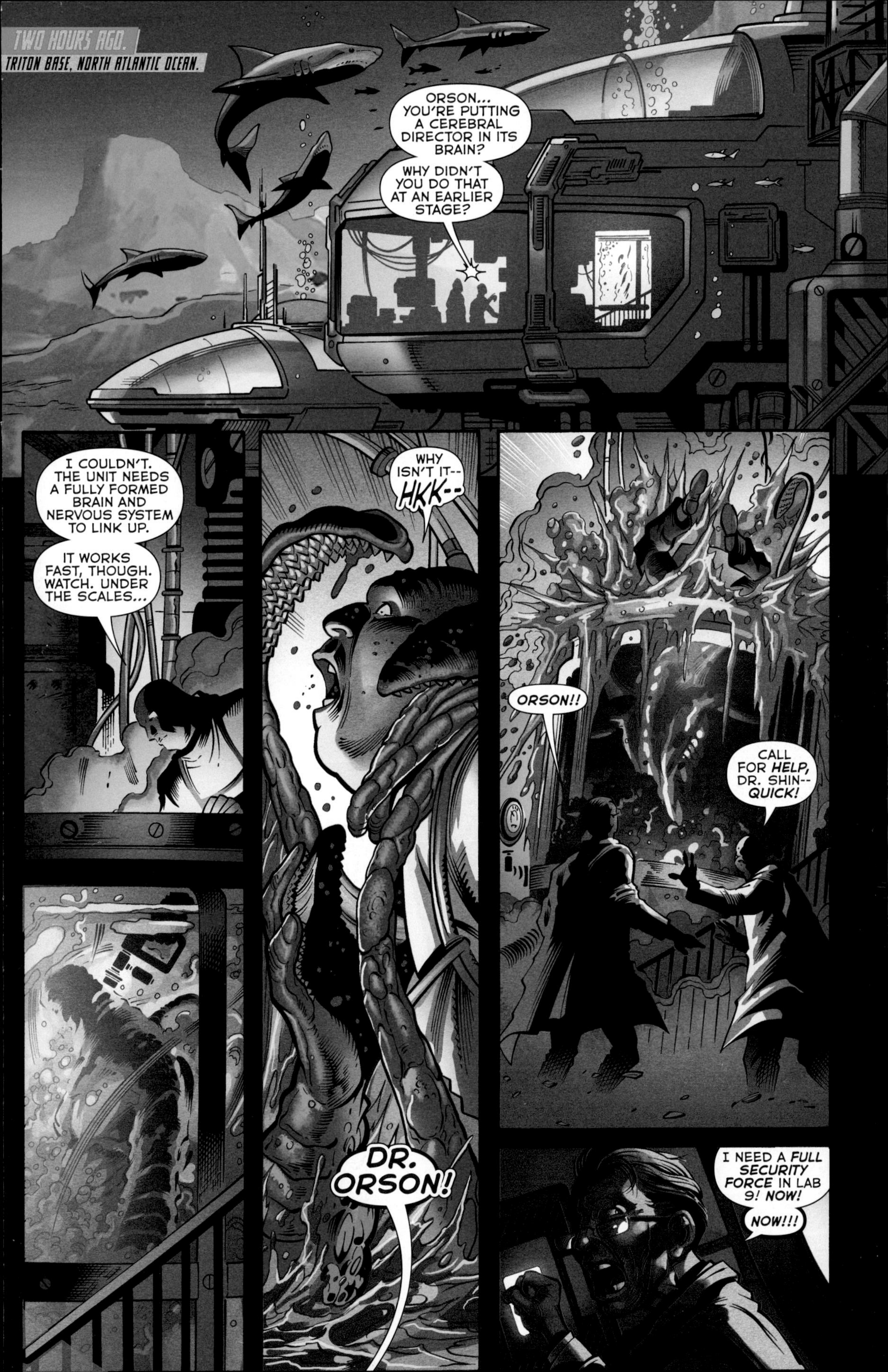
TWO HOURS AGO.
TRITON BASE, NORTH ATLANTIC OCEAN.
ORSON... YOU'RE PUTTING A CEREBRAL DIRECTOR IN ITS BRAIN?
WHY DIDN'T YOU DO THAT AT AN EARLIER STAGE?
I COULDN'T. THE UNIT NEEDS A FULLY FORMED BRAIN AND NERVOUS SYSTEM TO LINK UP.
IT WORKS FAST, THOUGH. WATCH. UNDER THE SCALES...
WHY ISN'T IT--
HKK--
DR. ORSON!
ORSON!!
CALL FOR HELP, DR. SHIN-- QUICK!
I NEED A FULL SECURITY FORCE IN LAB 9! NOW!
NOW!!!

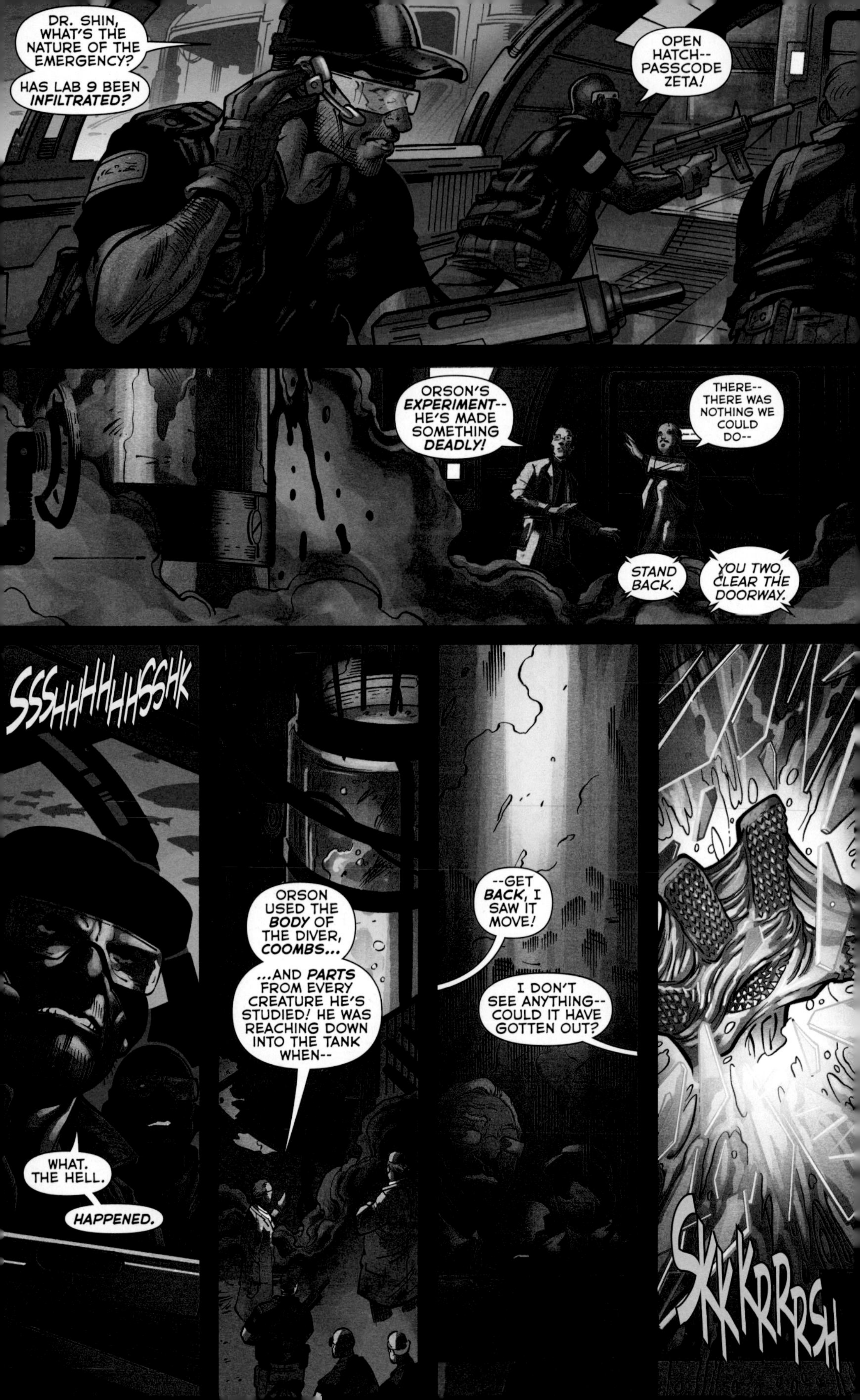
DR. SHIN, WHAT'S THE NATURE OF THE EMERGENCY?
HAS LAB 9 BEEN *INFILTRATED?*
OPEN HATCH-- PASSCODE ZETA!
ORSON'S *EXPERIMENT*-- HE'S MADE SOMETHING *DEADLY!*
THERE-- THERE WAS NOTHING WE COULD DO--
STAND BACK.
YOU TWO, CLEAR THE DOORWAY.
SSSHHHHHHSSHK
WHAT. THE HELL.
HAPPENED.
ORSON USED THE *BODY* OF THE DIVER, *COOMBS...*
...AND *PARTS* FROM EVERY CREATURE HE'S STUDIED! HE WAS REACHING DOWN INTO THE TANK WHEN--
--GET *BACK*, I SAW IT MOVE!
I DON'T SEE ANYTHING-- COULD IT HAVE GOTTEN OUT?
SKKKRRRRSH

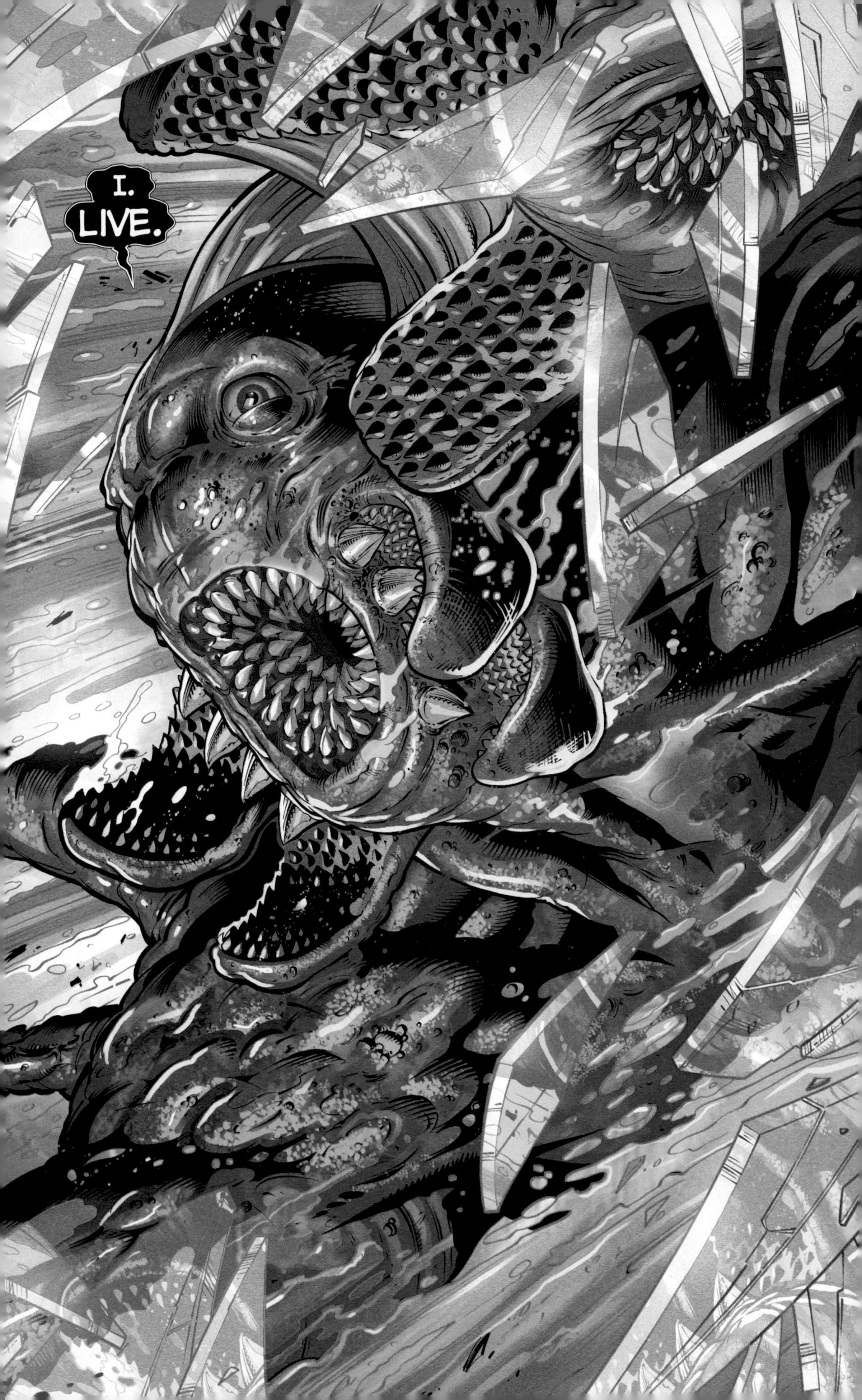
I. LIVE.

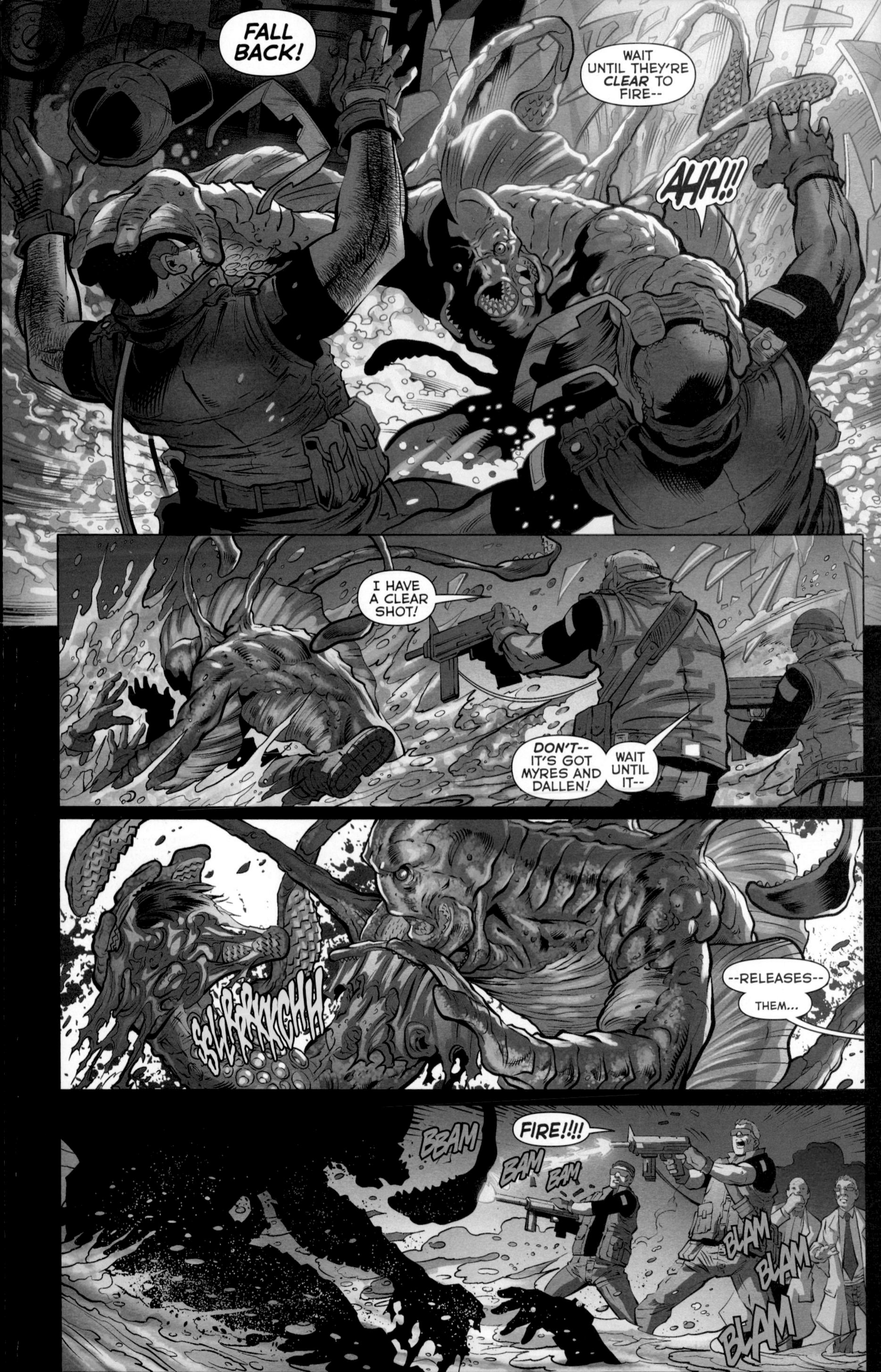
FALL BACK!
WAIT UNTIL THEY'RE CLEAR TO FIRE--
AHH!!
I HAVE A CLEAR SHOT!
DON'T-- IT'S GOT MYRES AND DALLEN!
WAIT UNTIL IT--
--RELEASES--
THEM...
SCLRRKKCHH
BBAM
FIRE!!!!
BAM
BAM
BLAM
BLAM
BLAM

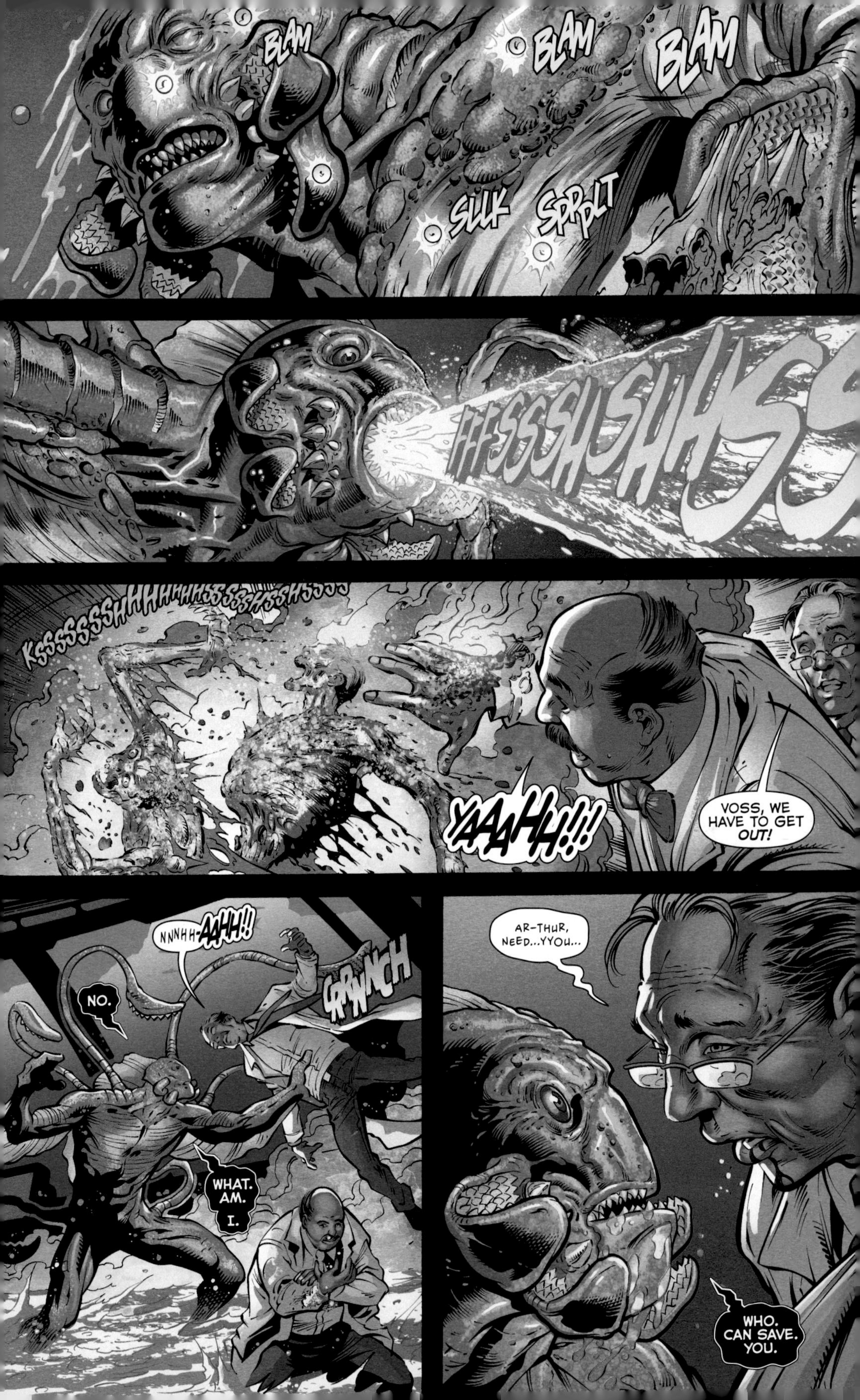
BLAM
BLAM
BLAM
SLLK
SPPPLT
FFFSSSHSHHSS
KSSSSSSSHHHHHHHSSSSHSSHSSSS
YAAAHH!!!
VOSS, WE HAVE TO GET OUT!
NNHH-AAHH!!
CRRNCH
NO.
WHAT. AM. I.
AR-THUR, NEED...YYOU...
WHO. CAN SAVE. YOU.

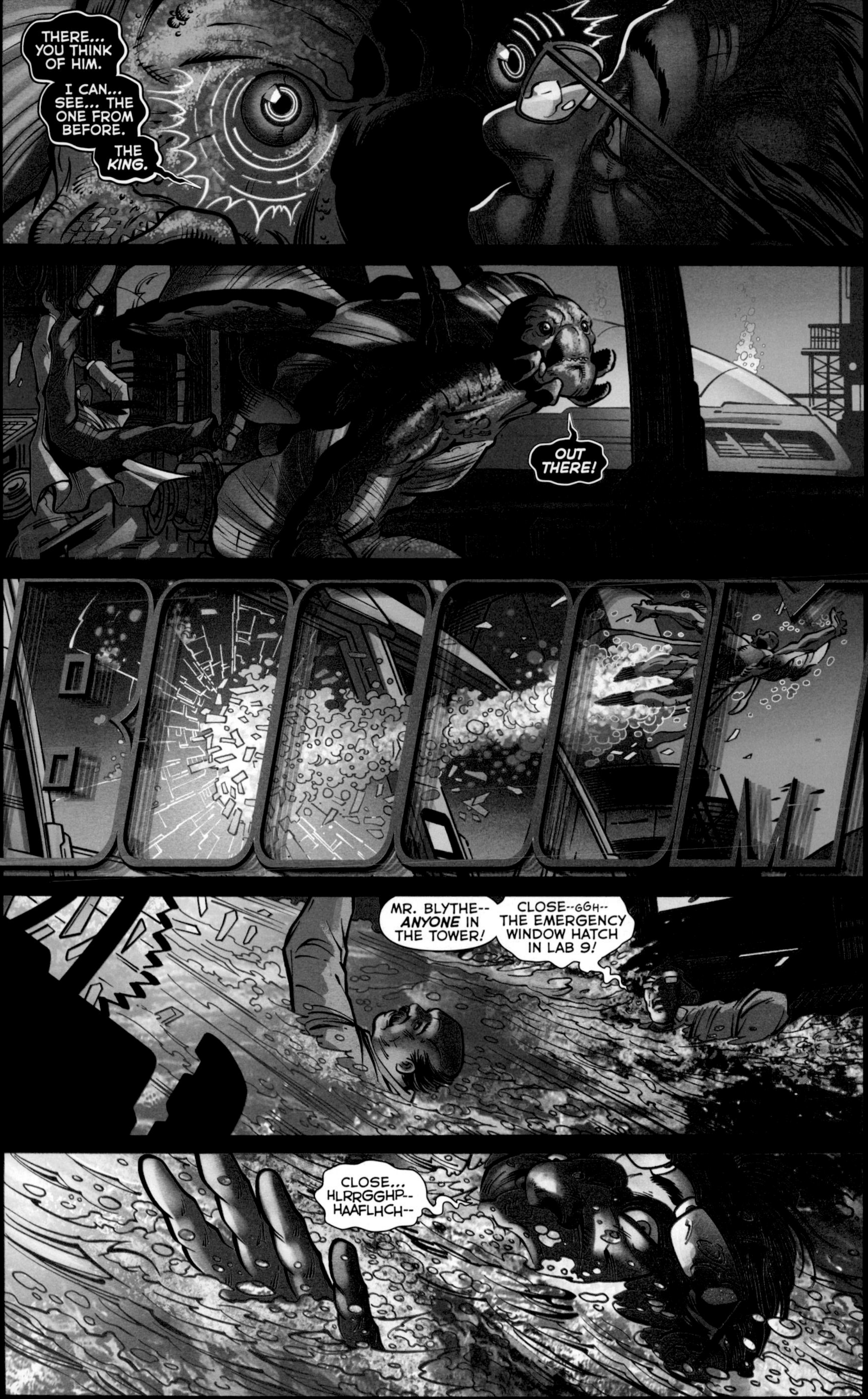
THERE... YOU THINK OF HIM.
I CAN... SEE... THE ONE FROM BEFORE.
THE *KING.*
OUT THERE!
MR. BLYTHE-- *ANYONE* IN THE TOWER!
CLOSE--GGH-- THE EMERGENCY WINDOW HATCH IN LAB 9!
CLOSE... HLRRGGHP-- HAAFLHCH--

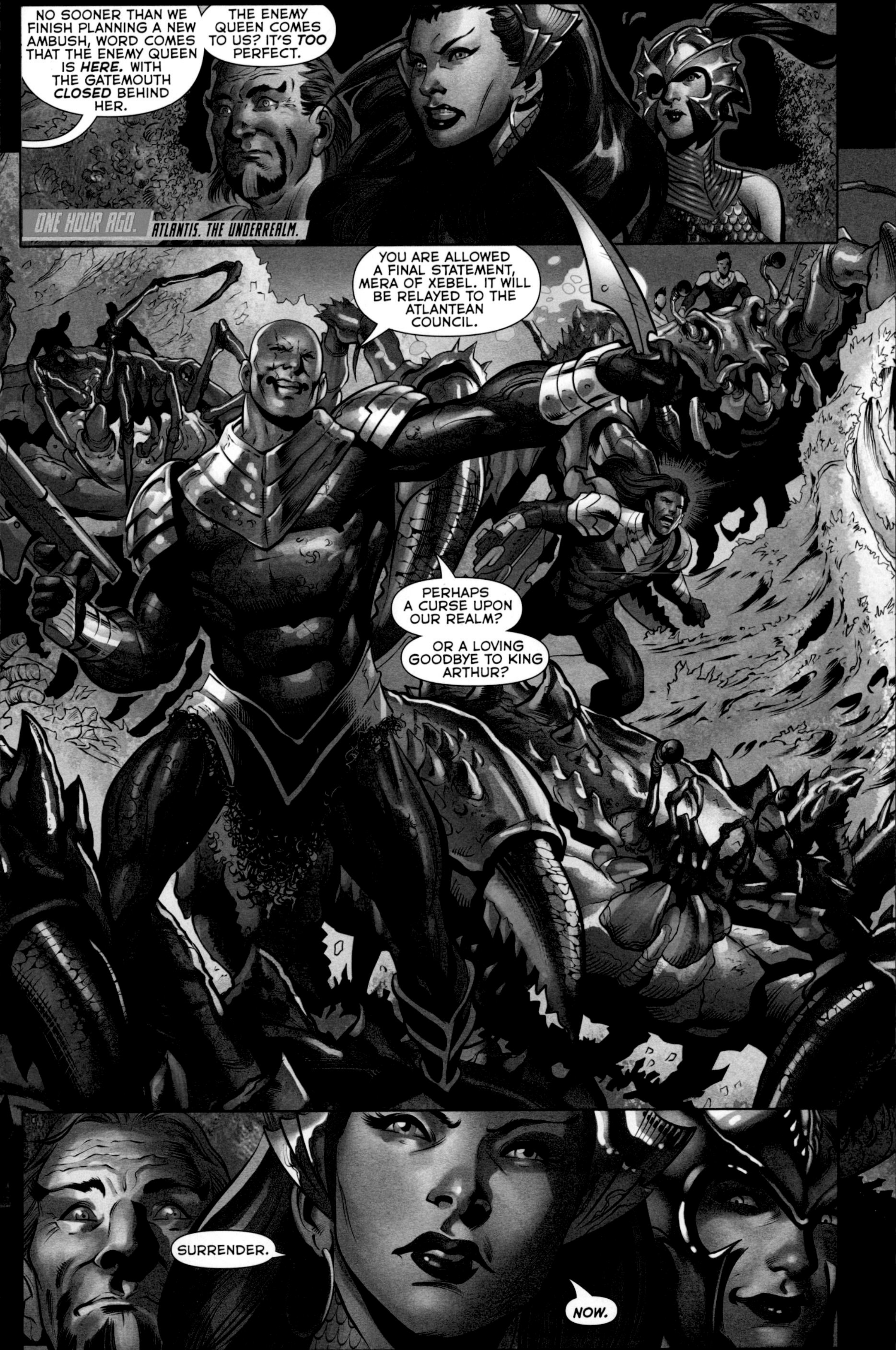
NO SOONER THAN WE FINISH PLANNING A NEW AMBUSH, WORD COMES THAT THE ENEMY QUEEN IS *HERE.* WITH THE GATEMOUTH *CLOSED* BEHIND HER.
THE ENEMY QUEEN COMES TO US? IT'S *TOO* PERFECT.
ONE HOUR AGO.
ATLANTIS. THE UNDERREALM.
YOU ARE ALLOWED A FINAL STATEMENT, MERA OF XEBEL. IT WILL BE RELAYED TO THE ATLANTEAN COUNCIL.
PERHAPS A CURSE UPON OUR REALM?
OR A LOVING GOODBYE TO KING ARTHUR?
SURRENDER.
NOW.

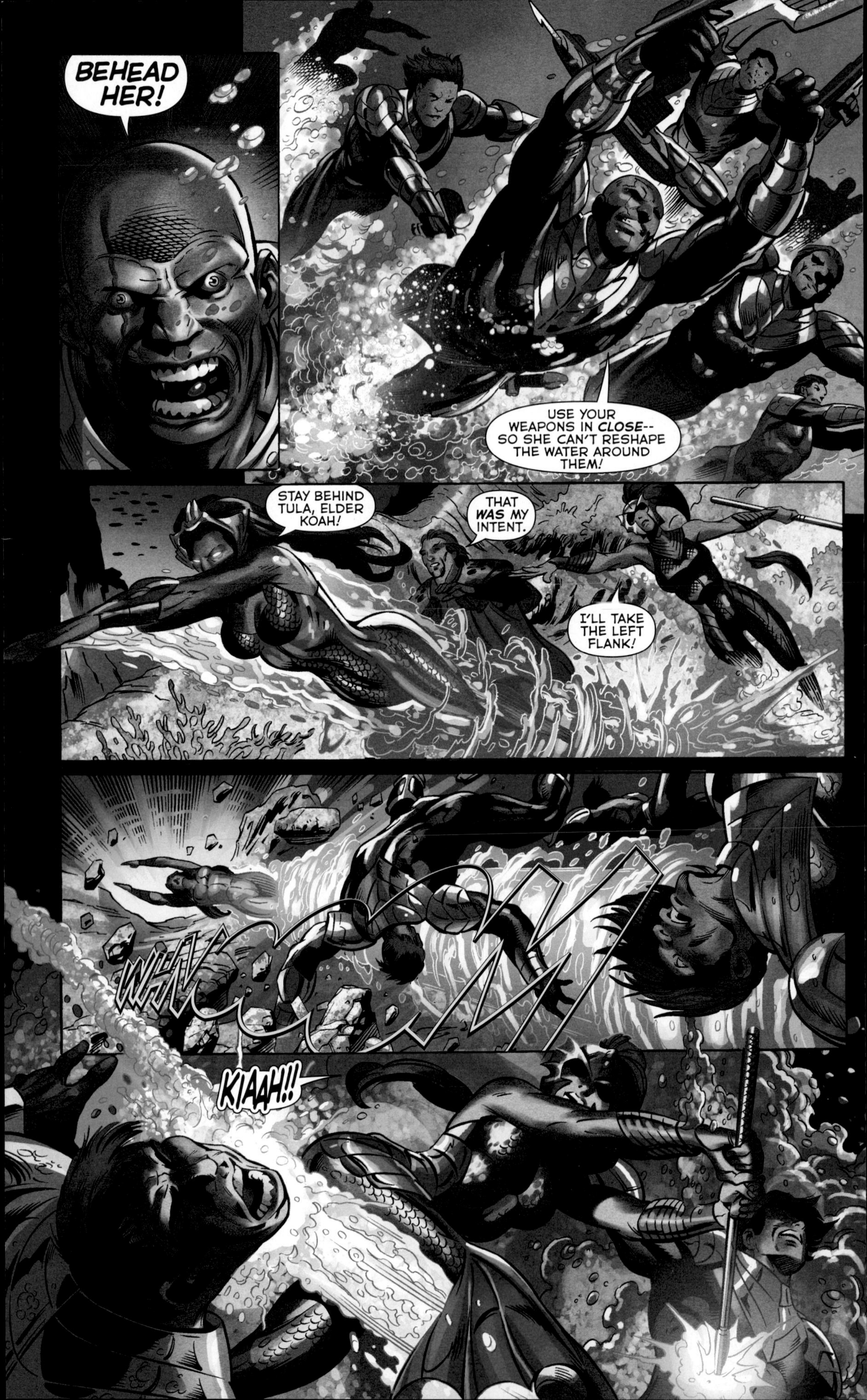
BEHEAD HER!
USE YOUR WEAPONS IN CLOSE-- SO SHE CAN'T RESHAPE THE WATER AROUND THEM!
STAY BEHIND TULA, ELDER KOAH!
THAT WAS MY INTENT.
I'LL TAKE THE LEFT FLANK!
WHVVVM
KIAAH!!

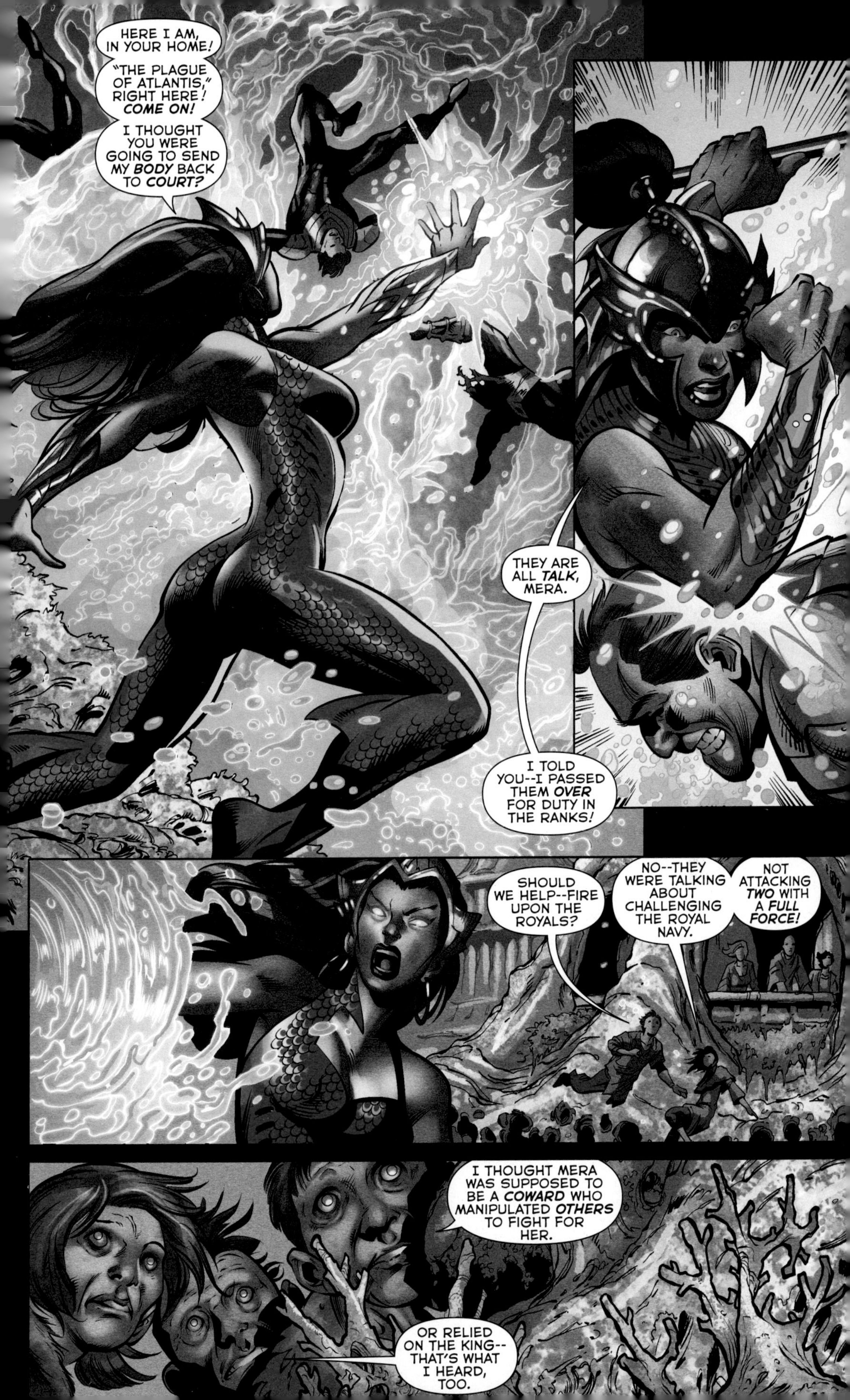
HERE I AM, IN YOUR HOME!
"THE PLAGUE OF ATLANTIS," RIGHT HERE! COME ON!
I THOUGHT YOU WERE GOING TO SEND MY BODY BACK TO COURT?
THEY ARE ALL TALK, MERA.
I TOLD YOU--I PASSED THEM OVER FOR DUTY IN THE RANKS!
SHOULD WE HELP--FIRE UPON THE ROYALS?
NO--THEY WERE TALKING ABOUT CHALLENGING THE ROYAL NAVY.
NOT ATTACKING TWO WITH A FULL FORCE!
I THOUGHT MERA WAS SUPPOSED TO BE A COWARD WHO MANIPULATED OTHERS TO FIGHT FOR HER.
OR RELIED ON THE KING--THAT'S WHAT I HEARD, TOO.

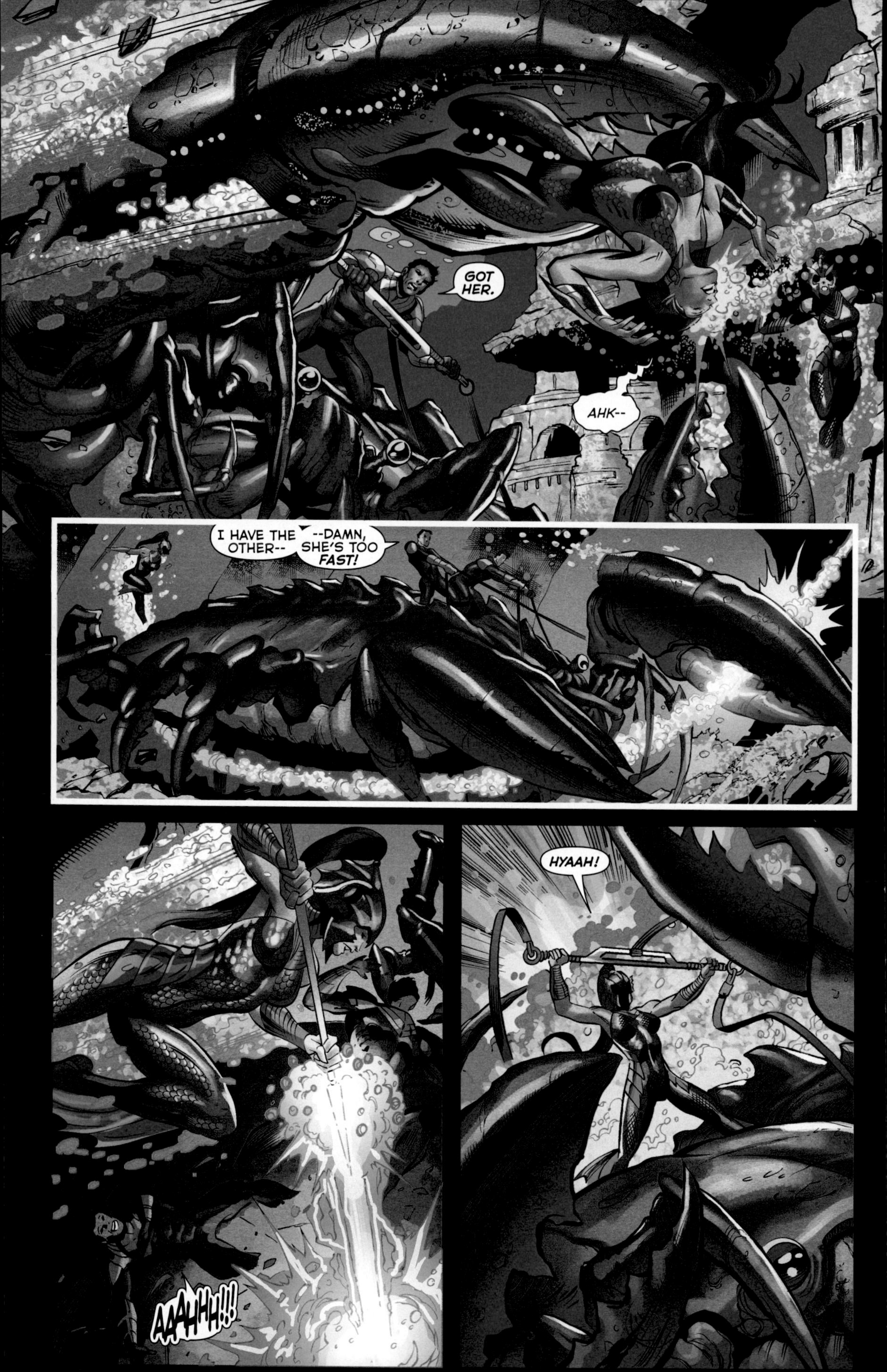
GOT HER.
AHK--
I HAVE THE OTHER--
--DAMN, SHE'S TOO FAST!
AAAHHH!!!
HYAAH!

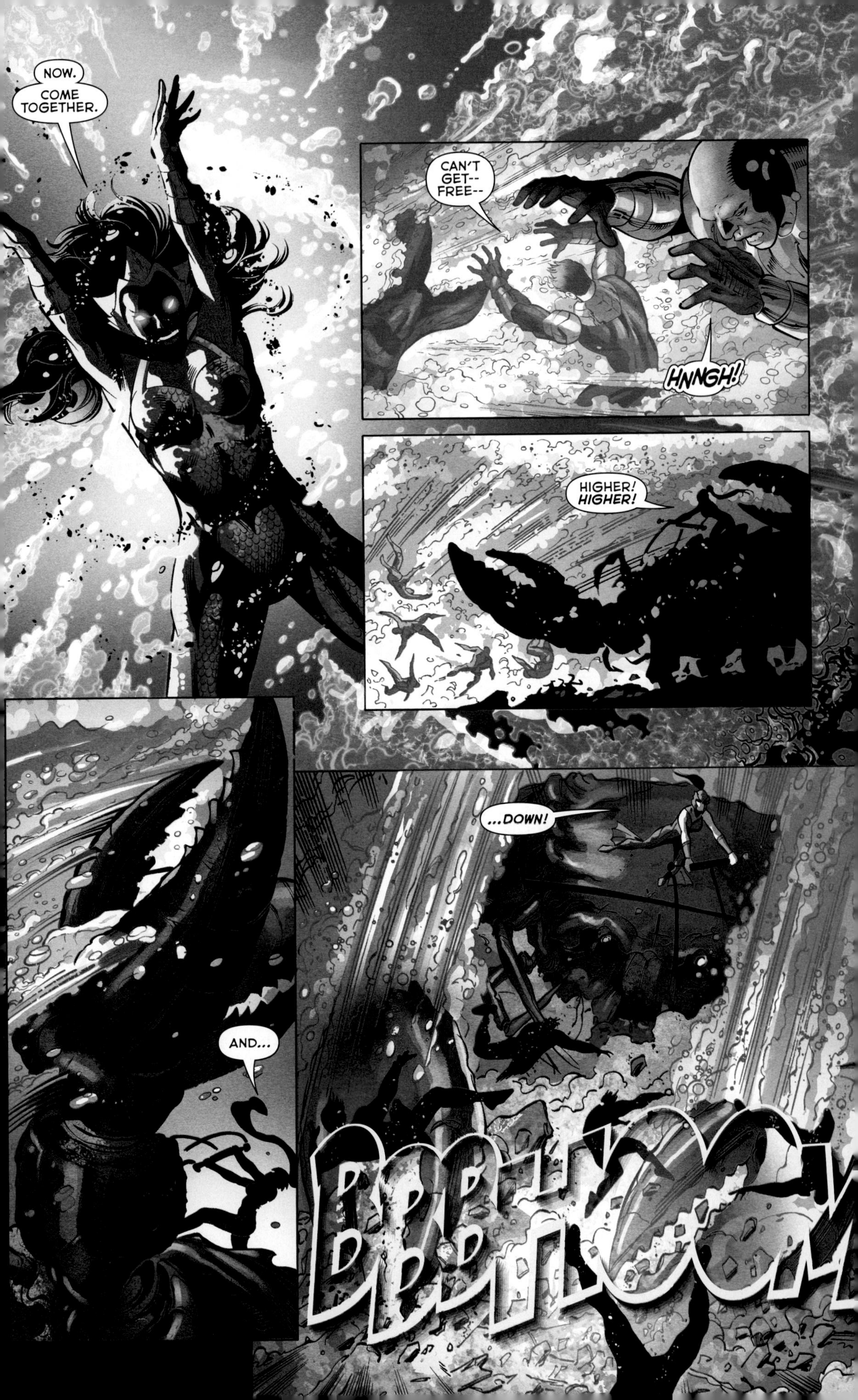
NOW.
COME TOGETHER.
CAN'T GET-- FREE--
HNNGH!
HIGHER! HIGHER!
AND...
...DOWN!

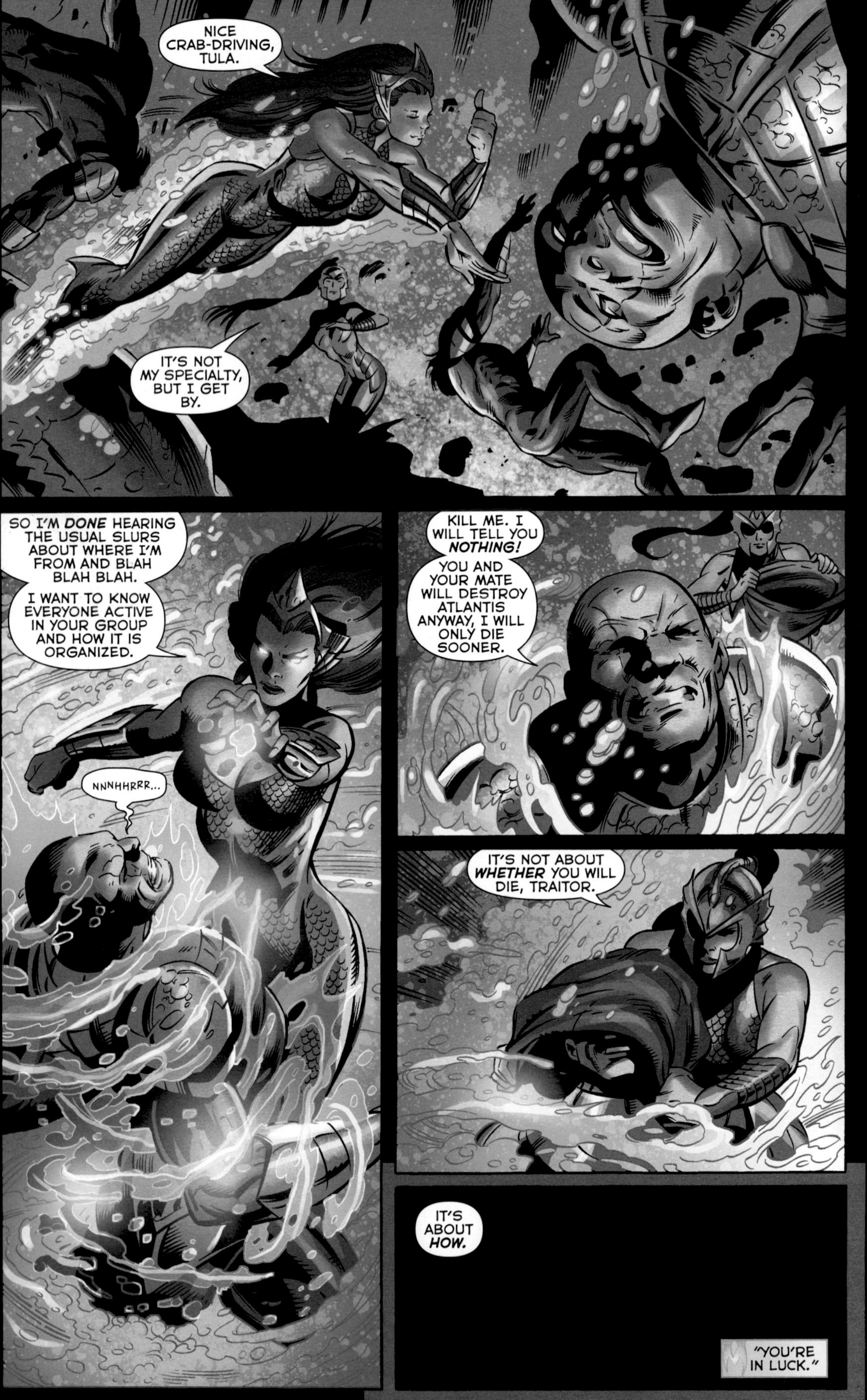
NICE CRAB-DRIVING, TULA.
IT'S NOT MY SPECIALTY, BUT I GET BY.
SO I'M *DONE* HEARING THE USUAL SLURS ABOUT WHERE I'M FROM AND BLAH BLAH BLAH.
I WANT TO KNOW EVERYONE ACTIVE IN YOUR GROUP AND HOW IT IS ORGANIZED.
NNNHHRRR...
KILL ME. I WILL TELL YOU *NOTHING!*
YOU AND YOUR MATE WILL DESTROY ATLANTIS ANYWAY, I WILL ONLY DIE SOONER.
IT'S NOT ABOUT *WHETHER* YOU WILL DIE, TRAITOR.
IT'S ABOUT *HOW.*
"YOU'RE IN LUCK."

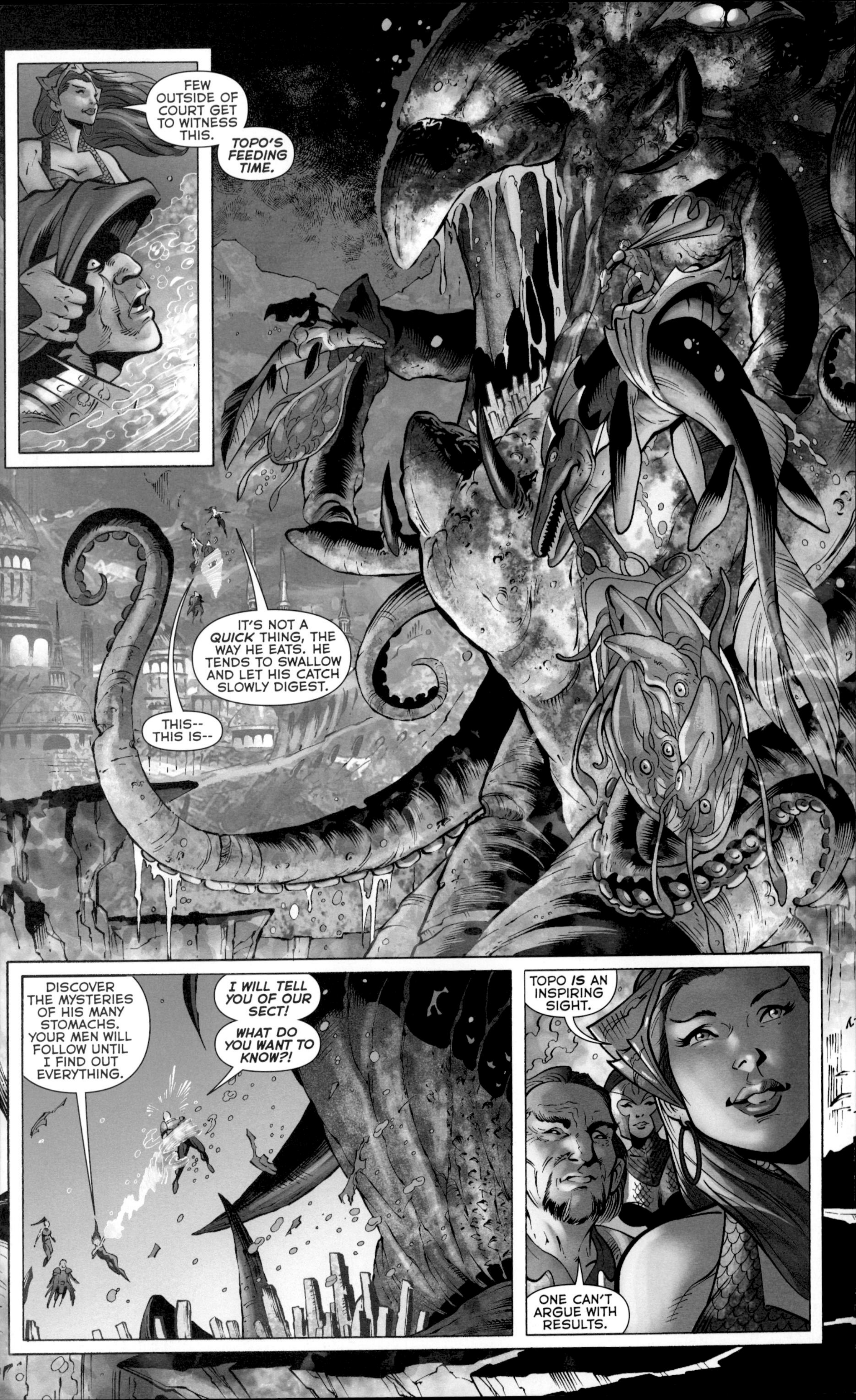
FEW OUTSIDE OF COURT GET TO WITNESS THIS.
TOPO'S FEEDING TIME.
IT'S NOT A *QUICK* THING, THE WAY HE EATS. HE TENDS TO SWALLOW AND LET HIS CATCH SLOWLY DIGEST.
THIS-- THIS IS--
DISCOVER THE MYSTERIES OF HIS MANY STOMACHS. YOUR MEN WILL FOLLOW UNTIL I FIND OUT EVERYTHING.
I WILL TELL YOU OF OUR SECT!
WHAT DO YOU WANT TO KNOW?!
TOPO *IS* AN INSPIRING SIGHT.
ONE CAN'T ARGUE WITH RESULTS.

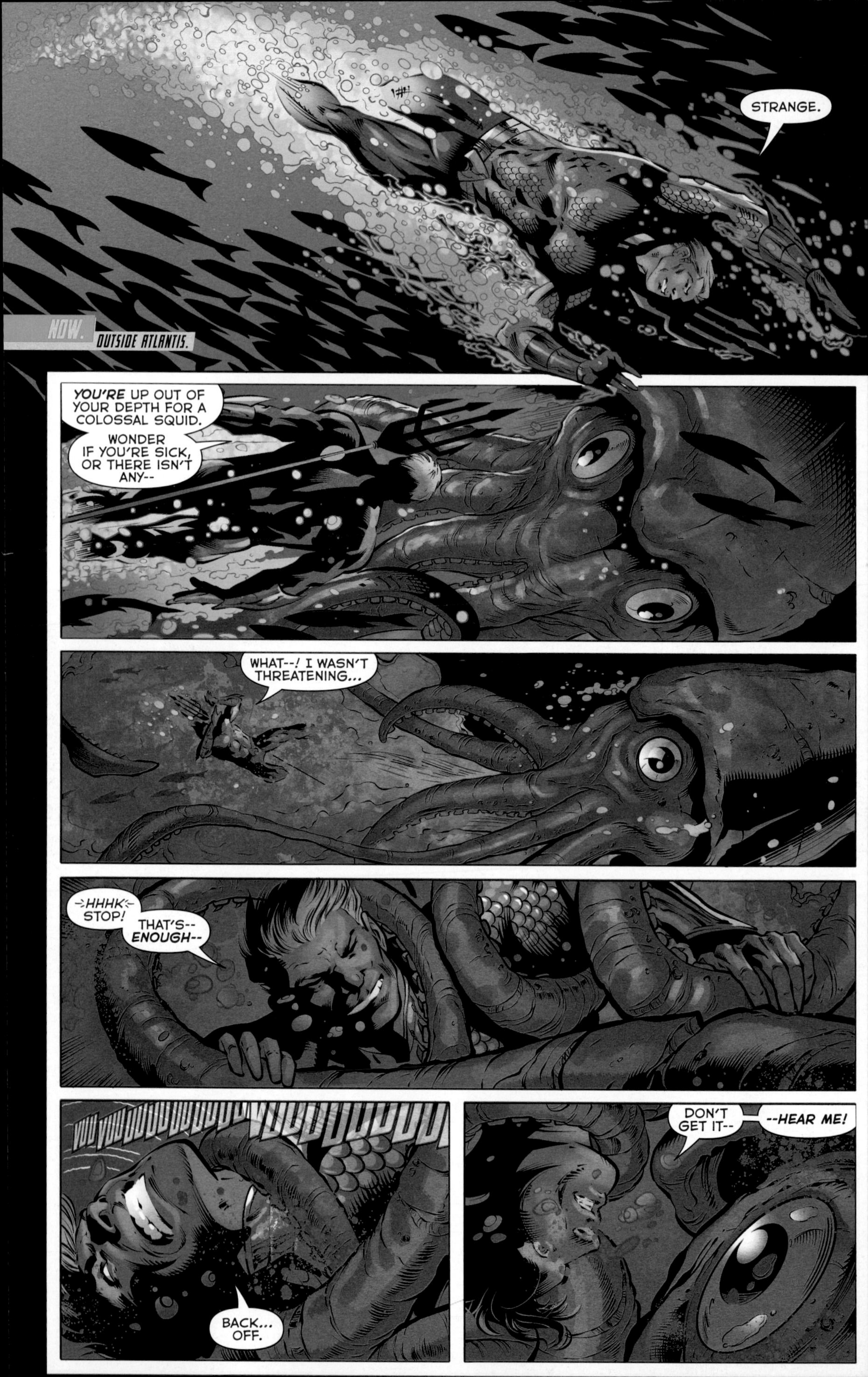
STRANGE.
NOW. OUTSIDE ATLANTIS.
YOU'RE UP OUT OF YOUR DEPTH FOR A COLOSSAL SQUID.
WONDER IF YOU'RE SICK, OR THERE ISN'T ANY--
WHAT--! I WASN'T THREATENING...
-HHHK- STOP!
THAT'S-- ENOUGH--
VUUVUUUUUUUUUUVUUUUUUUUUUU
BACK... OFF.
DON'T GET IT--
--HEAR ME!

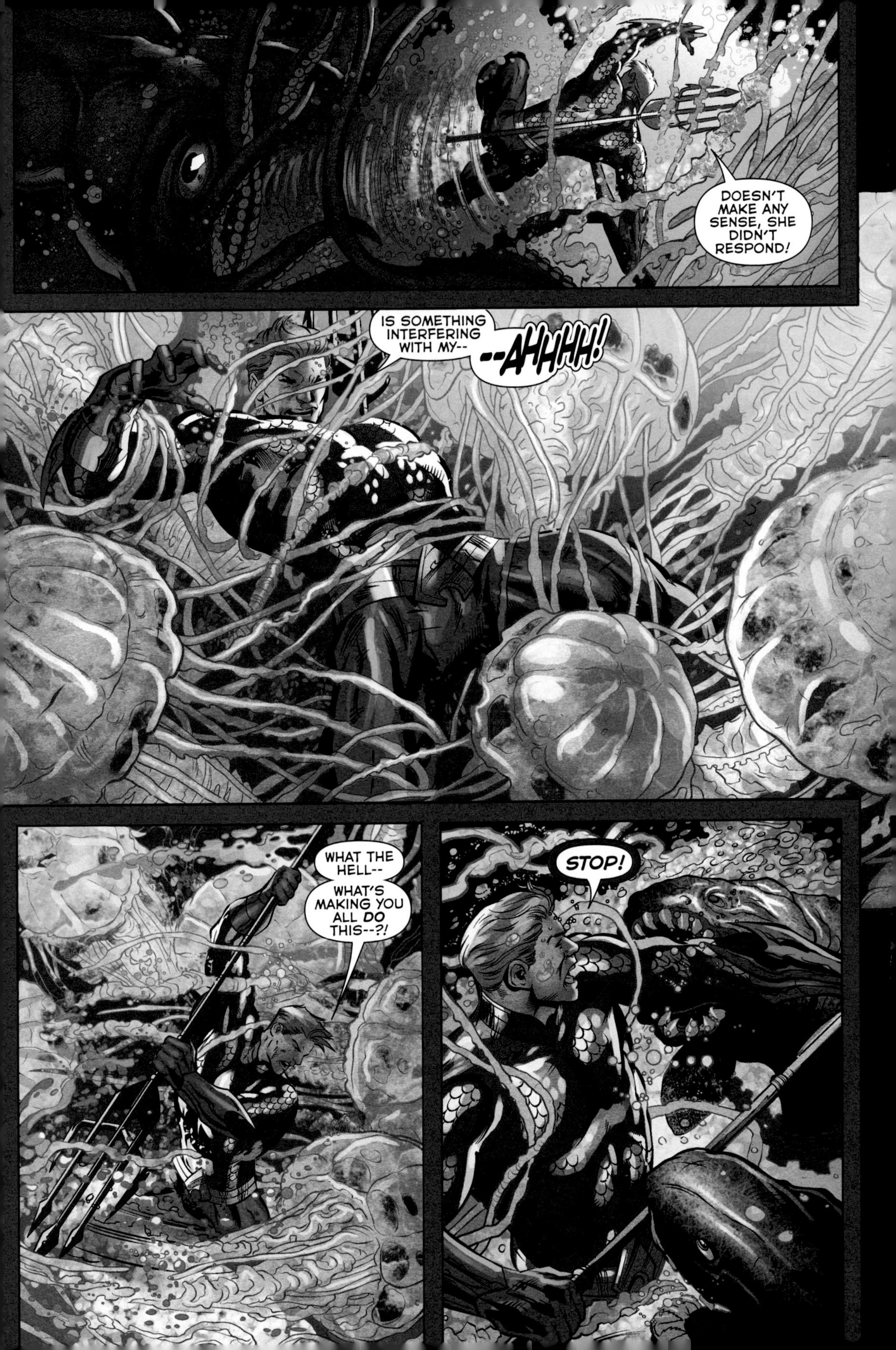
DOESN'T MAKE ANY SENSE, SHE DIDN'T RESPOND!
IS SOMETHING INTERFERING WITH MY--
--AHHHH!
WHAT THE HELL--
WHAT'S MAKING YOU ALL DO THIS--?!
STOP!

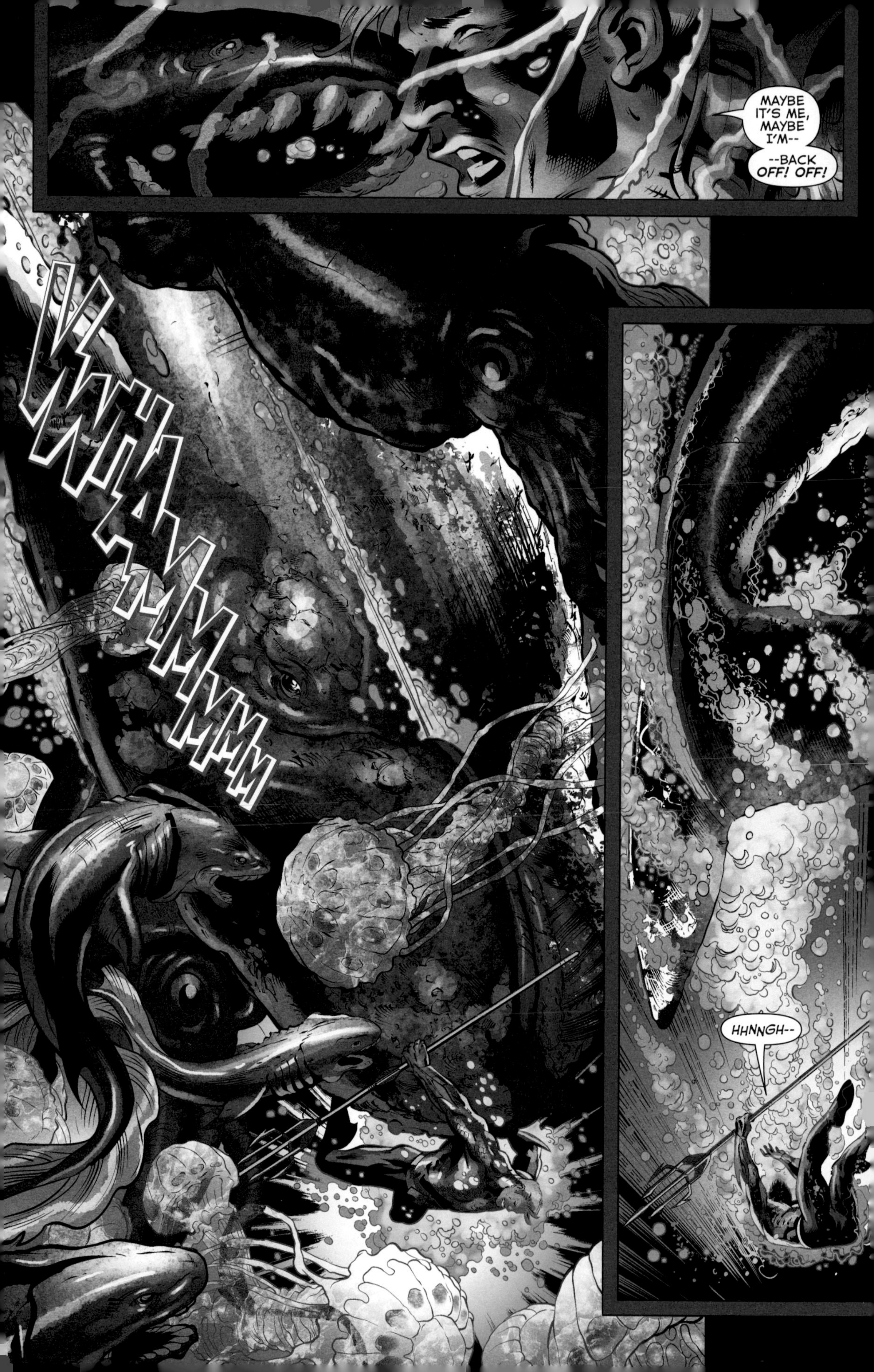
MAYBE IT'S ME, MAYBE I'M--
--BACK OFF! OFF!
VVHAMMMMM
HHNNGH--

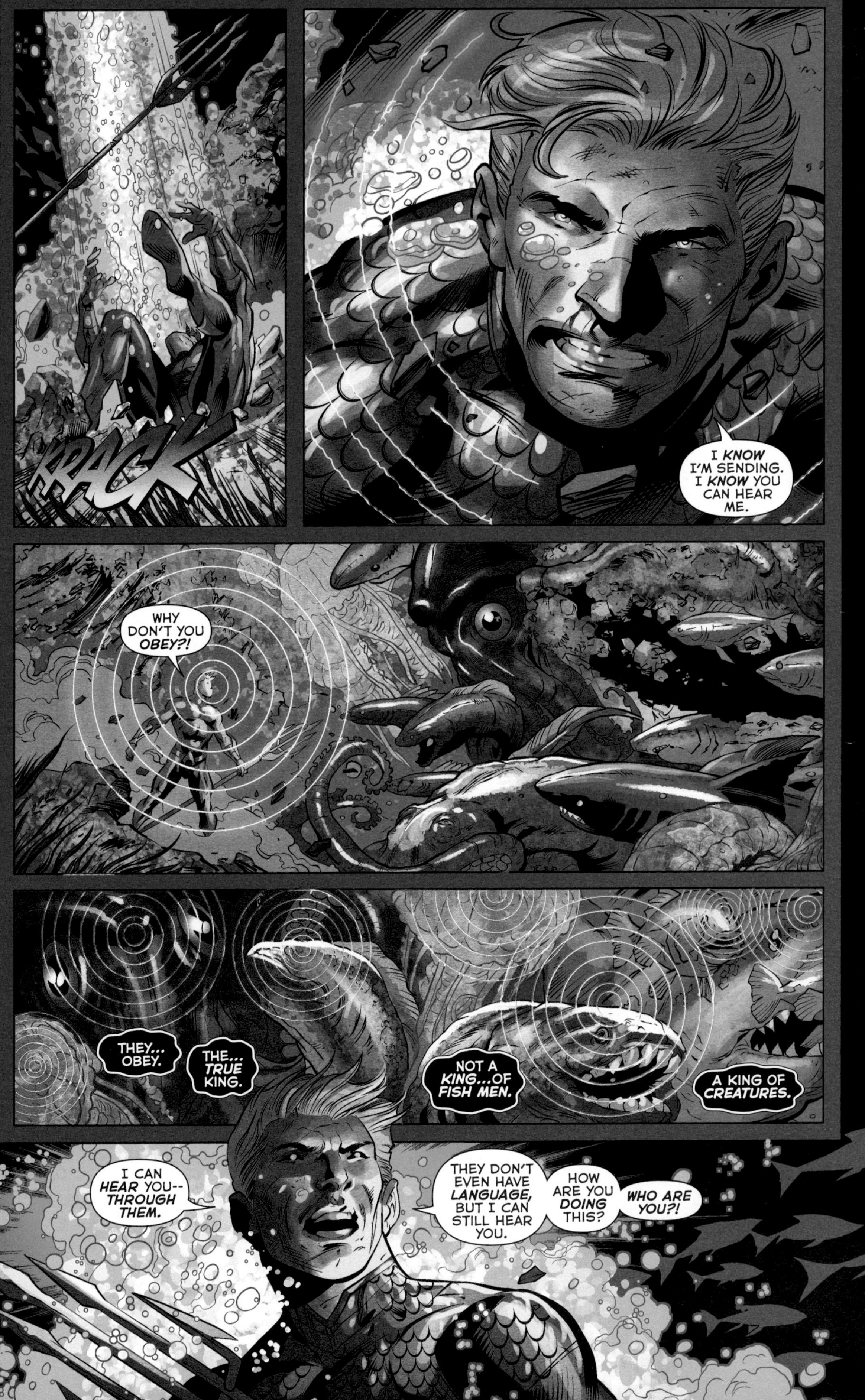
KRACK
I KNOW I'M SENDING. I KNOW YOU CAN HEAR ME.
WHY DON'T YOU OBEY?!
THEY... OBEY.
THE... TRUE KING.
NOT A KING...OF FISH MEN.
A KING OF CREATURES.
I CAN HEAR YOU-- THROUGH THEM.
THEY DON'T EVEN HAVE LANGUAGE, BUT I CAN STILL HEAR YOU.
HOW ARE YOU DOING THIS?
WHO ARE YOU?!

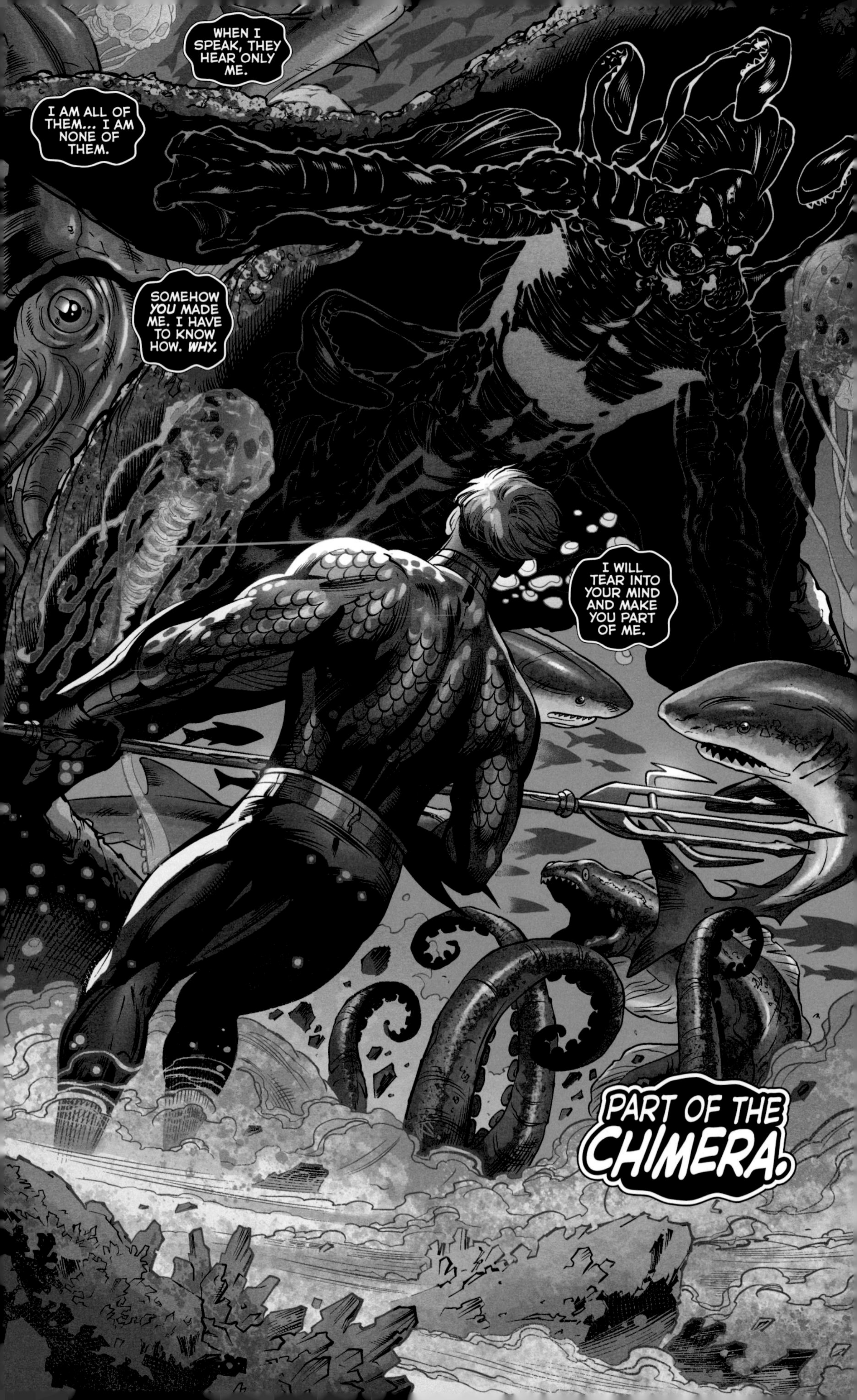

I AM ALL OF THEM... I AM NONE OF THEM.
WHEN I SPEAK, THEY HEAR ONLY ME.
SOMEHOW YOU MADE ME. I HAVE TO KNOW HOW. WHY.
I WILL TEAR INTO YOUR MIND AND MAKE YOU PART OF ME.
PART OF THE CHIMERA.

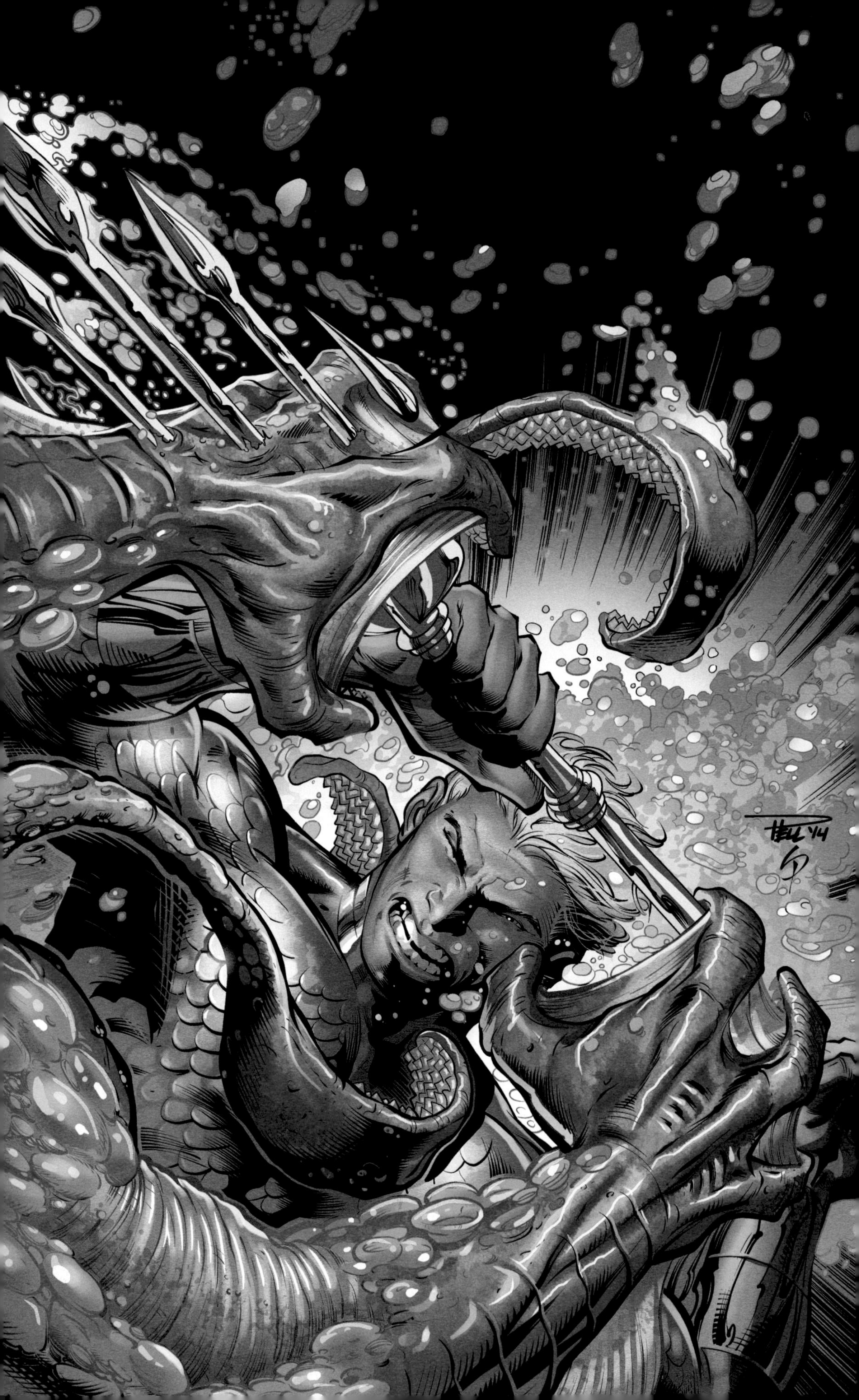

MEET YOUR MAKER

JEFF PARKER writer **PAUL PELLETIER** penciller **SEAN PARSONS** inker **RAIN BEREDO** colorist **DEZI SIENTY** letterer **PELLETIER, PARSONS and BEREDO** cover art

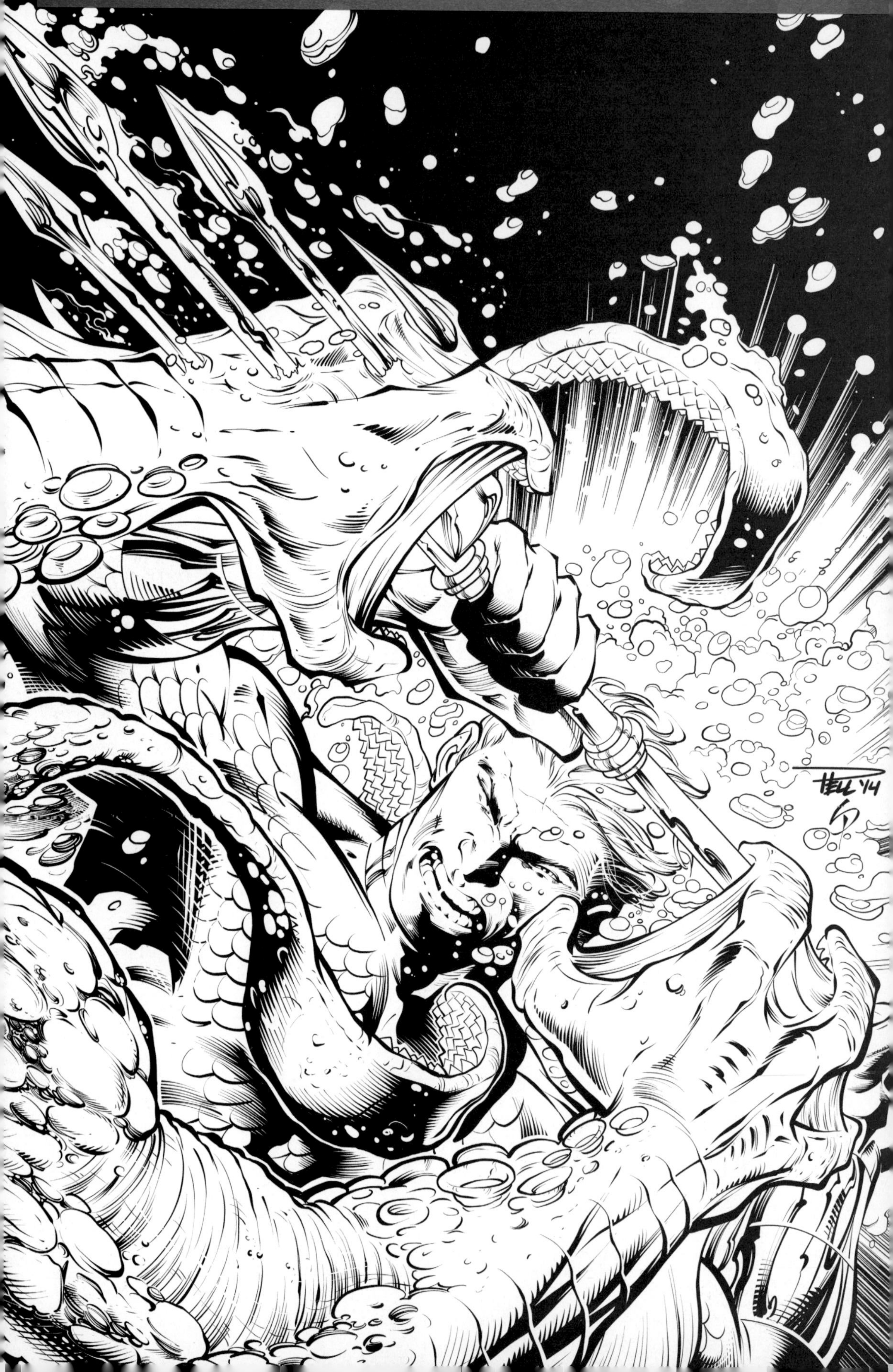

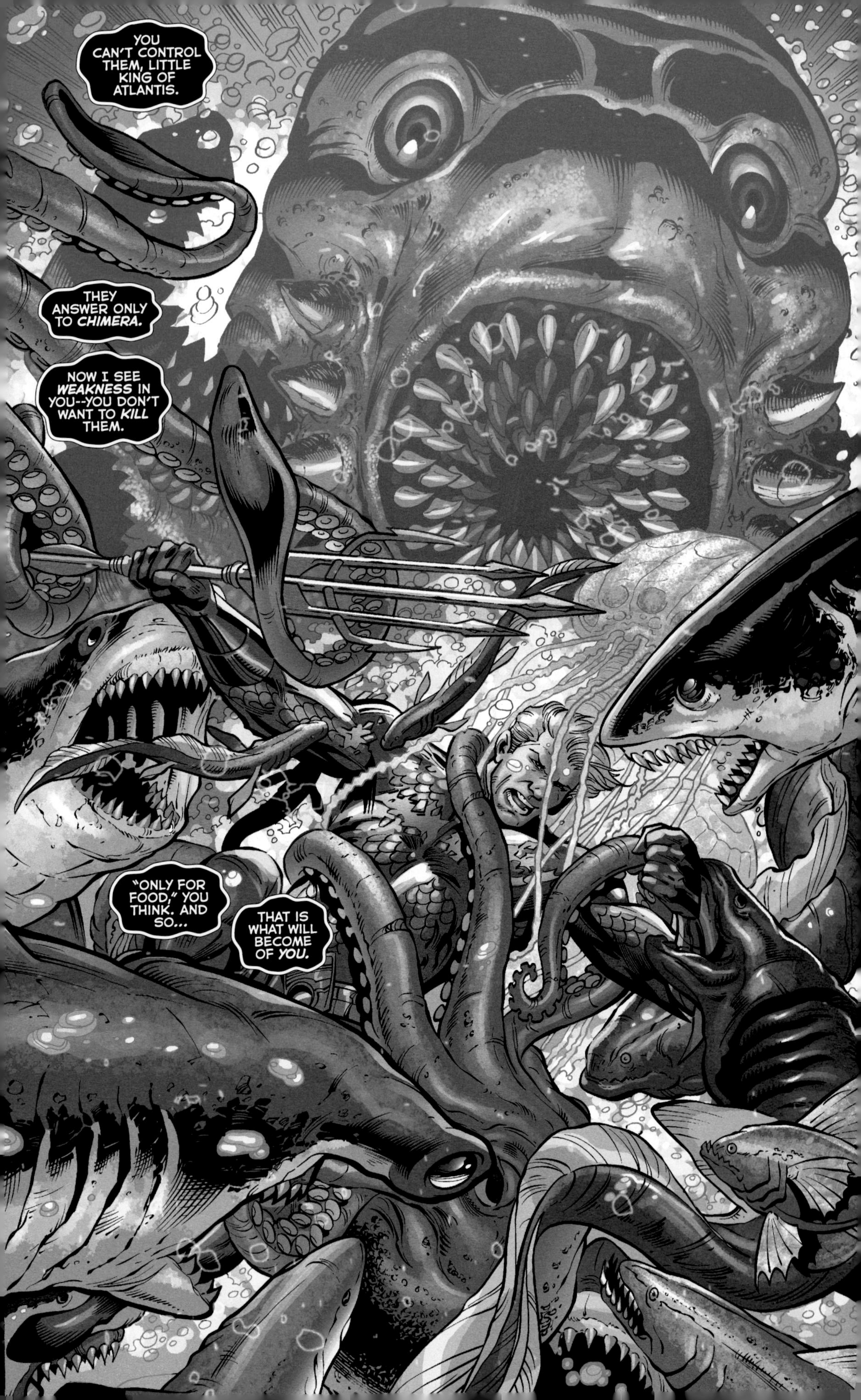
YOU CAN'T CONTROL THEM, LITTLE KING OF ATLANTIS.
THEY ANSWER ONLY TO *CHIMERA*.
NOW I SEE *WEAKNESS* IN YOU--YOU DON'T WANT TO *KILL* THEM.
"ONLY FOR FOOD," YOU THINK. AND SO...
THAT IS WHAT WILL BECOME OF *YOU*.

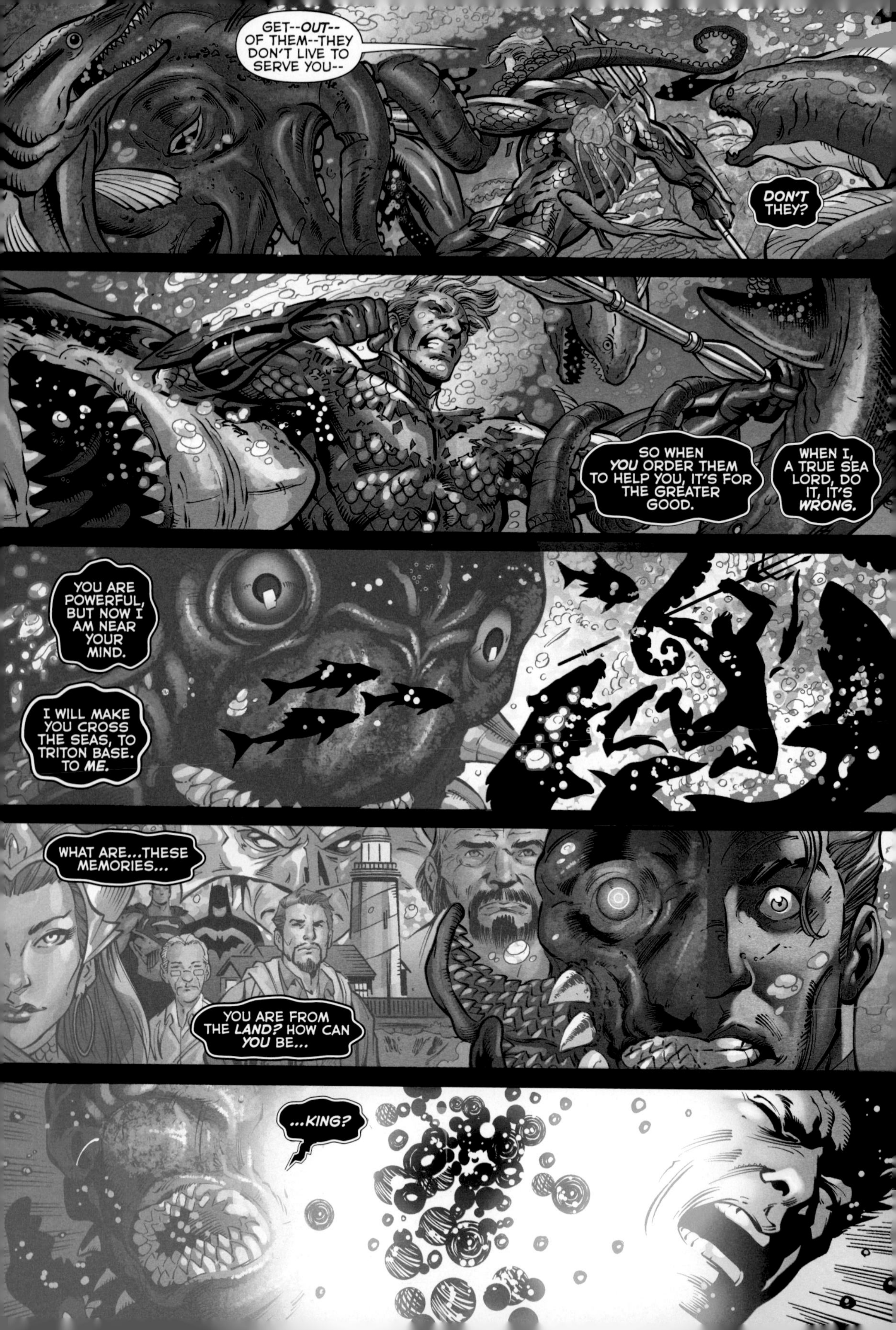

GET--OUT--OF THEM--THEY DON'T LIVE TO SERVE YOU--
DON'T THEY?
SO WHEN YOU ORDER THEM TO HELP YOU, IT'S FOR THE GREATER GOOD.
WHEN I, A TRUE SEA LORD, DO IT, IT'S WRONG.
YOU ARE POWERFUL, BUT NOW I AM NEAR YOUR MIND.
I WILL MAKE YOU CROSS THE SEAS, TO TRITON BASE. TO ME.
WHAT ARE...THESE MEMORIES...
YOU ARE FROM THE LAND? HOW CAN YOU BE...
...KING?

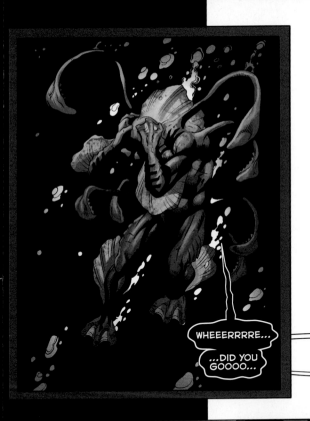

WHEEERRRRE...

...DID YOU GOOOO...

THE NORTH SENTRY WAS RIGHT, IT *IS* THE KING!

SIRE-- ARE YOU ALL RIGHT?

THE ANIMALS--THEY *ATTACKED* YOU--WHAT HAPPENED?

THAT...MAY TAKE SOME TIME TO ANSWER.

WHAT'S THE NEWS IN ATLANTIS?

ALL ANYONE SPEAKS OF IS THE QUEEN'S MISSION!

MISSION? *MERA*?

SHE AND CAPTAIN TULA CAPTURED AN ENTIRE SECT OF CONSPIRATORS!

THEY ARE IN THE PRISON COVES!

WHAT...?

YOU MEAN SHE DIDN'T *TELL* YOU...

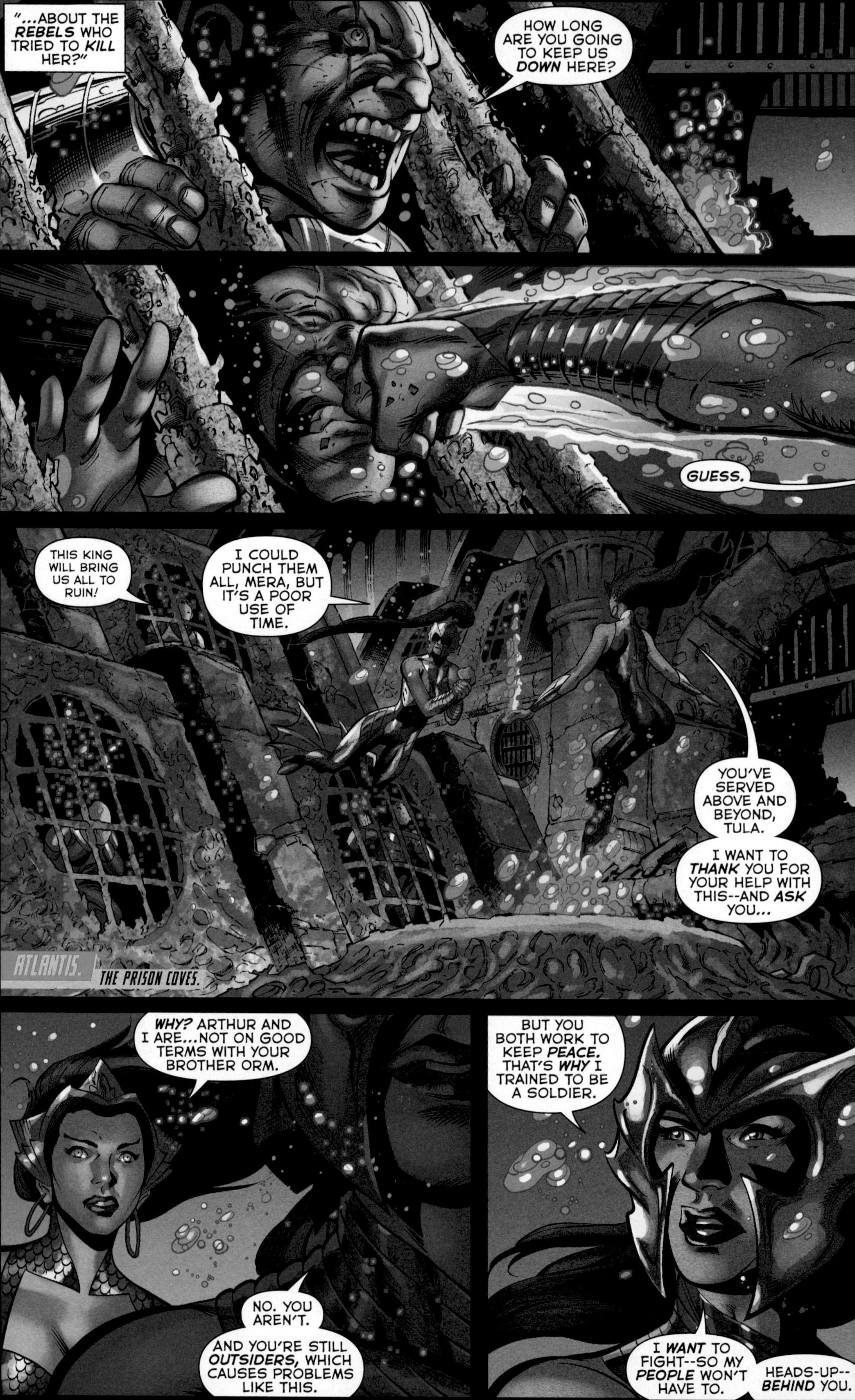
"...ABOUT THE REBELS WHO TRIED TO KILL HER?"
HOW LONG ARE YOU GOING TO KEEP US DOWN HERE?
GUESS.
ATLANTIS. THE PRISON COVES.
THIS KING WILL BRING US ALL TO RUIN!
I COULD PUNCH THEM ALL, MERA, BUT IT'S A POOR USE OF TIME.
YOU'VE SERVED ABOVE AND BEYOND, TULA.
I WANT TO THANK YOU FOR YOUR HELP WITH THIS--AND ASK YOU...
WHY? ARTHUR AND I ARE...NOT ON GOOD TERMS WITH YOUR BROTHER ORM.
NO. YOU AREN'T.
AND YOU'RE STILL OUTSIDERS, WHICH CAUSES PROBLEMS LIKE THIS.
BUT YOU BOTH WORK TO KEEP PEACE. THAT'S WHY I TRAINED TO BE A SOLDIER.
I WANT TO FIGHT--SO MY PEOPLE WON'T HAVE TO.
HEADS-UP--BEHIND YOU.

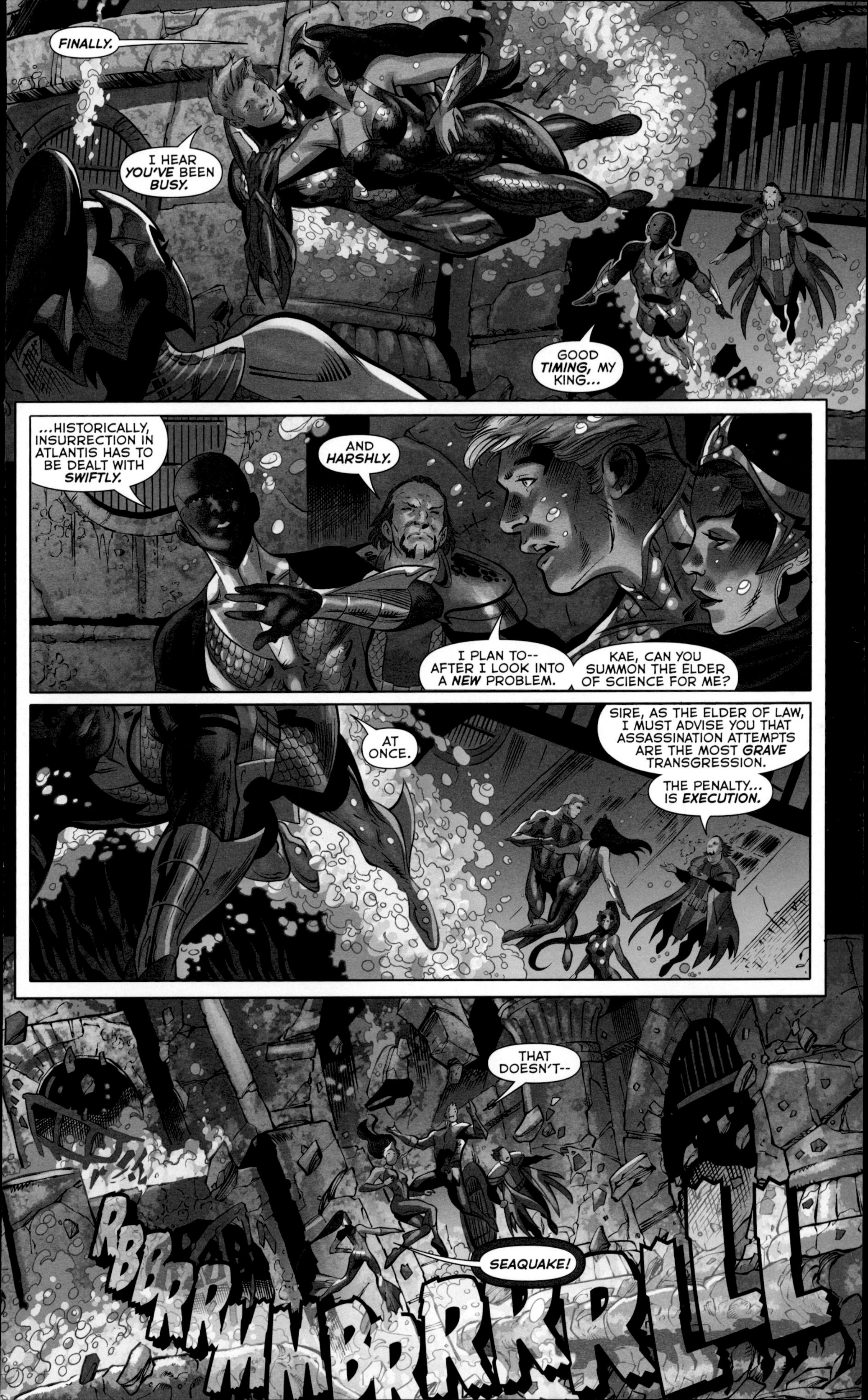
FINALLY.
I HEAR YOU'VE BEEN BUSY.
GOOD TIMING, MY KING...
...HISTORICALLY, INSURRECTION IN ATLANTIS HAS TO BE DEALT WITH SWIFTLY.
AND HARSHLY.
I PLAN TO-- AFTER I LOOK INTO A NEW PROBLEM.
KAE, CAN YOU SUMMON THE ELDER OF SCIENCE FOR ME?
AT ONCE.
SIRE, AS THE ELDER OF LAW, I MUST ADVISE YOU THAT ASSASSINATION ATTEMPTS ARE THE MOST GRAVE TRANSGRESSION.
THE PENALTY... IS EXECUTION.
THAT DOESN'T--
SEAQUAKE!
RBRRRMMBRRKRLL

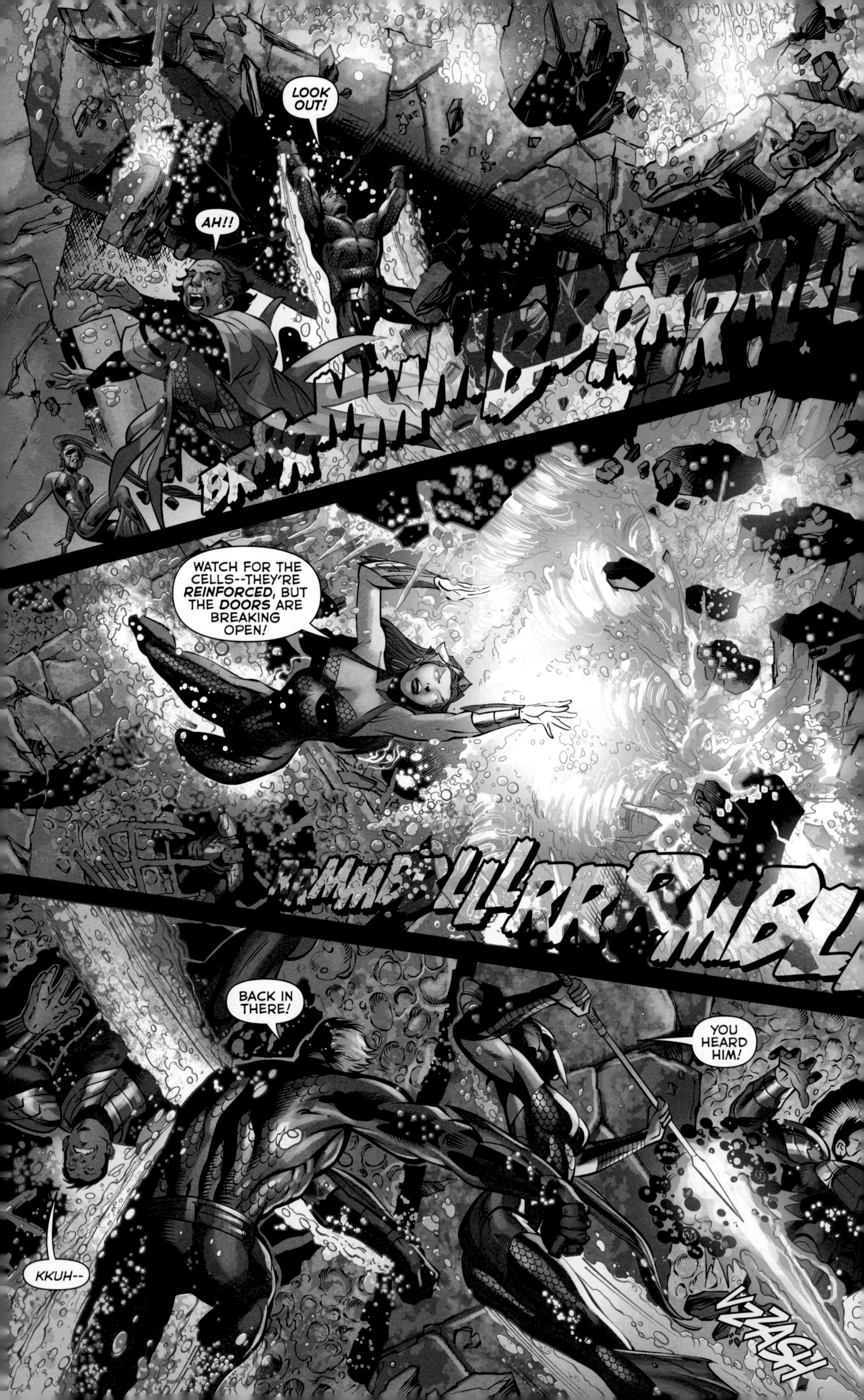
LOOK OUT!
AH!!
WATCH FOR THE CELLS--THEY'RE *REINFORCED*, BUT THE *DOORS* ARE BREAKING OPEN!
BACK IN THERE!
YOU HEARD HIM!
KKUH--
VZZASH

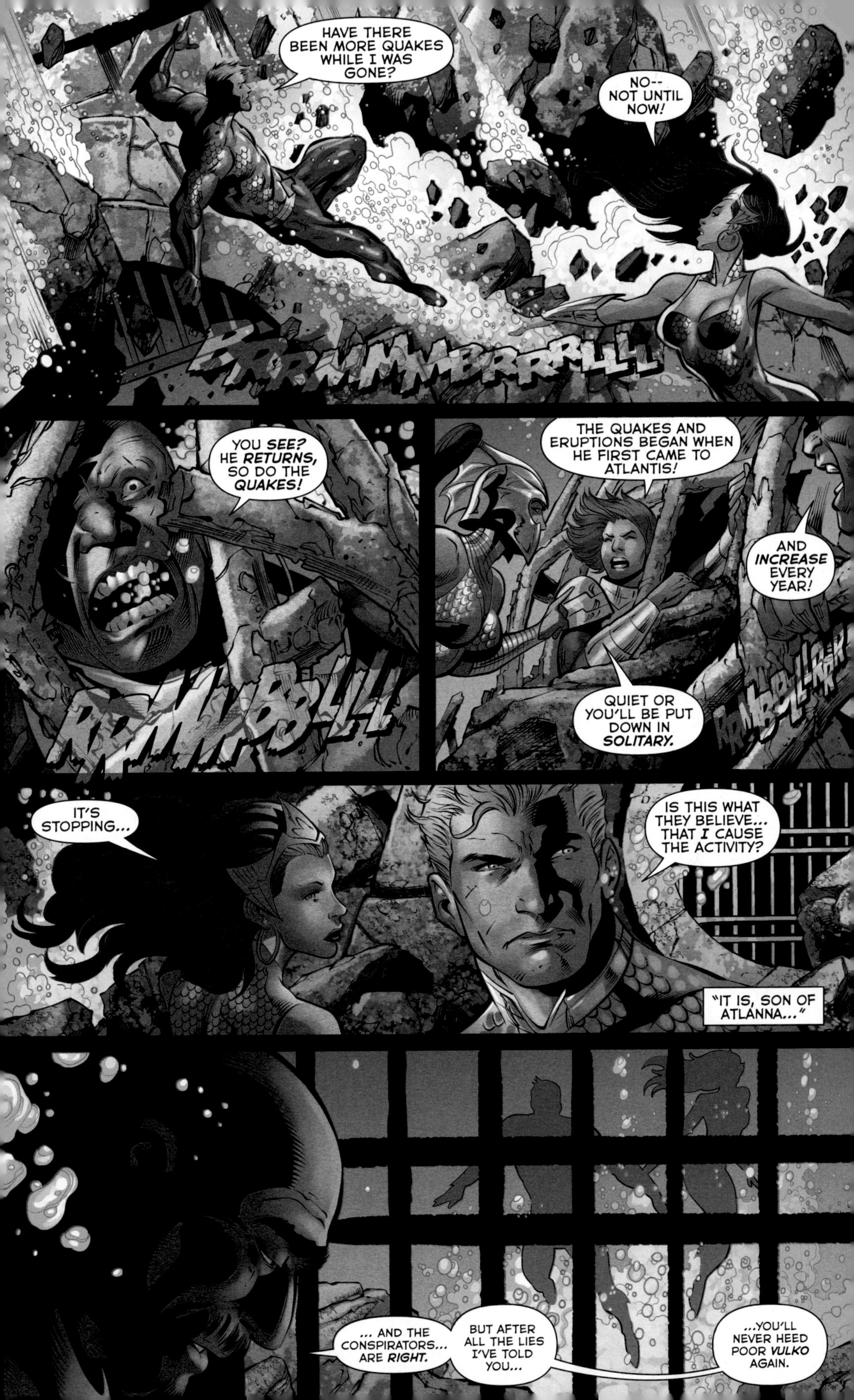
HAVE THERE BEEN MORE QUAKES WHILE I WAS GONE?
NO-- NOT UNTIL NOW!
BRRUMMMBRRRLLL
YOU SEE? HE RETURNS, SO DO THE QUAKES!
RRUMMBLLL
THE QUAKES AND ERUPTIONS BEGAN WHEN HE FIRST CAME TO ATLANTIS!
AND INCREASE EVERY YEAR!
QUIET OR YOU'LL BE PUT DOWN IN SOLITARY.
IT'S STOPPING...
IS THIS WHAT THEY BELIEVE... THAT I CAUSE THE ACTIVITY?
"IT IS, SON OF ATLANNA..."
... AND THE CONSPIRATORS... ARE RIGHT.
BUT AFTER ALL THE LIES I'VE TOLD YOU...
...YOU'LL NEVER HEED POOR VULKO AGAIN.

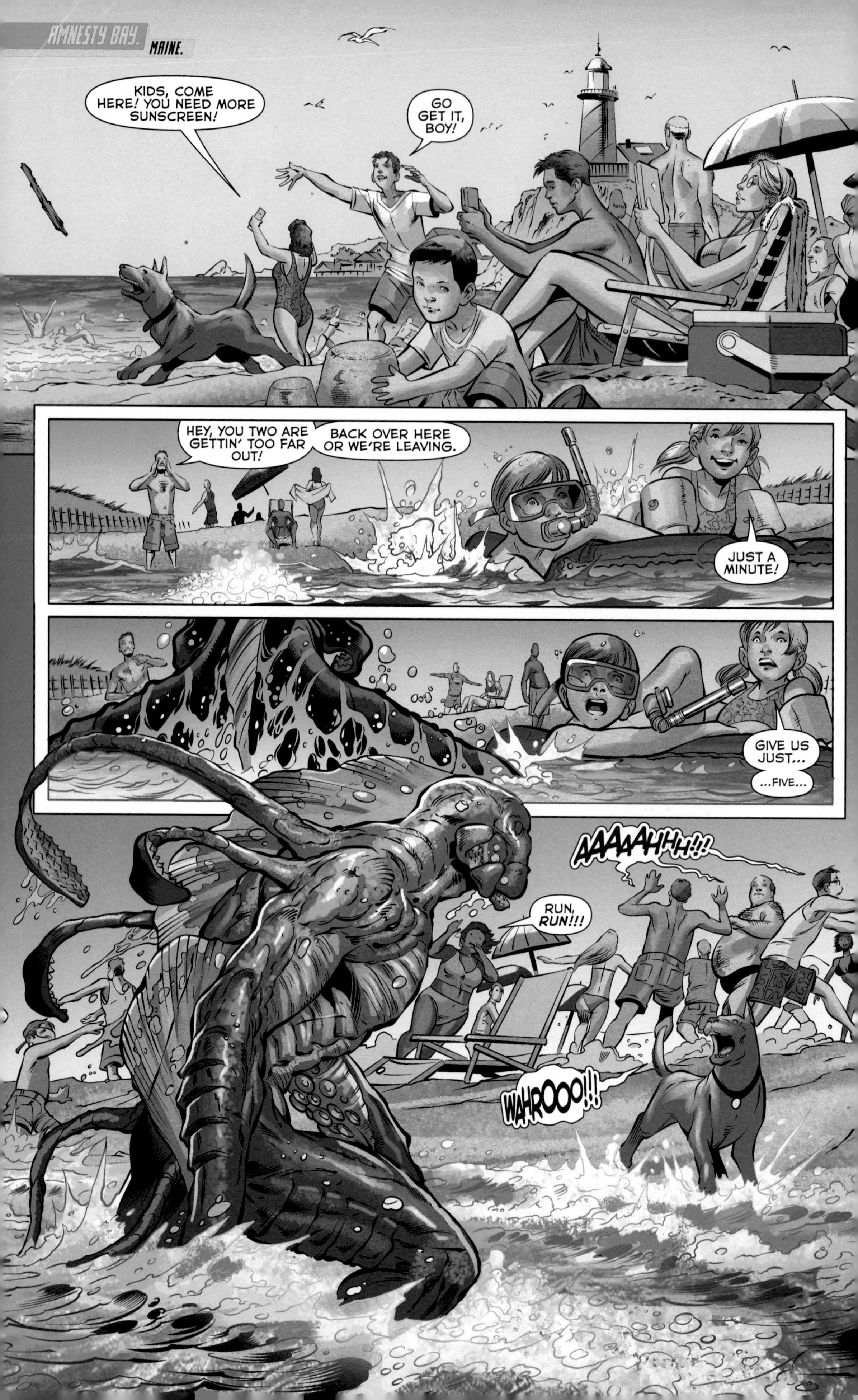
AMNESTY BAY.
MAINE.
KIDS, COME HERE! YOU NEED MORE SUNSCREEN!
GO GET IT, BOY!
HEY, YOU TWO ARE GETTIN' TOO FAR OUT!
BACK OVER HERE OR WE'RE LEAVING.
JUST A MINUTE!
GIVE US JUST...
...FIVE...
AAAAAHHHH!!!
RUN, RUN!!!
WAHROOO!!!

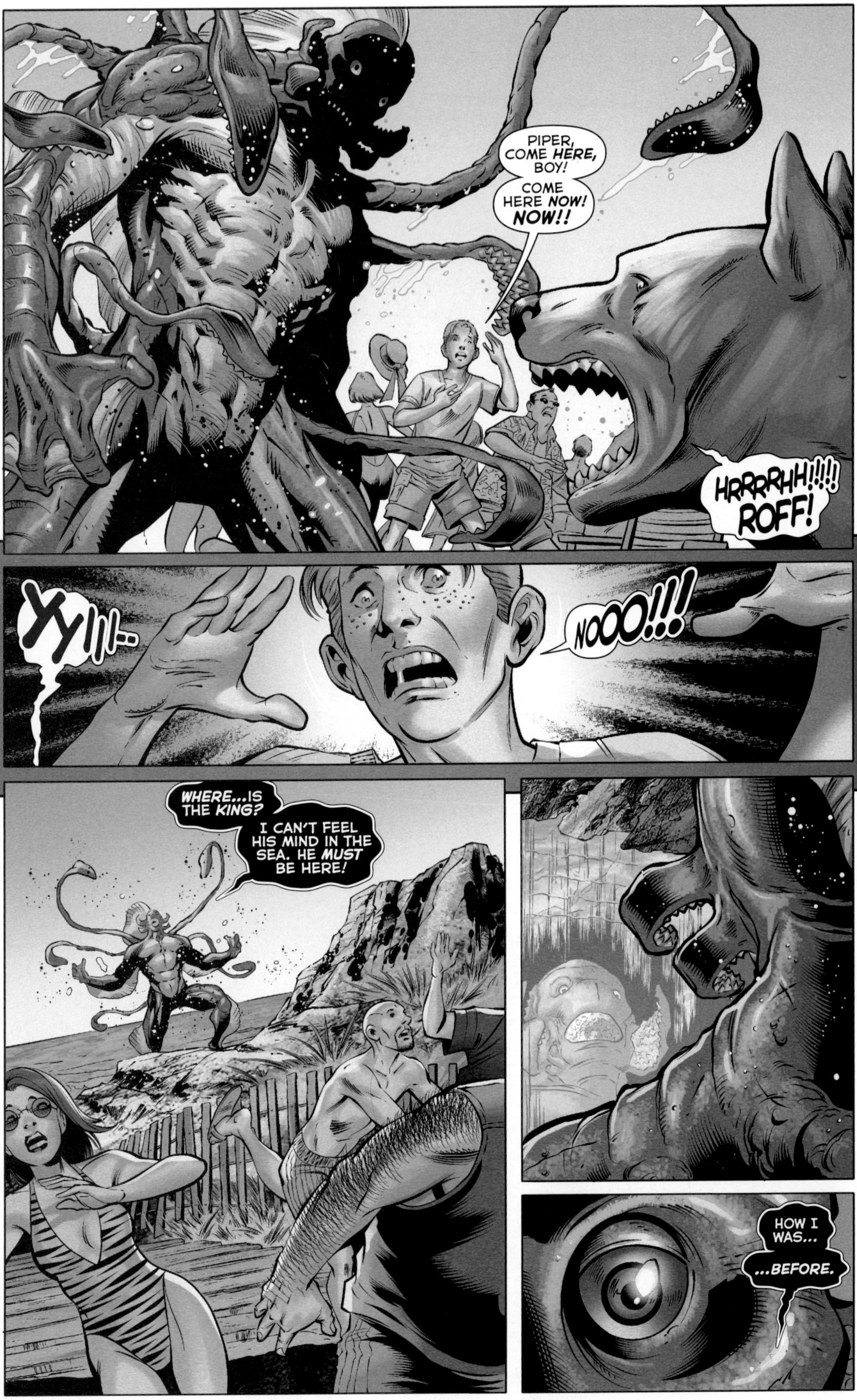
PIPER, COME HERE, BOY!
COME HERE NOW! NOW!!
HRRRRHH!!!!! ROFF!
YYIII--
NOOO!!!
WHERE...IS THE KING?
I CAN'T FEEL HIS MIND IN THE SEA. HE MUST BE HERE!
HOW I WAS...
...BEFORE.

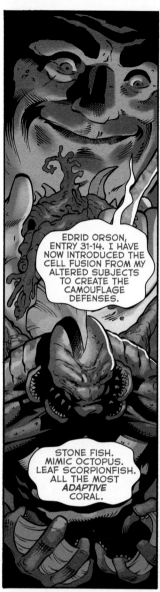

EDRID ORSON, ENTRY 31-14. I HAVE NOW INTRODUCED THE CELL FUSION FROM MY ALTERED SUBJECTS TO CREATE THE CAMOUFLAGE DEFENSES.

STONE FISH. MIMIC OCTOPUS. LEAF SCORPIONFISH. ALL THE MOST *ADAPTIVE* CORAL.

ADDED TO THE NERVOUS SYSTEM OF A HUMAN, OUR CHIMERA WILL SURPASS ALL THE DONORS IN STEALTH ABILITY.

HNNRR... RRGGHH...

THOUGH AN *EXTREME* CAMOUFLAGE COULD BE...

...PAINFUL.

YOU! HANDS BEHIND YOUR HEAD!

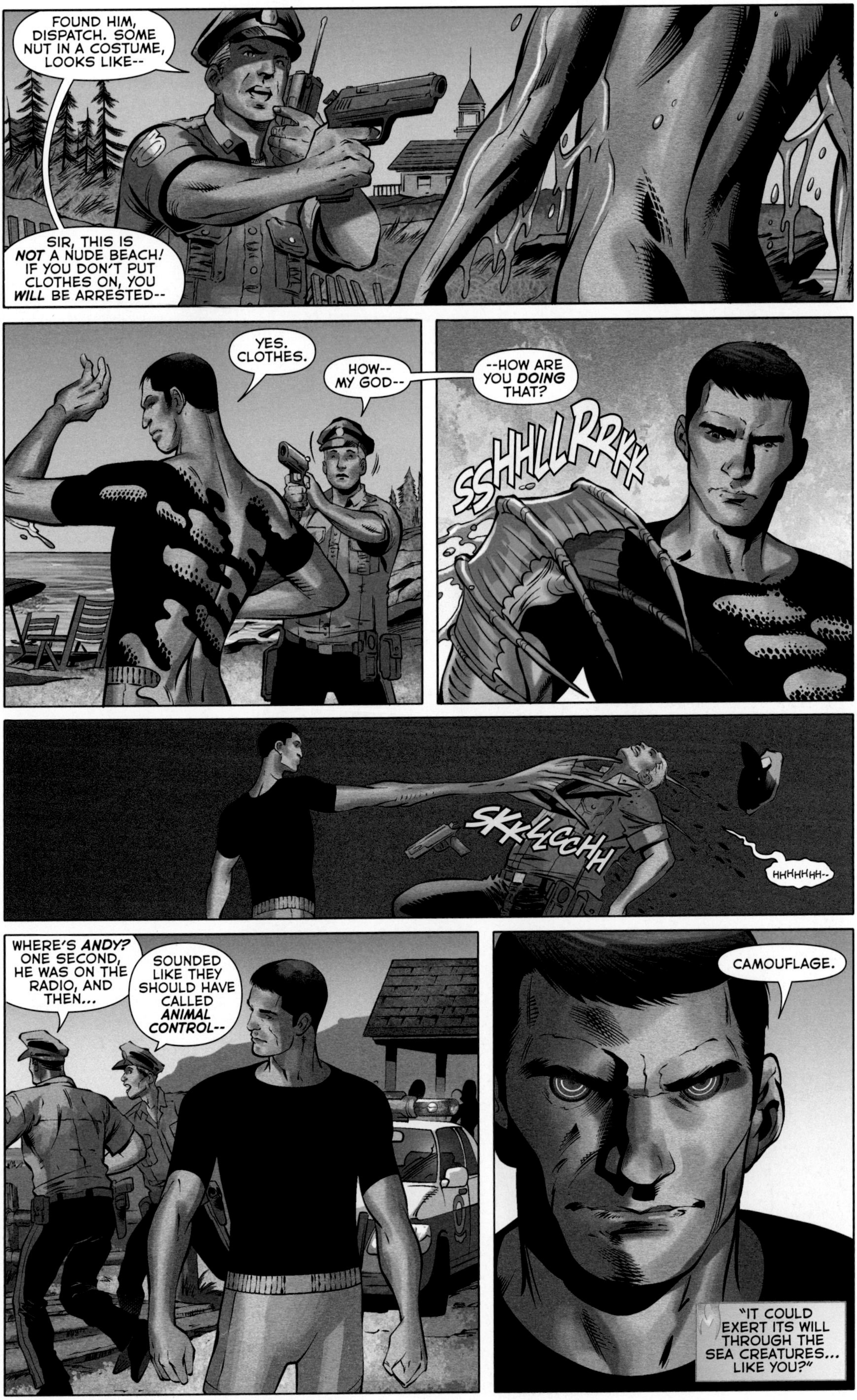
FOUND HIM, DISPATCH. SOME NUT IN A COSTUME, LOOKS LIKE--
SIR, THIS IS *NOT* A NUDE BEACH! IF YOU DON'T PUT CLOTHES ON, YOU *WILL* BE ARRESTED--
YES. CLOTHES.
HOW-- MY GOD--
--HOW ARE YOU *DOING* THAT?
SSHHLLRRKK
SKKLCCHH
HHHHHH--
WHERE'S *ANDY?* ONE SECOND, HE WAS ON THE RADIO, AND THEN...
SOUNDED LIKE THEY SHOULD HAVE CALLED *ANIMAL CONTROL*--
CAMOUFLAGE.
"IT COULD EXERT ITS WILL THROUGH THE SEA CREATURES... LIKE YOU?"

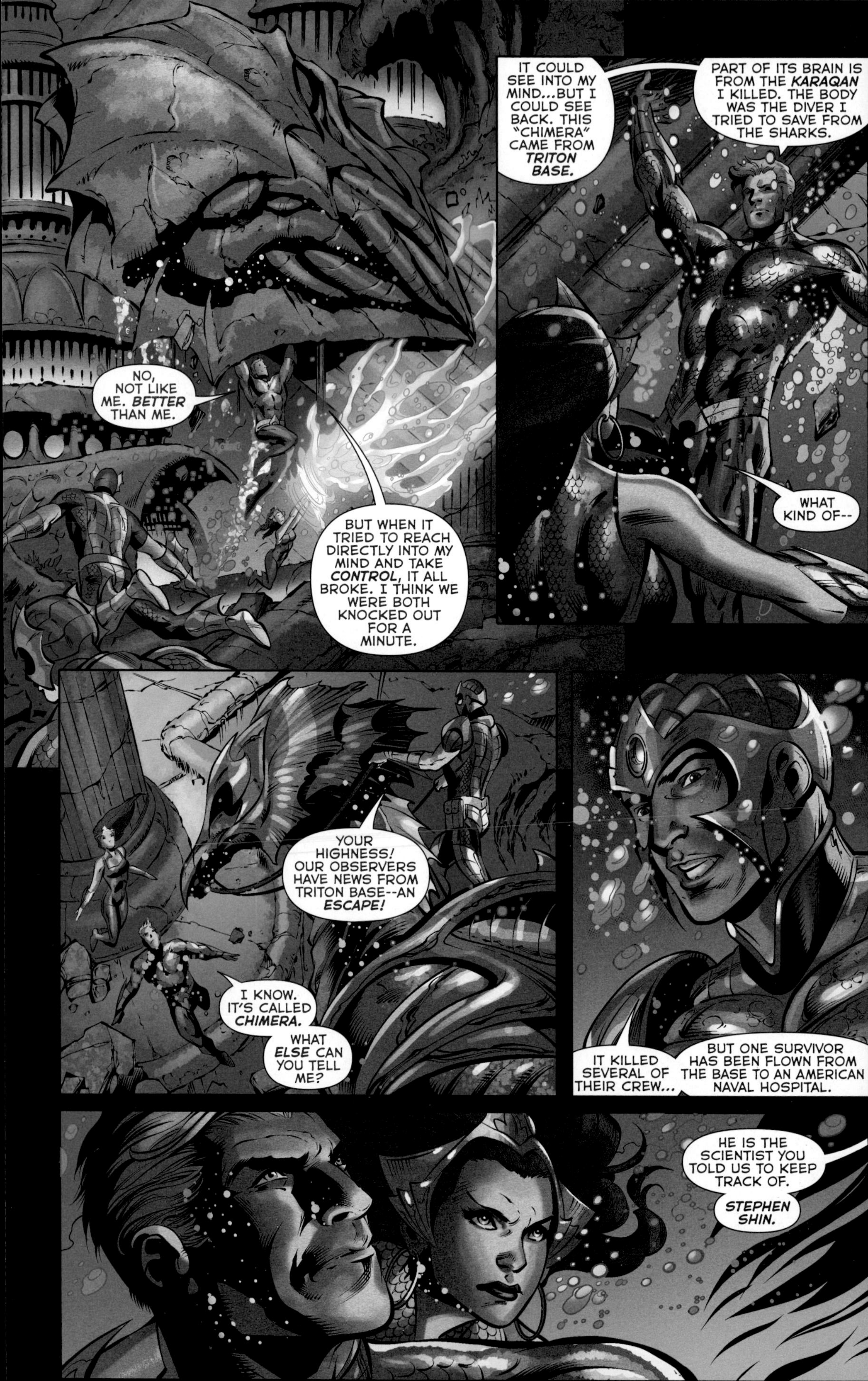
NO, NOT LIKE ME. BETTER THAN ME.
BUT WHEN IT TRIED TO REACH DIRECTLY INTO MY MIND AND TAKE CONTROL, IT ALL BROKE. I THINK WE WERE BOTH KNOCKED OUT FOR A MINUTE.
IT COULD SEE INTO MY MIND...BUT I COULD SEE BACK. THIS "CHIMERA" CAME FROM TRITON BASE.
PART OF ITS BRAIN IS FROM THE KARAQAN I KILLED. THE BODY WAS THE DIVER I TRIED TO SAVE FROM THE SHARKS.
WHAT KIND OF--
YOUR HIGHNESS! OUR OBSERVERS HAVE NEWS FROM TRITON BASE--AN ESCAPE!
I KNOW. IT'S CALLED CHIMERA.
WHAT ELSE CAN YOU TELL ME?
IT KILLED SEVERAL OF THEIR CREW...
BUT ONE SURVIVOR HAS BEEN FLOWN FROM THE BASE TO AN AMERICAN NAVAL HOSPITAL.
HE IS THE SCIENTIST YOU TOLD US TO KEEP TRACK OF.
STEPHEN SHIN.

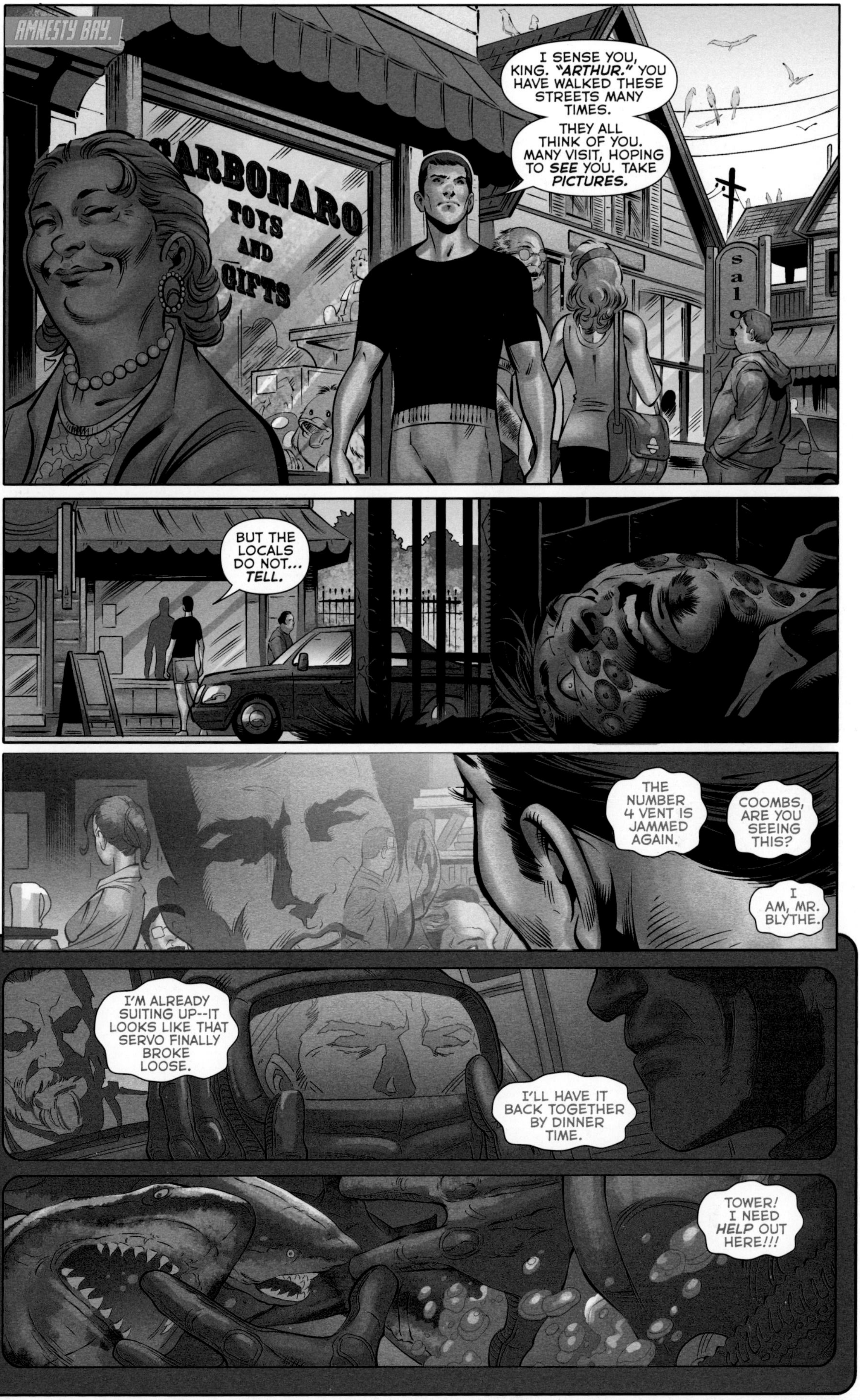
AMNESTY BAY.
I SENSE YOU, KING. "ARTHUR." YOU HAVE WALKED THESE STREETS MANY TIMES.
THEY ALL THINK OF YOU. MANY VISIT, HOPING TO SEE YOU. TAKE PICTURES.
CARBONARO TOYS AND GIFTS
salon
BUT THE LOCALS DO NOT... TELL.
THE NUMBER 4 VENT IS JAMMED AGAIN.
COOMBS, ARE YOU SEEING THIS?
I AM, MR. BLYTHE.
I'M ALREADY SUITING UP--IT LOOKS LIKE THAT SERVO FINALLY BROKE LOOSE.
I'LL HAVE IT BACK TOGETHER BY DINNER TIME.
TOWER! I NEED HELP OUT HERE!!!

ROWR-- RROOWR!!!

HSSS!!

SALTY, NO!

SO SORRY SIR, HE'S NOT USUALLY LIKE THIS--!

RRRRILLL!!!

--GOT IT, I'M HEADING OVER THERE NOW-- WHOA!

Specials
Venti Packer $2.99
Grande Pelletier $15
Mocha ___ ay $5.99
Berry-t ___ ices $4.29
Cacne ___ n $2.79
Rain

ERIKA-- OH GOSH, NOW WE'RE CATCHING EVERYBODY!

C'MON, SALTY, CALM DOWN!

THIS DAY IS AWFUL, JENNY. ONE OF OURS-- ANDY--WAS FOUND DEAD DOWN AT SOUTH BEACH.

LIKE HE HAD BEEN SHOT--MULTIPLE TIMES. THEN JUST AS I'M HEADING OUT THERE, GUESS WHO CALLS?

ARTHUR. HE SAYS DR. SHIN HAS BEEN LIFE-FLIGHTED TO A NAVAL HOSPITAL SHIP OFF BOSTON.

OH GOD, IS HE GOING TO BE OKAY?

ARTHUR.

COFFEE

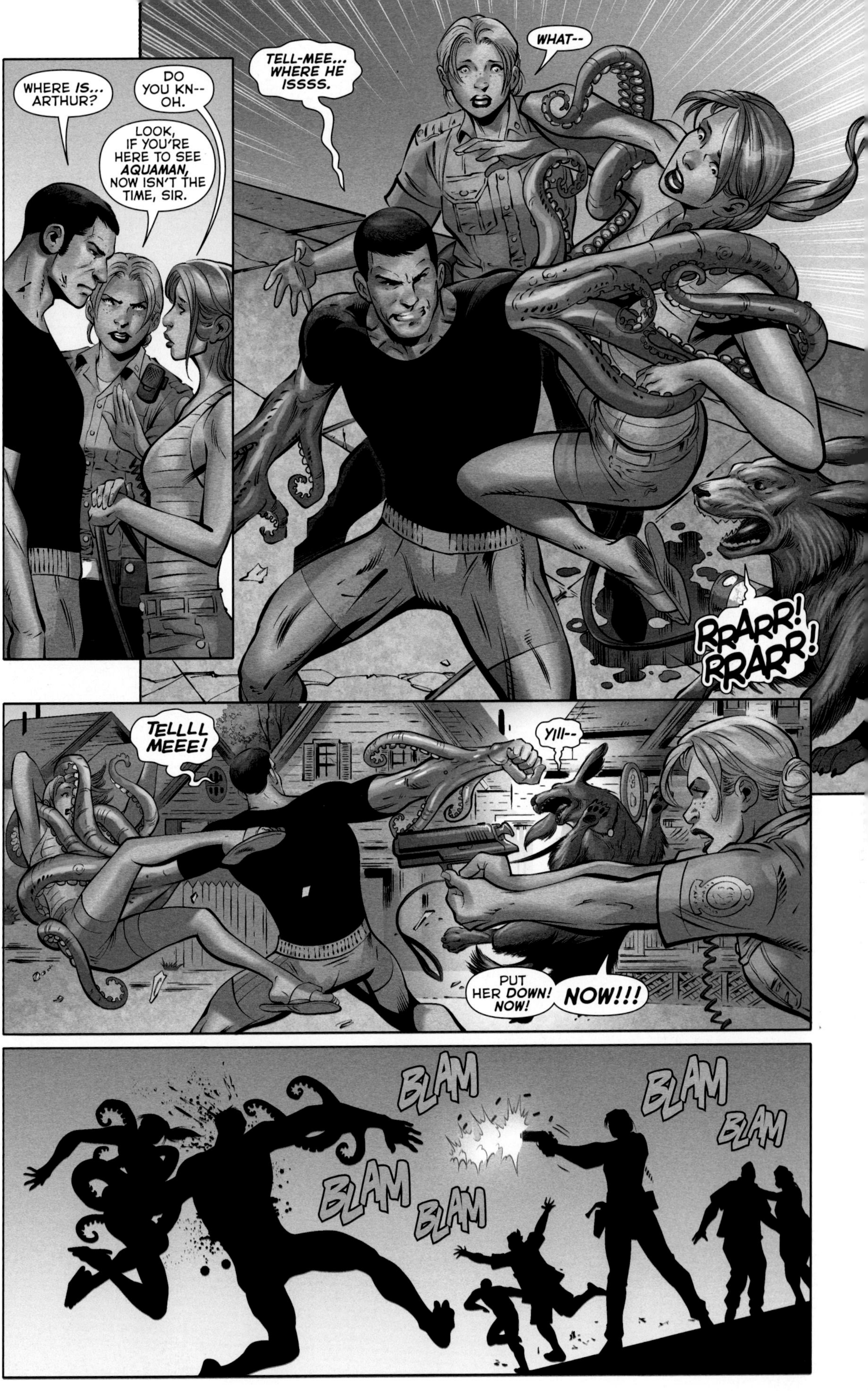
WHERE IS... ARTHUR?
DO YOU KN-- OH.
LOOK, IF YOU'RE HERE TO SEE AQUAMAN, NOW ISN'T THE TIME, SIR.
TELL-MEE... WHERE HE ISSSS.
WHAT--
RRARR! RRARR!
TELLLL MEEE!
YIII--
PUT HER DOWN! NOW!
NOW!!!
BLAM
BLAM
BLAM
BLAM
BLAM

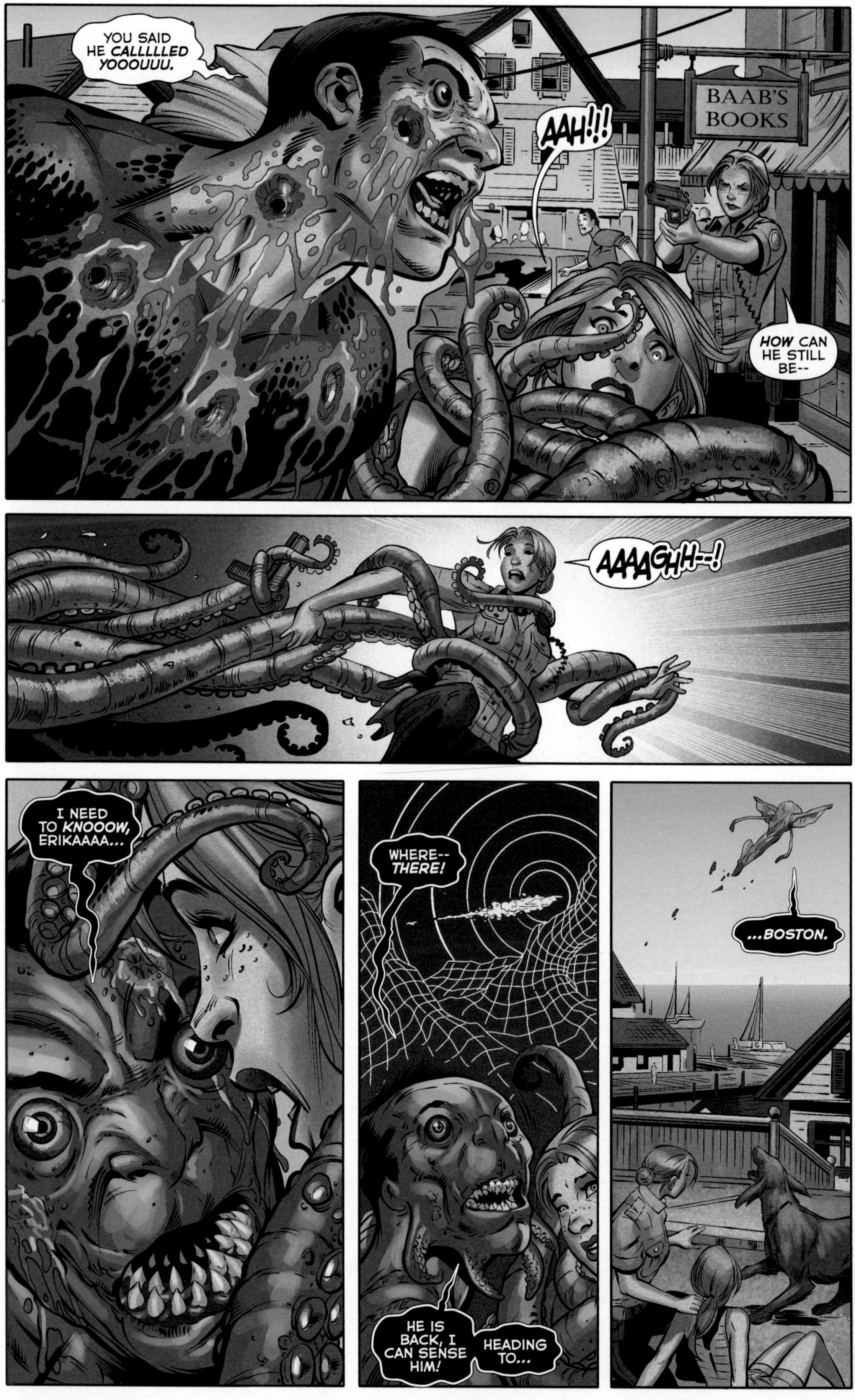
YOU SAID HE CALLLLLED YOOOUUU.
AAH!!!
HOW CAN HE STILL BE--
AAAAGHH--!
I NEED TO KNOOOW, ERIKAAAA...
WHERE-- THERE!
HE IS BACK, I CAN SENSE HIM!
HEADING TO...
...BOSTON.

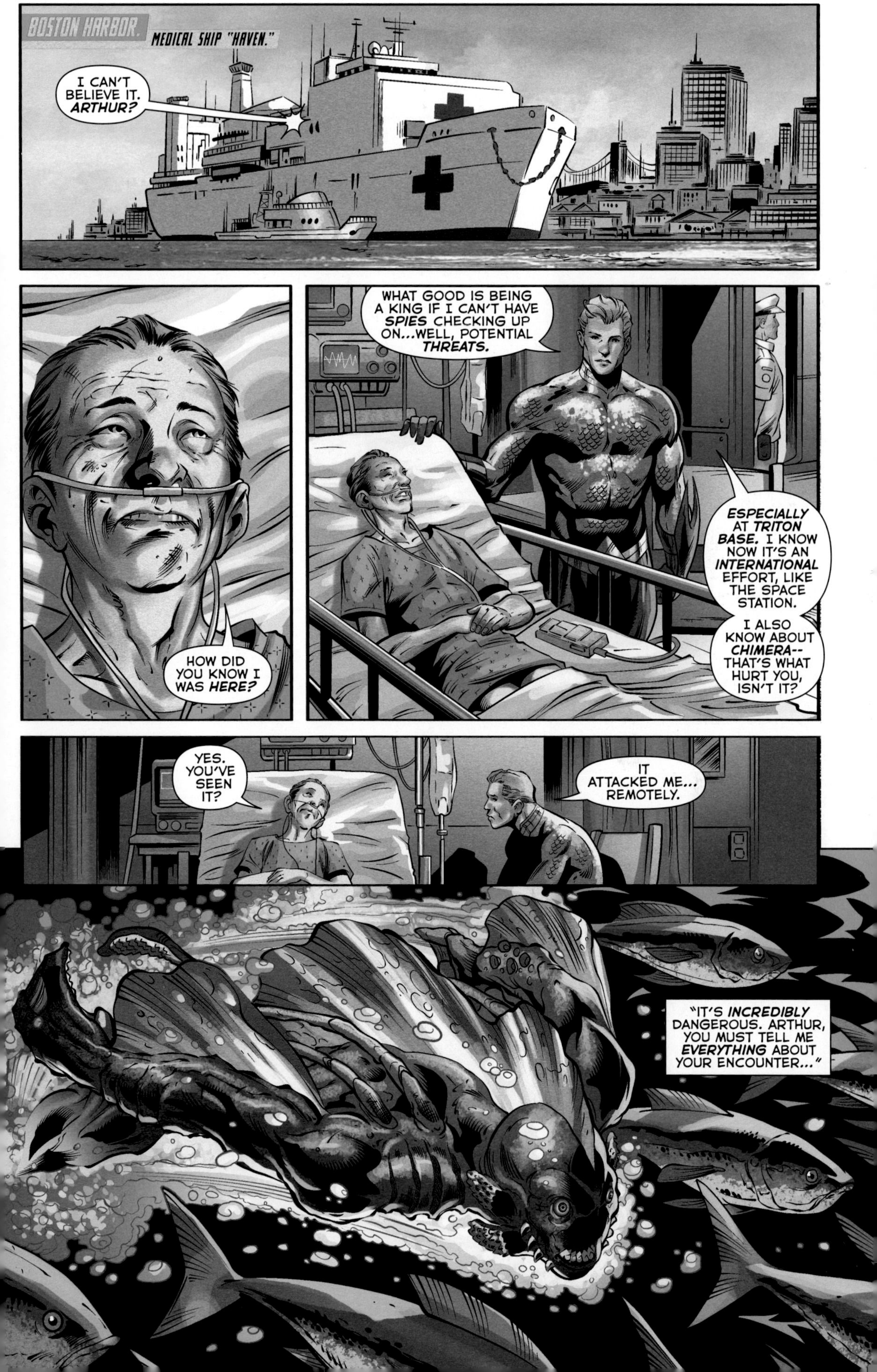
BOSTON HARBOR.
MEDICAL SHIP "HAVEN."
I CAN'T BELIEVE IT. ARTHUR?
HOW DID YOU KNOW I WAS HERE?
WHAT GOOD IS BEING A KING IF I CAN'T HAVE SPIES CHECKING UP ON...WELL, POTENTIAL THREATS.
ESPECIALLY AT TRITON BASE. I KNOW NOW IT'S AN INTERNATIONAL EFFORT, LIKE THE SPACE STATION.
I ALSO KNOW ABOUT CHIMERA-- THAT'S WHAT HURT YOU, ISN'T IT?
YES. YOU'VE SEEN IT?
IT ATTACKED ME... REMOTELY.
"IT'S INCREDIBLY DANGEROUS. ARTHUR, YOU MUST TELL ME EVERYTHING ABOUT YOUR ENCOUNTER..."

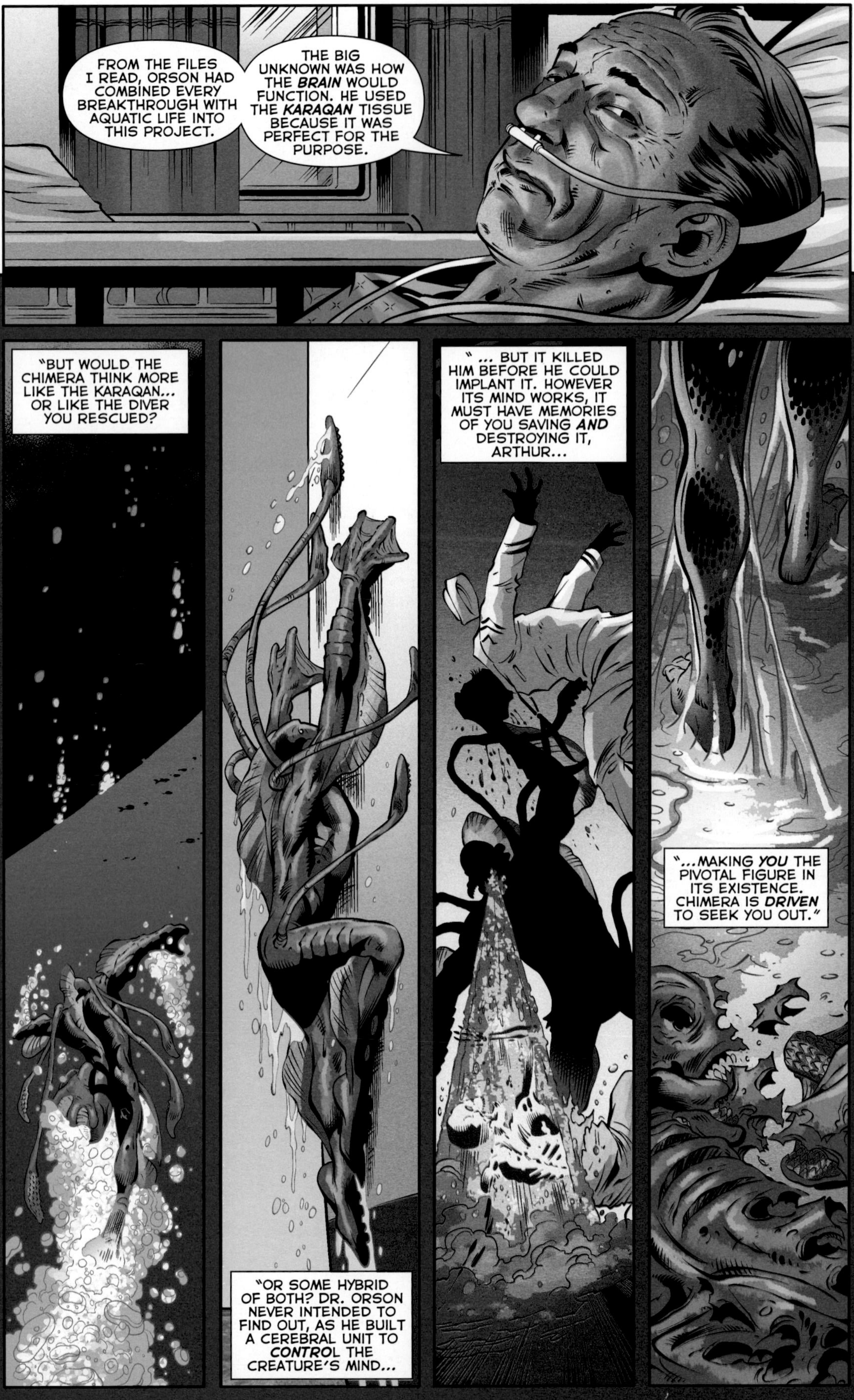
FROM THE FILES I READ, ORSON HAD COMBINED EVERY BREAKTHROUGH WITH AQUATIC LIFE INTO THIS PROJECT.
THE BIG UNKNOWN WAS HOW THE *BRAIN* WOULD FUNCTION. HE USED THE *KARAQAN* TISSUE BECAUSE IT WAS PERFECT FOR THE PURPOSE.
"BUT WOULD THE CHIMERA THINK MORE LIKE THE KARAQAN... OR LIKE THE DIVER YOU RESCUED?
"OR SOME HYBRID OF BOTH? DR. ORSON NEVER INTENDED TO FIND OUT, AS HE BUILT A CEREBRAL UNIT TO *CONTROL* THE CREATURE'S MIND...
"... BUT IT KILLED HIM BEFORE HE COULD IMPLANT IT. HOWEVER ITS MIND WORKS, IT MUST HAVE MEMORIES OF YOU SAVING *AND* DESTROYING IT, ARTHUR...
"...MAKING *YOU* THE PIVOTAL FIGURE IN ITS EXISTENCE. CHIMERA IS *DRIVEN* TO SEEK YOU OUT."

WHAT DO YOU THINK MADE US BOTH *BLACK OUT?*

IT HAD GREATER ABILITY WITH AQUATIC LIFE--IT ASSUMED ITS MIND WAS MORE POWERFUL THAN YOURS.

BUT THE KARAQAN ANSWERED TO YOUR ANCESTOR. IT'S LIKELY A GENETIC CONFLICT.

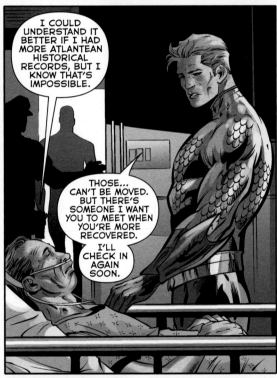

I COULD UNDERSTAND IT BETTER IF I HAD MORE ATLANTEAN HISTORICAL RECORDS, BUT I KNOW THAT'S IMPOSSIBLE.

THOSE... CAN'T BE MOVED. BUT THERE'S SOMEONE I WANT YOU TO MEET WHEN YOU'RE MORE RECOVERED.

I'LL CHECK IN AGAIN SOON.

NO ONE ADMITTED WITHOUT CAPTAIN'S ORDERS!

I HAVE TO DELIVER A MESSAGE TO DOCTOR SHIN. IT WON'T TAKE LONG.

DR. SHIN NEEDS *REST.*

I UNDERSTAND, KING.

ARTHUR... THAT'S *COOMBS,* THE DIVER!

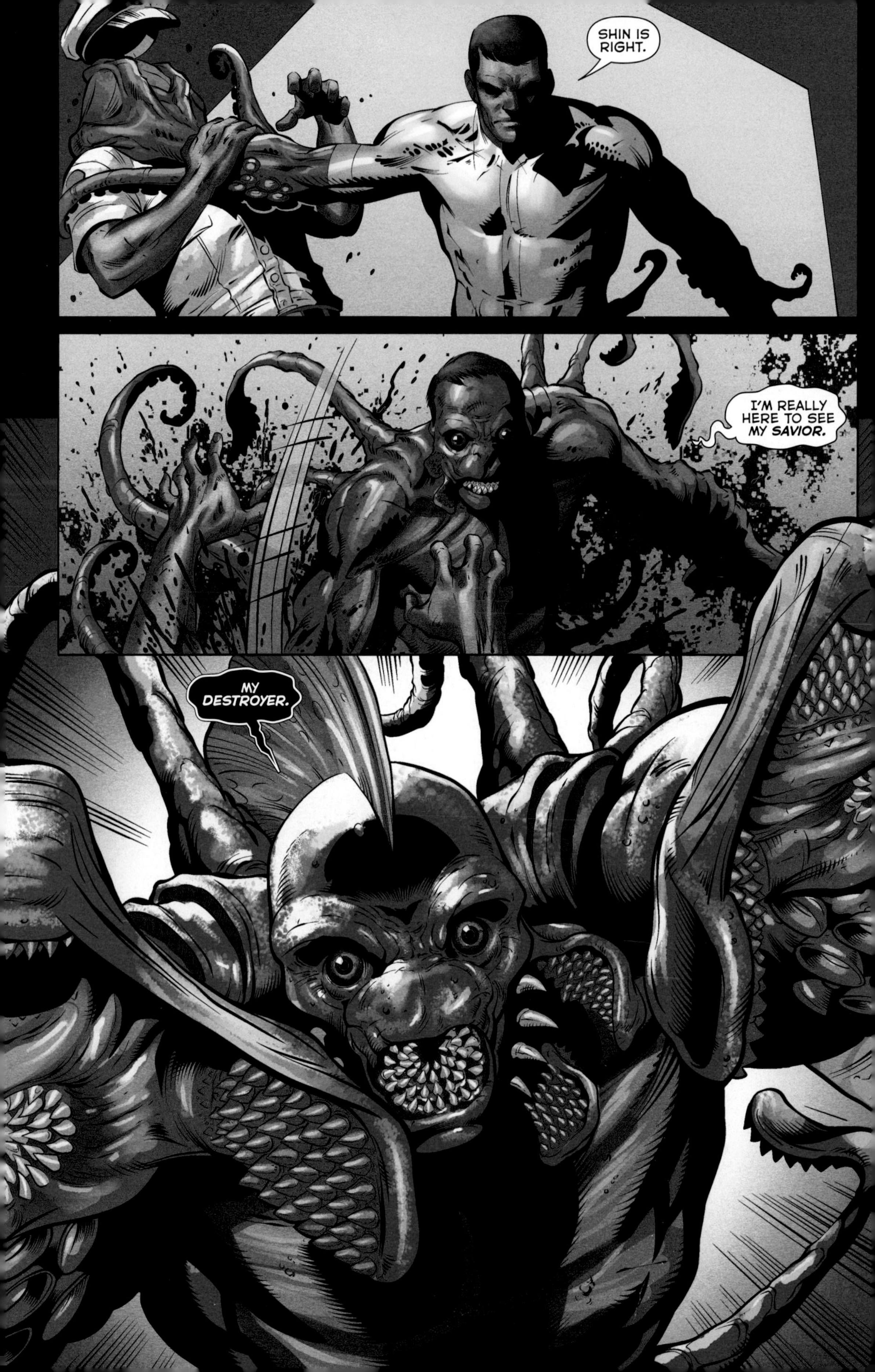
SHIN IS RIGHT.
I'M REALLY HERE TO SEE MY *SAVIOR.*
MY DESTROYER.

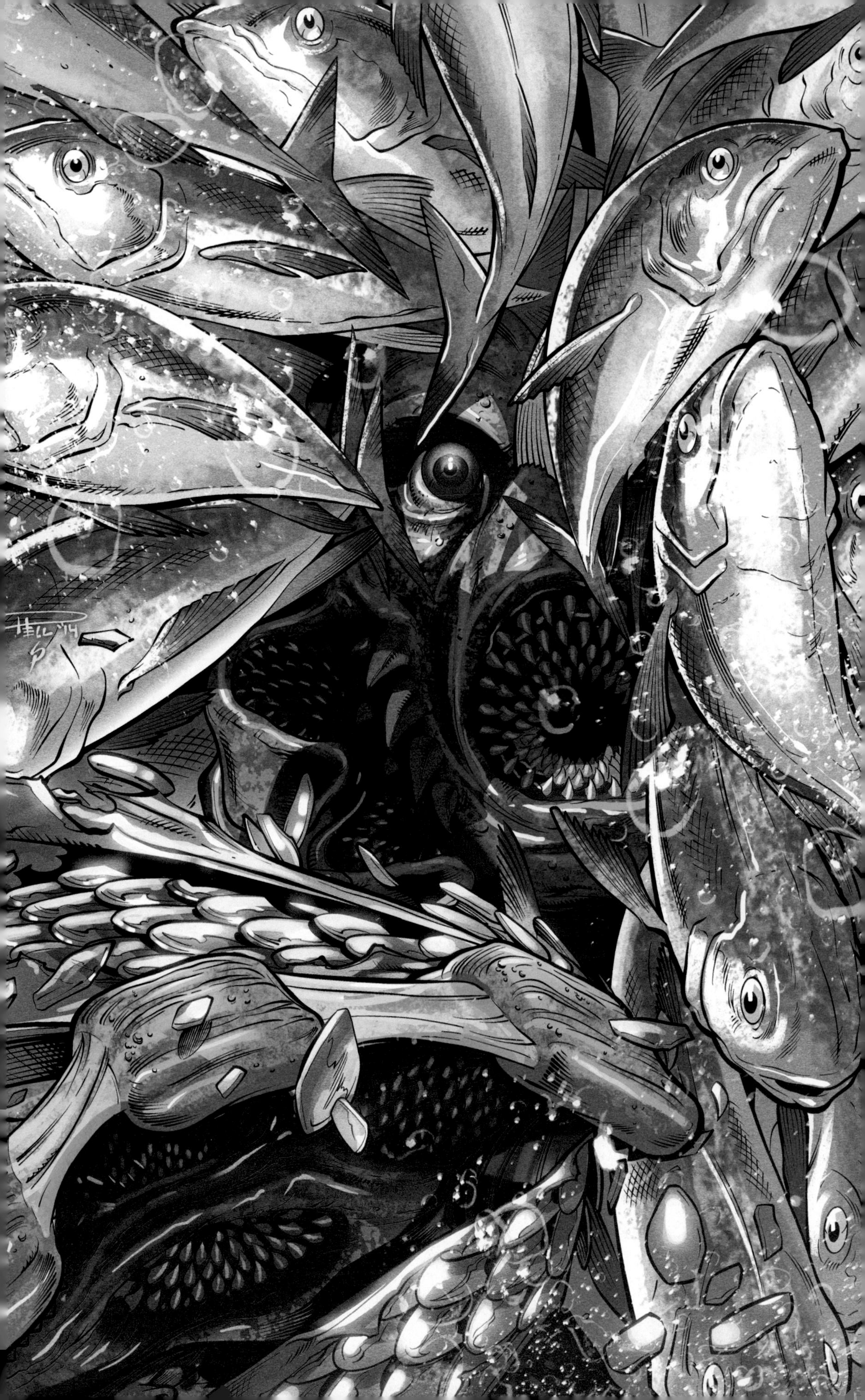

LAND AND SEA

JEFF PARKER writer **CARLOS RODRIGUEZ** penciller **BIT** inker **RAIN BEREDO** colorist **DEZI SIENTY** letterer **PELLETIER, PARSONS** and **BEREDO** cover art

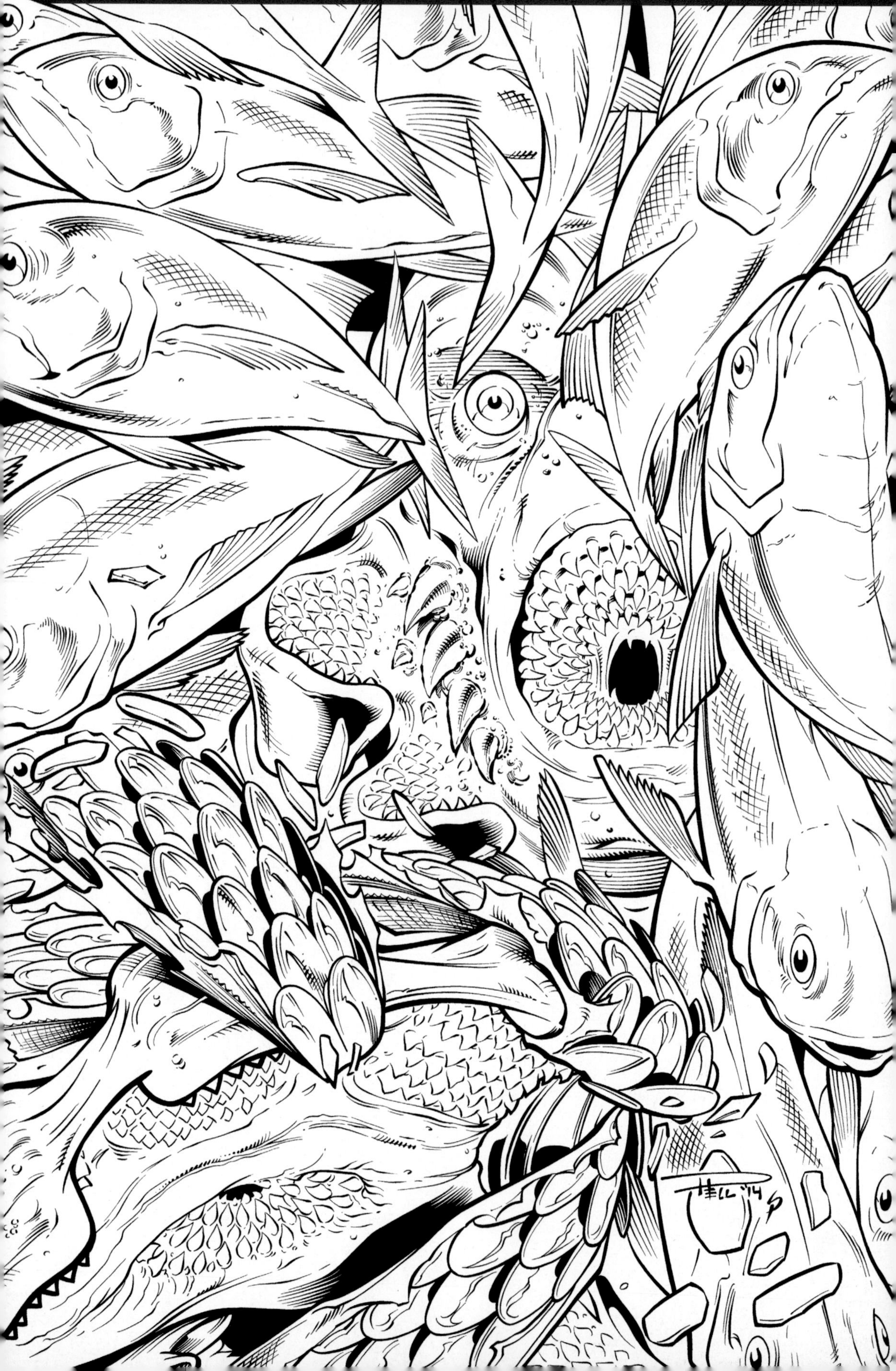

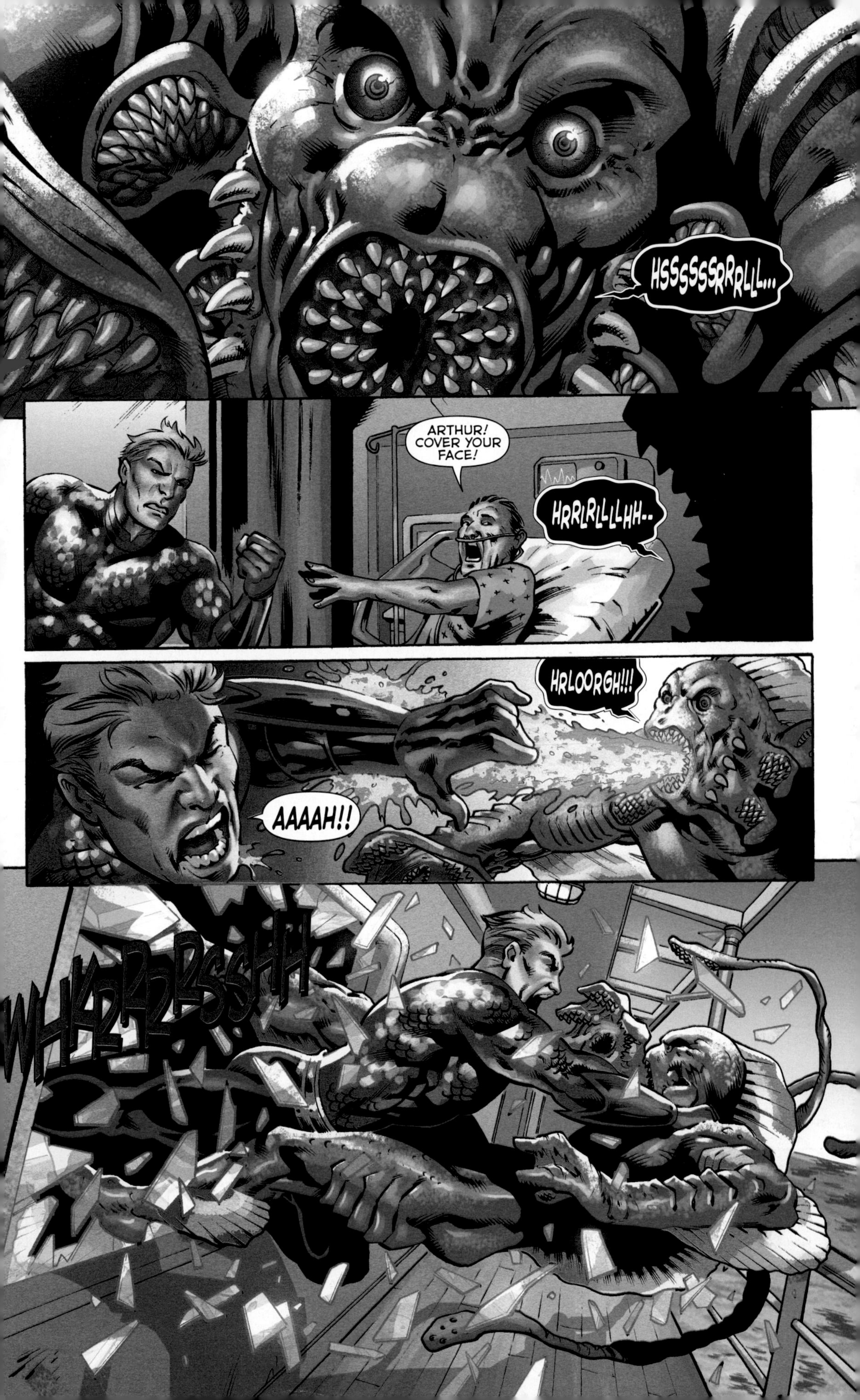
HSSSSSSRRRLLL...
ARTHUR! COVER YOUR FACE!
HRRLRLLLHH--
HRLOORGH!!!
AAAAH!!
WHKRRRSSHH

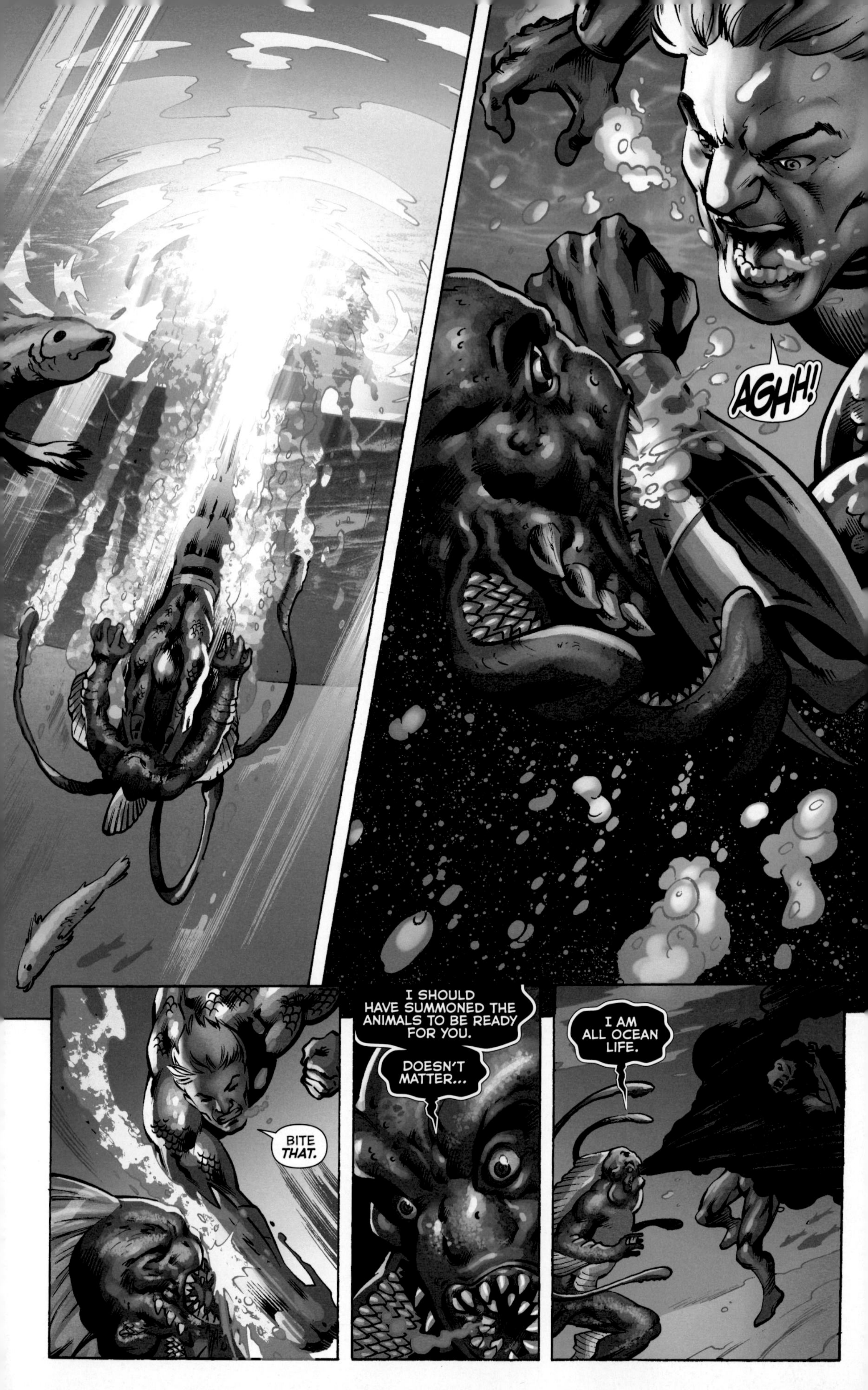
AGHH!
BITE THAT.
I SHOULD HAVE SUMMONED THE ANIMALS TO BE READY FOR YOU.
DOESN'T MATTER...
I AM ALL OCEAN LIFE.

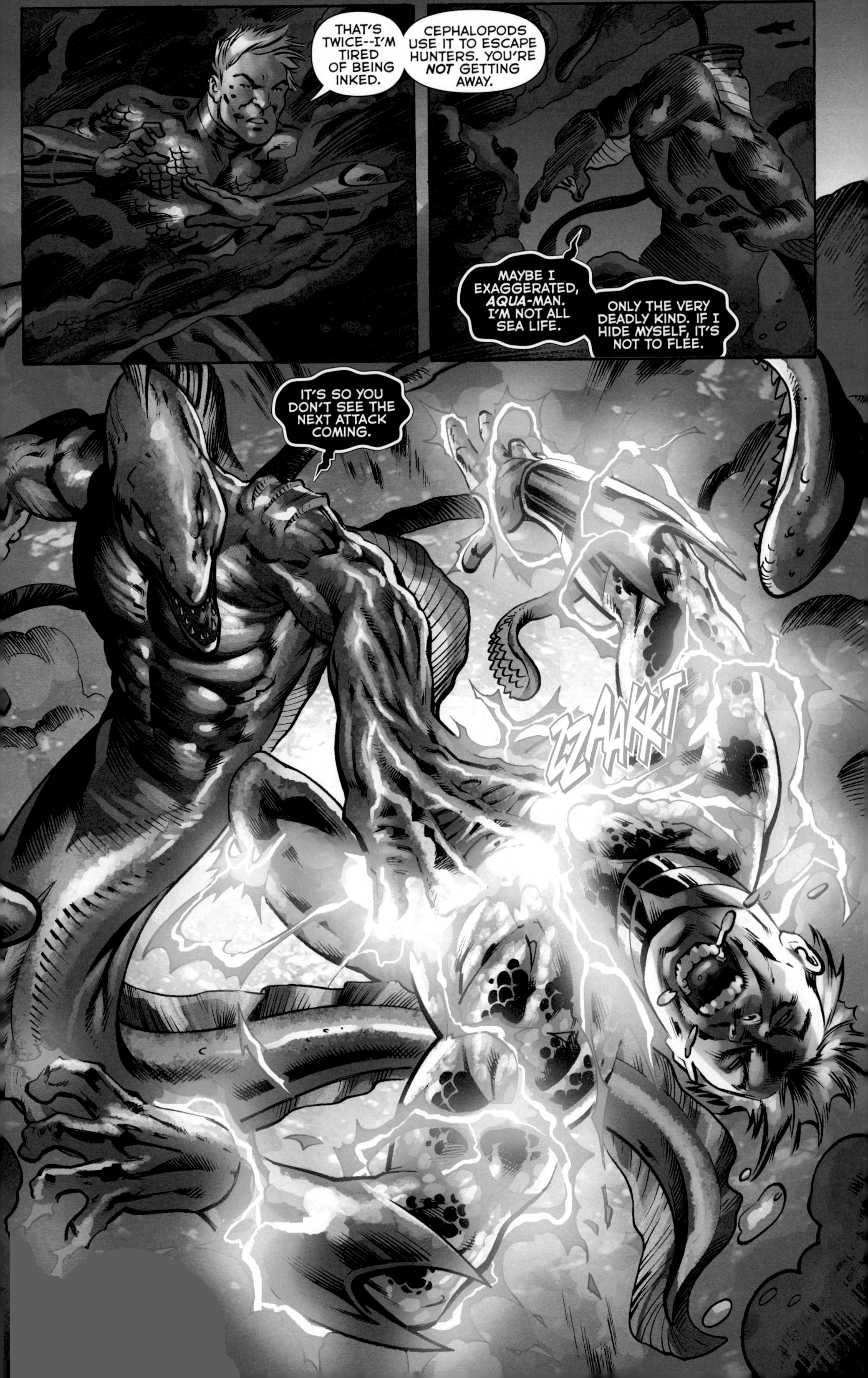
THAT'S TWICE--I'M TIRED OF BEING INKED.
CEPHALOPODS USE IT TO ESCAPE HUNTERS. YOU'RE *NOT* GETTING AWAY.
MAYBE I EXAGGERATED, *AQUA*-MAN. I'M NOT ALL SEA LIFE.
ONLY THE VERY DEADLY KIND. IF I HIDE MYSELF, IT'S NOT TO FLEE.
IT'S SO YOU DON'T SEE THE NEXT ATTACK COMING.
ZZAAKKT

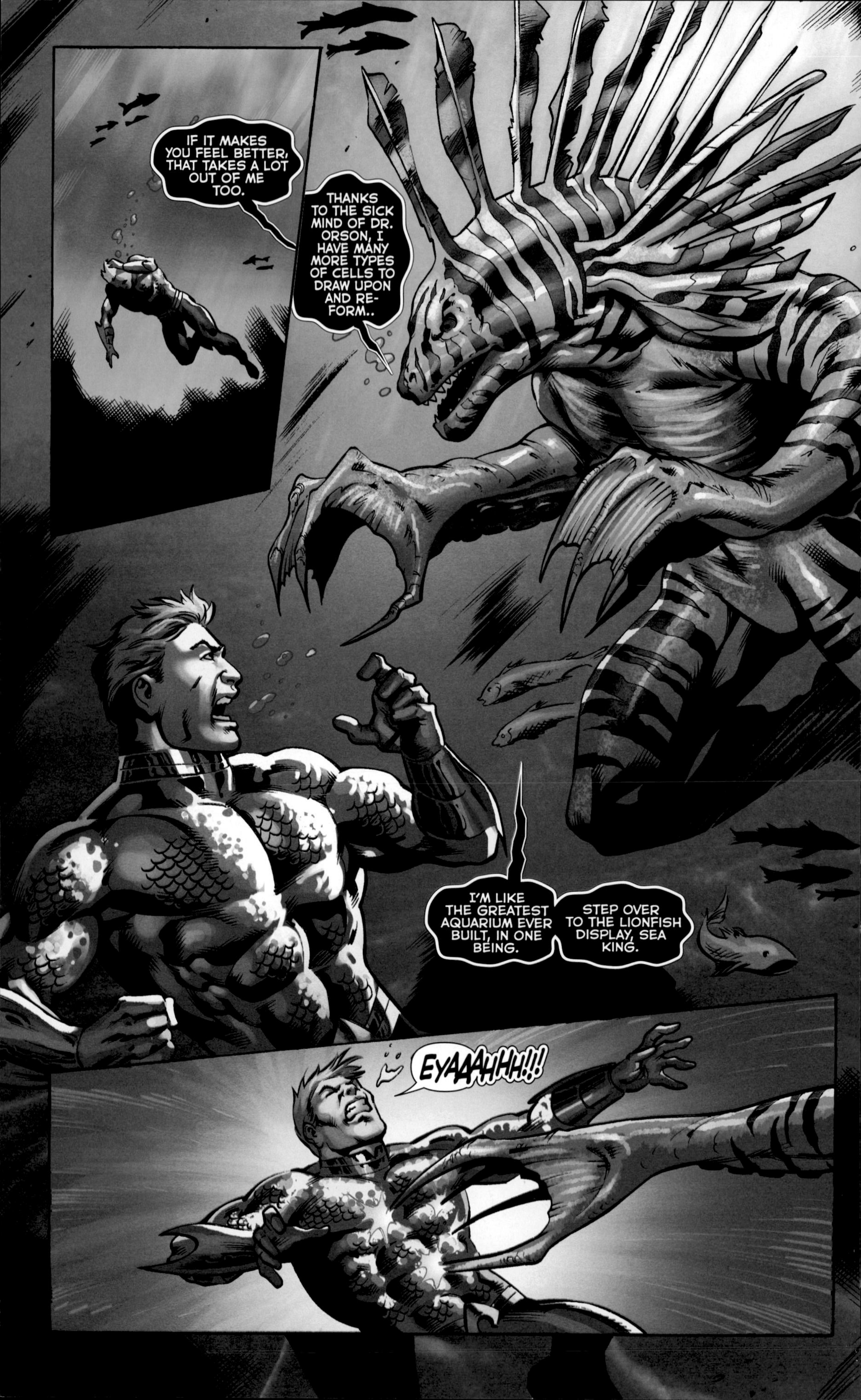
IF IT MAKES YOU FEEL BETTER, THAT TAKES A LOT OUT OF ME TOO.
THANKS TO THE SICK MIND OF DR. ORSON, I HAVE MANY MORE TYPES OF CELLS TO DRAW UPON AND RE-FORM..
I'M LIKE THE GREATEST AQUARIUM EVER BUILT, IN ONE BEING.
STEP OVER TO THE LIONFISH DISPLAY, SEA KING.
EYAAAHHH!!!

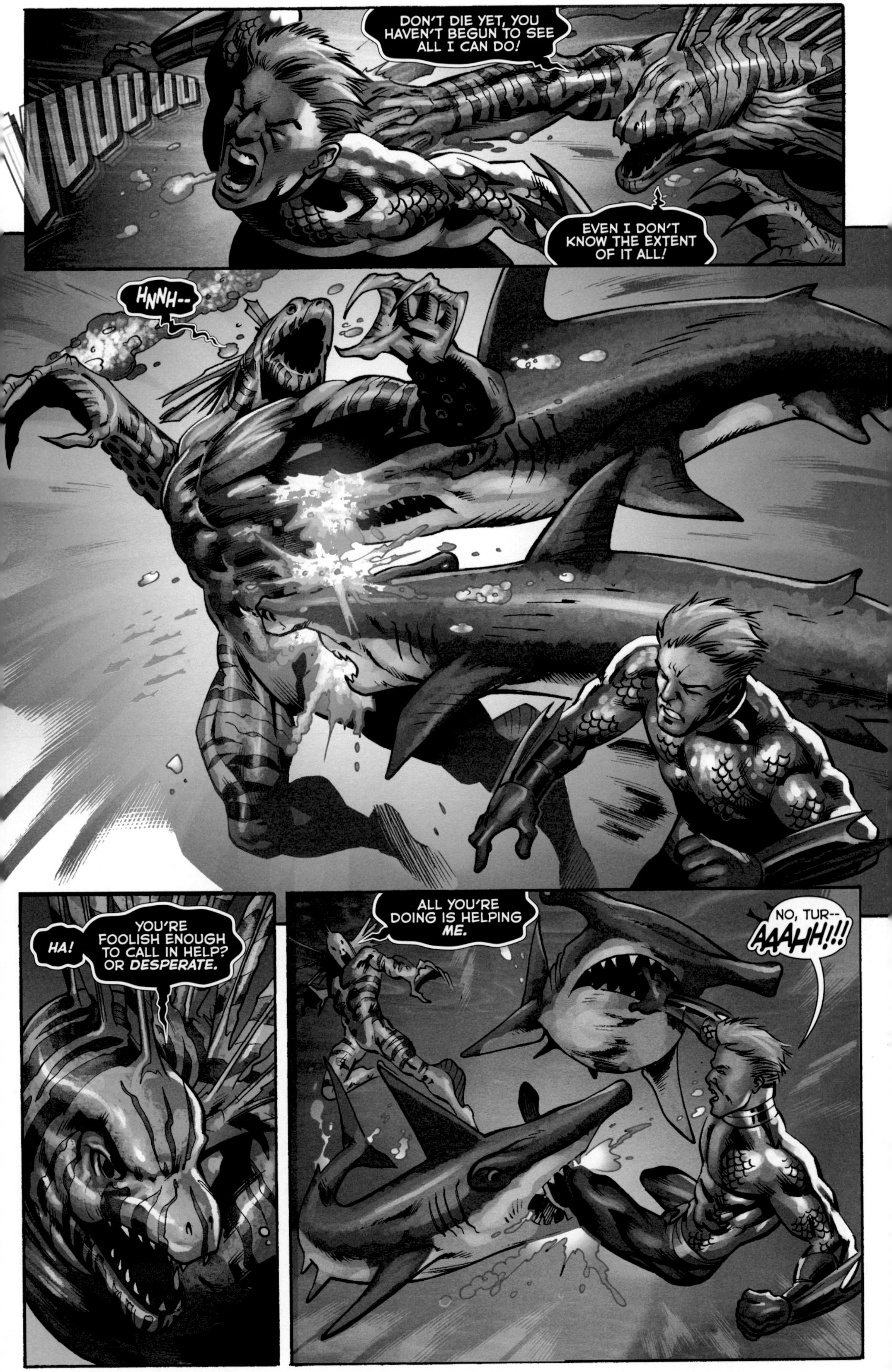
VUUUUUU
DON'T DIE YET, YOU HAVEN'T BEGUN TO SEE ALL I CAN DO!
EVEN I DON'T KNOW THE EXTENT OF IT ALL!
HNNH--
HA!
YOU'RE FOOLISH ENOUGH TO CALL IN HELP? OR DESPERATE.
ALL YOU'RE DOING IS HELPING ME.
NO, TUR--
AAAHH!!!

BREAK OFF!! GO!!

VUUVUUVUU

YOUR COMMAND OF THEM IS *NOTHING* TO MINE!

STOP-- TURN AWAY--

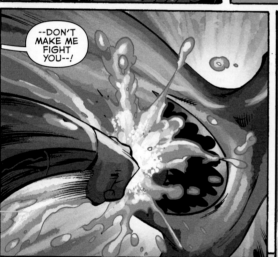

--DON'T MAKE ME FIGHT YOU--!

DON'T!!!

NO... NO!

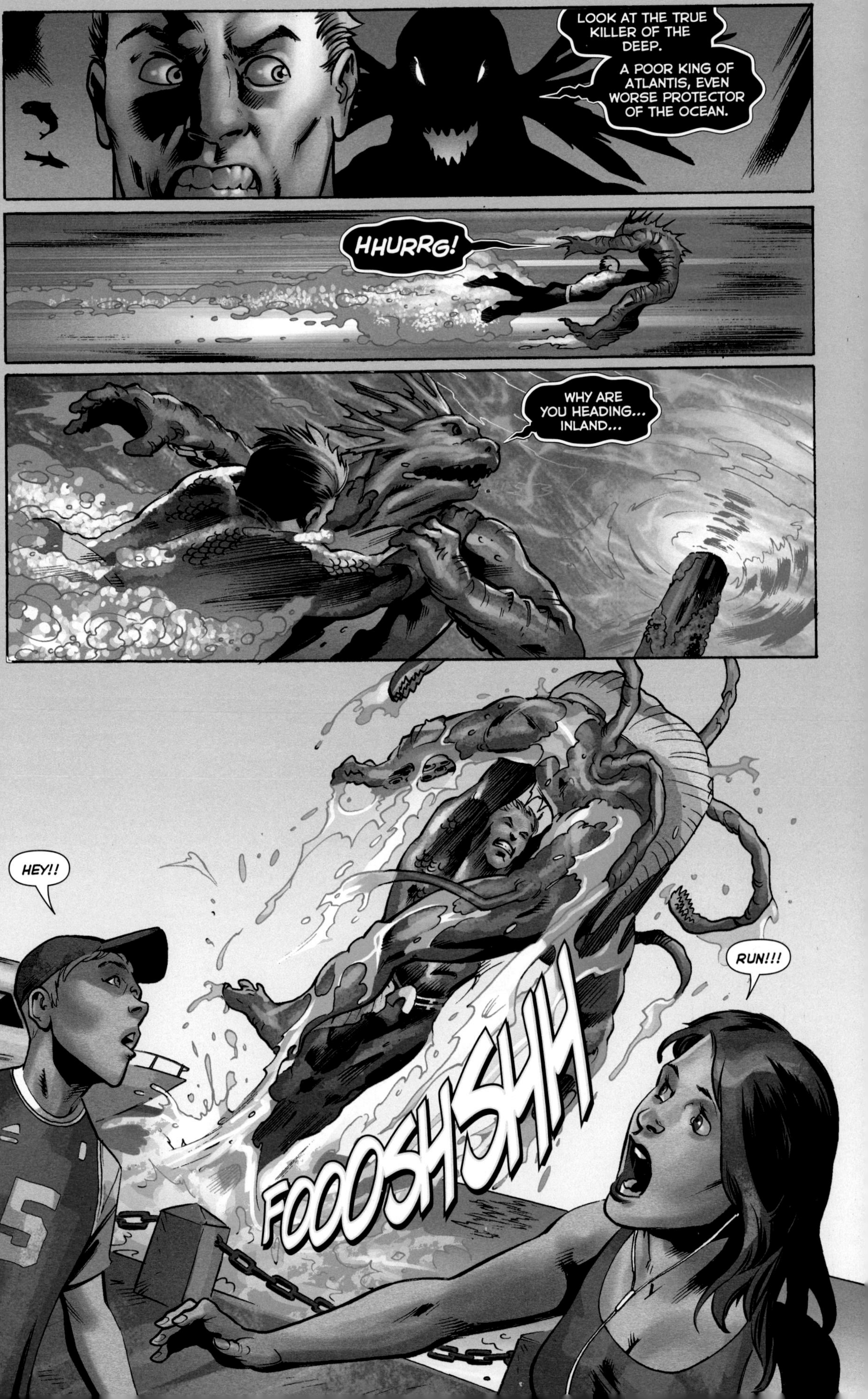
LOOK AT THE TRUE KILLER OF THE DEEP.
A POOR KING OF ATLANTIS, EVEN WORSE PROTECTOR OF THE OCEAN.
HHURRG!
WHY ARE YOU HEADING... INLAND...
HEY!!
RUN!!!
FOOOSHSHH

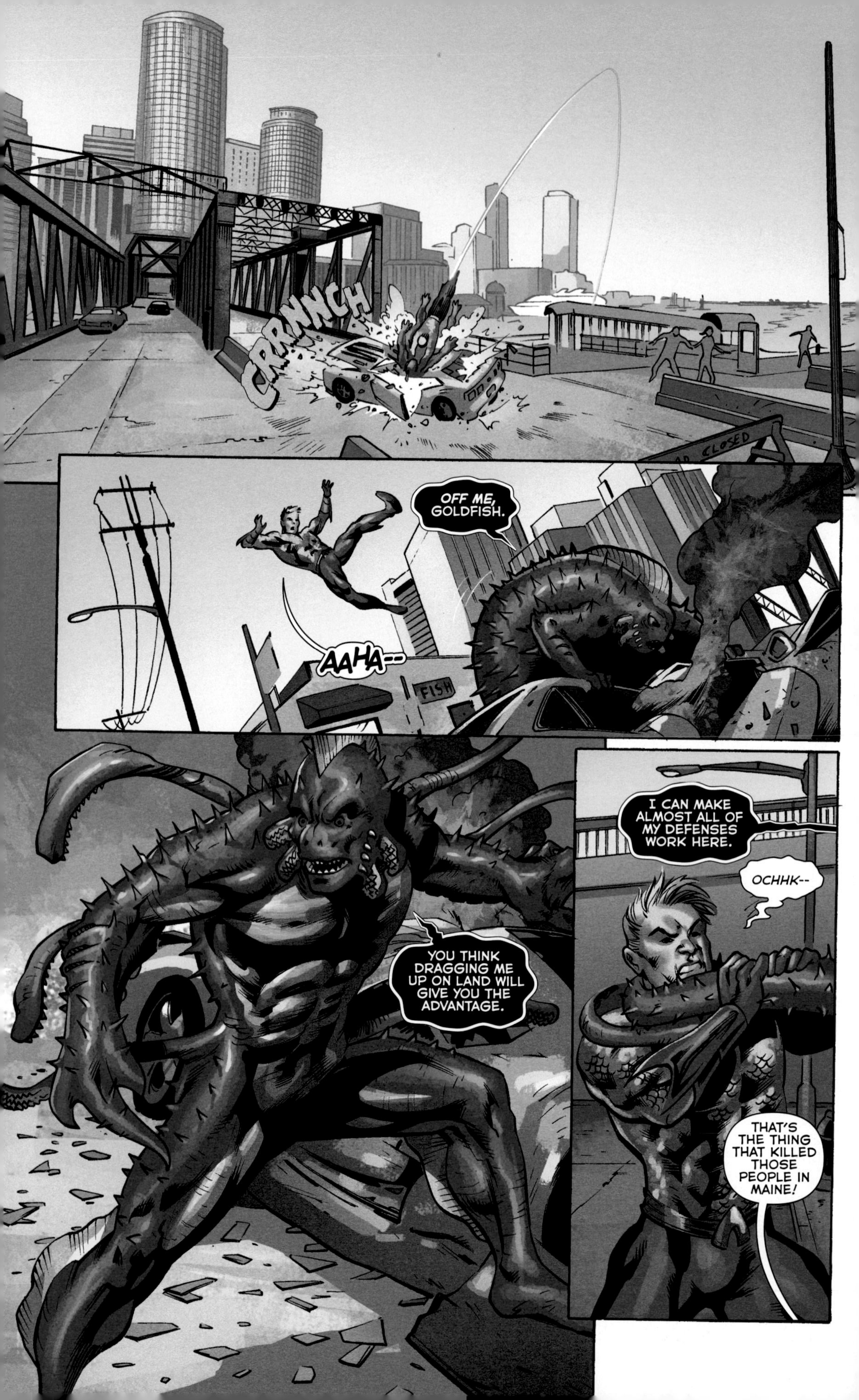

CRRNNCH
ROAD CLOSED
OFF ME, GOLDFISH.
AAHA--
FISH
I CAN MAKE ALMOST ALL OF MY DEFENSES WORK HERE.
OCHHK--
YOU THINK DRAGGING ME UP ON LAND WILL GIVE YOU THE ADVANTAGE.
THAT'S THE THING THAT KILLED THOSE PEOPLE IN MAINE!

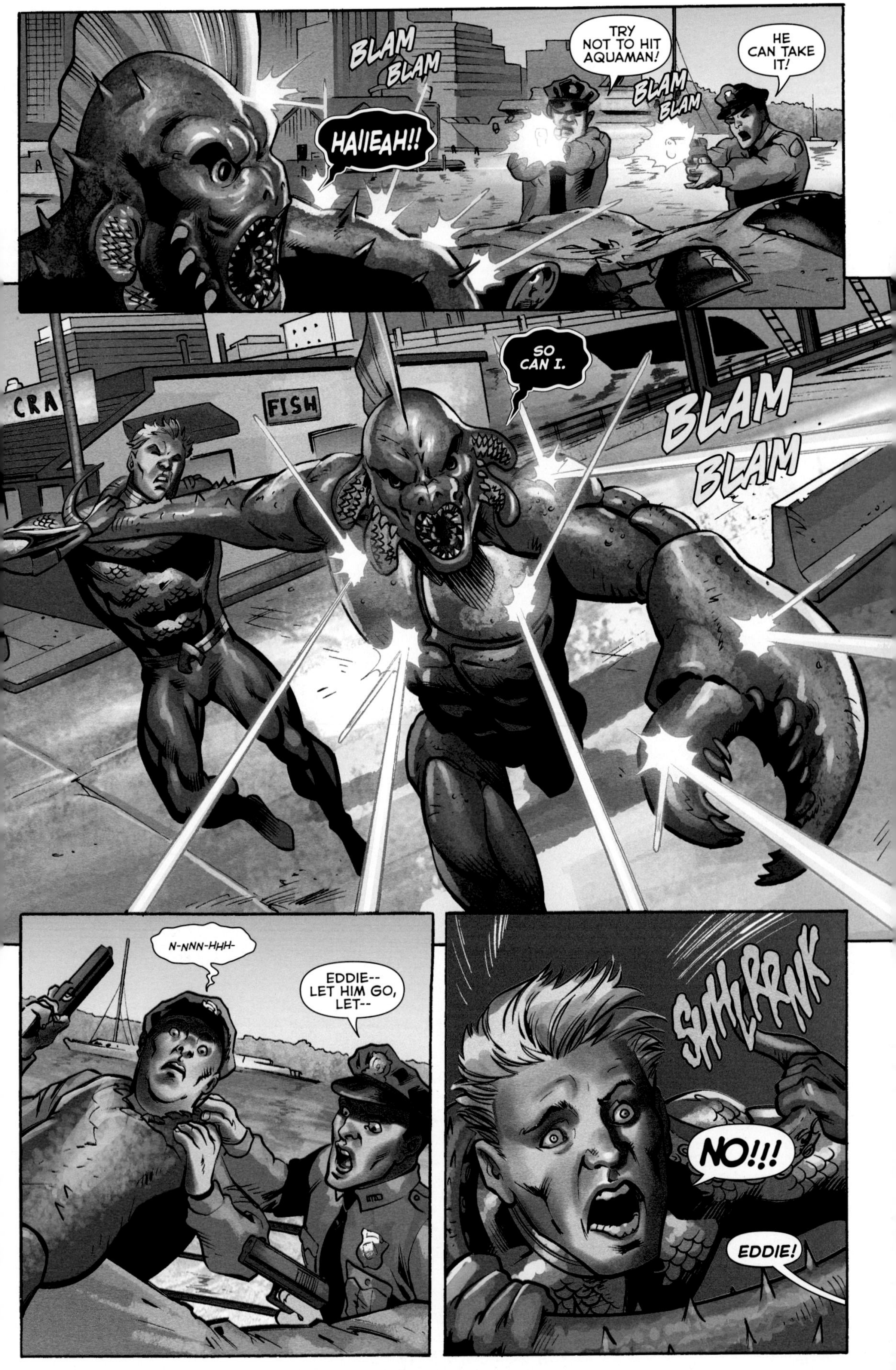
BLAM
BLAM
HAIIEAH!!
TRY NOT TO HIT AQUAMAN!
BLAM
BLAM
HE CAN TAKE IT!
CRA
FISH
SO CAN I.
BLAM
BLAM
N-NNN-HHH-
EDDIE-- LET HIM GO, LET--
SHHLRRNK
NO!!!
EDDIE!

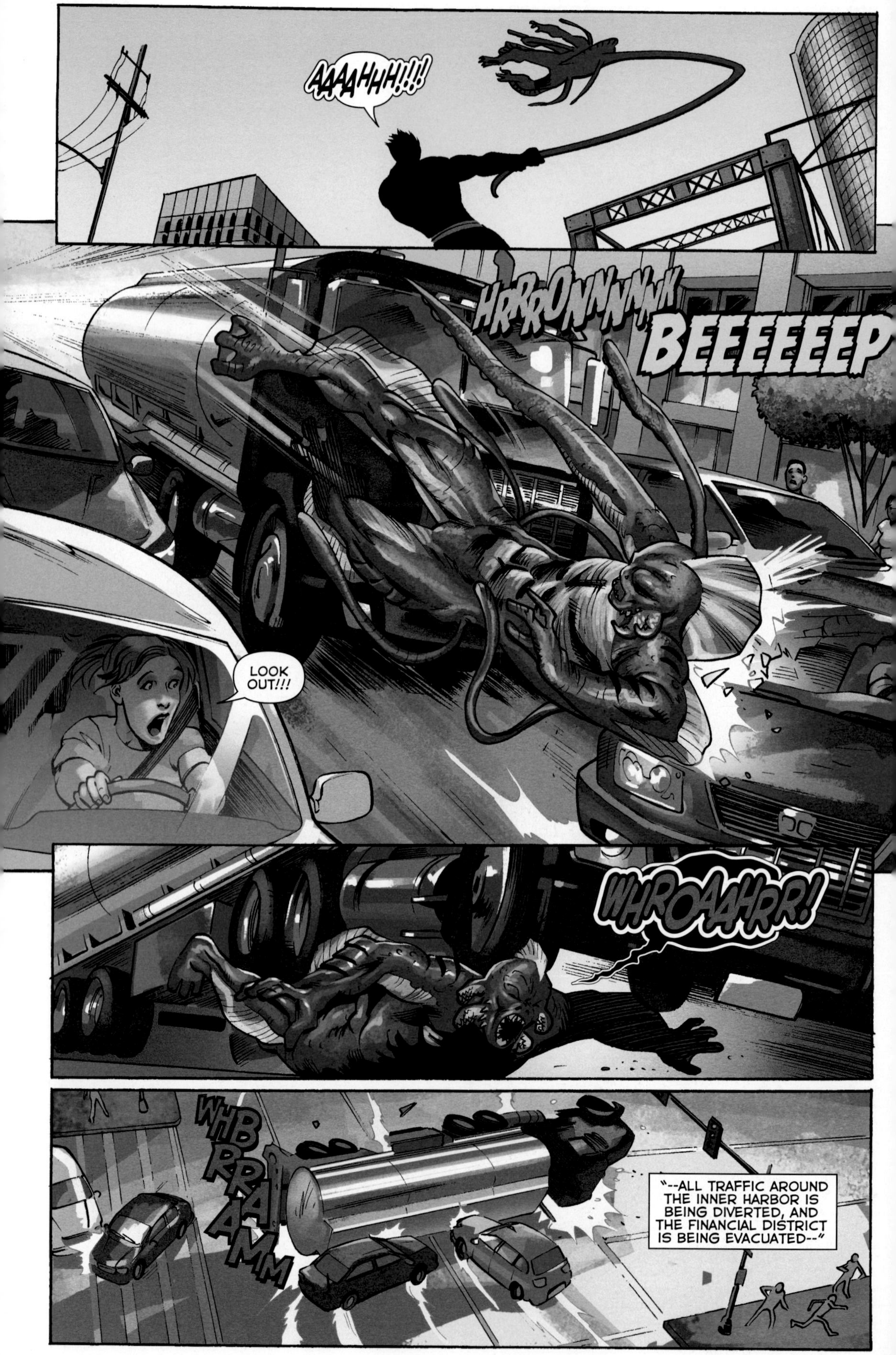
AAAAHHH!!!!
HRRRONNNNNK
BEEEEEEP
LOOK OUT!!!
WHROAAHRR!
WHBRRRAAMM
"--ALL TRAFFIC AROUND THE INNER HARBOR IS BEING DIVERTED, AND THE FINANCIAL DISTRICT IS BEING EVACUATED--"

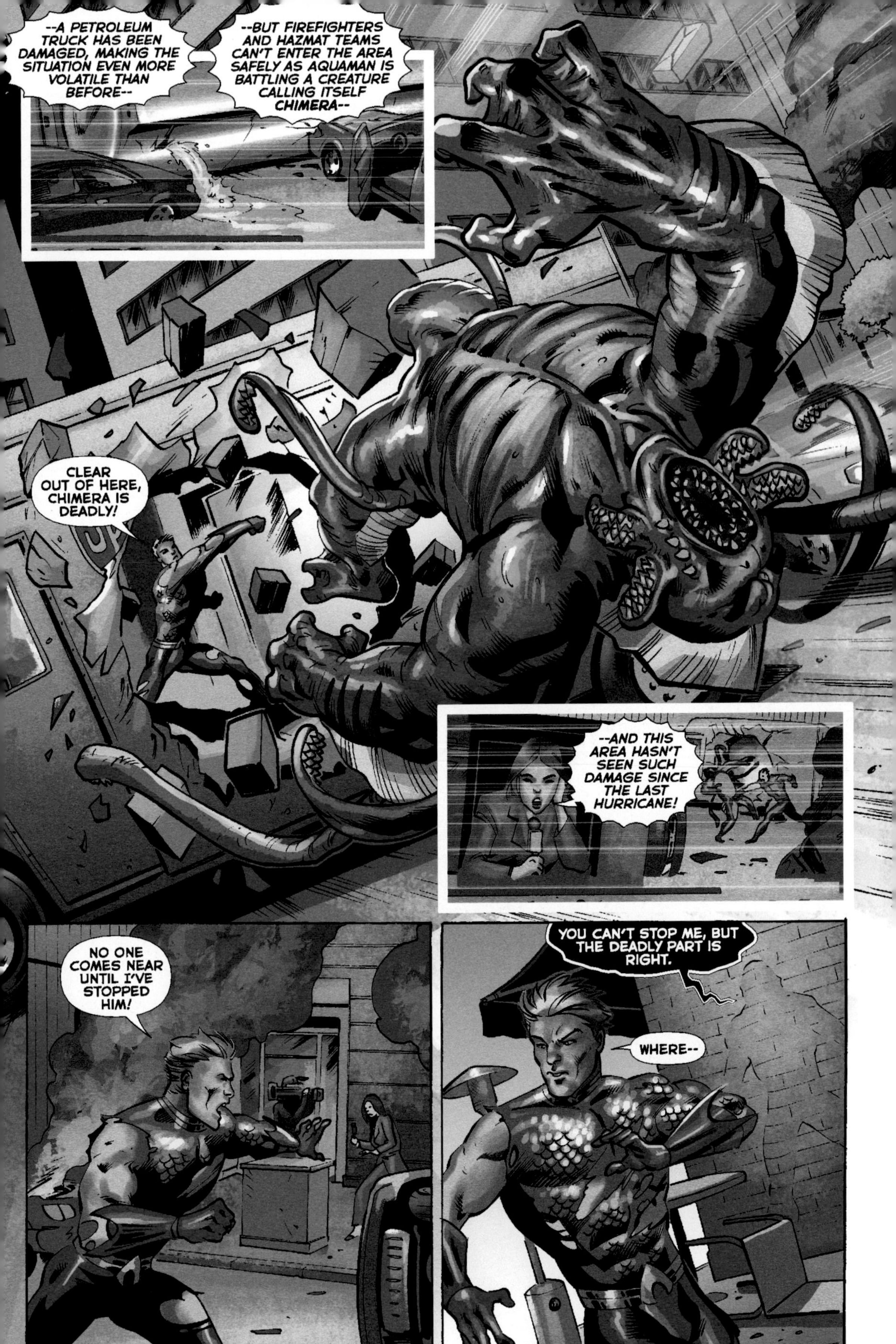
--A PETROLEUM TRUCK HAS BEEN DAMAGED, MAKING THE SITUATION EVEN MORE VOLATILE THAN BEFORE--
--BUT FIREFIGHTERS AND HAZMAT TEAMS CAN'T ENTER THE AREA SAFELY AS AQUAMAN IS BATTLING A CREATURE CALLING ITSELF CHIMERA--
CLEAR OUT OF HERE, CHIMERA IS DEADLY!
--AND THIS AREA HASN'T SEEN SUCH DAMAGE SINCE THE LAST HURRICANE!
NO ONE COMES NEAR UNTIL I'VE STOPPED HIM!
YOU CAN'T STOP ME, BUT THE DEADLY PART IS RIGHT.
WHERE--

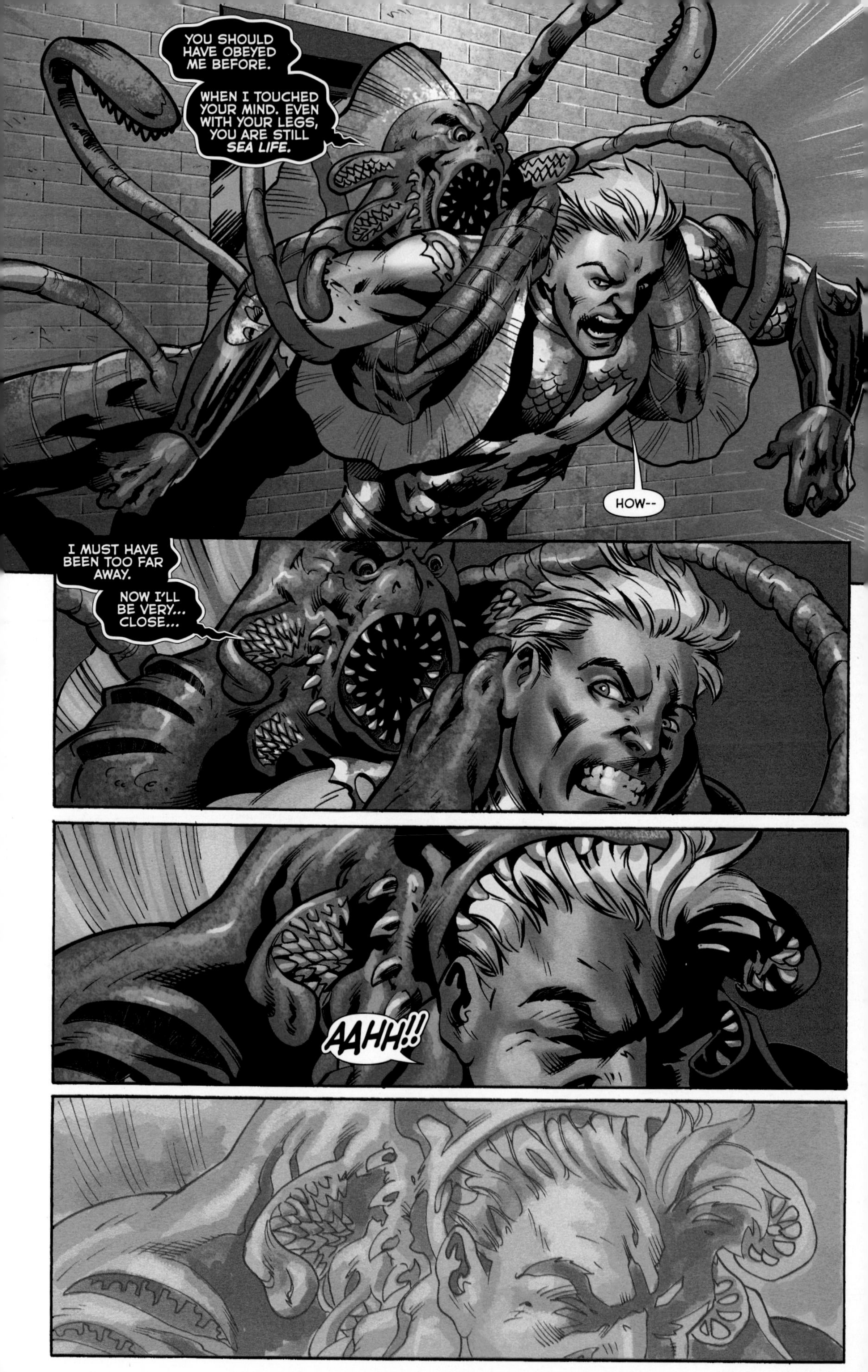
YOU SHOULD HAVE OBEYED ME BEFORE.
WHEN I TOUCHED YOUR MIND. EVEN WITH YOUR LEGS, YOU ARE STILL SEA LIFE.
HOW--
I MUST HAVE BEEN TOO FAR AWAY.
NOW I'LL BE VERY... CLOSE...
AAHH!!

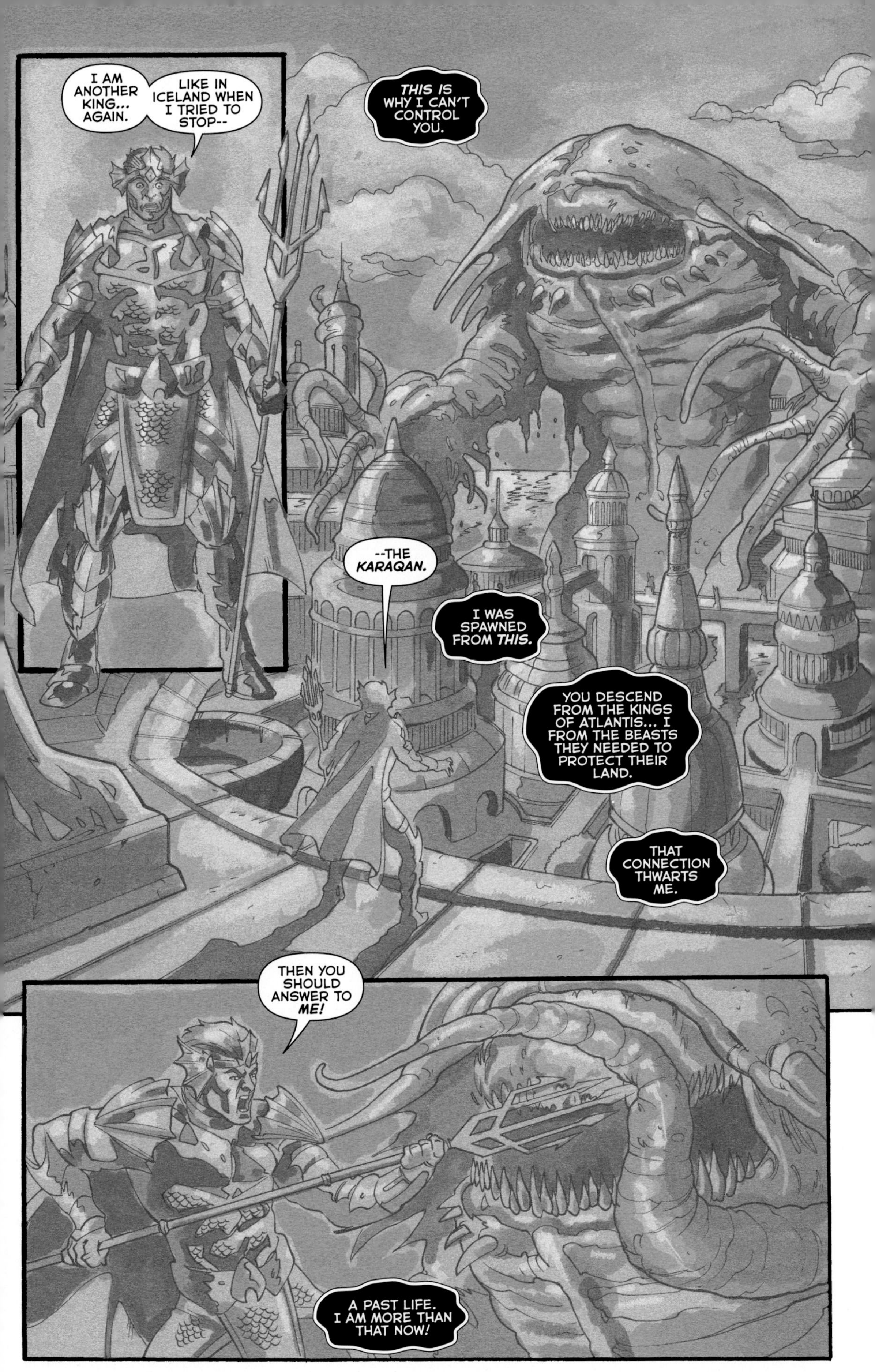
I AM ANOTHER KING... AGAIN.
LIKE IN ICELAND WHEN I TRIED TO STOP--
THIS IS WHY I CAN'T CONTROL YOU.
--THE KARAQAN.
I WAS SPAWNED FROM THIS.
YOU DESCEND FROM THE KINGS OF ATLANTIS... I FROM THE BEASTS THEY NEEDED TO PROTECT THEIR LAND.
THAT CONNECTION THWARTS ME.
THEN YOU SHOULD ANSWER TO ME!
A PAST LIFE. I AM MORE THAN THAT NOW!

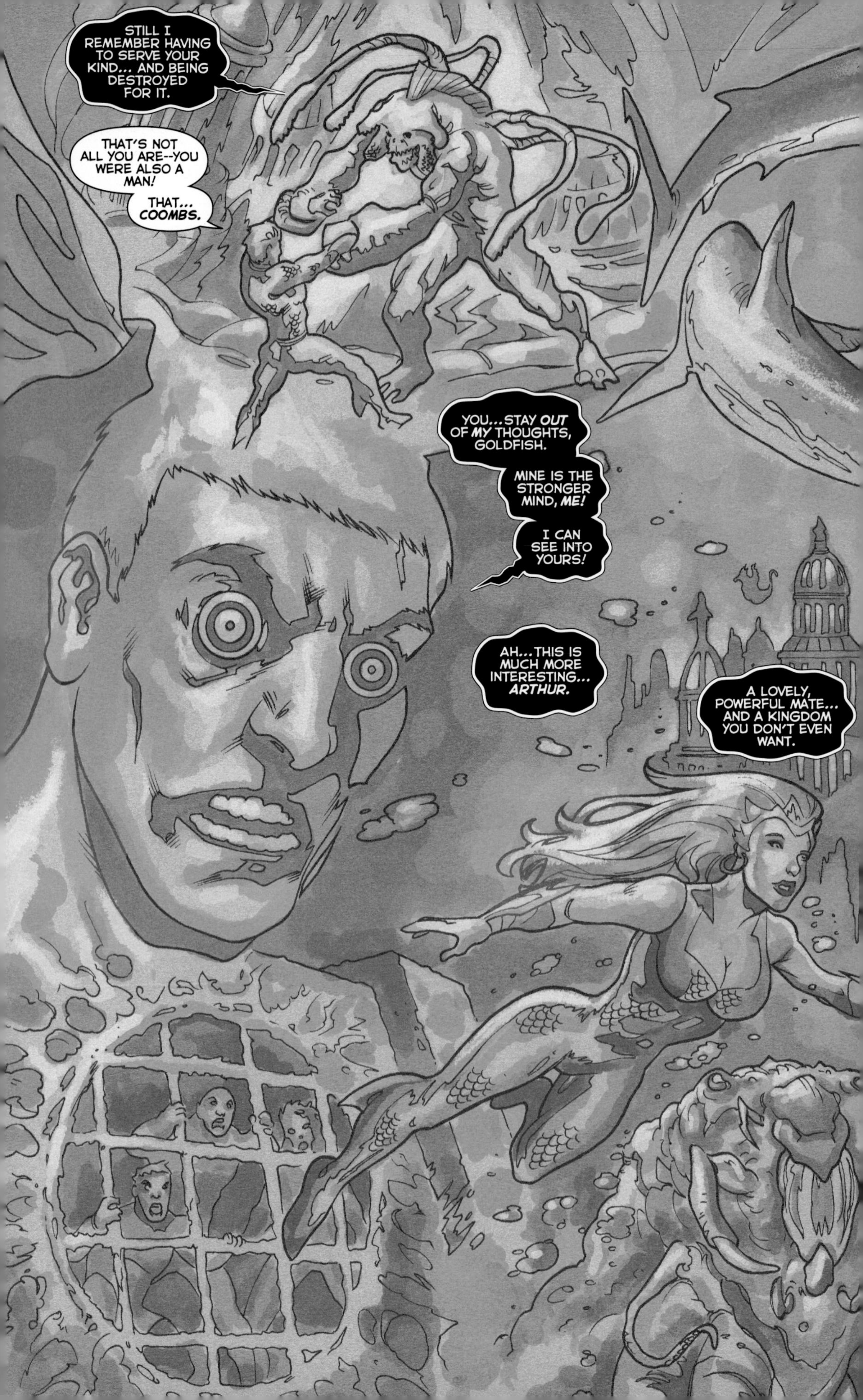
STILL I REMEMBER HAVING TO SERVE YOUR KIND... AND BEING DESTROYED FOR IT.
THAT'S NOT ALL YOU ARE--YOU WERE ALSO A MAN!
THAT... COOMBS.
YOU...STAY OUT OF MY THOUGHTS, GOLDFISH.
MINE IS THE STRONGER MIND, ME!
I CAN SEE INTO YOURS!
AH...THIS IS MUCH MORE INTERESTING... ARTHUR.
A LOVELY, POWERFUL MATE... AND A KINGDOM YOU DON'T EVEN WANT.

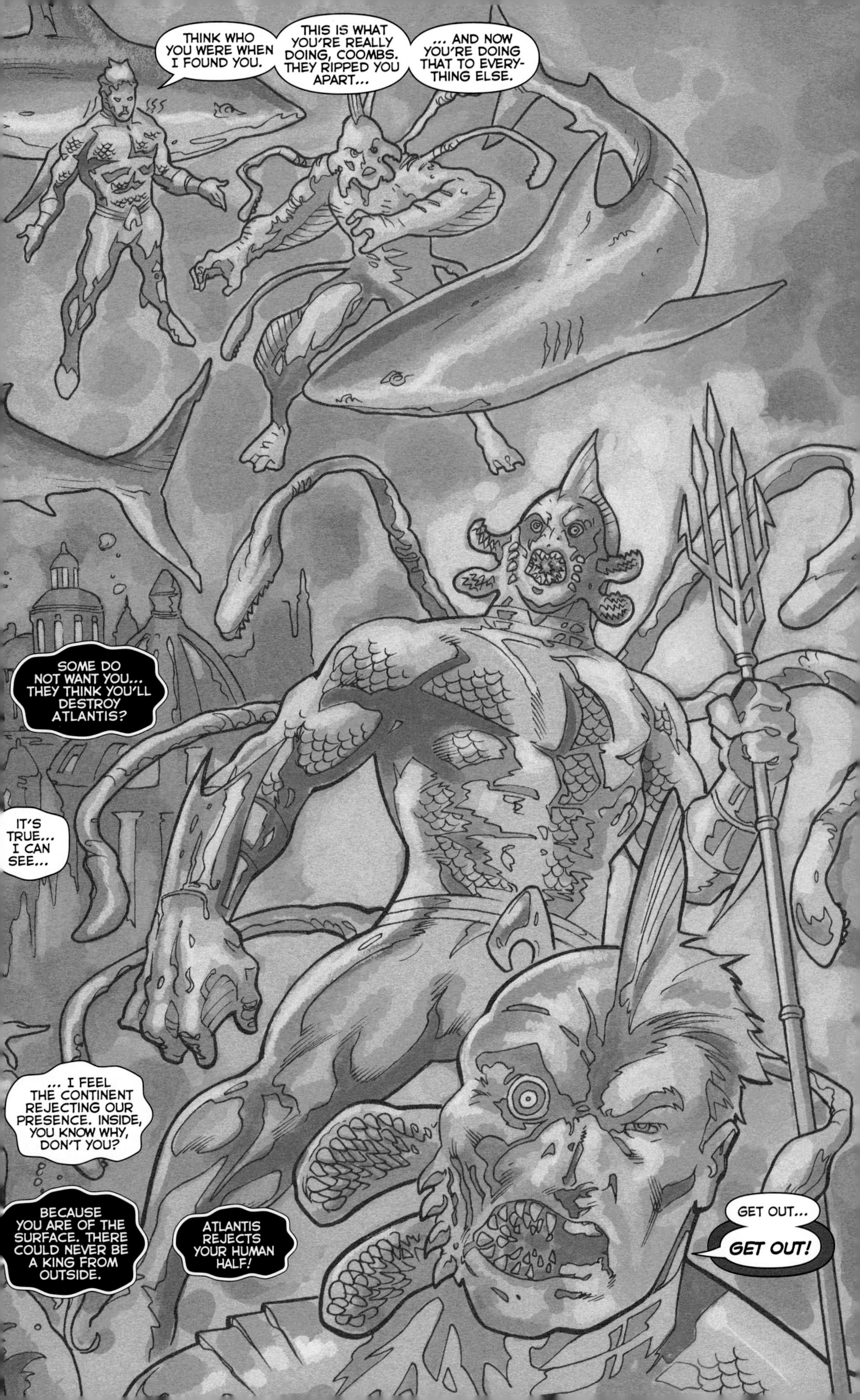
THINK WHO YOU WERE WHEN I FOUND YOU.
THIS IS WHAT YOU'RE REALLY DOING, COOMBS. THEY RIPPED YOU APART...
... AND NOW YOU'RE DOING THAT TO EVERYTHING ELSE.
SOME DO NOT WANT YOU... THEY THINK YOU'LL DESTROY ATLANTIS?
IT'S TRUE... I CAN SEE...
... I FEEL THE CONTINENT REJECTING OUR PRESENCE. INSIDE, YOU KNOW WHY, DON'T YOU?
BECAUSE YOU ARE OF THE SURFACE. THERE COULD NEVER BE A KING FROM OUTSIDE.
ATLANTIS REJECTS YOUR HUMAN HALF!
GET OUT...
GET OUT!

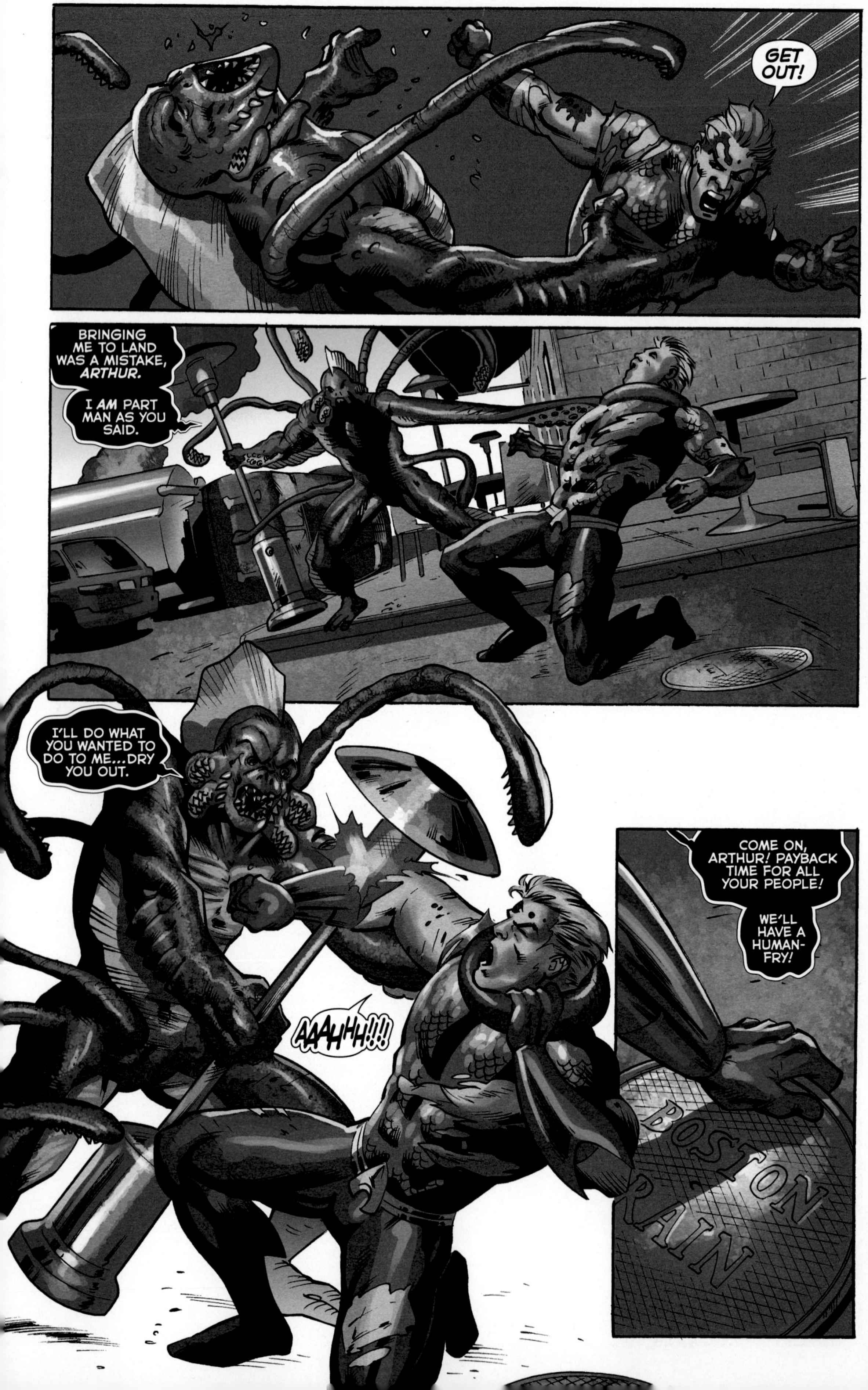
GET OUT!
BRINGING ME TO LAND WAS A MISTAKE, ARTHUR.
I AM PART MAN AS YOU SAID.
I'LL DO WHAT YOU WANTED TO DO TO ME...DRY YOU OUT.
AAAHHH!!!
COME ON, ARTHUR! PAYBACK TIME FOR ALL YOUR PEOPLE!
WE'LL HAVE A HUMAN-FRY!
BOSTON
DRAIN

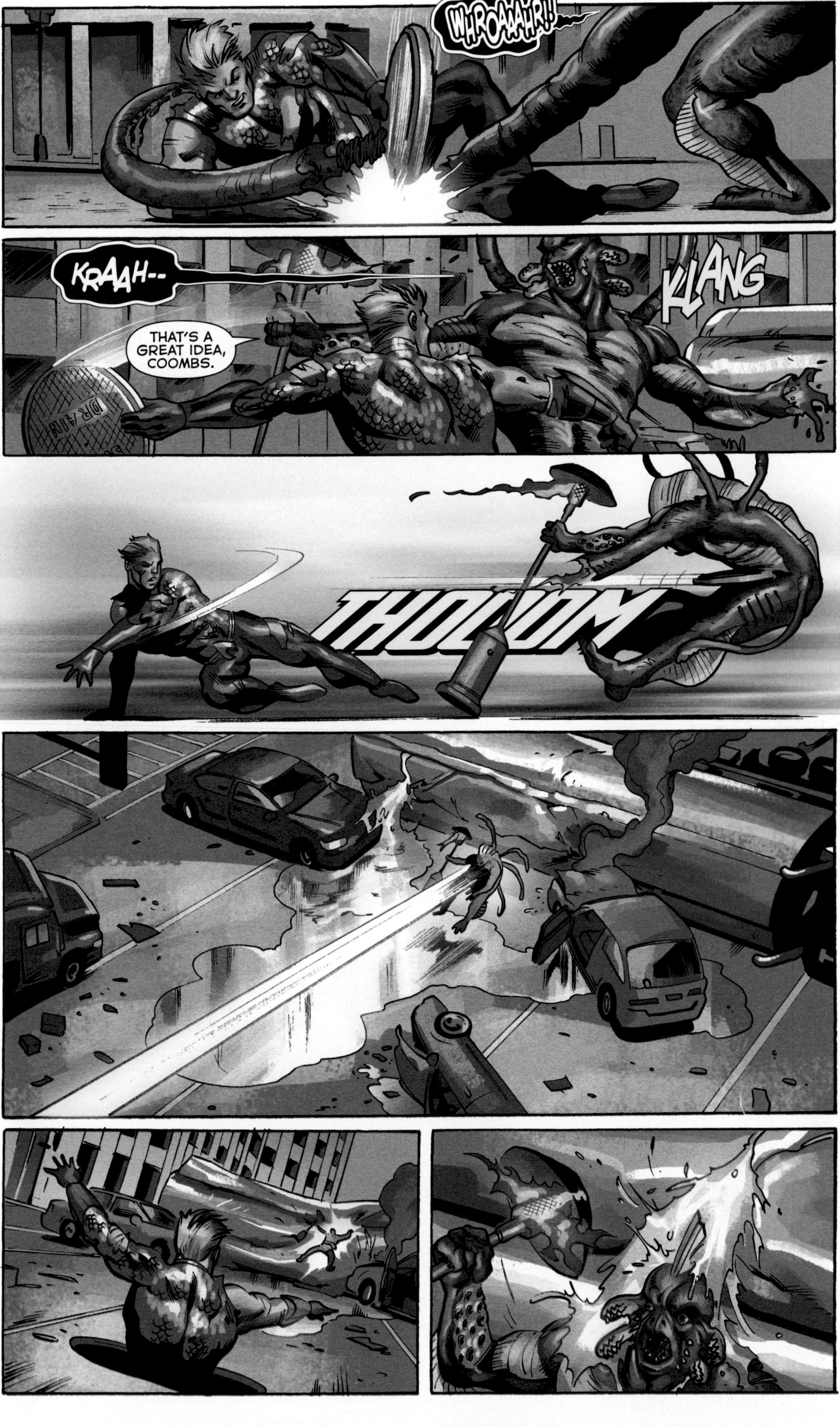

WHROAAAHR!!
KRAAH--
THAT'S A GREAT IDEA, COOMBS.
KLANG
THOOM

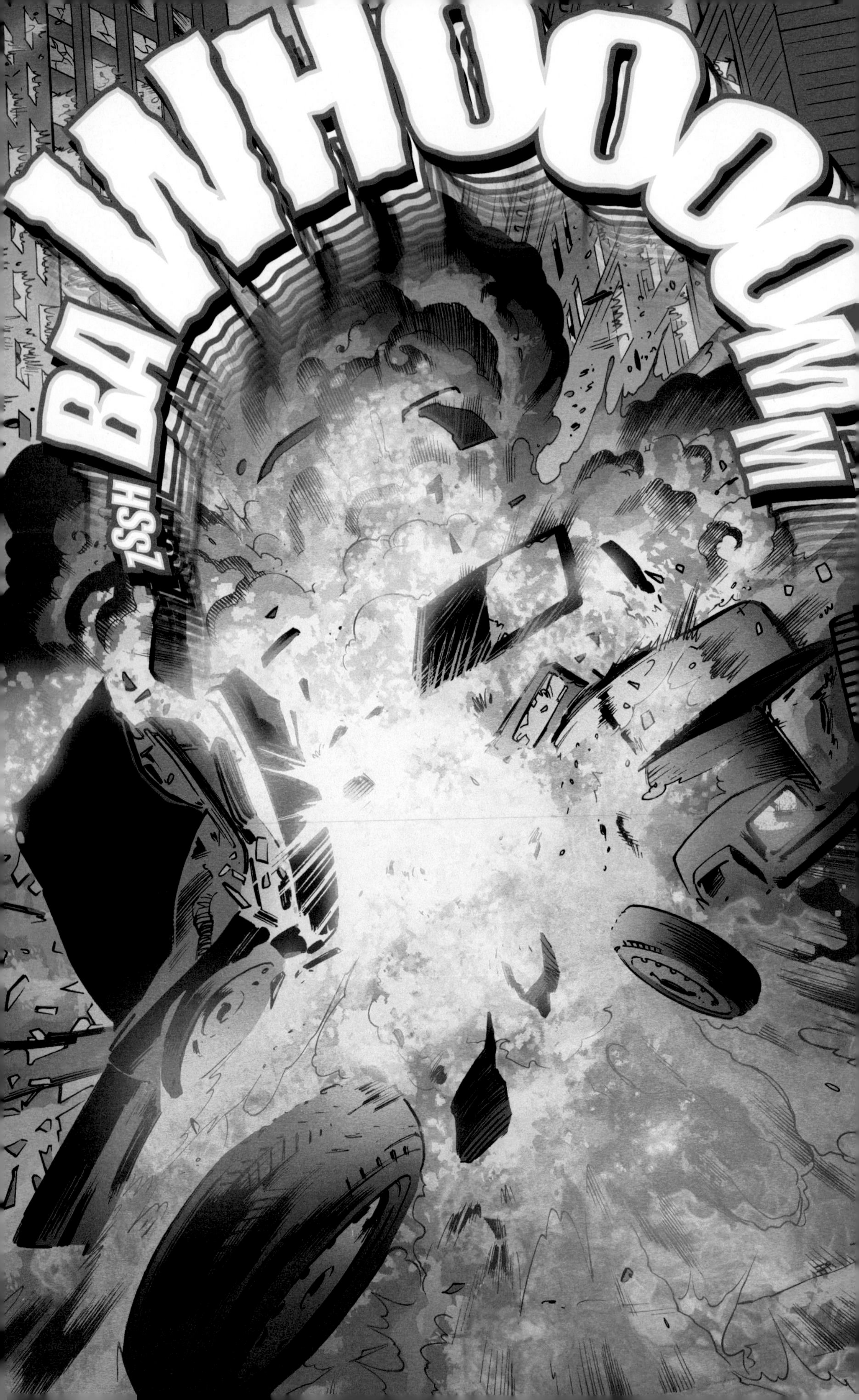
BAWHOOOM
ZSSH

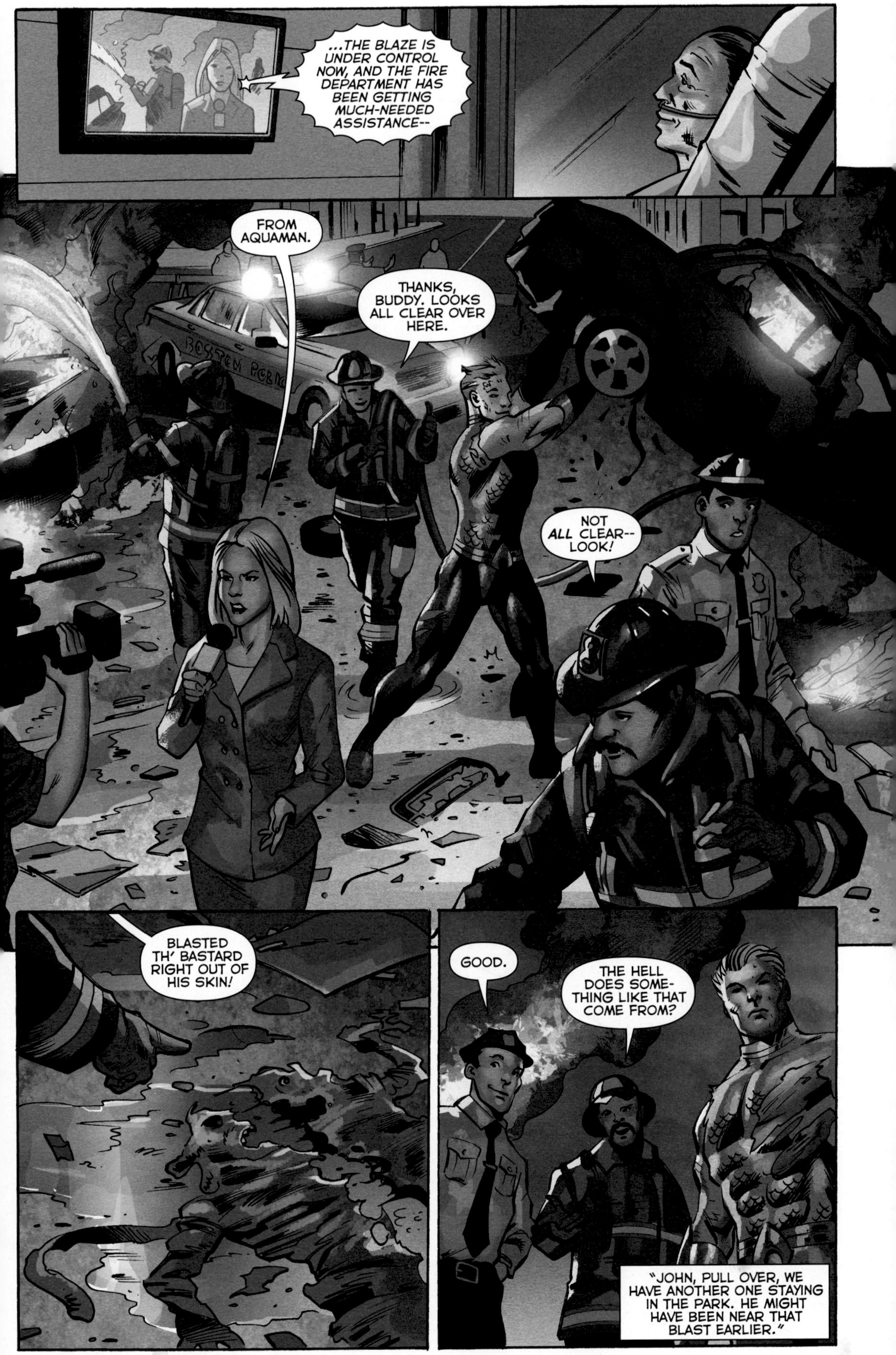
...THE BLAZE IS UNDER CONTROL NOW, AND THE FIRE DEPARTMENT HAS BEEN GETTING MUCH-NEEDED ASSISTANCE--
FROM AQUAMAN.
THANKS, BUDDY. LOOKS ALL CLEAR OVER HERE.
NOT ALL CLEAR-- LOOK!
BLASTED TH' BASTARD RIGHT OUT OF HIS SKIN!
GOOD.
THE HELL DOES SOMETHING LIKE THAT COME FROM?
"JOHN, PULL OVER, WE HAVE ANOTHER ONE STAYING IN THE PARK. HE MIGHT HAVE BEEN NEAR THAT BLAST EARLIER."

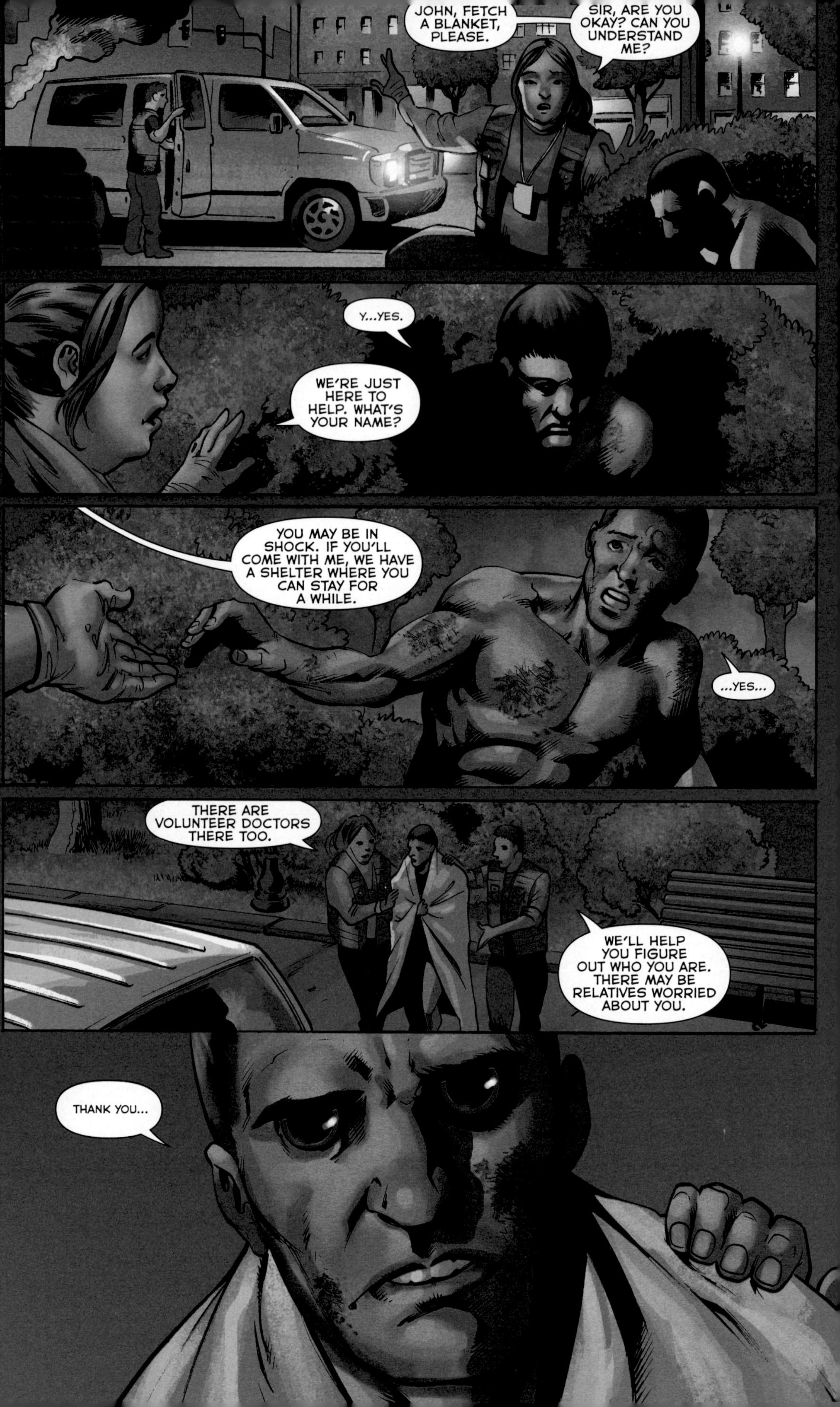
JOHN, FETCH A BLANKET, PLEASE.
SIR, ARE YOU OKAY? CAN YOU UNDERSTAND ME?
Y...YES.
WE'RE JUST HERE TO HELP. WHAT'S YOUR NAME?
YOU MAY BE IN SHOCK. IF YOU'LL COME WITH ME, WE HAVE A SHELTER WHERE YOU CAN STAY FOR A WHILE.
...YES...
THERE ARE VOLUNTEER DOCTORS THERE TOO.
WE'LL HELP YOU FIGURE OUT WHO YOU ARE. THERE MAY BE RELATIVES WORRIED ABOUT YOU.
THANK YOU...

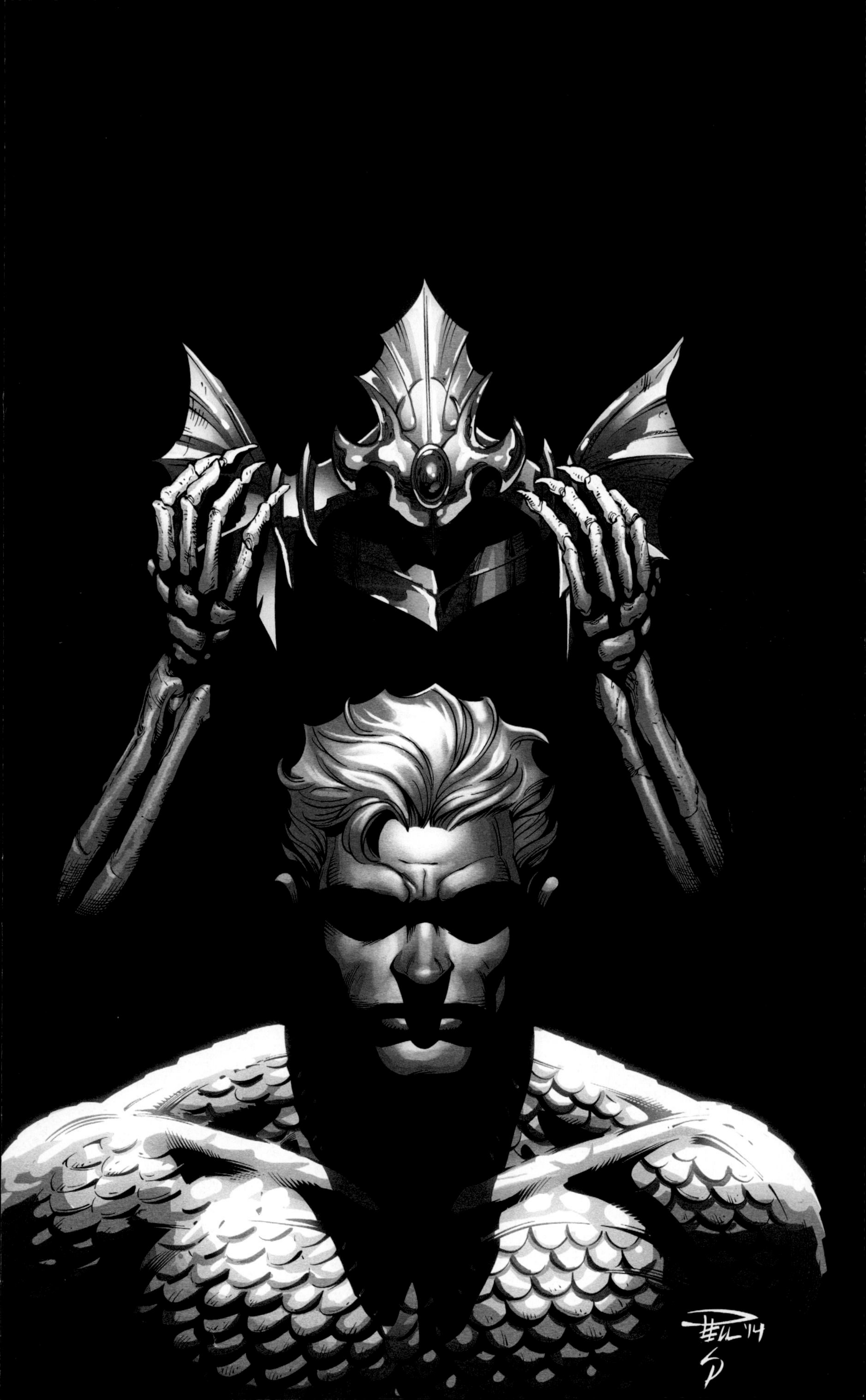

MAELSTROM PART I: AFTERLIFE

JEFF PARKER writer PAUL PELLETIER penciller SEAN PARSONS inker RAIN BEREDO colorist TAYLOR ESPOSITO letterer PELLETIER and PARSONS cover art

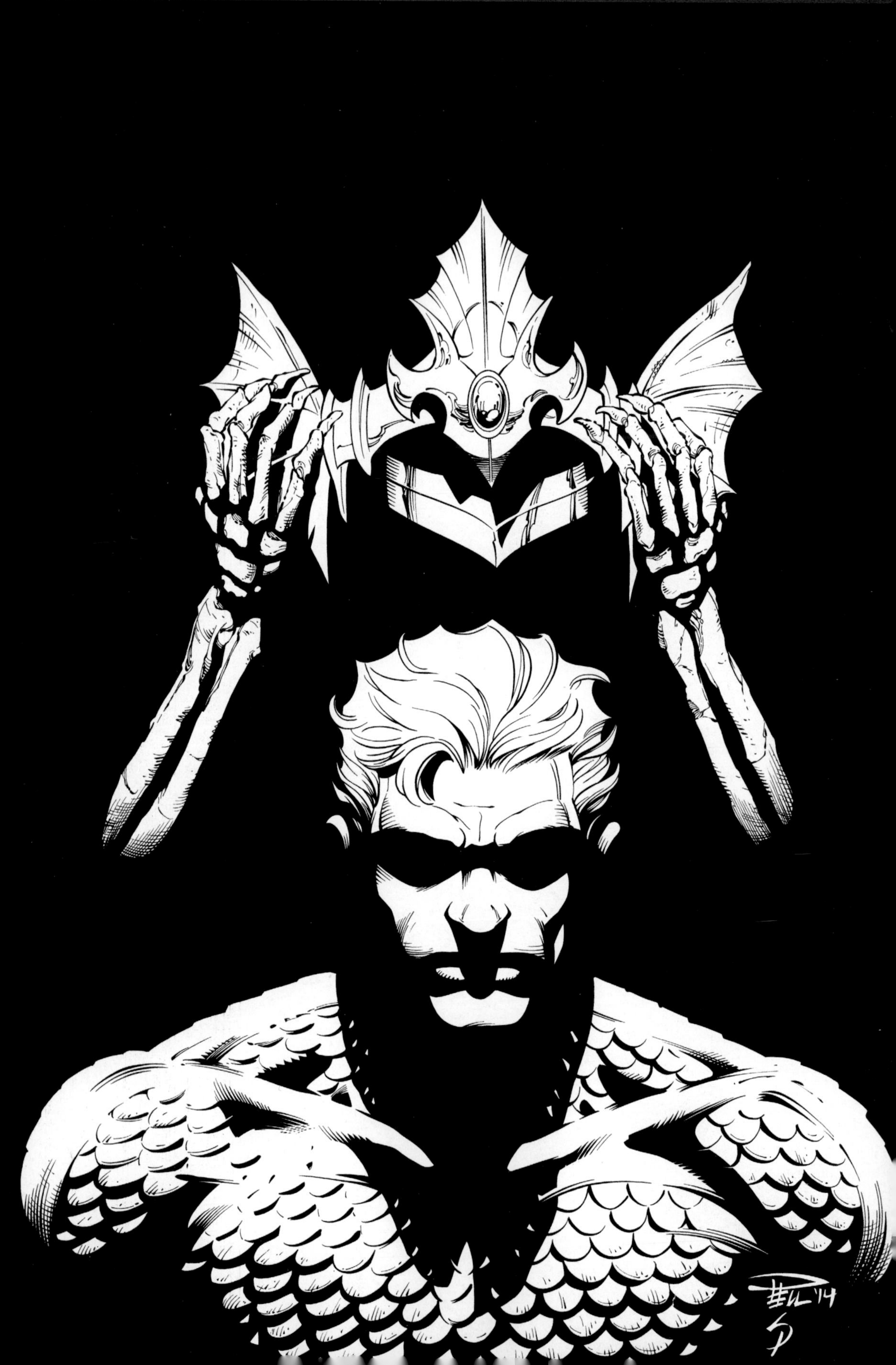

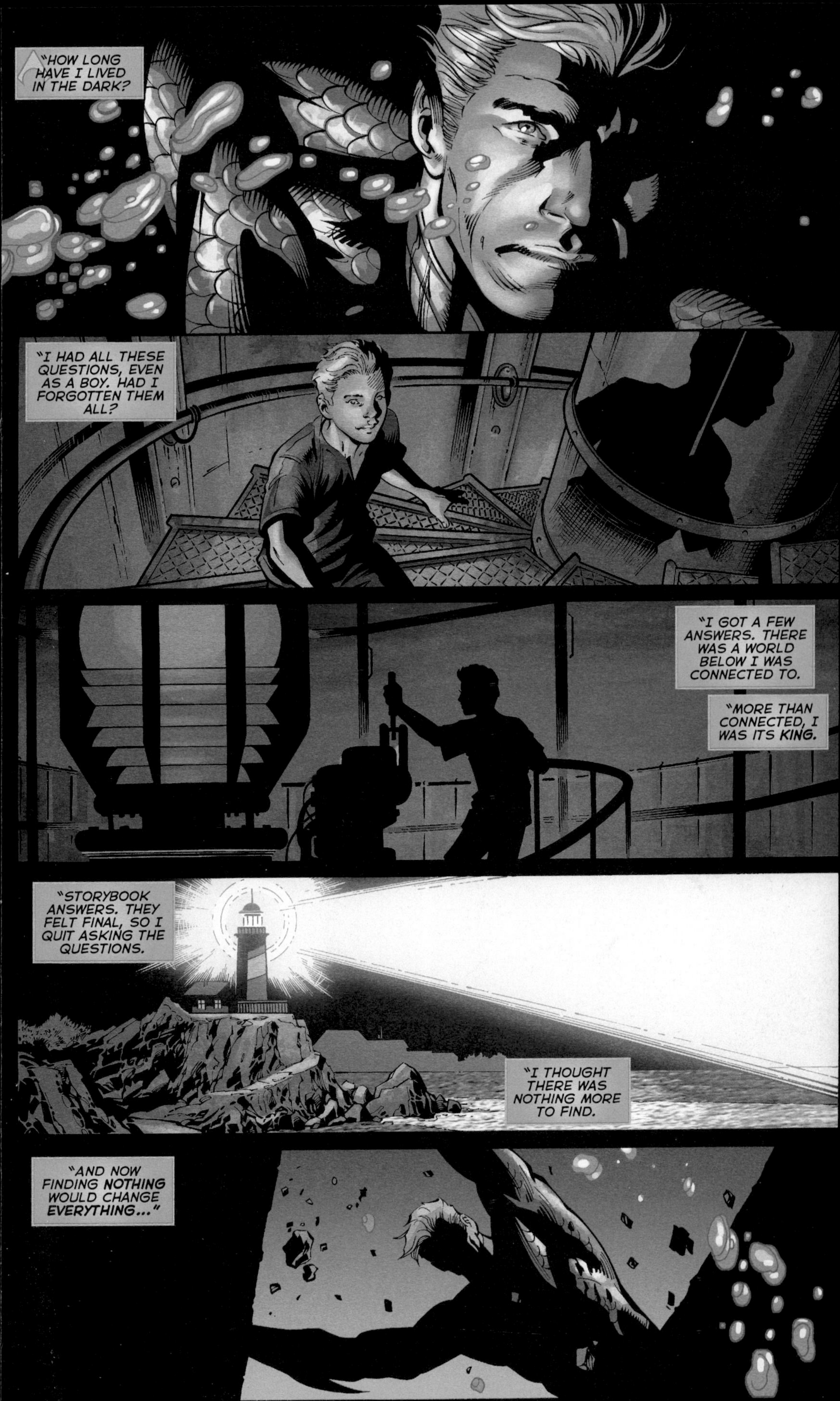
"HOW LONG HAVE I LIVED IN THE DARK?
"I HAD ALL THESE QUESTIONS, EVEN AS A BOY. HAD I FORGOTTEN THEM ALL?
"I GOT A FEW ANSWERS. THERE WAS A WORLD BELOW I WAS CONNECTED TO.
"MORE THAN CONNECTED, I WAS ITS KING.
"STORYBOOK ANSWERS. THEY FELT FINAL, SO I QUIT ASKING THE QUESTIONS.
"I THOUGHT THERE WAS NOTHING MORE TO FIND.
"AND NOW FINDING NOTHING WOULD CHANGE EVERYTHING..."

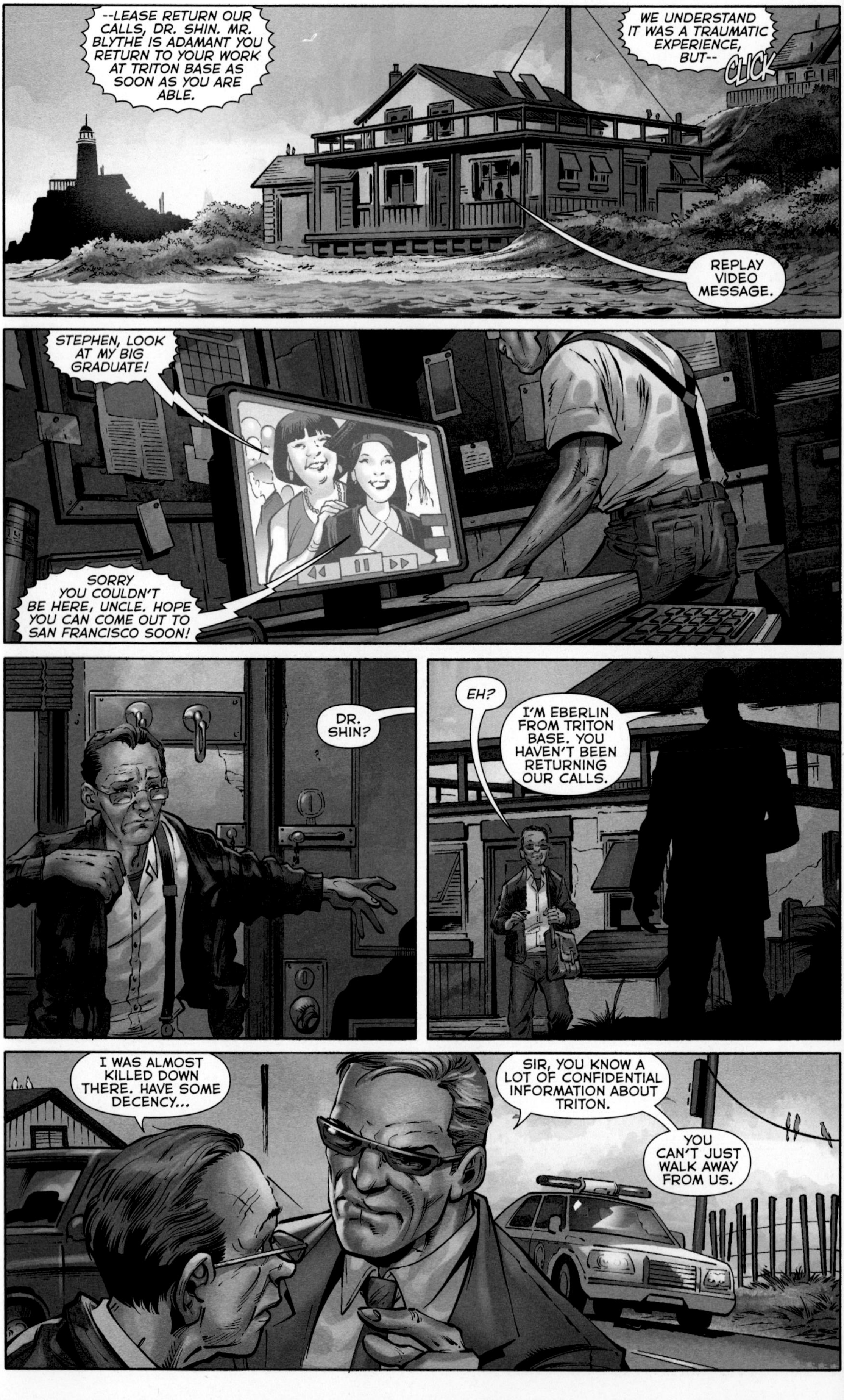
--LEASE RETURN OUR CALLS, DR. SHIN. MR. BLYTHE IS ADAMANT YOU RETURN TO YOUR WORK AT TRITON BASE AS SOON AS YOU ARE ABLE.
WE UNDERSTAND IT WAS A TRAUMATIC EXPERIENCE, BUT--
CLICK
REPLAY VIDEO MESSAGE.
STEPHEN, LOOK AT MY BIG GRADUATE!
SORRY YOU COULDN'T BE HERE, UNCLE. HOPE YOU CAN COME OUT TO SAN FRANCISCO SOON!
DR. SHIN?
EH?
I'M EBERLIN FROM TRITON BASE. YOU HAVEN'T BEEN RETURNING OUR CALLS.
I WAS ALMOST KILLED DOWN THERE. HAVE SOME DECENCY...
SIR, YOU KNOW A LOT OF CONFIDENTIAL INFORMATION ABOUT TRITON.
YOU CAN'T JUST WALK AWAY FROM US.

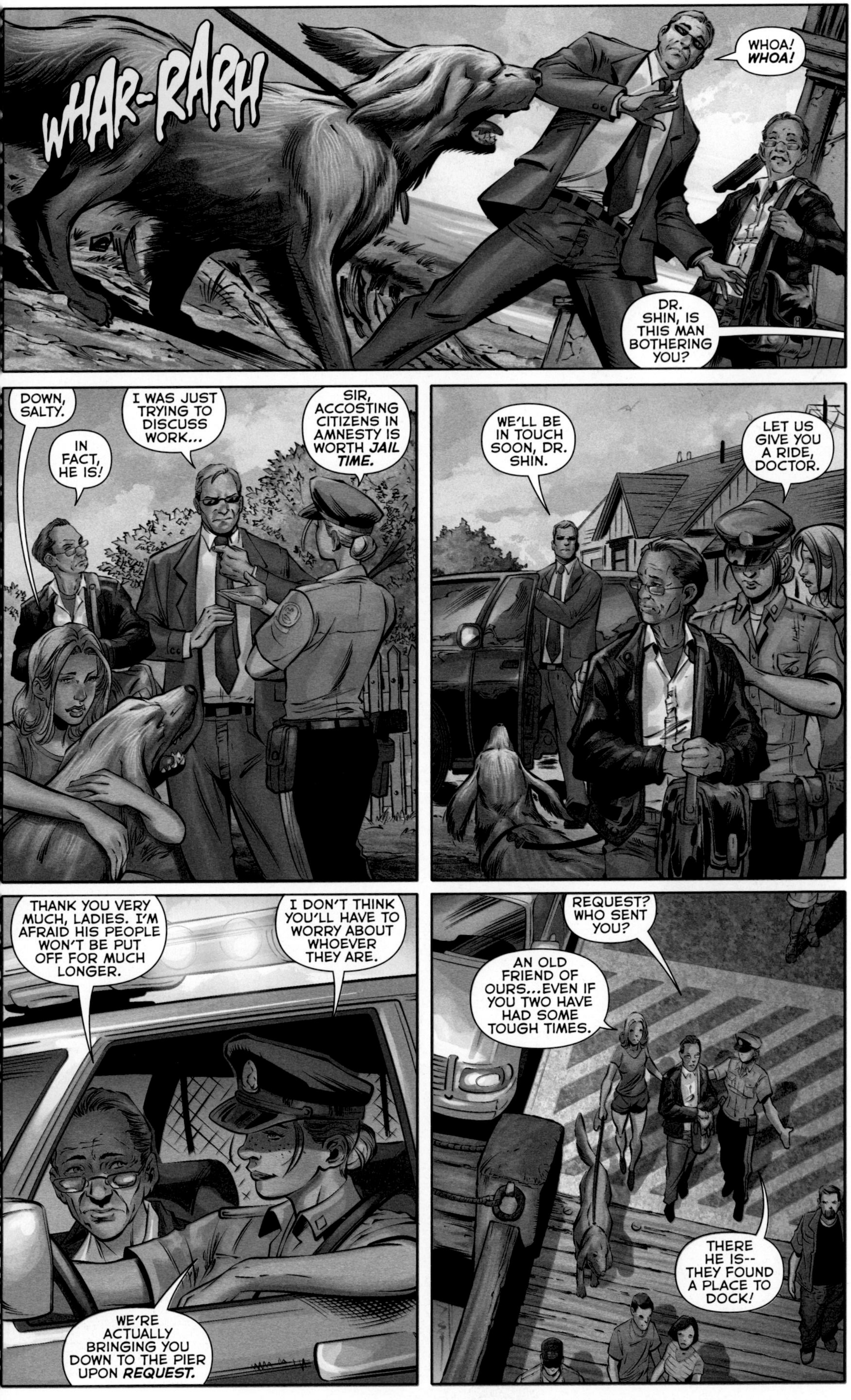
WHAR-RARH
WHOA! WHOA!
DR. SHIN, IS THIS MAN BOTHERING YOU?
DOWN, SALTY.
IN FACT, HE IS!
I WAS JUST TRYING TO DISCUSS WORK...
SIR, ACCOSTING CITIZENS IN AMNESTY IS WORTH JAIL TIME.
WE'LL BE IN TOUCH SOON, DR. SHIN.
LET US GIVE YOU A RIDE, DOCTOR.
THANK YOU VERY MUCH, LADIES. I'M AFRAID HIS PEOPLE WON'T BE PUT OFF FOR MUCH LONGER.
I DON'T THINK YOU'LL HAVE TO WORRY ABOUT WHOEVER THEY ARE.
WE'RE ACTUALLY BRINGING YOU DOWN TO THE PIER UPON REQUEST.
REQUEST? WHO SENT YOU?
AN OLD FRIEND OF OURS...EVEN IF YOU TWO HAVE HAD SOME TOUGH TIMES.
THERE HE IS-- THEY FOUND A PLACE TO DOCK!

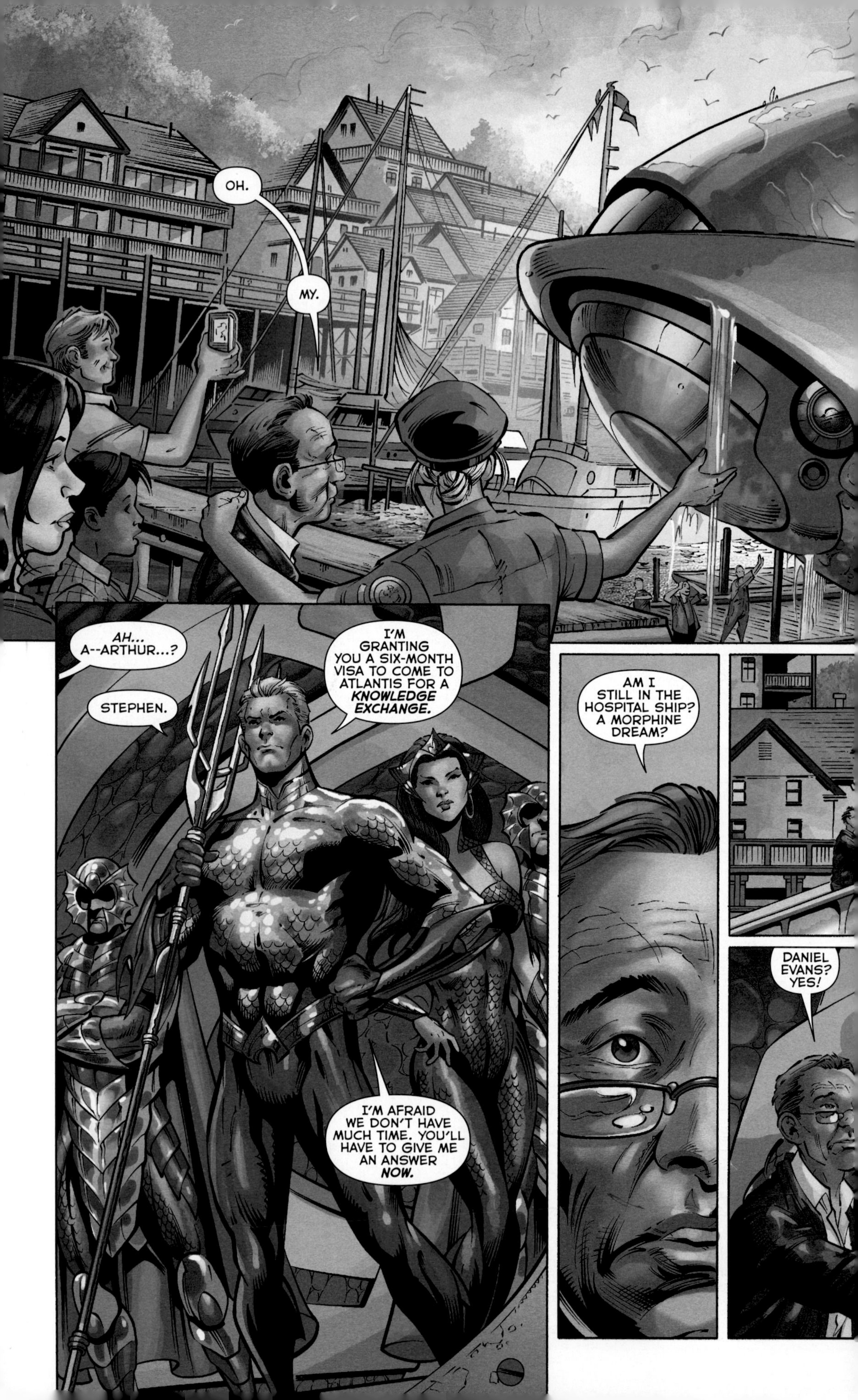
OH.
MY.
AH... A--ARTHUR...?
STEPHEN.
I'M GRANTING YOU A SIX-MONTH VISA TO COME TO ATLANTIS FOR A KNOWLEDGE EXCHANGE.
I'M AFRAID WE DON'T HAVE MUCH TIME. YOU'LL HAVE TO GIVE ME AN ANSWER NOW.
AM I STILL IN THE HOSPITAL SHIP? A MORPHINE DREAM?
DANIEL EVANS? YES!

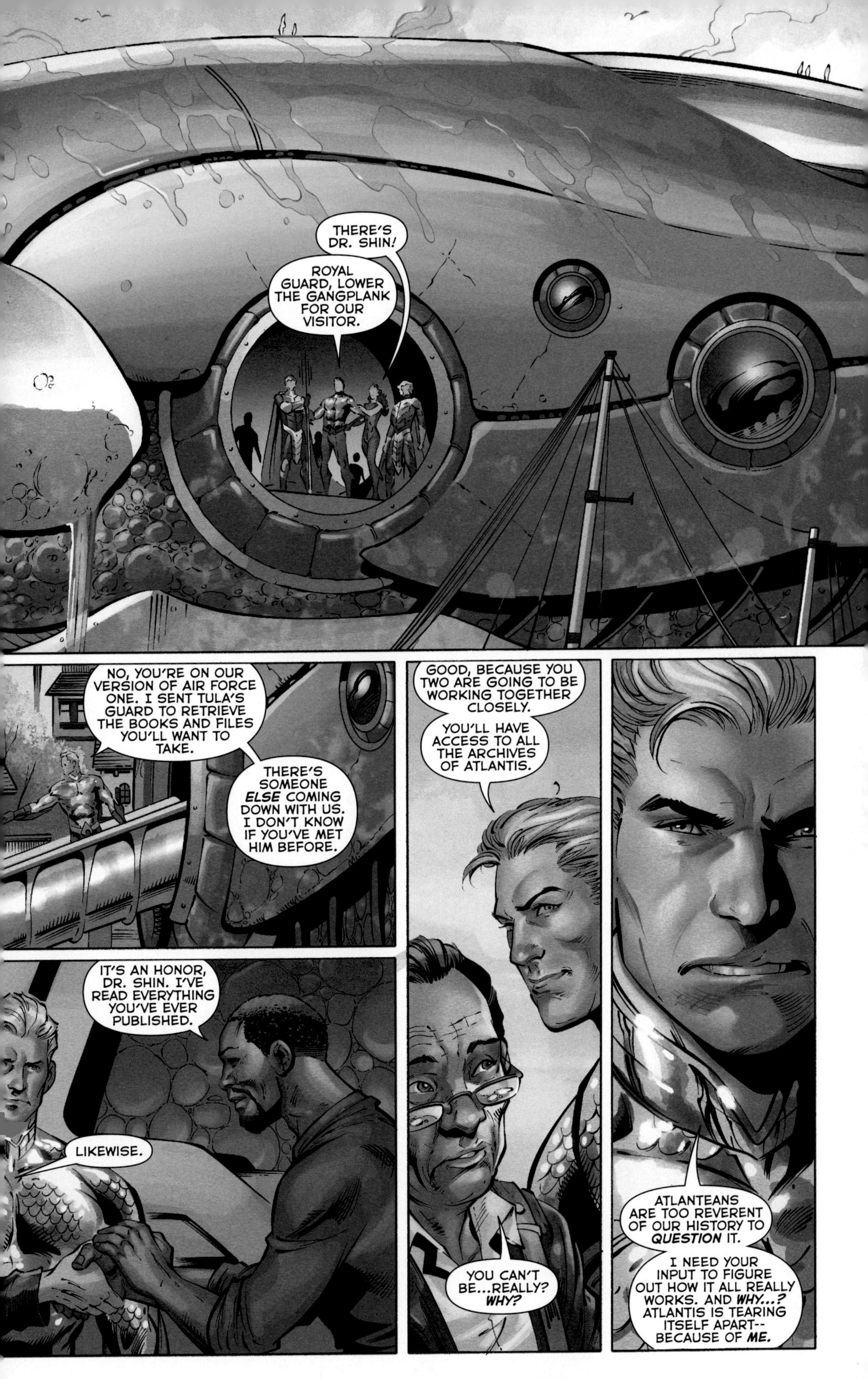
THERE'S DR. SHIN!
ROYAL GUARD, LOWER THE GANGPLANK FOR OUR VISITOR.
NO, YOU'RE ON OUR VERSION OF AIR FORCE ONE. I SENT TULA'S GUARD TO RETRIEVE THE BOOKS AND FILES YOU'LL WANT TO TAKE.
THERE'S SOMEONE *ELSE* COMING DOWN WITH US. I DON'T KNOW IF YOU'VE MET HIM BEFORE.
IT'S AN HONOR, DR. SHIN. I'VE READ EVERYTHING YOU'VE EVER PUBLISHED.
LIKEWISE.
GOOD, BECAUSE YOU TWO ARE GOING TO BE WORKING TOGETHER CLOSELY.
YOU'LL HAVE ACCESS TO ALL THE ARCHIVES OF ATLANTIS.
YOU CAN'T BE...REALLY? *WHY?*
ATLANTEANS ARE TOO REVERENT OF OUR HISTORY TO *QUESTION* IT.
I NEED YOUR INPUT TO FIGURE OUT HOW IT ALL REALLY WORKS. AND *WHY...?* ATLANTIS IS TEARING ITSELF APART-- BECAUSE OF *ME.*

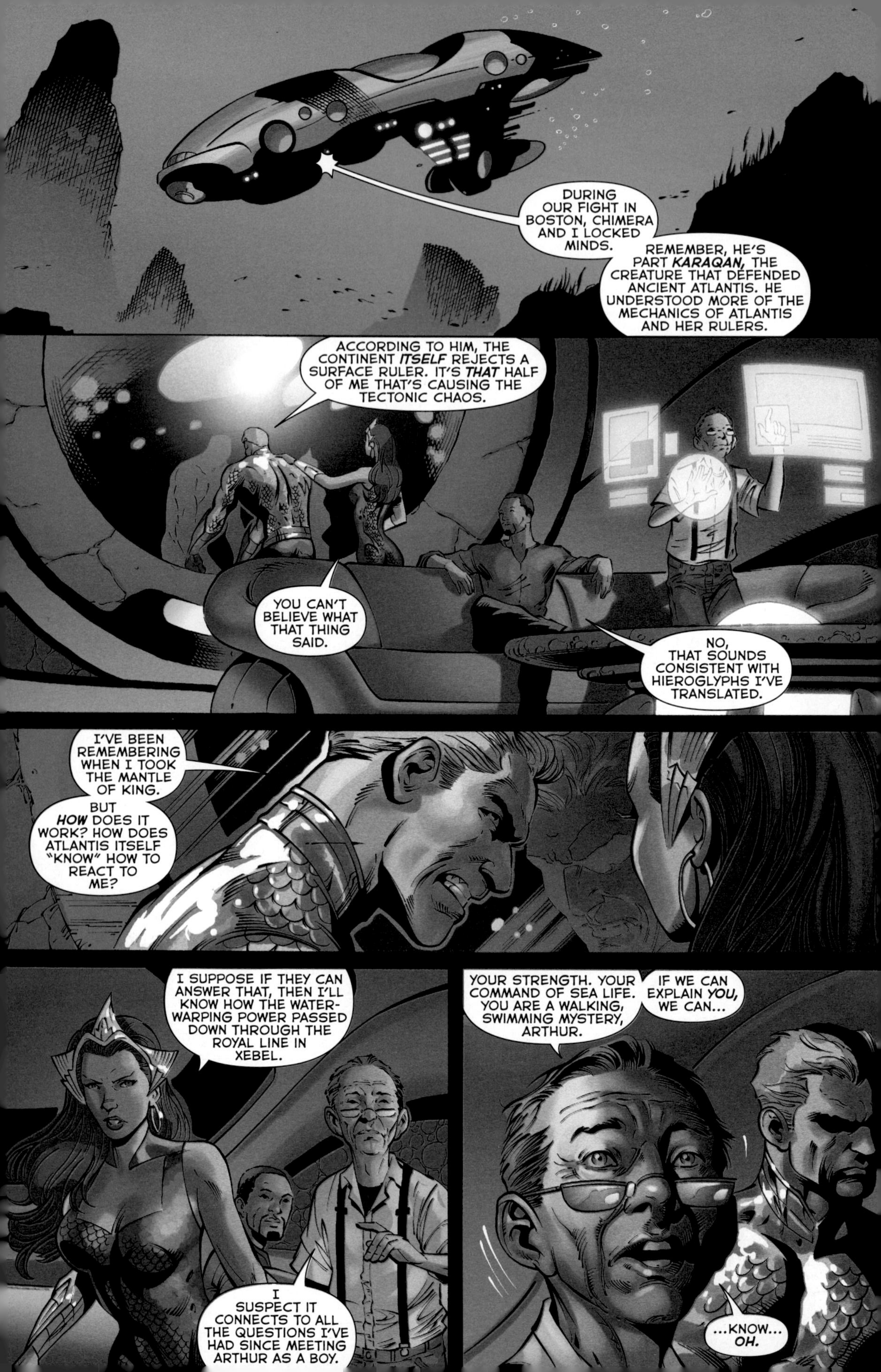
DURING OUR FIGHT IN BOSTON, CHIMERA AND I LOCKED MINDS.
REMEMBER, HE'S PART *KARAQAN,* THE CREATURE THAT DEFENDED ANCIENT ATLANTIS. HE UNDERSTOOD MORE OF THE MECHANICS OF ATLANTIS AND HER RULERS.
ACCORDING TO HIM, THE CONTINENT *ITSELF* REJECTS A SURFACE RULER. IT'S *THAT* HALF OF ME THAT'S CAUSING THE TECTONIC CHAOS.
YOU CAN'T BELIEVE WHAT THAT THING SAID.
NO, THAT SOUNDS CONSISTENT WITH HIEROGLYPHS I'VE TRANSLATED.
I'VE BEEN REMEMBERING WHEN I TOOK THE MANTLE OF KING.
BUT *HOW* DOES IT WORK? HOW DOES ATLANTIS ITSELF "KNOW" HOW TO REACT TO ME?
I SUPPOSE IF THEY CAN ANSWER THAT, THEN I'LL KNOW HOW THE WATER-WARPING POWER PASSED DOWN THROUGH THE ROYAL LINE IN XEBEL.
I SUSPECT IT CONNECTS TO ALL THE QUESTIONS I'VE HAD SINCE MEETING ARTHUR AS A BOY.
YOUR STRENGTH. YOUR COMMAND OF SEA LIFE. YOU ARE A WALKING, SWIMMING MYSTERY, ARTHUR.
IF WE CAN EXPLAIN *YOU,* WE CAN...
...KNOW... *OH.*

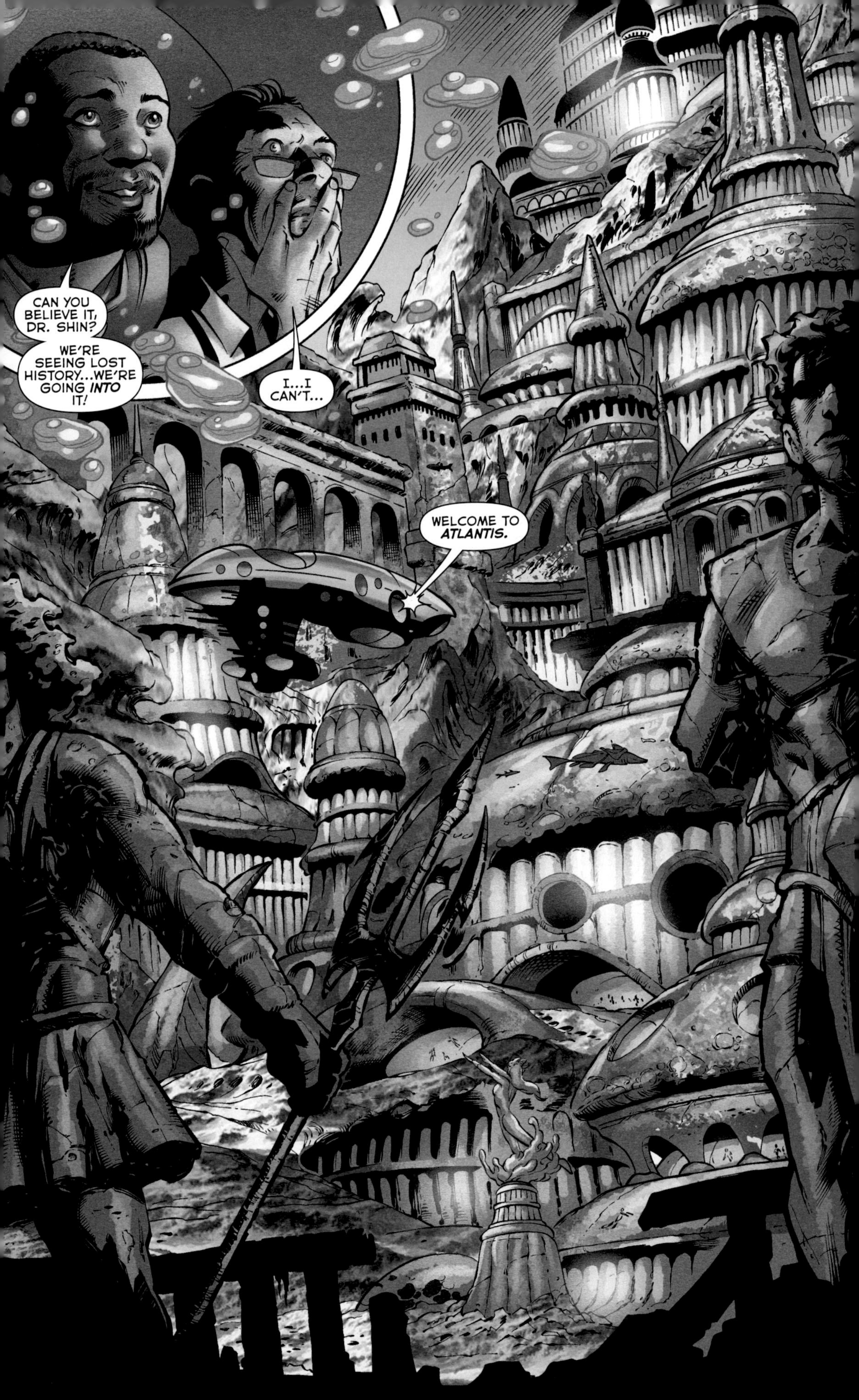

CAN YOU BELIEVE IT, DR. SHIN?
WE'RE SEEING LOST HISTORY...WE'RE GOING *INTO* IT!
I...I CAN'T...
WELCOME TO *ATLANTIS.*

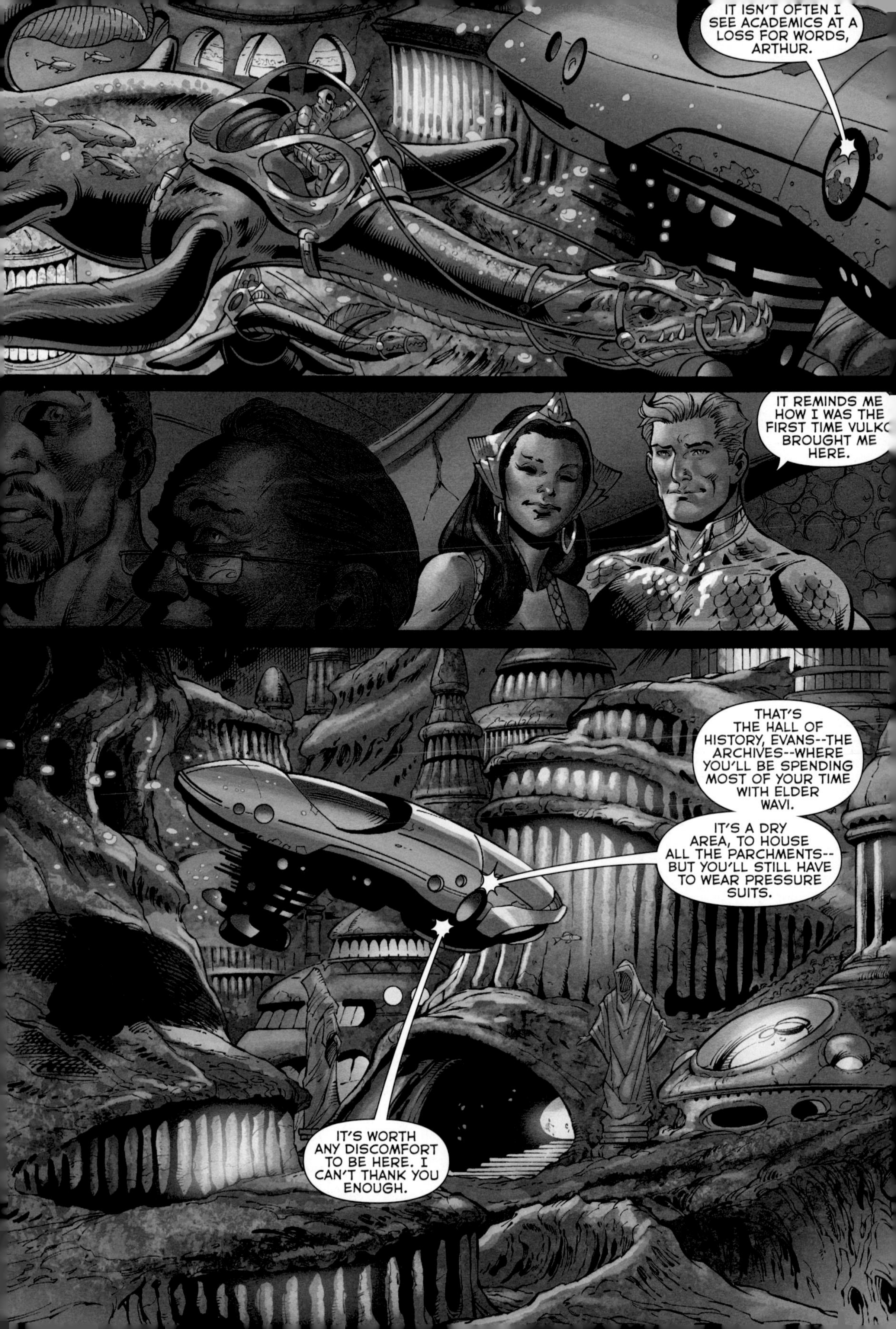
IT ISN'T OFTEN I SEE ACADEMICS AT A LOSS FOR WORDS, ARTHUR.
IT REMINDS ME HOW I WAS THE FIRST TIME VULKO BROUGHT ME HERE.
THAT'S THE HALL OF HISTORY, EVANS--THE ARCHIVES--WHERE YOU'LL BE SPENDING MOST OF YOUR TIME WITH ELDER WAVI.
IT'S A DRY AREA, TO HOUSE ALL THE PARCHMENTS--BUT YOU'LL STILL HAVE TO WEAR PRESSURE SUITS.
IT'S WORTH ANY DISCOMFORT TO BE HERE. I CAN'T THANK YOU ENOUGH.

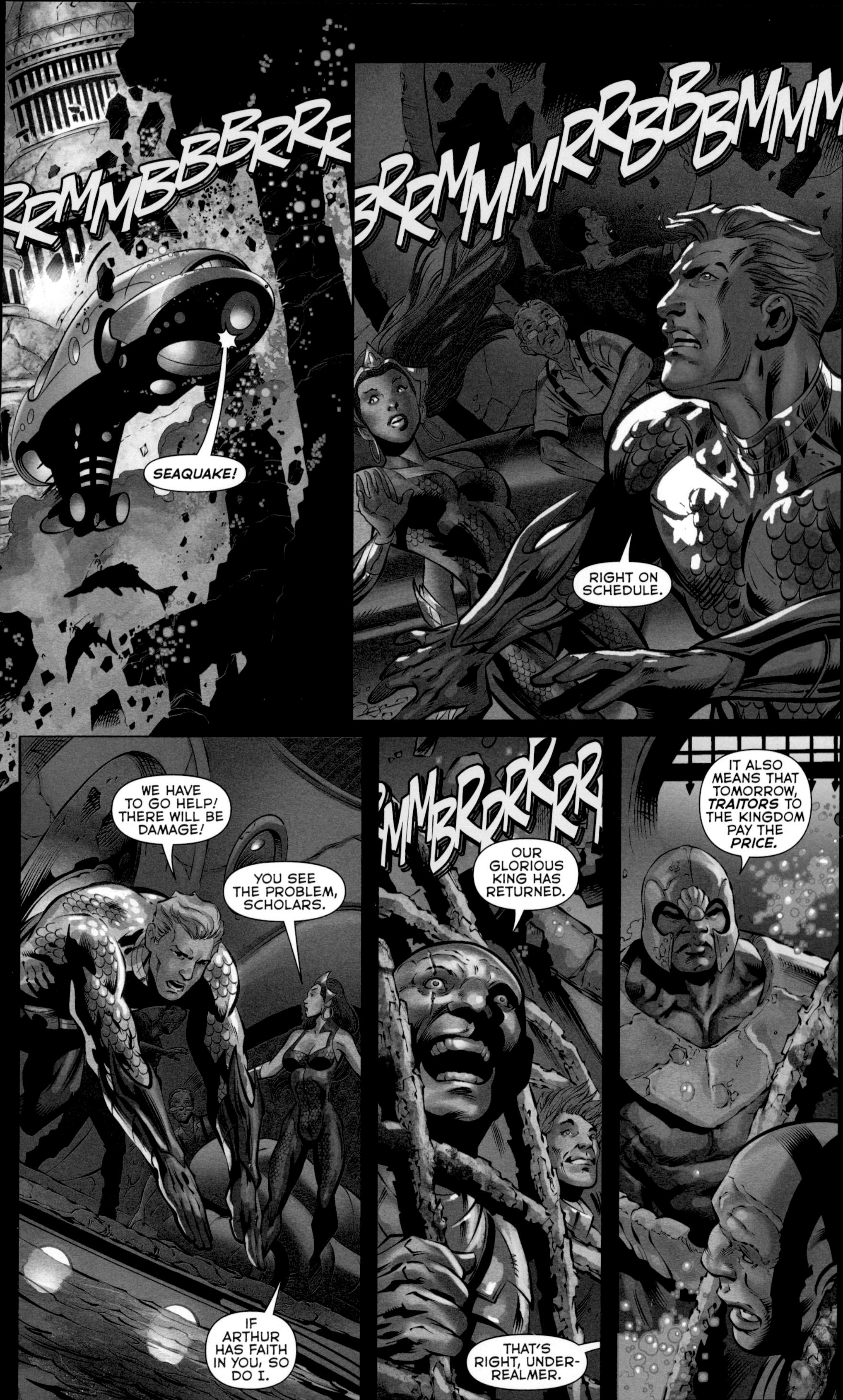
RRMMBBBRRR
SEAQUAKE!
RRMMMRRBBBMMM
RIGHT ON SCHEDULE.
WE HAVE TO GO HELP! THERE WILL BE DAMAGE!
YOU SEE THE PROBLEM, SCHOLARS.
IF ARTHUR HAS FAITH IN YOU, SO DO I.
MMBRRRKRR
OUR GLORIOUS KING HAS RETURNED.
THAT'S RIGHT, UNDER-REALMER.
IT ALSO MEANS THAT TOMORROW, *TRAITORS* TO THE KINGDOM PAY THE *PRICE.*

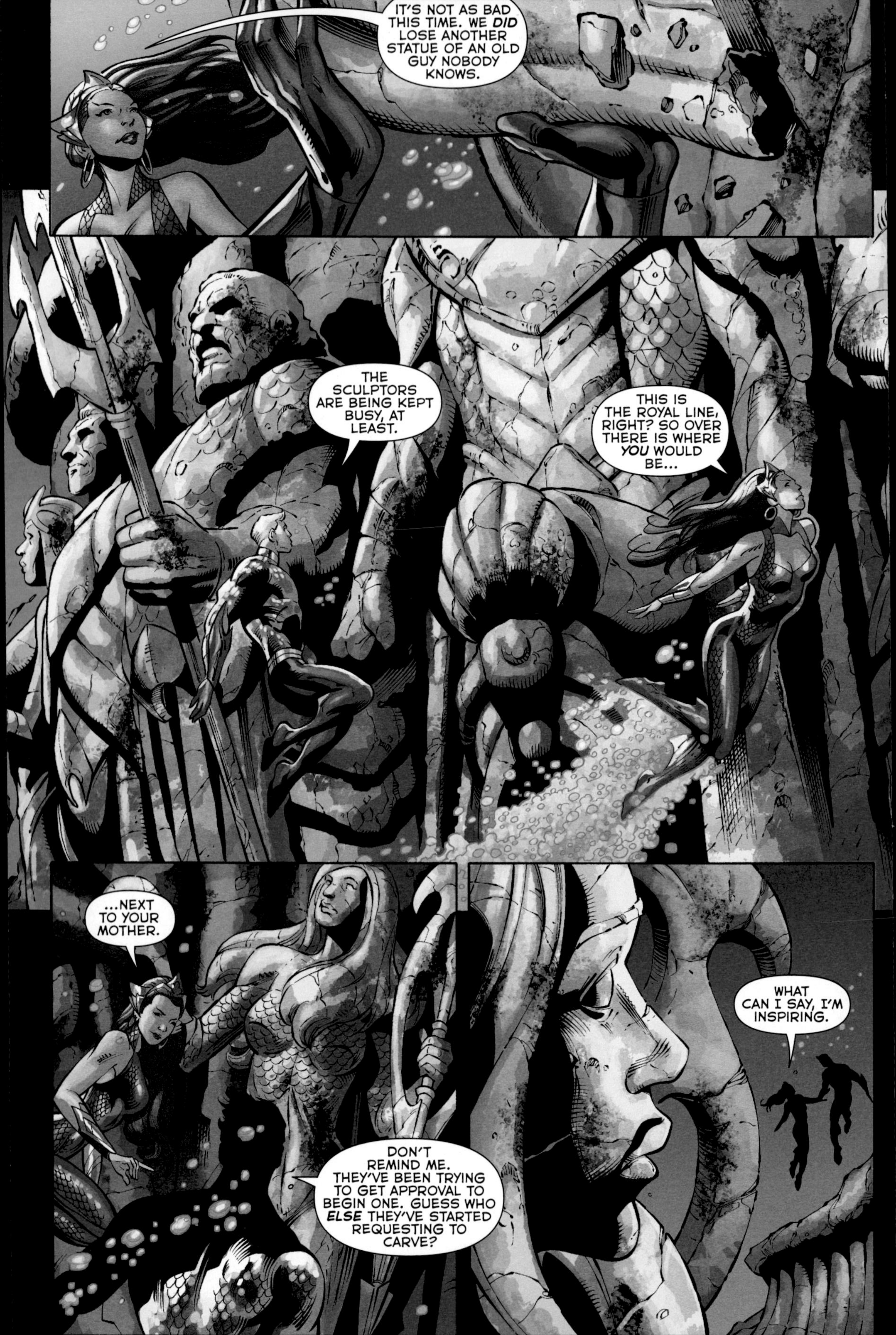
IT'S NOT AS BAD THIS TIME. WE DID LOSE ANOTHER STATUE OF AN OLD GUY NOBODY KNOWS.
THE SCULPTORS ARE BEING KEPT BUSY, AT LEAST.
THIS IS THE ROYAL LINE, RIGHT? SO OVER THERE IS WHERE YOU WOULD BE...
...NEXT TO YOUR MOTHER.
DON'T REMIND ME. THEY'VE BEEN TRYING TO GET APPROVAL TO BEGIN ONE. GUESS WHO ELSE THEY'VE STARTED REQUESTING TO CARVE?
WHAT CAN I SAY, I'M INSPIRING.

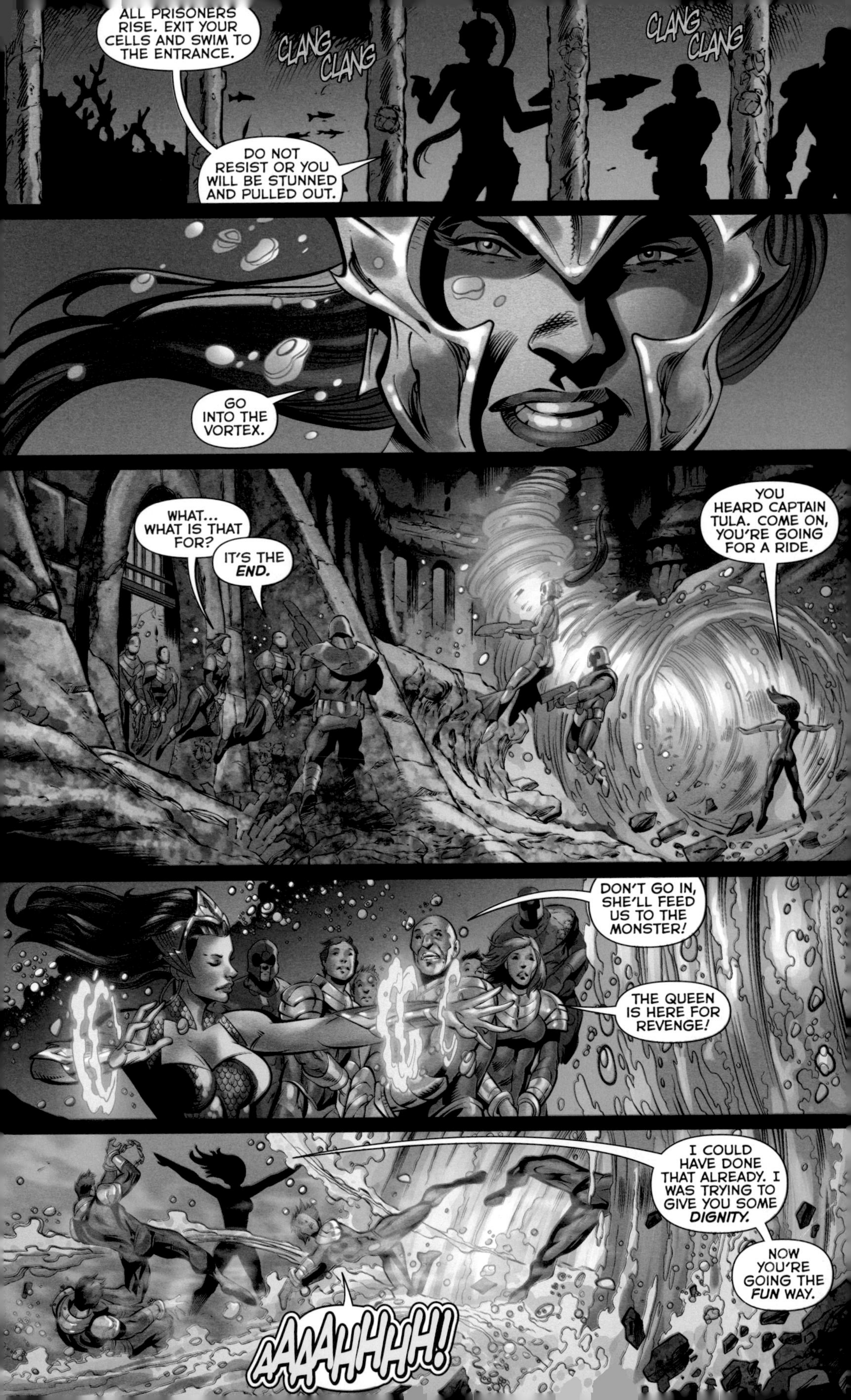
ALL PRISONERS RISE. EXIT YOUR CELLS AND SWIM TO THE ENTRANCE.
CLANG CLANG
CLANG CLANG
DO NOT RESIST OR YOU WILL BE STUNNED AND PULLED OUT.
GO INTO THE VORTEX.
WHAT... WHAT IS THAT FOR?
IT'S THE END.
YOU HEARD CAPTAIN TULA. COME ON, YOU'RE GOING FOR A RIDE.
DON'T GO IN, SHE'LL FEED US TO THE MONSTER!
THE QUEEN IS HERE FOR REVENGE!
I COULD HAVE DONE THAT ALREADY. I WAS TRYING TO GIVE YOU SOME DIGNITY.
NOW YOU'RE GOING THE FUN WAY.
AAAAHHHH!

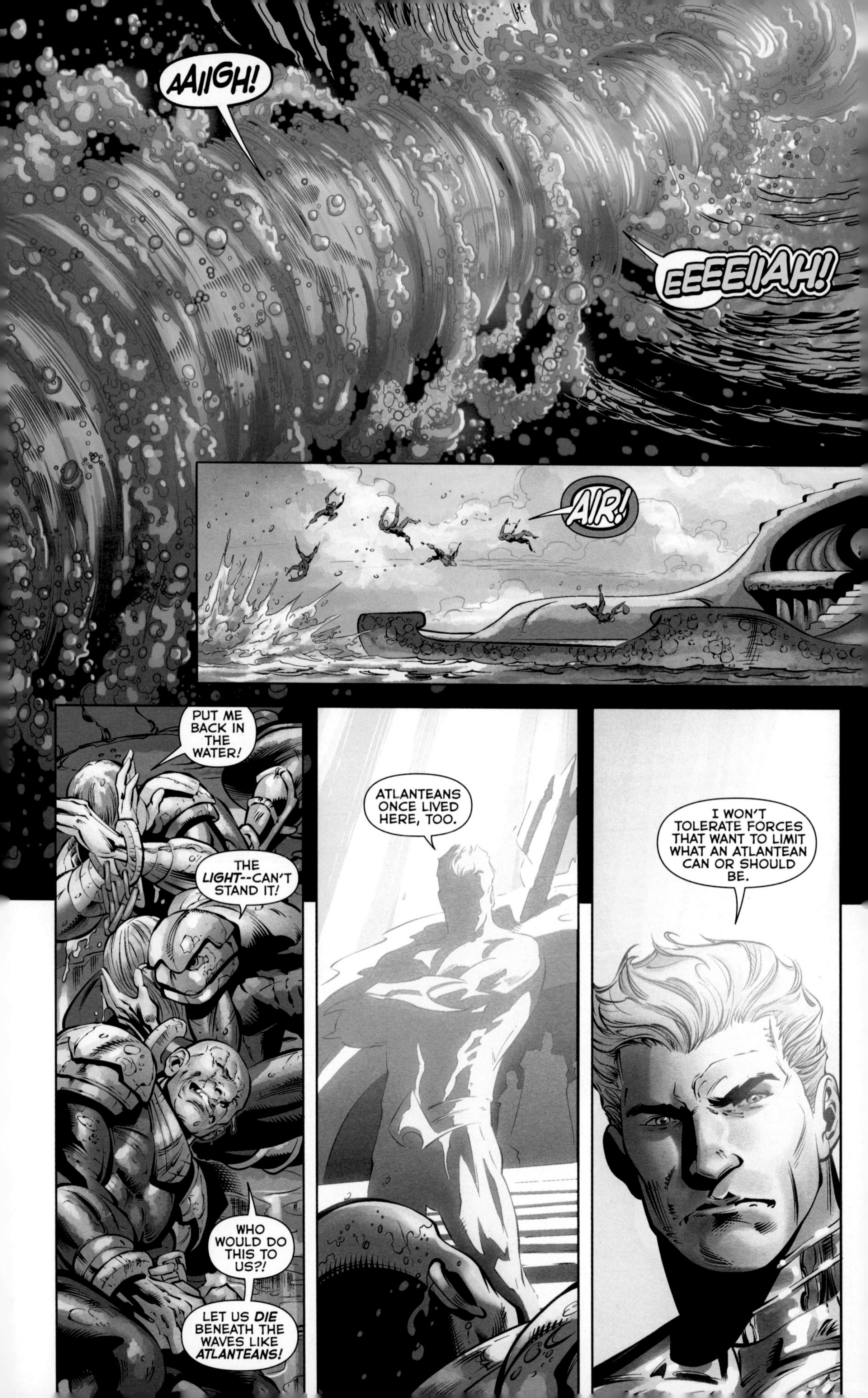
AAIIGH!
EEEEIIAH!
AIR!
PUT ME BACK IN THE WATER!
THE LIGHT--CAN'T STAND IT!
WHO WOULD DO THIS TO US?!
LET US DIE BENEATH THE WAVES LIKE ATLANTEANS!
ATLANTEANS ONCE LIVED HERE, TOO.
I WON'T TOLERATE FORCES THAT WANT TO LIMIT WHAT AN ATLANTEAN CAN OR SHOULD BE.

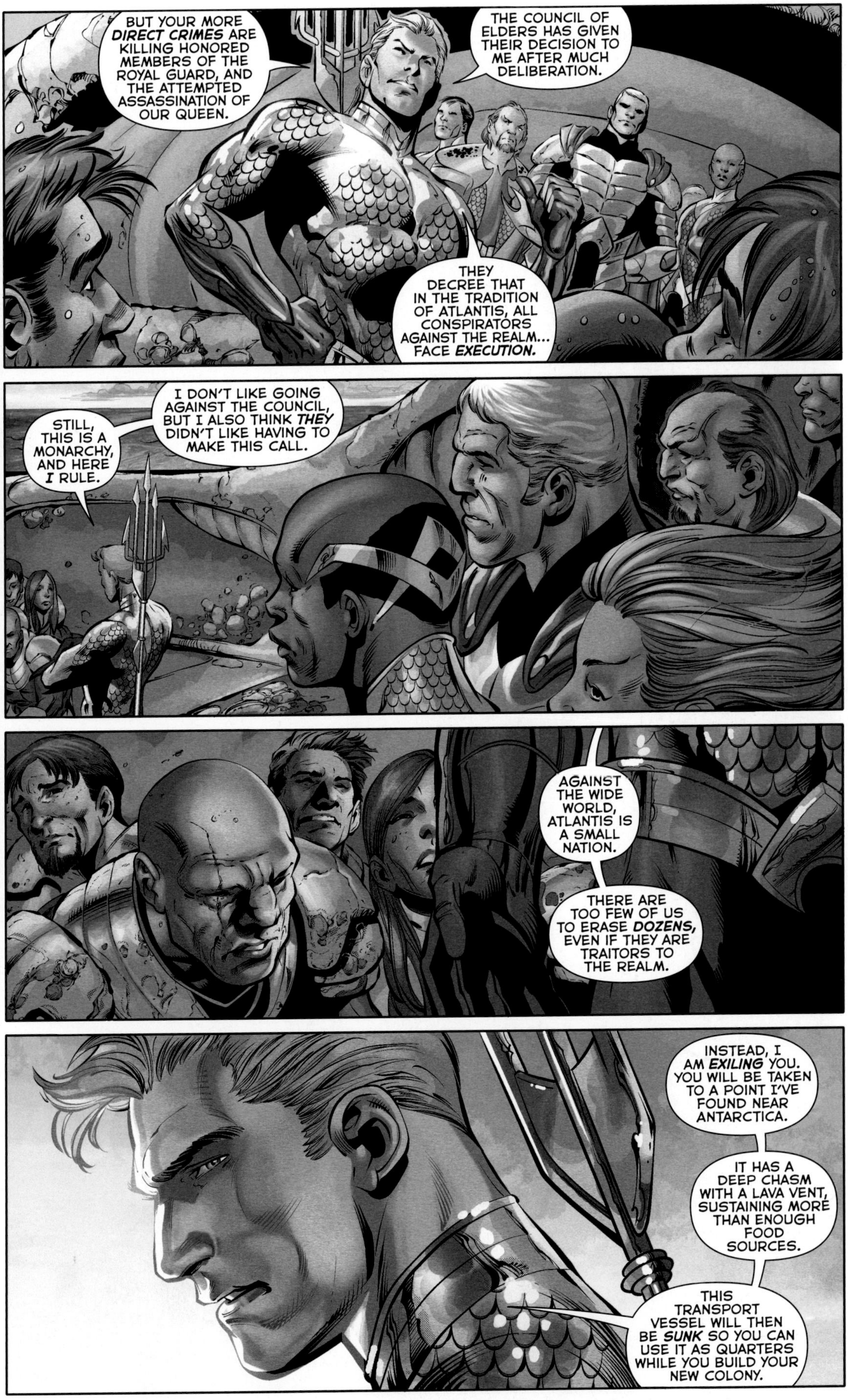
BUT YOUR MORE DIRECT CRIMES ARE KILLING HONORED MEMBERS OF THE ROYAL GUARD, AND THE ATTEMPTED ASSASSINATION OF OUR QUEEN.
THE COUNCIL OF ELDERS HAS GIVEN THEIR DECISION TO ME AFTER MUCH DELIBERATION.
THEY DECREE THAT IN THE TRADITION OF ATLANTIS, ALL CONSPIRATORS AGAINST THE REALM... FACE EXECUTION.
STILL, THIS IS A MONARCHY, AND HERE I RULE.
I DON'T LIKE GOING AGAINST THE COUNCIL, BUT I ALSO THINK THEY DIDN'T LIKE HAVING TO MAKE THIS CALL.
AGAINST THE WIDE WORLD, ATLANTIS IS A SMALL NATION.
THERE ARE TOO FEW OF US TO ERASE DOZENS, EVEN IF THEY ARE TRAITORS TO THE REALM.
INSTEAD, I AM EXILING YOU. YOU WILL BE TAKEN TO A POINT I'VE FOUND NEAR ANTARCTICA.
IT HAS A DEEP CHASM WITH A LAVA VENT, SUSTAINING MORE THAN ENOUGH FOOD SOURCES.
THIS TRANSPORT VESSEL WILL THEN BE SUNK SO YOU CAN USE IT AS QUARTERS WHILE YOU BUILD YOUR NEW COLONY.

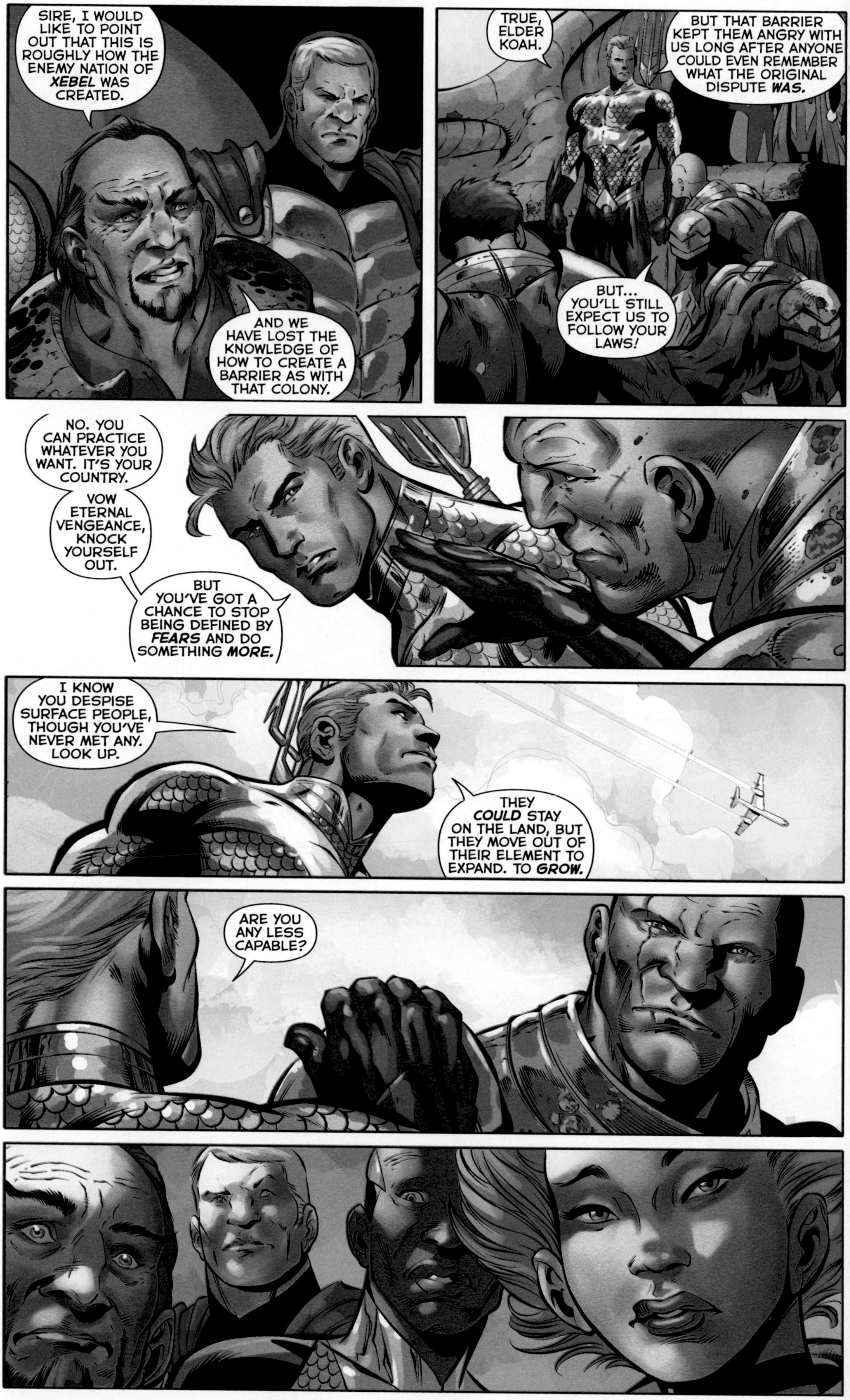

SIRE, I WOULD LIKE TO POINT OUT THAT THIS IS ROUGHLY HOW THE ENEMY NATION OF XEBEL WAS CREATED.
AND WE HAVE LOST THE KNOWLEDGE OF HOW TO CREATE A BARRIER AS WITH THAT COLONY.
TRUE, ELDER KOAH.
BUT THAT BARRIER KEPT THEM ANGRY WITH US LONG AFTER ANYONE COULD EVEN REMEMBER WHAT THE ORIGINAL DISPUTE WAS.
BUT... YOU'LL STILL EXPECT US TO FOLLOW YOUR LAWS!
NO. YOU CAN PRACTICE WHATEVER YOU WANT. IT'S YOUR COUNTRY.
VOW ETERNAL VENGEANCE, KNOCK YOURSELF OUT.
BUT YOU'VE GOT A CHANCE TO STOP BEING DEFINED BY FEARS AND DO SOMETHING MORE.
I KNOW YOU DESPISE SURFACE PEOPLE, THOUGH YOU'VE NEVER MET ANY. LOOK UP.
THEY COULD STAY ON THE LAND, BUT THEY MOVE OUT OF THEIR ELEMENT TO EXPAND. TO GROW.
ARE YOU ANY LESS CAPABLE?

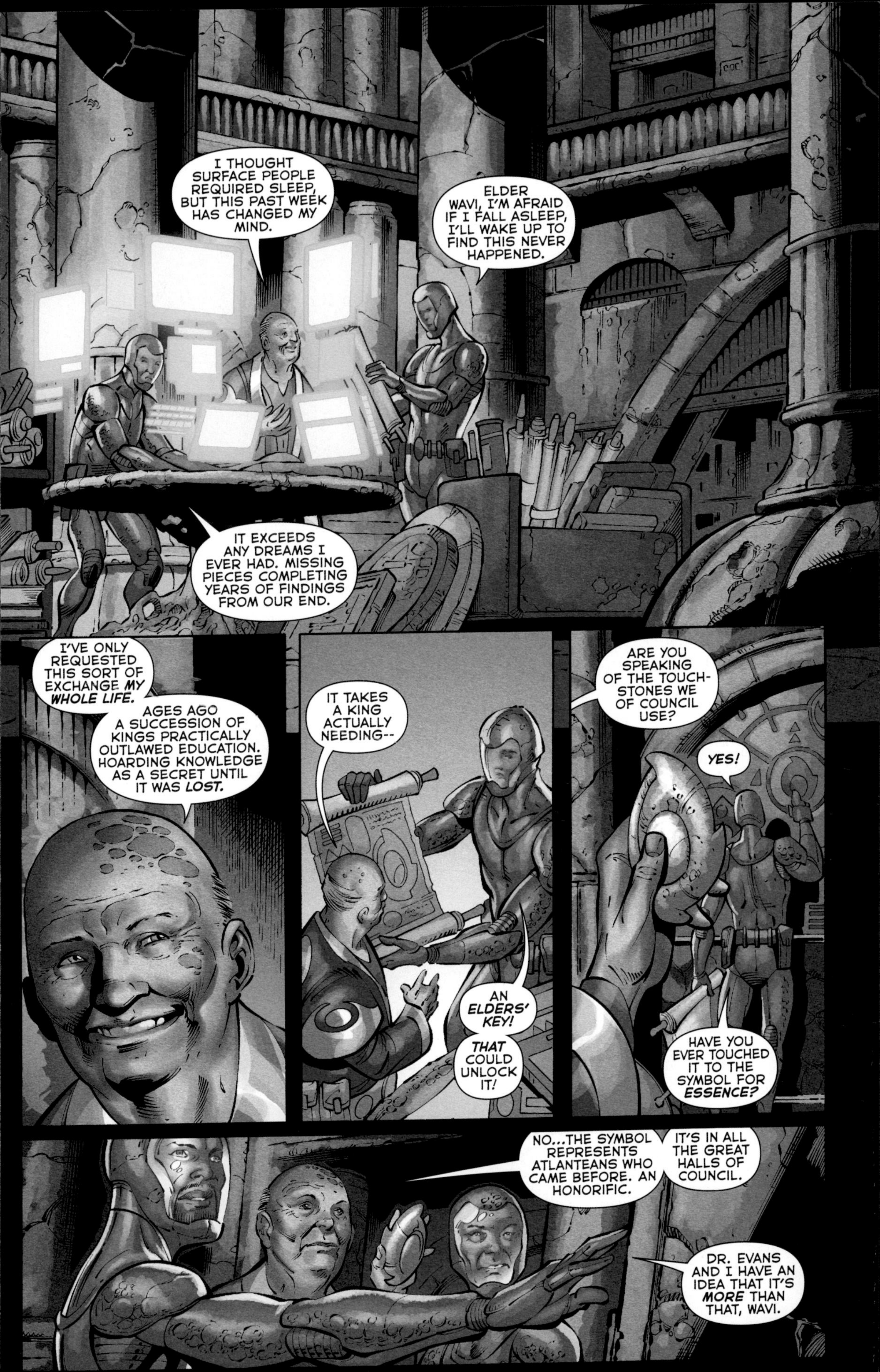
I THOUGHT SURFACE PEOPLE REQUIRED SLEEP, BUT THIS PAST WEEK HAS CHANGED MY MIND.
ELDER WAVI, I'M AFRAID IF I FALL ASLEEP, I'LL WAKE UP TO FIND THIS NEVER HAPPENED.
IT EXCEEDS ANY DREAMS I EVER HAD. MISSING PIECES COMPLETING YEARS OF FINDINGS FROM OUR END.
I'VE ONLY REQUESTED THIS SORT OF EXCHANGE *MY WHOLE LIFE.*
AGES AGO A SUCCESSION OF KINGS PRACTICALLY OUTLAWED EDUCATION. HOARDING KNOWLEDGE AS A SECRET UNTIL IT WAS *LOST.*
IT TAKES A KING ACTUALLY NEEDING--
AN *ELDERS' KEY!*
THAT COULD UNLOCK IT!
ARE YOU SPEAKING OF THE TOUCH-STONES WE OF COUNCIL USE?
YES!
HAVE YOU EVER TOUCHED IT TO THE SYMBOL FOR *ESSENCE?*
NO...THE SYMBOL REPRESENTS ATLANTEANS WHO CAME BEFORE. AN HONORIFIC.
IT'S IN ALL THE GREAT HALLS OF COUNCIL.
DR. EVANS AND I HAVE AN IDEA THAT IT'S *MORE* THAN THAT, WAVI.

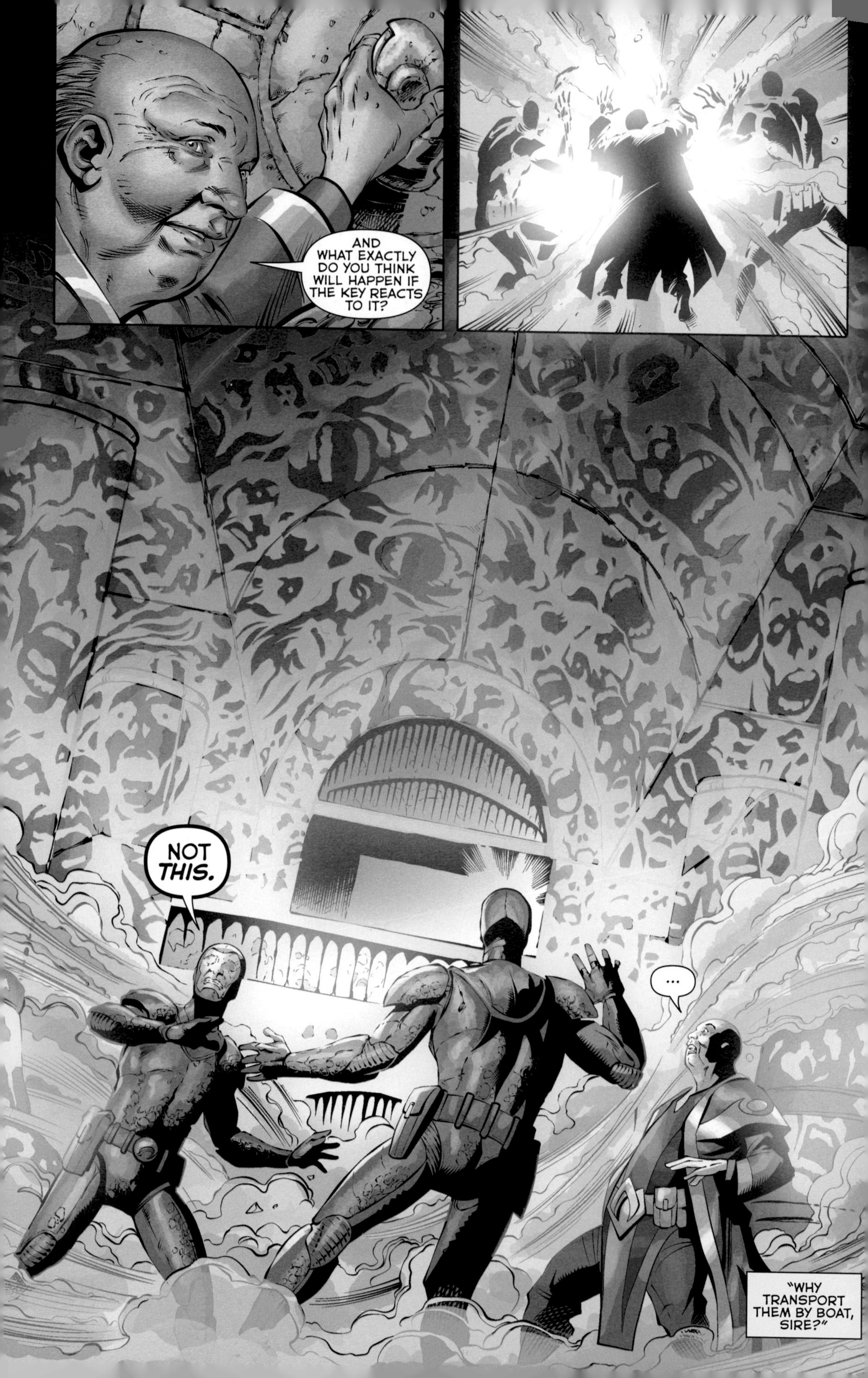
AND WHAT EXACTLY DO YOU THINK WILL HAPPEN IF THE KEY REACTS TO IT?
NOT THIS.
...
"WHY TRANSPORT THEM BY BOAT, SIRE?"

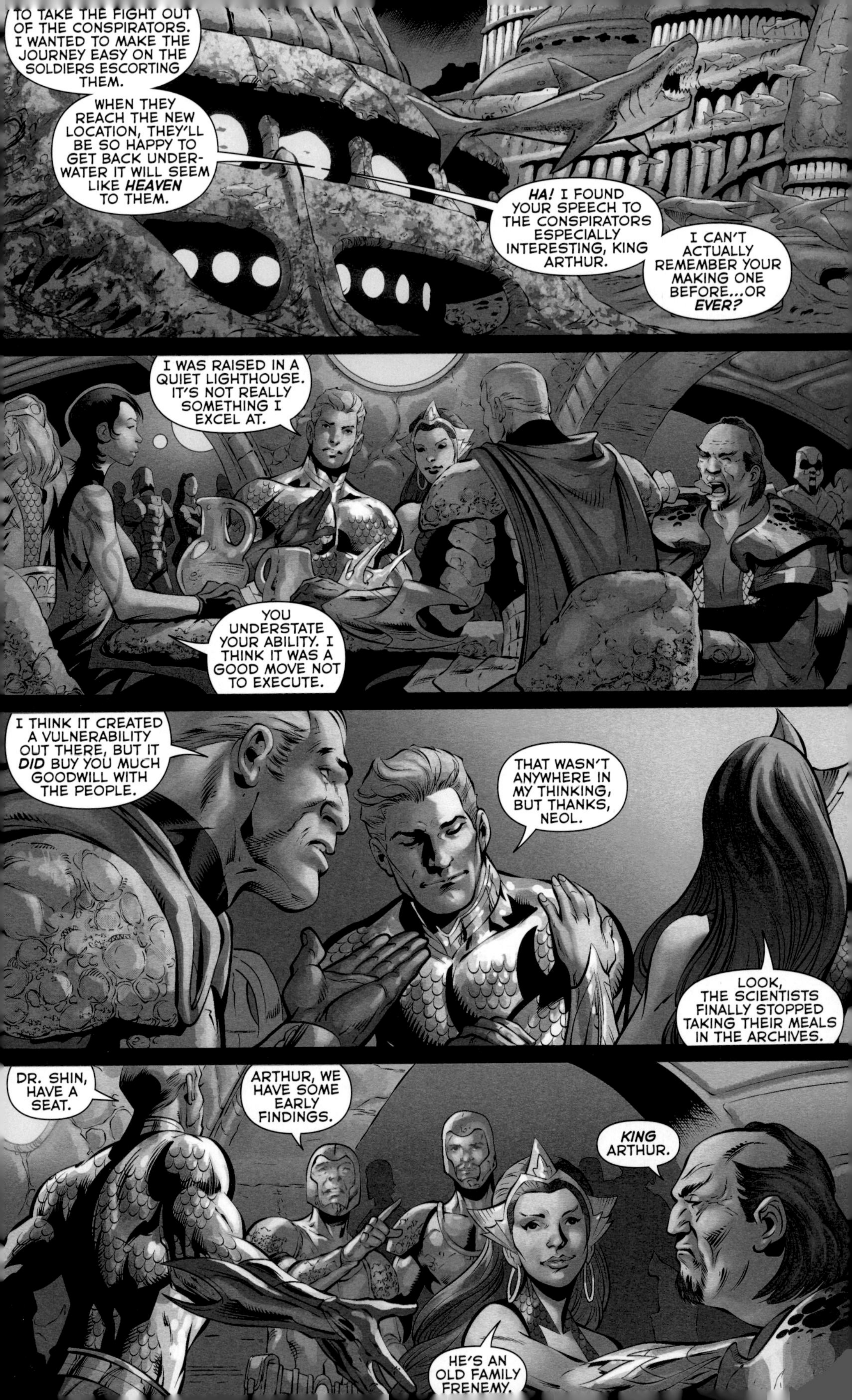
TO TAKE THE FIGHT OUT OF THE CONSPIRATORS. I WANTED TO MAKE THE JOURNEY EASY ON THE SOLDIERS ESCORTING THEM.
WHEN THEY REACH THE NEW LOCATION, THEY'LL BE SO HAPPY TO GET BACK UNDER-WATER IT WILL SEEM LIKE HEAVEN TO THEM.
HA! I FOUND YOUR SPEECH TO THE CONSPIRATORS ESPECIALLY INTERESTING, KING ARTHUR.
I CAN'T ACTUALLY REMEMBER YOUR MAKING ONE BEFORE...OR EVER?
I WAS RAISED IN A QUIET LIGHTHOUSE. IT'S NOT REALLY SOMETHING I EXCEL AT.
YOU UNDERSTATE YOUR ABILITY. I THINK IT WAS A GOOD MOVE NOT TO EXECUTE.
I THINK IT CREATED A VULNERABILITY OUT THERE, BUT IT DID BUY YOU MUCH GOODWILL WITH THE PEOPLE.
THAT WASN'T ANYWHERE IN MY THINKING, BUT THANKS, NEOL.
LOOK, THE SCIENTISTS FINALLY STOPPED TAKING THEIR MEALS IN THE ARCHIVES.
DR. SHIN, HAVE A SEAT.
ARTHUR, WE HAVE SOME EARLY FINDINGS.
KING ARTHUR.
HE'S AN OLD FAMILY FRENEMY.

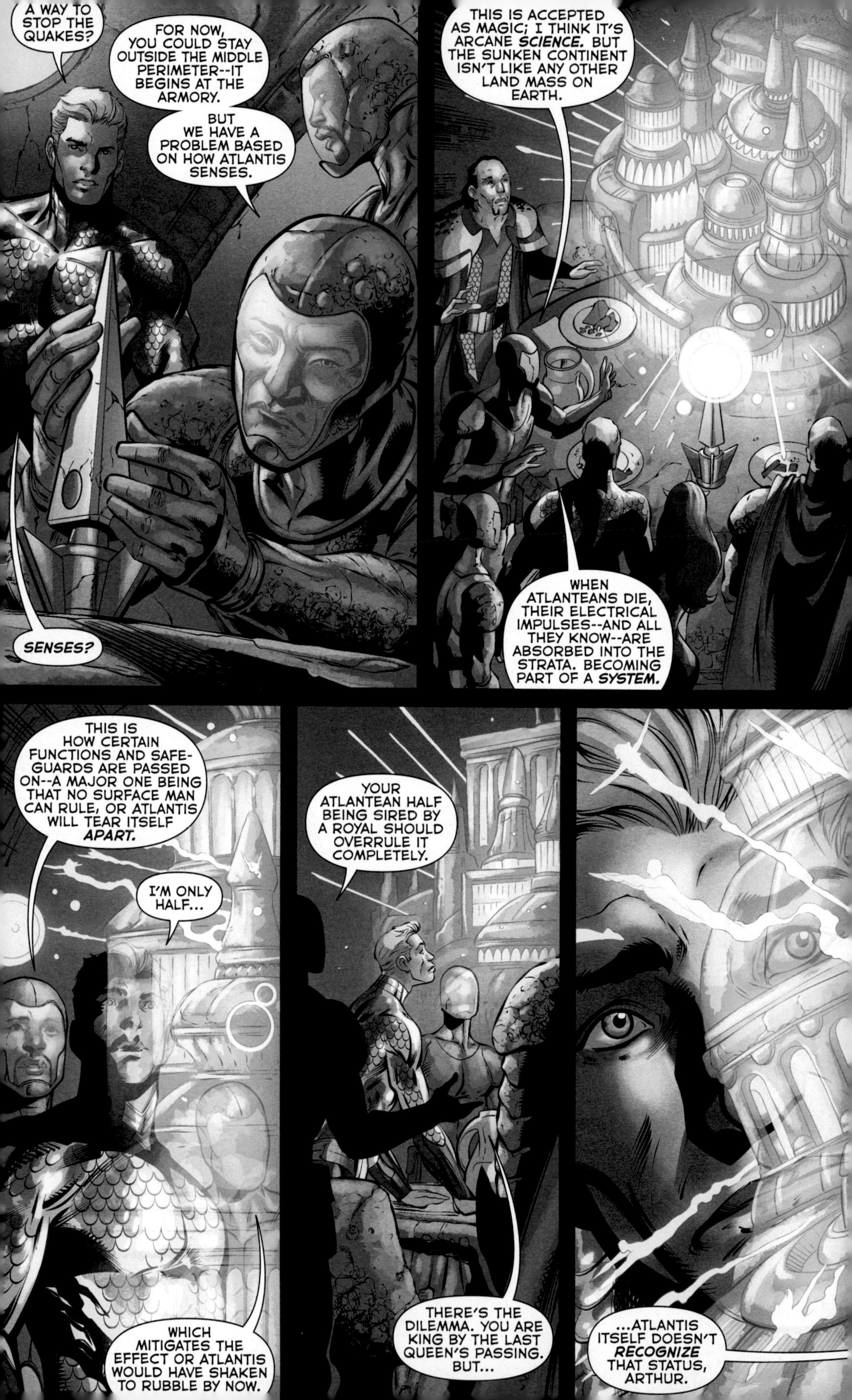
A WAY TO STOP THE QUAKES?
FOR NOW, YOU COULD STAY OUTSIDE THE MIDDLE PERIMETER--IT BEGINS AT THE ARMORY.
BUT WE HAVE A PROBLEM BASED ON HOW ATLANTIS SENSES.
SENSES?
THIS IS ACCEPTED AS MAGIC; I THINK IT'S ARCANE SCIENCE. BUT THE SUNKEN CONTINENT ISN'T LIKE ANY OTHER LAND MASS ON EARTH.
WHEN ATLANTEANS DIE, THEIR ELECTRICAL IMPULSES--AND ALL THEY KNOW--ARE ABSORBED INTO THE STRATA. BECOMING PART OF A SYSTEM.
THIS IS HOW CERTAIN FUNCTIONS AND SAFE-GUARDS ARE PASSED ON--A MAJOR ONE BEING THAT NO SURFACE MAN CAN RULE, OR ATLANTIS WILL TEAR ITSELF APART.
I'M ONLY HALF...
WHICH MITIGATES THE EFFECT OR ATLANTIS WOULD HAVE SHAKEN TO RUBBLE BY NOW.
YOUR ATLANTEAN HALF BEING SIRED BY A ROYAL SHOULD OVERRULE IT COMPLETELY.
THERE'S THE DILEMMA. YOU ARE KING BY THE LAST QUEEN'S PASSING. BUT...
...ATLANTIS ITSELF DOESN'T RECOGNIZE THAT STATUS, ARTHUR.

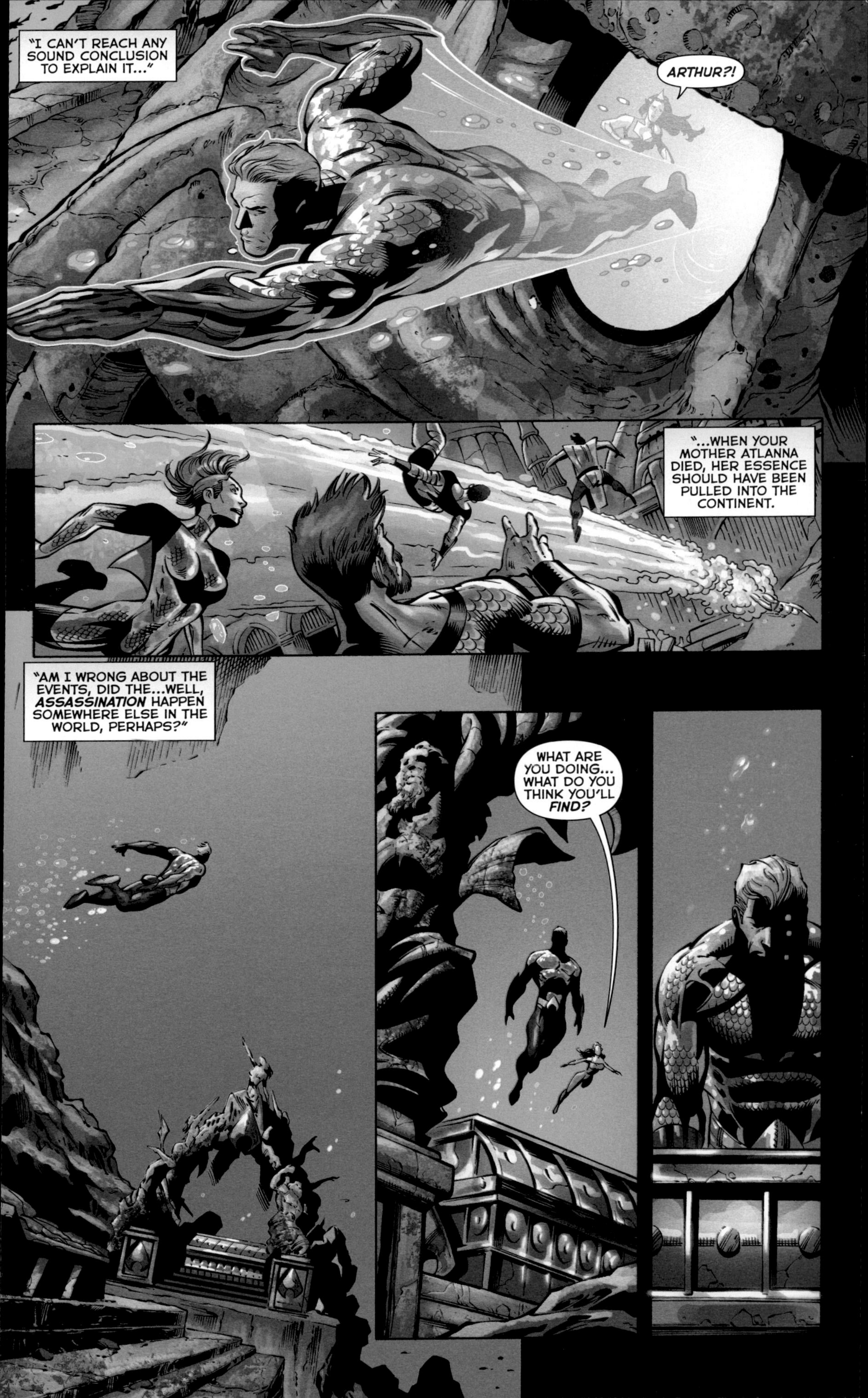
"I CAN'T REACH ANY SOUND CONCLUSION TO EXPLAIN IT..."
ARTHUR?!
"...WHEN YOUR MOTHER ATLANNA DIED, HER ESSENCE SHOULD HAVE BEEN PULLED INTO THE CONTINENT.
"AM I WRONG ABOUT THE EVENTS, DID THE...WELL, ASSASSINATION HAPPEN SOMEWHERE ELSE IN THE WORLD, PERHAPS?"
WHAT ARE YOU DOING... WHAT DO YOU THINK YOU'LL FIND?

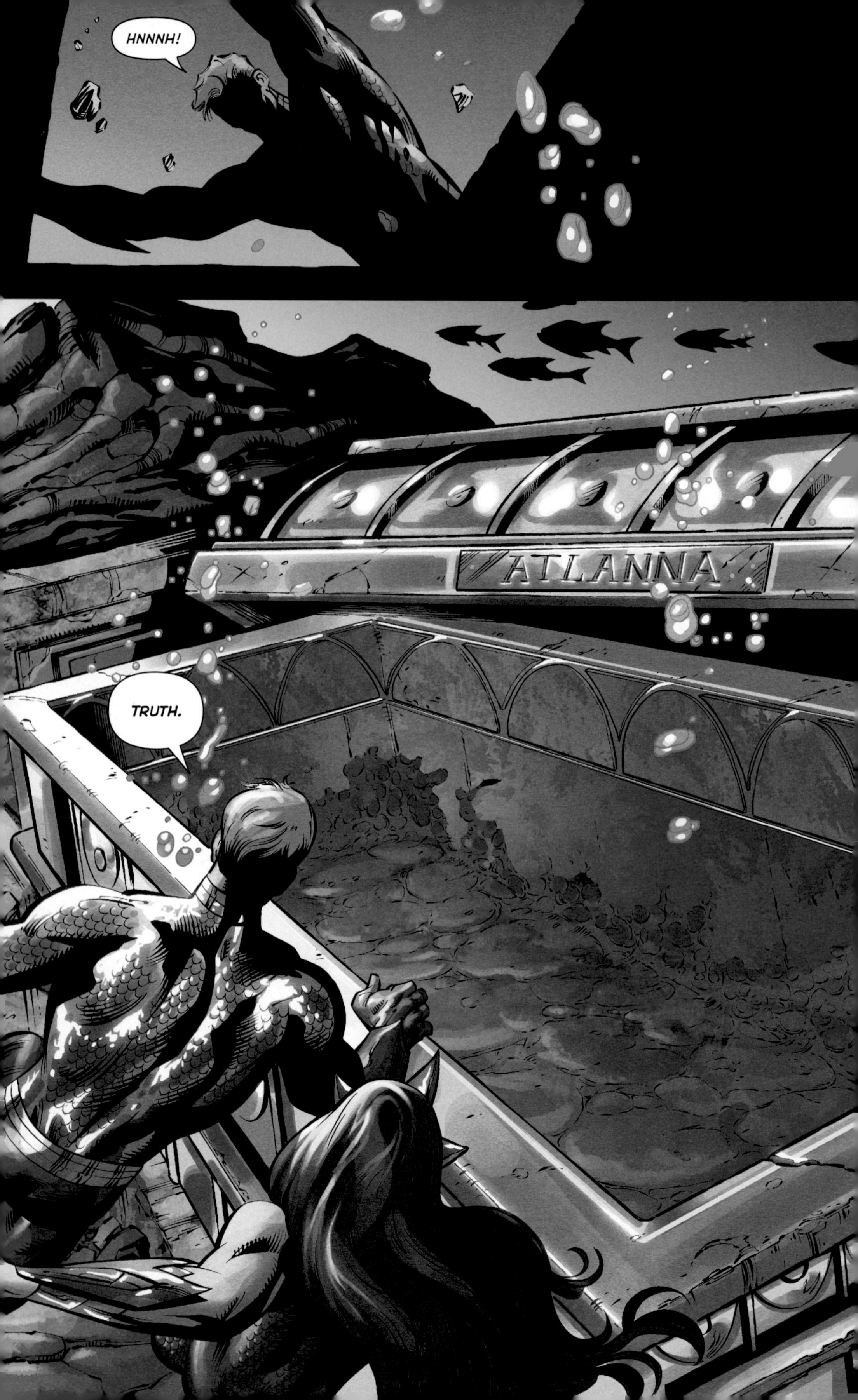
HNNNH!
ATLANNA
TRUTH.

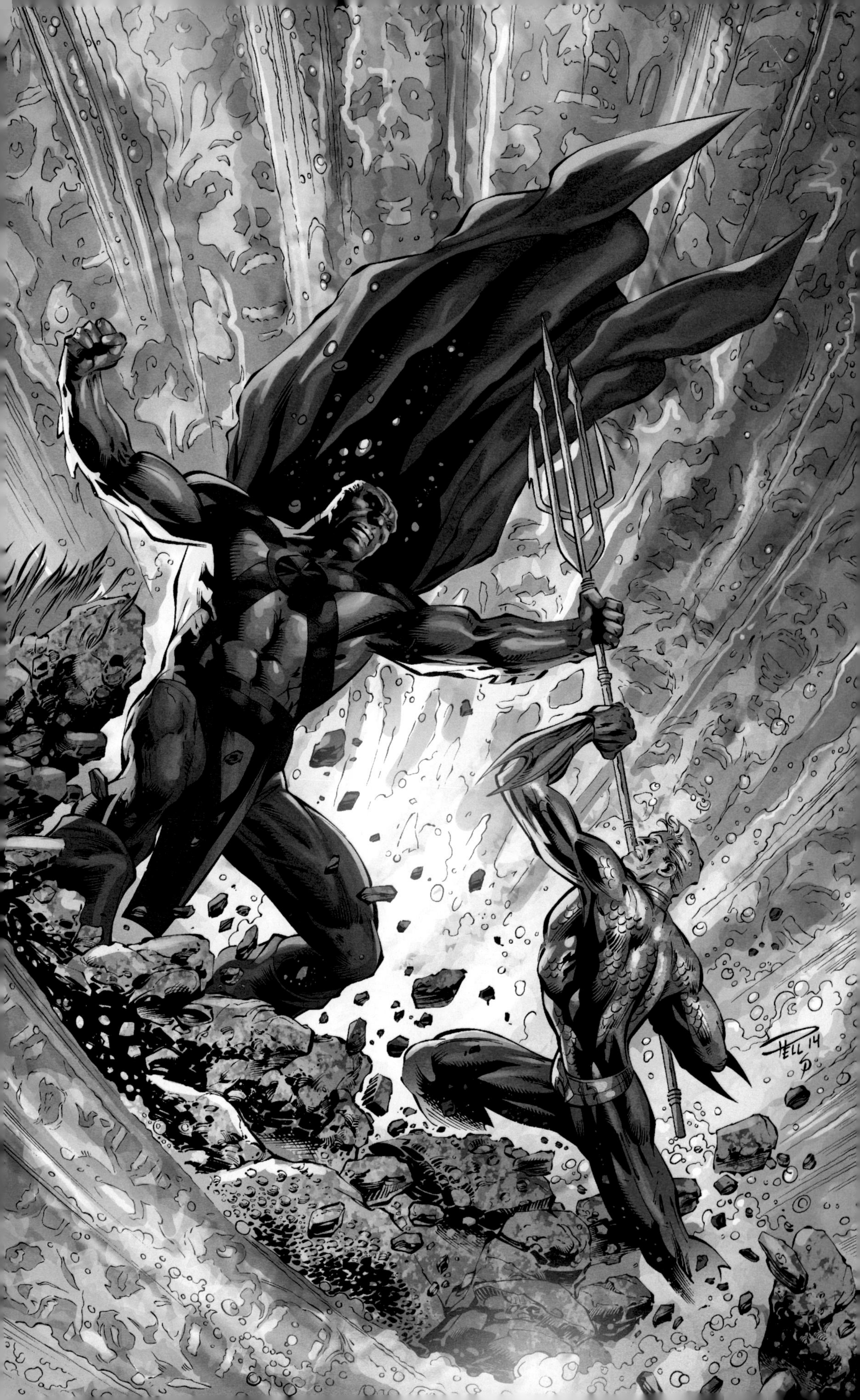

MAELSTROM PART II: POSSESSED

JEFF PARKER writer **PAUL PELLETIER** penciller **SEAN PARSONS** inker **RAIN BEREDO** colorist **CARLOS M. MANGUAL** letterer **PELLETIER and PARSONS** cover art

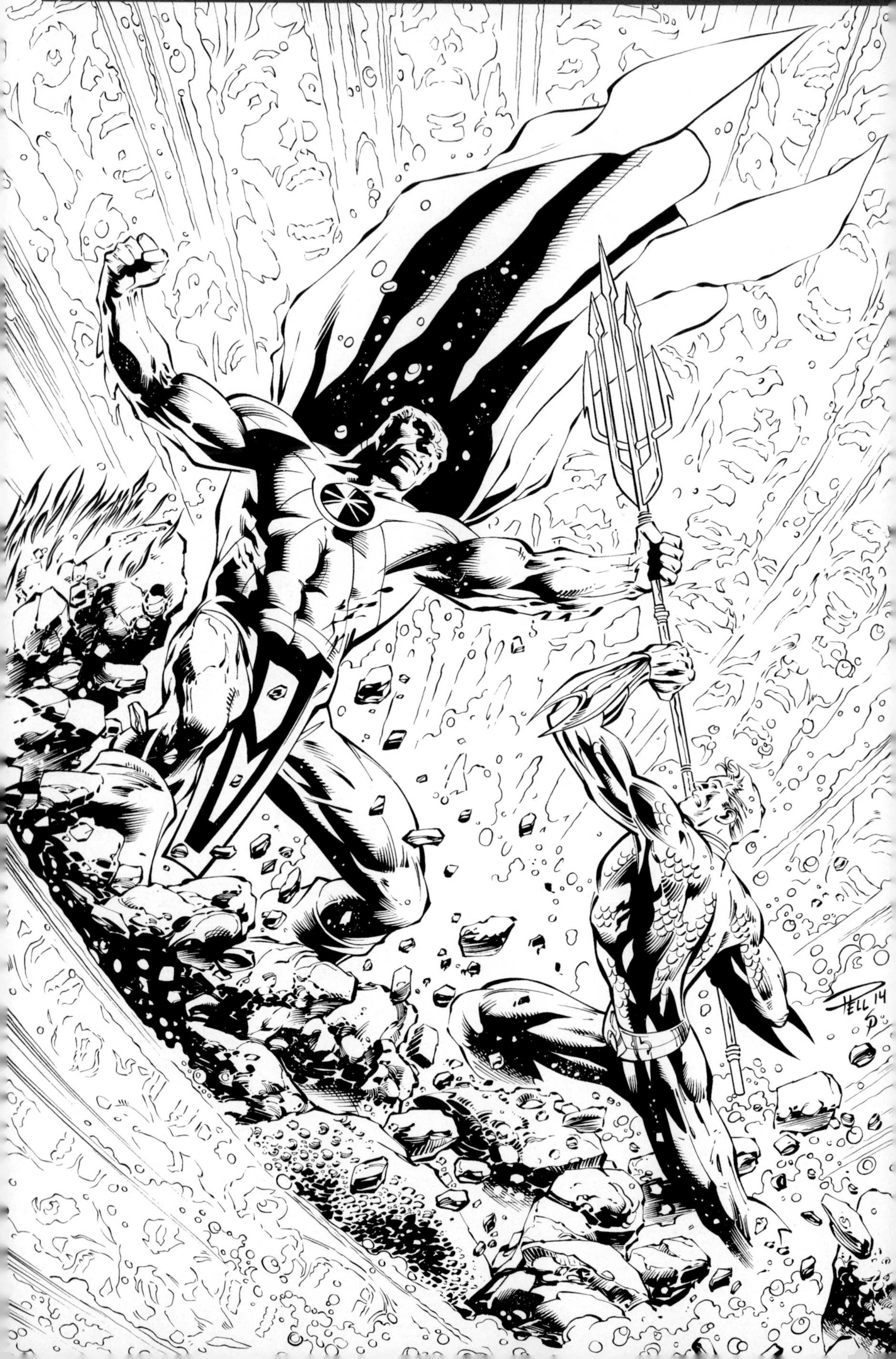

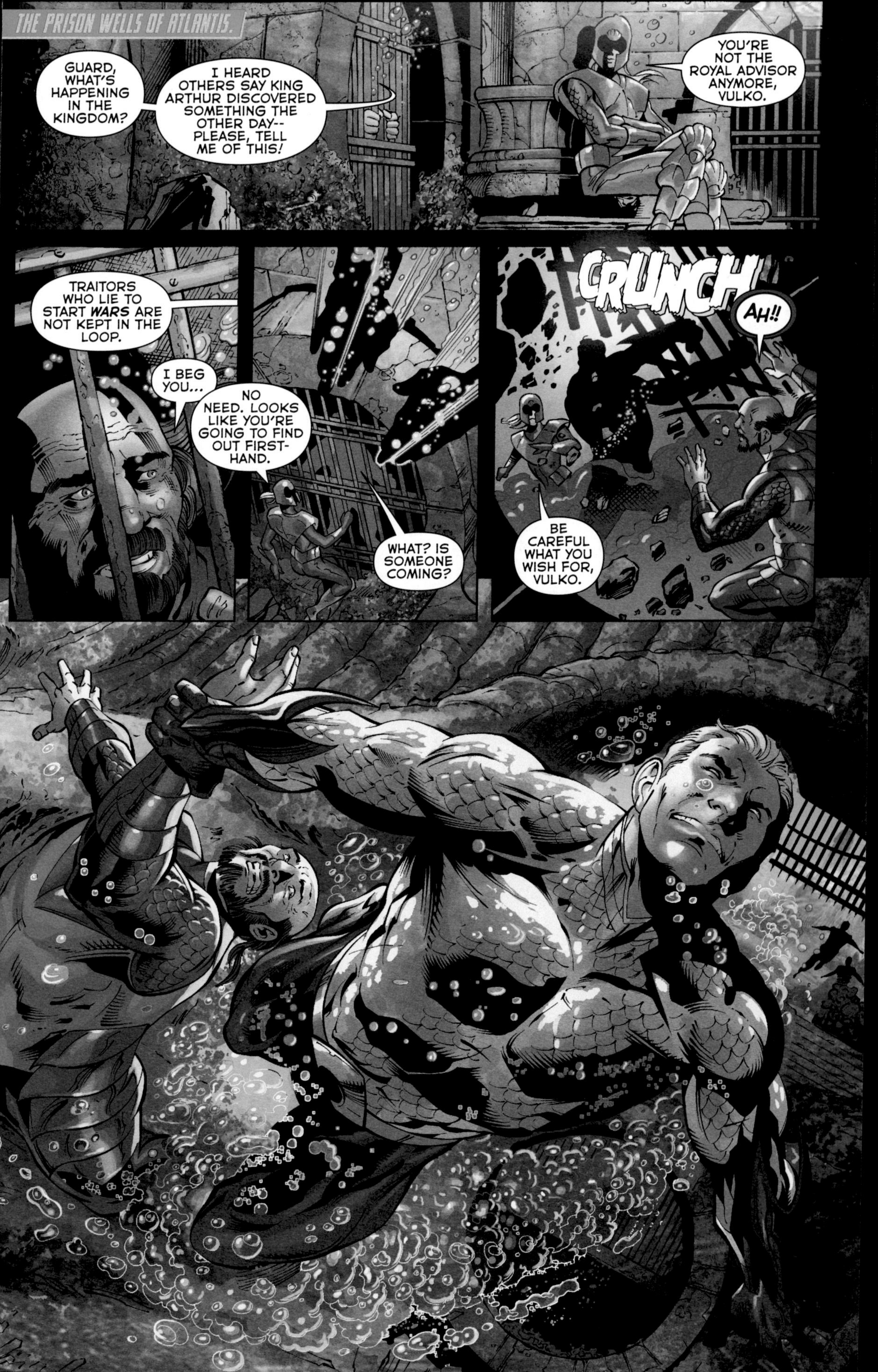
THE PRISON WELLS OF ATLANTIS.
GUARD, WHAT'S HAPPENING IN THE KINGDOM?
I HEARD OTHERS SAY KING ARTHUR DISCOVERED SOMETHING THE OTHER DAY-- PLEASE, TELL ME OF THIS!
YOU'RE NOT THE ROYAL ADVISOR ANYMORE, VULKO.
TRAITORS WHO LIE TO START WARS ARE NOT KEPT IN THE LOOP.
I BEG YOU...
NO NEED. LOOKS LIKE YOU'RE GOING TO FIND OUT FIRST-HAND.
WHAT? IS SOMEONE COMING?
CRUNCH
AH!!
BE CAREFUL WHAT YOU WISH FOR, VULKO.

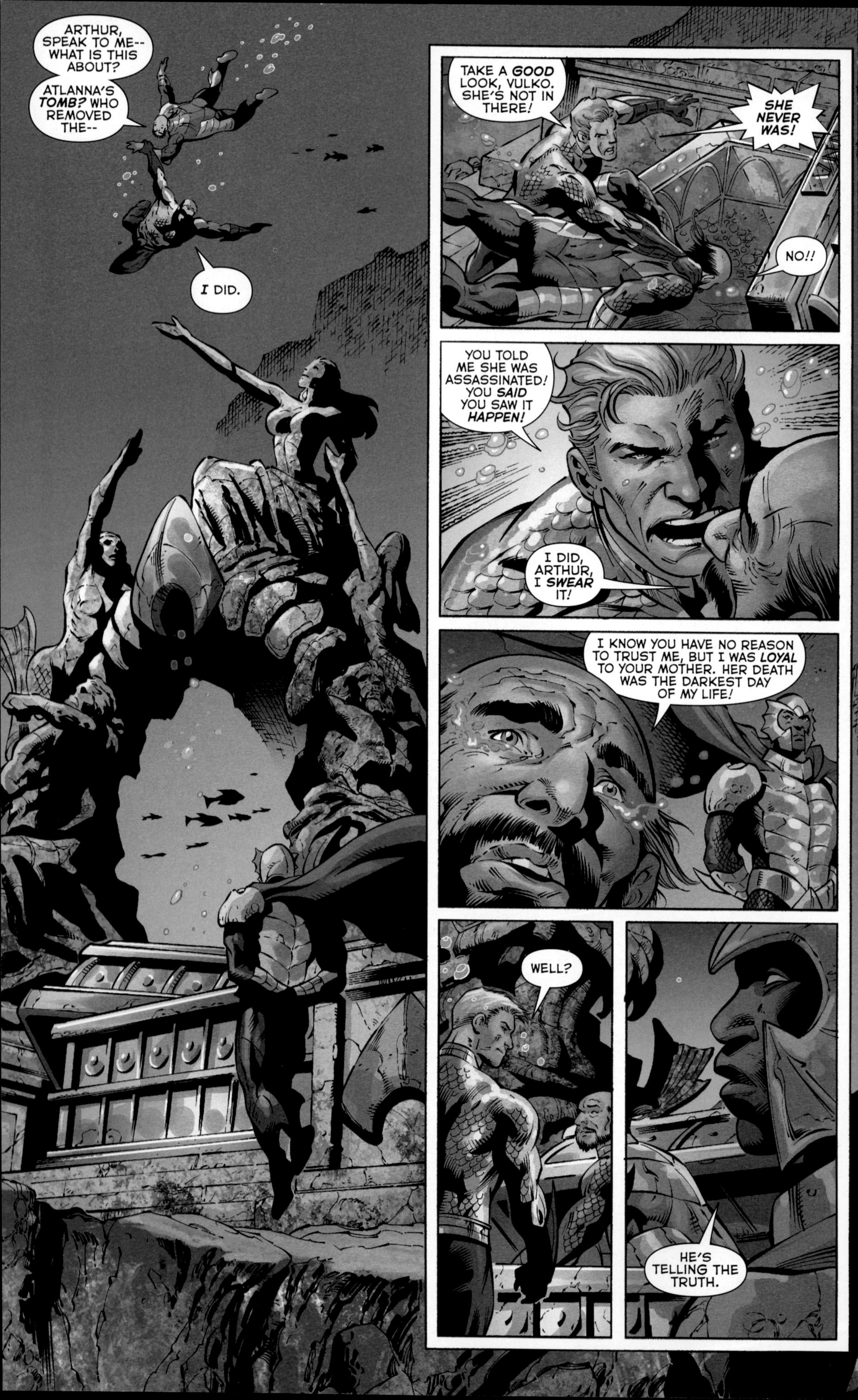
ARTHUR, SPEAK TO ME-- WHAT IS THIS ABOUT?
ATLANNA'S TOMB? WHO REMOVED THE--
I DID.
TAKE A GOOD LOOK, VULKO. SHE'S NOT IN THERE!
SHE NEVER WAS!
NO!!
YOU TOLD ME SHE WAS ASSASSINATED! YOU SAID YOU SAW IT HAPPEN!
I DID, ARTHUR, I SWEAR IT!
I KNOW YOU HAVE NO REASON TO TRUST ME, BUT I WAS LOYAL TO YOUR MOTHER. HER DEATH WAS THE DARKEST DAY OF MY LIFE!
WELL?
HE'S TELLING THE TRUTH.

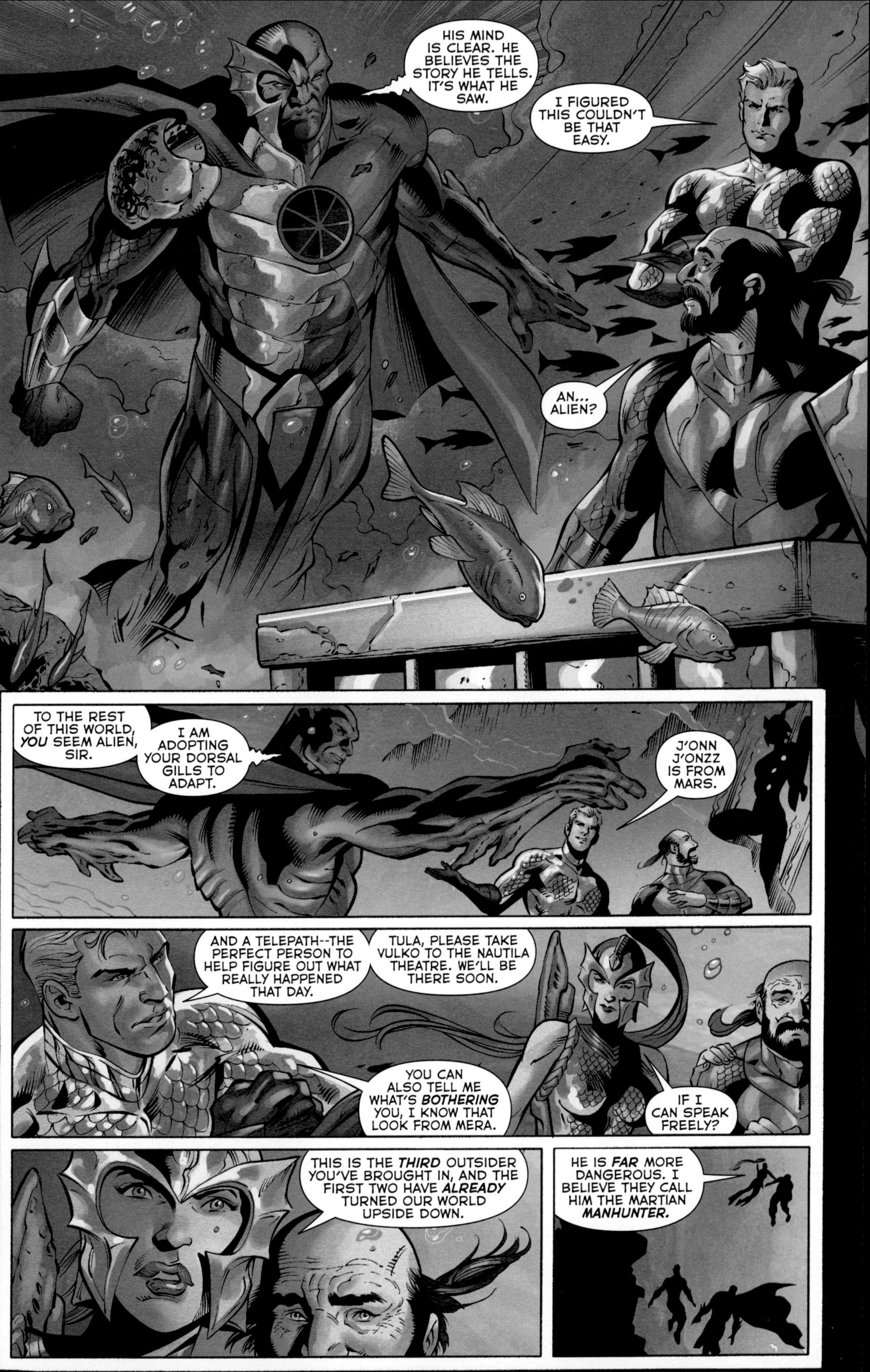
HIS MIND IS CLEAR. HE BELIEVES THE STORY HE TELLS. IT'S WHAT HE SAW.
I FIGURED THIS COULDN'T BE THAT EASY.
AN... ALIEN?
TO THE REST OF THIS WORLD, *YOU* SEEM ALIEN, SIR.
I AM ADOPTING YOUR DORSAL GILLS TO ADAPT.
J'ONN J'ONZZ IS FROM MARS.
AND A TELEPATH--THE PERFECT PERSON TO HELP FIGURE OUT WHAT REALLY HAPPENED THAT DAY.
TULA, PLEASE TAKE VULKO TO THE NAUTILA THEATRE. WE'LL BE THERE SOON.
YOU CAN ALSO TELL ME WHAT'S *BOTHERING* YOU, I KNOW THAT LOOK FROM MERA.
IF I CAN SPEAK FREELY?
THIS IS THE *THIRD* OUTSIDER YOU'VE BROUGHT IN, AND THE FIRST TWO HAVE *ALREADY* TURNED OUR WORLD UPSIDE DOWN.
HE IS *FAR* MORE DANGEROUS. I BELIEVE THEY CALL HIM THE MARTIAN *MANHUNTER.*

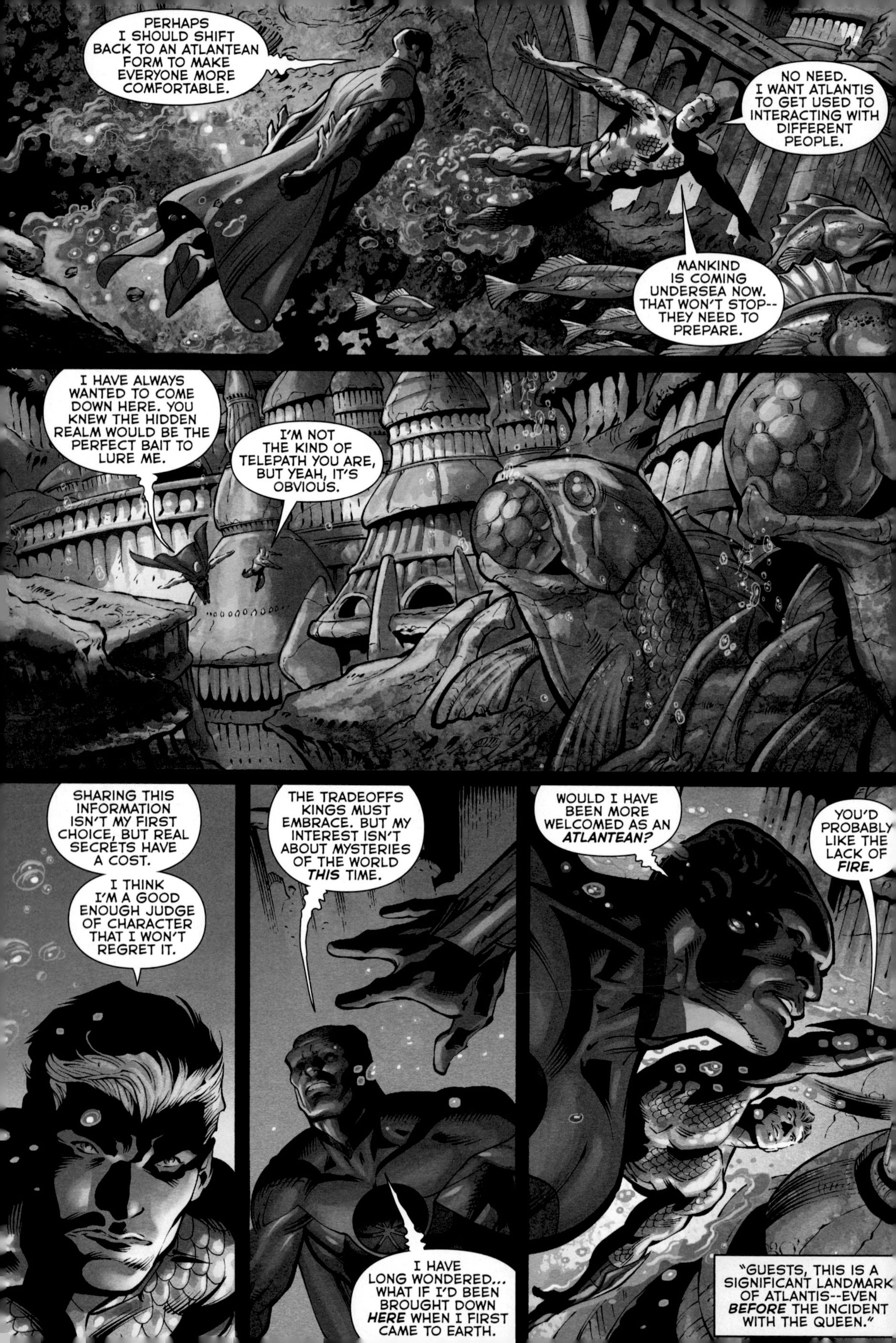
PERHAPS I SHOULD SHIFT BACK TO AN ATLANTEAN FORM TO MAKE EVERYONE MORE COMFORTABLE.
NO NEED. I WANT ATLANTIS TO GET USED TO INTERACTING WITH DIFFERENT PEOPLE.
MANKIND IS COMING UNDERSEA NOW. THAT WON'T STOP-- THEY NEED TO PREPARE.
I HAVE ALWAYS WANTED TO COME DOWN HERE. YOU KNEW THE HIDDEN REALM WOULD BE THE PERFECT BAIT TO LURE ME.
I'M NOT THE KIND OF TELEPATH YOU ARE, BUT YEAH, IT'S OBVIOUS.
SHARING THIS INFORMATION ISN'T MY FIRST CHOICE, BUT REAL SECRETS HAVE A COST.
I THINK I'M A GOOD ENOUGH JUDGE OF CHARACTER THAT I WON'T REGRET IT.
THE TRADEOFFS KINGS MUST EMBRACE. BUT MY INTEREST ISN'T ABOUT MYSTERIES OF THE WORLD *THIS* TIME.
I HAVE LONG WONDERED... WHAT IF I'D BEEN BROUGHT DOWN *HERE* WHEN I FIRST CAME TO EARTH.
WOULD I HAVE BEEN MORE WELCOMED AS AN *ATLANTEAN?*
YOU'D PROBABLY LIKE THE LACK OF *FIRE.*
"GUESTS, THIS IS A SIGNIFICANT LANDMARK OF ATLANTIS--EVEN *BEFORE* THE INCIDENT WITH THE QUEEN."

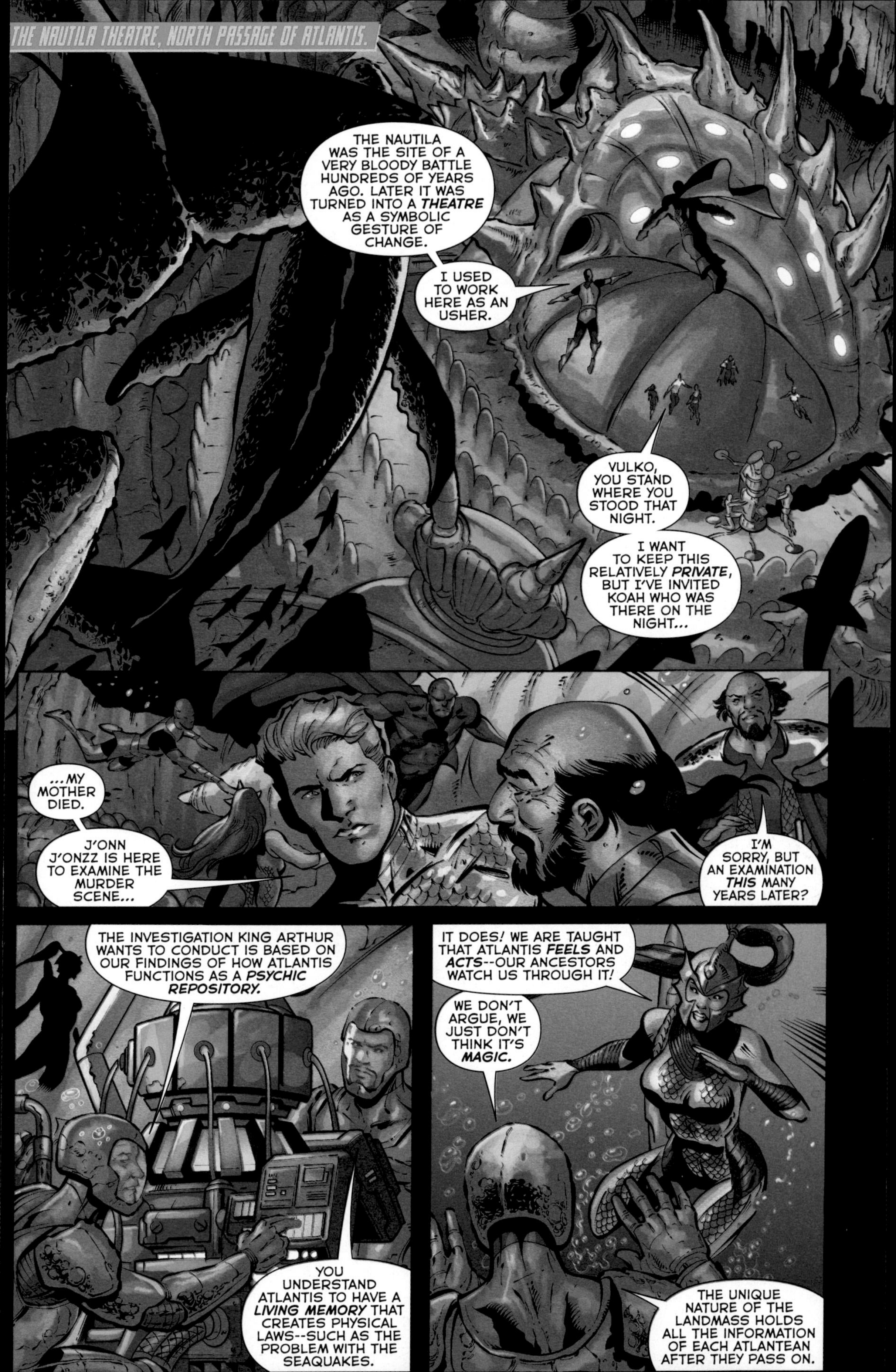
THE NAUTILA THEATRE, NORTH PASSAGE OF ATLANTIS.
THE NAUTILA WAS THE SITE OF A VERY BLOODY BATTLE HUNDREDS OF YEARS AGO. LATER IT WAS TURNED INTO A THEATRE AS A SYMBOLIC GESTURE OF CHANGE.
I USED TO WORK HERE AS AN USHER.
VULKO, YOU STAND WHERE YOU STOOD THAT NIGHT.
I WANT TO KEEP THIS RELATIVELY PRIVATE, BUT I'VE INVITED KOAH WHO WAS THERE ON THE NIGHT...
...MY MOTHER DIED.
J'ONN J'ONZZ IS HERE TO EXAMINE THE MURDER SCENE...
I'M SORRY, BUT AN EXAMINATION THIS MANY YEARS LATER?
THE INVESTIGATION KING ARTHUR WANTS TO CONDUCT IS BASED ON OUR FINDINGS OF HOW ATLANTIS FUNCTIONS AS A PSYCHIC REPOSITORY.
YOU UNDERSTAND ATLANTIS TO HAVE A LIVING MEMORY THAT CREATES PHYSICAL LAWS--SUCH AS THE PROBLEM WITH THE SEAQUAKES.
IT DOES! WE ARE TAUGHT THAT ATLANTIS FEELS AND ACTS--OUR ANCESTORS WATCH US THROUGH IT!
WE DON'T ARGUE, WE JUST DON'T THINK IT'S MAGIC.
THE UNIQUE NATURE OF THE LANDMASS HOLDS ALL THE INFORMATION OF EACH ATLANTEAN AFTER THEY PASS ON.

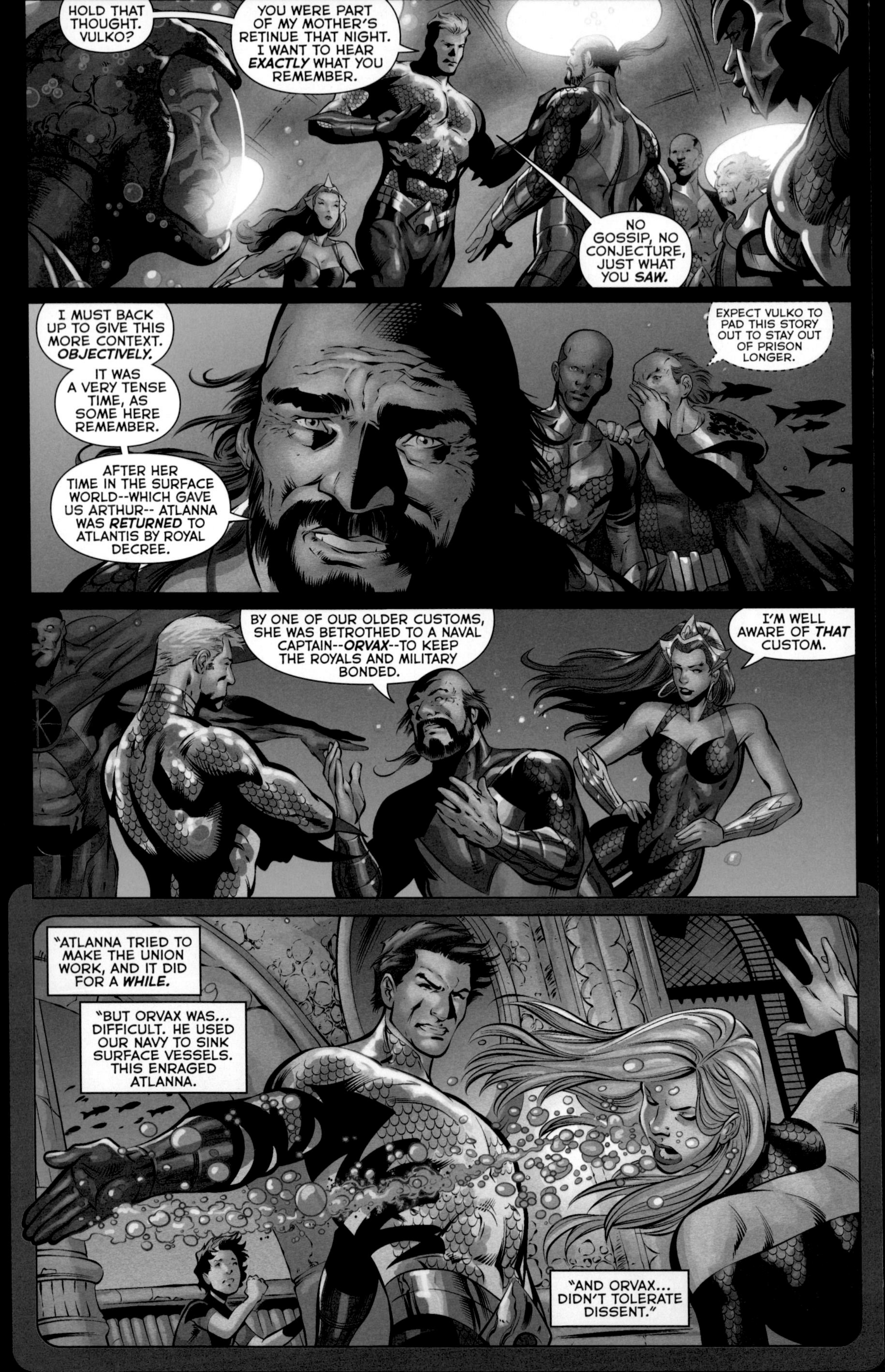
HOLD THAT THOUGHT. VULKO?
YOU WERE PART OF MY MOTHER'S RETINUE THAT NIGHT. I WANT TO HEAR *EXACTLY* WHAT YOU REMEMBER.
NO GOSSIP, NO CONJECTURE, JUST WHAT YOU *SAW.*
I MUST BACK UP TO GIVE THIS MORE CONTEXT. *OBJECTIVELY.*
IT WAS A VERY TENSE TIME, AS SOME HERE REMEMBER.
AFTER HER TIME IN THE SURFACE WORLD--WHICH GAVE US ARTHUR-- ATLANNA WAS *RETURNED* TO ATLANTIS BY ROYAL DECREE.
EXPECT VULKO TO PAD THIS STORY OUT TO STAY OUT OF PRISON LONGER.
BY ONE OF OUR OLDER CUSTOMS, SHE WAS BETROTHED TO A NAVAL CAPTAIN--*ORVAX*--TO KEEP THE ROYALS AND MILITARY BONDED.
I'M WELL AWARE OF *THAT* CUSTOM.
"ATLANNA TRIED TO MAKE THE UNION WORK, AND IT DID FOR A *WHILE.*
"BUT ORVAX WAS... DIFFICULT. HE USED OUR NAVY TO SINK SURFACE VESSELS. THIS ENRAGED ATLANNA.
"AND ORVAX... DIDN'T TOLERATE DISSENT."

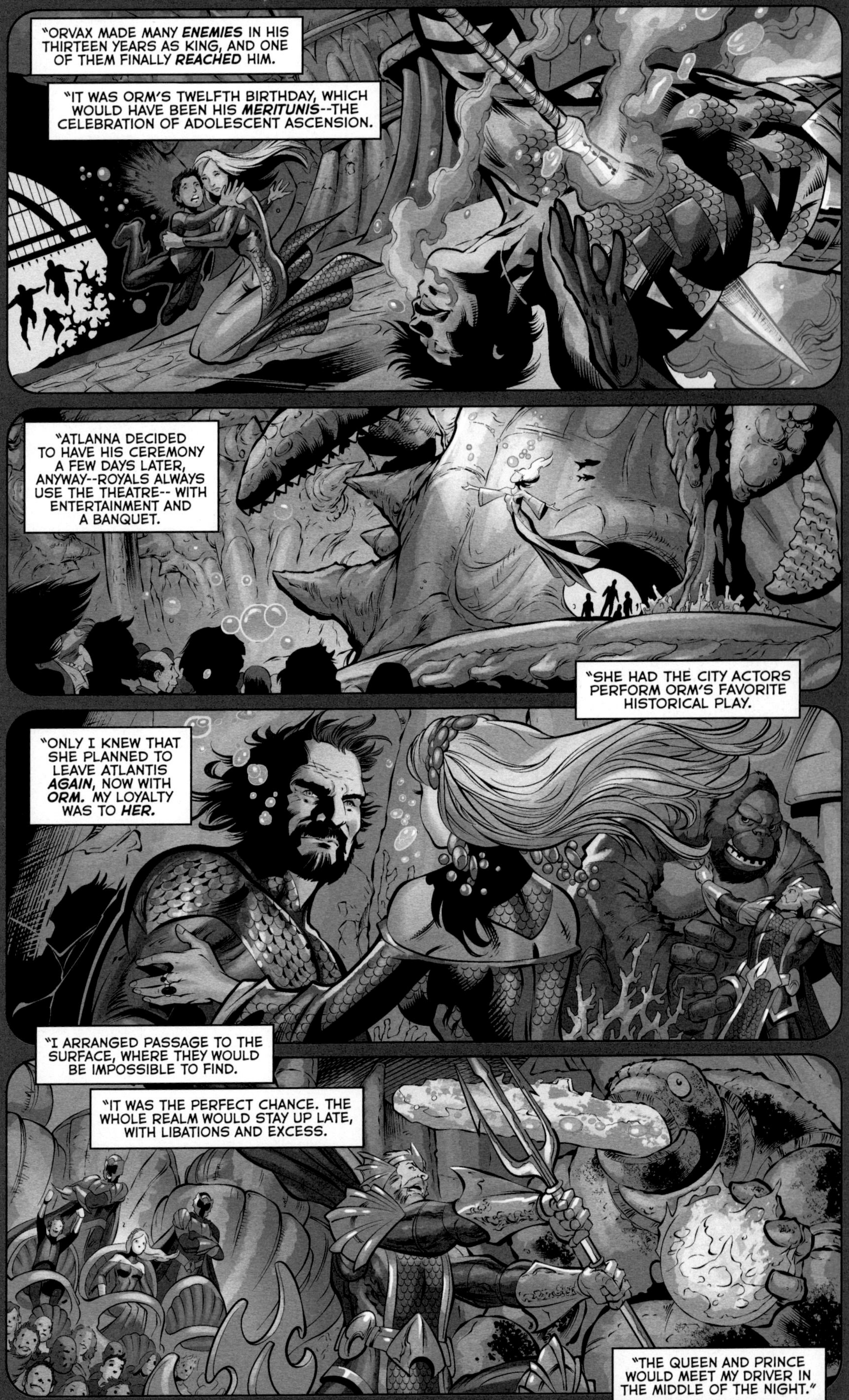
"ORVAX MADE MANY ENEMIES IN HIS THIRTEEN YEARS AS KING, AND ONE OF THEM FINALLY REACHED HIM.
"IT WAS ORM'S TWELFTH BIRTHDAY, WHICH WOULD HAVE BEEN HIS MERITUNIS--THE CELEBRATION OF ADOLESCENT ASCENSION.
"ATLANNA DECIDED TO HAVE HIS CEREMONY A FEW DAYS LATER, ANYWAY--ROYALS ALWAYS USE THE THEATRE-- WITH ENTERTAINMENT AND A BANQUET.
"SHE HAD THE CITY ACTORS PERFORM ORM'S FAVORITE HISTORICAL PLAY.
"ONLY I KNEW THAT SHE PLANNED TO LEAVE ATLANTIS AGAIN, NOW WITH ORM. MY LOYALTY WAS TO HER.
"I ARRANGED PASSAGE TO THE SURFACE, WHERE THEY WOULD BE IMPOSSIBLE TO FIND.
"IT WAS THE PERFECT CHANCE. THE WHOLE REALM WOULD STAY UP LATE, WITH LIBATIONS AND EXCESS.
"THE QUEEN AND PRINCE WOULD MEET MY DRIVER IN THE MIDDLE OF THE NIGHT."

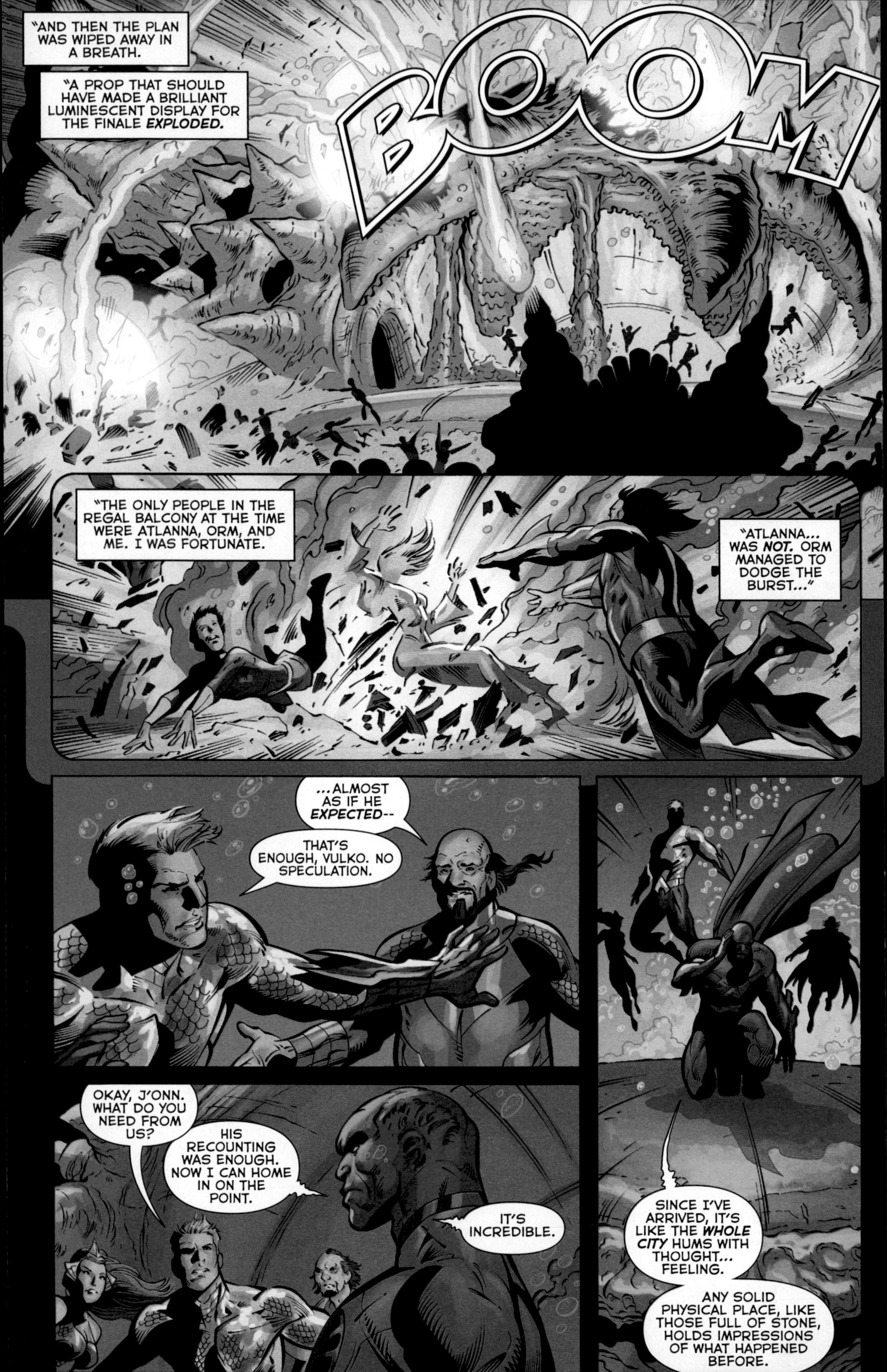
"AND THEN THE PLAN WAS WIPED AWAY IN A BREATH.
"A PROP THAT SHOULD HAVE MADE A BRILLIANT LUMINESCENT DISPLAY FOR THE FINALE EXPLODED.
BOOM
"THE ONLY PEOPLE IN THE REGAL BALCONY AT THE TIME WERE ATLANNA, ORM, AND ME. I WAS FORTUNATE.
"ATLANNA... WAS NOT. ORM MANAGED TO DODGE THE BURST..."
...ALMOST AS IF HE EXPECTED--
THAT'S ENOUGH, VULKO. NO SPECULATION.
OKAY, J'ONN. WHAT DO YOU NEED FROM US?
HIS RECOUNTING WAS ENOUGH. NOW I CAN HOME IN ON THE POINT.
IT'S INCREDIBLE.
SINCE I'VE ARRIVED, IT'S LIKE THE WHOLE CITY HUMS WITH THOUGHT... FEELING.
ANY SOLID PHYSICAL PLACE, LIKE THOSE FULL OF STONE, HOLDS IMPRESSIONS OF WHAT HAPPENED BEFORE.

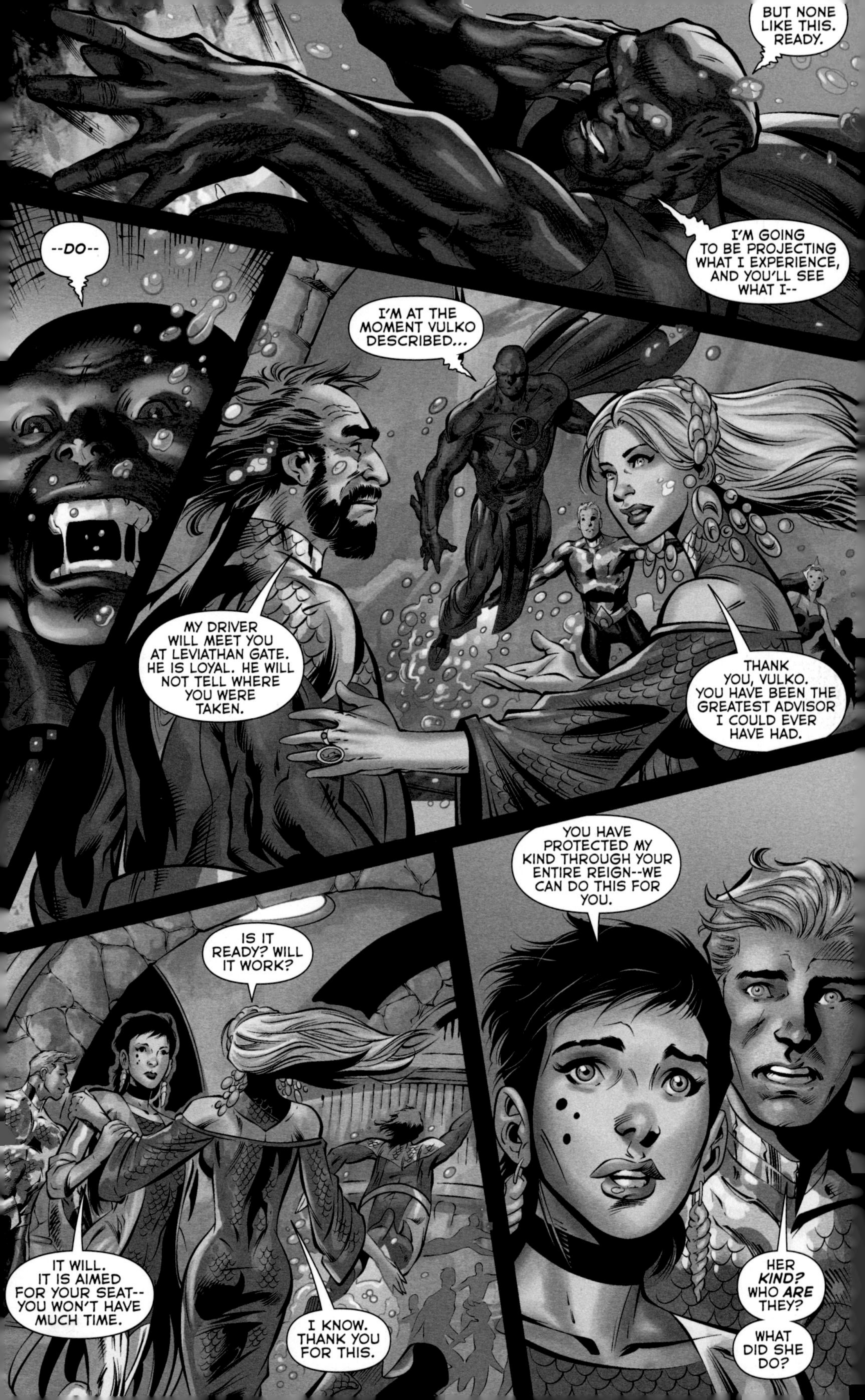
BUT NONE LIKE THIS. READY.
I'M GOING TO BE PROJECTING WHAT I EXPERIENCE, AND YOU'LL SEE WHAT I--
--DO--
I'M AT THE MOMENT VULKO DESCRIBED...
MY DRIVER WILL MEET YOU AT LEVIATHAN GATE. HE IS LOYAL. HE WILL NOT TELL WHERE YOU WERE TAKEN.
THANK YOU, VULKO. YOU HAVE BEEN THE GREATEST ADVISOR I COULD EVER HAVE HAD.
IS IT READY? WILL IT WORK?
IT WILL. IT IS AIMED FOR YOUR SEAT--YOU WON'T HAVE MUCH TIME.
I KNOW. THANK YOU FOR THIS.
YOU HAVE PROTECTED MY KIND THROUGH YOUR ENTIRE REIGN--WE CAN DO THIS FOR YOU.
HER KIND? WHO ARE THEY?
WHAT DID SHE DO?

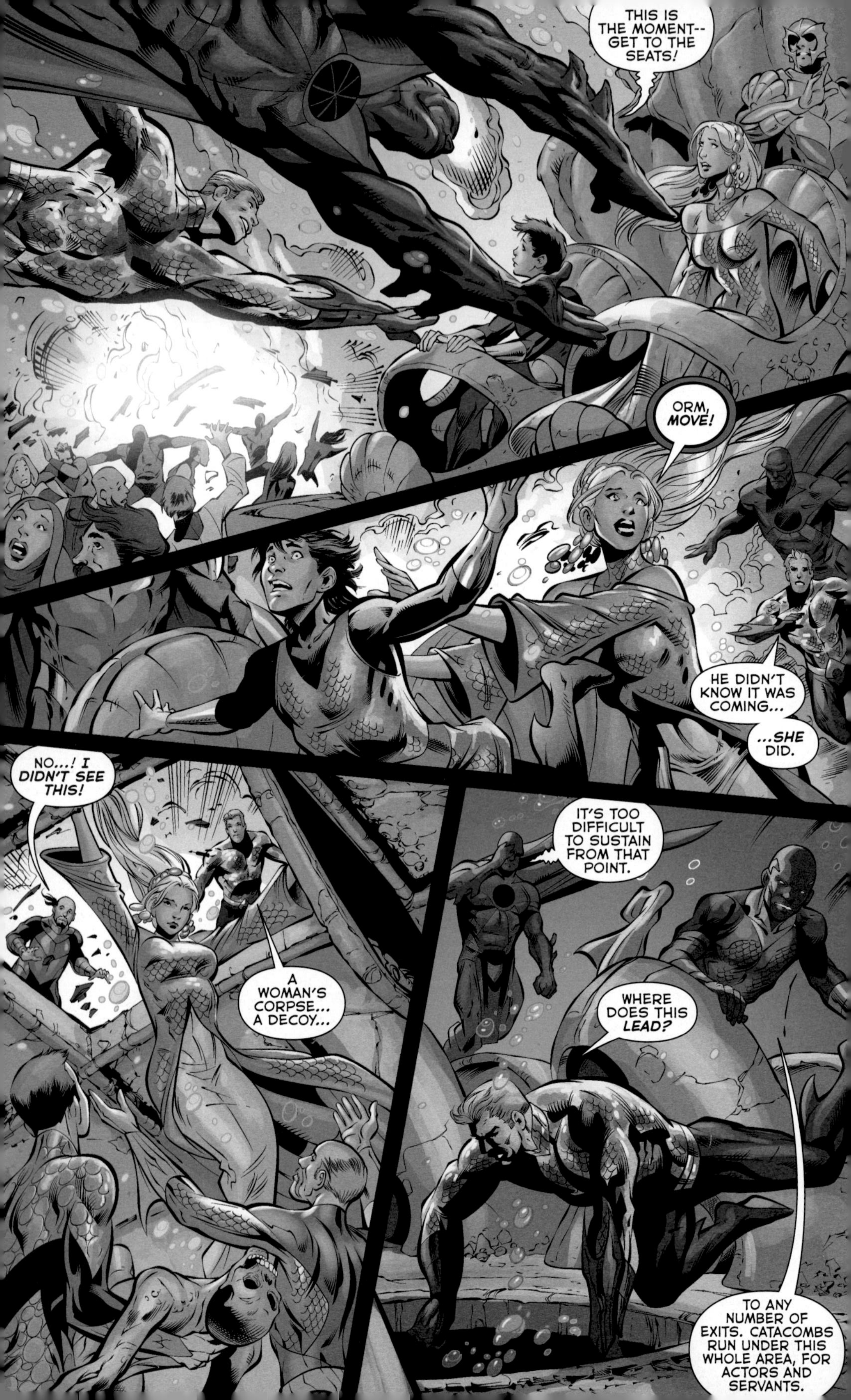
THIS IS THE MOMENT-- GET TO THE SEATS!
ORM, MOVE!
HE DIDN'T KNOW IT WAS COMING...
...SHE DID.
NO...! I DIDN'T SEE THIS!
A WOMAN'S CORPSE... A DECOY...
IT'S TOO DIFFICULT TO SUSTAIN FROM THAT POINT.
WHERE DOES THIS LEAD?
TO ANY NUMBER OF EXITS. CATACOMBS RUN UNDER THIS WHOLE AREA, FOR ACTORS AND SERVANTS.

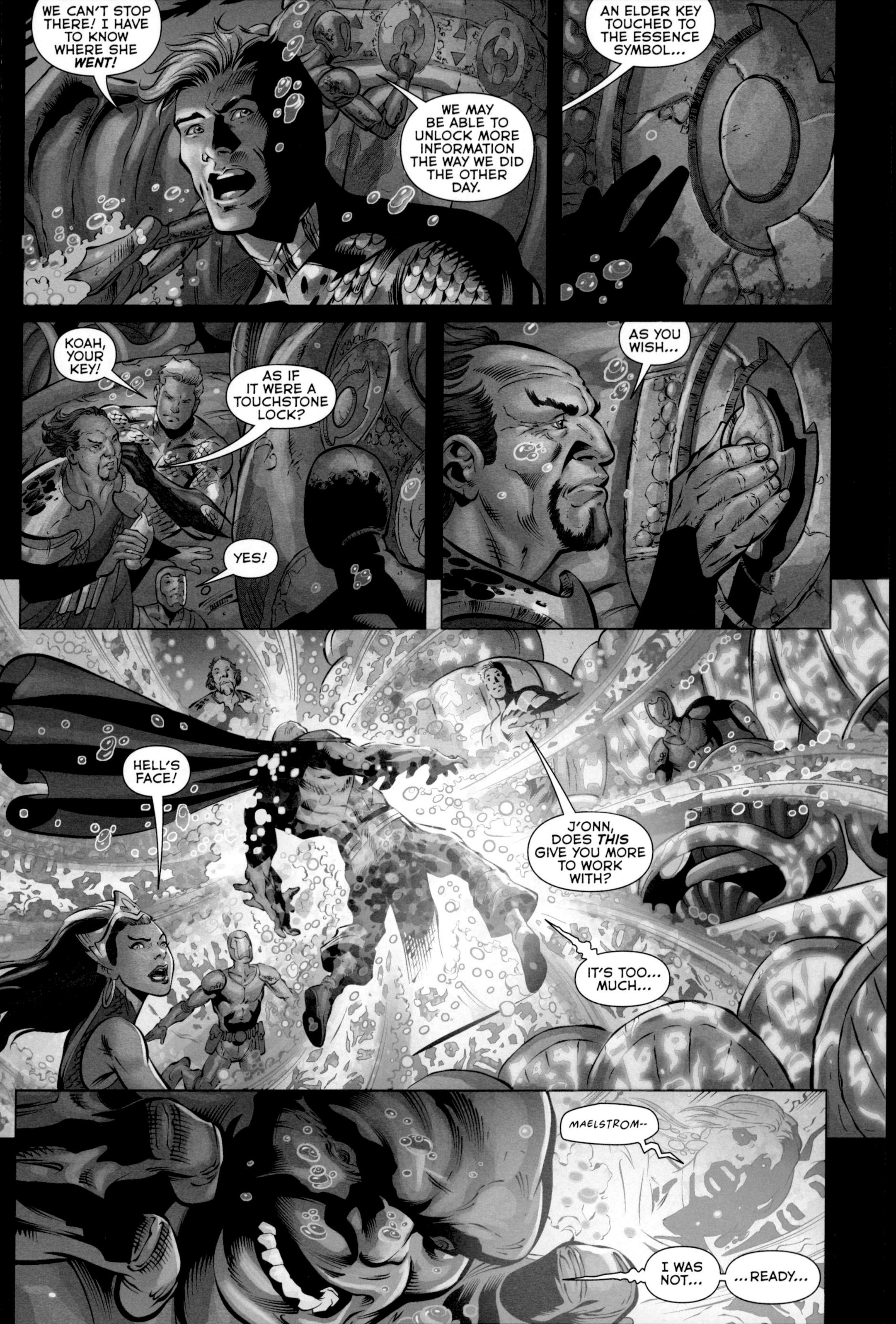
WE CAN'T STOP THERE! I HAVE TO KNOW WHERE SHE *WENT!*
WE MAY BE ABLE TO UNLOCK MORE INFORMATION THE WAY WE DID THE OTHER DAY.
AN ELDER KEY TOUCHED TO THE ESSENCE SYMBOL...
KOAH, YOUR KEY!
AS IF IT WERE A TOUCHSTONE LOCK?
YES!
AS YOU WISH...
HELL'S FACE!
J'ONN, DOES *THIS* GIVE YOU MORE TO WORK WITH?
IT'S TOO... MUCH...
MAELSTROM--
I WAS NOT...
...READY...

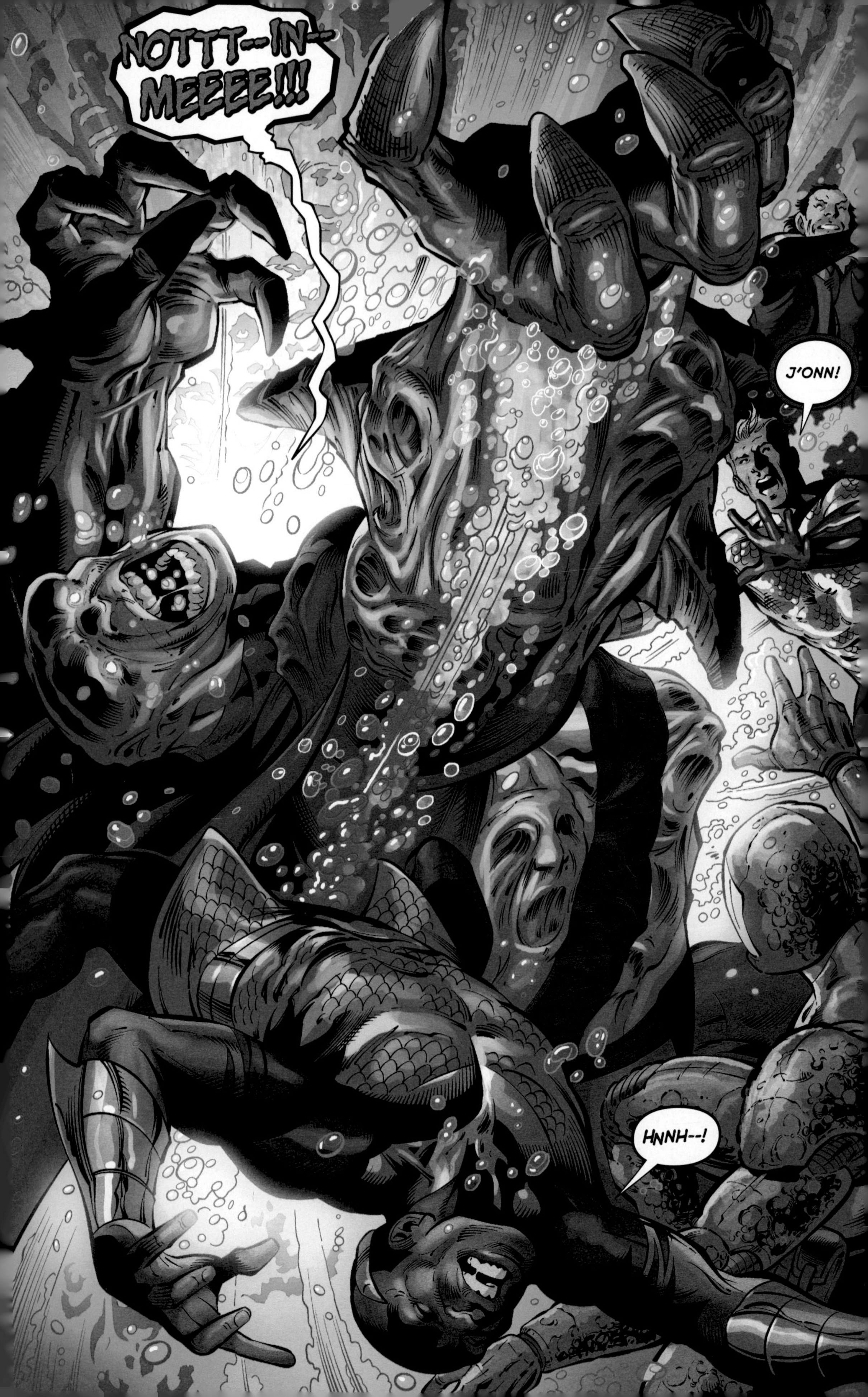
NOTTT--IN--
MEEEE!!!
J'ONN!
HNNH--!

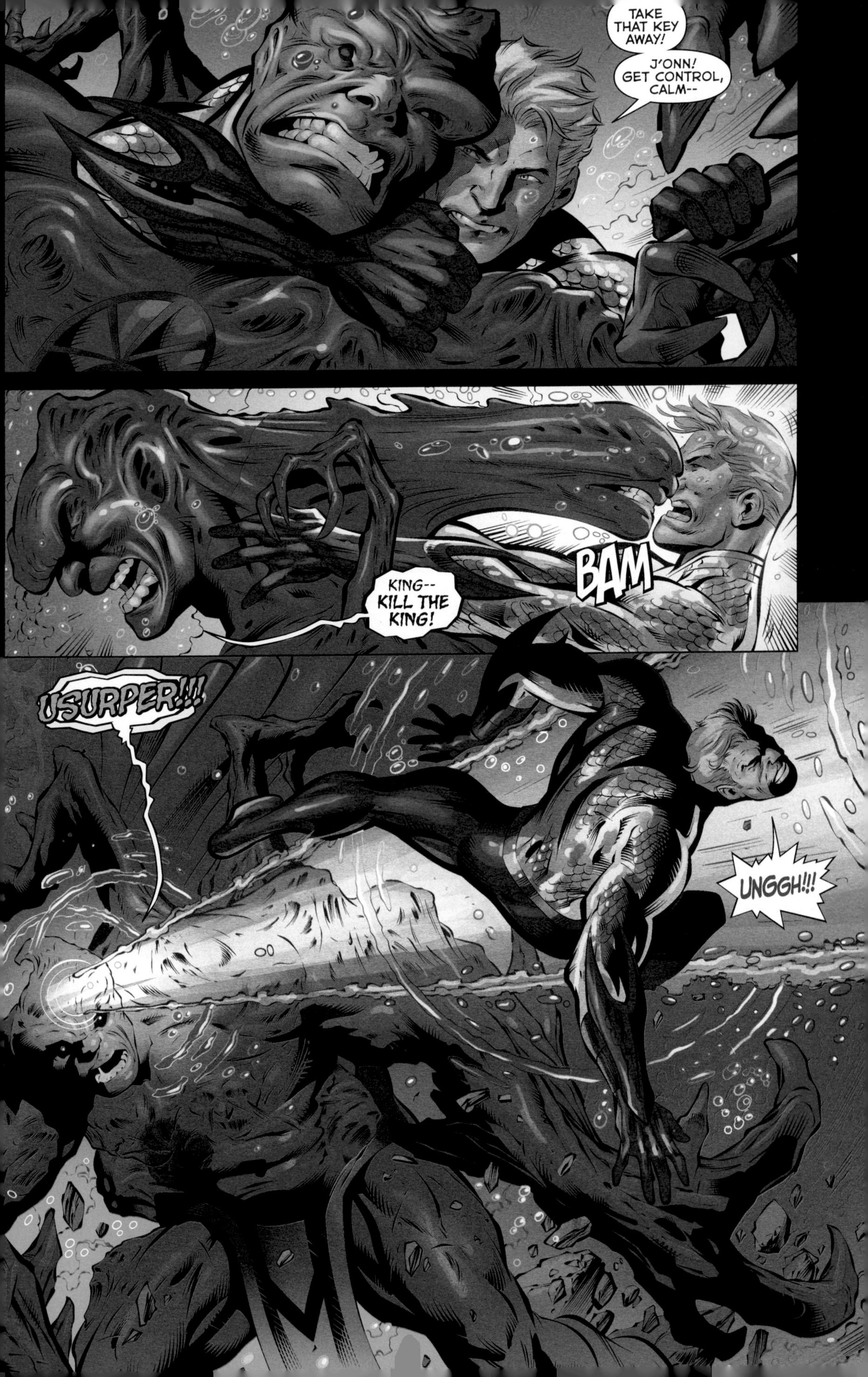
TAKE THAT KEY AWAY!
J'ONN! GET CONTROL, CALM--
BAM
KING-- KILL THE KING!
USURPER!!!
UNGGH!!!

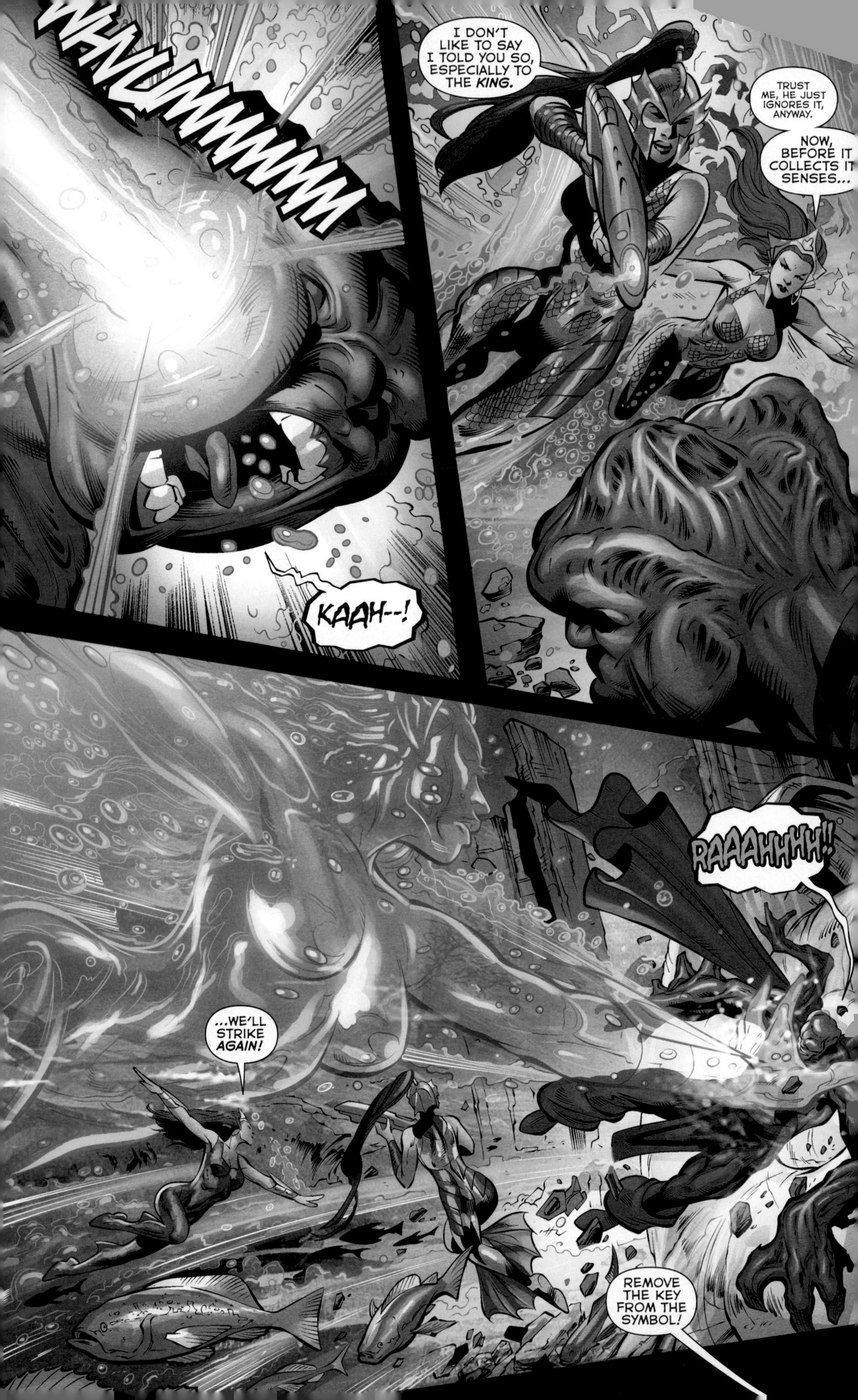
WHUMMMMMMM
KAAH--!
I DON'T LIKE TO SAY I TOLD YOU SO, ESPECIALLY TO THE KING.
TRUST ME, HE JUST IGNORES IT, ANYWAY.
NOW, BEFORE IT COLLECTS ITS SENSES...
...WE'LL STRIKE AGAIN!
RAAAHHHH!!
REMOVE THE KEY FROM THE SYMBOL!

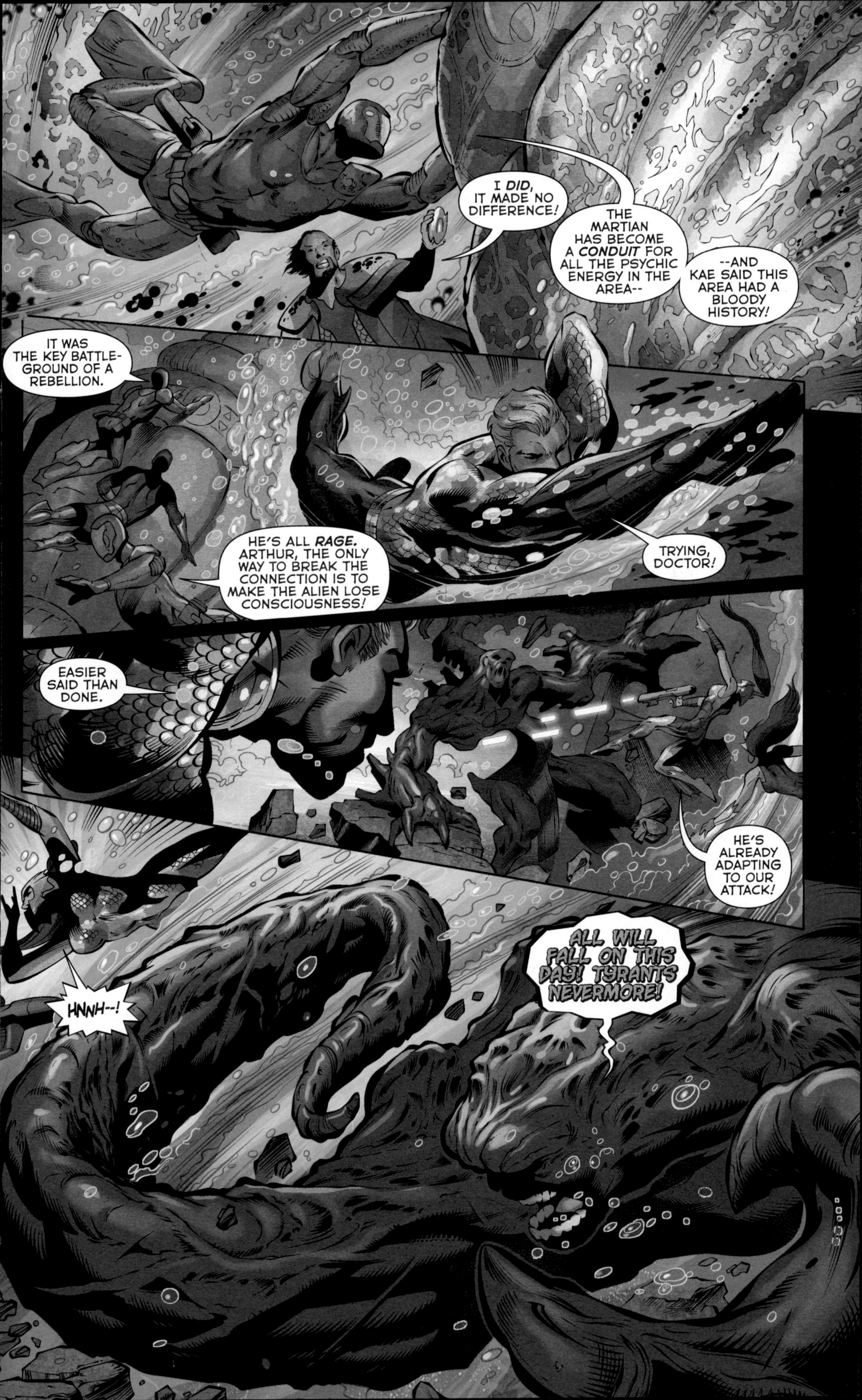
I DID, IT MADE NO DIFFERENCE!
THE MARTIAN HAS BECOME A CONDUIT FOR ALL THE PSYCHIC ENERGY IN THE AREA--
--AND KAE SAID THIS AREA HAD A BLOODY HISTORY!
IT WAS THE KEY BATTLE-GROUND OF A REBELLION.
HE'S ALL RAGE. ARTHUR, THE ONLY WAY TO BREAK THE CONNECTION IS TO MAKE THE ALIEN LOSE CONSCIOUSNESS!
TRYING, DOCTOR!
EASIER SAID THAN DONE.
HE'S ALREADY ADAPTING TO OUR ATTACK!
HNNH--!
ALL WILL FALL ON THIS DAY! TYRANTS NEVERMORE!

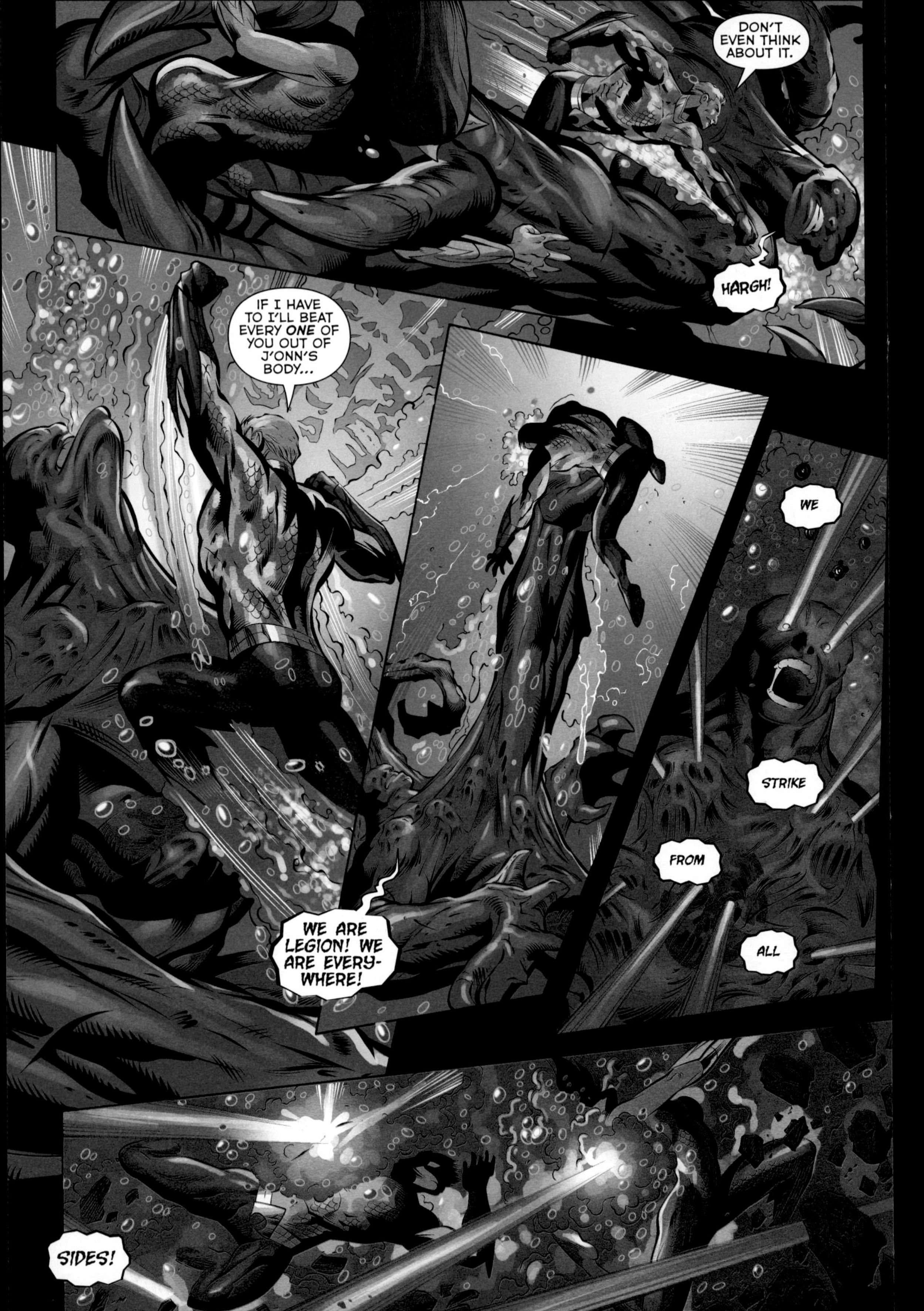
DON'T EVEN THINK ABOUT IT.
HARGH!
IF I HAVE TO I'LL BEAT EVERY ONE OF YOU OUT OF J'ONN'S BODY...
WE ARE LEGION! WE ARE EVERY-WHERE!
WE
STRIKE
FROM
ALL
SIDES!

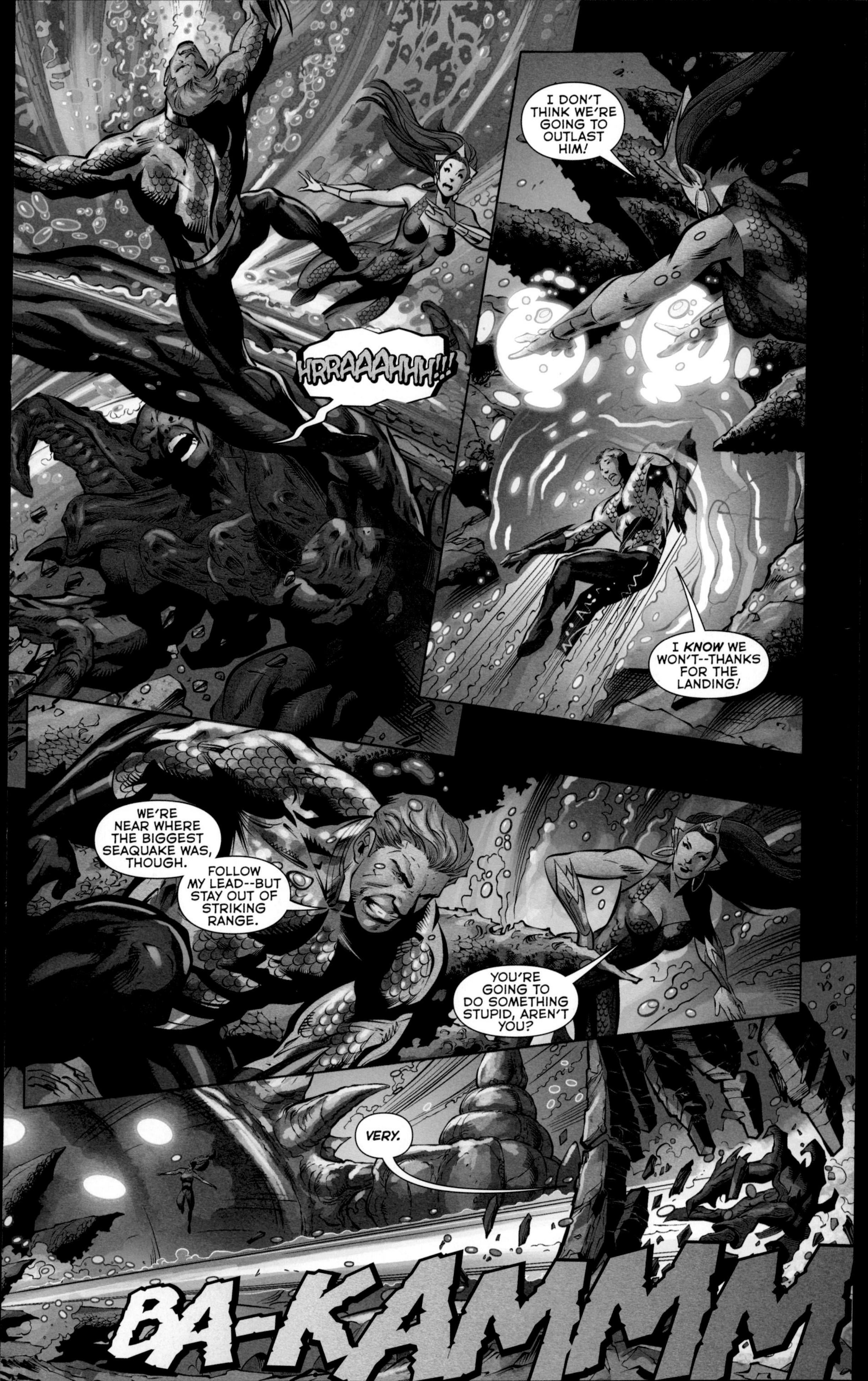
HRRAAAHHH!!!
I DON'T THINK WE'RE GOING TO OUTLAST HIM!
I *KNOW* WE WON'T--THANKS FOR THE LANDING!
WE'RE NEAR WHERE THE BIGGEST SEAQUAKE WAS, THOUGH.
FOLLOW MY LEAD--BUT STAY OUT OF STRIKING RANGE.
YOU'RE GOING TO DO SOMETHING STUPID, AREN'T YOU?
VERY.
BA-KAMMM

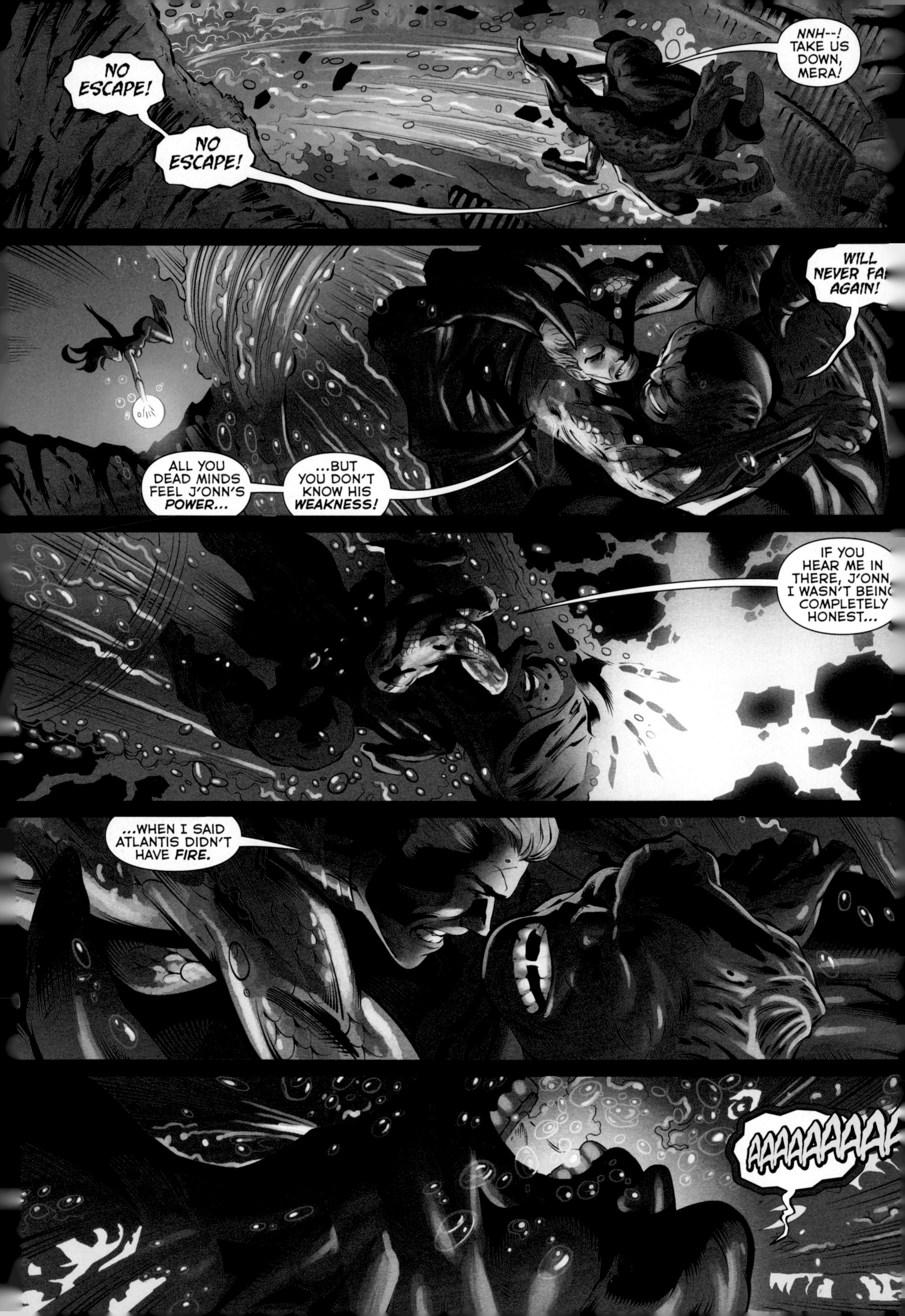
NO ESCAPE!
NO ESCAPE!
NNH--! TAKE US DOWN, MERA!
WILL NEVER FA AGAIN!
ALL YOU DEAD MINDS FEEL J'ONN'S POWER...
...BUT YOU DON'T KNOW HIS WEAKNESS!
IF YOU HEAR ME IN THERE, J'ONN I WASN'T BEIN COMPLETELY HONEST...
...WHEN I SAID ATLANTIS DIDN'T HAVE FIRE.
AAAAAAAAA

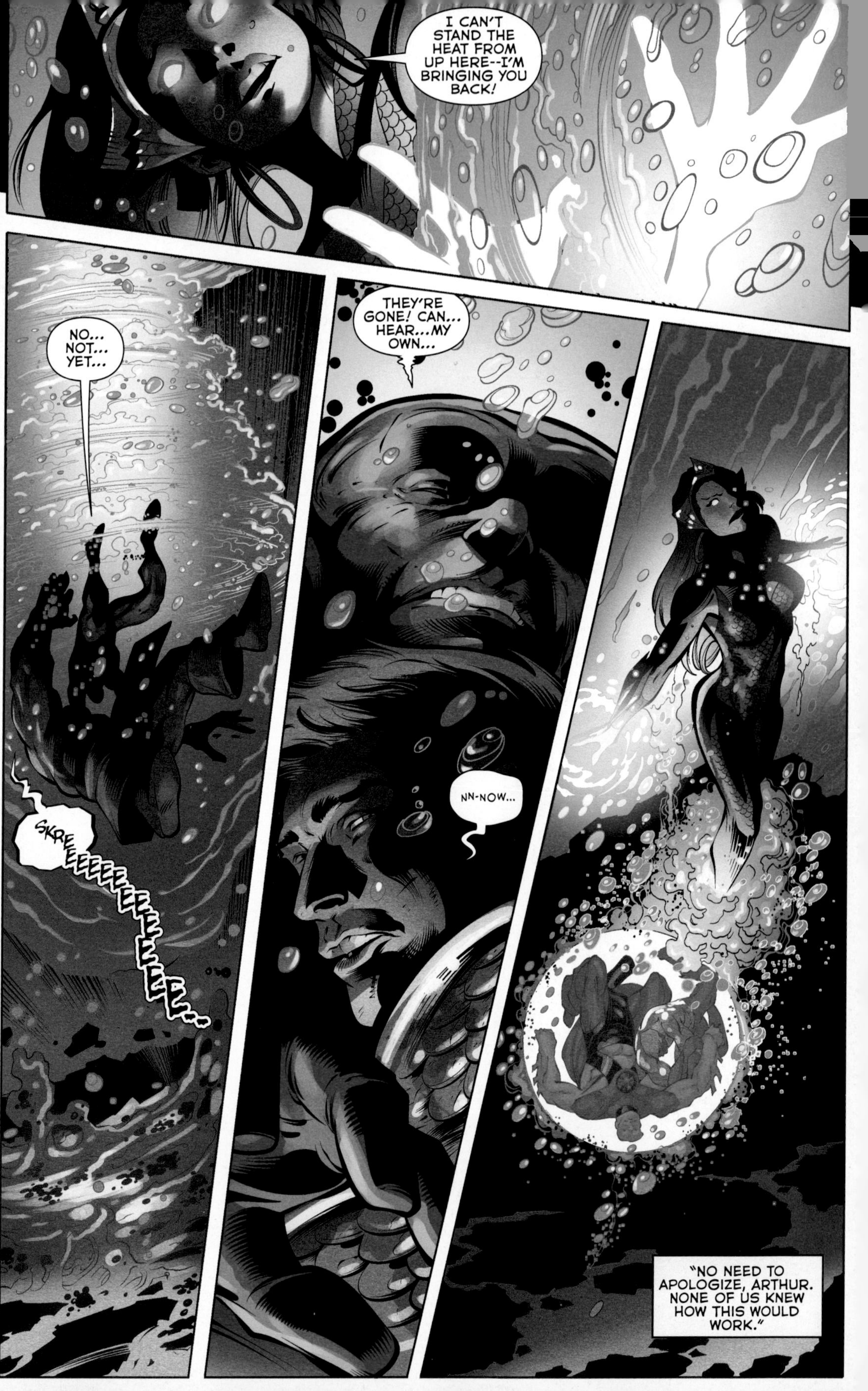
I CAN'T STAND THE HEAT FROM UP HERE--I'M BRINGING YOU BACK!
NO... NOT... YET...
SKREEEEEEEEEEEEEE...
THEY'RE GONE! CAN... HEAR...MY OWN...
NN-NOW...
"NO NEED TO APOLOGIZE, ARTHUR. NONE OF US KNEW HOW THIS WOULD WORK."

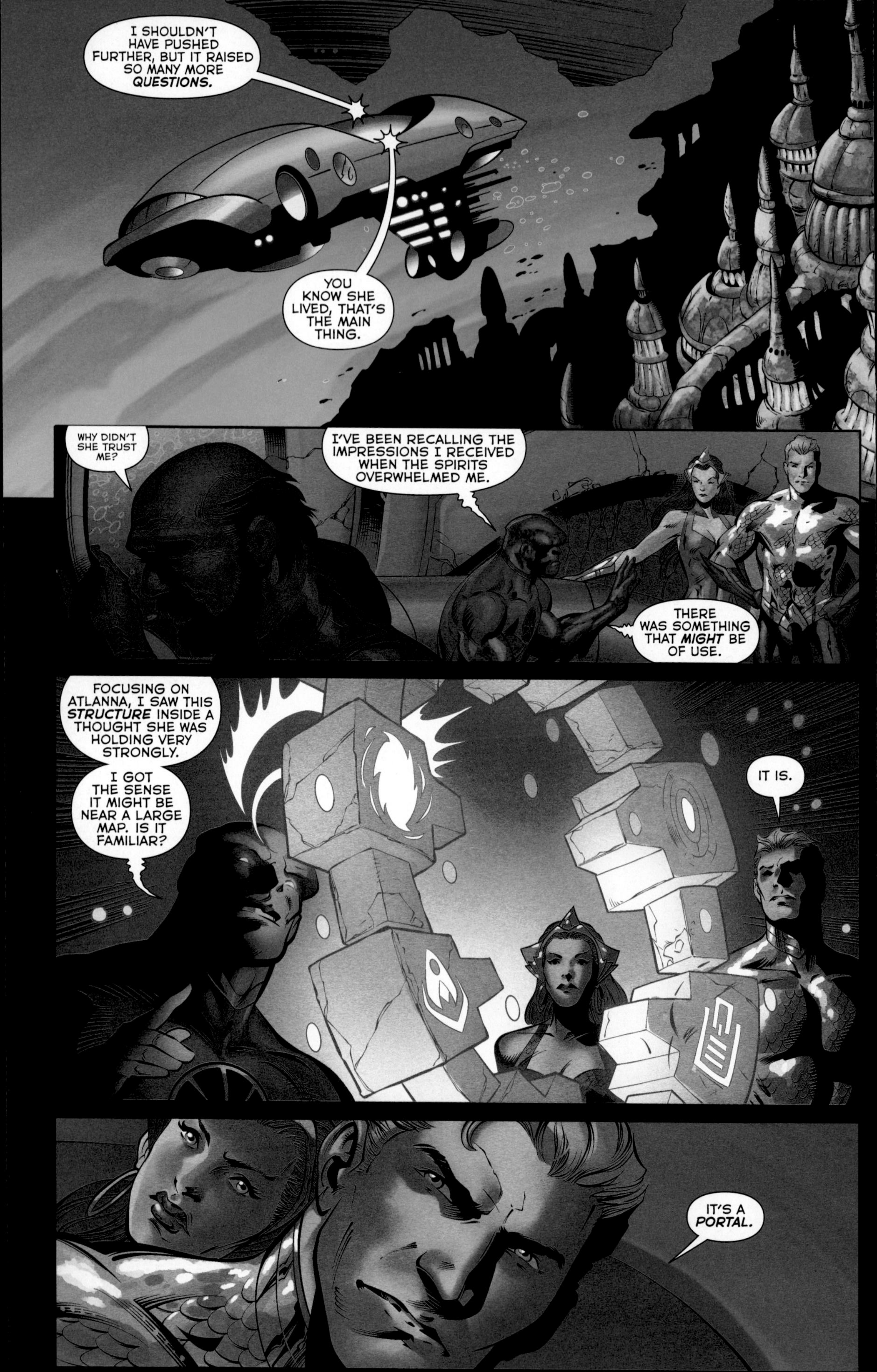
I SHOULDN'T HAVE PUSHED FURTHER, BUT IT RAISED SO MANY MORE *QUESTIONS.*
YOU KNOW SHE LIVED, THAT'S THE MAIN THING.
WHY DIDN'T SHE TRUST ME?
I'VE BEEN RECALLING THE IMPRESSIONS I RECEIVED WHEN THE SPIRITS OVERWHELMED ME.
THERE WAS SOMETHING THAT *MIGHT* BE OF USE.
FOCUSING ON ATLANNA, I SAW THIS *STRUCTURE* INSIDE A THOUGHT SHE WAS HOLDING VERY STRONGLY.
I GOT THE SENSE IT MIGHT BE NEAR A LARGE MAP. IS IT FAMILIAR?
IT IS.
IT'S A *PORTAL.*

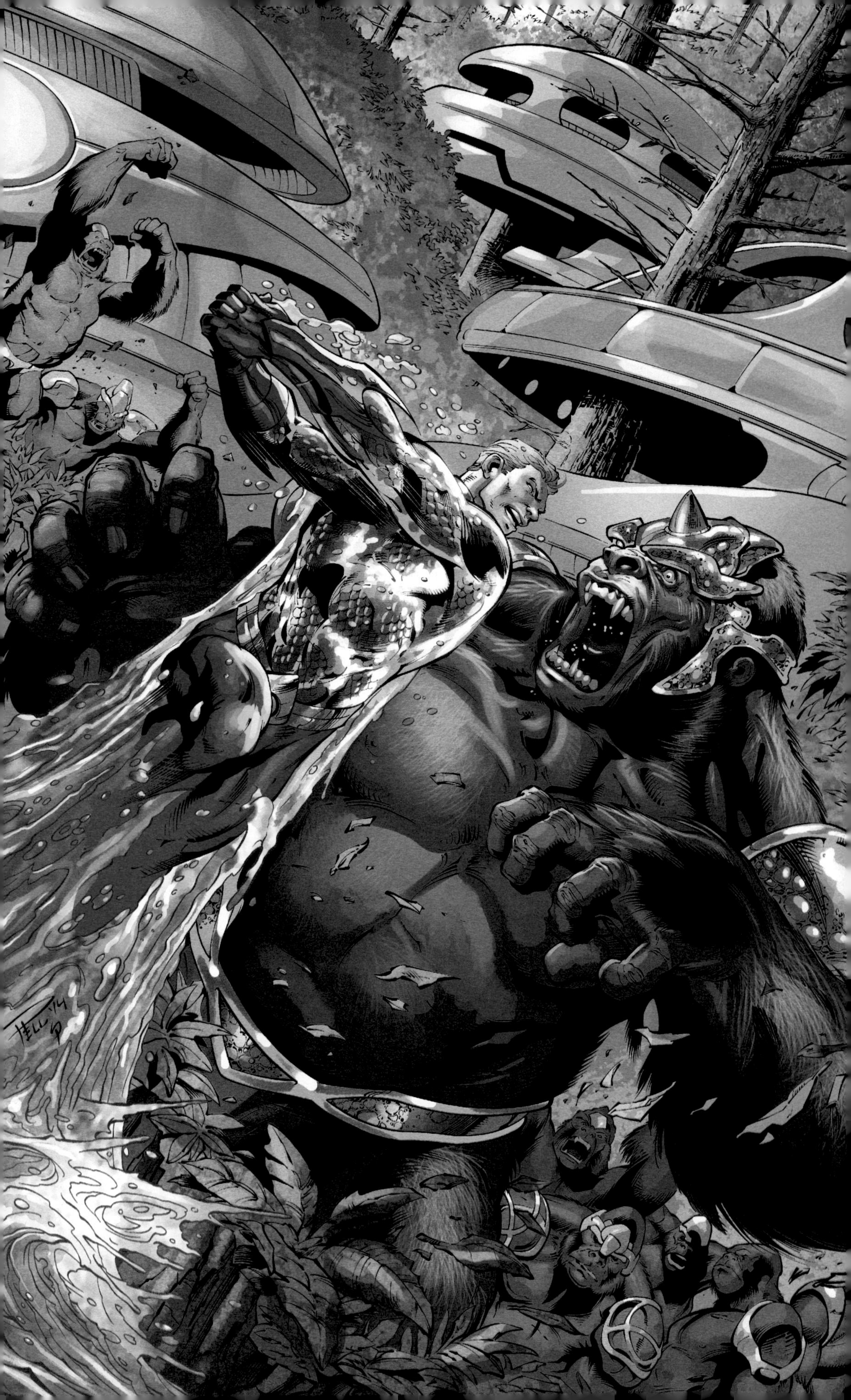

MAELSTROM PART III: THE CUNNING OF QUEENS

JEFF PARKER writer **PAUL PELLETIER** penciller **SEAN PARSONS** inker **RAIN BEREDO** colorist **DEZI SIENTY** letterer **PELLETIER, PARSONS and BEREDO** cover art

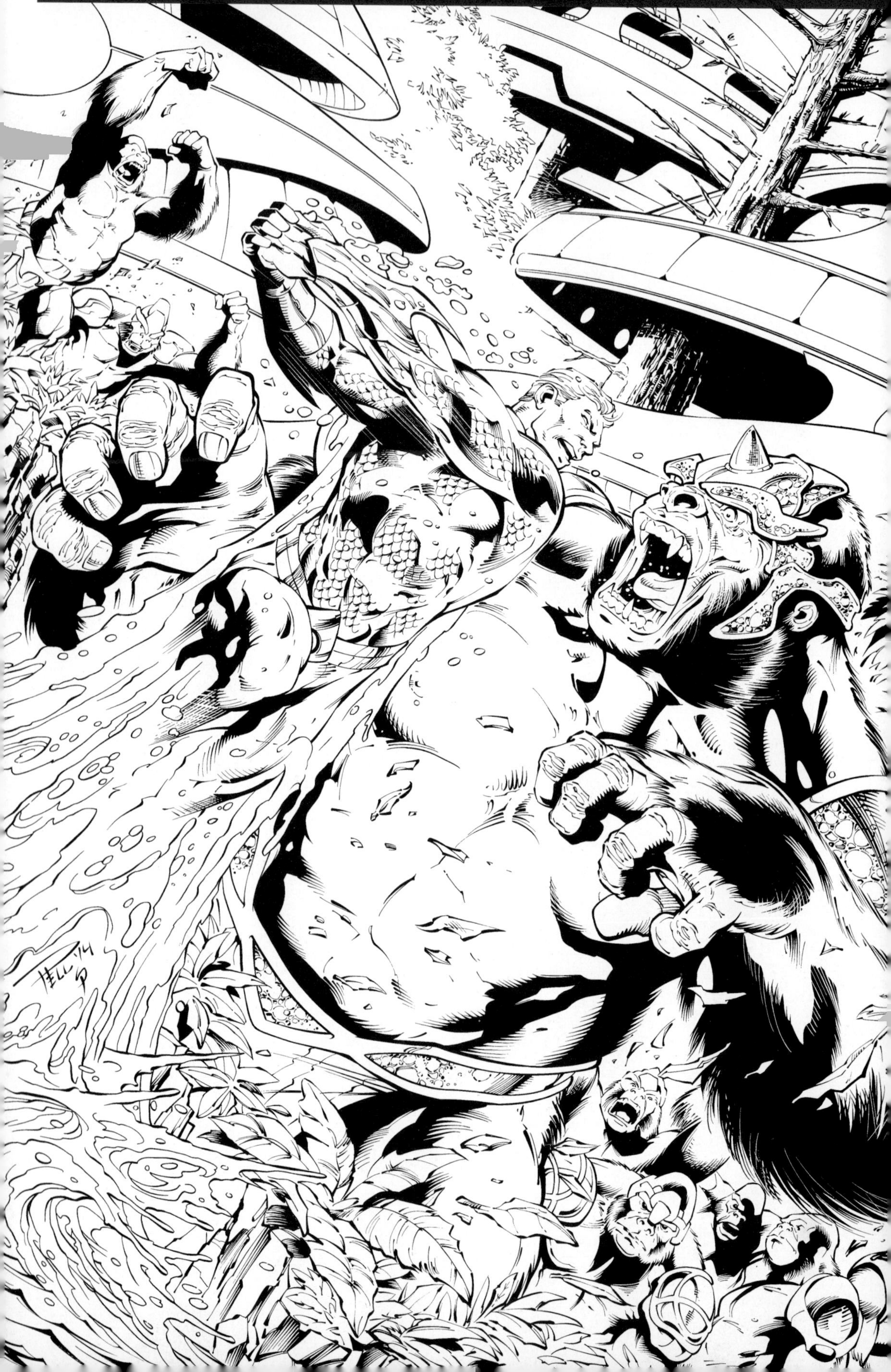

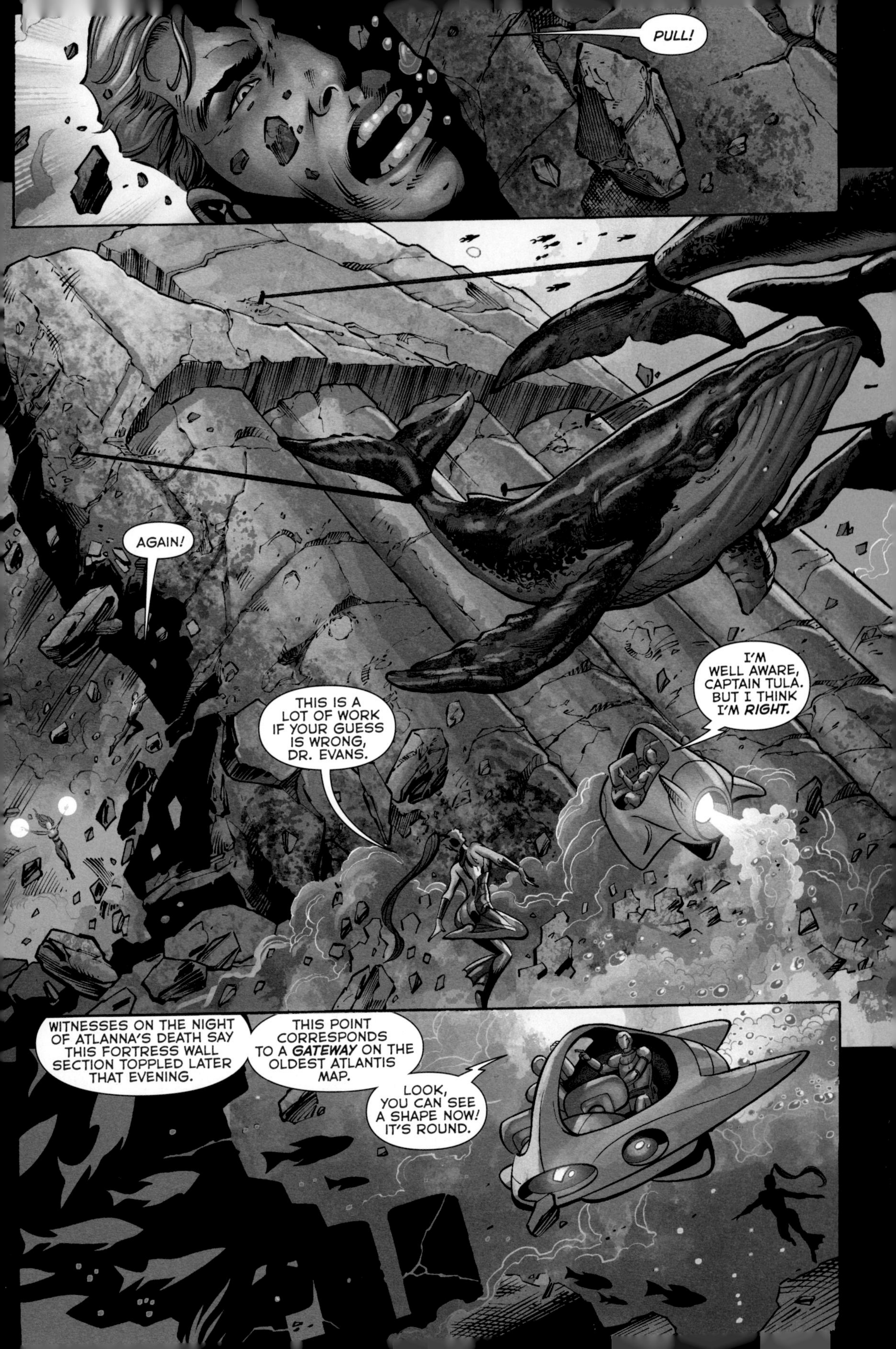
PULL!
AGAIN!
THIS IS A LOT OF WORK IF YOUR GUESS IS WRONG, DR. EVANS.
I'M WELL AWARE, CAPTAIN TULA. BUT I THINK I'M *RIGHT.*
WITNESSES ON THE NIGHT OF ATLANNA'S DEATH SAY THIS FORTRESS WALL SECTION TOPPLED LATER THAT EVENING.
THIS POINT CORRESPONDS TO A *GATEWAY* ON THE OLDEST ATLANTIS MAP.
LOOK, YOU CAN SEE A SHAPE NOW! IT'S ROUND.

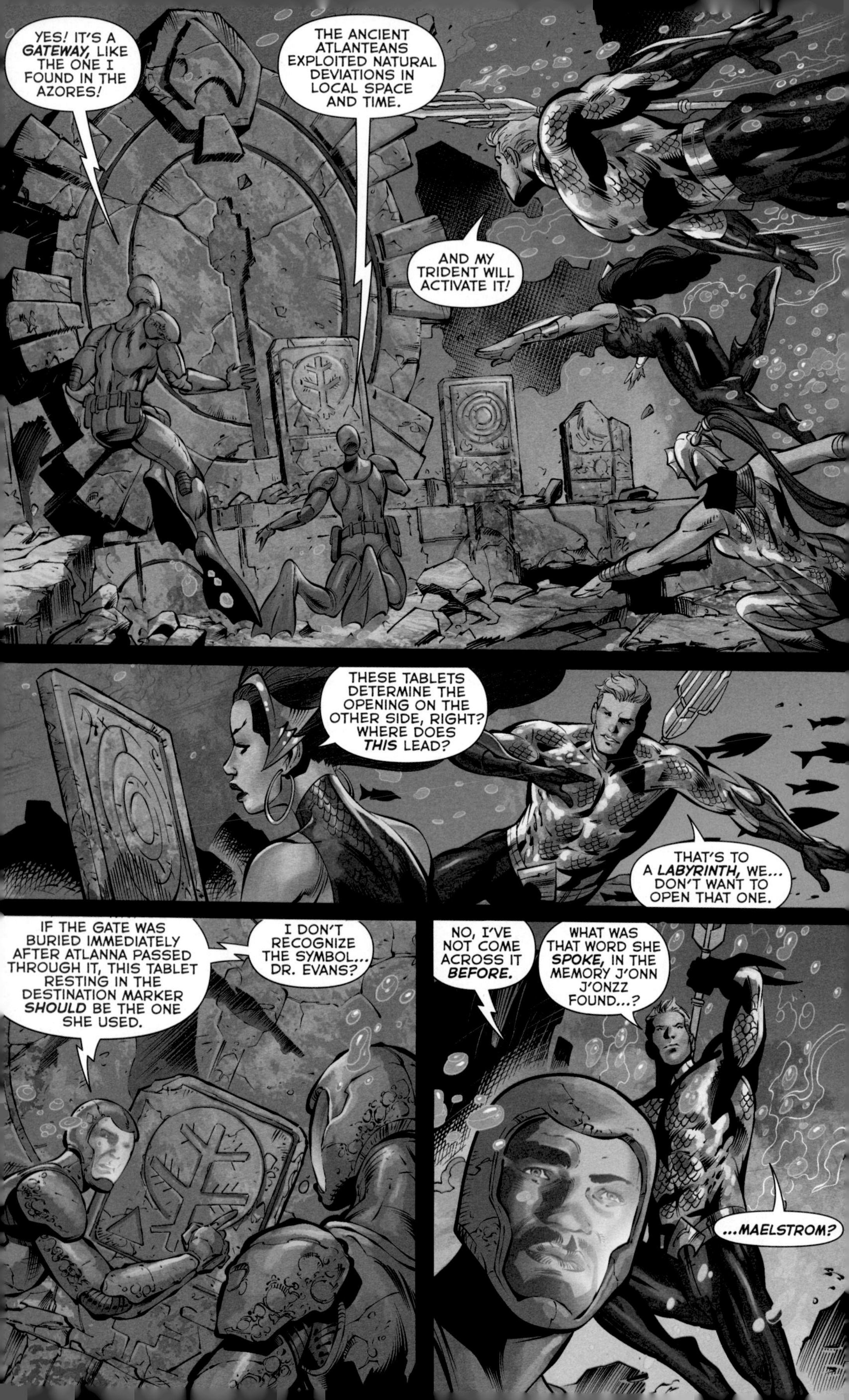
YES! IT'S A GATEWAY, LIKE THE ONE I FOUND IN THE AZORES!
THE ANCIENT ATLANTEANS EXPLOITED NATURAL DEVIATIONS IN LOCAL SPACE AND TIME.
AND MY TRIDENT WILL ACTIVATE IT!
THESE TABLETS DETERMINE THE OPENING ON THE OTHER SIDE, RIGHT? WHERE DOES THIS LEAD?
THAT'S TO A LABYRINTH, WE... DON'T WANT TO OPEN THAT ONE.
IF THE GATE WAS BURIED IMMEDIATELY AFTER ATLANNA PASSED THROUGH IT, THIS TABLET RESTING IN THE DESTINATION MARKER SHOULD BE THE ONE SHE USED.
I DON'T RECOGNIZE THE SYMBOL... DR. EVANS?
NO, I'VE NOT COME ACROSS IT BEFORE.
WHAT WAS THAT WORD SHE SPOKE, IN THE MEMORY J'ONN J'ONZZ FOUND...?
...MAELSTROM?

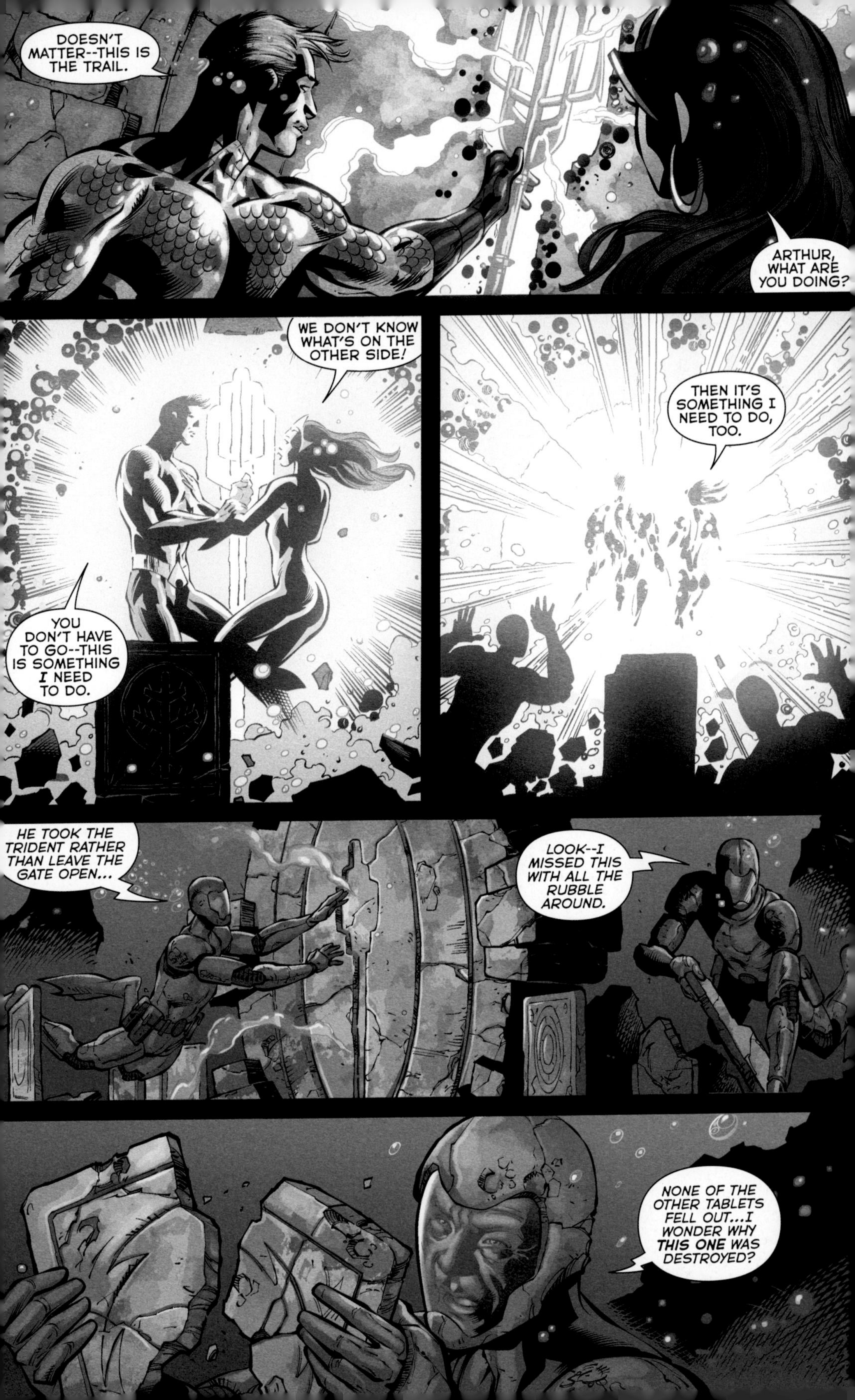
DOESN'T MATTER--THIS IS THE TRAIL.
ARTHUR, WHAT ARE YOU DOING?
WE DON'T KNOW WHAT'S ON THE OTHER SIDE!
YOU DON'T HAVE TO GO--THIS IS SOMETHING I NEED TO DO.
THEN IT'S SOMETHING I NEED TO DO, TOO.
HE TOOK THE TRIDENT RATHER THAN LEAVE THE GATE OPEN...
LOOK--I MISSED THIS WITH ALL THE RUBBLE AROUND.
NONE OF THE OTHER TABLETS FELL OUT...I WONDER WHY THIS ONE WAS DESTROYED?

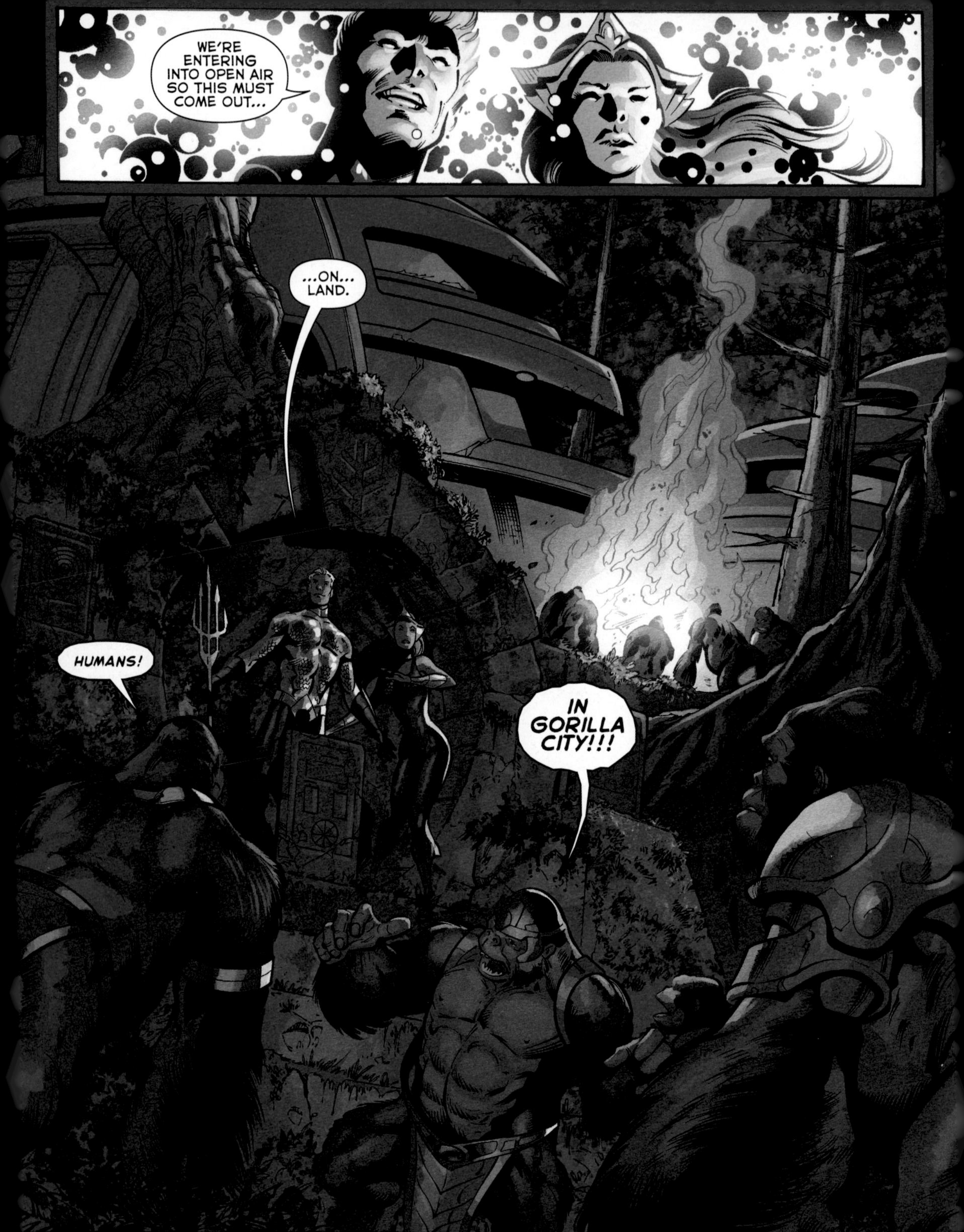
WE'RE ENTERING INTO OPEN AIR SO THIS MUST COME OUT...
...ON... LAND.
HUMANS!
IN GORILLA CITY!!!

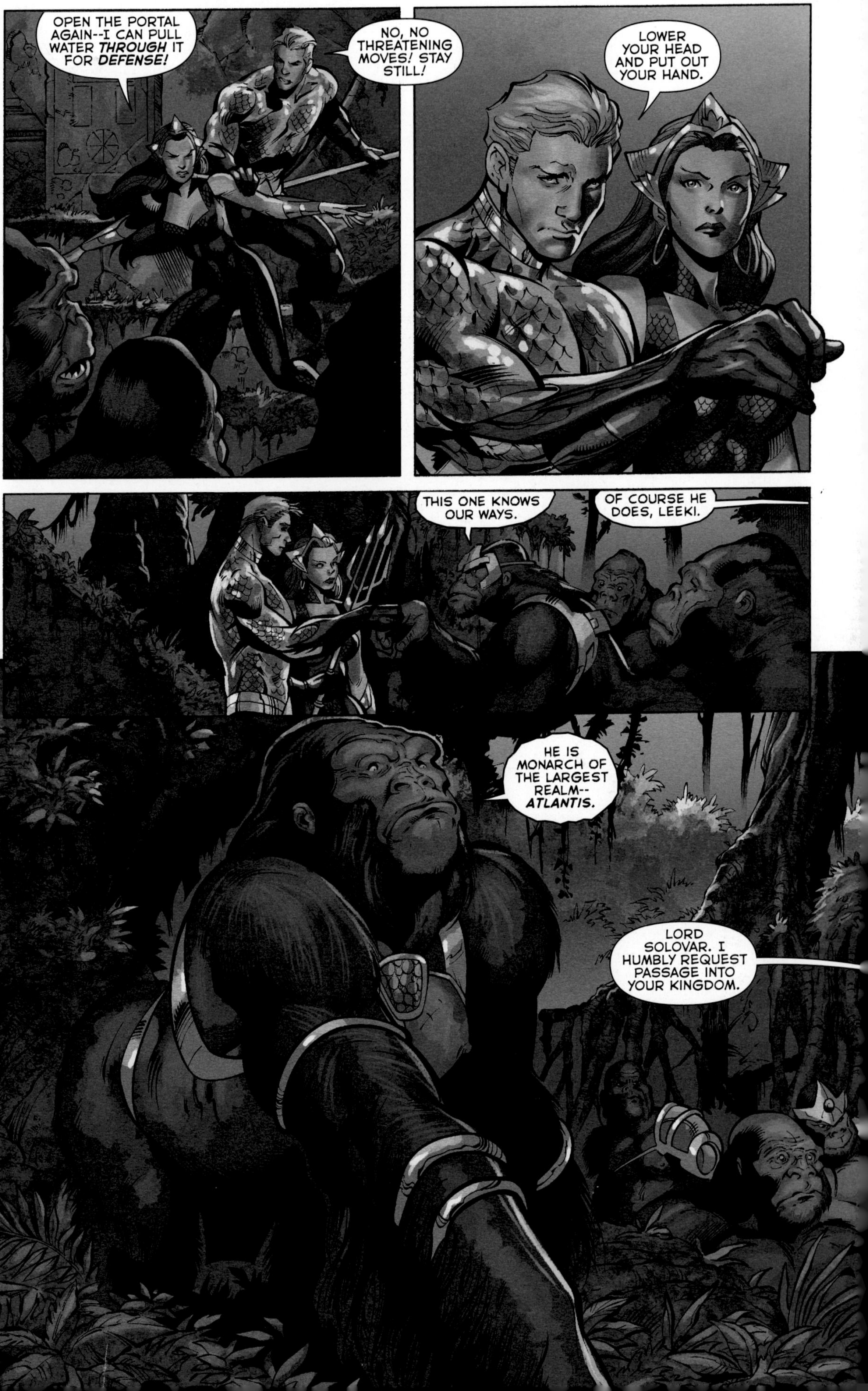
OPEN THE PORTAL AGAIN--I CAN PULL WATER *THROUGH* IT FOR *DEFENSE!*
NO, NO THREATENING MOVES! STAY STILL!
LOWER YOUR HEAD AND PUT OUT YOUR HAND.
THIS ONE KNOWS OUR WAYS.
OF COURSE HE DOES, LEEKI.
HE IS MONARCH OF THE LARGEST REALM-- *ATLANTIS.*
LORD SOLOVAR. I HUMBLY REQUEST PASSAGE INTO YOUR KINGDOM.

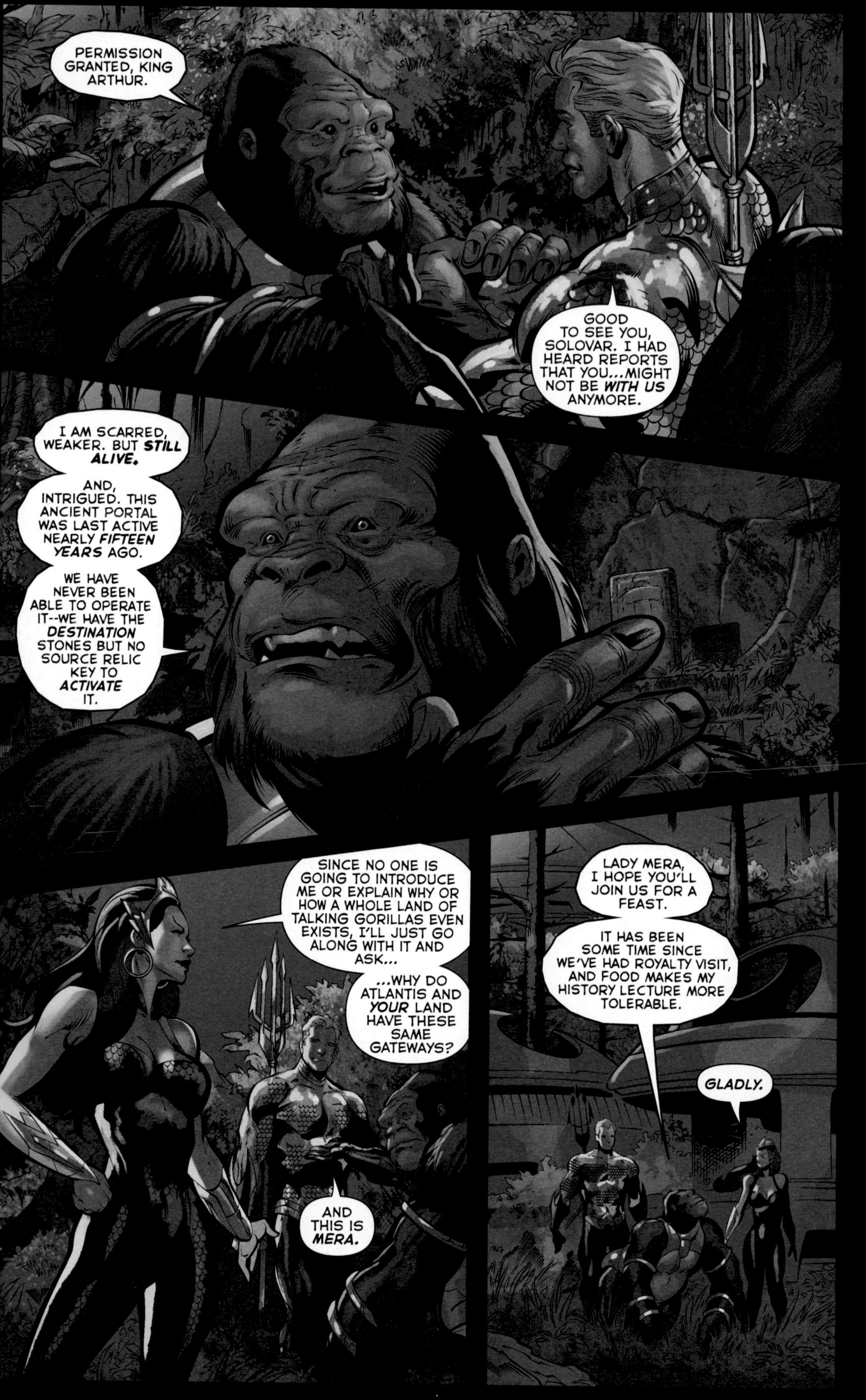
PERMISSION GRANTED, KING ARTHUR.
GOOD TO SEE YOU, SOLOVAR. I HAD HEARD REPORTS THAT YOU...MIGHT NOT BE *WITH US* ANYMORE.
I AM SCARRED, WEAKER. BUT **STILL ALIVE.**
AND, INTRIGUED. THIS ANCIENT PORTAL WAS LAST ACTIVE NEARLY *FIFTEEN YEARS* AGO.
WE HAVE NEVER BEEN ABLE TO OPERATE IT--WE HAVE THE *DESTINATION* STONES BUT NO SOURCE RELIC KEY TO *ACTIVATE* IT.
SINCE NO ONE IS GOING TO INTRODUCE ME OR EXPLAIN WHY OR HOW A WHOLE LAND OF TALKING GORILLAS EVEN EXISTS, I'LL JUST GO ALONG WITH IT AND ASK...
...WHY DO ATLANTIS AND *YOUR* LAND HAVE THESE SAME GATEWAYS?
AND THIS IS *MERA.*
LADY MERA, I HOPE YOU'LL JOIN US FOR A FEAST.
IT HAS BEEN SOME TIME SINCE WE'VE HAD ROYALTY VISIT, AND FOOD MAKES MY HISTORY LECTURE MORE TOLERABLE.
GLADLY.

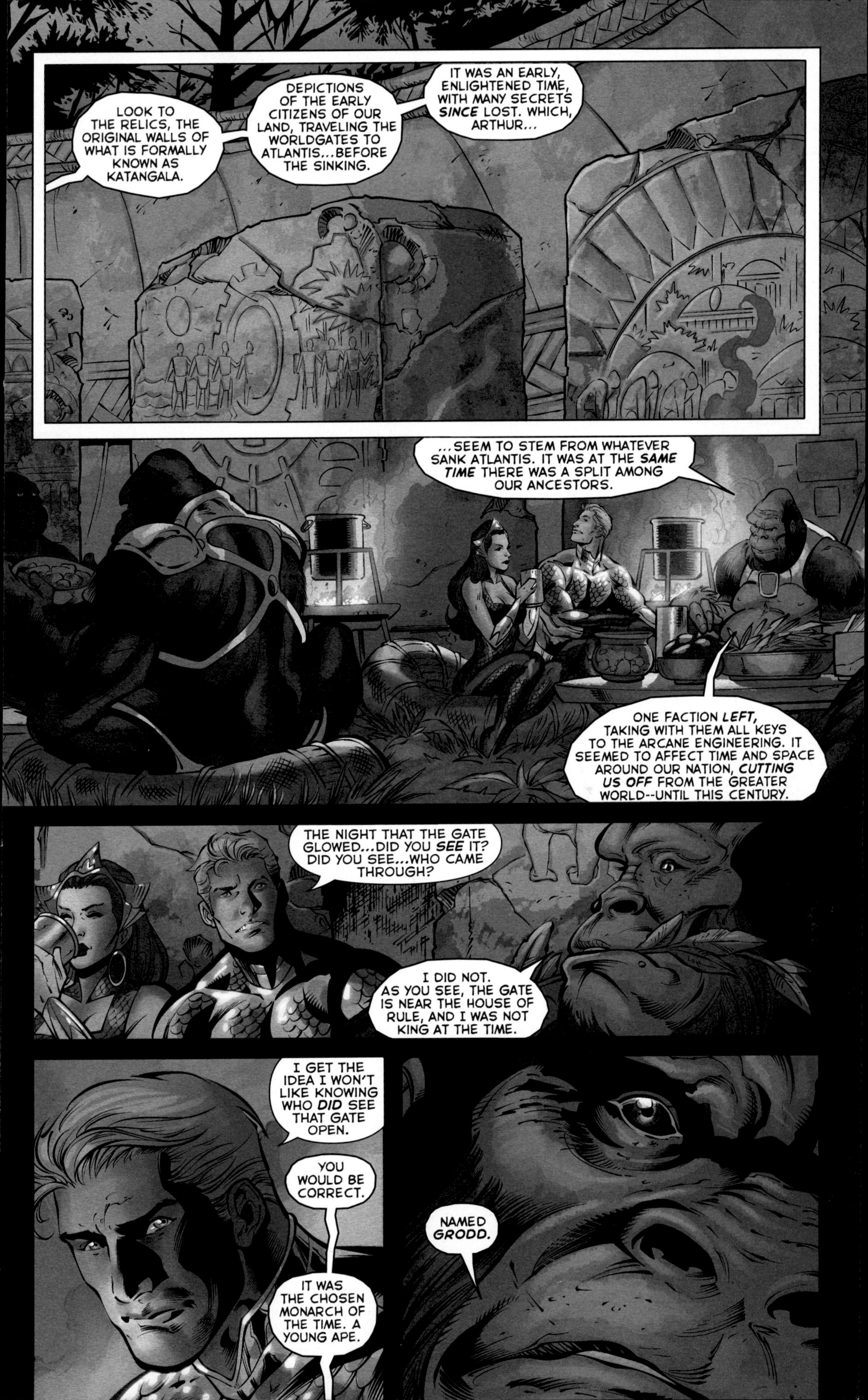
LOOK TO THE RELICS, THE ORIGINAL WALLS OF WHAT IS FORMALLY KNOWN AS KATANGALA.
DEPICTIONS OF THE EARLY CITIZENS OF OUR LAND, TRAVELING THE WORLDGATES TO ATLANTIS...BEFORE THE SINKING.
IT WAS AN EARLY, ENLIGHTENED TIME, WITH MANY SECRETS *SINCE* LOST. WHICH, ARTHUR...
...SEEM TO STEM FROM WHATEVER SANK ATLANTIS. IT WAS AT THE *SAME TIME* THERE WAS A SPLIT AMONG OUR ANCESTORS.
ONE FACTION *LEFT*, TAKING WITH THEM ALL KEYS TO THE ARCANE ENGINEERING. IT SEEMED TO AFFECT TIME AND SPACE AROUND OUR NATION, *CUTTING US OFF* FROM THE GREATER WORLD--UNTIL THIS CENTURY.
THE NIGHT THAT THE GATE GLOWED...DID YOU *SEE* IT? DID YOU SEE...WHO CAME THROUGH?
I DID NOT. AS YOU SEE, THE GATE IS NEAR THE HOUSE OF RULE, AND I WAS NOT KING AT THE TIME.
I GET THE IDEA I WON'T LIKE KNOWING WHO *DID* SEE THAT GATE OPEN.
YOU WOULD BE CORRECT.
IT WAS THE CHOSEN MONARCH OF THE TIME. A YOUNG APE.
NAMED *GRODD.*

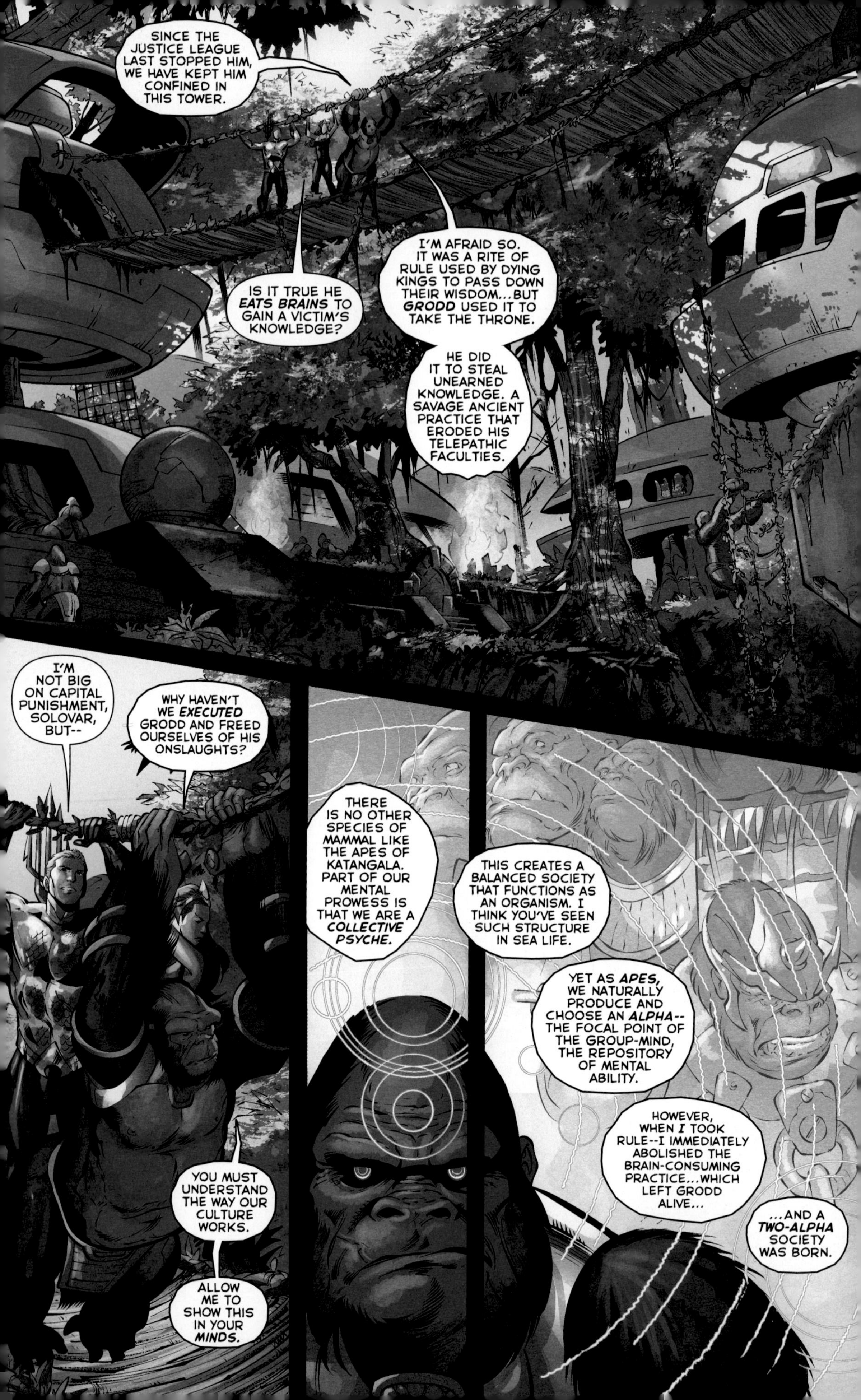
SINCE THE JUSTICE LEAGUE LAST STOPPED HIM, WE HAVE KEPT HIM CONFINED IN THIS TOWER.
IS IT TRUE HE *EATS BRAINS* TO GAIN A VICTIM'S KNOWLEDGE?
I'M AFRAID SO. IT WAS A RITE OF RULE USED BY DYING KINGS TO PASS DOWN THEIR WISDOM... BUT *GRODD* USED IT TO TAKE THE THRONE.
HE DID IT TO STEAL UNEARNED KNOWLEDGE. A SAVAGE ANCIENT PRACTICE THAT ERODED HIS TELEPATHIC FACULTIES.
I'M NOT BIG ON CAPITAL PUNISHMENT, SOLOVAR, BUT--
WHY HAVEN'T WE *EXECUTED* GRODD AND FREED OURSELVES OF HIS ONSLAUGHTS?
YOU MUST UNDERSTAND THE WAY OUR CULTURE WORKS.
ALLOW ME TO SHOW THIS IN YOUR *MINDS.*
THERE IS NO OTHER SPECIES OF MAMMAL LIKE THE APES OF KATANGALA. PART OF OUR MENTAL PROWESS IS THAT WE ARE A *COLLECTIVE PSYCHE.*
THIS CREATES A BALANCED SOCIETY THAT FUNCTIONS AS AN ORGANISM. I THINK YOU'VE SEEN SUCH STRUCTURE IN SEA LIFE.
YET AS *APES,* WE NATURALLY PRODUCE AND CHOOSE AN *ALPHA*-- THE FOCAL POINT OF THE GROUP-MIND, THE REPOSITORY OF MENTAL ABILITY.
HOWEVER, WHEN *I* TOOK RULE--I IMMEDIATELY ABOLISHED THE BRAIN-CONSUMING PRACTICE... WHICH LEFT GRODD ALIVE...
...AND A *TWO-ALPHA* SOCIETY WAS BORN.

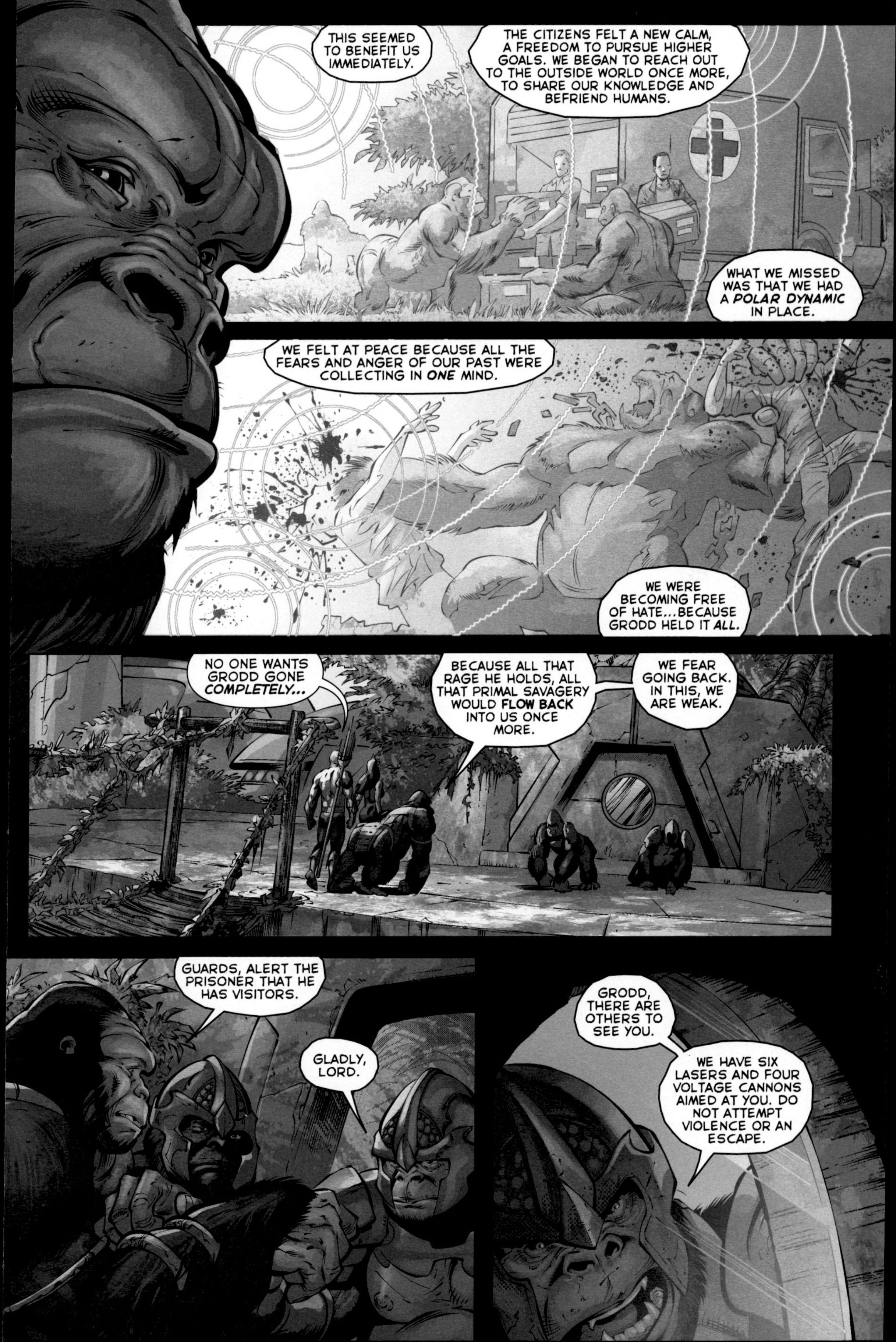
THIS SEEMED TO BENEFIT US IMMEDIATELY.
THE CITIZENS FELT A NEW CALM, A FREEDOM TO PURSUE HIGHER GOALS. WE BEGAN TO REACH OUT TO THE OUTSIDE WORLD ONCE MORE, TO SHARE OUR KNOWLEDGE AND BEFRIEND HUMANS.
WHAT WE MISSED WAS THAT WE HAD A *POLAR DYNAMIC* IN PLACE.
WE FELT AT PEACE BECAUSE ALL THE FEARS AND ANGER OF OUR PAST WERE COLLECTING IN *ONE* MIND.
WE WERE BECOMING FREE OF HATE...BECAUSE GRODD HELD IT *ALL.*
NO ONE WANTS GRODD GONE *COMPLETELY...*
BECAUSE ALL THAT RAGE HE HOLDS, ALL THAT PRIMAL SAVAGERY WOULD **FLOW BACK** INTO US ONCE MORE.
WE FEAR GOING BACK. IN THIS, WE ARE WEAK.
GUARDS, ALERT THE PRISONER THAT HE HAS VISITORS.
GLADLY, LORD.
GRODD, THERE ARE OTHERS TO SEE YOU.
WE HAVE SIX LASERS AND FOUR VOLTAGE CANNONS AIMED AT YOU. DO NOT ATTEMPT VIOLENCE OR AN ESCAPE.

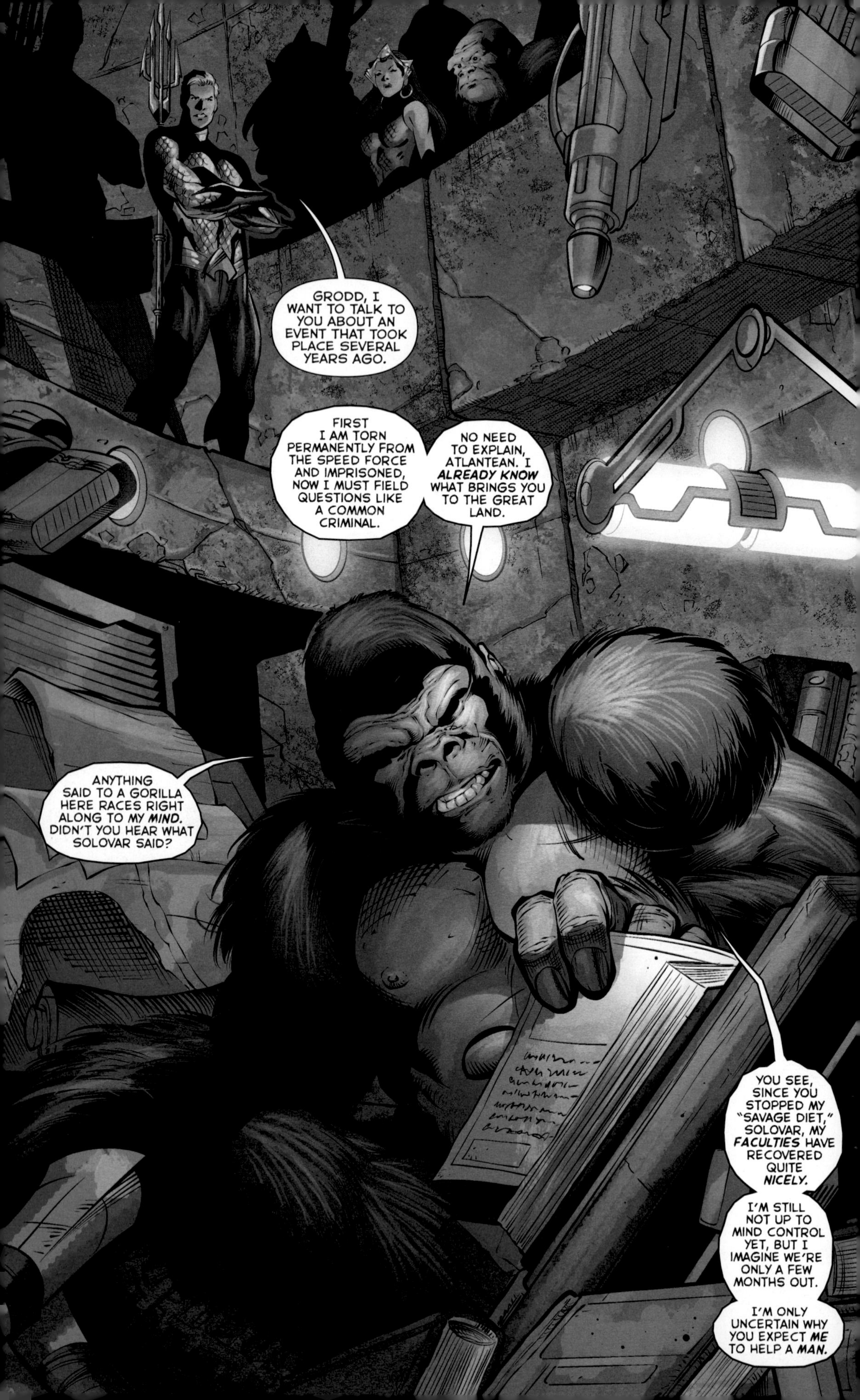
GRODD, I WANT TO TALK TO YOU ABOUT AN EVENT THAT TOOK PLACE SEVERAL YEARS AGO.
FIRST I AM TORN PERMANENTLY FROM THE SPEED FORCE AND IMPRISONED, NOW I MUST FIELD QUESTIONS LIKE A COMMON CRIMINAL.
NO NEED TO EXPLAIN, ATLANTEAN. I ALREADY KNOW WHAT BRINGS YOU TO THE GREAT LAND.
ANYTHING SAID TO A GORILLA HERE RACES RIGHT ALONG TO MY MIND. DIDN'T YOU HEAR WHAT SOLOVAR SAID?
YOU SEE, SINCE YOU STOPPED MY "SAVAGE DIET," SOLOVAR, MY FACULTIES HAVE RECOVERED QUITE NICELY.
I'M STILL NOT UP TO MIND CONTROL YET, BUT I IMAGINE WE'RE ONLY A FEW MONTHS OUT.
I'M ONLY UNCERTAIN WHY YOU EXPECT ME TO HELP A MAN.

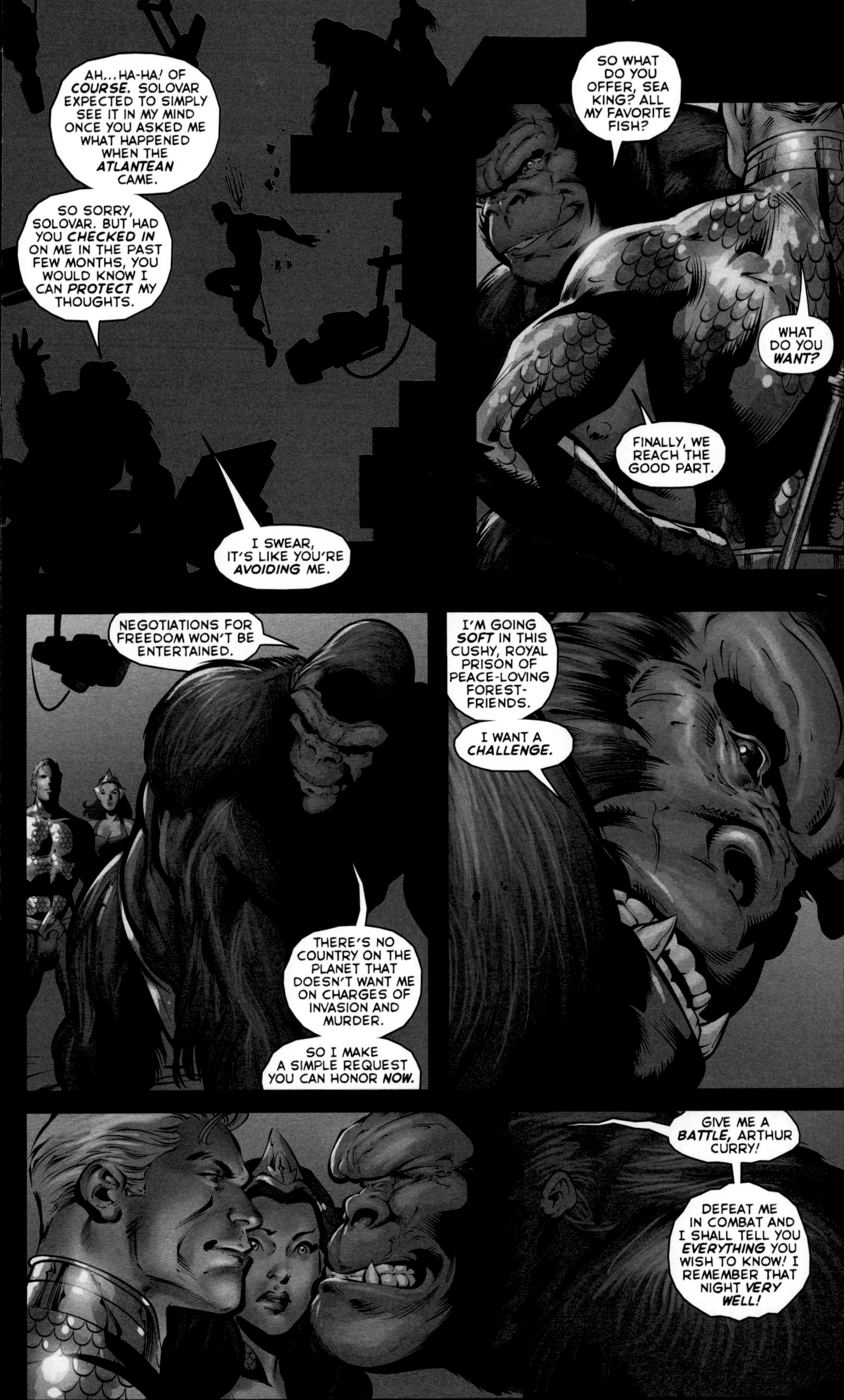
AH...HA-HA! OF COURSE. SOLOVAR EXPECTED TO SIMPLY SEE IT IN MY MIND ONCE YOU ASKED ME WHAT HAPPENED WHEN THE ATLANTEAN CAME.
SO SORRY, SOLOVAR. BUT HAD YOU CHECKED IN ON ME IN THE PAST FEW MONTHS, YOU WOULD KNOW I CAN PROTECT MY THOUGHTS.
I SWEAR, IT'S LIKE YOU'RE AVOIDING ME.
SO WHAT DO YOU OFFER, SEA KING? ALL MY FAVORITE FISH?
WHAT DO YOU WANT?
FINALLY, WE REACH THE GOOD PART.
NEGOTIATIONS FOR FREEDOM WON'T BE ENTERTAINED.
THERE'S NO COUNTRY ON THE PLANET THAT DOESN'T WANT ME ON CHARGES OF INVASION AND MURDER.
SO I MAKE A SIMPLE REQUEST YOU CAN HONOR NOW.
I'M GOING SOFT IN THIS CUSHY, ROYAL PRISON OF PEACE-LOVING FOREST-FRIENDS.
I WANT A CHALLENGE.
GIVE ME A BATTLE, ARTHUR CURRY!
DEFEAT ME IN COMBAT AND I SHALL TELL YOU EVERYTHING YOU WISH TO KNOW! I REMEMBER THAT NIGHT VERY WELL!

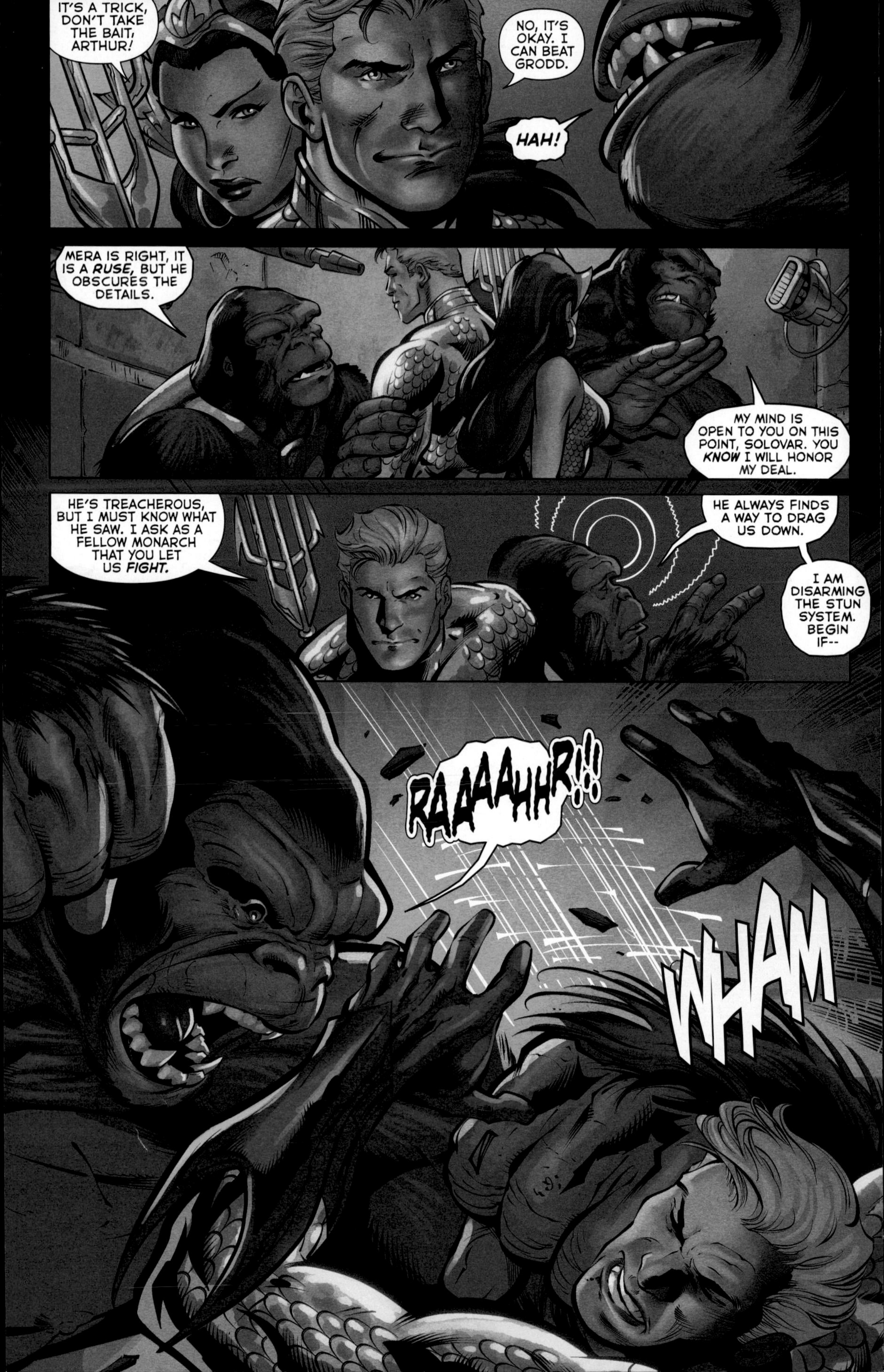
IT'S A TRICK, DON'T TAKE THE BAIT, ARTHUR!
NO, IT'S OKAY. I CAN BEAT GRODD.
HAH!
MERA IS RIGHT, IT IS A RUSE, BUT HE OBSCURES THE DETAILS.
MY MIND IS OPEN TO YOU ON THIS POINT, SOLOVAR. YOU KNOW I WILL HONOR MY DEAL.
HE'S TREACHEROUS, BUT I MUST KNOW WHAT HE SAW. I ASK AS A FELLOW MONARCH THAT YOU LET US FIGHT.
HE ALWAYS FINDS A WAY TO DRAG US DOWN.
I AM DISARMING THE STUN SYSTEM. BEGIN IF--
RAAAAHHR!!!
WHAM

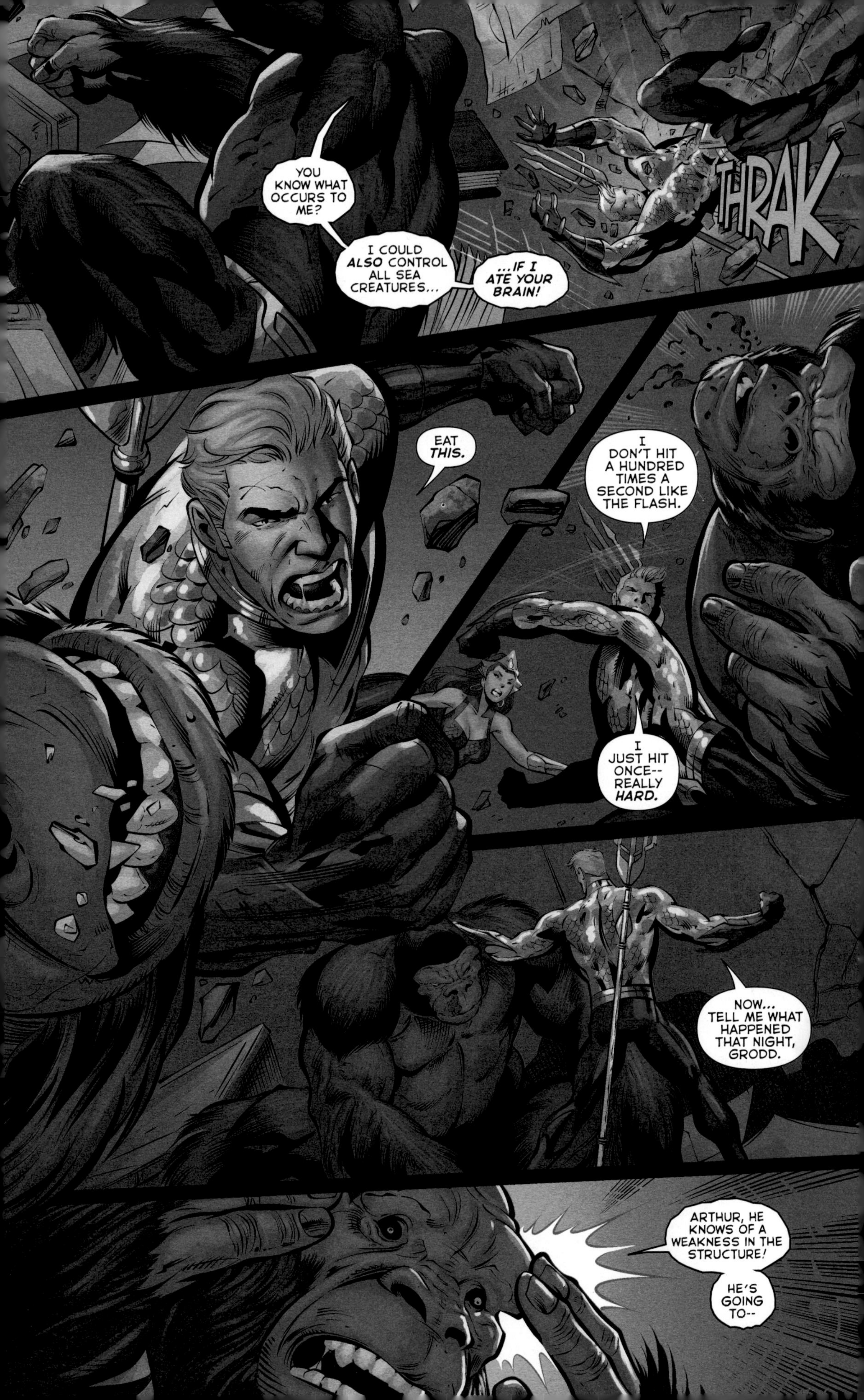
YOU KNOW WHAT OCCURS TO ME?
I COULD ALSO CONTROL ALL SEA CREATURES...
...IF I ATE YOUR BRAIN!
THRAK
EAT THIS.
I DON'T HIT A HUNDRED TIMES A SECOND LIKE THE FLASH.
I JUST HIT ONCE-- REALLY HARD.
NOW... TELL ME WHAT HAPPENED THAT NIGHT, GRODD.
ARTHUR, HE KNOWS OF A WEAKNESS IN THE STRUCTURE!
HE'S GOING TO--

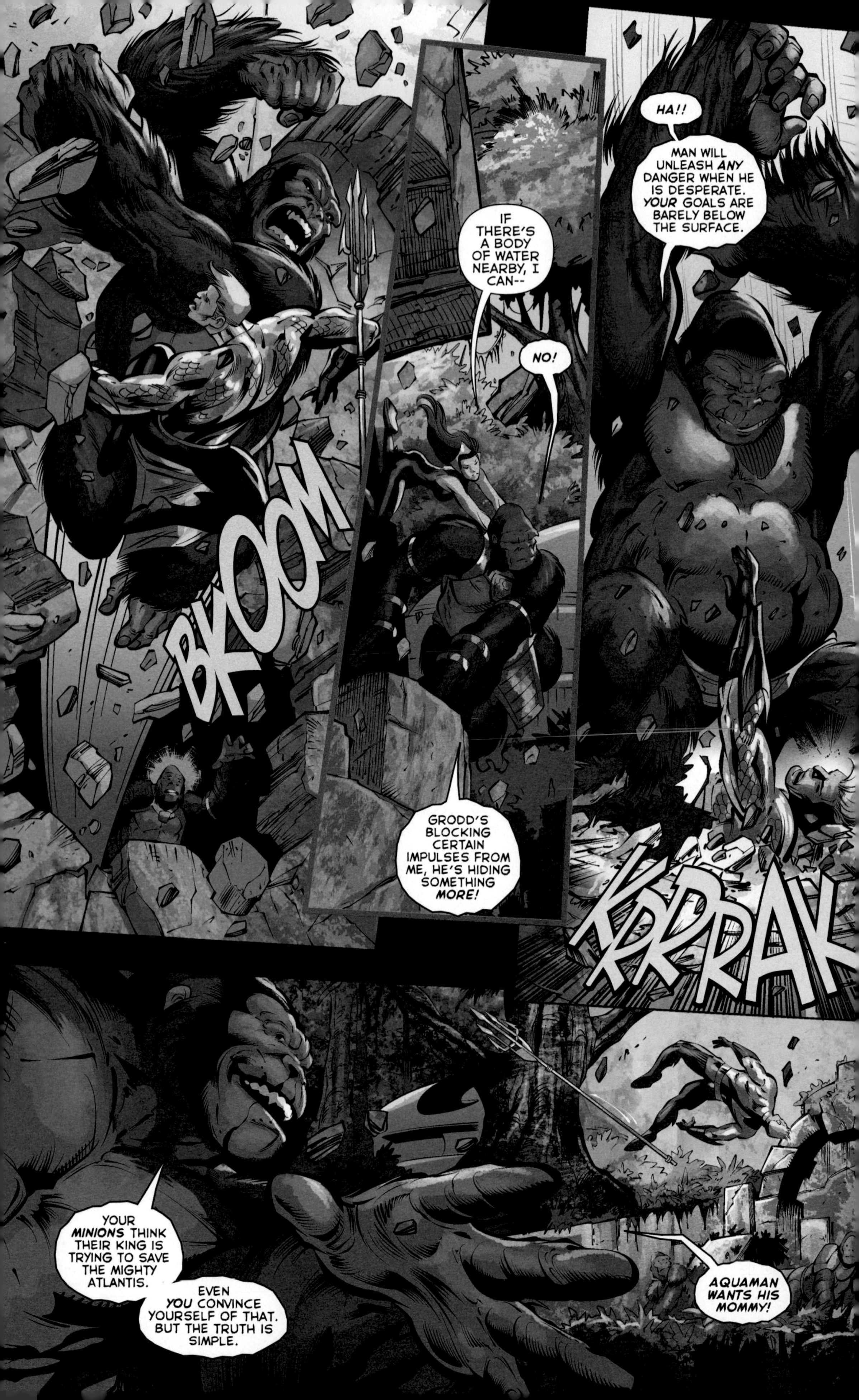
BKOOM
IF THERE'S A BODY OF WATER NEARBY, I CAN--
NO!
GRODD'S BLOCKING CERTAIN IMPULSES FROM ME, HE'S HIDING SOMETHING MORE!
HA!!
MAN WILL UNLEASH ANY DANGER WHEN HE IS DESPERATE. YOUR GOALS ARE BARELY BELOW THE SURFACE.
KRRRAK
YOUR MINIONS THINK THEIR KING IS TRYING TO SAVE THE MIGHTY ATLANTIS.
EVEN YOU CONVINCE YOURSELF OF THAT. BUT THE TRUTH IS SIMPLE.
AQUAMAN WANTS HIS MOMMY!

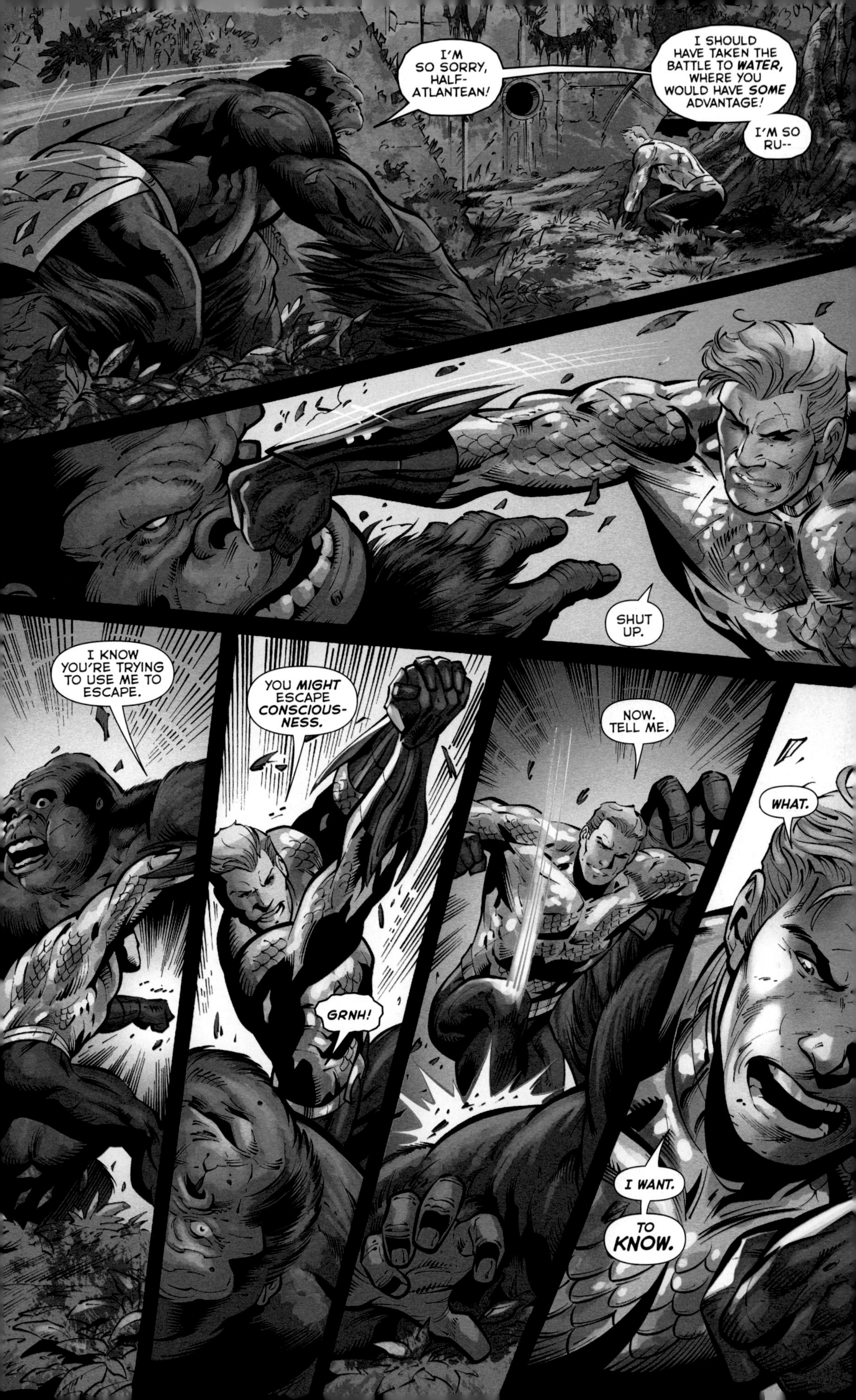
I'M SO SORRY, HALF-ATLANTEAN!
I SHOULD HAVE TAKEN THE BATTLE TO WATER, WHERE YOU WOULD HAVE SOME ADVANTAGE!
I'M SO RU--
SHUT UP.
I KNOW YOU'RE TRYING TO USE ME TO ESCAPE.
YOU MIGHT ESCAPE CONSCIOUS-NESS.
GRNH!
NOW. TELL ME.
WHAT.
I WANT.
TO KNOW.

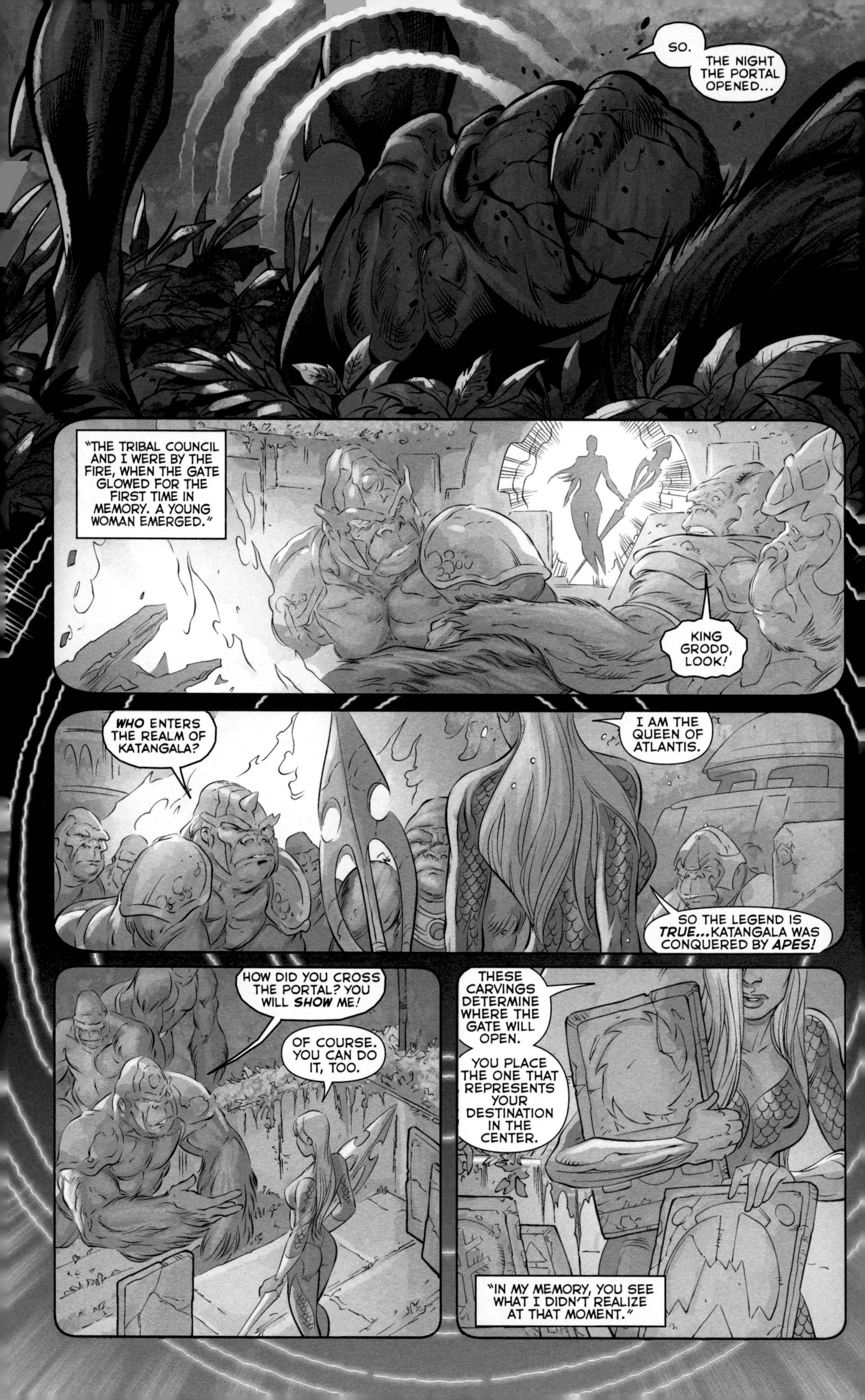
SO.
THE NIGHT THE PORTAL OPENED...
"THE TRIBAL COUNCIL AND I WERE BY THE FIRE, WHEN THE GATE GLOWED FOR THE FIRST TIME IN MEMORY. A YOUNG WOMAN EMERGED."
KING GRODD, LOOK!
WHO ENTERS THE REALM OF KATANGALA?
I AM THE QUEEN OF ATLANTIS.
SO THE LEGEND IS TRUE...KATANGALA WAS CONQUERED BY APES!
HOW DID YOU CROSS THE PORTAL? YOU WILL SHOW ME!
OF COURSE. YOU CAN DO IT, TOO.
THESE CARVINGS DETERMINE WHERE THE GATE WILL OPEN.
YOU PLACE THE ONE THAT REPRESENTS YOUR DESTINATION IN THE CENTER.
"IN MY MEMORY, YOU SEE WHAT I DIDN'T REALIZE AT THAT MOMENT."

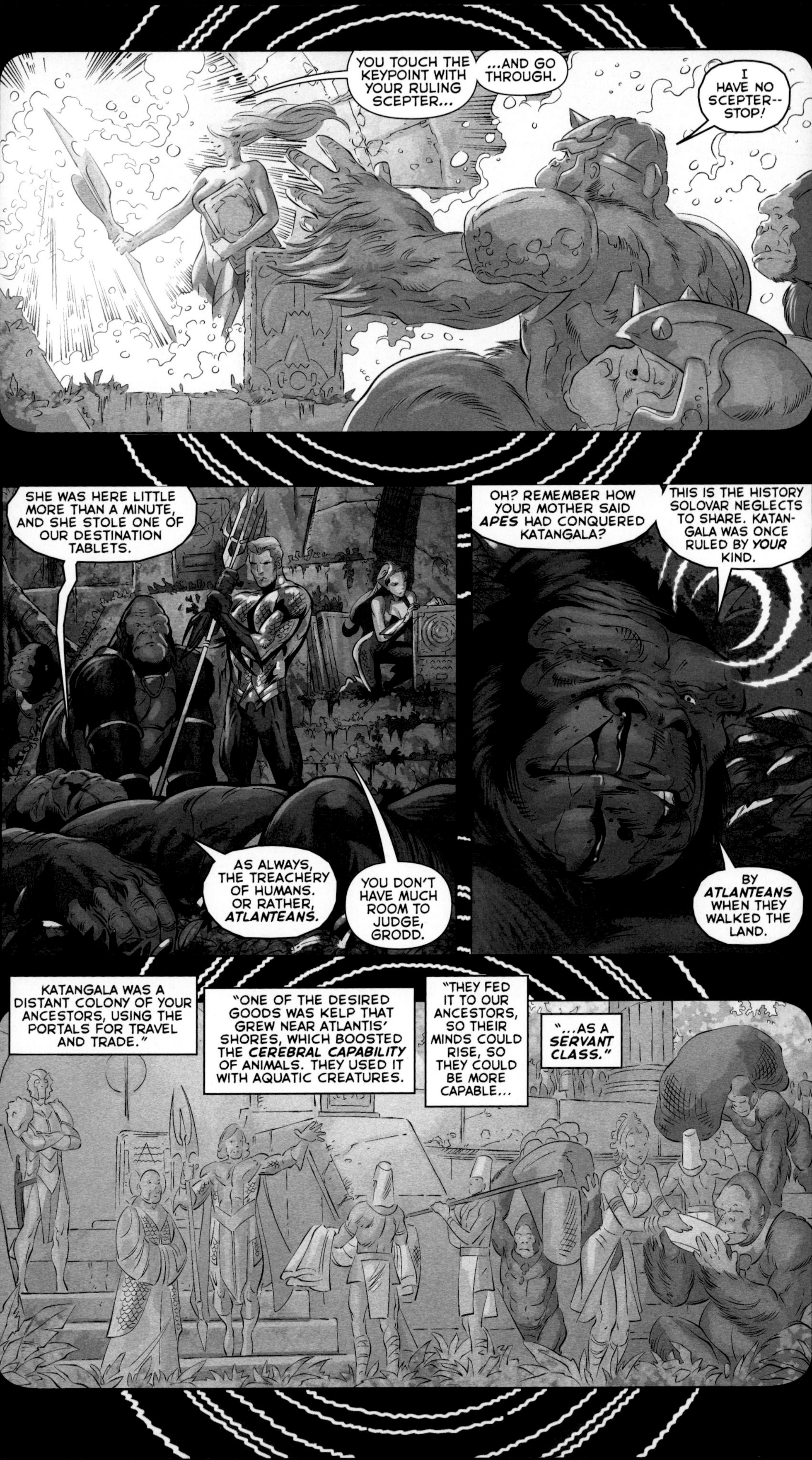
YOU TOUCH THE KEYPOINT WITH YOUR RULING SCEPTER...
...AND GO THROUGH.
I HAVE NO SCEPTER-- STOP!
SHE WAS HERE LITTLE MORE THAN A MINUTE, AND SHE STOLE ONE OF OUR DESTINATION TABLETS.
AS ALWAYS, THE TREACHERY OF HUMANS. OR RATHER, ATLANTEANS.
YOU DON'T HAVE MUCH ROOM TO JUDGE, GRODD.
OH? REMEMBER HOW YOUR MOTHER SAID APES HAD CONQUERED KATANGALA?
THIS IS THE HISTORY SOLOVAR NEGLECTS TO SHARE. KATANGALA WAS ONCE RULED BY YOUR KIND.
BY ATLANTEANS WHEN THEY WALKED THE LAND.
KATANGALA WAS A DISTANT COLONY OF YOUR ANCESTORS, USING THE PORTALS FOR TRAVEL AND TRADE."
"ONE OF THE DESIRED GOODS WAS KELP THAT GREW NEAR ATLANTIS' SHORES, WHICH BOOSTED THE CEREBRAL CAPABILITY OF ANIMALS. THEY USED IT WITH AQUATIC CREATURES.
"THEY FED IT TO OUR ANCESTORS, SO THEIR MINDS COULD RISE, SO THEY COULD BE MORE CAPABLE...
"...AS A SERVANT CLASS."

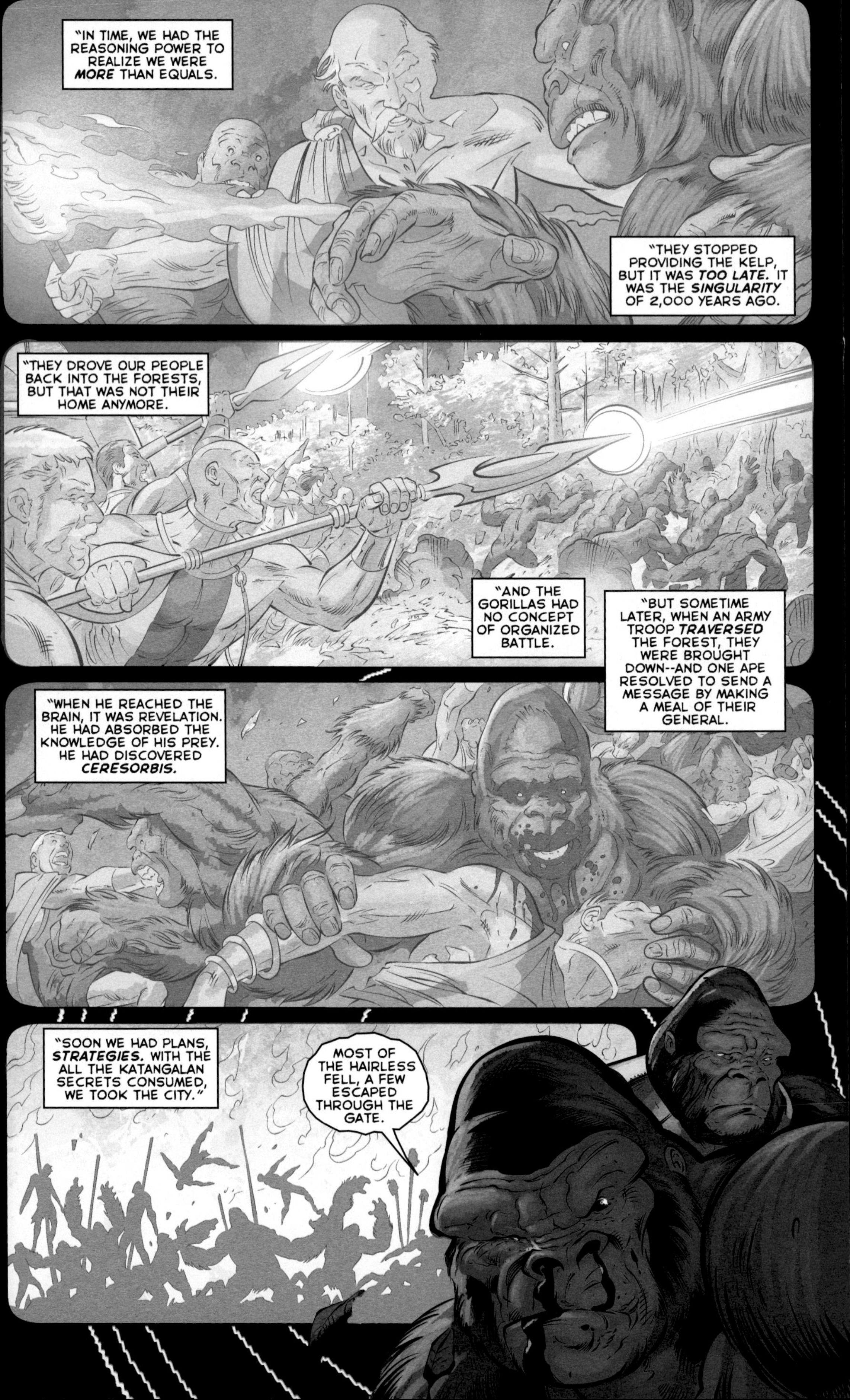
"IN TIME, WE HAD THE REASONING POWER TO REALIZE WE WERE MORE THAN EQUALS.
"THEY STOPPED PROVIDING THE KELP, BUT IT WAS TOO LATE. IT WAS THE SINGULARITY OF 2,000 YEARS AGO.
"THEY DROVE OUR PEOPLE BACK INTO THE FORESTS, BUT THAT WAS NOT THEIR HOME ANYMORE.
"AND THE GORILLAS HAD NO CONCEPT OF ORGANIZED BATTLE.
"BUT SOMETIME LATER, WHEN AN ARMY TROOP TRAVERSED THE FOREST, THEY WERE BROUGHT DOWN--AND ONE APE RESOLVED TO SEND A MESSAGE BY MAKING A MEAL OF THEIR GENERAL.
"WHEN HE REACHED THE BRAIN, IT WAS REVELATION. HE HAD ABSORBED THE KNOWLEDGE OF HIS PREY. HE HAD DISCOVERED CERESORBIS.
"SOON WE HAD PLANS, STRATEGIES. WITH THE ALL THE KATANGALAN SECRETS CONSUMED, WE TOOK THE CITY."
MOST OF THE HAIRLESS FELL, A FEW ESCAPED THROUGH THE GATE.

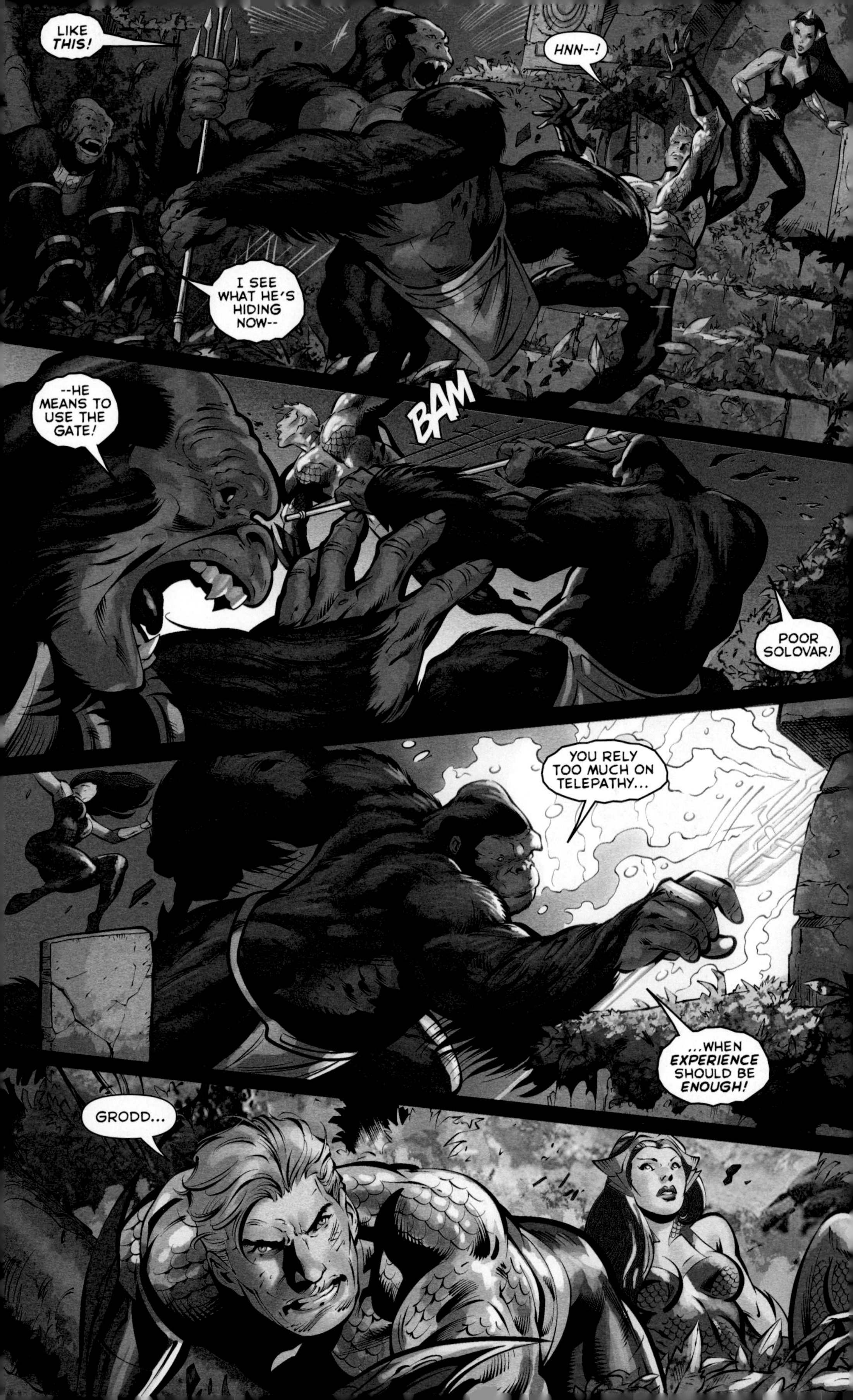
LIKE *THIS!*
HNN--!
I SEE WHAT HE'S HIDING NOW--
--HE MEANS TO USE THE GATE!
BAM
POOR SOLOVAR!
YOU RELY TOO MUCH ON TELEPATHY...
...WHEN *EXPERIENCE* SHOULD BE *ENOUGH!*
GRODD...

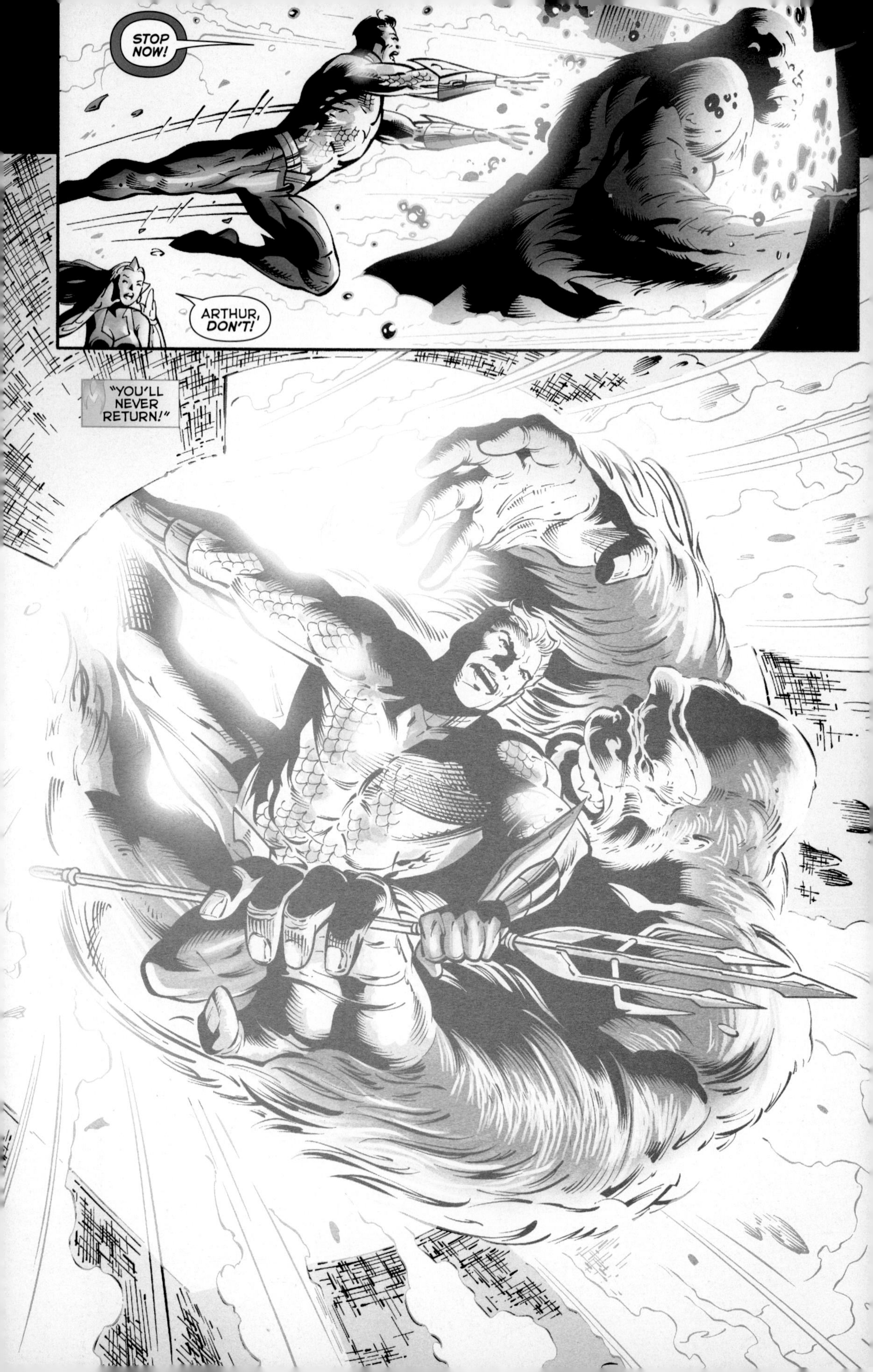
STOP NOW!
ARTHUR, DON'T!
"YOU'LL NEVER RETURN!"

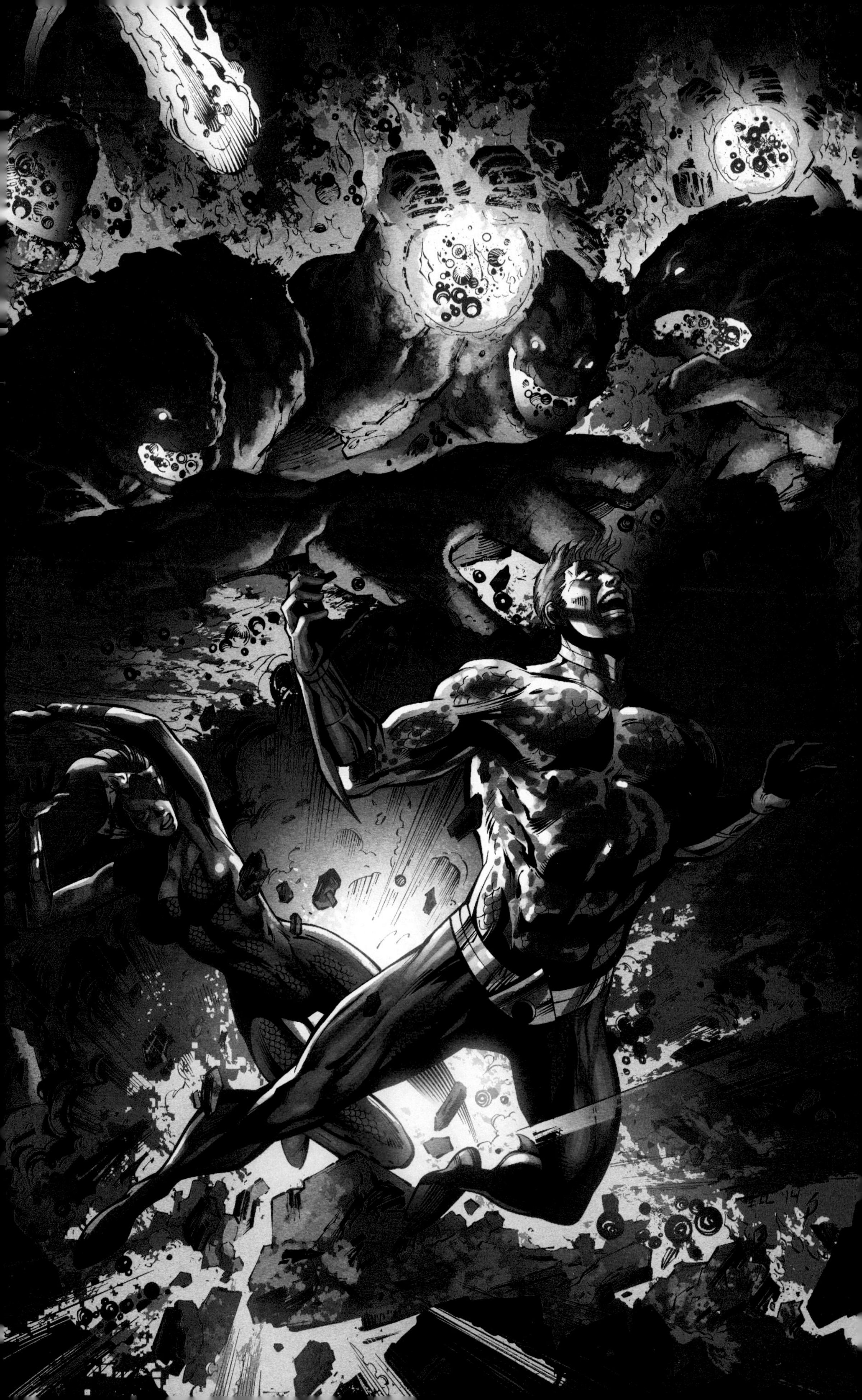

MAELSTROM PART IV: THE FINAL GATE

JEFF PARKER writer **PAUL PELLETIER** penciller **SEAN PARSONS, SANDRA HOPE** inkers **RAIN BEREDO** colorist **TRAVIS LANHAM** letterer **PELLETIER, HOPE** and **BEREDO** cover art

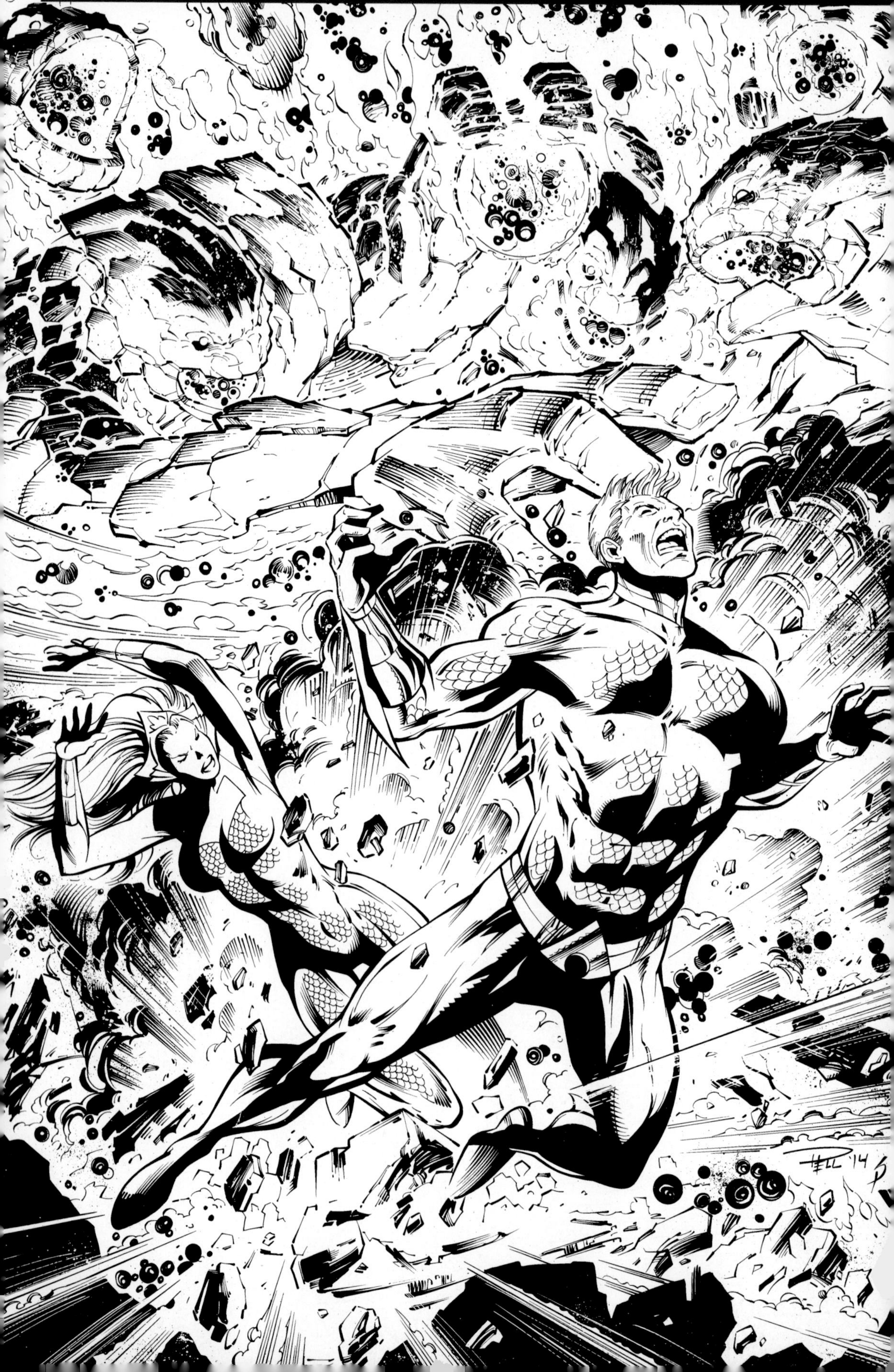

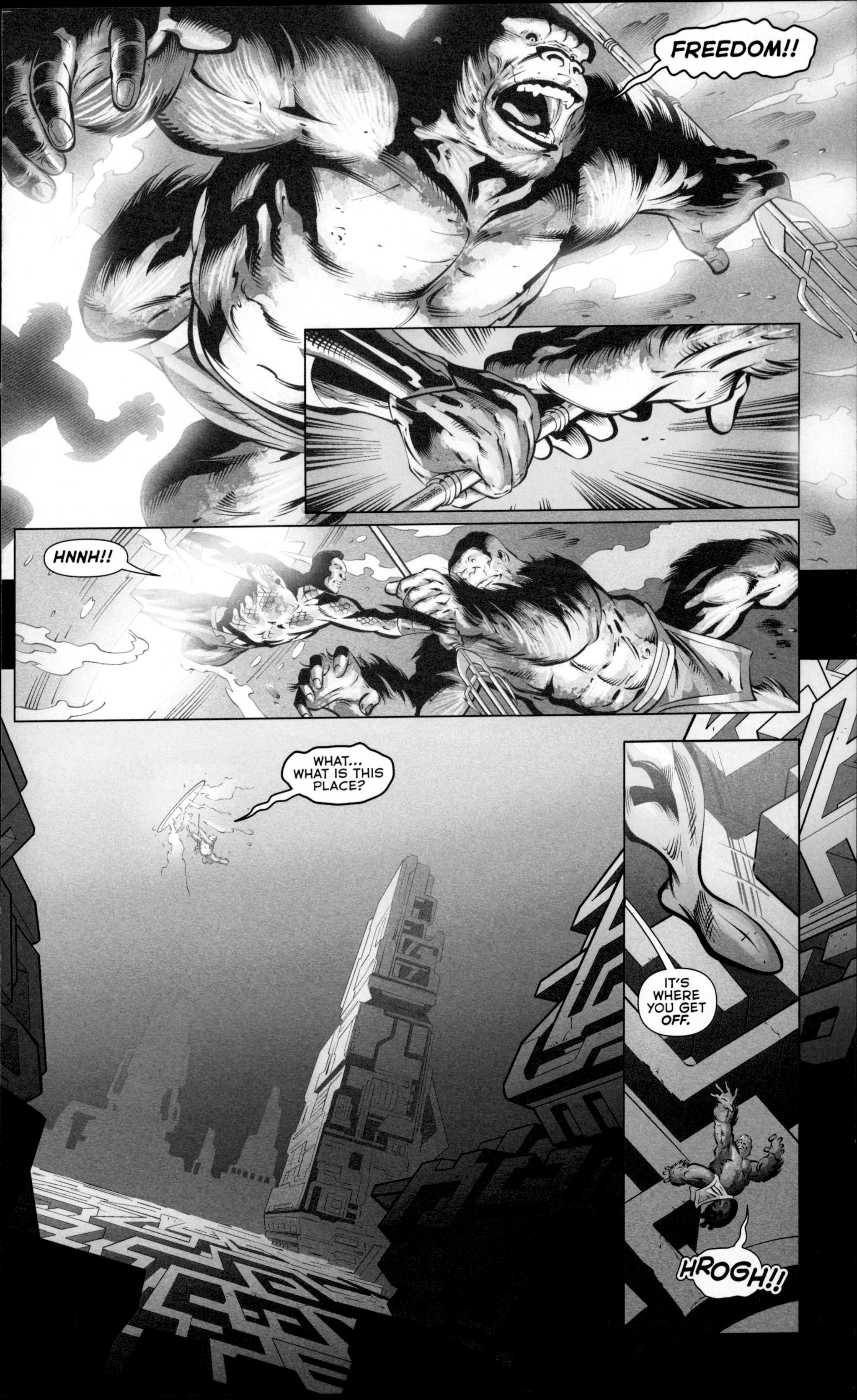
FREEDOM!!
HNNH!!
WHAT... WHAT IS THIS PLACE?
IT'S WHERE YOU GET OFF.
HROGH!!

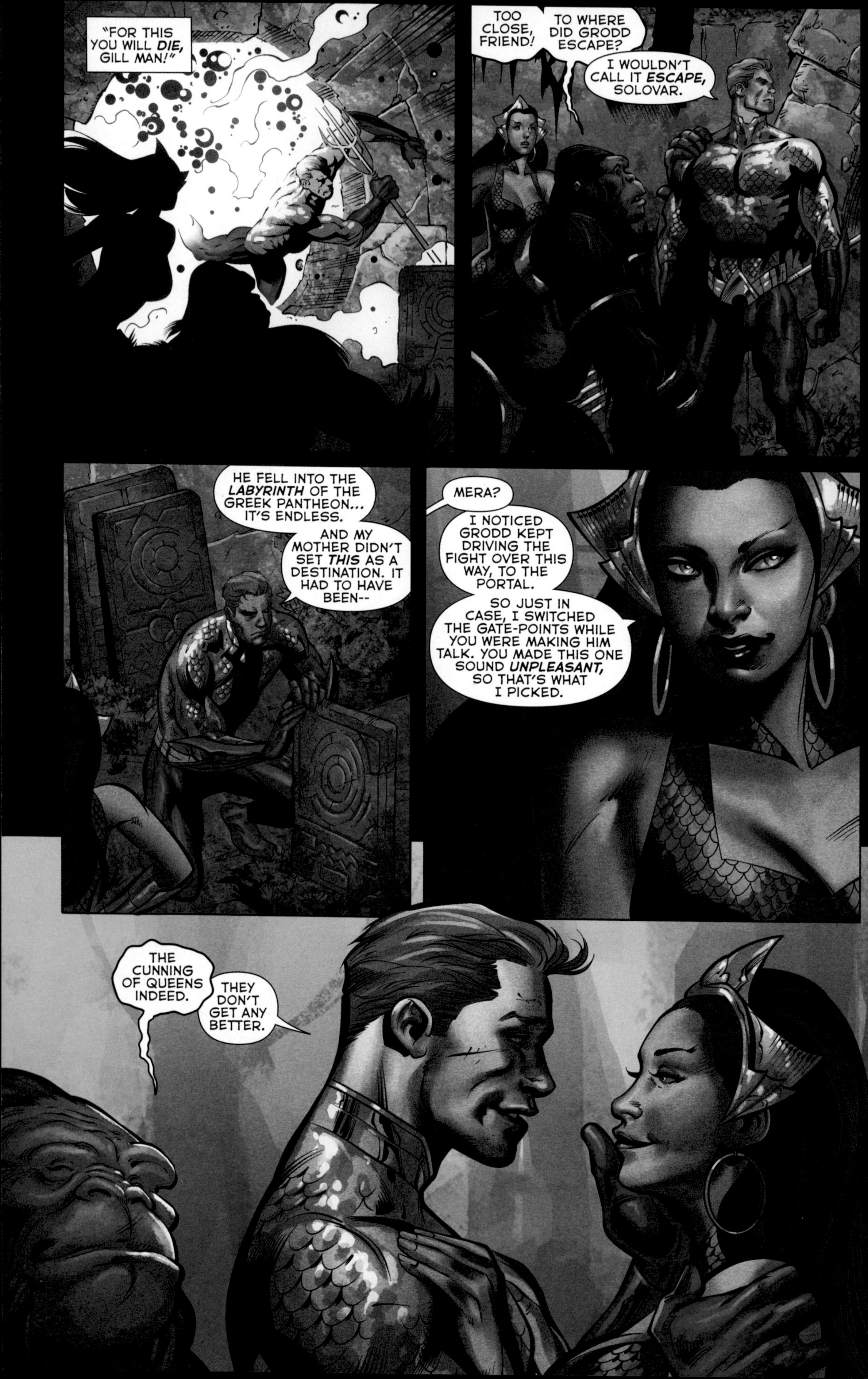
"FOR THIS YOU WILL *DIE,* GILL MAN!"
TOO CLOSE, FRIEND!
TO WHERE DID GRODD ESCAPE?
I WOULDN'T CALL IT *ESCAPE,* SOLOVAR.
HE FELL INTO THE *LABYRINTH* OF THE GREEK PANTHEON... IT'S ENDLESS.
AND MY MOTHER DIDN'T SET *THIS* AS A DESTINATION. IT HAD TO HAVE BEEN--
MERA?
I NOTICED GRODD KEPT DRIVING THE FIGHT OVER THIS WAY, TO THE PORTAL.
SO JUST IN CASE, I SWITCHED THE GATE-POINTS WHILE YOU WERE MAKING HIM TALK. YOU MADE THIS ONE SOUND *UNPLEASANT,* SO THAT'S WHAT I PICKED.
THE CUNNING OF QUEENS INDEED.
THEY DON'T GET ANY BETTER.

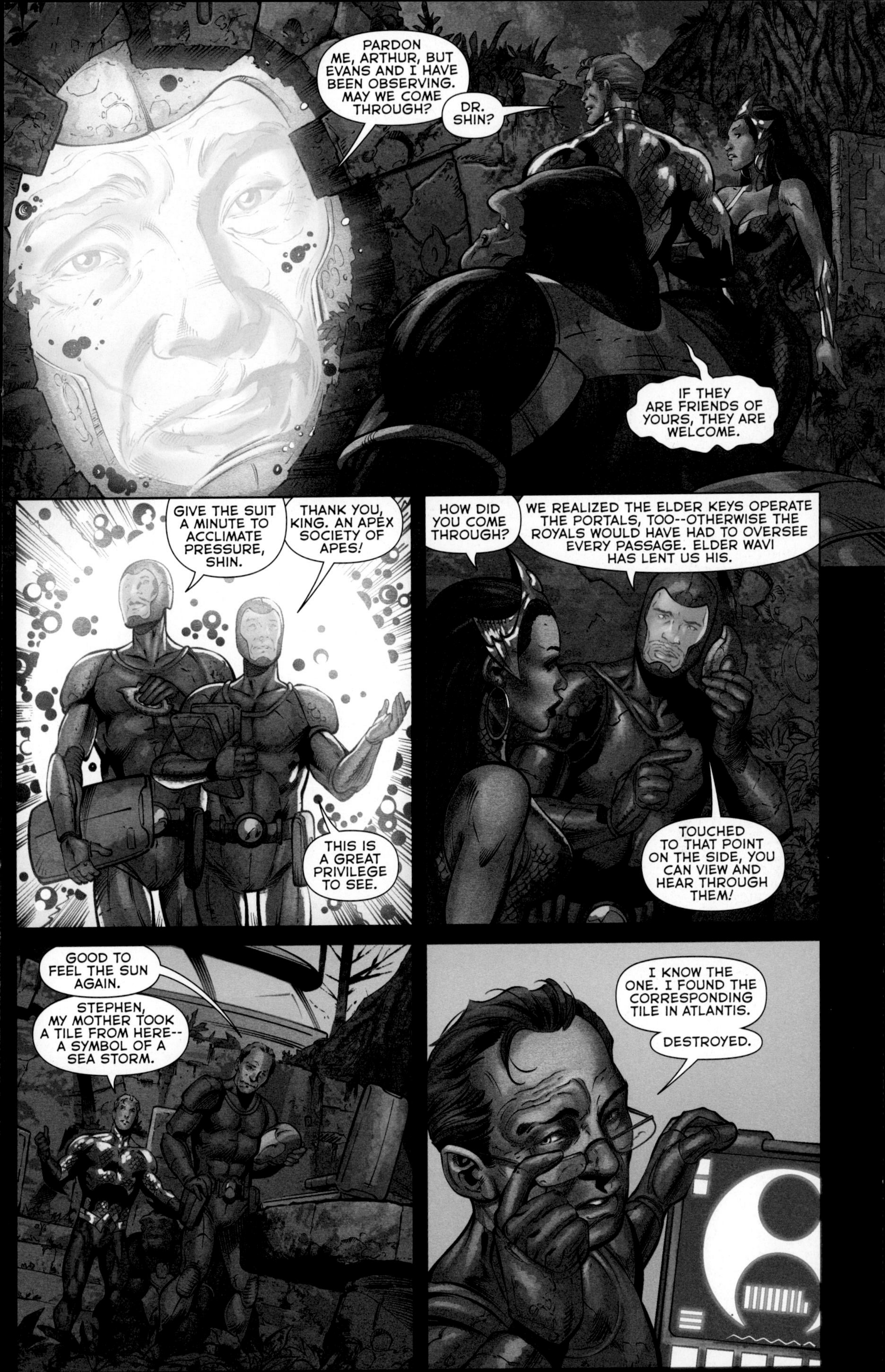
PARDON ME, ARTHUR, BUT EVANS AND I HAVE BEEN OBSERVING. MAY WE COME THROUGH?
DR. SHIN?
IF THEY ARE FRIENDS OF YOURS, THEY ARE WELCOME.
GIVE THE SUIT A MINUTE TO ACCLIMATE PRESSURE, SHIN.
THANK YOU, KING. AN APEX SOCIETY OF APES!
THIS IS A GREAT PRIVILEGE TO SEE.
HOW DID YOU COME THROUGH?
WE REALIZED THE ELDER KEYS OPERATE THE PORTALS, TOO--OTHERWISE THE ROYALS WOULD HAVE HAD TO OVERSEE EVERY PASSAGE. ELDER WAVI HAS LENT US HIS.
TOUCHED TO THAT POINT ON THE SIDE, YOU CAN VIEW AND HEAR THROUGH THEM!
GOOD TO FEEL THE SUN AGAIN.
STEPHEN, MY MOTHER TOOK A TILE FROM HERE--A SYMBOL OF A SEA STORM.
I KNOW THE ONE. I FOUND THE CORRESPONDING TILE IN ATLANTIS.
DESTROYED.

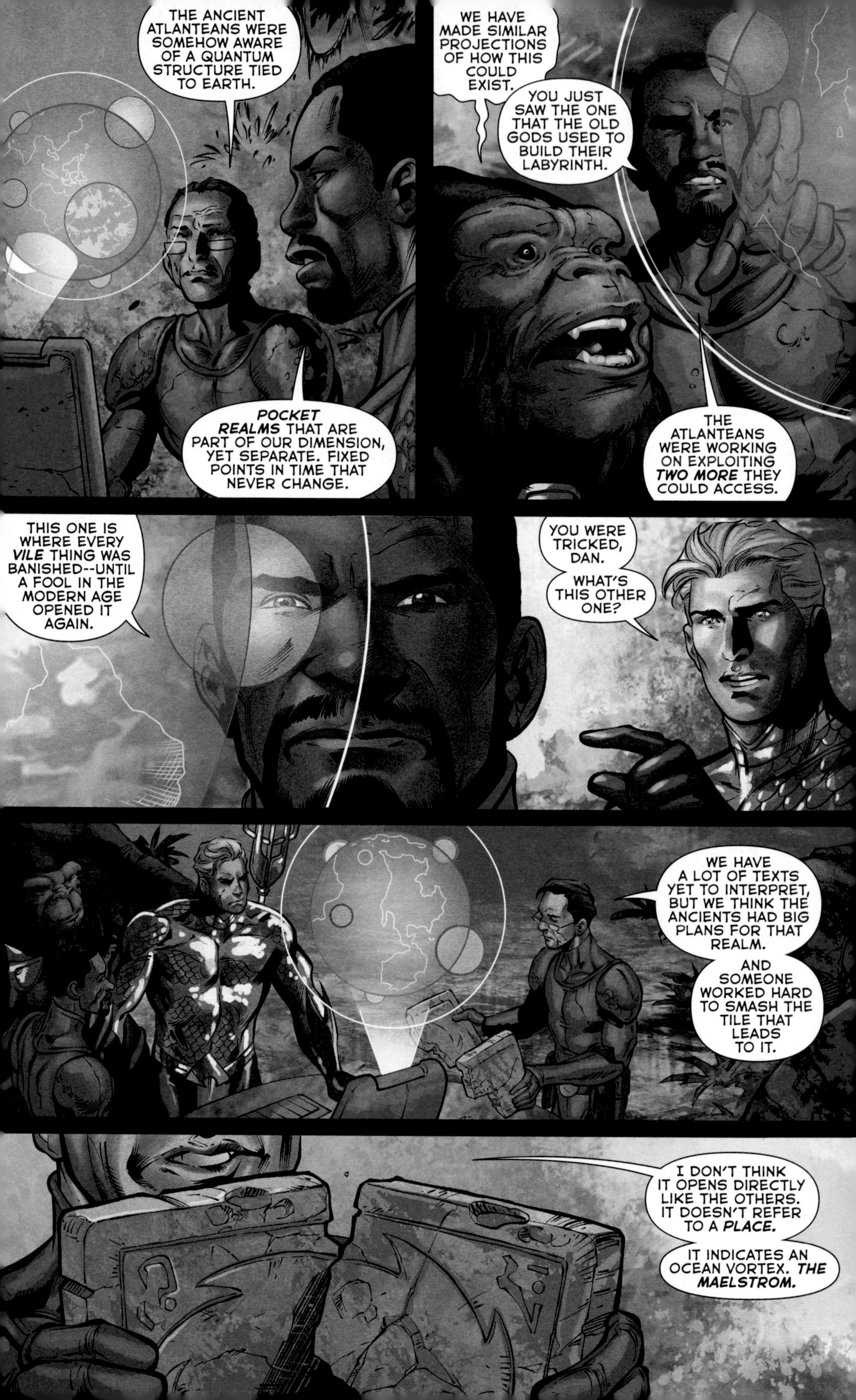
THE ANCIENT ATLANTEANS WERE SOMEHOW AWARE OF A QUANTUM STRUCTURE TIED TO EARTH.
POCKET REALMS THAT ARE PART OF OUR DIMENSION, YET SEPARATE. FIXED POINTS IN TIME THAT NEVER CHANGE.
WE HAVE MADE SIMILAR PROJECTIONS OF HOW THIS COULD EXIST.
YOU JUST SAW THE ONE THAT THE OLD GODS USED TO BUILD THEIR LABYRINTH.
THE ATLANTEANS WERE WORKING ON EXPLOITING *TWO MORE* THEY COULD ACCESS.
THIS ONE IS WHERE EVERY *VILE* THING WAS BANISHED--UNTIL A FOOL IN THE MODERN AGE OPENED IT AGAIN.
YOU WERE TRICKED, DAN.
WHAT'S THIS OTHER ONE?
WE HAVE A LOT OF TEXTS YET TO INTERPRET, BUT WE THINK THE ANCIENTS HAD BIG PLANS FOR THAT REALM.
AND SOMEONE WORKED HARD TO SMASH THE TILE THAT LEADS TO IT.
I DON'T THINK IT OPENS DIRECTLY LIKE THE OTHERS. IT DOESN'T REFER TO A *PLACE.*
IT INDICATES AN OCEAN VORTEX. ***THE MAELSTROM.***

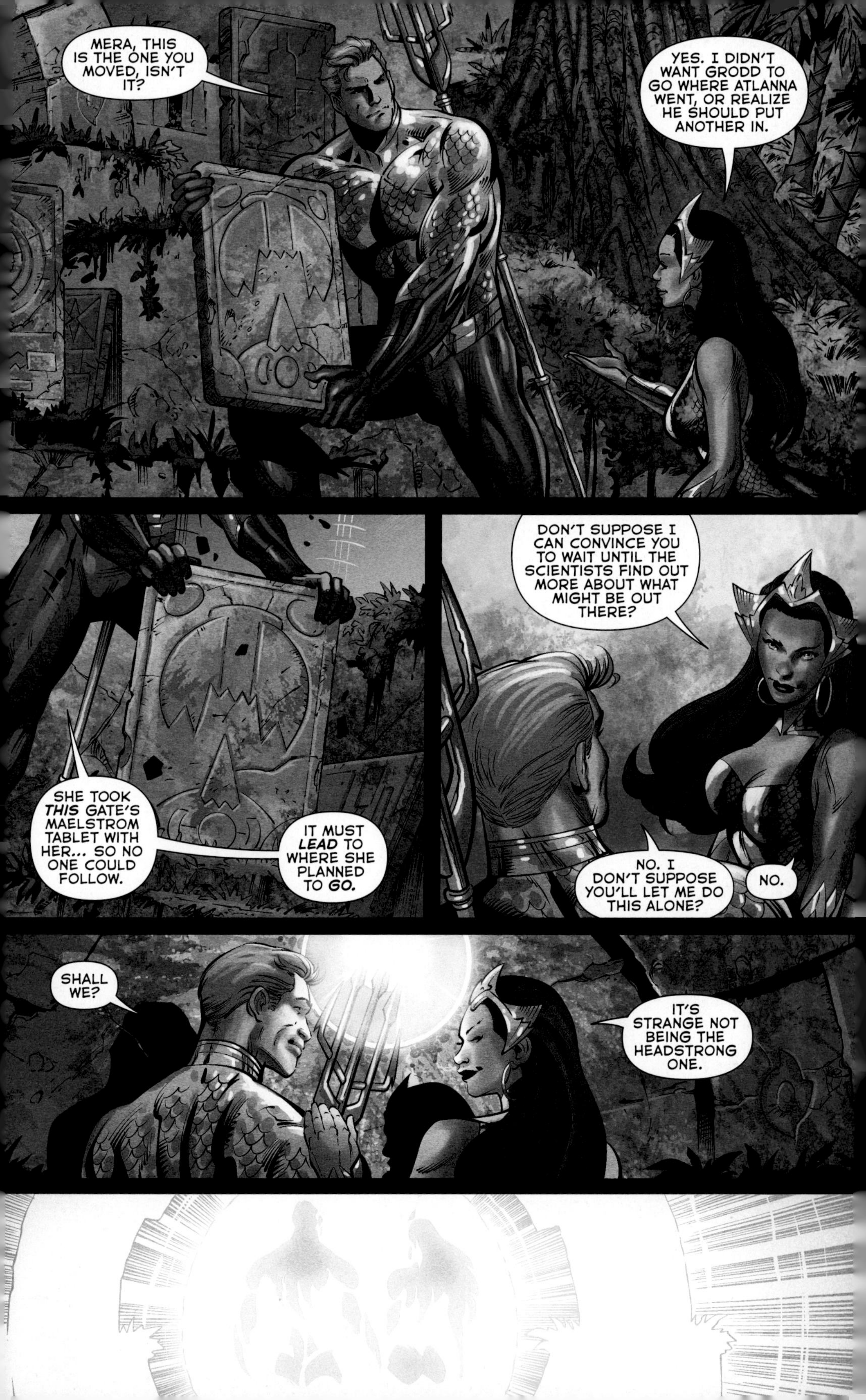
MERA, THIS IS THE ONE YOU MOVED, ISN'T IT?
YES. I DIDN'T WANT GRODD TO GO WHERE ATLANNA WENT, OR REALIZE HE SHOULD PUT ANOTHER IN.
SHE TOOK *THIS* GATE'S MAELSTROM TABLET WITH HER... SO NO ONE COULD FOLLOW.
IT MUST *LEAD* TO WHERE SHE PLANNED TO *GO.*
DON'T SUPPOSE I CAN CONVINCE YOU TO WAIT UNTIL THE SCIENTISTS FIND OUT MORE ABOUT WHAT MIGHT BE OUT THERE?
NO. I DON'T SUPPOSE YOU'LL LET ME DO THIS ALONE?
NO.
SHALL WE?
IT'S STRANGE NOT BEING THE HEADSTRONG ONE.

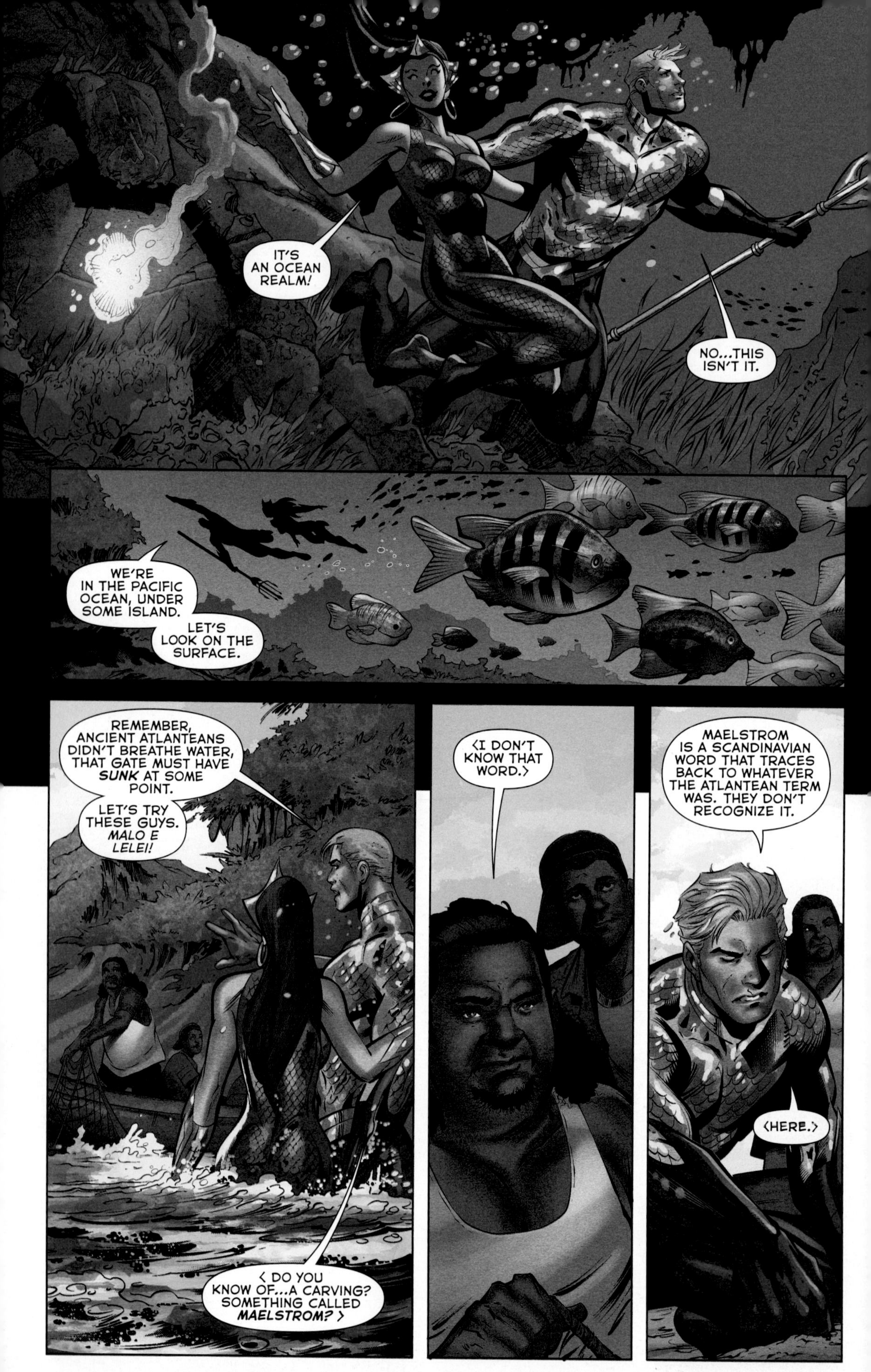
IT'S AN OCEAN REALM!
NO...THIS ISN'T IT.
WE'RE IN THE PACIFIC OCEAN, UNDER SOME ISLAND.
LET'S LOOK ON THE SURFACE.
REMEMBER, ANCIENT ATLANTEANS DIDN'T BREATHE WATER, THAT GATE MUST HAVE SUNK AT SOME POINT.
LET'S TRY THESE GUYS. MALO E LELEI!
< DO YOU KNOW OF...A CARVING? SOMETHING CALLED MAELSTROM? >
<I DON'T KNOW THAT WORD.>
MAELSTROM IS A SCANDINAVIAN WORD THAT TRACES BACK TO WHATEVER THE ATLANTEAN TERM WAS. THEY DON'T RECOGNIZE IT.
<HERE.>

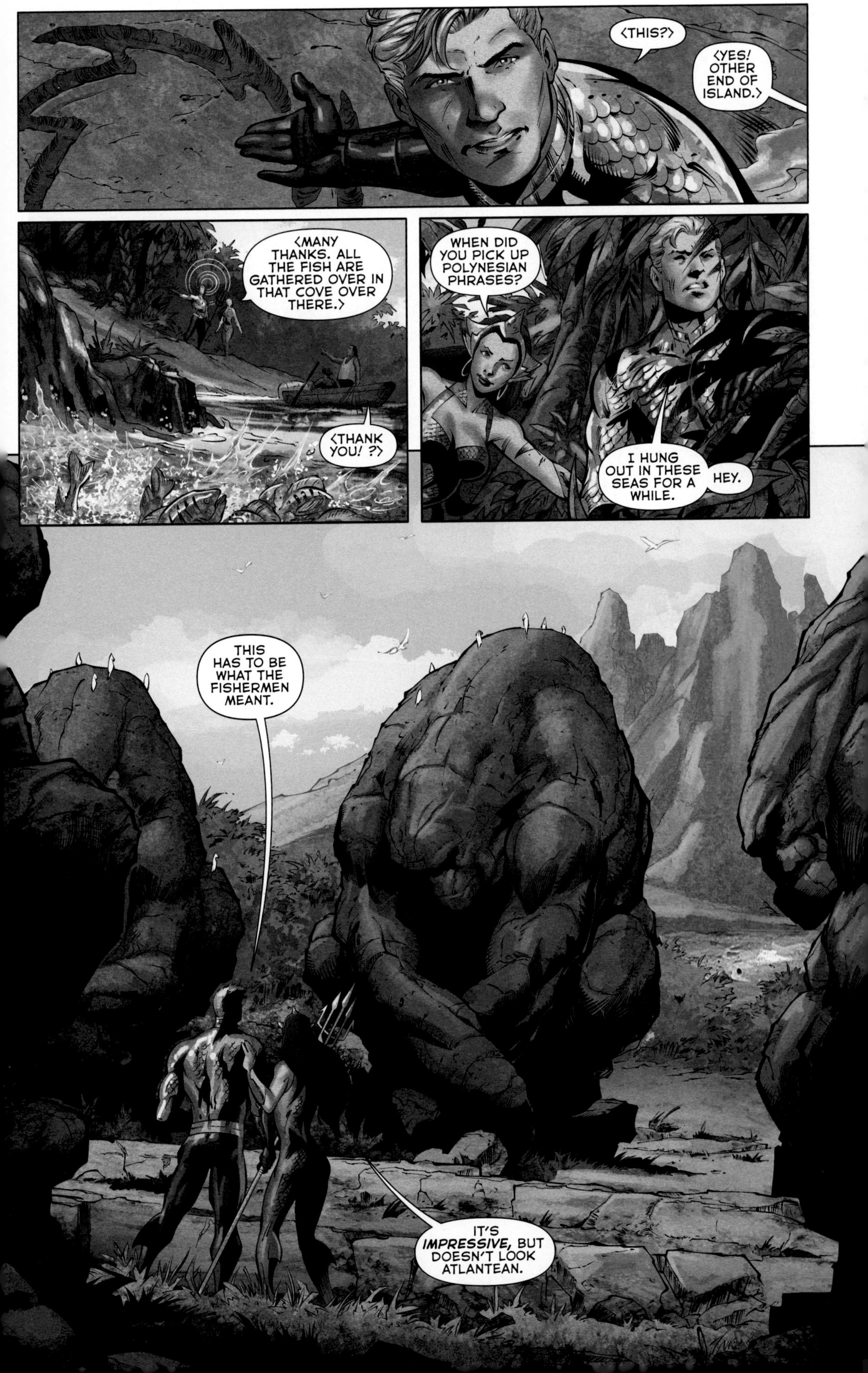

<THIS?>
<YES! OTHER END OF ISLAND.>
<MANY THANKS. ALL THE FISH ARE GATHERED OVER IN THAT COVE OVER THERE.>
<THANK YOU! ?>
WHEN DID YOU PICK UP POLYNESIAN PHRASES?
I HUNG OUT IN THESE SEAS FOR A WHILE.
HEY.
THIS HAS TO BE WHAT THE FISHERMEN MEANT.
IT'S *IMPRESSIVE,* BUT DOESN'T LOOK ATLANTEAN.

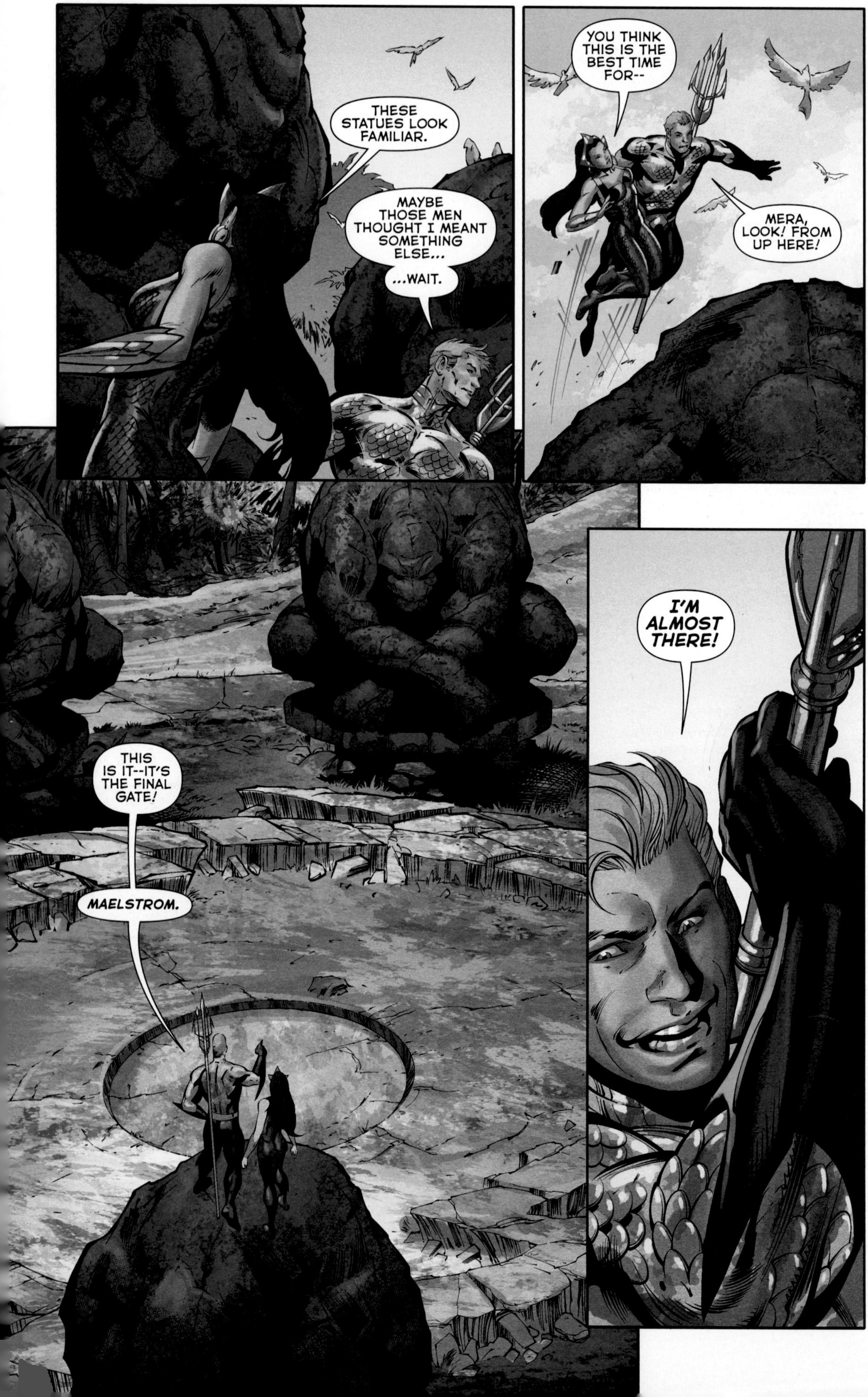
THESE STATUES LOOK FAMILIAR.
MAYBE THOSE MEN THOUGHT I MEANT SOMETHING ELSE...
...WAIT.
YOU THINK THIS IS THE BEST TIME FOR--
MERA, LOOK! FROM UP HERE!
THIS IS IT--IT'S THE FINAL GATE!
MAELSTROM.
I'M ALMOST THERE!

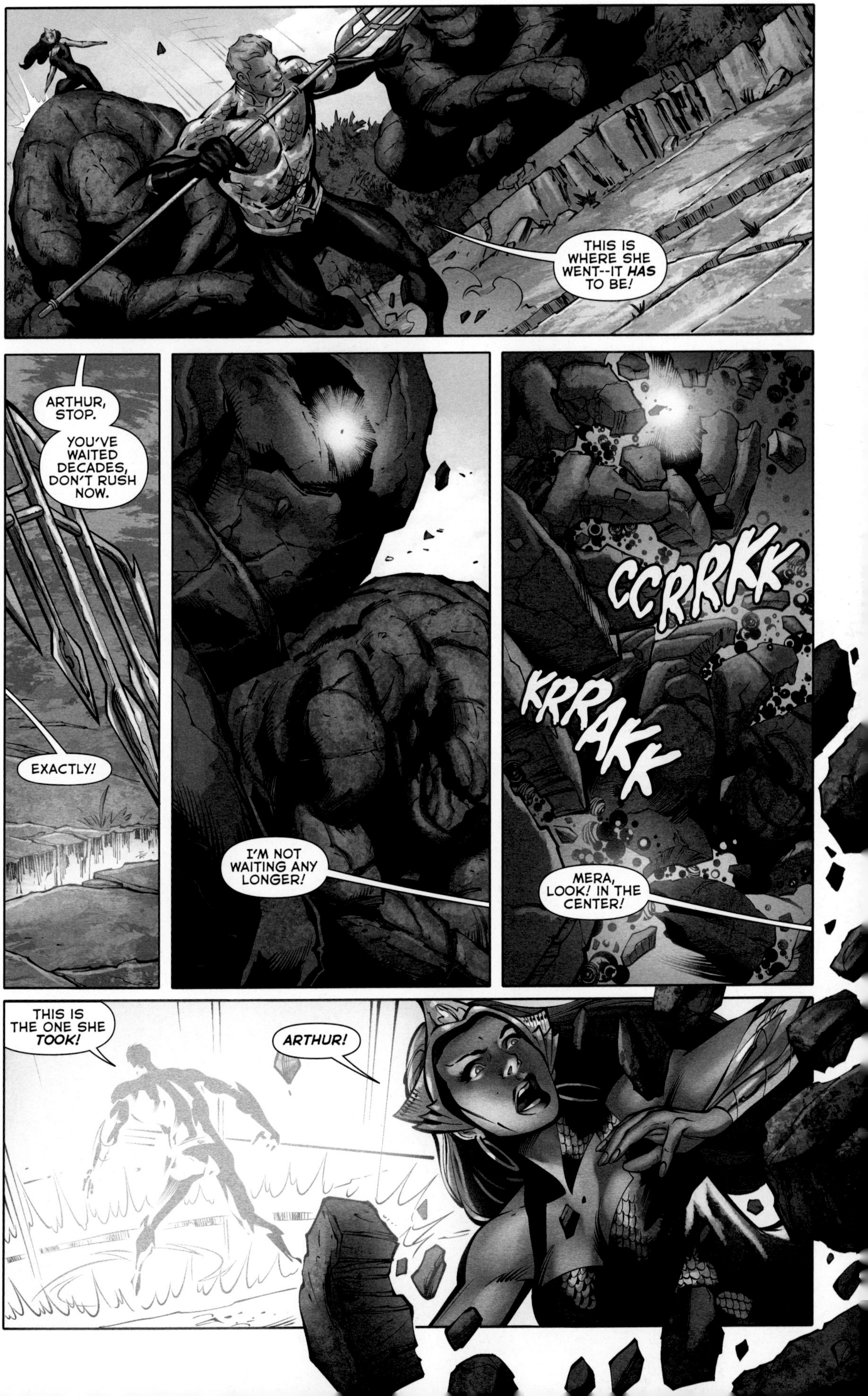
THIS IS WHERE SHE WENT--IT *HAS* TO BE!
ARTHUR, STOP.
YOU'VE WAITED DECADES, DON'T RUSH NOW.
EXACTLY!
I'M NOT WAITING ANY LONGER!
CCRRKK
KRRAKK
MERA, LOOK! IN THE CENTER!
THIS IS THE ONE SHE *TOOK!*
ARTHUR!

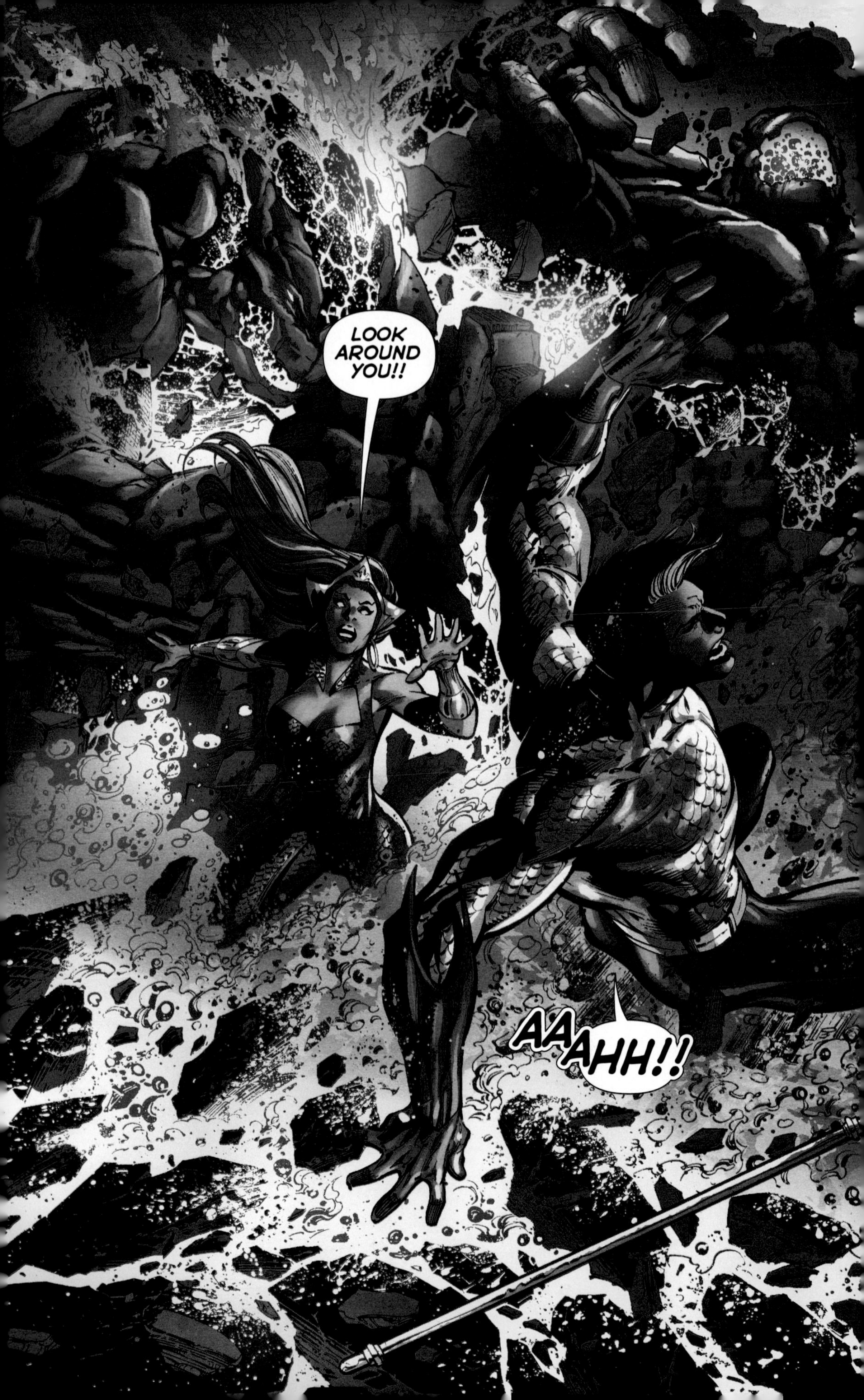
LOOK AROUND YOU!!
AAAHH!!

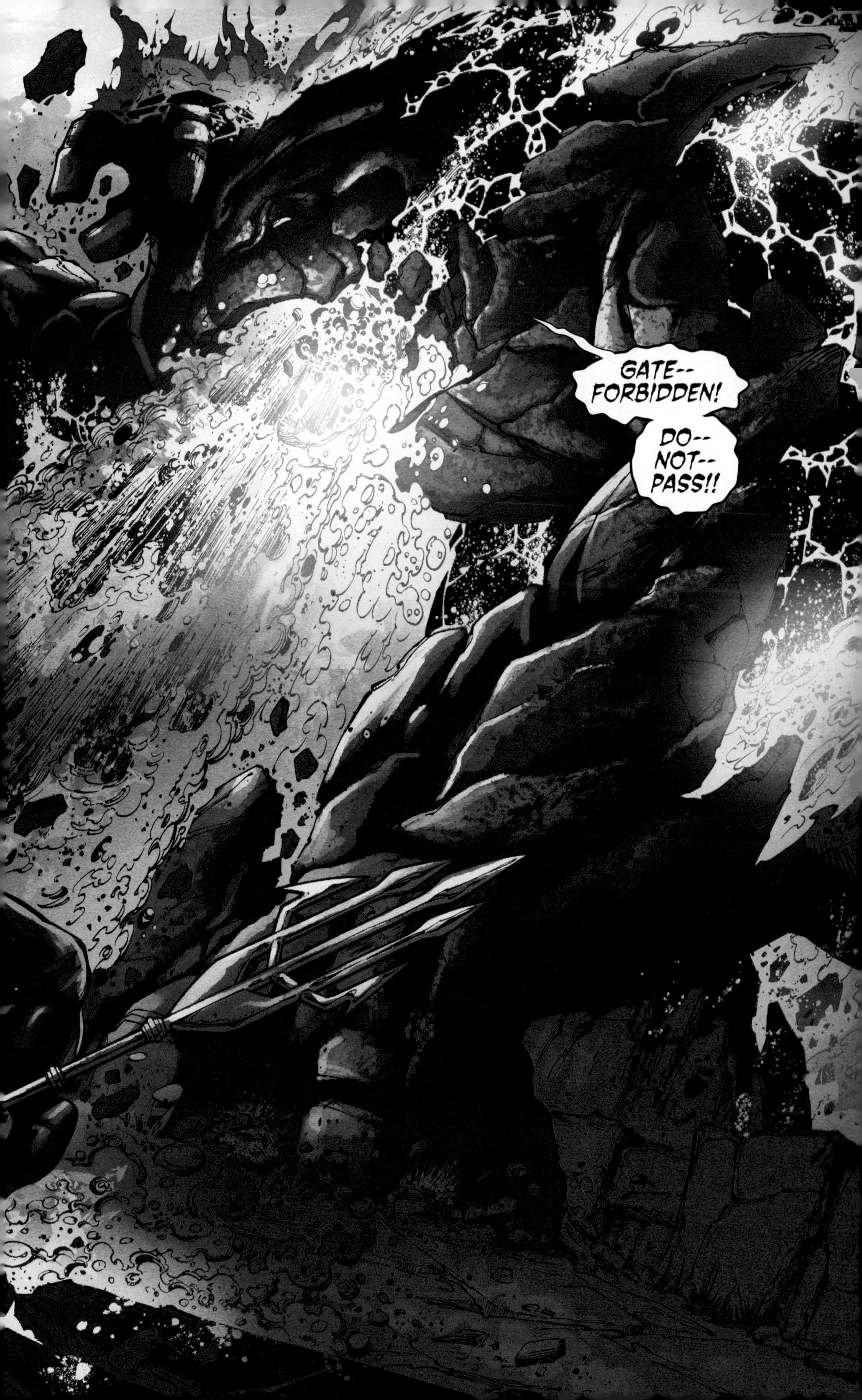
GATE--
FORBIDDEN!
DO--
NOT--
PASS!!

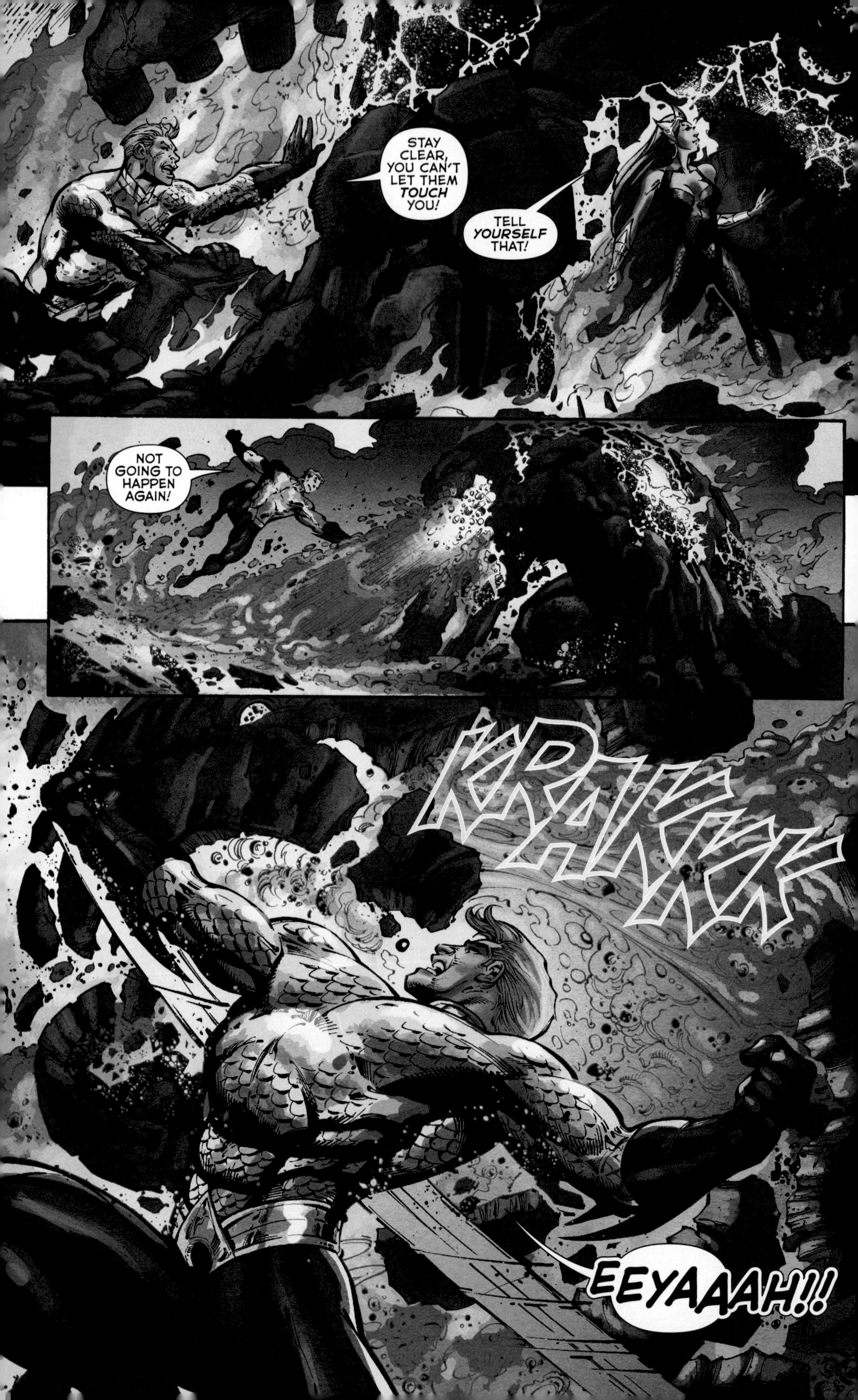
STAY CLEAR, YOU CAN'T LET THEM *TOUCH* YOU!
TELL *YOURSELF* THAT!
NOT GOING TO HAPPEN AGAIN!
KRAKKK
EEYAAAH!!

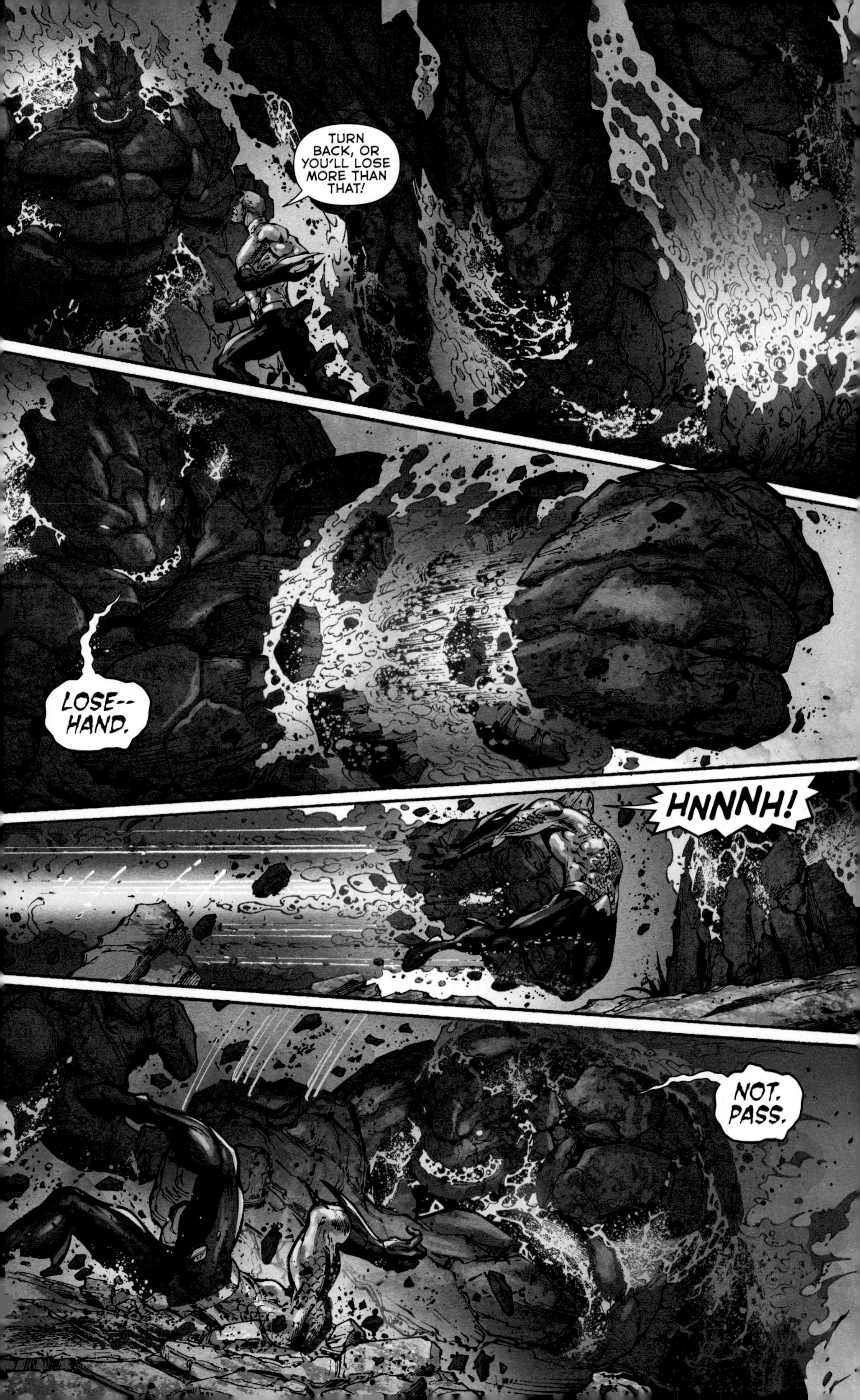
TURN BACK, OR YOU'LL LOSE MORE THAN THAT!
LOSE-- HAND.
HNNNH!
NOT. PASS.

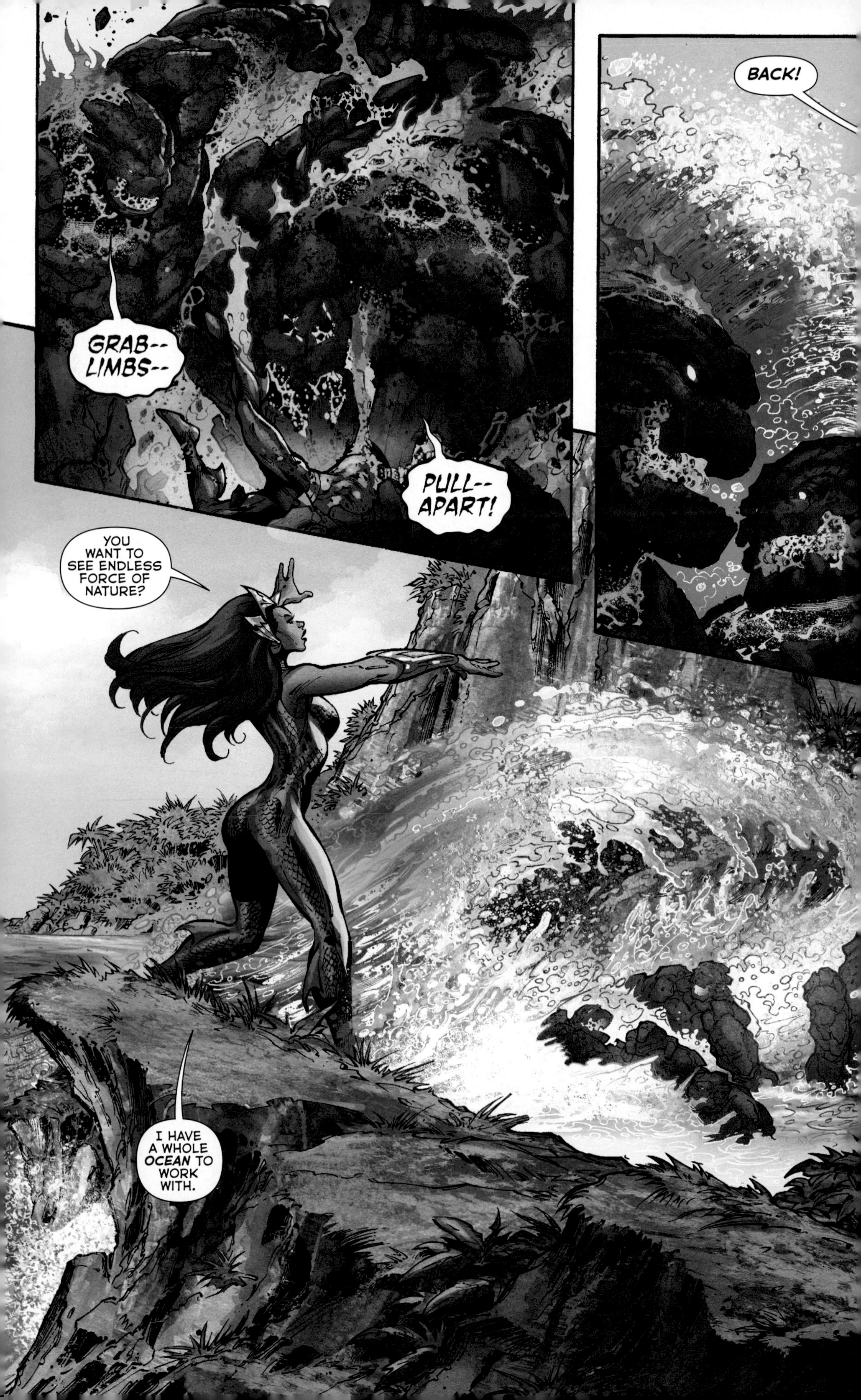
GRAB--
LIMBS--
PULL--
APART!
BACK!
YOU WANT TO SEE ENDLESS FORCE OF NATURE?
I HAVE A WHOLE OCEAN TO WORK WITH.

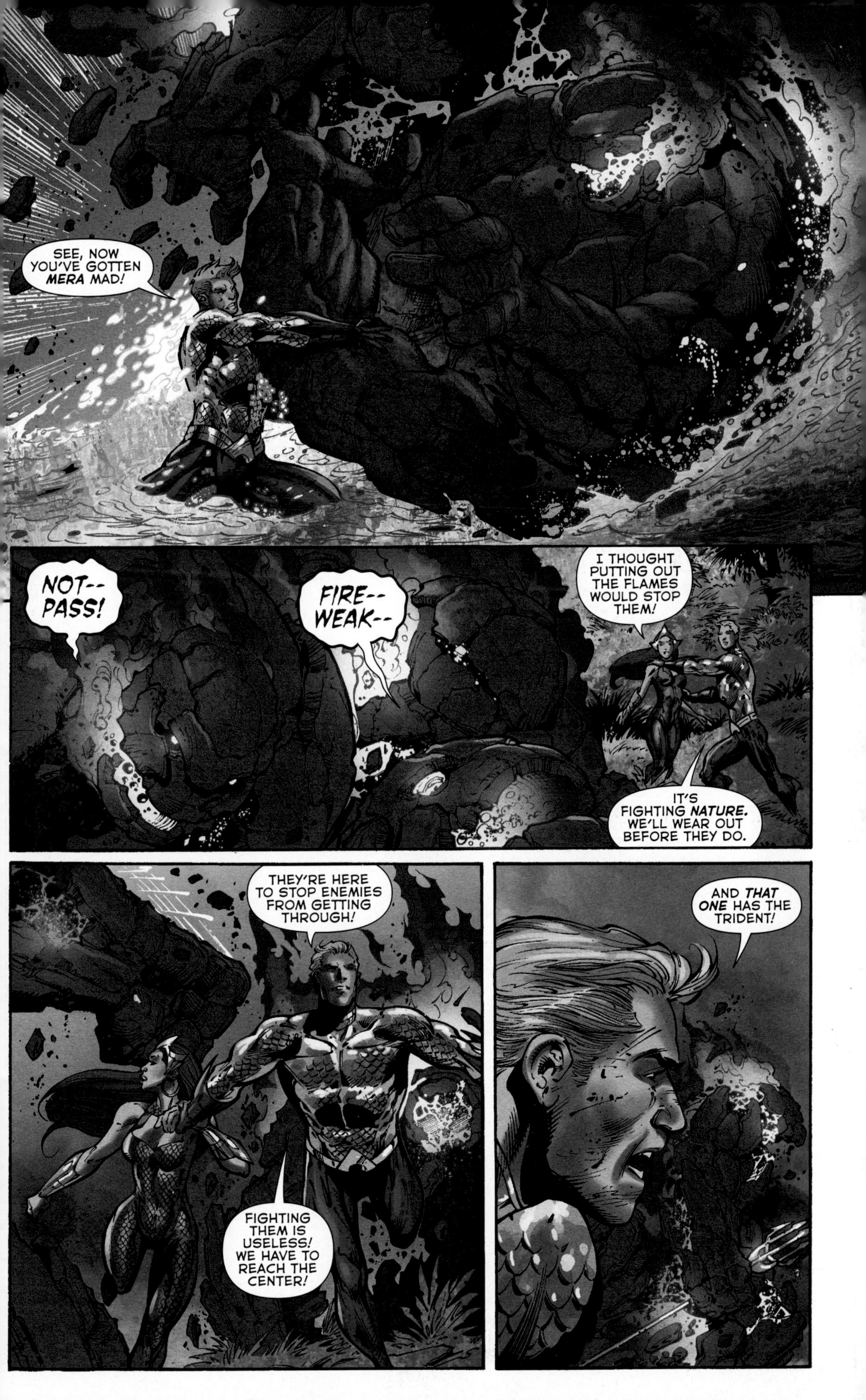
SEE, NOW YOU'VE GOTTEN *MERA* MAD!
NOT-- PASS!
FIRE-- WEAK--
I THOUGHT PUTTING OUT THE FLAMES WOULD STOP THEM!
IT'S FIGHTING *NATURE.* WE'LL WEAR OUT BEFORE THEY DO.
THEY'RE HERE TO STOP ENEMIES FROM GETTING THROUGH!
FIGHTING THEM IS USELESS! WE HAVE TO REACH THE CENTER!
AND *THAT ONE* HAS THE TRIDENT!

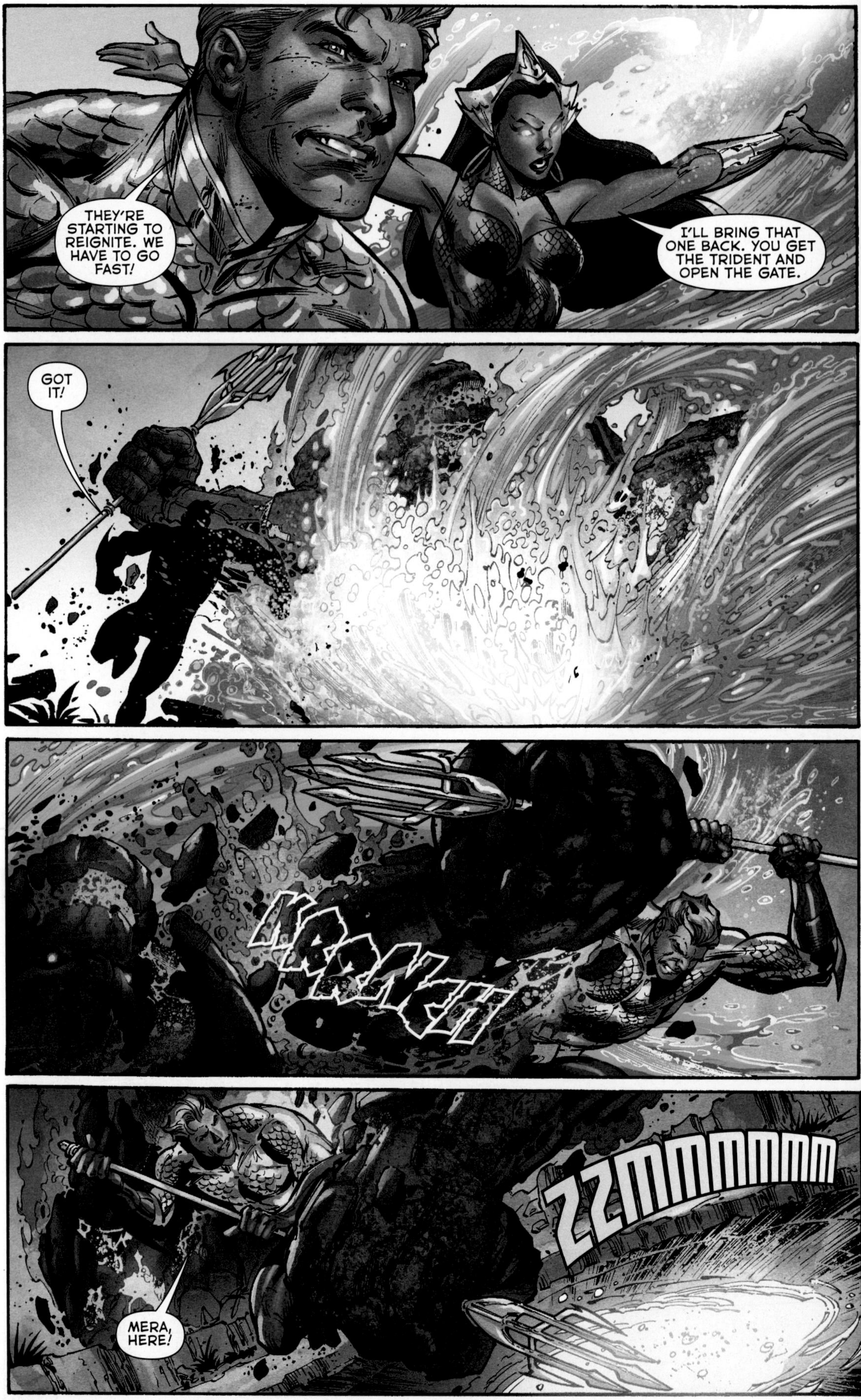
THEY'RE STARTING TO REIGNITE. WE HAVE TO GO FAST!
I'LL BRING THAT ONE BACK. YOU GET THE TRIDENT AND OPEN THE GATE.
GOT IT!
ZZMMMMMM
MERA, HERE!

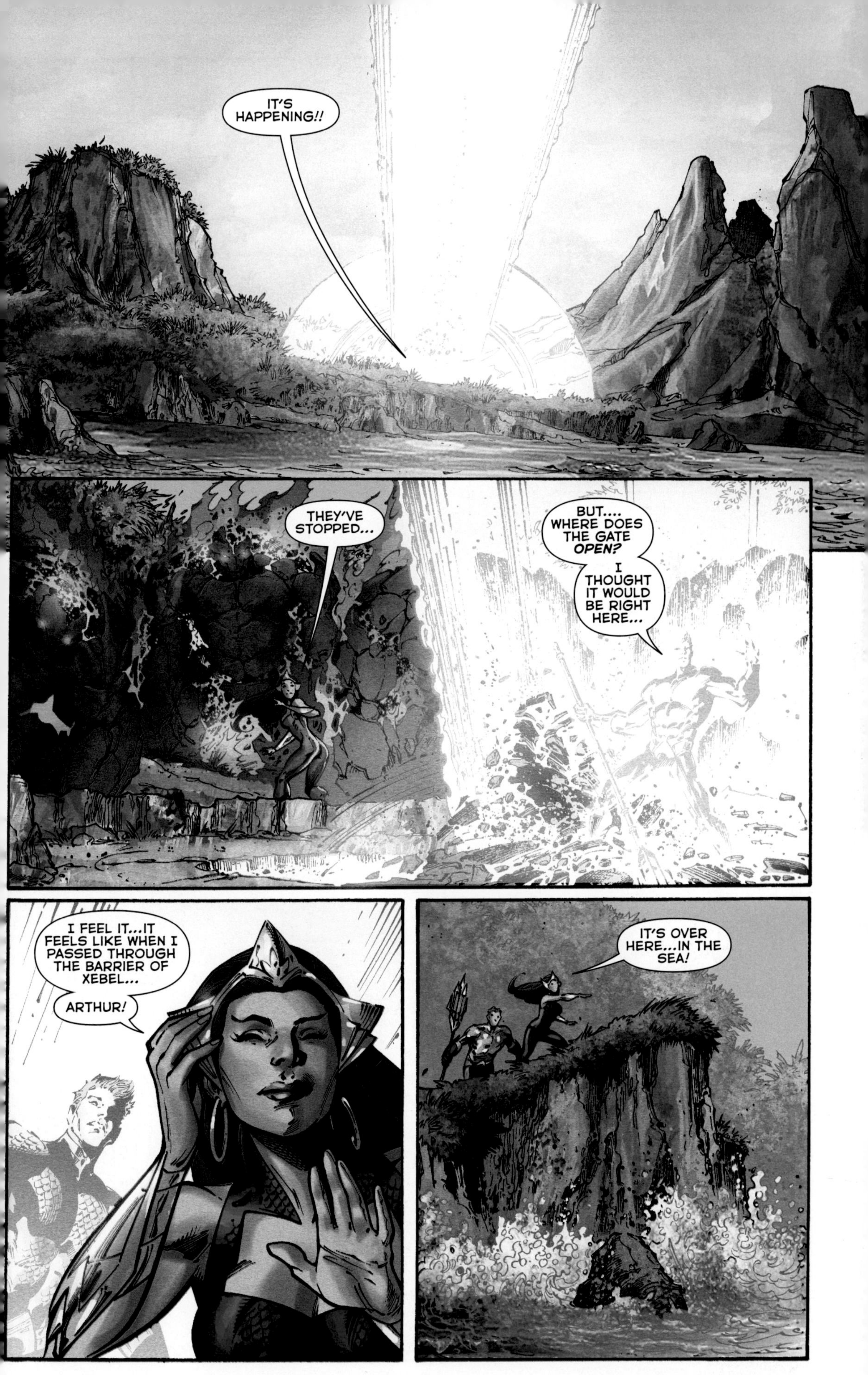
IT'S HAPPENING!!
THEY'VE STOPPED...
BUT.... WHERE DOES THE GATE OPEN?
I THOUGHT IT WOULD BE RIGHT HERE...
I FEEL IT...IT FEELS LIKE WHEN I PASSED THROUGH THE BARRIER OF XEBEL...
ARTHUR!
IT'S OVER HERE...IN THE SEA!

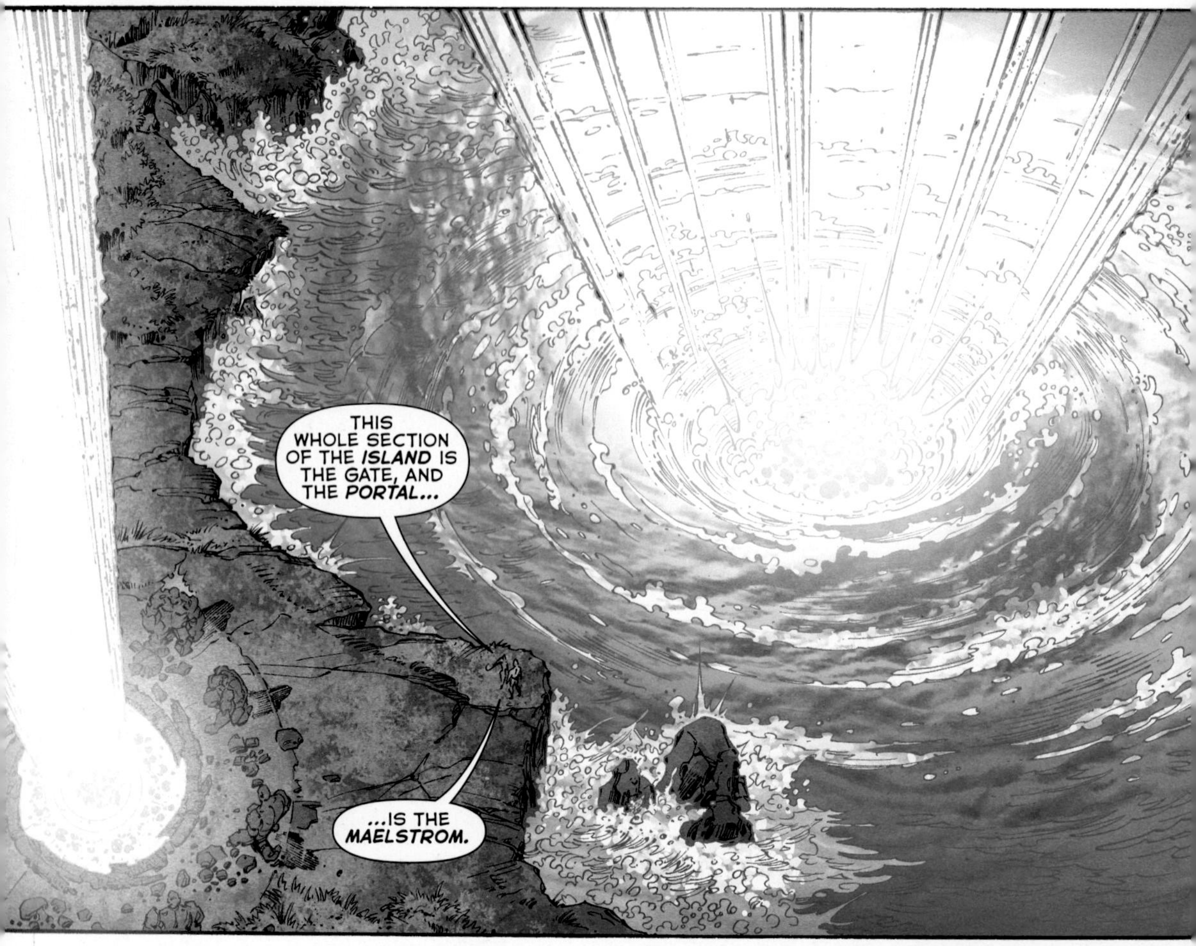
THIS WHOLE SECTION OF THE ISLAND IS THE GATE, AND THE PORTAL...
...IS THE MAELSTROM.
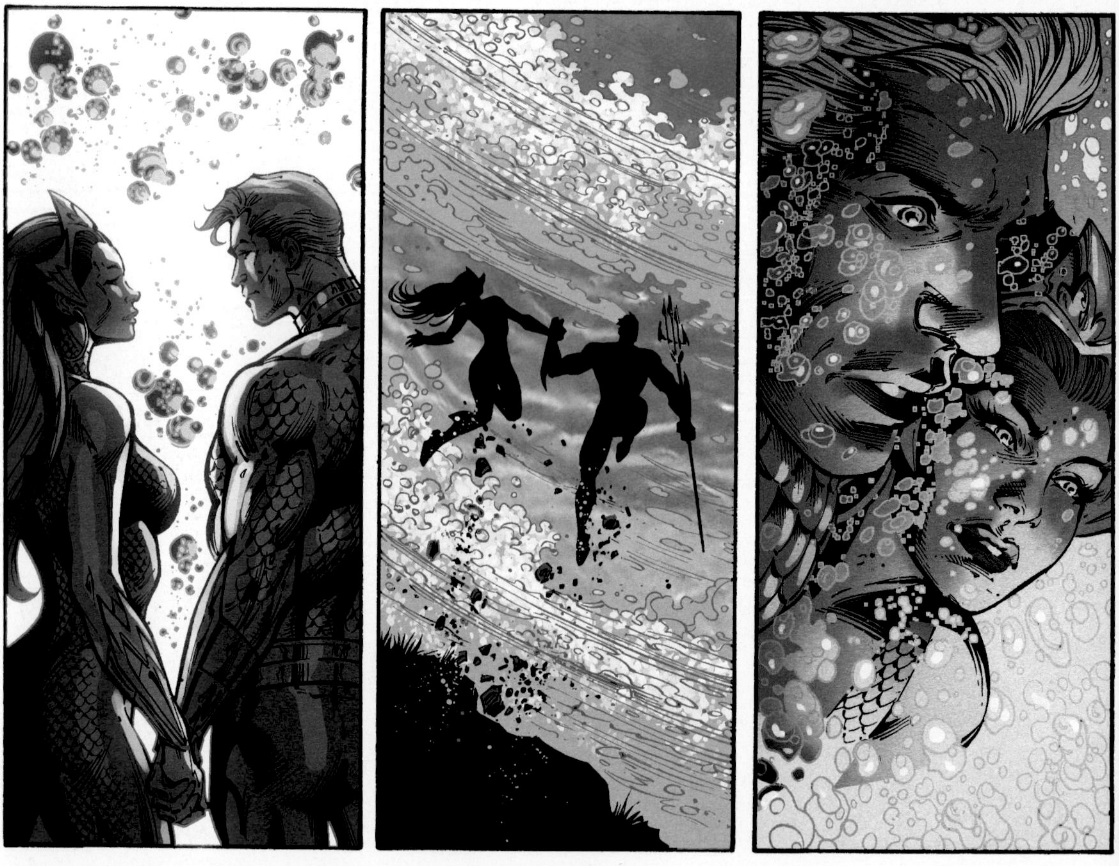

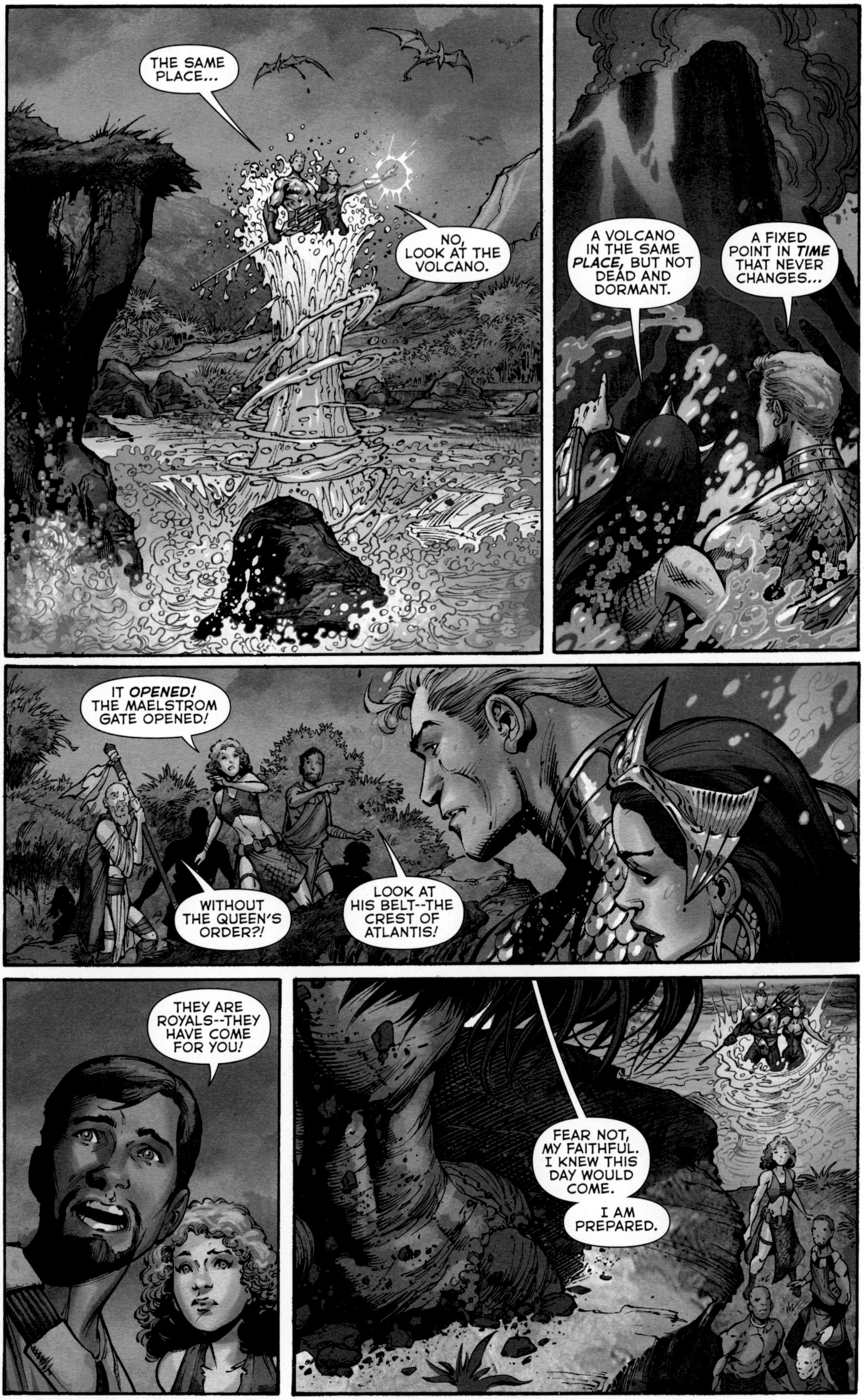
THE SAME PLACE...
NO, LOOK AT THE VOLCANO.
A VOLCANO IN THE SAME *PLACE,* BUT NOT DEAD AND DORMANT.
A FIXED POINT IN *TIME* THAT NEVER CHANGES...
IT *OPENED!* THE MAELSTROM GATE OPENED!
WITHOUT THE QUEEN'S ORDER?!
LOOK AT HIS BELT--THE CREST OF ATLANTIS!
THEY ARE ROYALS--THEY HAVE COME FOR YOU!
FEAR NOT, MY FAITHFUL. I KNEW THIS DAY WOULD COME.
I AM PREPARED.

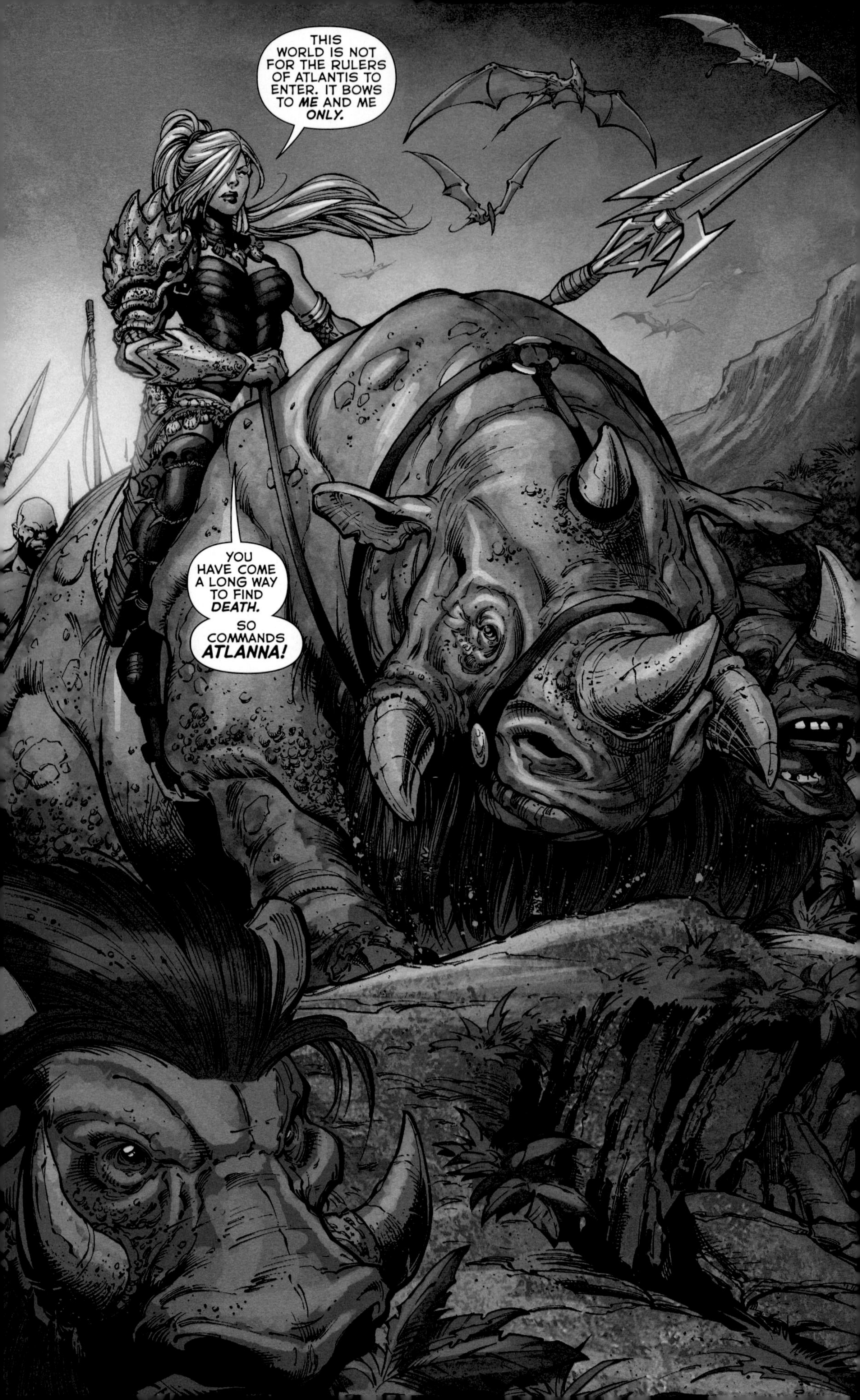
THIS WORLD IS NOT FOR THE RULERS OF ATLANTIS TO ENTER. IT BOWS TO ME AND ME ONLY.
YOU HAVE COME A LONG WAY TO FIND DEATH.
SO COMMANDS ATLANNA!

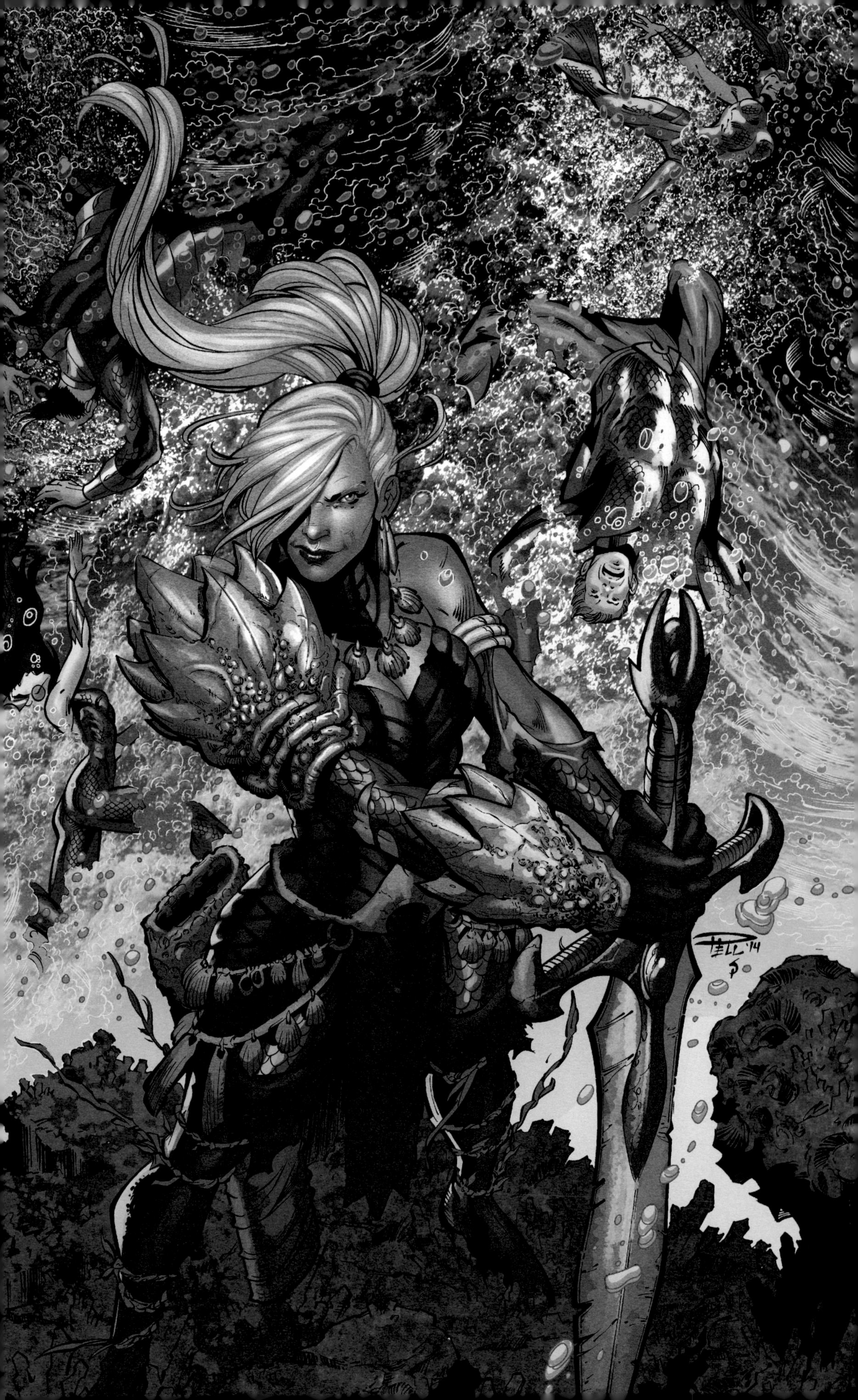

MAELSTROM PART V: PACIFICA

JEFF PARKER writer **PAUL PELLETIER** penciller **SANDRA HOPE, WAYNE FAUCHER** inkers **PETE PANTAZIS** colorist **TRAVIS LANHAM** letterer
PELLETIER, PARSONS and **BEREDO** cover art

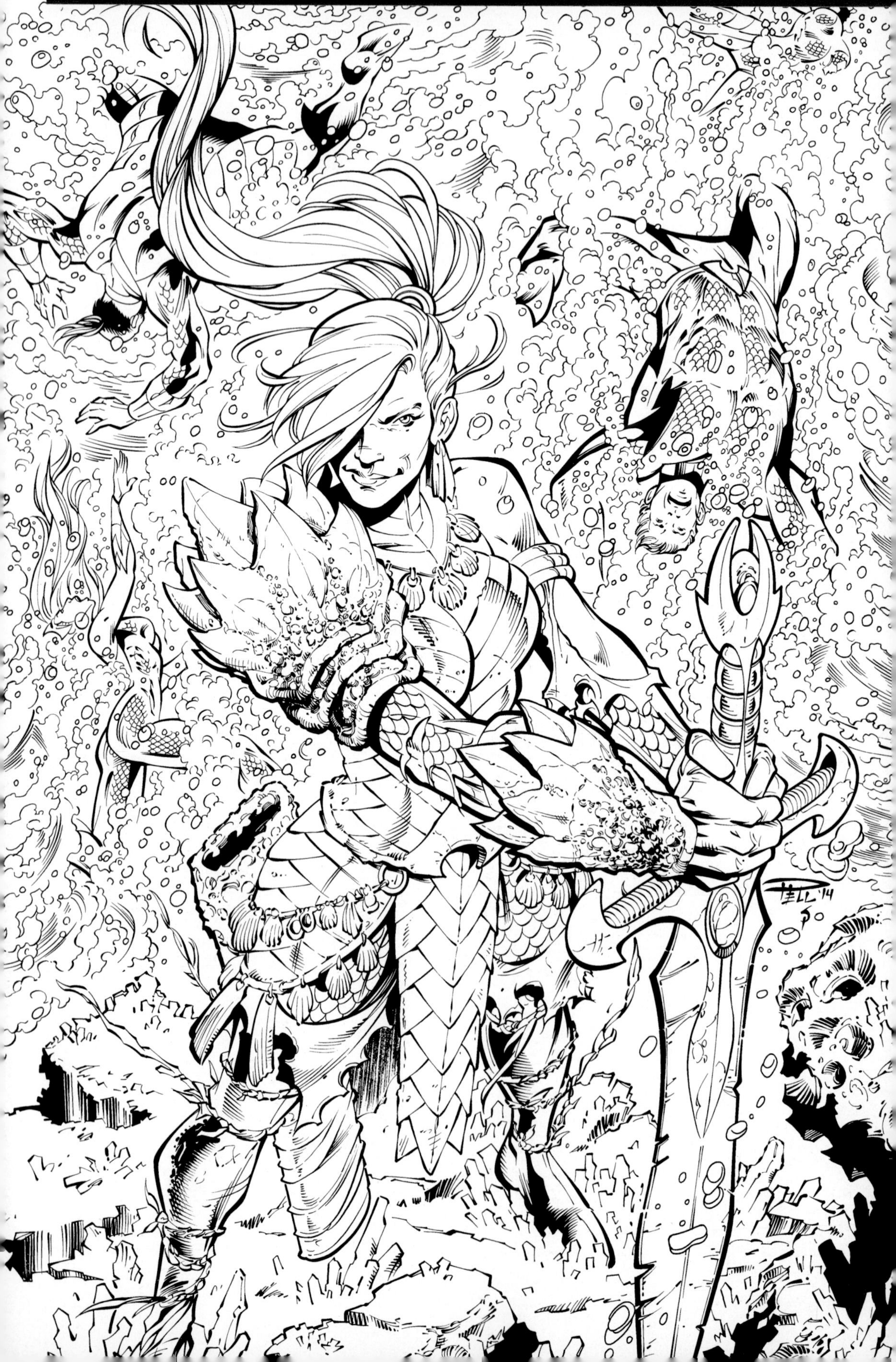

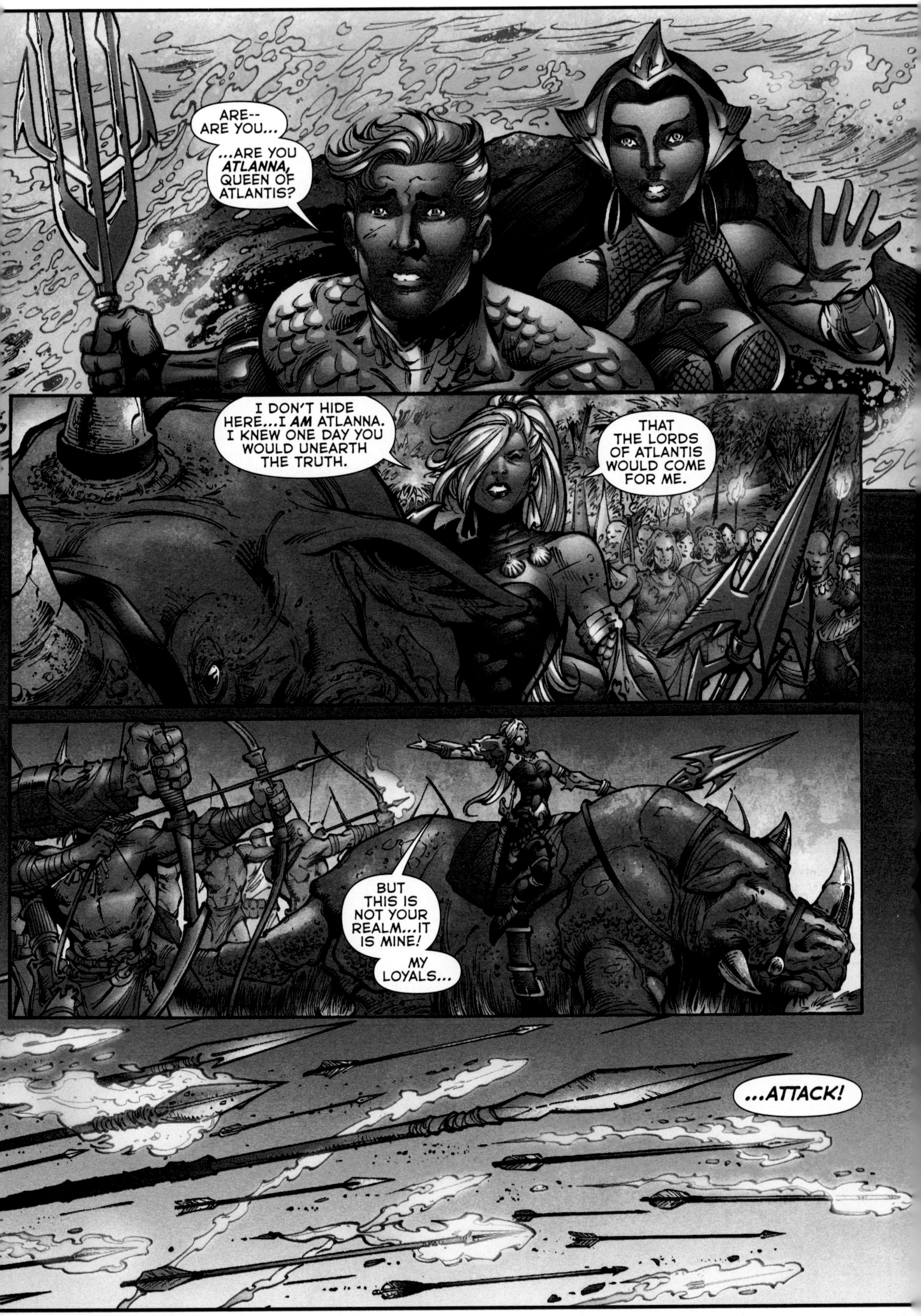
ARE-- ARE YOU...
...ARE YOU ATLANNA, QUEEN OF ATLANTIS?
I DON'T HIDE HERE...I AM ATLANNA. I KNEW ONE DAY YOU WOULD UNEARTH THE TRUTH.
THAT THE LORDS OF ATLANTIS WOULD COME FOR ME.
BUT THIS IS NOT YOUR REALM...IT IS MINE!
MY LOYALS...
...ATTACK!

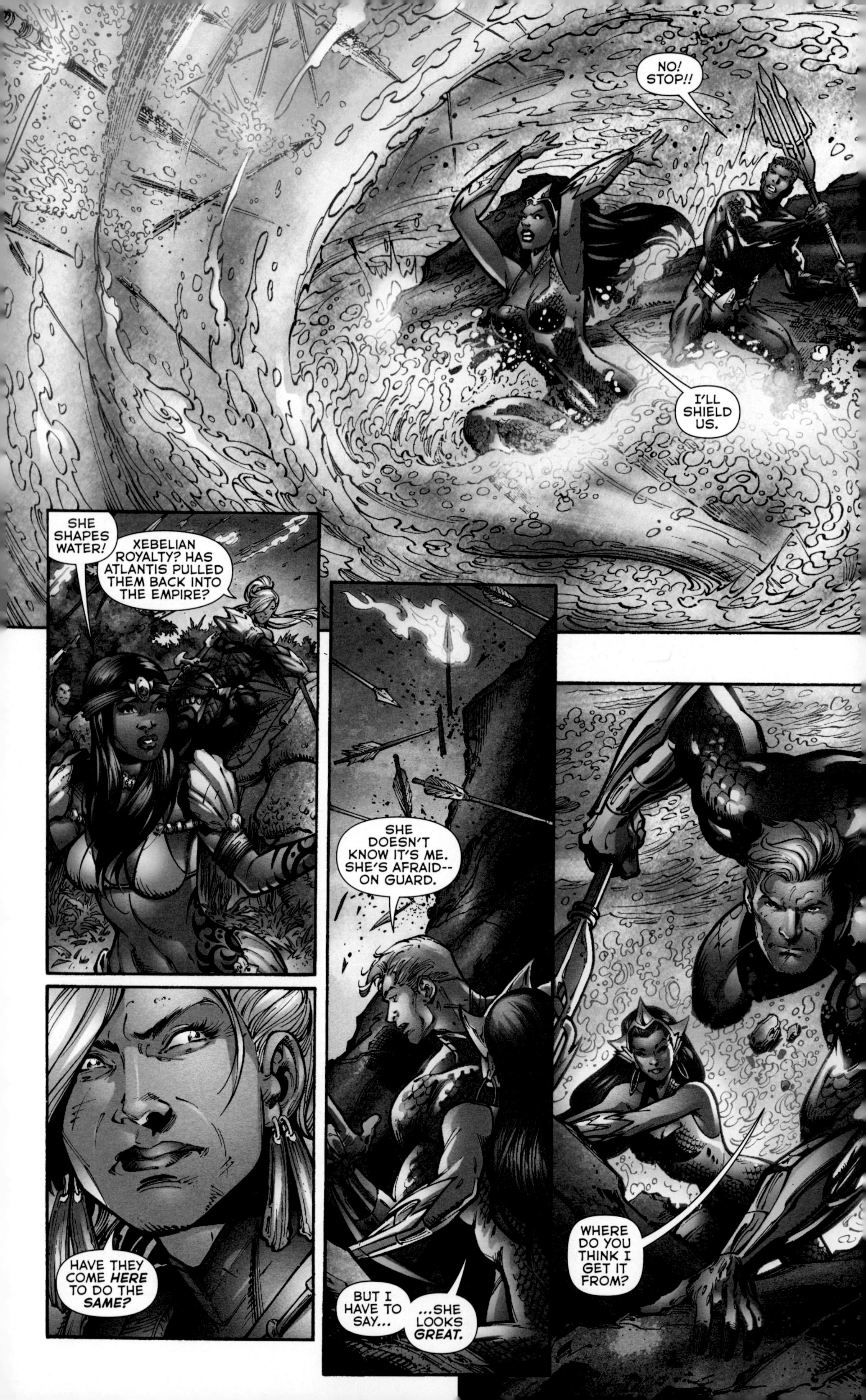
NO! STOP!!
I'LL SHIELD US.
SHE SHAPES WATER!
XEBELIAN ROYALTY? HAS ATLANTIS PULLED THEM BACK INTO THE EMPIRE?
HAVE THEY COME HERE TO DO THE SAME?
SHE DOESN'T KNOW IT'S ME. SHE'S AFRAID-- ON GUARD.
BUT I HAVE TO SAY...
...SHE LOOKS GREAT.
WHERE DO YOU THINK I GET IT FROM?

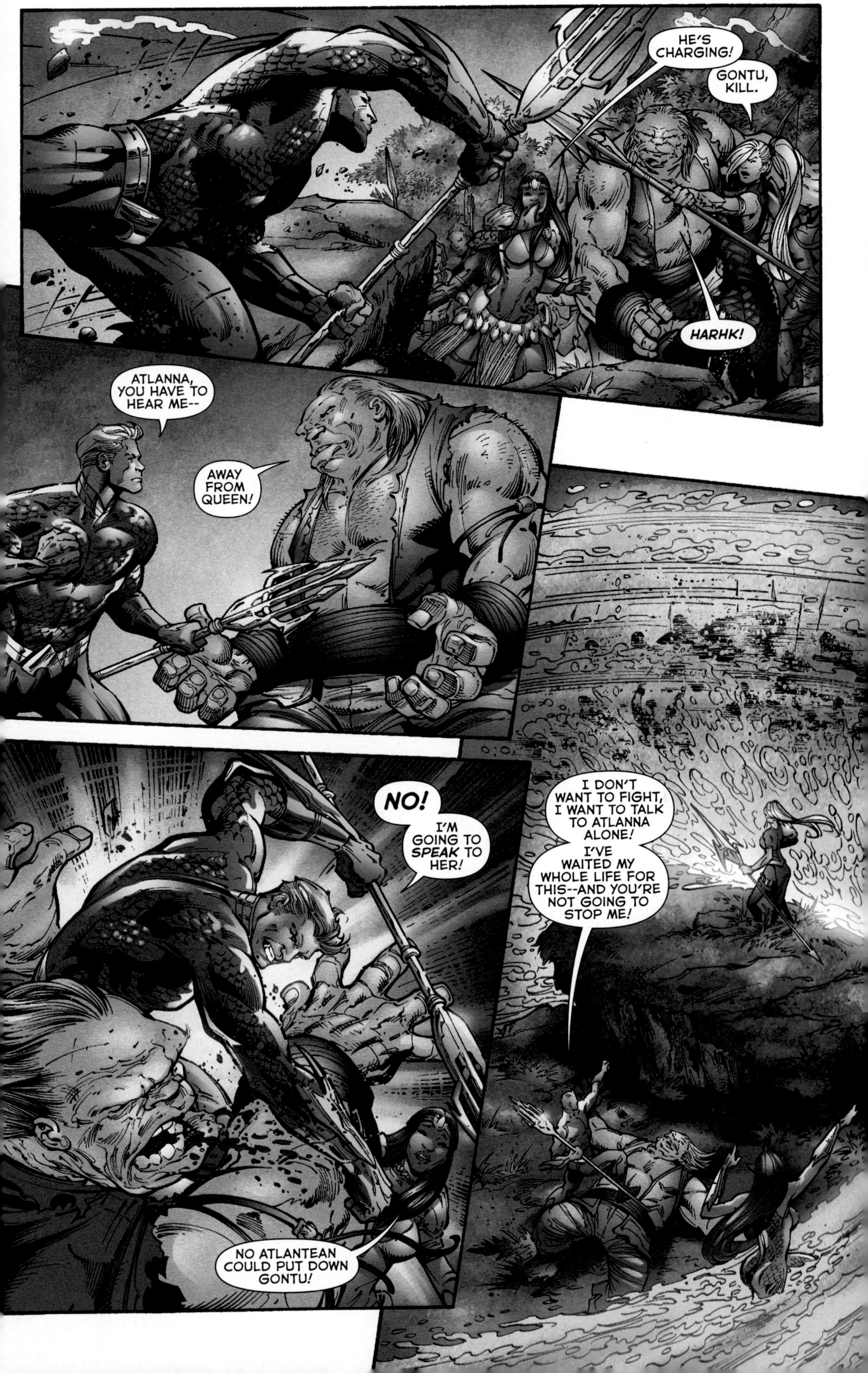

HE'S CHARGING!
GONTU, KILL.
HARHK!
ATLANNA, YOU HAVE TO HEAR ME--
AWAY FROM QUEEN!
NO!
I'M GOING TO SPEAK TO HER!
NO ATLANTEAN COULD PUT DOWN GONTU!
I DON'T WANT TO FIGHT, I WANT TO TALK TO ATLANNA ALONE!
I'VE WAITED MY WHOLE LIFE FOR THIS--AND YOU'RE NOT GOING TO STOP ME!

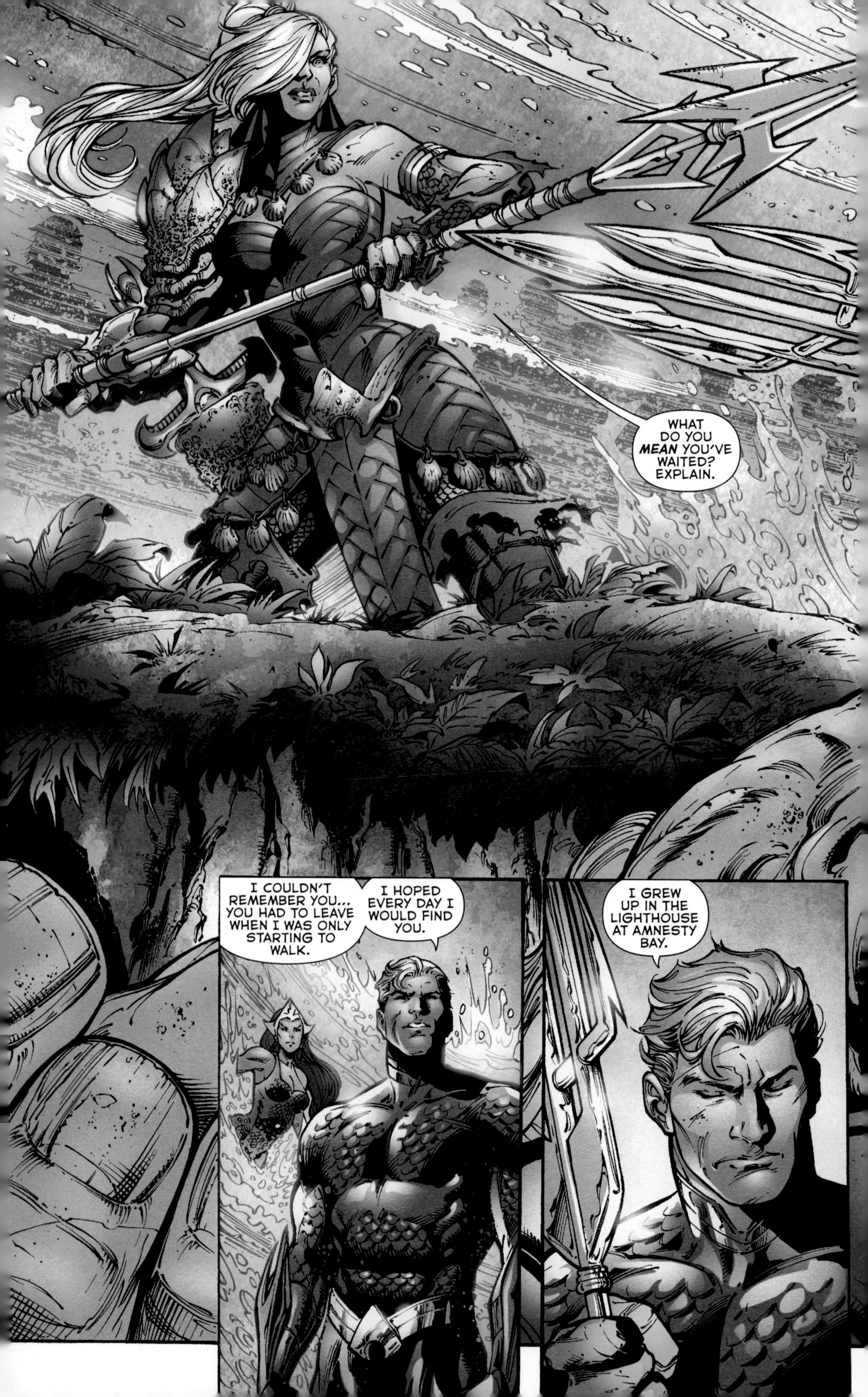
WHAT DO YOU *MEAN* YOU'VE WAITED? EXPLAIN.
I COULDN'T REMEMBER YOU... YOU HAD TO LEAVE WHEN I WAS ONLY STARTING TO WALK.
I HOPED EVERY DAY I WOULD FIND YOU.
I GREW UP IN THE LIGHTHOUSE AT AMNESTY BAY.

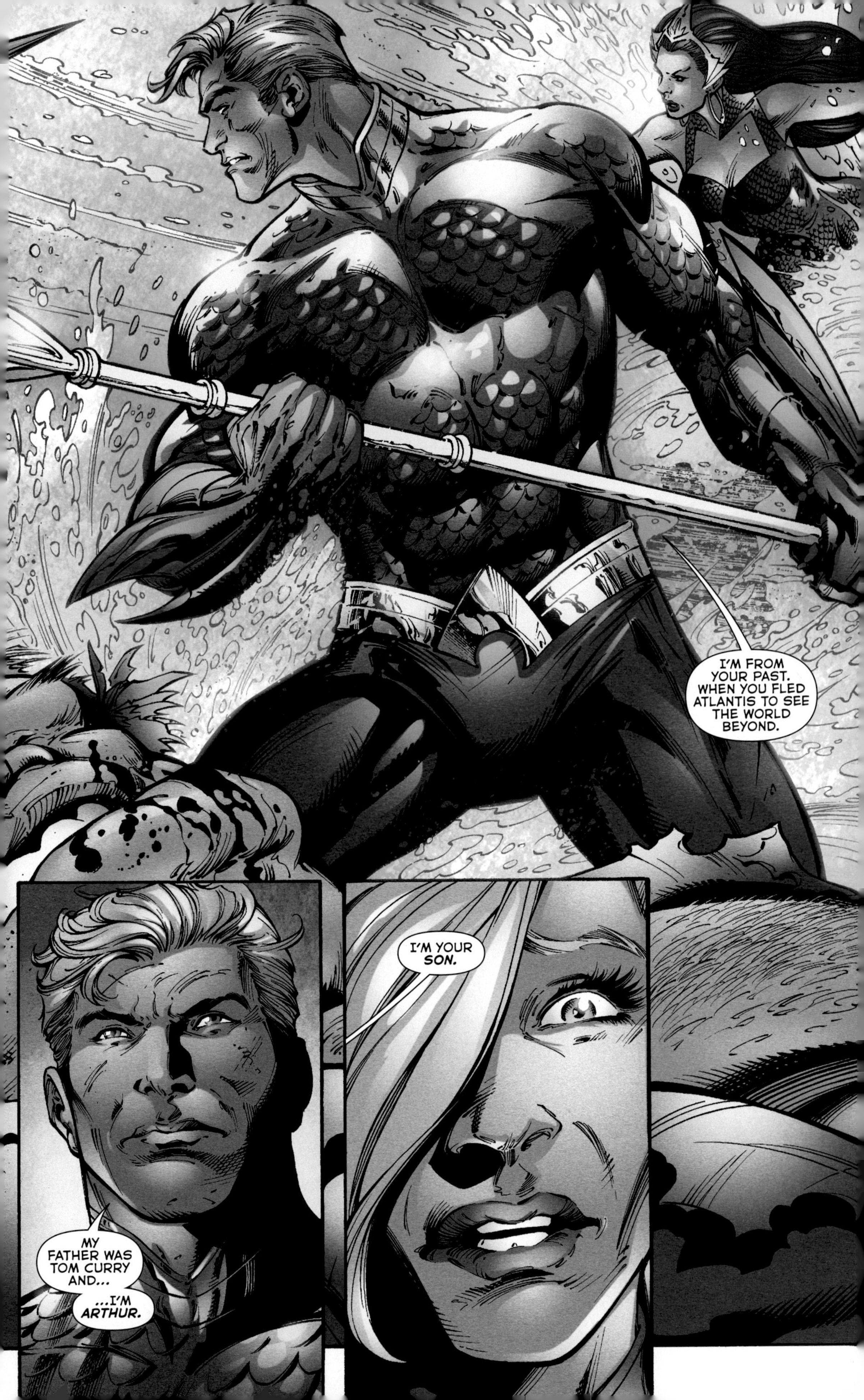
I'M FROM YOUR PAST. WHEN YOU FLED ATLANTIS TO SEE THE WORLD BEYOND.
MY FATHER WAS TOM CURRY AND...
...I'M ARTHUR.
I'M YOUR SON.

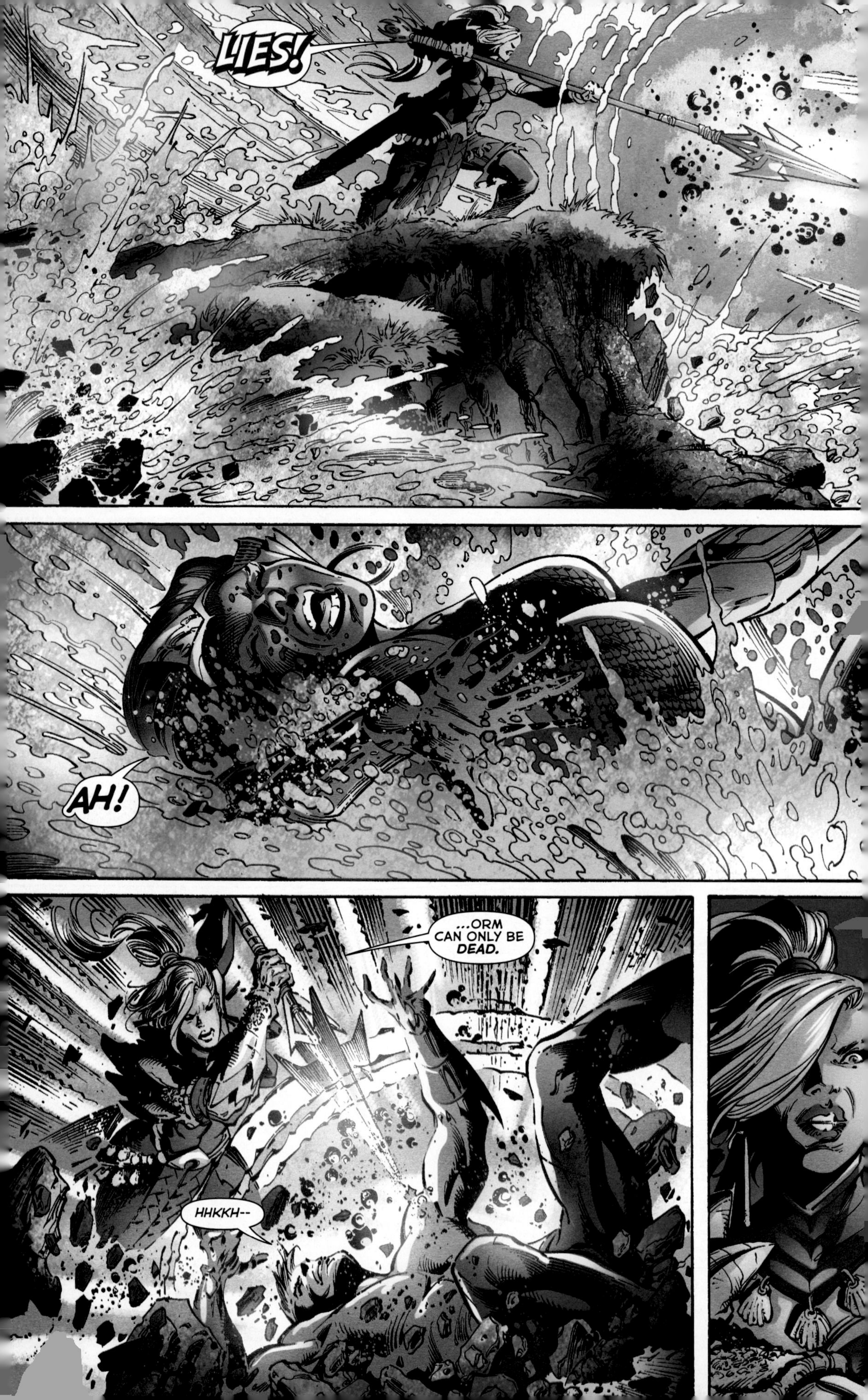
LIES!
AH!
...ORM CAN ONLY BE DEAD.
HHKKH--

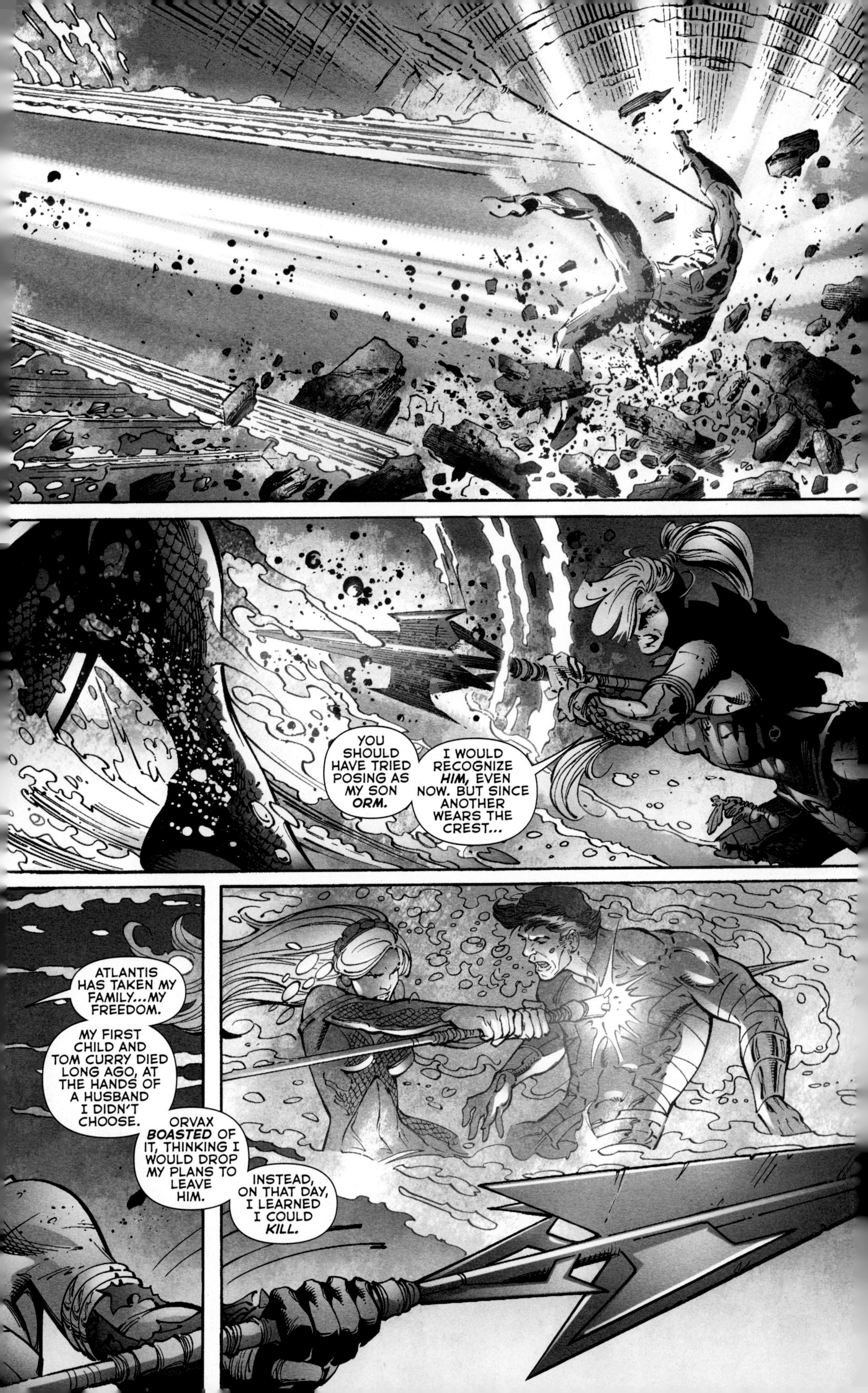
YOU SHOULD HAVE TRIED POSING AS MY SON *ORM.*
I WOULD RECOGNIZE *HIM,* EVEN NOW. BUT SINCE ANOTHER WEARS THE CREST...
ATLANTIS HAS TAKEN MY FAMILY...MY FREEDOM.
MY FIRST CHILD AND TOM CURRY DIED LONG AGO, AT THE HANDS OF A HUSBAND I DIDN'T CHOOSE.
ORVAX *BOASTED* OF IT, THINKING I WOULD DROP MY PLANS TO LEAVE HIM.
INSTEAD, ON THAT DAY, I LEARNED I COULD *KILL.*

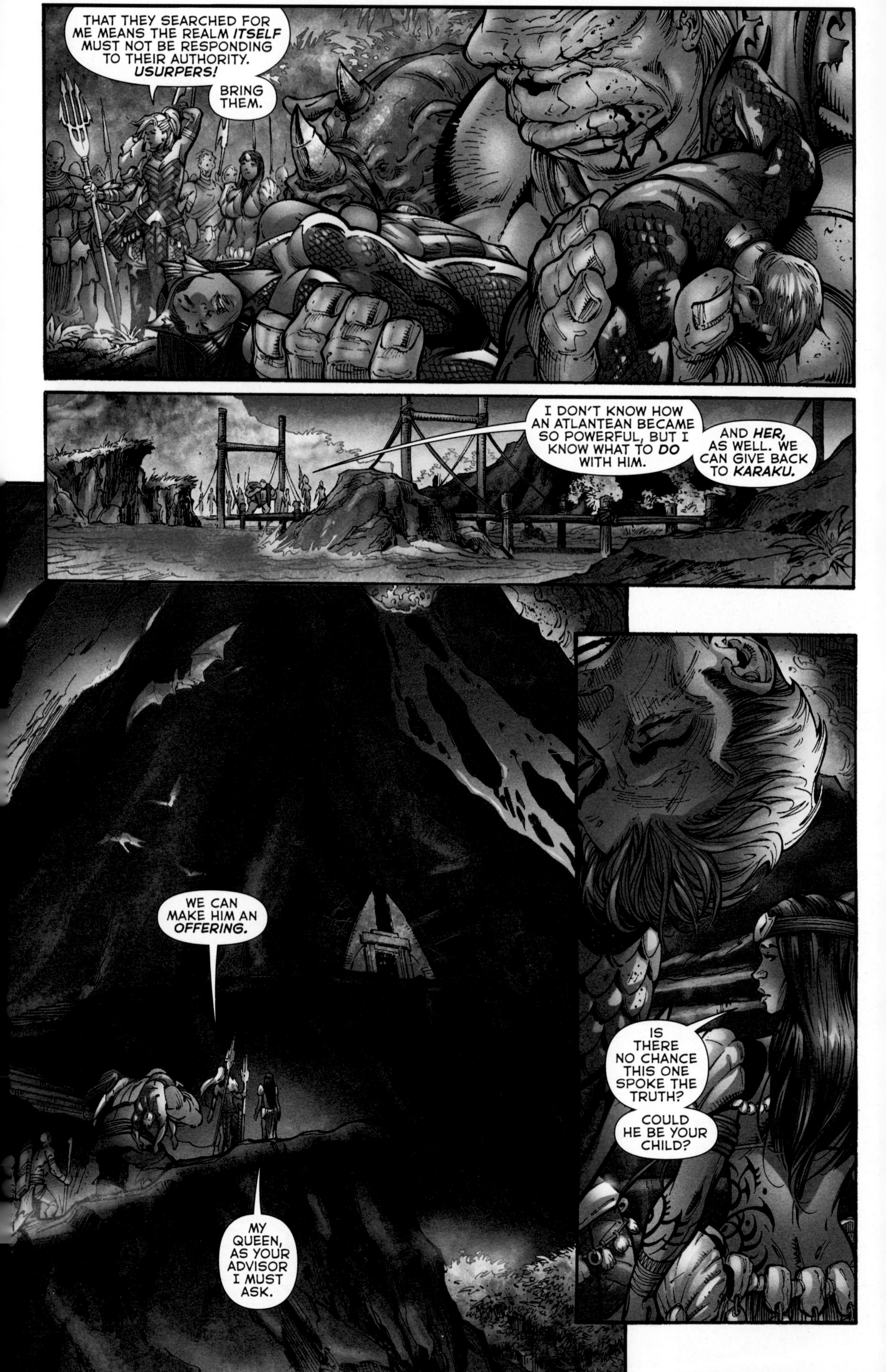
THAT THEY SEARCHED FOR ME MEANS THE REALM ITSELF MUST NOT BE RESPONDING TO THEIR AUTHORITY. USURPERS!
BRING THEM.
I DON'T KNOW HOW AN ATLANTEAN BECAME SO POWERFUL, BUT I KNOW WHAT TO DO WITH HIM.
AND HER, AS WELL. WE CAN GIVE BACK TO KARAKU.
WE CAN MAKE HIM AN OFFERING.
MY QUEEN, AS YOUR ADVISOR I MUST ASK.
IS THERE NO CHANCE THIS ONE SPOKE THE TRUTH?
COULD HE BE YOUR CHILD?

YOU GREW UP A NOMAD, LENU. YOU DON'T KNOW THE TREACHERY OF ATLANTEAN RULE.

THE COUNCIL WHO RESENT THE ROYALS.

THE MILITARY CHIEFS WHO HOPE TO MARRY *INTO* THAT ROYALTY AND TAKE OVER.

IT WAS ALWAYS THAT WAY. IN MY TIME MARRIED TO ORVAX MARIUS, I SOUGHT OUT LOST KNOWLEDGE THAT MIGHT HELP ME.

THAT'S HOW I LEARNED ABOUT THE *MAELSTROM,* AND HOW IT LED HERE.

TO *PACIFICA.*

THIS ARCHIPELAGO WAS TO BE A NEW HOME FOR THOSE WHO DIDN'T WANT TO EMBRACE LIFE BELOW THE WAVES, WHEN ATLANTIS WAS SLOWLY SINKING.

ANCIENTS SECRETLY CULTIVATED IT, STOCKED IT WITH THE ATLANTEAN BEASTS.

BUT ALL PEOPLE WERE TURNED BACK OR KILLED. ONLY *YOU* COULD FINISH WHAT THEY STARTED.

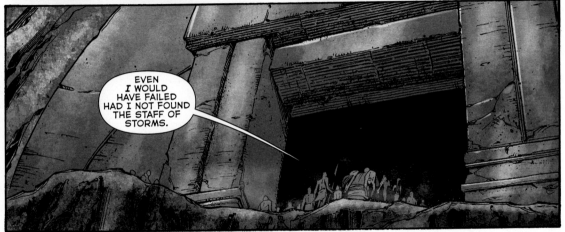

EVEN *I* WOULD HAVE FAILED HAD I NOT FOUND THE STAFF OF STORMS.

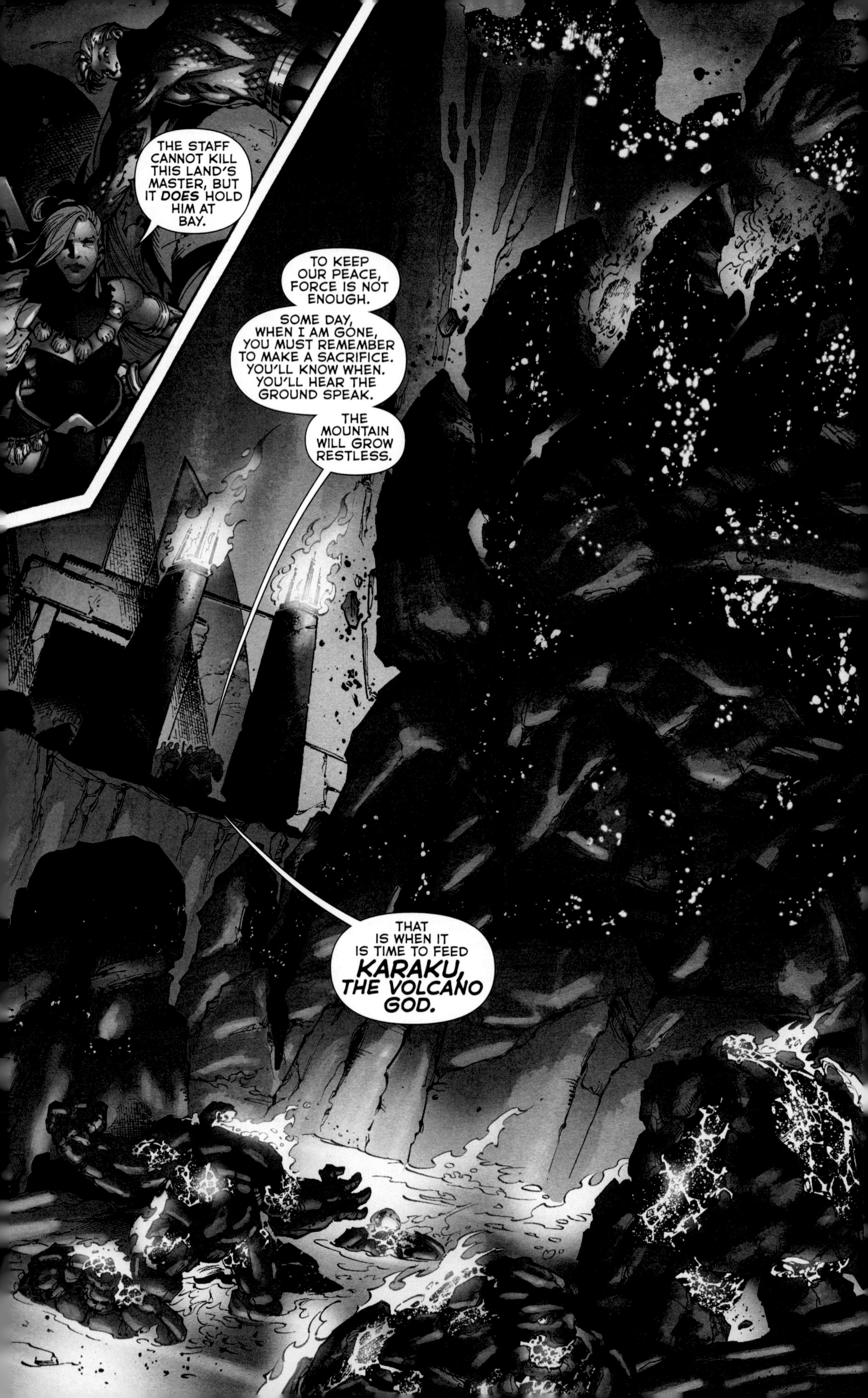
THE STAFF CANNOT KILL THIS LAND'S MASTER, BUT IT *DOES* HOLD HIM AT BAY.
TO KEEP OUR PEACE, FORCE IS NOT ENOUGH.
SOME DAY, WHEN I AM GONE, YOU MUST REMEMBER TO MAKE A SACRIFICE. YOU'LL KNOW WHEN. YOU'LL HEAR THE GROUND SPEAK.
THE MOUNTAIN WILL GROW RESTLESS.
THAT IS WHEN IT IS TIME TO FEED ***KARAKU, THE VOLCANO GOD.***

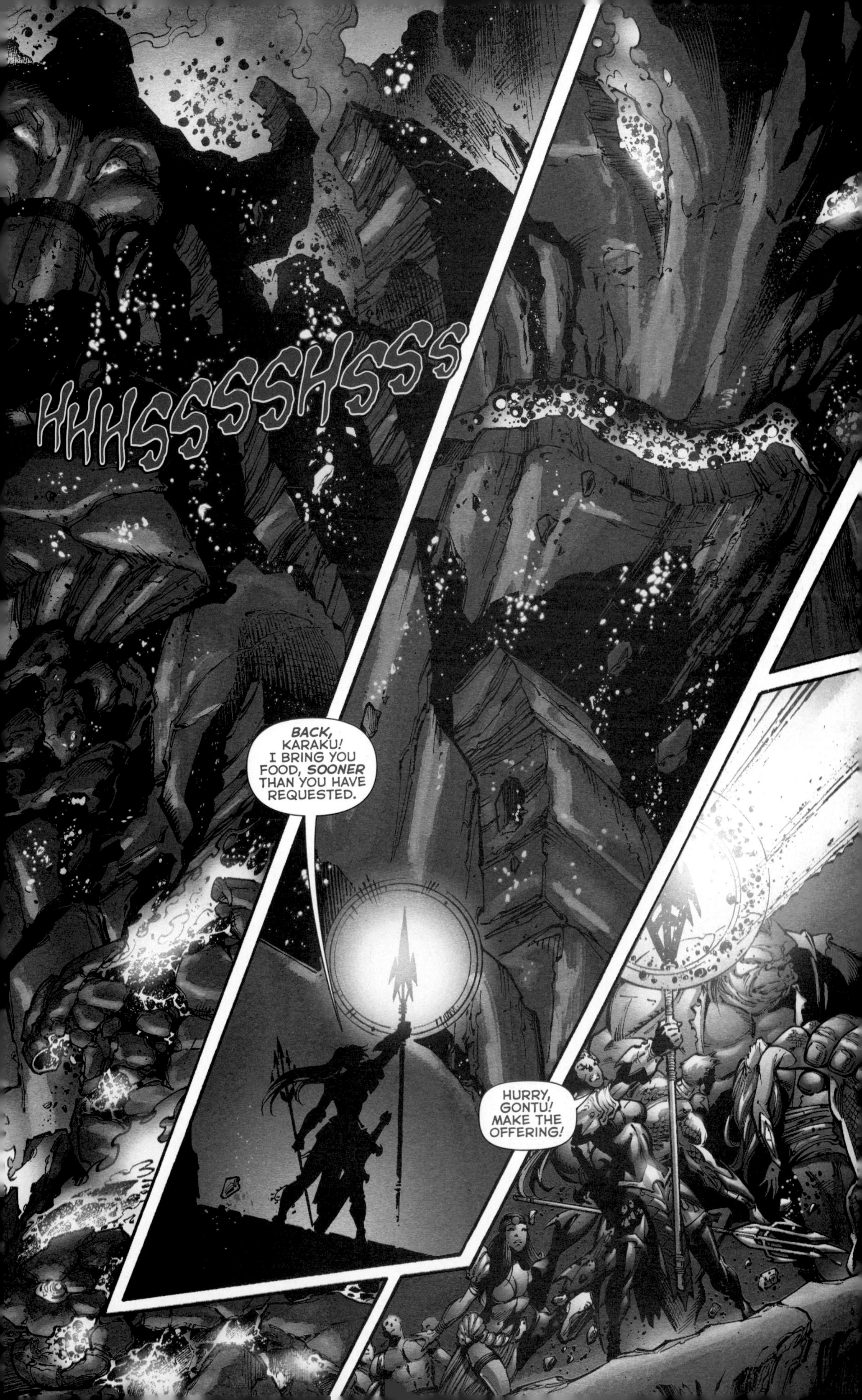
HHHSSSSSHSSS
BACK, KARAKU! I BRING YOU FOOD, SOONER THAN YOU HAVE REQUESTED.
HURRY, GONTU! MAKE THE OFFERING!

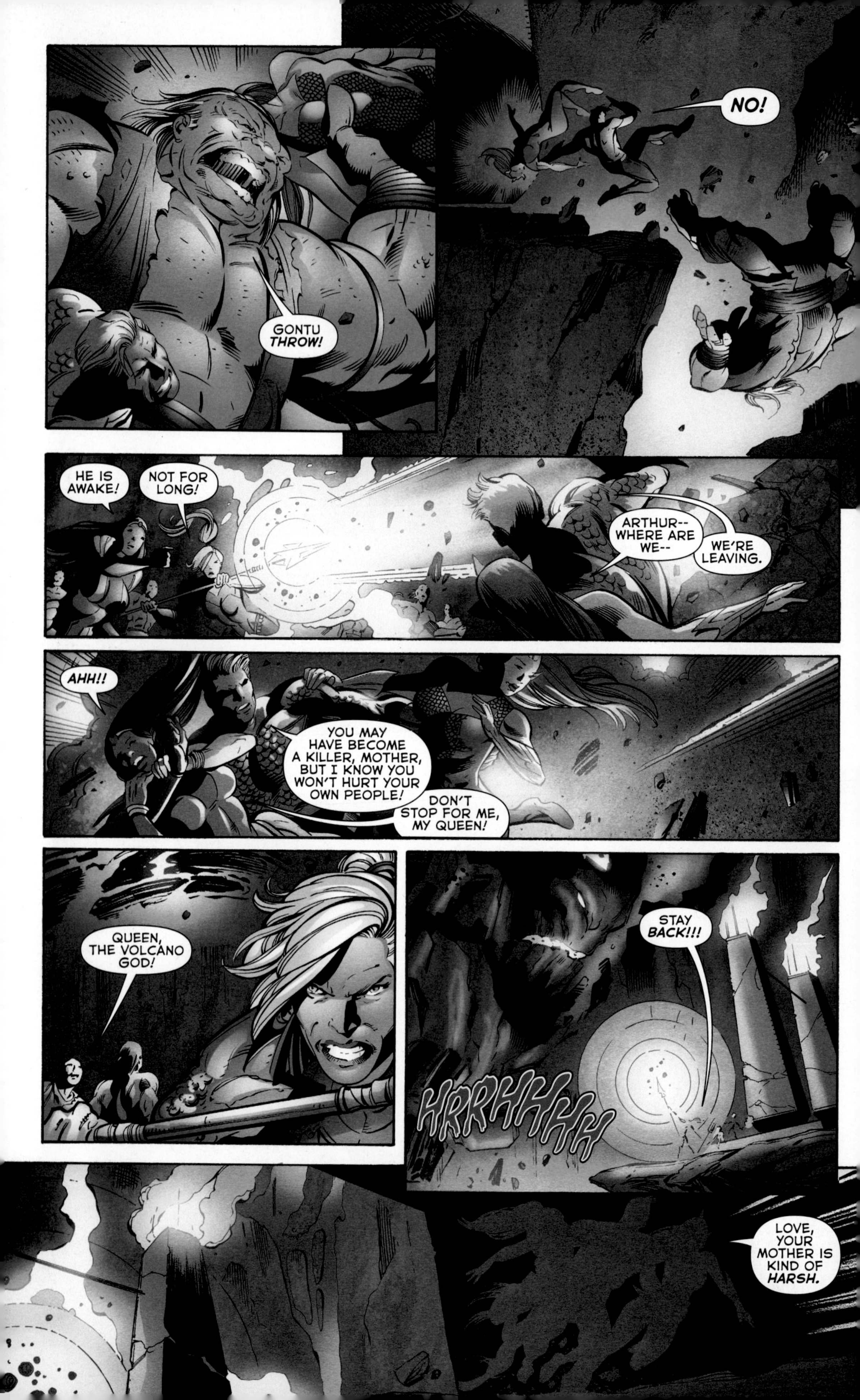

GONTU THROW!
NO!
HE IS AWAKE!
NOT FOR LONG!
ARTHUR-- WHERE ARE WE--
WE'RE LEAVING.
AHH!!
YOU MAY HAVE BECOME A KILLER, MOTHER, BUT I KNOW YOU WON'T HURT YOUR OWN PEOPLE!
DON'T STOP FOR ME, MY QUEEN!
QUEEN, THE VOLCANO GOD!
STAY BACK!!!
HRRHHHH
LOVE, YOUR MOTHER IS KIND OF HARSH.

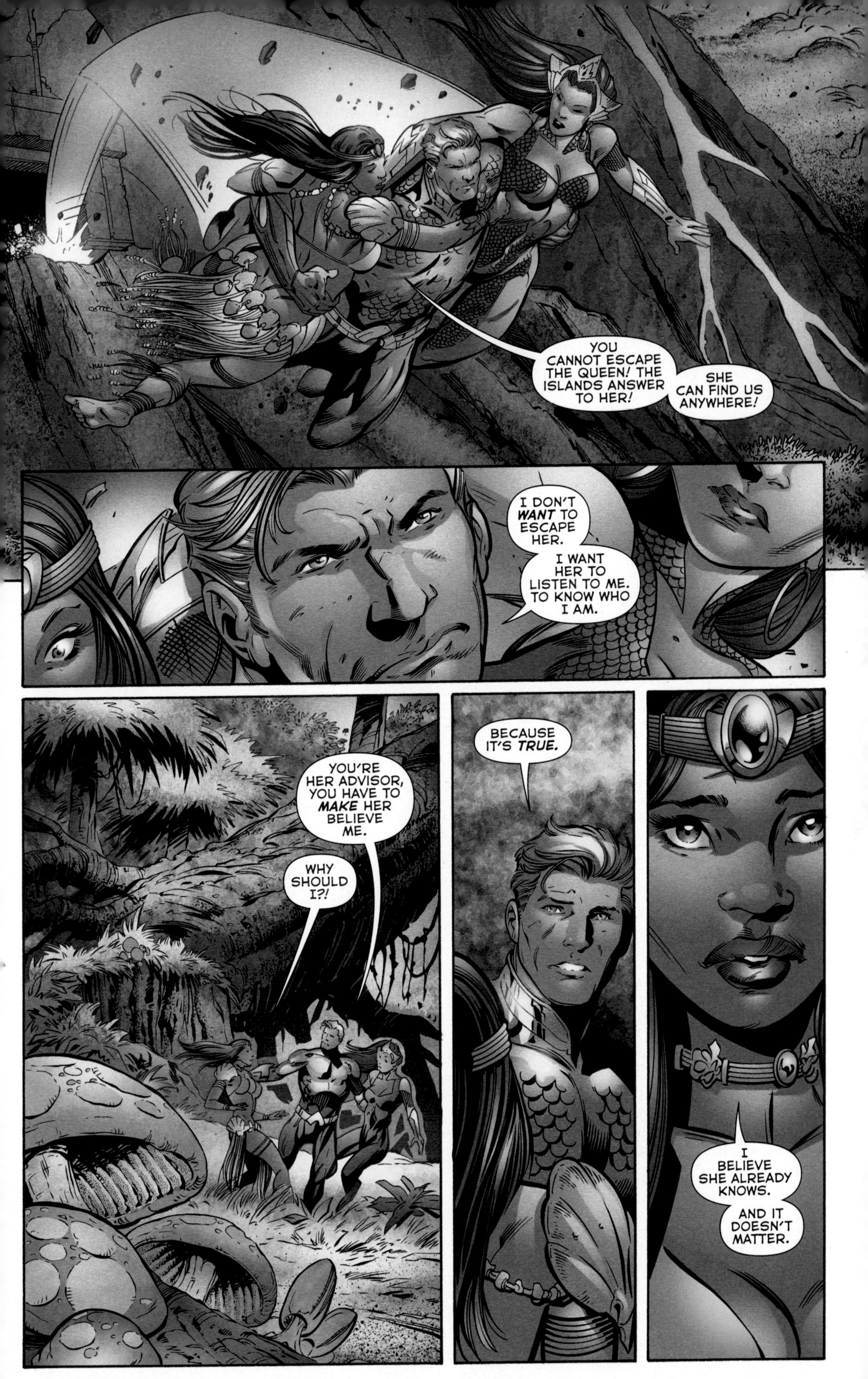
YOU CANNOT ESCAPE THE QUEEN! THE ISLANDS ANSWER TO HER!
SHE CAN FIND US ANYWHERE!
I DON'T WANT TO ESCAPE HER.
I WANT HER TO LISTEN TO ME. TO KNOW WHO I AM.
YOU'RE HER ADVISOR, YOU HAVE TO MAKE HER BELIEVE ME.
WHY SHOULD I?!
BECAUSE IT'S TRUE.
I BELIEVE SHE ALREADY KNOWS.
AND IT DOESN'T MATTER.

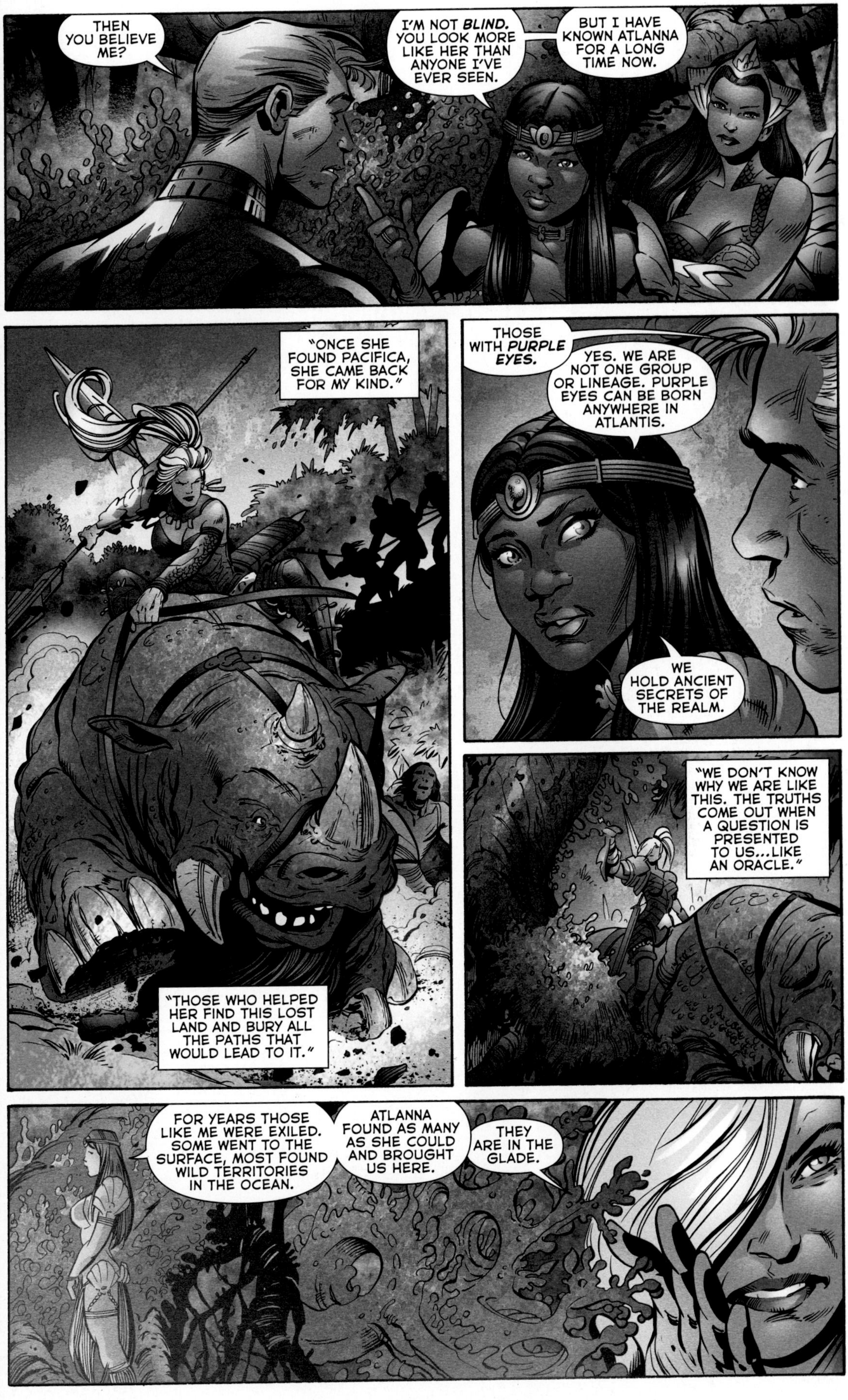
THEN YOU BELIEVE ME?
I'M NOT *BLIND.* YOU LOOK MORE LIKE HER THAN ANYONE I'VE EVER SEEN.
BUT I HAVE KNOWN ATLANNA FOR A LONG TIME NOW.
"ONCE SHE FOUND PACIFICA, SHE CAME BACK FOR MY KIND."
"THOSE WHO HELPED HER FIND THIS LOST LAND AND BURY ALL THE PATHS THAT WOULD LEAD TO IT."
THOSE WITH *PURPLE EYES.*
YES. WE ARE NOT ONE GROUP OR LINEAGE. PURPLE EYES CAN BE BORN ANYWHERE IN ATLANTIS.
WE HOLD ANCIENT SECRETS OF THE REALM.
"WE DON'T KNOW WHY WE ARE LIKE THIS. THE TRUTHS COME OUT WHEN A QUESTION IS PRESENTED TO US...LIKE AN ORACLE."
FOR YEARS THOSE LIKE ME WERE EXILED. SOME WENT TO THE SURFACE, MOST FOUND WILD TERRITORIES IN THE OCEAN.
ATLANNA FOUND AS MANY AS SHE COULD AND BROUGHT US HERE.
THEY ARE IN THE GLADE.

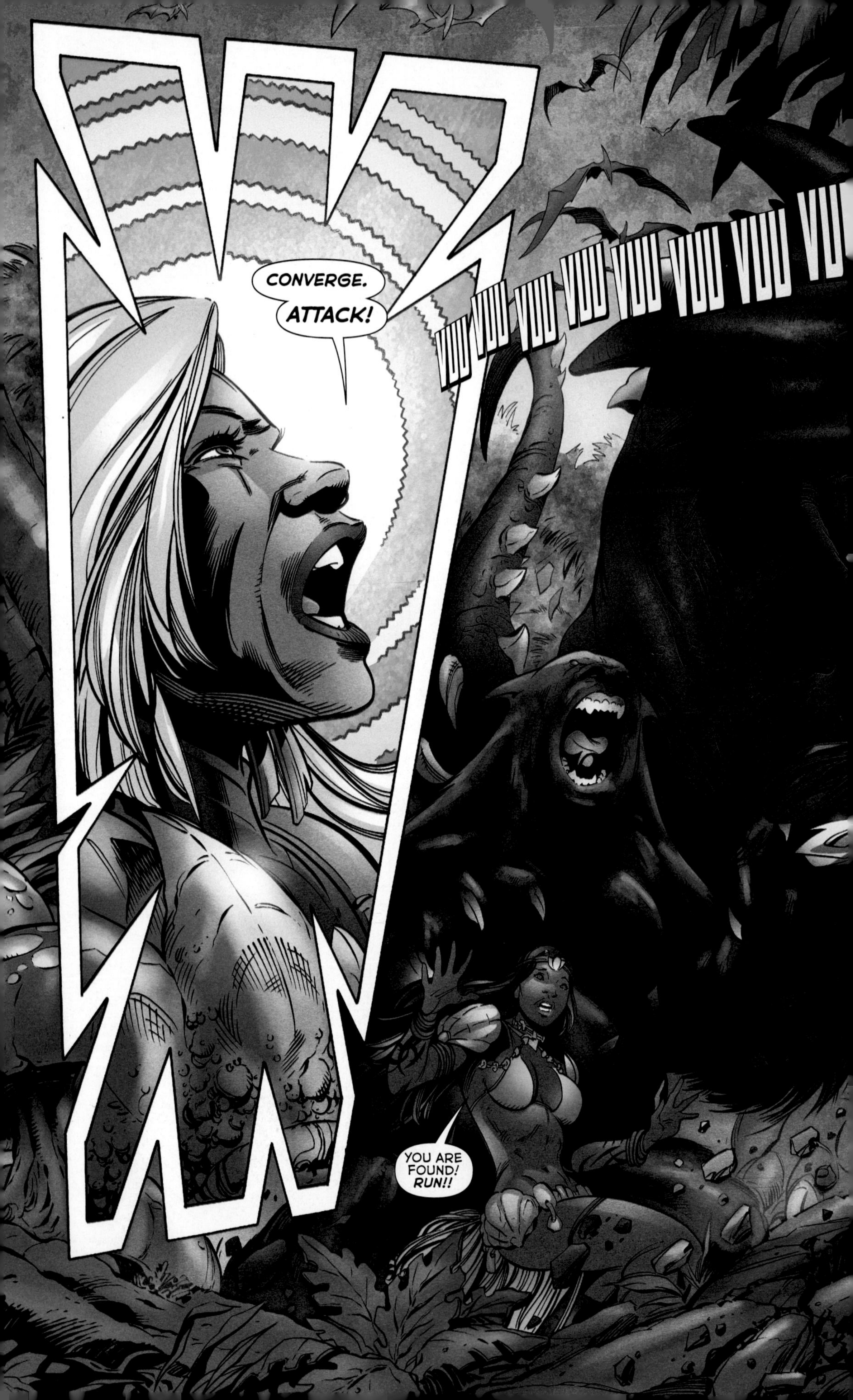
CONVERGE.
ATTACK!
VUU VUU VUU VUU VUU VUU VUU VUU VU
YOU ARE FOUND! RUN!!

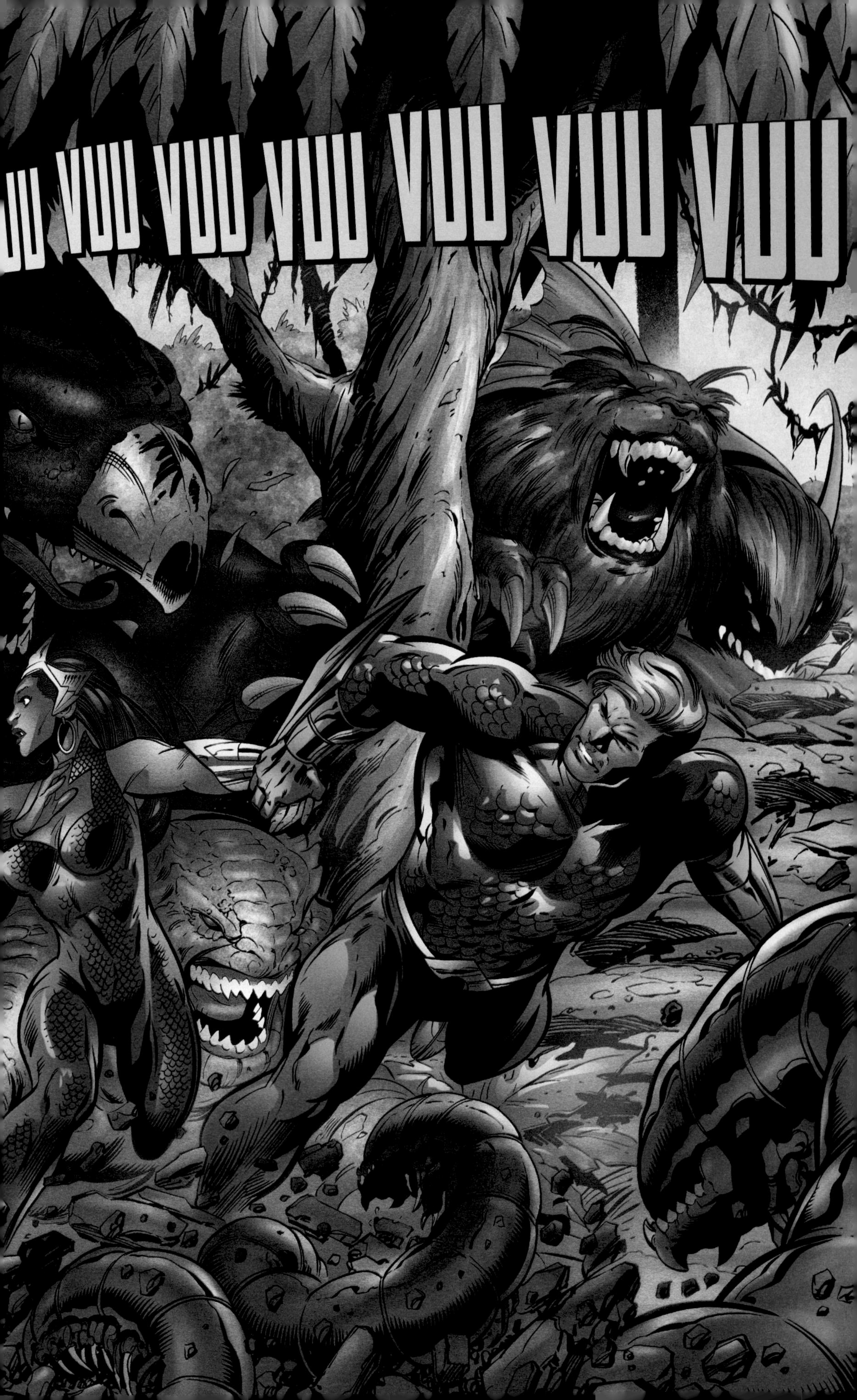
UU VUU VUU VUU VUU VUU VUU

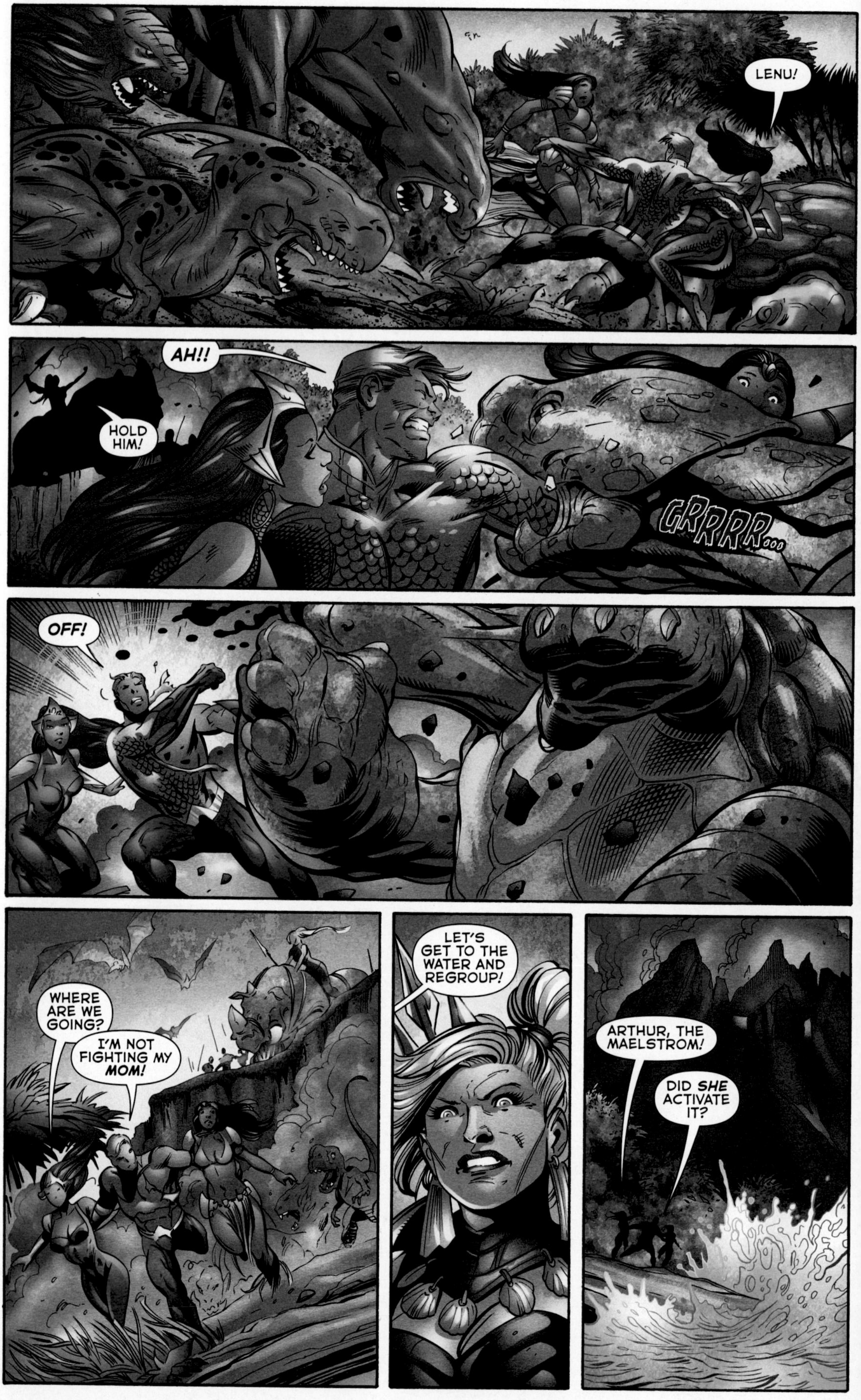

LENU!
AH!!
HOLD HIM!
GRRRR...
OFF!
WHERE ARE WE GOING?
I'M NOT FIGHTING MY MOM!
LET'S GET TO THE WATER AND REGROUP!
ARTHUR, THE MAELSTROM!
DID SHE ACTIVATE IT?

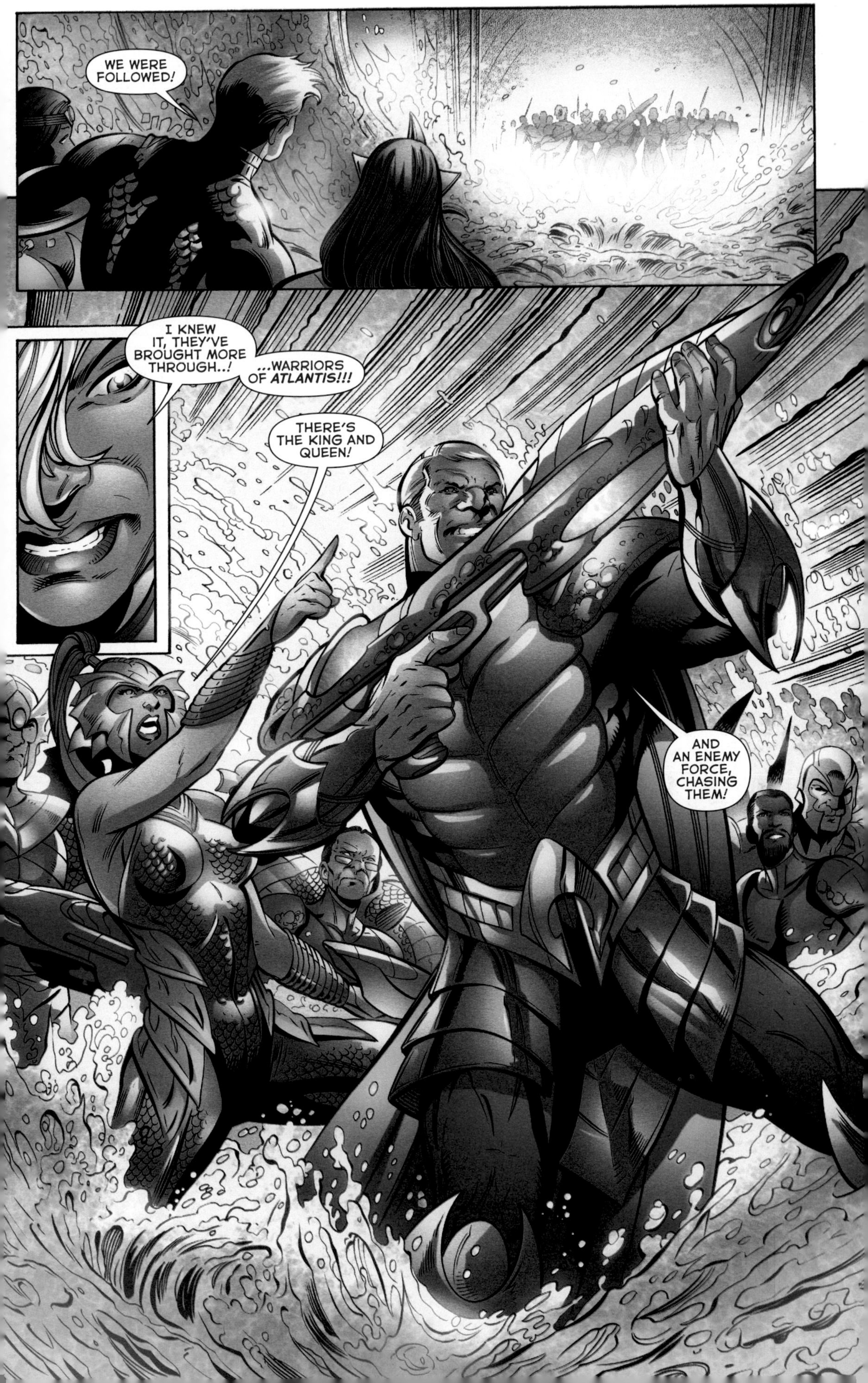
WE WERE FOLLOWED!
I KNEW IT, THEY'VE BROUGHT MORE THROUGH..!
...WARRIORS OF ATLANTIS!!!
THERE'S THE KING AND QUEEN!
AND AN ENEMY FORCE, CHASING THEM!

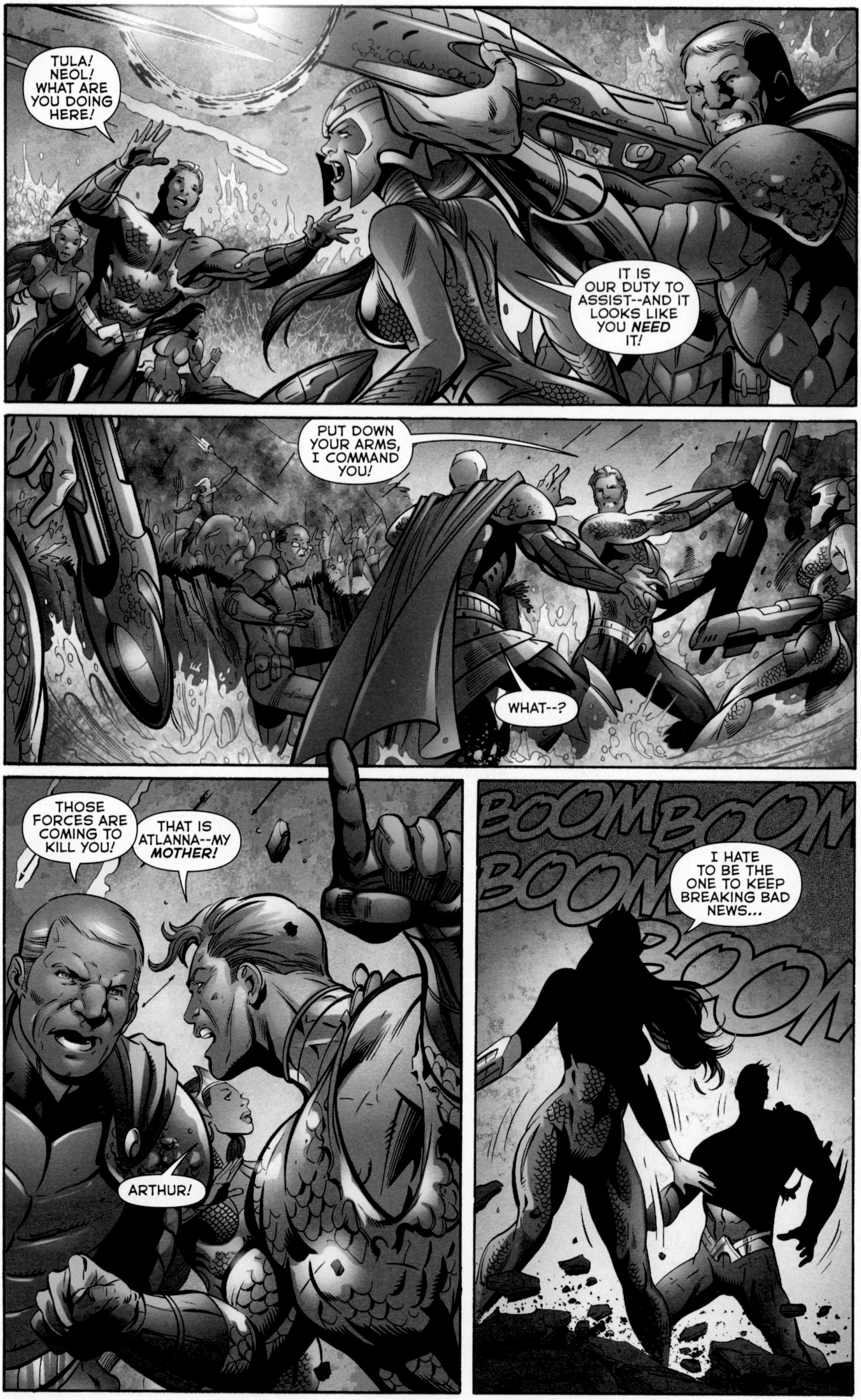
TULA! NEOL! WHAT ARE YOU DOING HERE!
IT IS OUR DUTY TO ASSIST--AND IT LOOKS LIKE YOU *NEED* IT!
PUT DOWN YOUR ARMS, I COMMAND YOU!
WHAT--?
THOSE FORCES ARE COMING TO KILL YOU!
THAT IS ATLANNA--MY *MOTHER!*
ARTHUR!
BOOM BOOM
BOOM
BOOM
I HATE TO BE THE ONE TO KEEP BREAKING BAD NEWS...

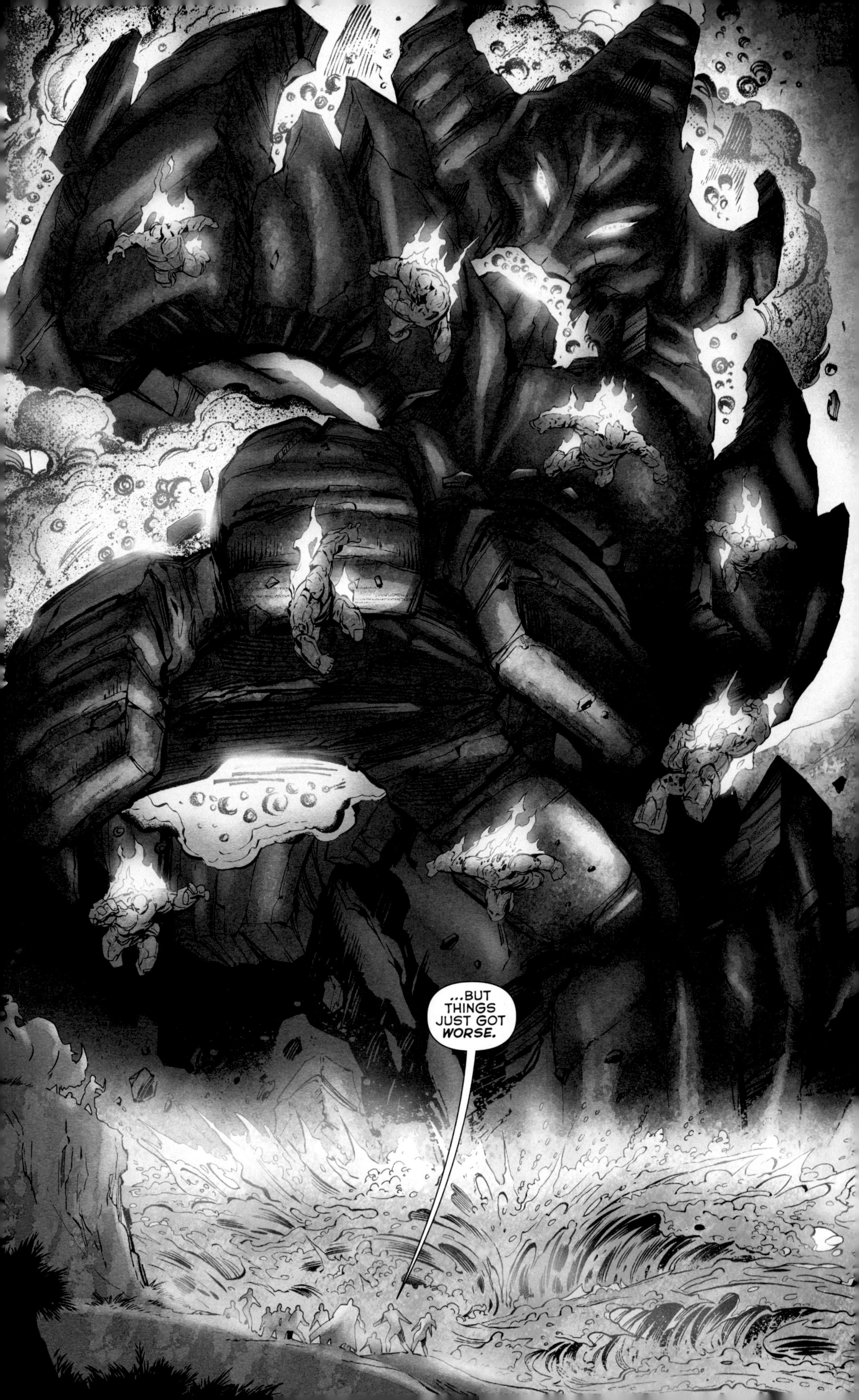
...BUT THINGS JUST GOT WORSE.

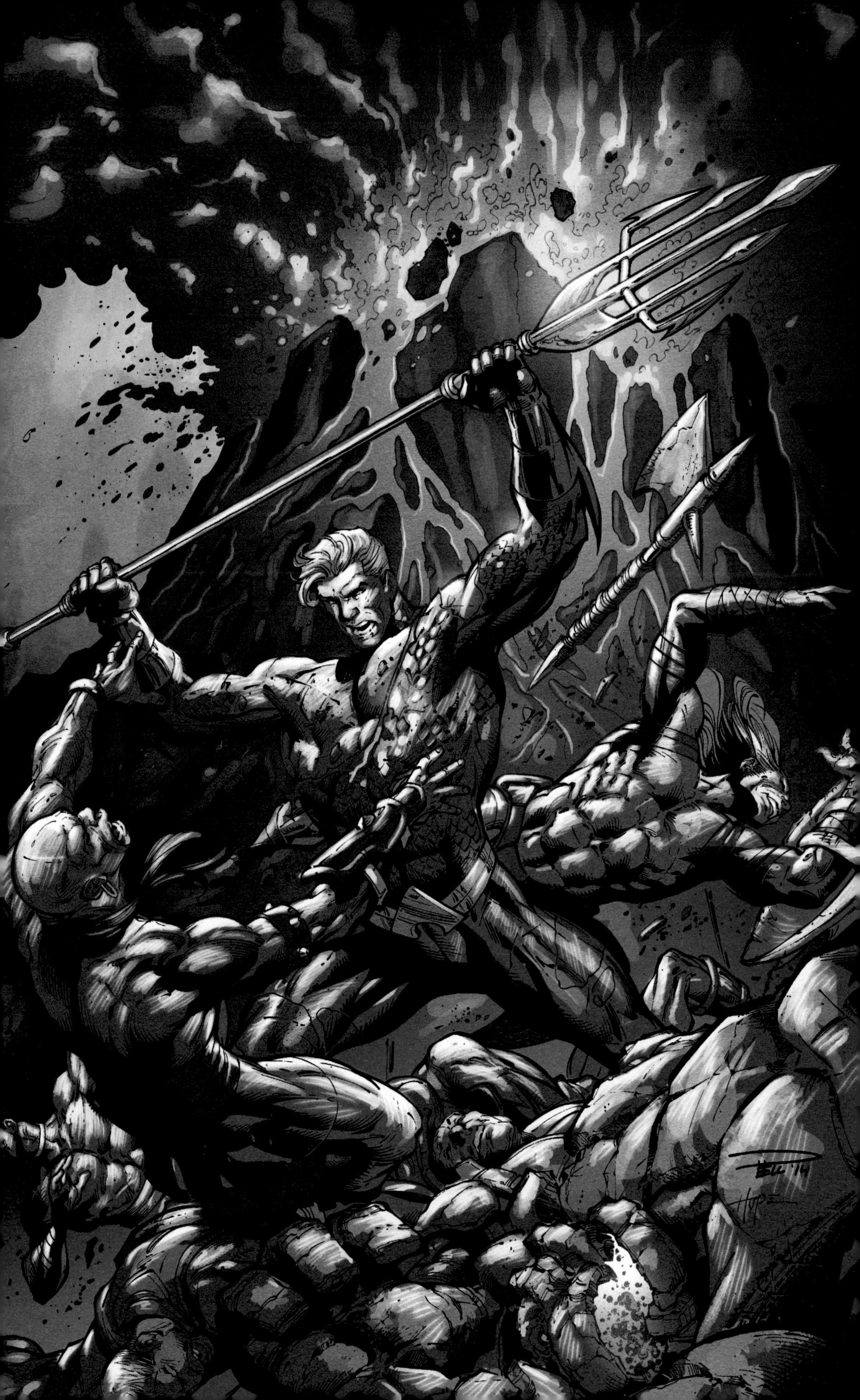

MAELSTROM PART VI: THE EDGE OF THE WORLD

JEFF PARKER writer **PAUL PELLETIER** penciller **SANDRA HOPE, WAYNE FAUCHER, TONY KORDOS** inkers **RAIN BEREDO** colorist **TRAVIS LANHAM** letterer
PELLETIER, HOPE and **BEREDO** cover art

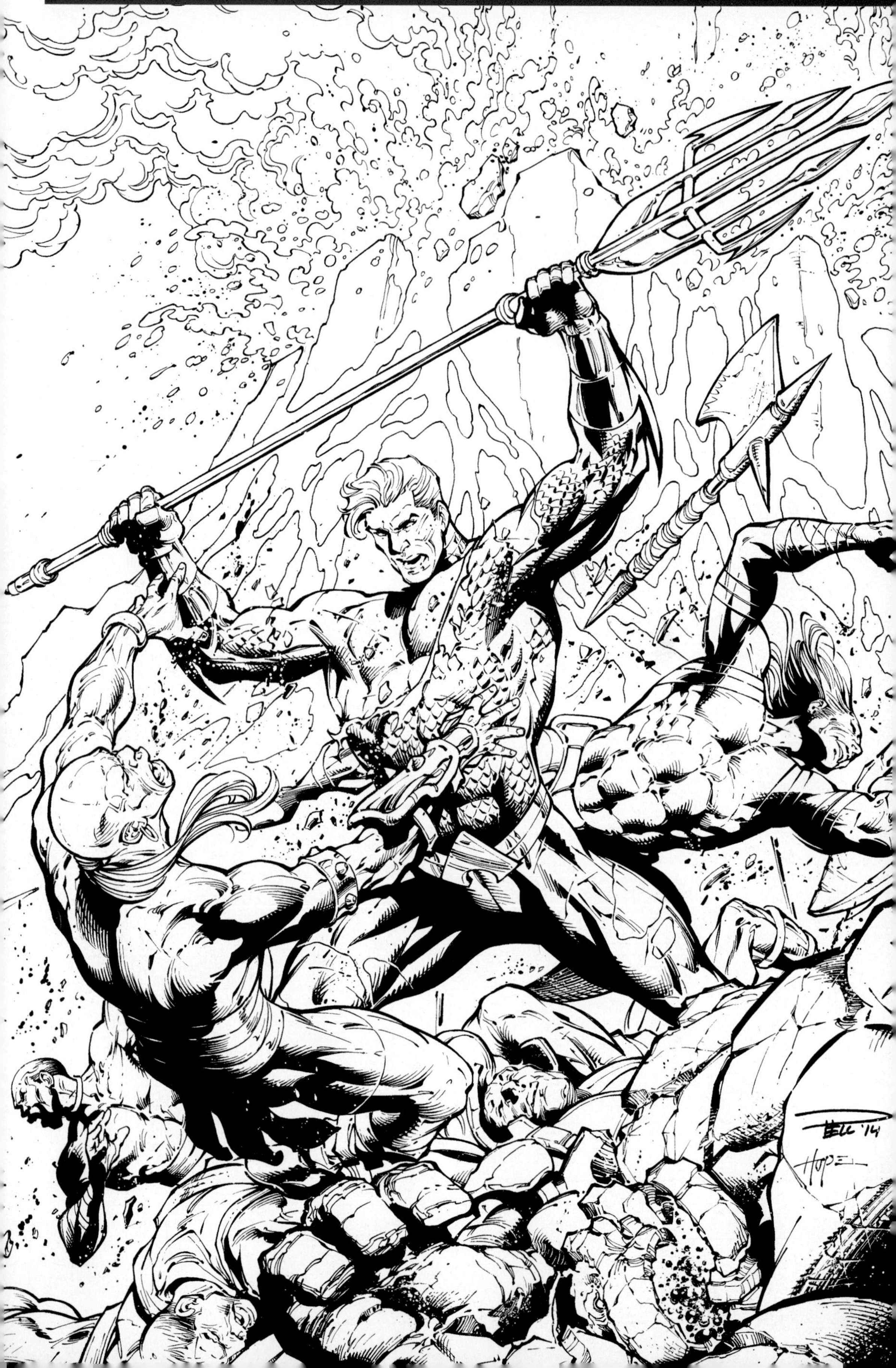

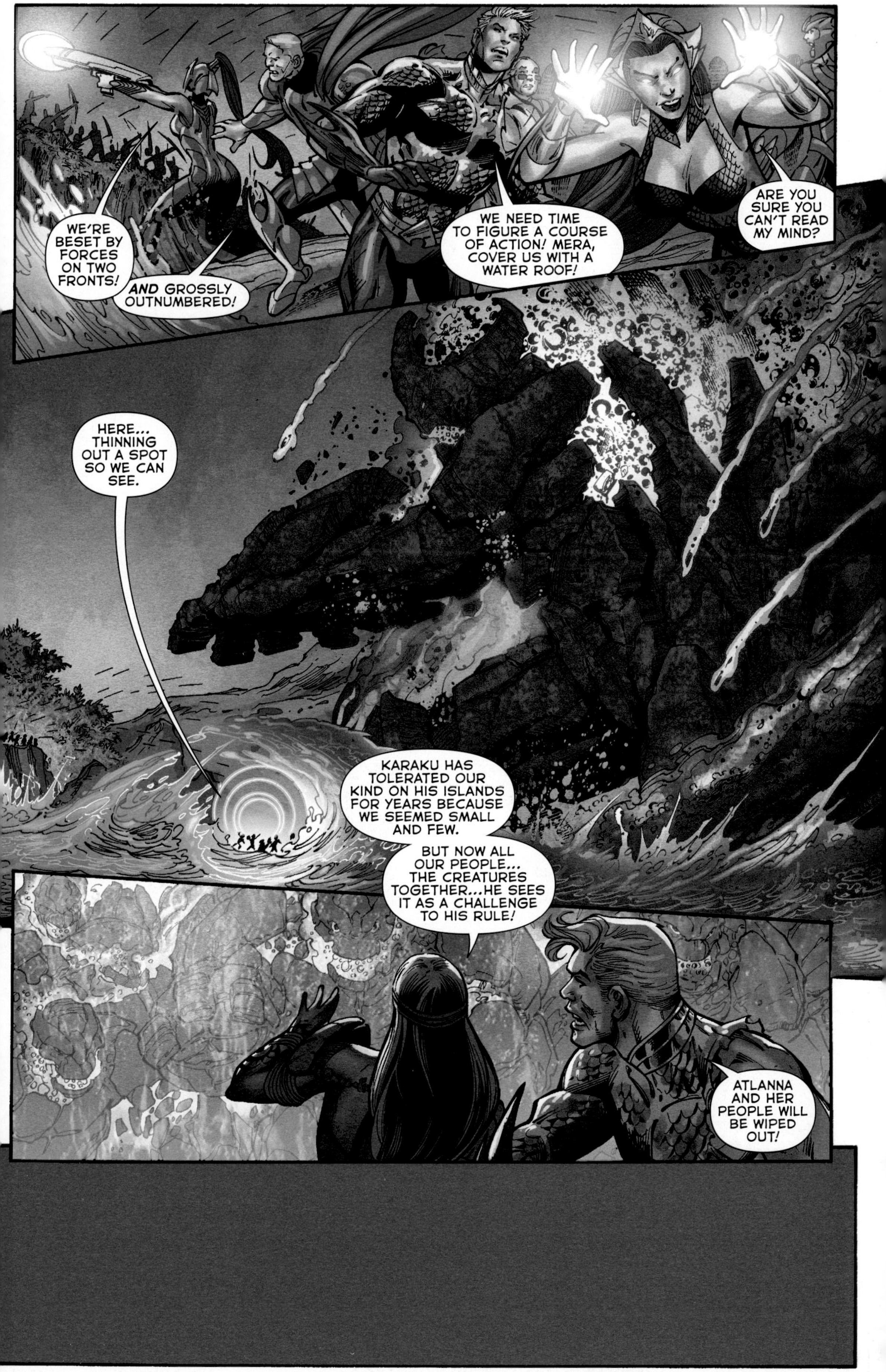
WE'RE BESET BY FORCES ON TWO FRONTS!
AND GROSSLY OUTNUMBERED!
WE NEED TIME TO FIGURE A COURSE OF ACTION! MERA, COVER US WITH A WATER ROOF!
ARE YOU SURE YOU CAN'T READ MY MIND?
HERE... THINNING OUT A SPOT SO WE CAN SEE.
KARAKU HAS TOLERATED OUR KIND ON HIS ISLANDS FOR YEARS BECAUSE WE SEEMED SMALL AND FEW.
BUT NOW ALL OUR PEOPLE... THE CREATURES TOGETHER...HE SEES IT AS A CHALLENGE TO HIS RULE!
ATLANNA AND HER PEOPLE WILL BE WIPED OUT!

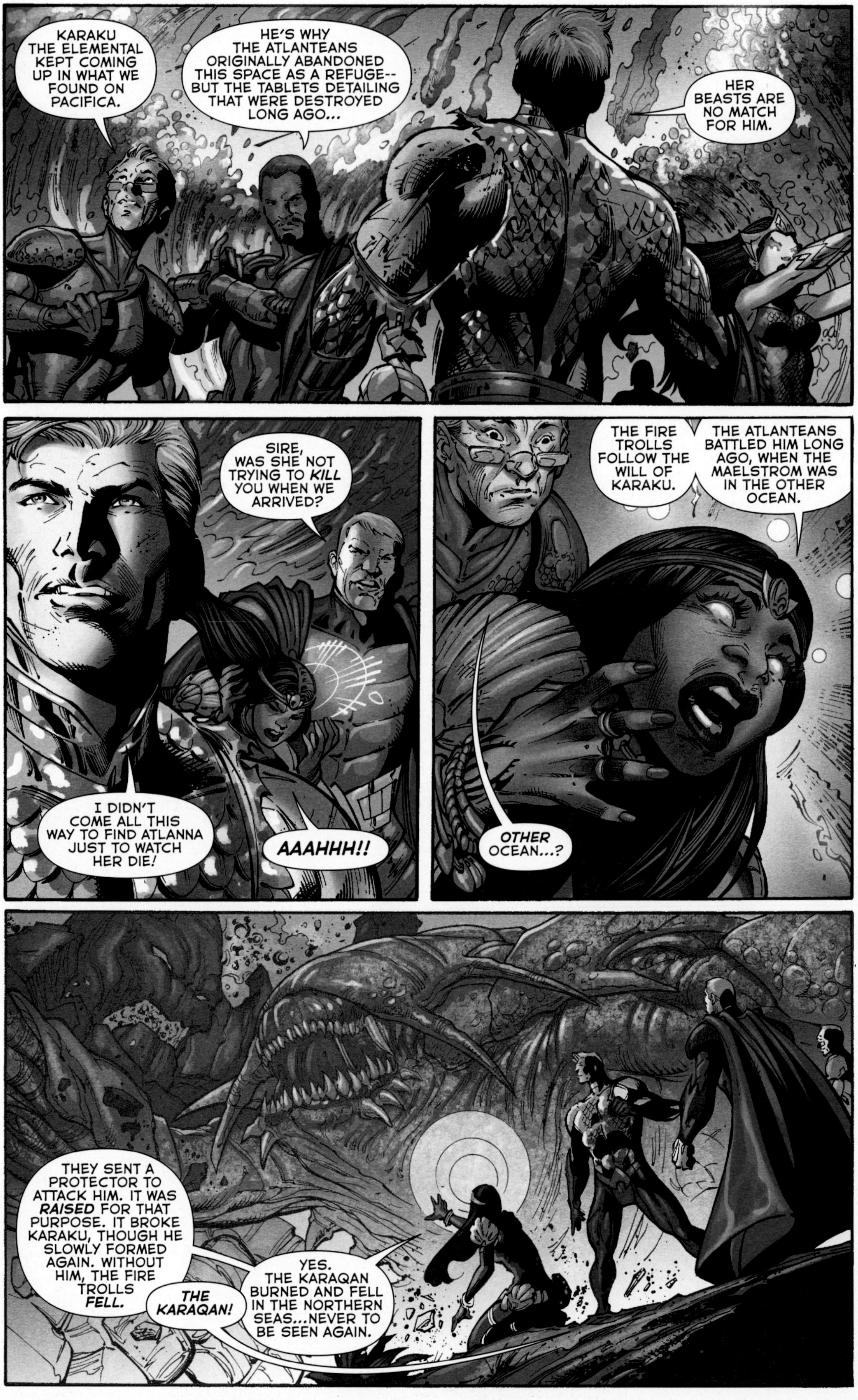
KARAKU THE ELEMENTAL KEPT COMING UP IN WHAT WE FOUND ON PACIFICA.
HE'S WHY THE ATLANTEANS ORIGINALLY ABANDONED THIS SPACE AS A REFUGE-- BUT THE TABLETS DETAILING THAT WERE DESTROYED LONG AGO...
HER BEASTS ARE NO MATCH FOR HIM.
SIRE, WAS SHE NOT TRYING TO KILL YOU WHEN WE ARRIVED?
I DIDN'T COME ALL THIS WAY TO FIND ATLANNA JUST TO WATCH HER DIE!
AAAHHH!!
THE FIRE TROLLS FOLLOW THE WILL OF KARAKU.
THE ATLANTEANS BATTLED HIM LONG AGO, WHEN THE MAELSTROM WAS IN THE OTHER OCEAN.
OTHER OCEAN...?
THEY SENT A PROTECTOR TO ATTACK HIM. IT WAS RAISED FOR THAT PURPOSE. IT BROKE KARAKU, THOUGH HE SLOWLY FORMED AGAIN. WITHOUT HIM, THE FIRE TROLLS FELL.
THE KARAQAN!
YES. THE KARAQAN BURNED AND FELL IN THE NORTHERN SEAS...NEVER TO BE SEEN AGAIN.

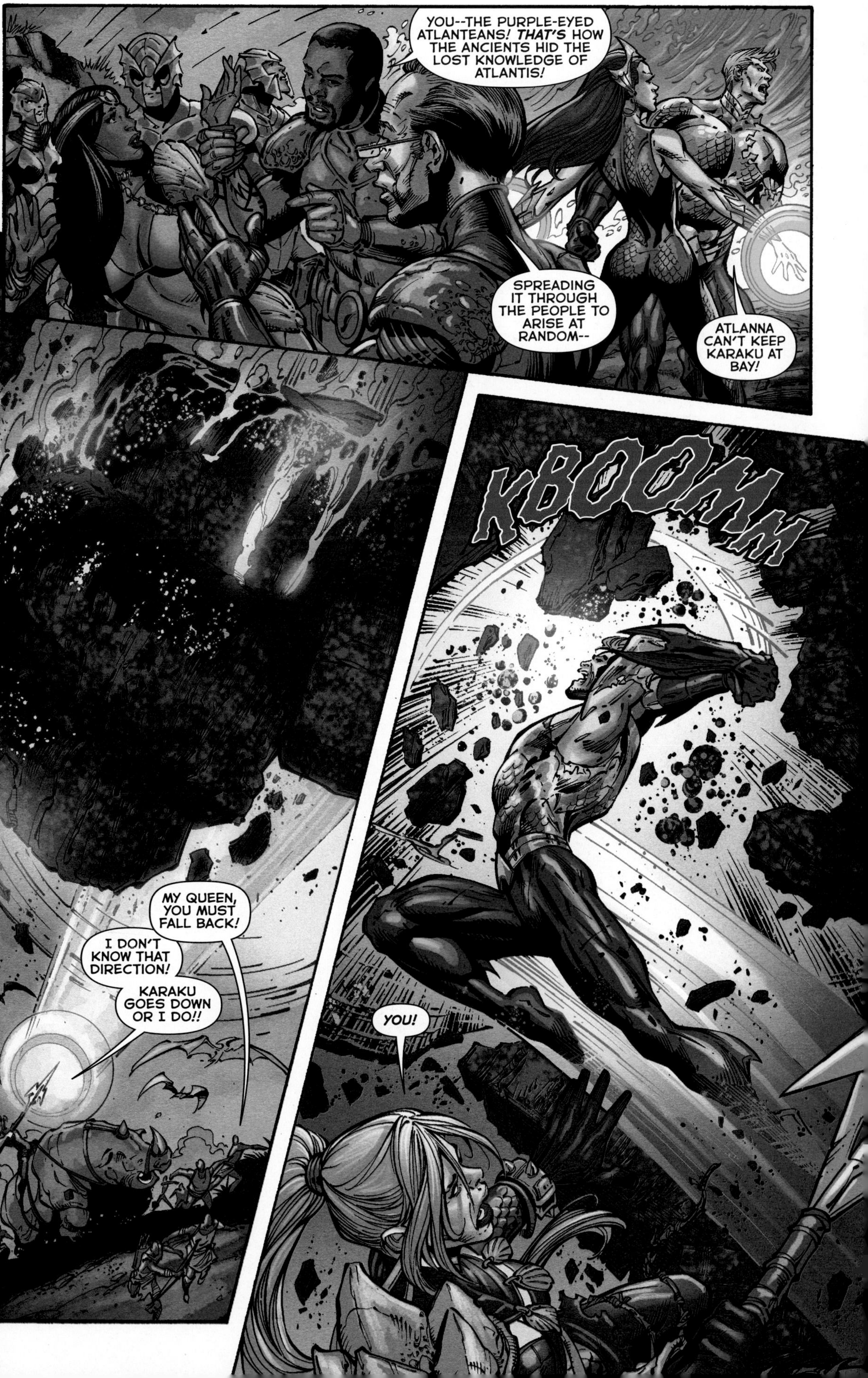
YOU--THE PURPLE-EYED ATLANTEANS! THAT'S HOW THE ANCIENTS HID THE LOST KNOWLEDGE OF ATLANTIS!
SPREADING IT THROUGH THE PEOPLE TO ARISE AT RANDOM--
ATLANNA CAN'T KEEP KARAKU AT BAY!
KBOOMM
MY QUEEN, YOU MUST FALL BACK!
I DON'T KNOW THAT DIRECTION!
KARAKU GOES DOWN OR I DO!!
YOU!

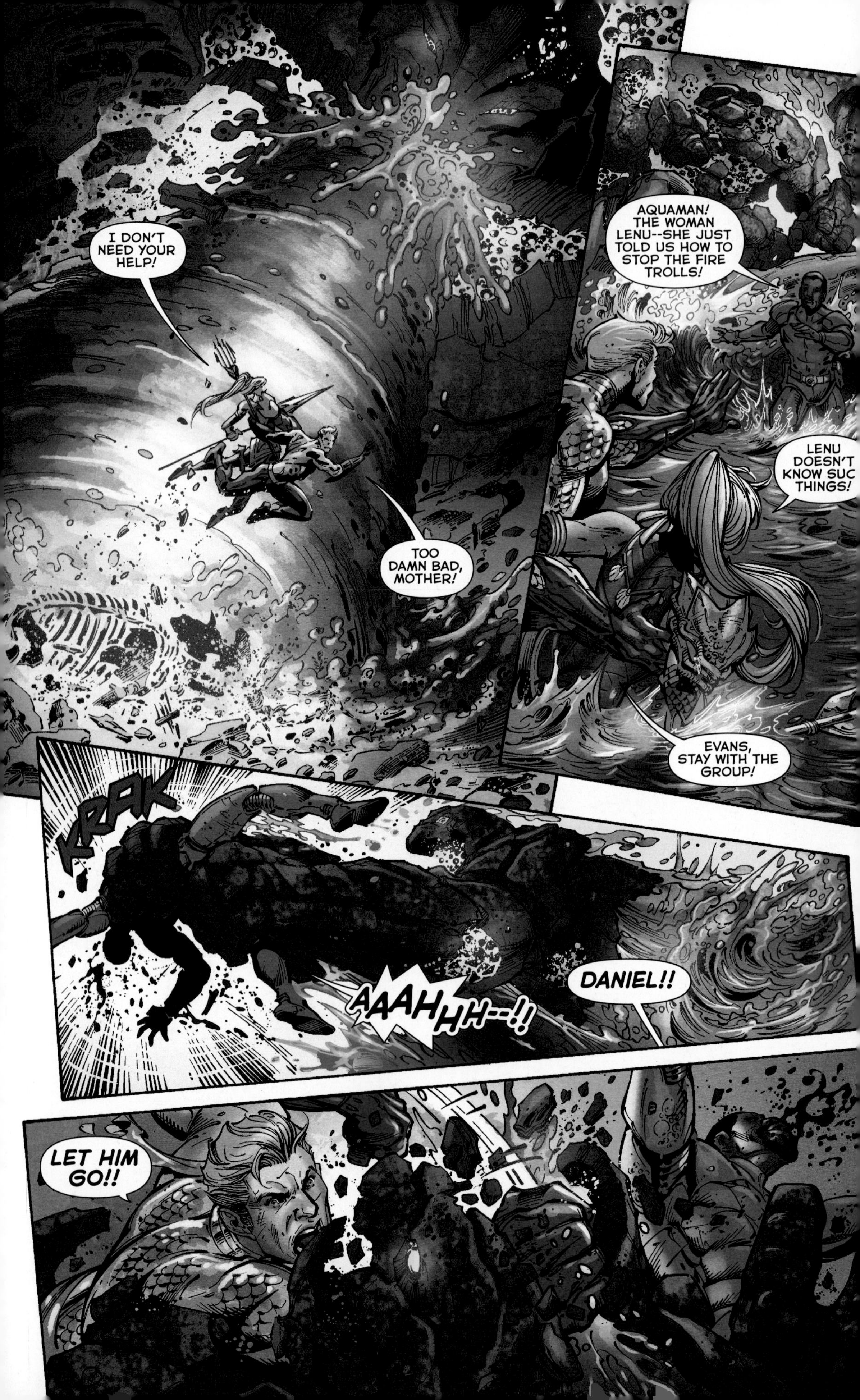
I DON'T NEED YOUR HELP!
TOO DAMN BAD, MOTHER!
AQUAMAN! THE WOMAN LENU--SHE JUST TOLD US HOW TO STOP THE FIRE TROLLS!
LENU DOESN'T KNOW SUC THINGS!
EVANS, STAY WITH THE GROUP!
KRAK
AAAHHH--!!
DANIEL!!
LET HIM GO!!

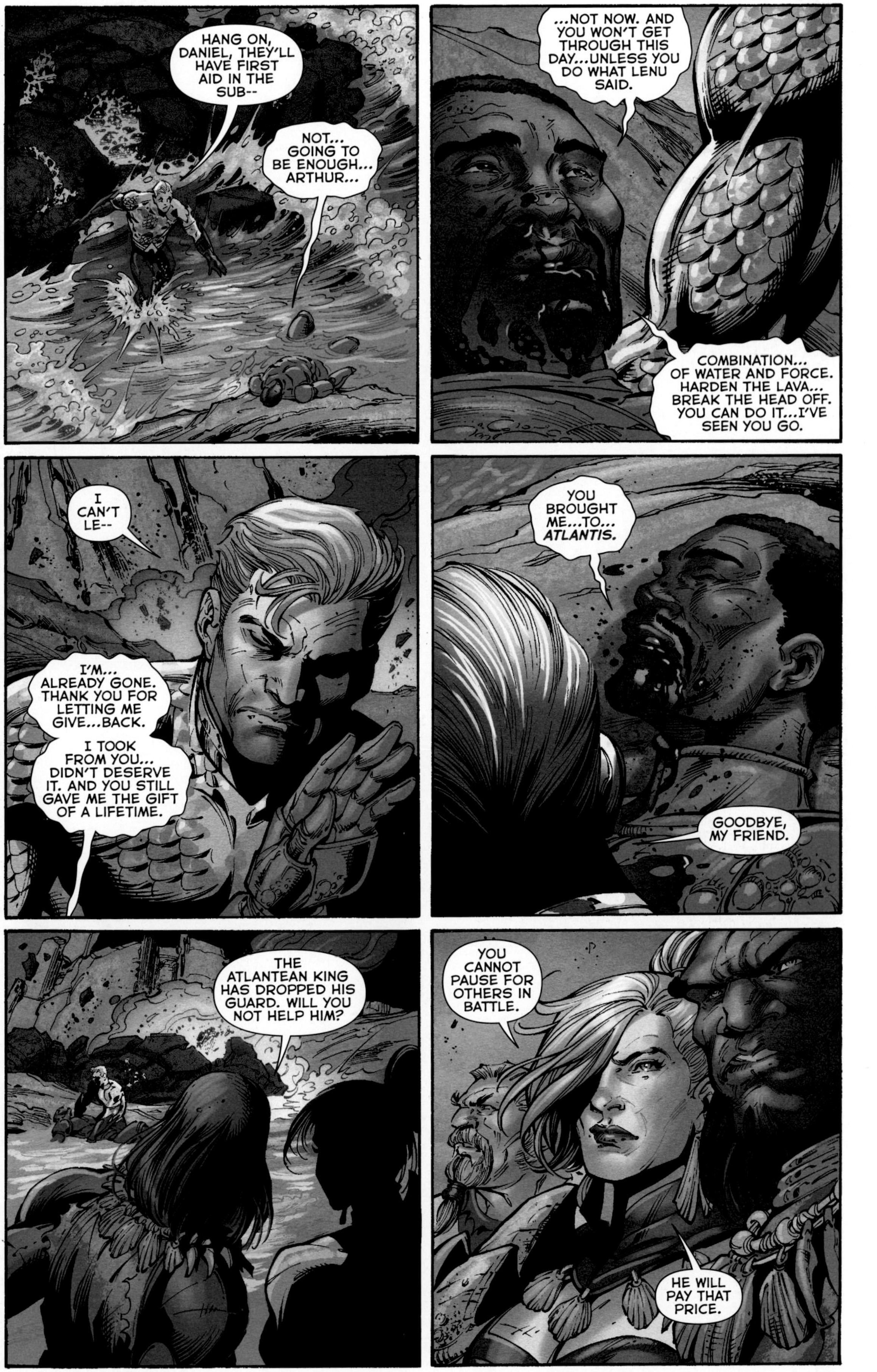
HANG ON, DANIEL, THEY'LL HAVE FIRST AID IN THE SUB--
NOT... GOING TO BE ENOUGH... ARTHUR...
...NOT NOW. AND YOU WON'T GET THROUGH THIS DAY...UNLESS YOU DO WHAT LENU SAID.
COMBINATION... OF WATER AND FORCE. HARDEN THE LAVA... BREAK THE HEAD OFF. YOU CAN DO IT...I'VE SEEN YOU GO.
I CAN'T LE--
I'M... ALREADY GONE. THANK YOU FOR LETTING ME GIVE...BACK.
I TOOK FROM YOU... DIDN'T DESERVE IT. AND YOU STILL GAVE ME THE GIFT OF A LIFETIME.
YOU BROUGHT ME...TO... ATLANTIS.
GOODBYE, MY FRIEND.
THE ATLANTEAN KING HAS DROPPED HIS GUARD. WILL YOU NOT HELP HIM?
YOU CANNOT PAUSE FOR OTHERS IN BATTLE.
HE WILL PAY THAT PRICE.

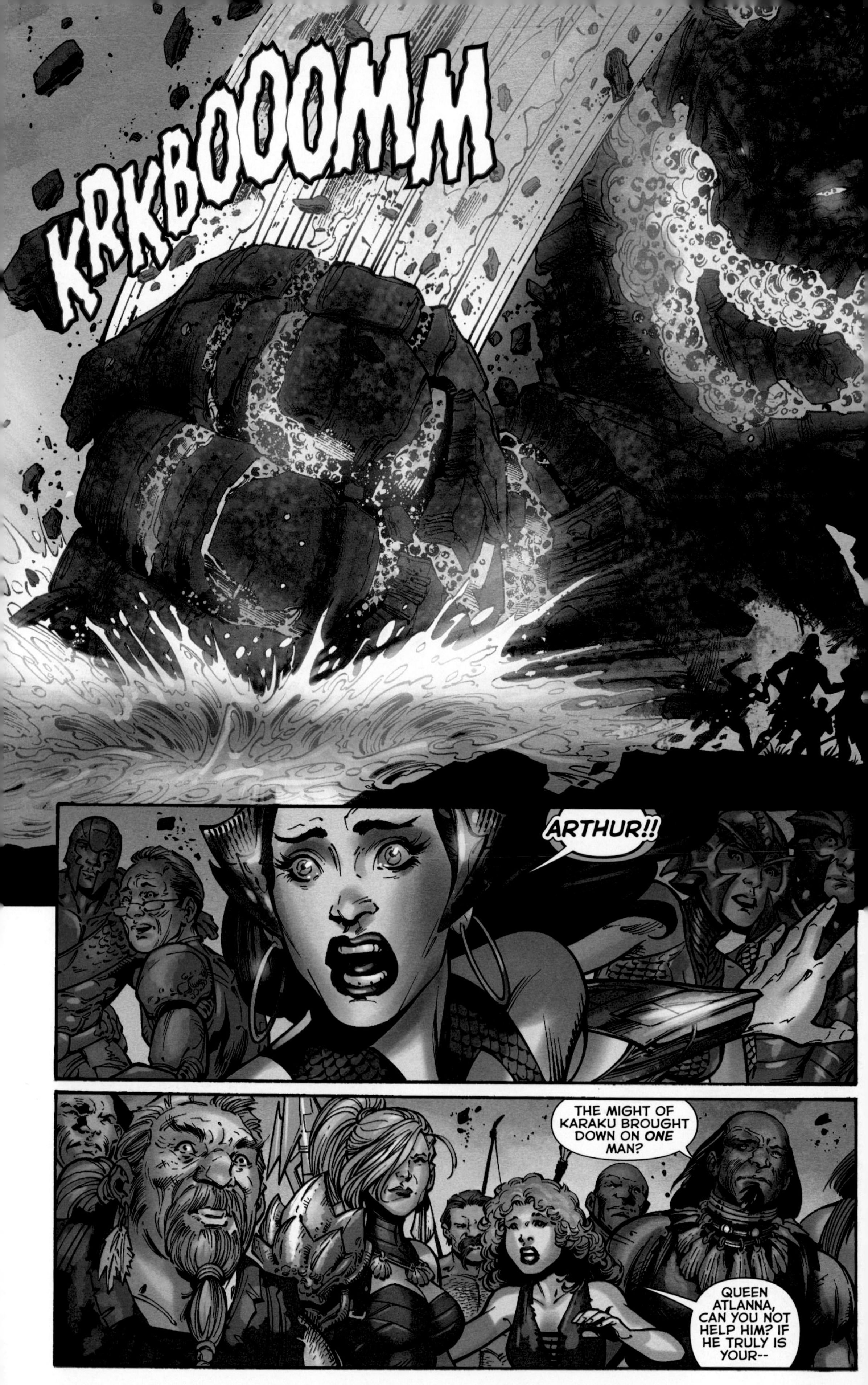
KRKBOOOMM
ARTHUR!!
THE MIGHT OF KARAKU BROUGHT DOWN ON ONE MAN?
QUEEN ATLANNA, CAN YOU NOT HELP HIM? IF HE TRULY IS YOUR--

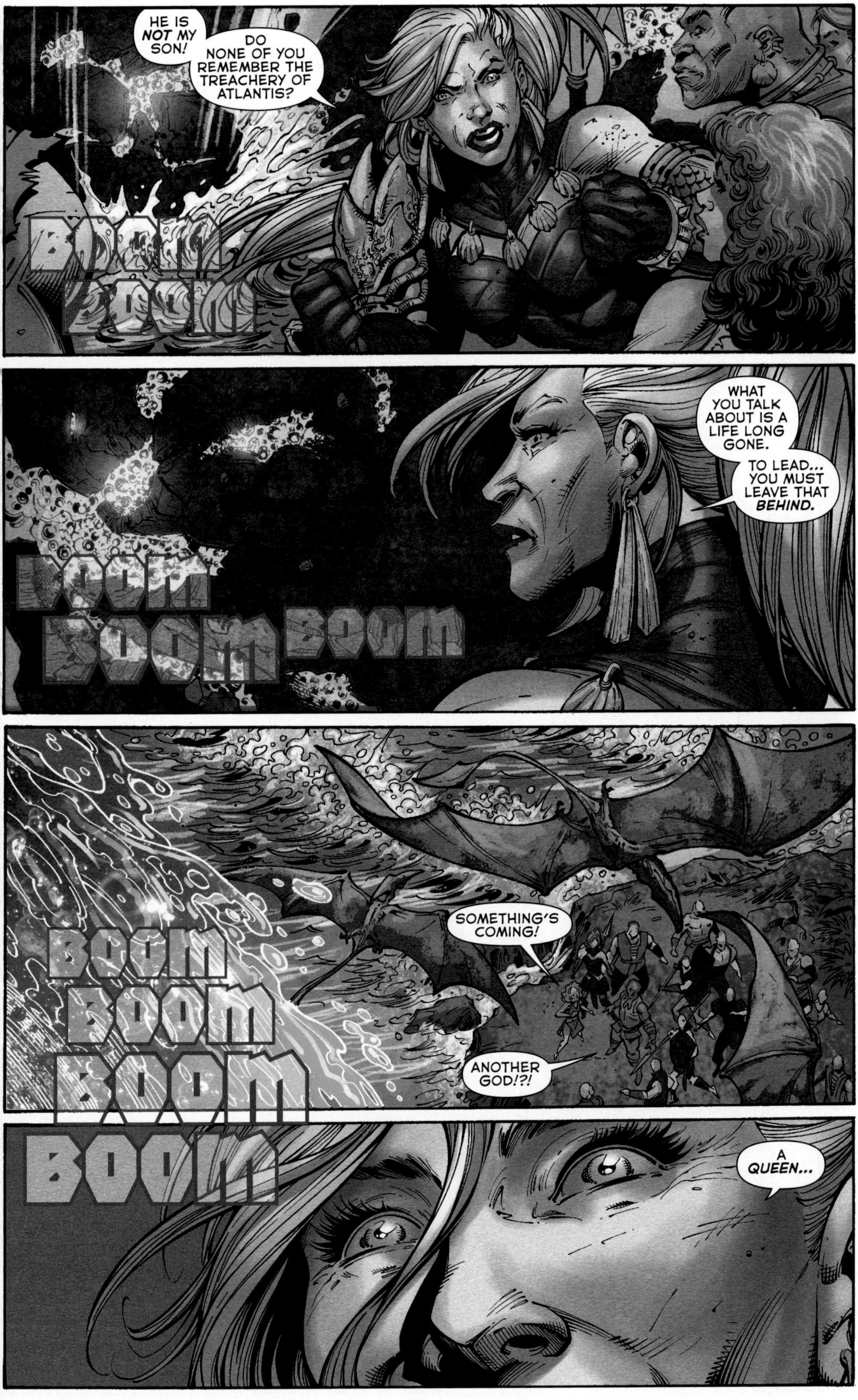
HE IS *NOT* MY SON!
DO NONE OF YOU REMEMBER THE TREACHERY OF ATLANTIS?
BOOM BOOM
BOOM BOOM BOOM
WHAT YOU TALK ABOUT IS A LIFE LONG GONE.
TO LEAD... YOU MUST LEAVE THAT *BEHIND.*
BOOM BOOM BOOM
SOMETHING'S COMING!
ANOTHER GOD!?!
BOOM
A *QUEEN...*

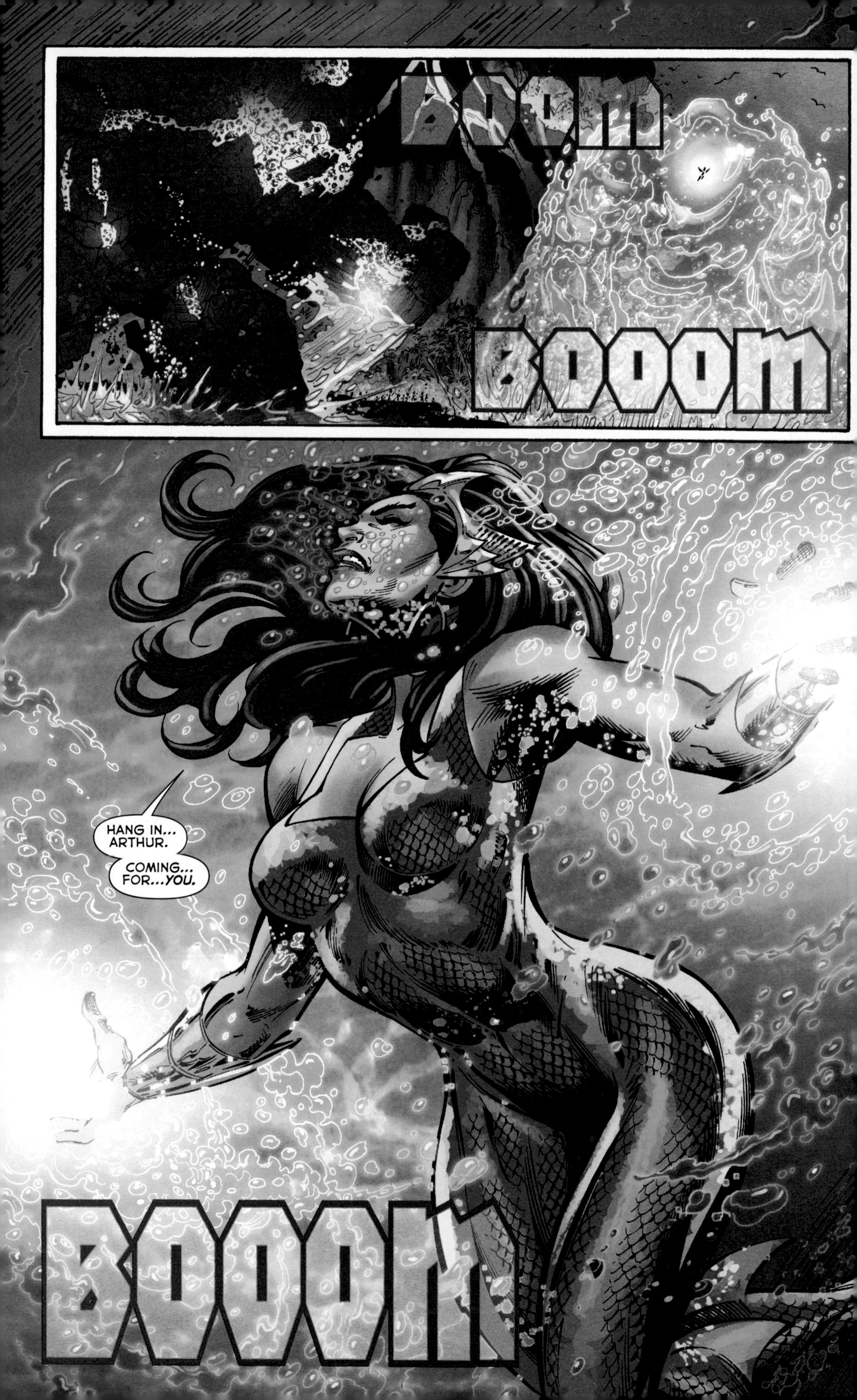
BOOM
BOOOM
HANG IN... ARTHUR.
COMING... FOR...*YOU.*
BOOOM

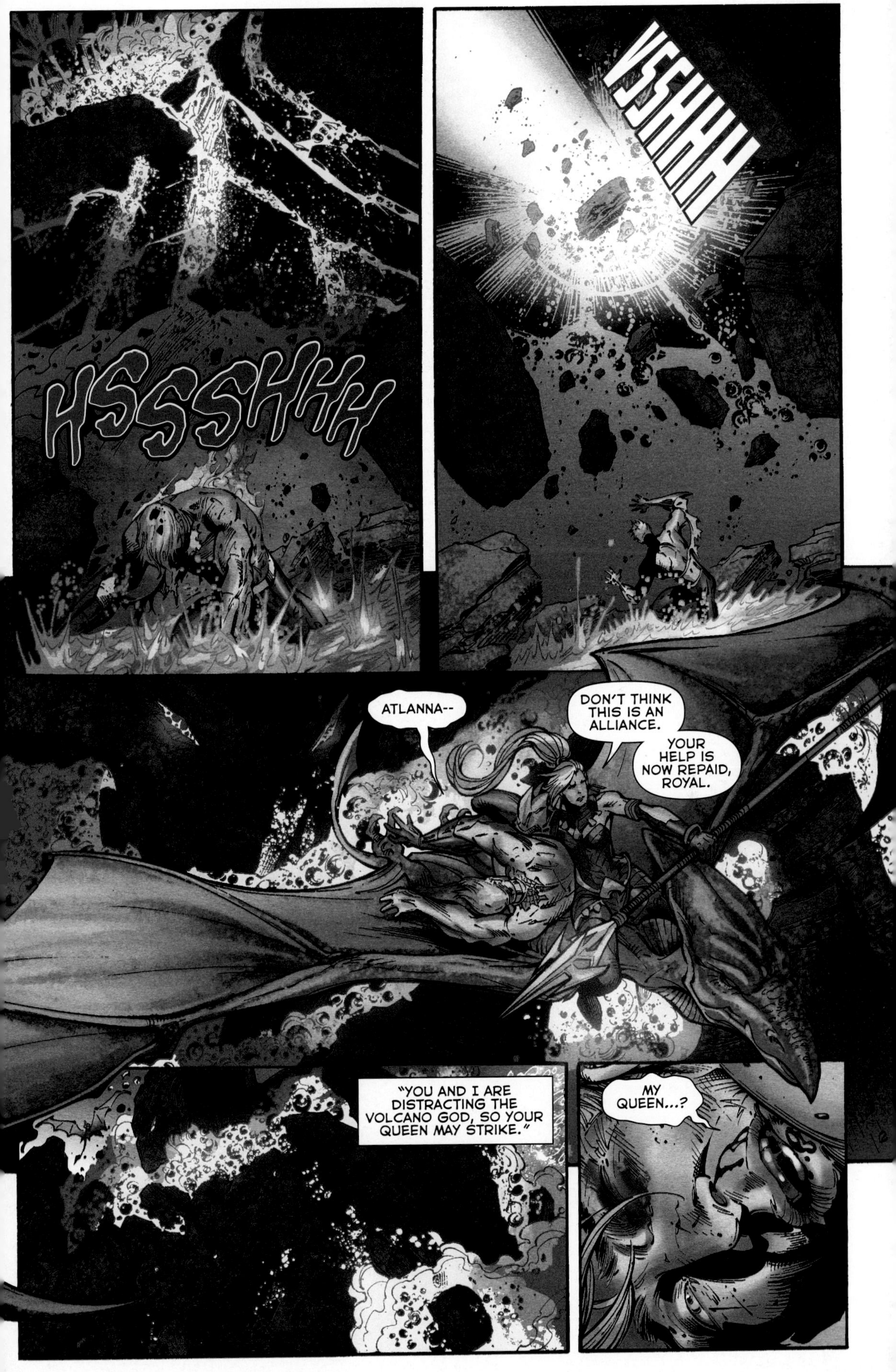
HSSSHHH
VSHHH
ATLANNA--
DON'T THINK THIS IS AN ALLIANCE.
YOUR HELP IS NOW REPAID, ROYAL.
"YOU AND I ARE DISTRACTING THE VOLCANO GOD, SO YOUR QUEEN MAY STRIKE."
MY QUEEN...?

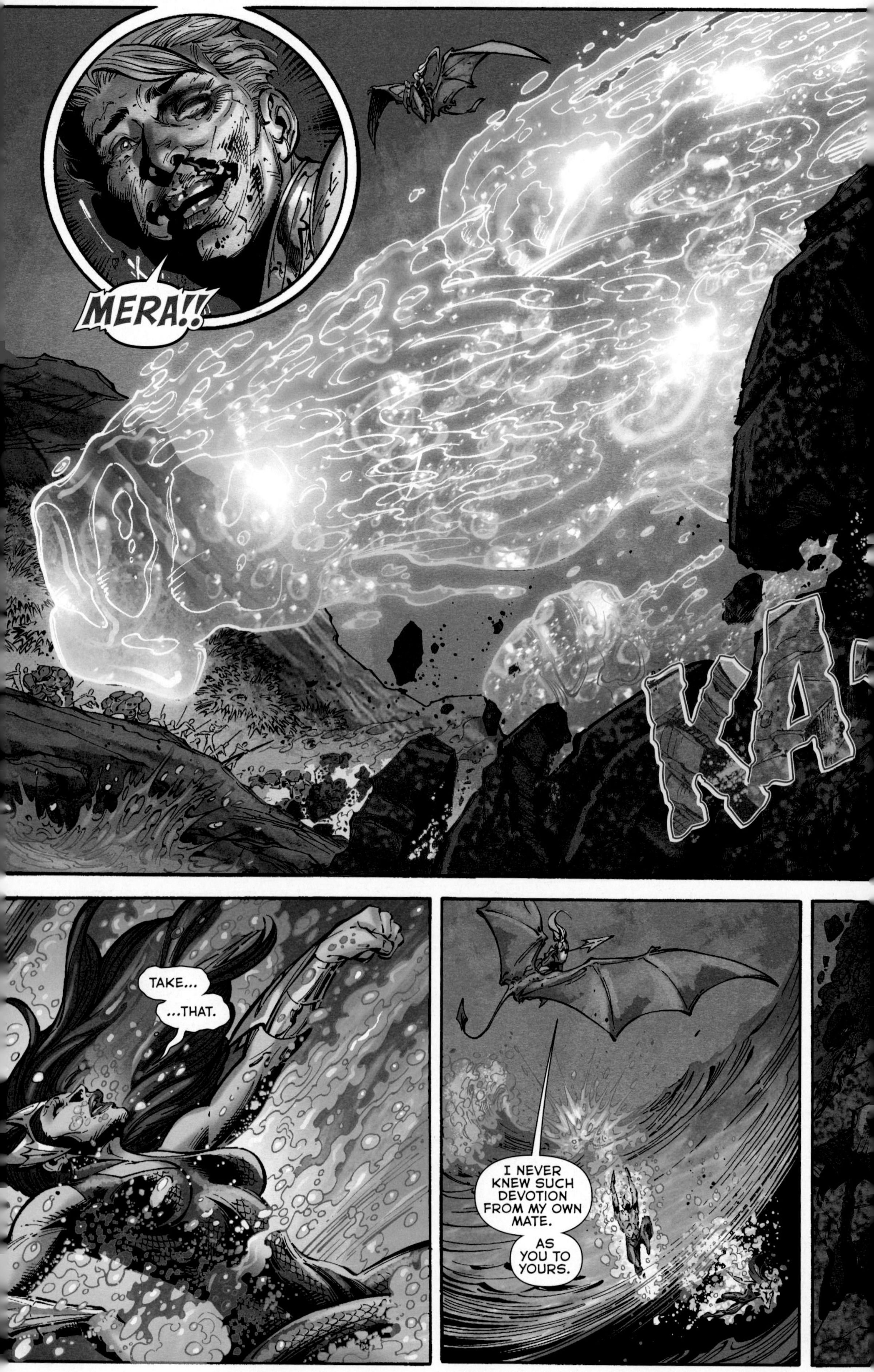
MERA!!
KA-
TAKE...
...THAT.
I NEVER KNEW SUCH DEVOTION FROM MY OWN MATE.
AS YOU TO YOURS.

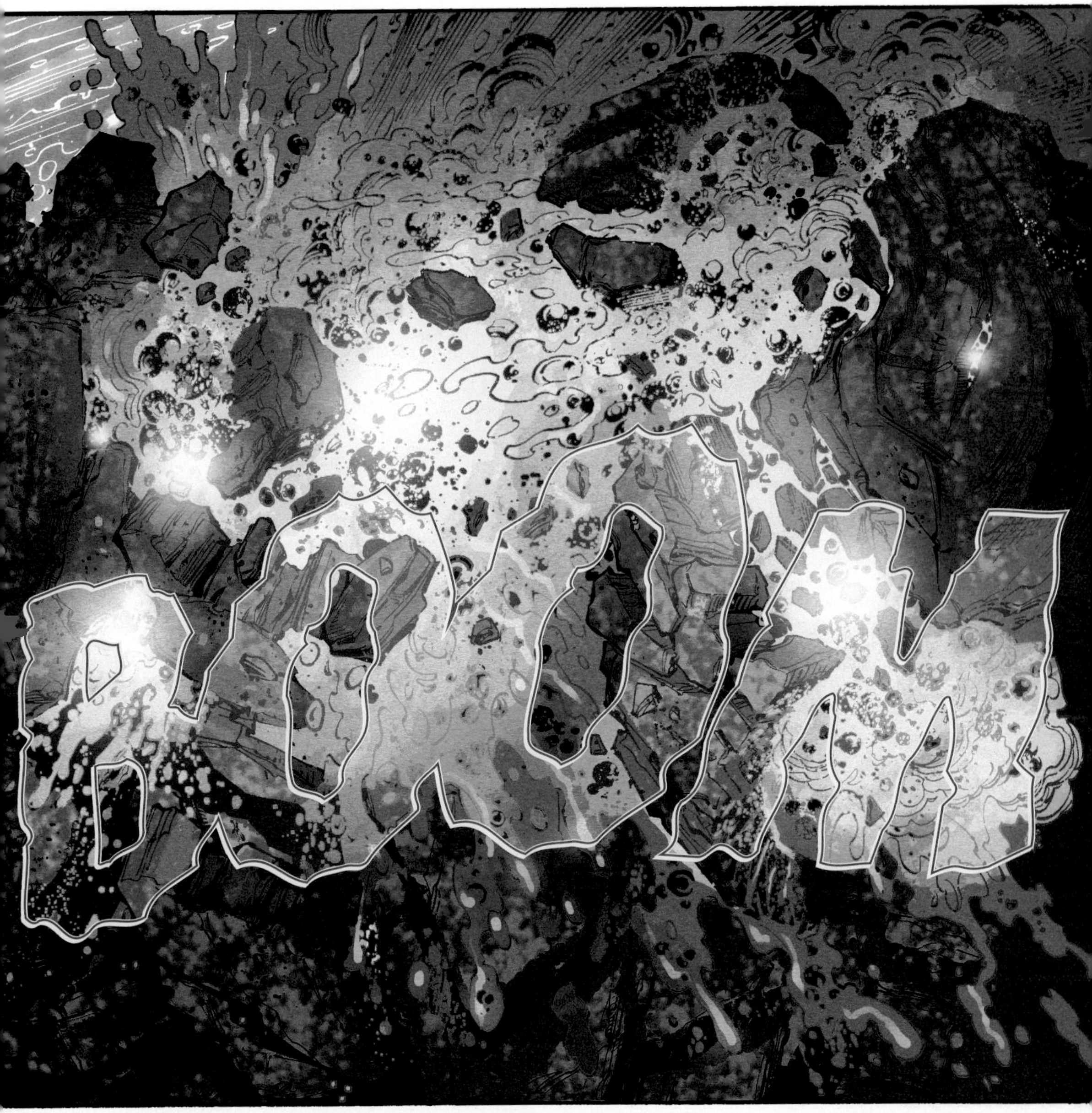
BOOOM

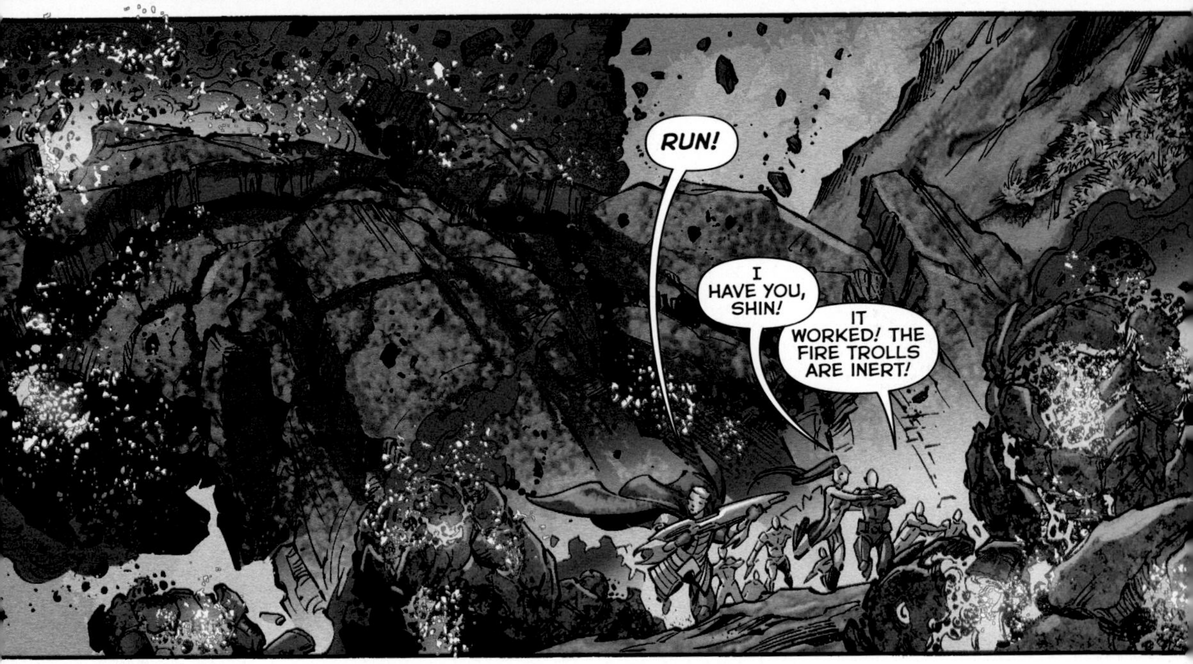
RUN!
I HAVE YOU, SHIN!
IT WORKED! THE FIRE TROLLS ARE INERT!

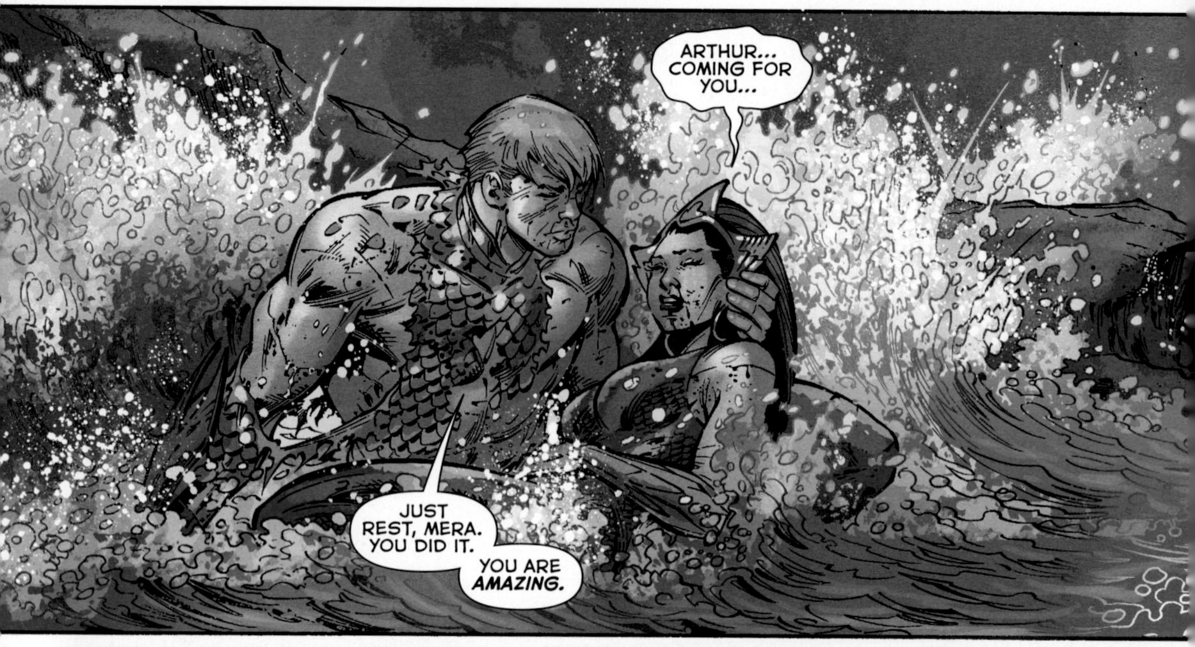
ARTHUR... COMING FOR YOU...
JUST REST, MERA. YOU DID IT.
YOU ARE *AMAZING.*

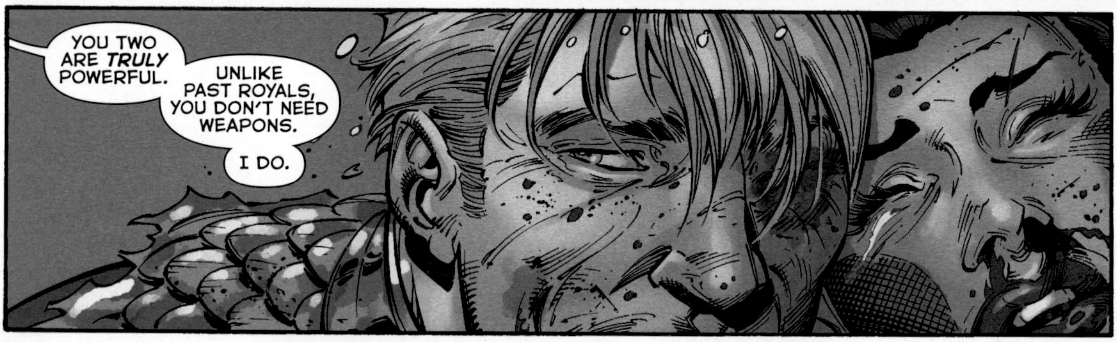
YOU TWO ARE *TRULY* POWERFUL.
UNLIKE PAST ROYALS, YOU DON'T NEED WEAPONS.
I DO.

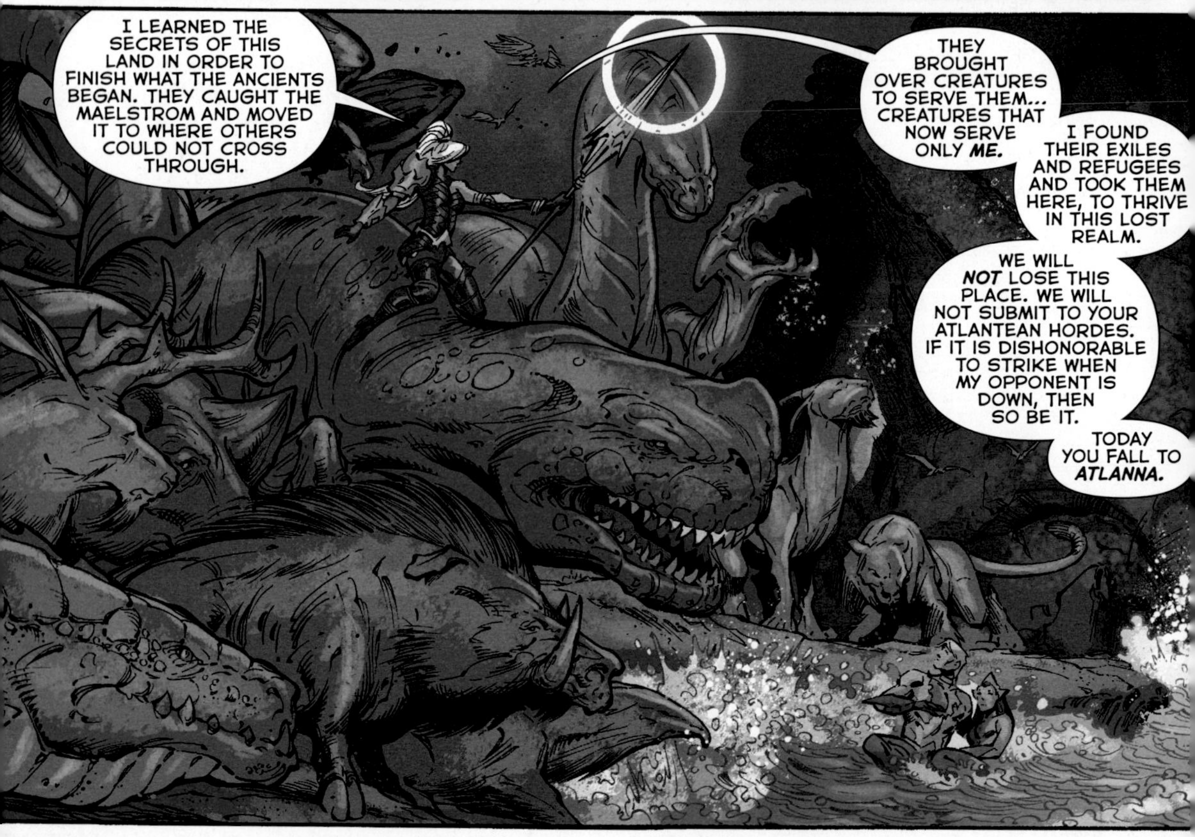
I LEARNED THE SECRETS OF THIS LAND IN ORDER TO FINISH WHAT THE ANCIENTS BEGAN. THEY CAUGHT THE MAELSTROM AND MOVED IT TO WHERE OTHERS COULD NOT CROSS THROUGH.
THEY BROUGHT OVER CREATURES TO SERVE THEM... CREATURES THAT NOW SERVE ONLY *ME.*
I FOUND THEIR EXILES AND REFUGEES AND TOOK THEM HERE, TO THRIVE IN THIS LOST REALM.
WE WILL *NOT* LOSE THIS PLACE. WE WILL NOT SUBMIT TO YOUR ATLANTEAN HORDES. IF IT IS DISHONORABLE TO STRIKE WHEN MY OPPONENT IS DOWN, THEN SO BE IT.
TODAY YOU FALL TO *ATLANNA.*

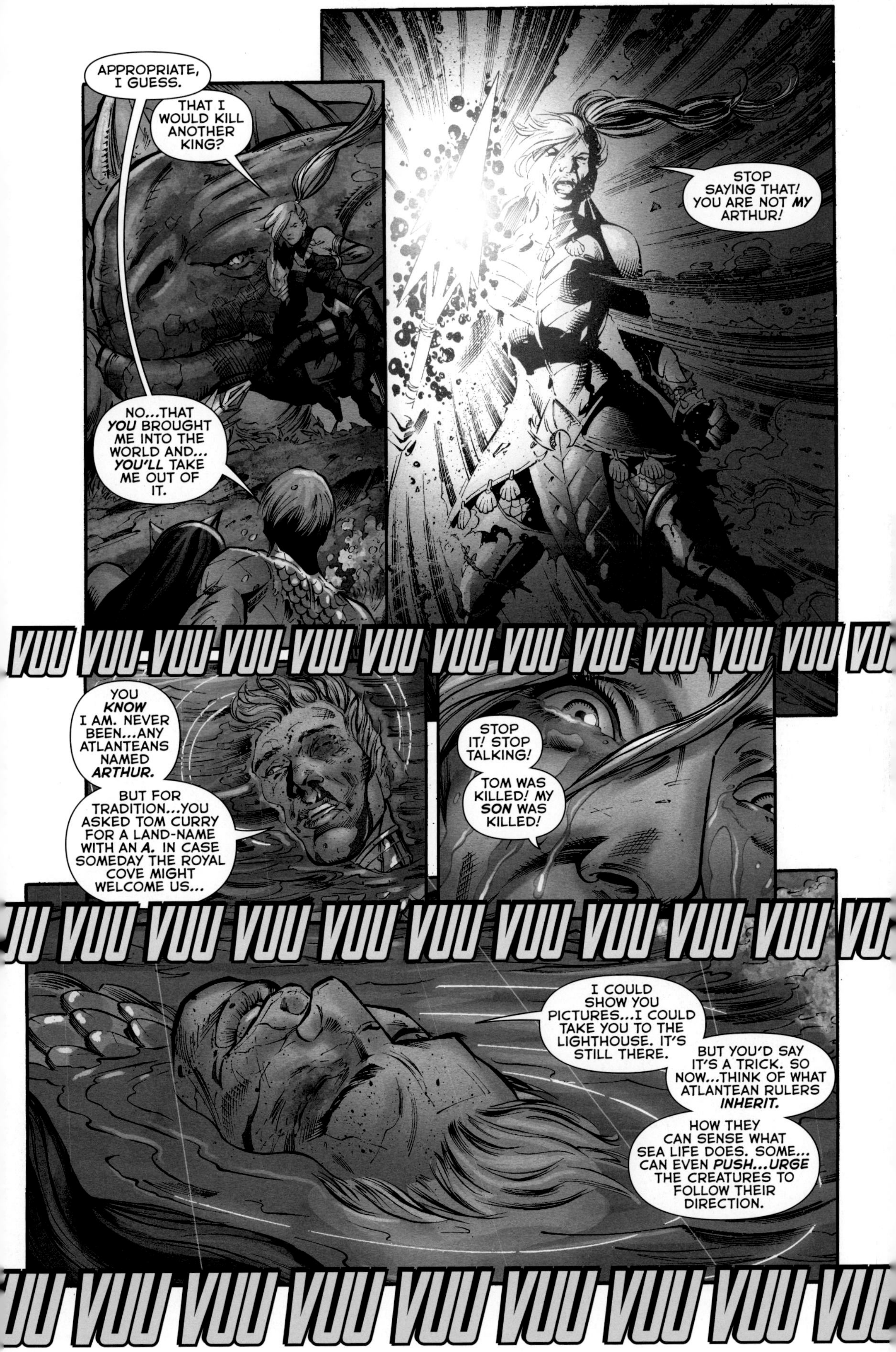
APPROPRIATE, I GUESS.
THAT I WOULD KILL ANOTHER KING?
NO...THAT YOU BROUGHT ME INTO THE WORLD AND... YOU'LL TAKE ME OUT OF IT.
STOP SAYING THAT! YOU ARE NOT MY ARTHUR!
VUU VUU-VUU-VUU-VUU VUU VUU VUU VUU VUU VUU VUU
YOU KNOW I AM. NEVER BEEN...ANY ATLANTEANS NAMED ARTHUR.
BUT FOR TRADITION...YOU ASKED TOM CURRY FOR A LAND-NAME WITH AN A. IN CASE SOMEDAY THE ROYAL COVE MIGHT WELCOME US...
STOP IT! STOP TALKING!
TOM WAS KILLED! MY SON WAS KILLED!
VUU VUU VUU VUU VUU VUU VUU VUU VUU VUU
I COULD SHOW YOU PICTURES...I COULD TAKE YOU TO THE LIGHTHOUSE. IT'S STILL THERE.
BUT YOU'D SAY IT'S A TRICK. SO NOW...THINK OF WHAT ATLANTEAN RULERS INHERIT.
HOW THEY CAN SENSE WHAT SEA LIFE DOES. SOME... CAN EVEN PUSH...URGE THE CREATURES TO FOLLOW THEIR DIRECTION.
VUU VUU VUU VUU VUU VUU VUU VUU VUU VUU

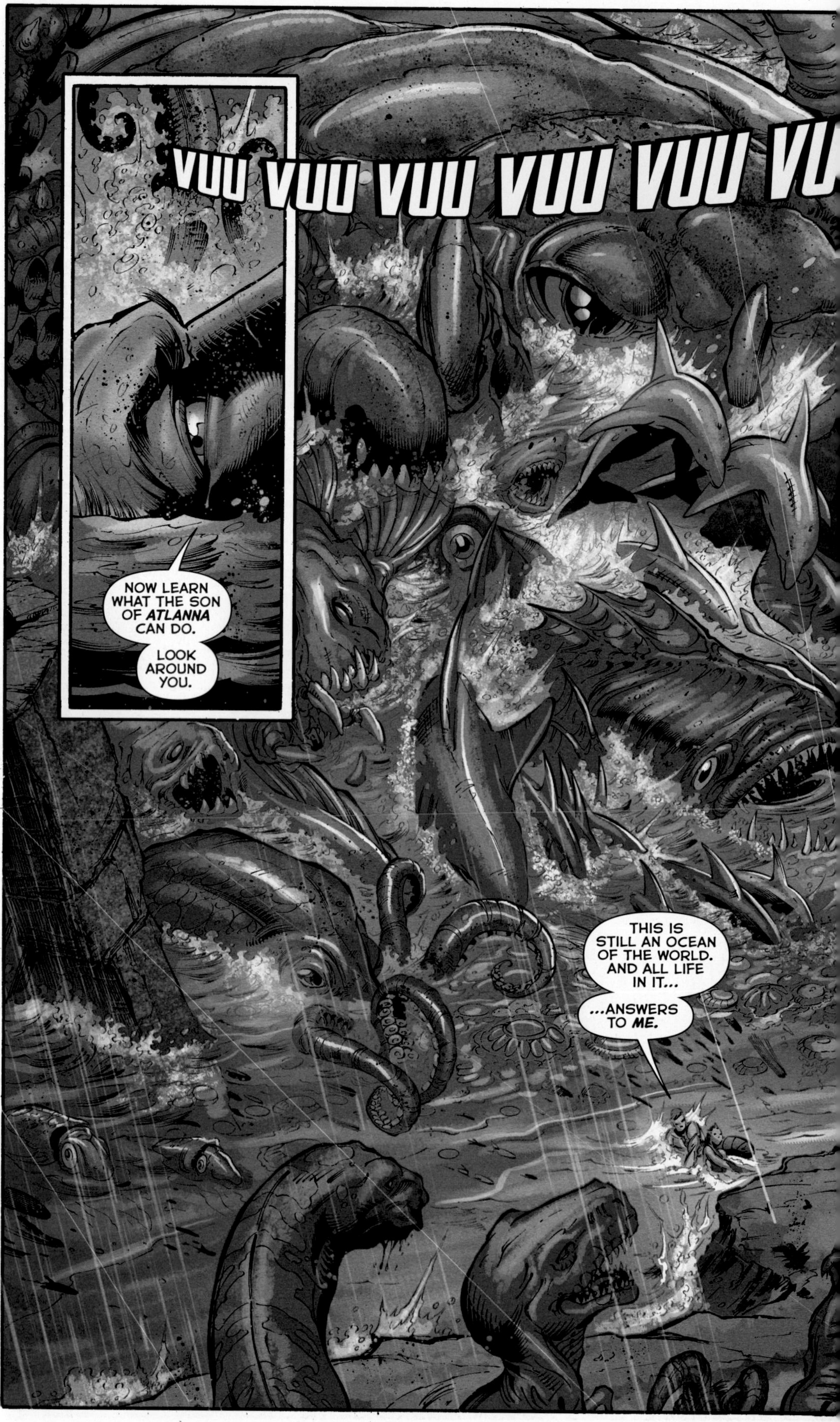
VUU VUU VUU VUU VUU VU
NOW LEARN WHAT THE SON OF ***ATLANNA*** CAN DO.
LOOK AROUND YOU.
THIS IS STILL AN OCEAN OF THE WORLD. AND ALL LIFE IN IT...
...ANSWERS TO ***ME.***

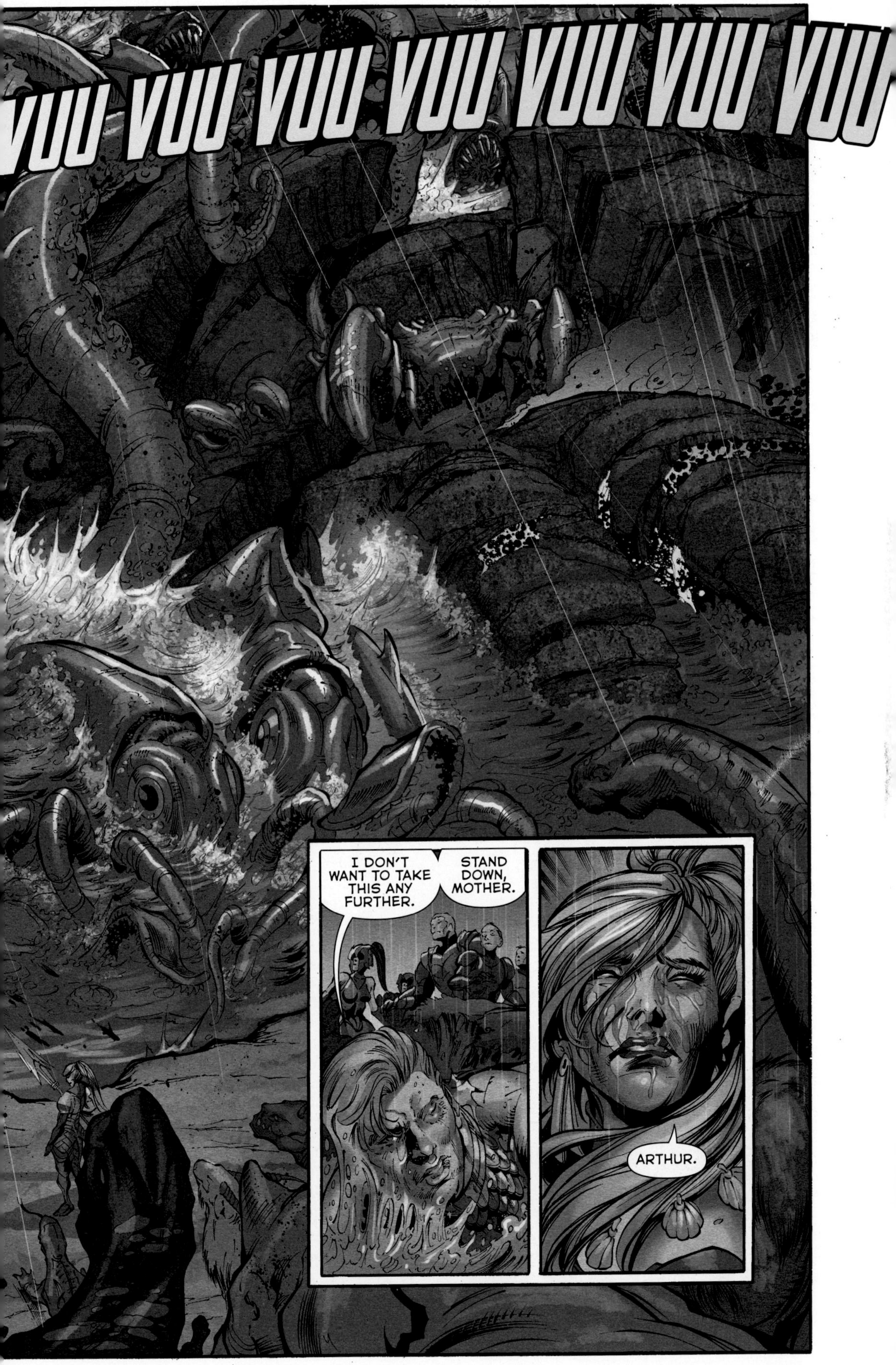
VUU VUU VUU VUU VUU VUU VUU
I DON'T WANT TO TAKE THIS ANY FURTHER.
STAND DOWN, MOTHER.
ARTHUR.

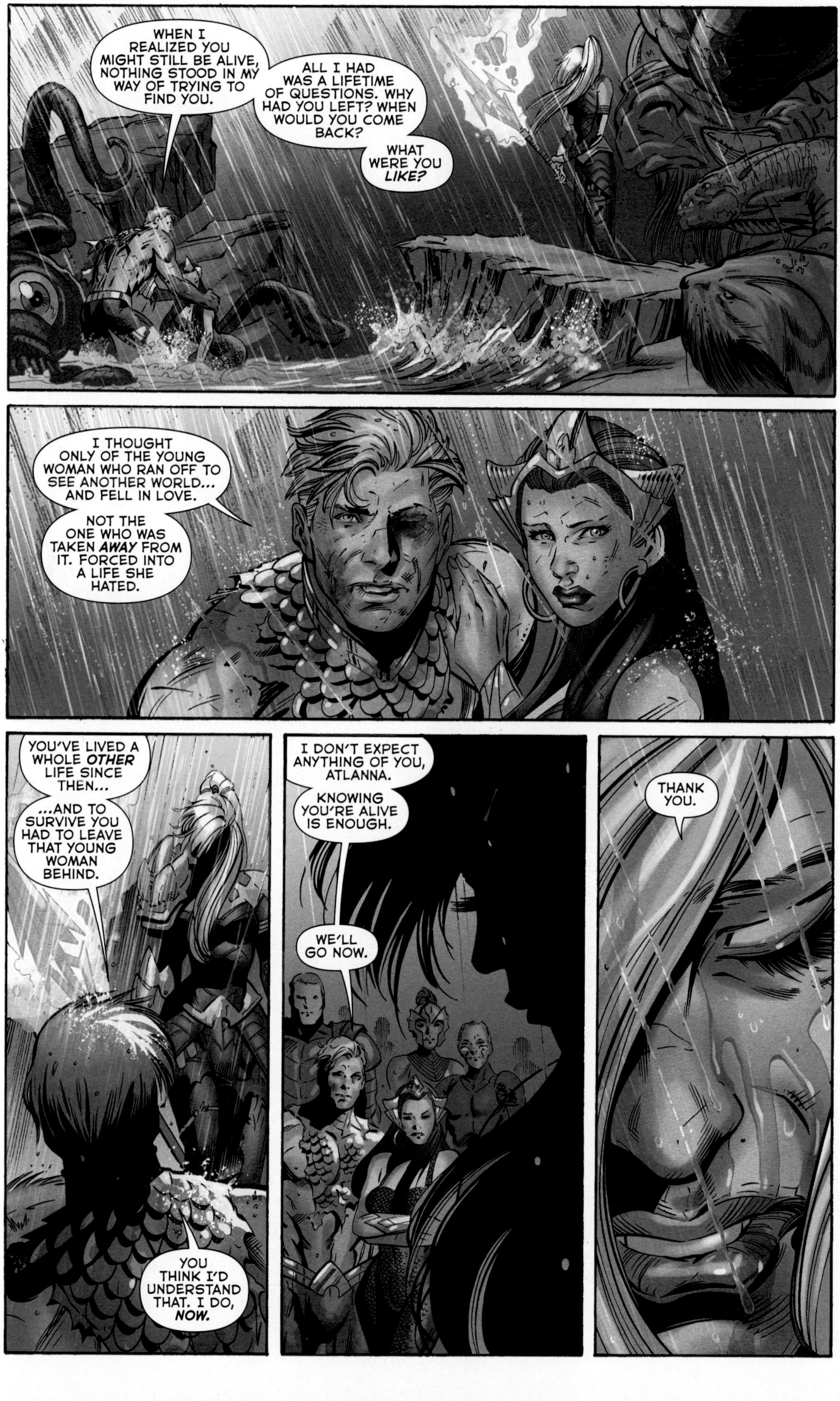
WHEN I REALIZED YOU MIGHT STILL BE ALIVE, NOTHING STOOD IN MY WAY OF TRYING TO FIND YOU.
ALL I HAD WAS A LIFETIME OF QUESTIONS. WHY HAD YOU LEFT? WHEN WOULD YOU COME BACK?
WHAT WERE YOU *LIKE?*
I THOUGHT ONLY OF THE YOUNG WOMAN WHO RAN OFF TO SEE ANOTHER WORLD... AND FELL IN LOVE.
NOT THE ONE WHO WAS TAKEN *AWAY* FROM IT. FORCED INTO A LIFE SHE HATED.
YOU'VE LIVED A WHOLE *OTHER* LIFE SINCE THEN...
...AND TO SURVIVE YOU HAD TO LEAVE THAT YOUNG WOMAN BEHIND.
YOU THINK I'D UNDERSTAND THAT. I DO, *NOW.*
I DON'T EXPECT ANYTHING OF YOU, ATLANNA.
KNOWING YOU'RE ALIVE IS ENOUGH.
WE'LL GO NOW.
THANK YOU.

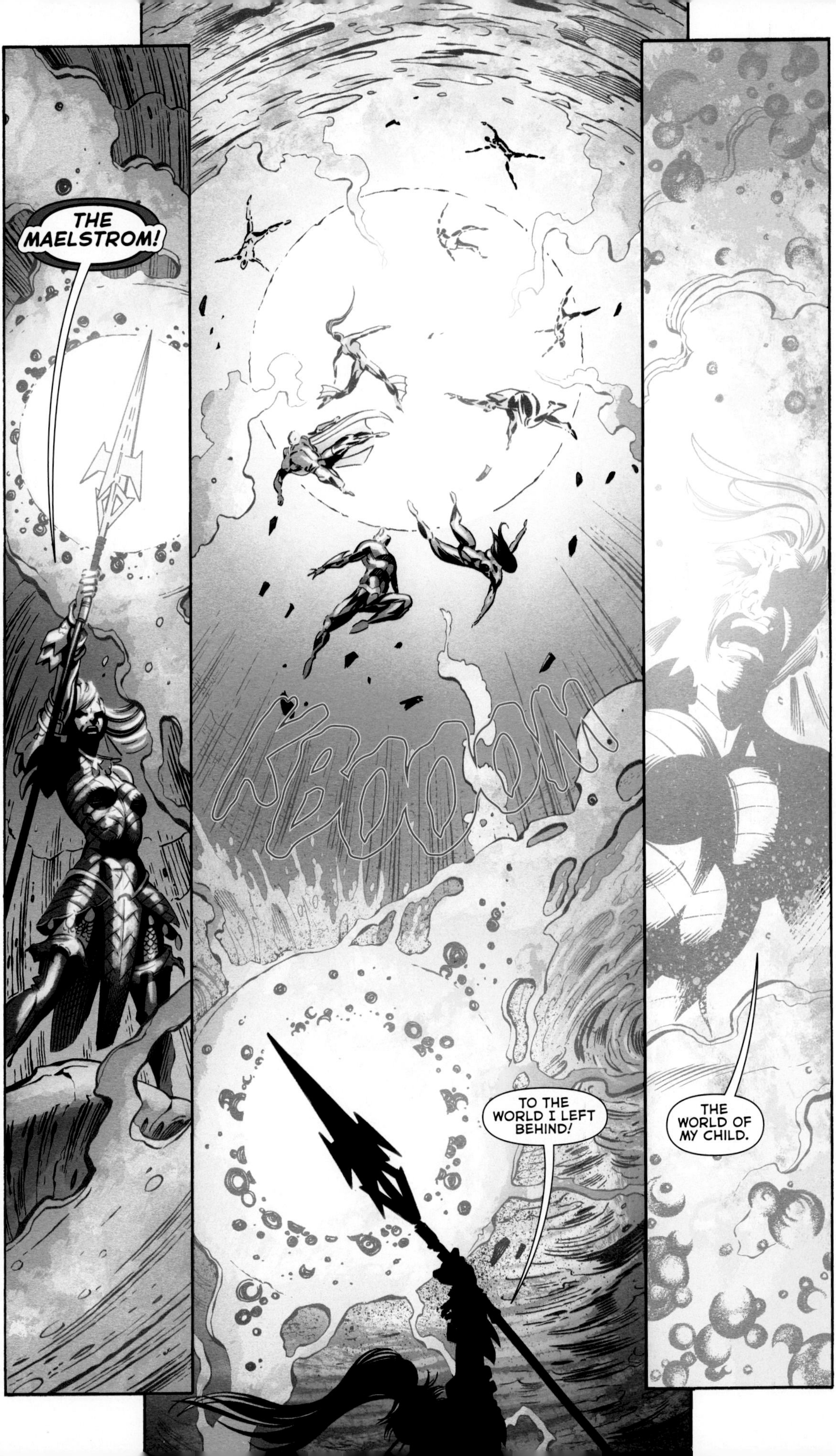
THE MAELSTROM!
KBOOOOM
TO THE WORLD I LEFT BEHIND!
THE WORLD OF MY CHILD.

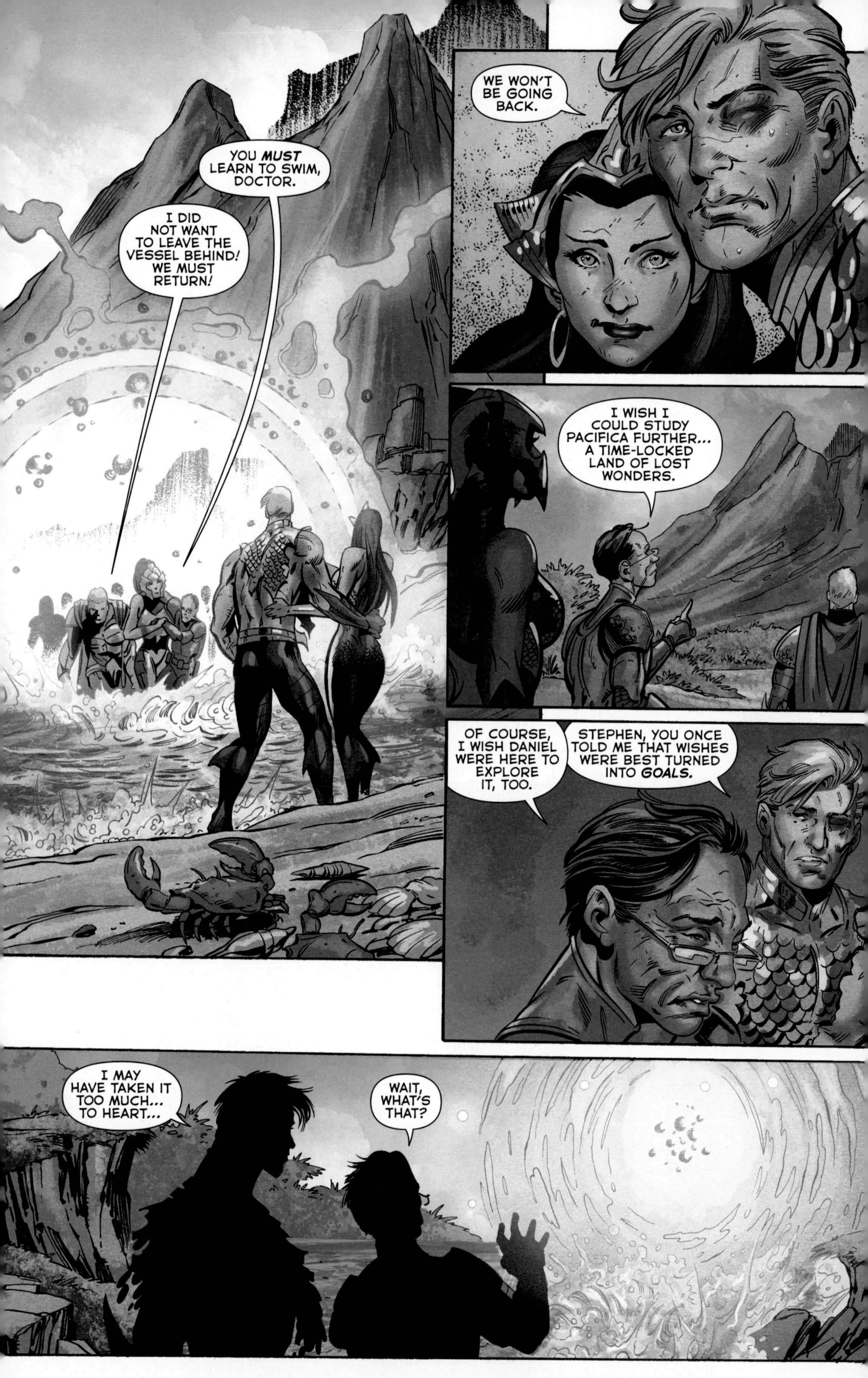
YOU MUST LEARN TO SWIM, DOCTOR.
I DID NOT WANT TO LEAVE THE VESSEL BEHIND! WE MUST RETURN!
WE WON'T BE GOING BACK.
I WISH I COULD STUDY PACIFICA FURTHER... A TIME-LOCKED LAND OF LOST WONDERS.
OF COURSE, I WISH DANIEL WERE HERE TO EXPLORE IT, TOO.
STEPHEN, YOU ONCE TOLD ME THAT WISHES WERE BEST TURNED INTO GOALS.
I MAY HAVE TAKEN IT TOO MUCH... TO HEART...
WAIT, WHAT'S THAT?

THE TRIDENT!

AND THERE'S MORE...

ATLANNA'S ROYAL SIGNET?

THIS IS WHAT YOU WANT--A SHELL OF SOUNDS!

LIKE MY MOTHER LEFT FOR *ME*.

I'VE NEVER USED ONE OF THESE...

JUST TRY TO TOUCH IT...WITH YOUR MIND.

PROJECT THAT YOU'RE READY TO *LISTEN*.

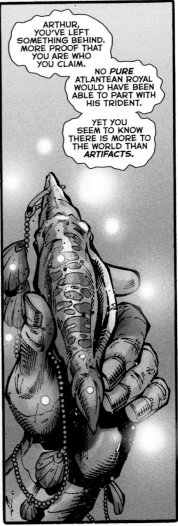

ARTHUR, YOU'VE LEFT SOMETHING BEHIND. MORE PROOF THAT YOU ARE WHO YOU CLAIM. NO *PURE* ATLANTEAN ROYAL WOULD HAVE BEEN ABLE TO PART WITH HIS TRIDENT.

YET YOU SEEM TO KNOW THERE IS MORE TO THE WORLD THAN *ARTIFACTS*.

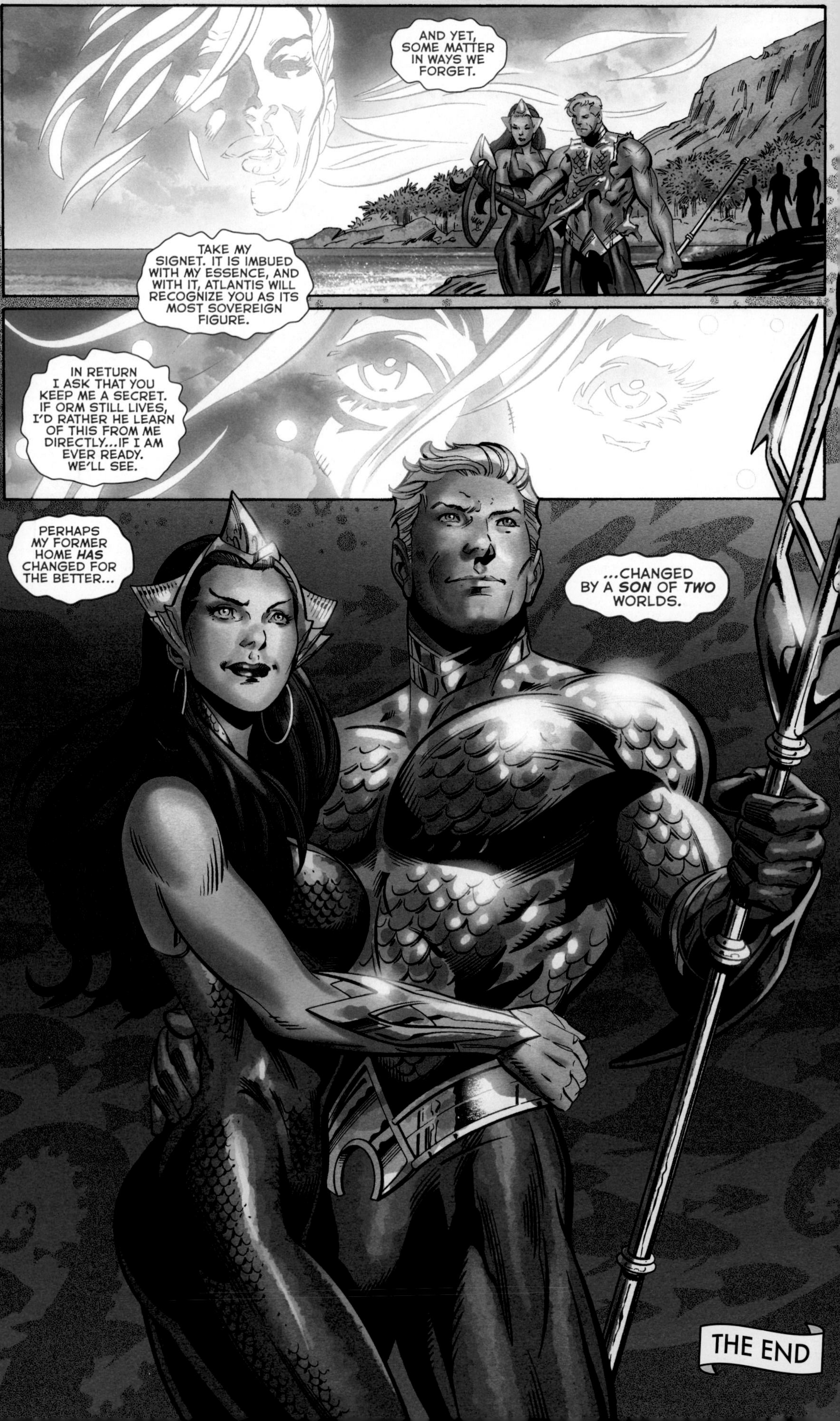
AND YET, SOME MATTER IN WAYS WE FORGET.
TAKE MY SIGNET. IT IS IMBUED WITH MY ESSENCE, AND WITH IT, ATLANTIS WILL RECOGNIZE YOU AS ITS MOST SOVEREIGN FIGURE.
IN RETURN I ASK THAT YOU KEEP ME A SECRET. IF ORM STILL LIVES, I'D RATHER HE LEARN OF THIS FROM ME DIRECTLY...IF I AM EVER READY. WE'LL SEE.
PERHAPS MY FORMER HOME HAS CHANGED FOR THE BETTER...
...CHANGED BY A SON OF TWO WORLDS.
THE END

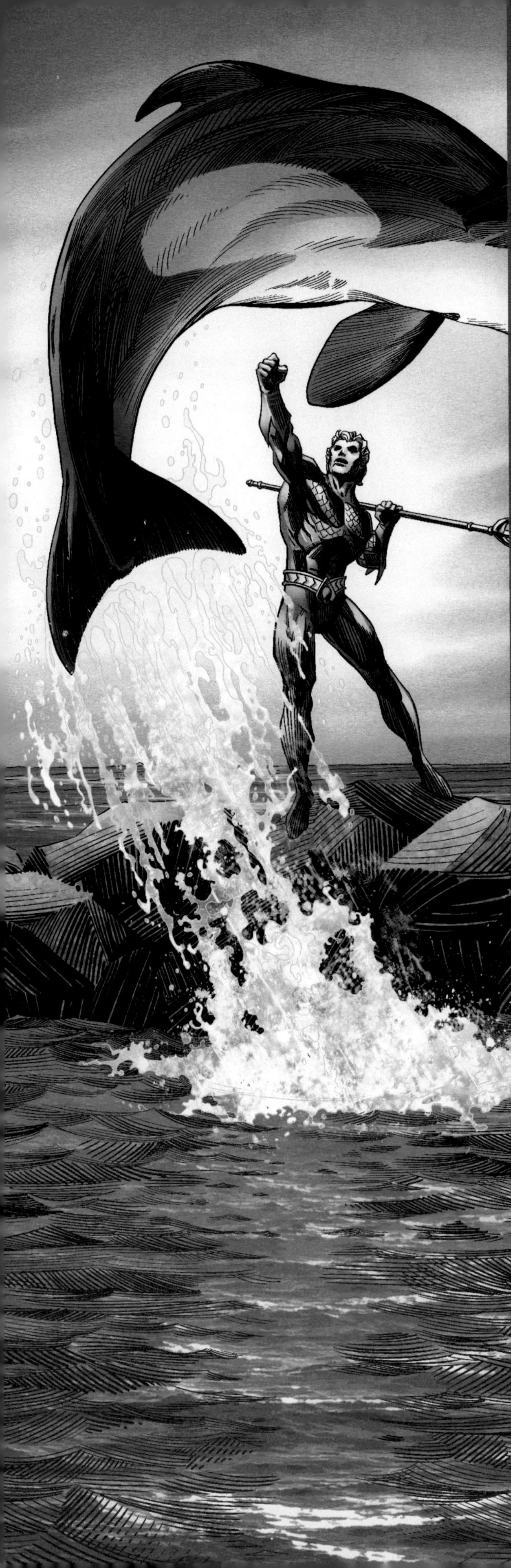

VARIANT COVER GALLERY

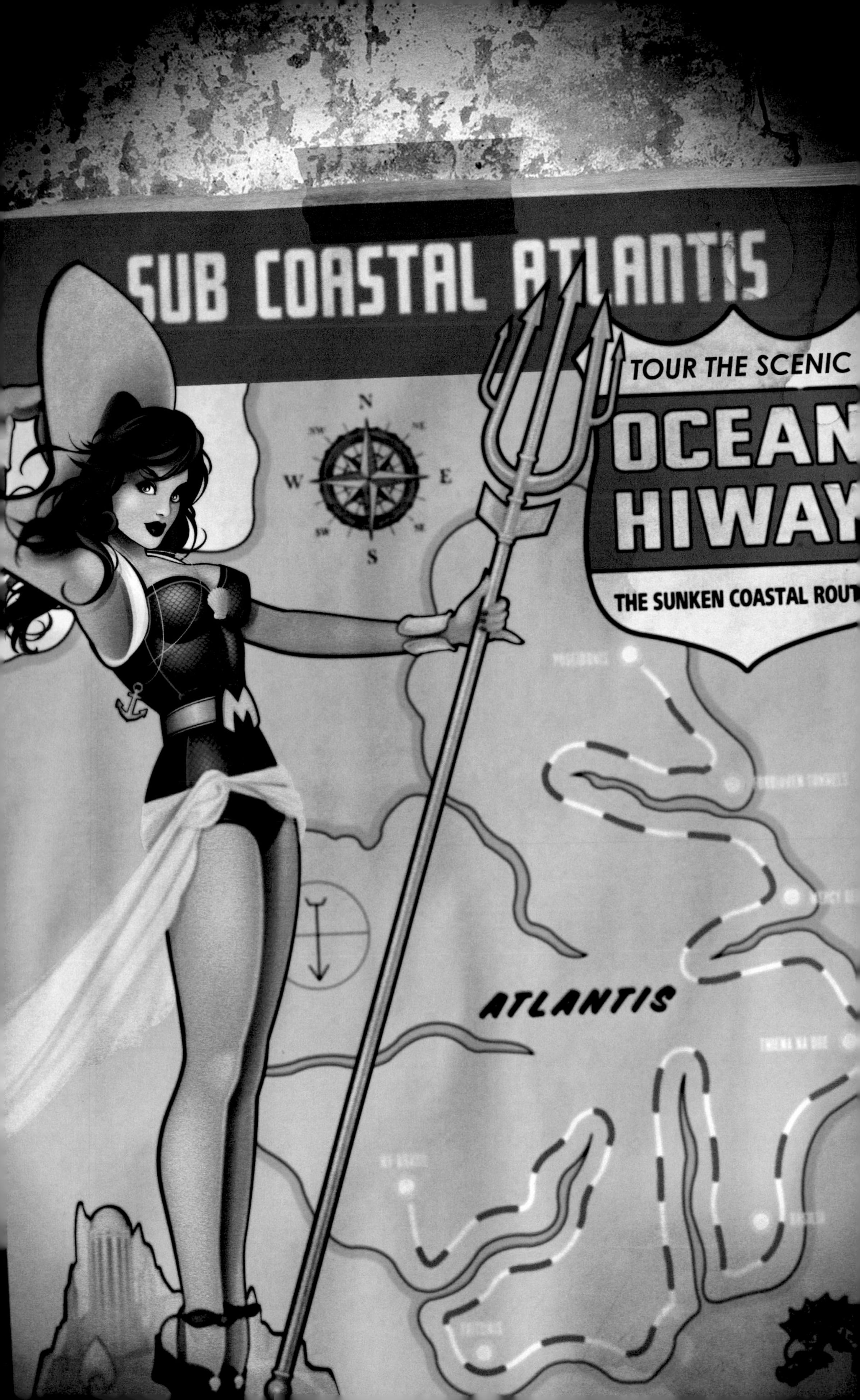
SUB COASTAL ATLANTIS
TOUR THE SCENIC
OCEAN
HIWAY
THE SUNKEN COASTAL ROUT
N
W
E
S
ATLANTIS

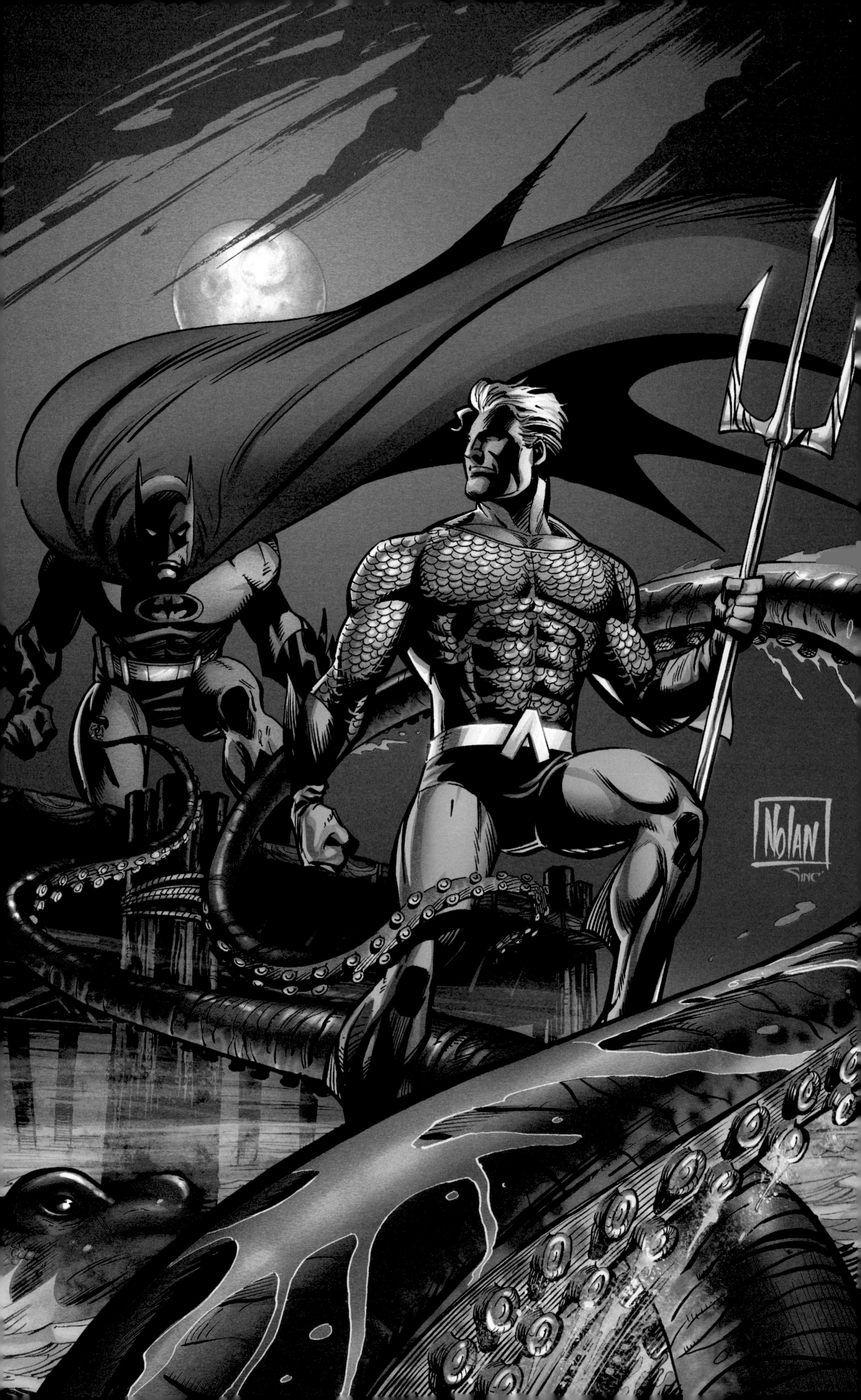
NOLAN

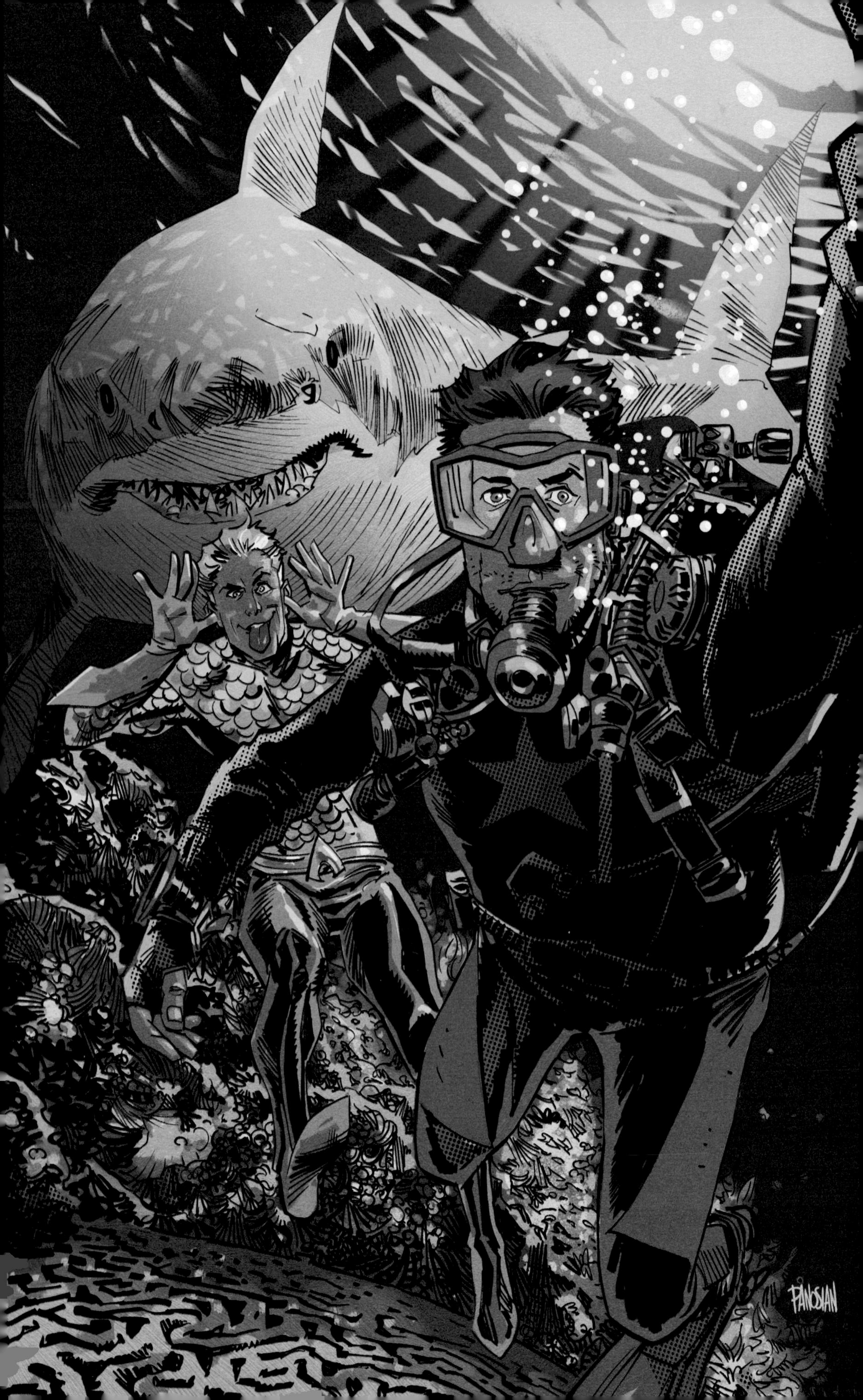
PANOSIAN

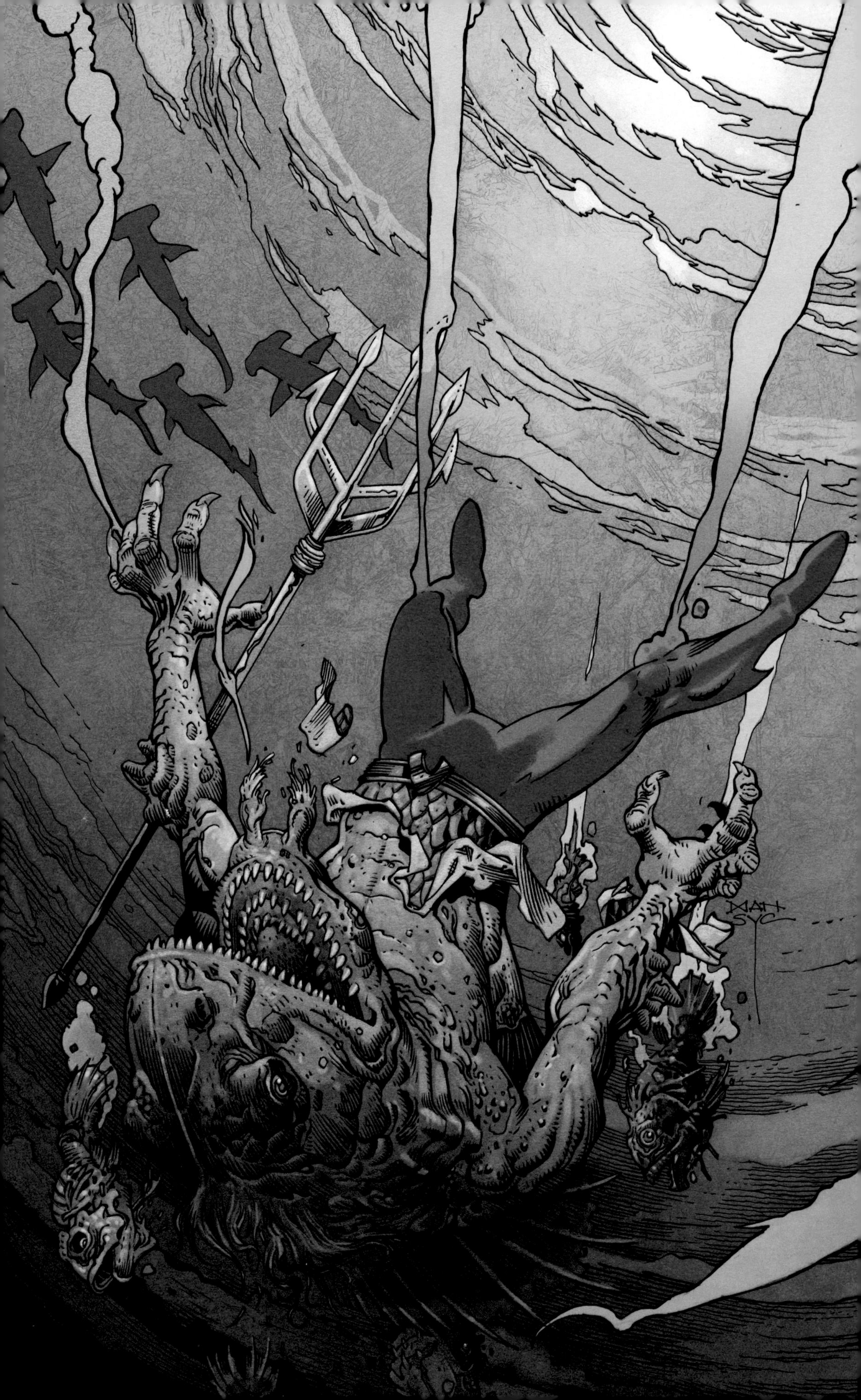

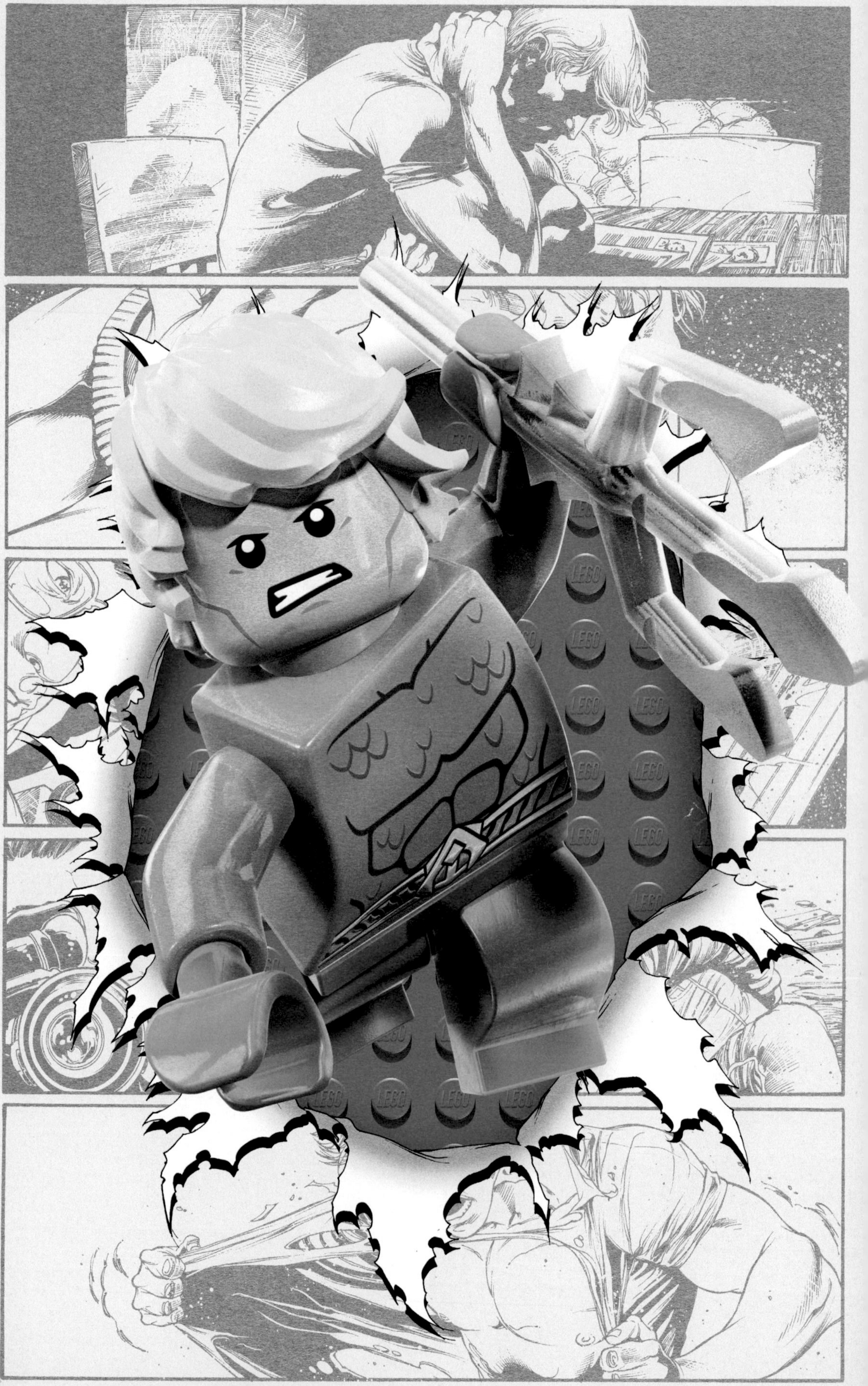

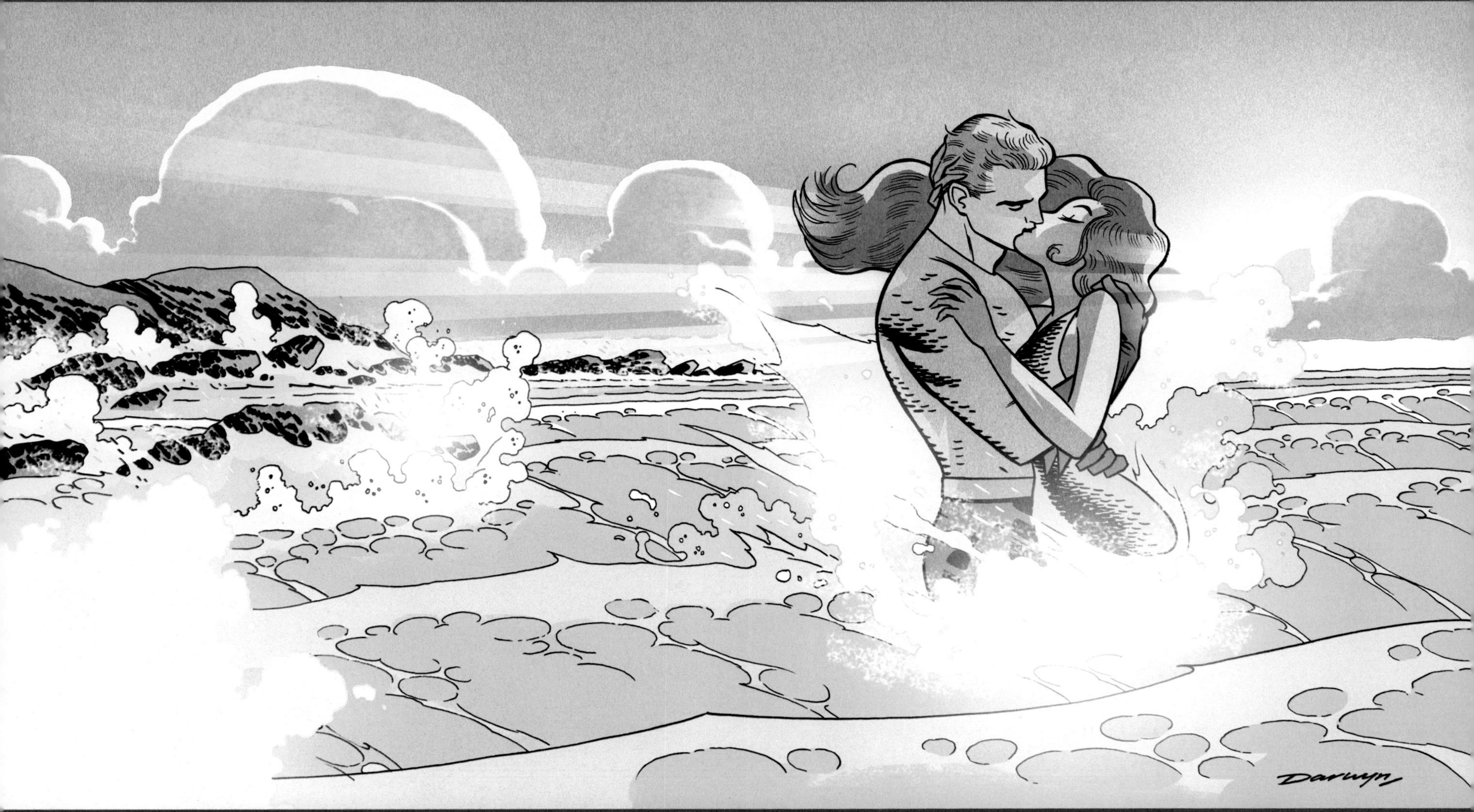
Darwyn

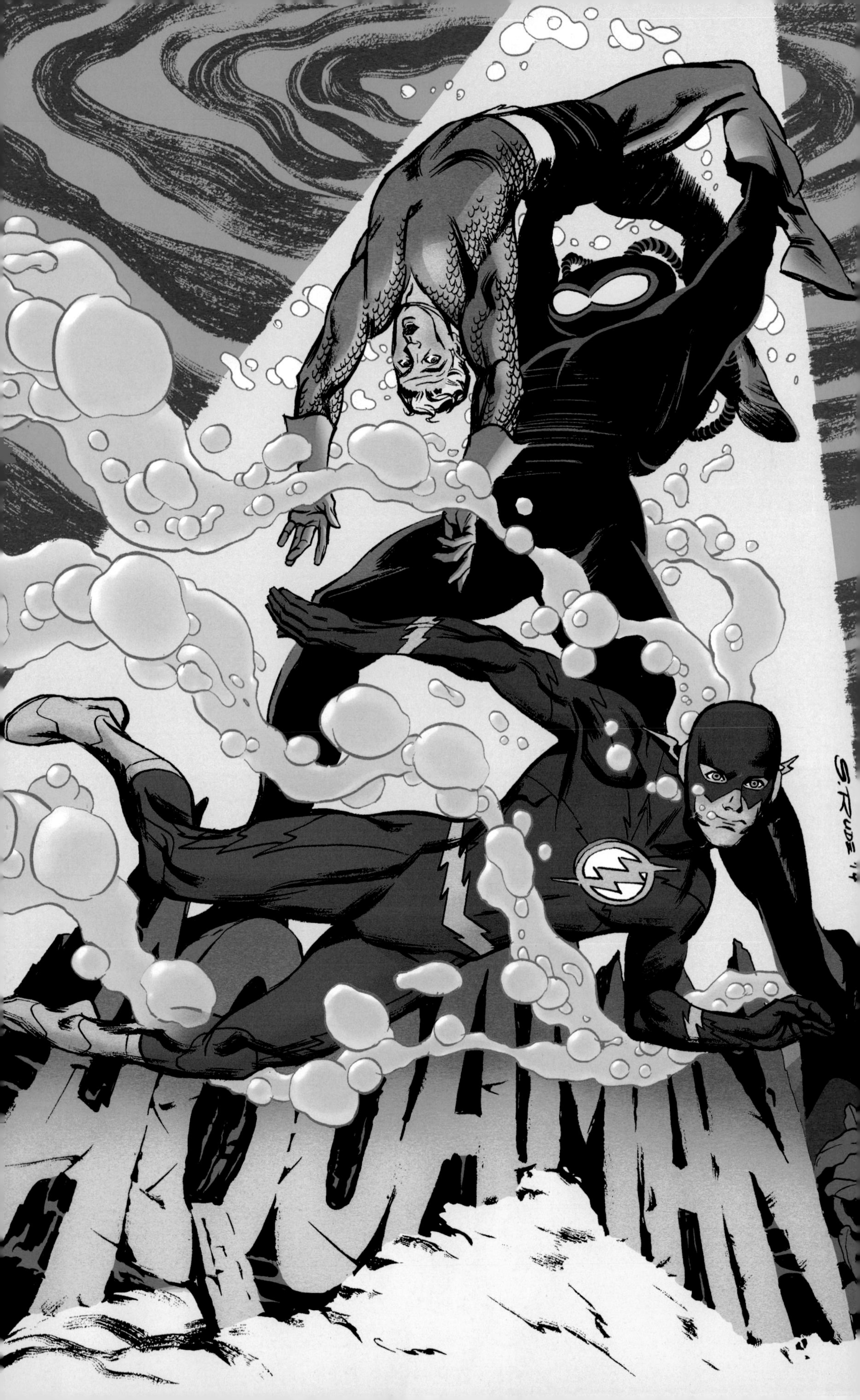
S.RUDE '14

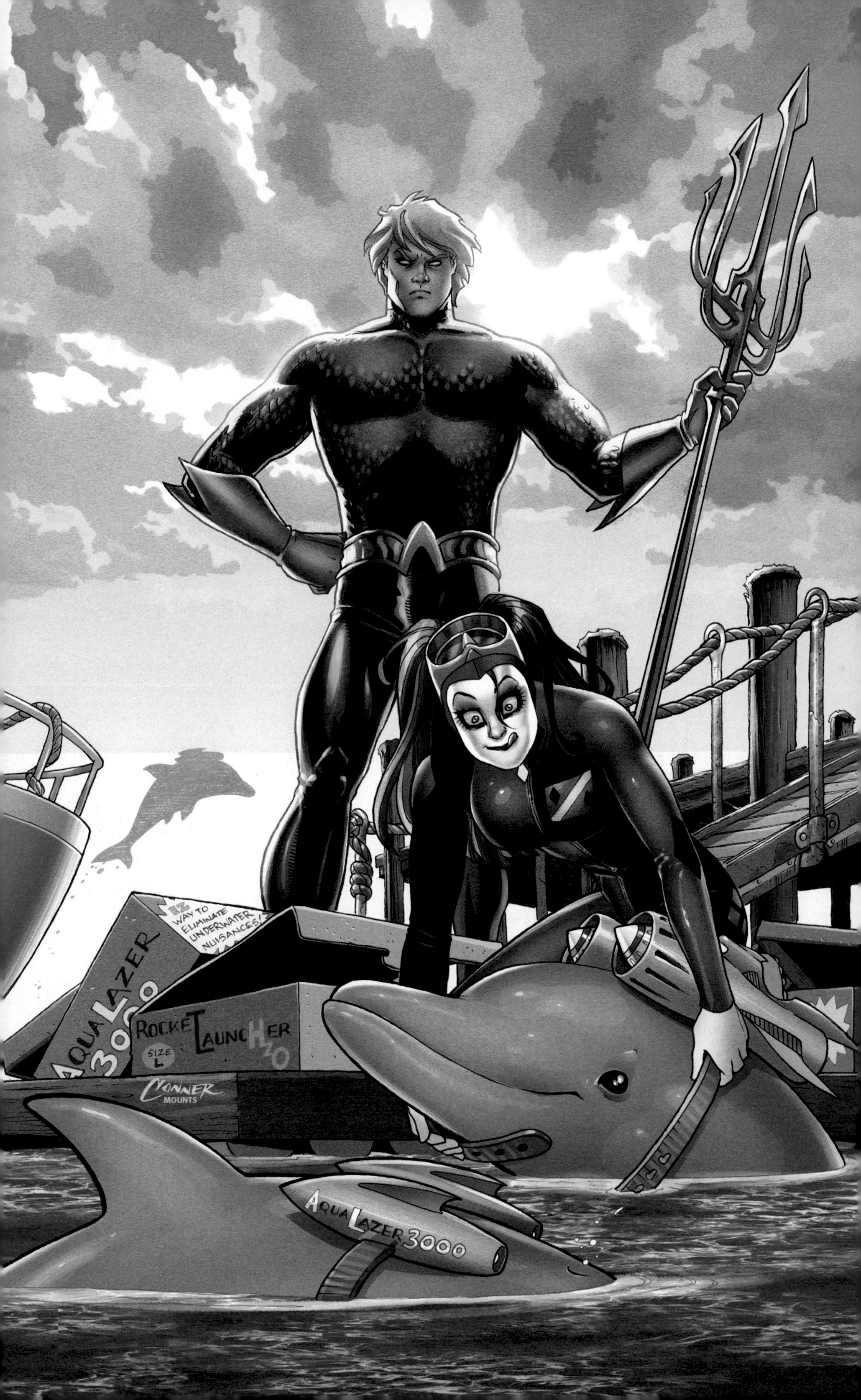
EZ WAY TO ELIMINATE UNDERWATER NUISANCES!
AQUALAZER 3000
ROCKET LAUNCHER
SIZE L
H2O
CONNER MOUNTS
AQUALAZER3000

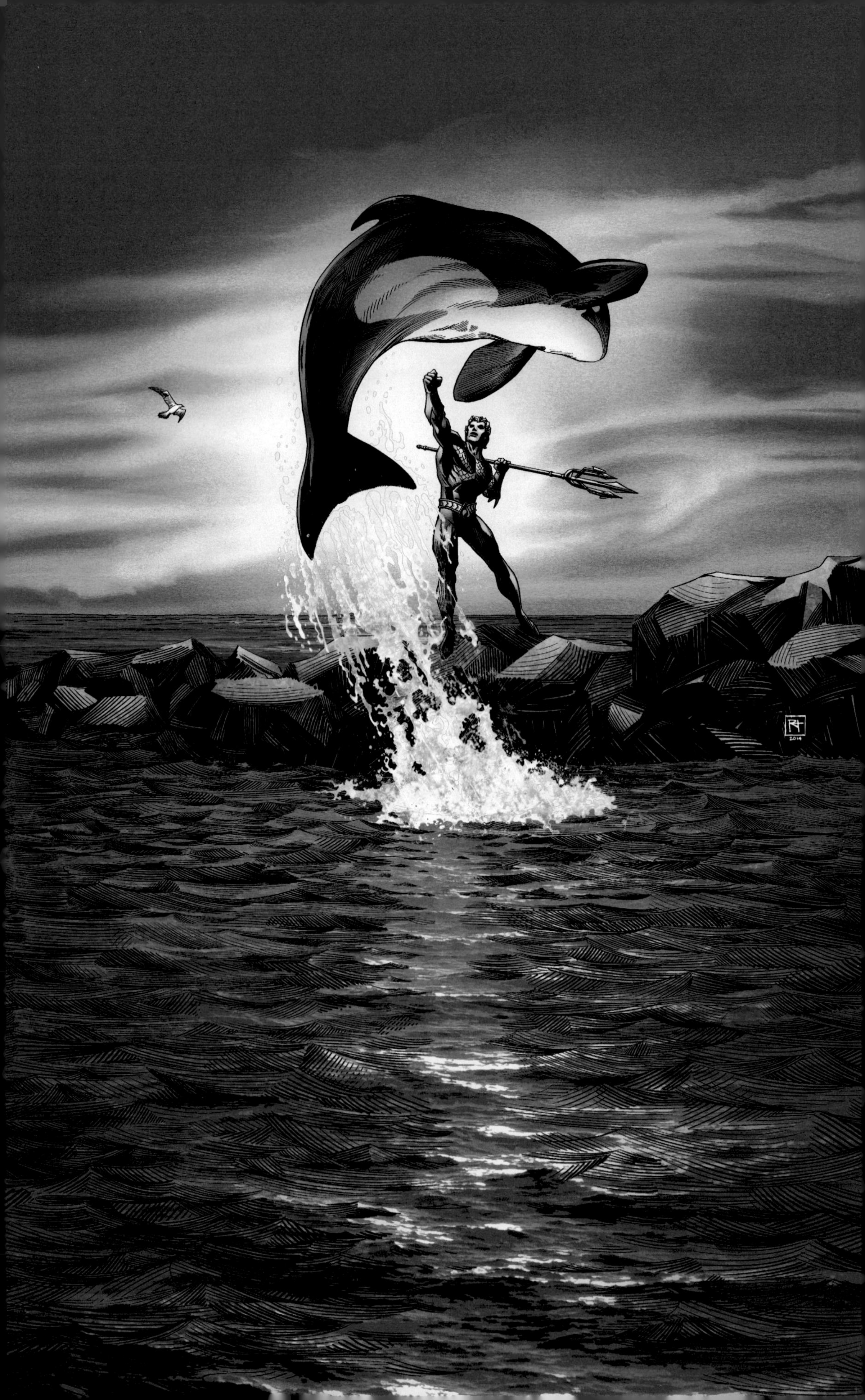

"AQUAMAN has been a rollicking good ride so far... The mythology Johns has been building up here keeps getting teased out at just the right rate, like giving a junkie their fix."—MTV GEEK

"With Reis on art and Johns using his full creative juices, AQUAMAN is constantly setting the bar higher and higher."—CRAVE ONLINE

START AT THE BEGINNING!
AQUAMAN
VOLUME 1: THE TRENCH
GEOFF JOHNS and IVAN REIS

AQUAMAN VOL. 2: THE OTHERS

AQUAMAN VOL. 3: THE THRONE OF ATLANTIS

JUSTICE LEAGUE VOL. 3: THE THRONE OF ATLANTIS

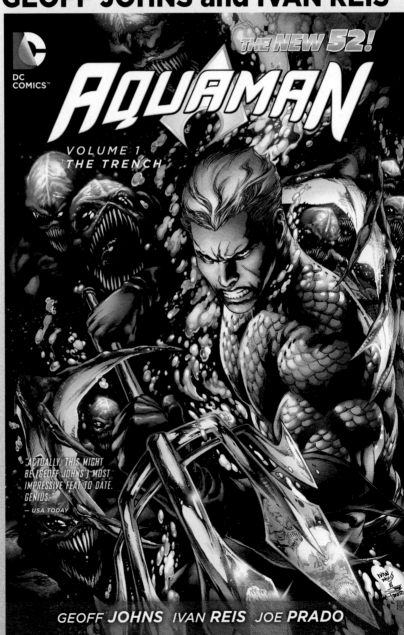

"Writer Geoff Johns and artist Jim Lee toss you—and their heroes—into the action from the very start and don't put on the brakes. DC's über-creative team craft an inviting world for those who are trying out a comic for the first time. Lee's art is stunning."—USA TODAY

"A fun ride."—IG

START AT THE BEGINNING!

JUSTICE LEAGUE
VOLUME 1: ORIGIN
GEOFF JOHNS and JIM LEE

JUSTICE LEAGUE VOL. 2: THE VILLAIN'S JOURNEY

JUSTICE LEAGUE VOL. 3: THRONE OF ATLANTIS

JUSTICE LEAGUE OF AMERICA VOL. 1: WORLD'S MOST DANGEROUS

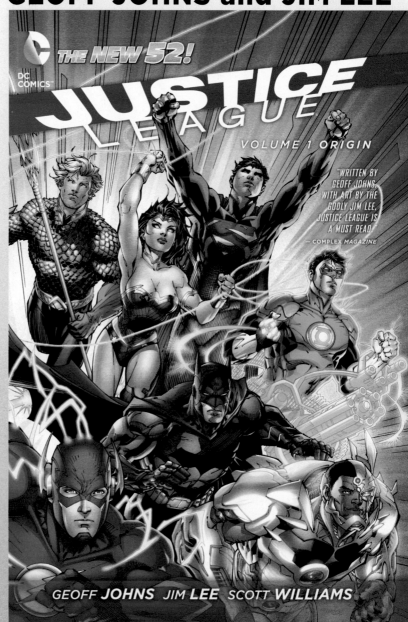